GW01018421

THE MOST HOLY PLACE

THE MOST HOLY PLACE

C. H. SPURGEON

CHRISTIAN FOCUS

ISBN 1 85792 195 X

This edition of *The Most Holy Place*
published in 1996
by
Christian Focus Publications,
Geanies House, Fearn, Ross-shire,
IV20 1TW, Great Britain.

Reprinted 2000

Cover design by Donna Macleod

Printed in Finland by WSOY

Contents

SERMON DETAILS

Sermon 1, BETTER THAN WINE (Song of Solomon 1:2), was preached at the Metropolitan Tabernacle, Newington, on Lord's Day evening, June 2nd, 1872.

Sermon 2, REJOICING AND REMEMBERING (Song of Solomon 1:4), was preached at the Metropolitan Tabernacle, Newington, on Lord's Day evening, April 4th, 1886.

Sermon 3, THE MEMORY OF CHRIST'S LOVE (Song of Solomon 1:4) was preached at the Metropolitan Tabernacle, Newington, on Lord's Day evening, November 2nd, 1890.

Sermon 4, SELF-HUMBLING AND SELF-SEARCHING (Song of Solomon 1:6) was preached at the Metropolitan Tabernacle, Newington.

Sermon 5, THE UNKEPT VINEYARD; OR, PERSONAL WORK NEGLECTED (Song of Solomon 1:6) was preached at the Metropolitan Tabernacle, Newington, on Lord's Day evening, September 19th, 1886.

Sermon 6, LOVE TO JESUS (Song of Solomon 1:7) was preached at Exeter Hall, Strand, on Lord's Day morning, September 30th, 1860.

Sermon 7, THE CHURCH'S LOVE TO HER LOVING LORD (Song of Solomon 1:7) was preached at the Metropolitan Tabernacle, Newington.

Sermon 8, THE GOOD SHEPHERDESS (Song of Solomon 1:7, 8) was preached at the Metropolitan Tabernacle, Newington, on Lord's Day morning, June 1st, 1873.

Sermon 9, A BUNDLE OF MYRRH (Song of Solomon 1:13) was preached at the Metropolitan Tabernacle, Newington, on Lord's Day morning, March 6th, 2nd, 1864.

Sermon 10, THE ROSE AND THE LILY (Song of Solomon 2:1) was preached at the Metropolitan Tabernacle, Newington, on Lord's Day morning, December 8th, 1867.

Sermon 11, THE BEST OF THE BEST (Song of Solomon 2:1) was preached at the Metropolitan Tabernacle, Newington, on Thursday evening, May 19th, 1881.

Sermon 12, THE LILY AMONG THORNS (Song of Solomon 2:2) was preached at the Metropolitan Tabernacle, Newington, on Lord's Day morning, February 29th, 1880.

Sermon 13, THE APPLE TREE IN THE WOOD (Song of Solomon 2:3), was preached at the Metropolitan Tabernacle, Newington, on Lord's Day morning, July 6th, 1873.

Sermon 14, THE ROES AND THE HINDS (Song of Solomon 2:7), was written at Mentone.

Sermon 15, A SERMON FOR SPRING (Song of Solomon 2:10-13), was preached at the Metropolitan Tabernacle, Newington, on Lord's Day morning, February 23rd, 1862.

Sermon 16, THE TENDER GRAPES (Song of Solomon 2:13), was

preached at the Metropolitan Tabernacle, Newington, on Lord's Day evening, August 8th, 1880.

Sermon 17, THE INTEREST OF CHRIST AND HIS PEOPLE IN EACH OTHER (Song of Solomon 2:16), was preached at the Metropolitan Tabernacle, Newington, on Good Friday evening, March 29th, 1861.

Sermon 18, A SONG AMONG THE LILIES (Song of Solomon 2:16) was preached at the Metropolitan Tabernacle, Newington, on Lord's Day morning, July 6th, 1873.

Sermon 19, LOVED AND LOVING (Song of Solomon 2:16), was preached at the Metropolitan Tabernacle, Newington, on Lord's Day morning, August 30th, 1874.

Sermon 20, 'MY BELOVED IS MINE' (Song of Solomon 2:16) was preached at the Metropolitan Tabernacle, Newington, on Lord's Day morning, July 6th, 1873.

Sermon 21, DARKNESS BEFORE THE DAWN (Song of Solomon 2:17), was preached at the Metropolitan Tabernacle, Newington, on Lord's Day evening, August 1st, 1886.

Sermon 22, LOVE'S VIGILANCE REWARDED (Song of Solomon 3:4) was preached at the Metropolitan Tabernacle, Newington, on Lord's Day evening, October 7th, 1877.

Sermon 23, THE REAL PRESENCE, THE GREAT WANT OF THE CHURCH (Song of Solomon 3:4, 5) was preached at the Metropolitan Tabernacle, Newington, on Lord's Day morning, February 11th, 1872..

Sermon 24, THE ROYAL PAIR IN THEIR GLORIOUS CHARIOT (Song of Solomon 3:6-11), was preached at the Metropolitan Tabernacle, Newington, on Lord's Day morning, November 30th, 1862.

Sermon 25, PAVED WITH LOVE (Song of Solomon 3:10), was preached at the Metropolitan Tabernacle, Newington, on Lord's Day morning, September 28th, 1873.

Sermon 26, CHRIST'S ESTIMATE OF HIS PEOPLE (Song of Solomon 4:10, 11), was preached at the Metropolitan Tabernacle, Newington, on Lord's Day evening, January 23rd, 1859.

Sermon 27, THE LORD'S OWN VIEW OF HIS CHURCH AND PEOPLE (Song of Solomon 4:12),was preached at the Metropolitan Tabernacle, Newington.

Sermon 28, A SECRET AND YET NO SECRET (Song of Solomon 4:12 and 15), was preached at the Metropolitan Tabernacle, Newington, on Lord's Day morning, January 26th, 1862.

Sermon 29, GRACE FOR COMMUNION (Song of Solomon 4:16) was a short address to a few friends at Mentone at the breaking of bread on Lord's Day afternoon, January 2nd, 1887.

Sermon 30, MY GARDEN – HIS GARDEN (Song of Solomon 4:16), was preached at the Metropolitan Tabernacle, Newington, on Thursday evening, July 20th, 1882.

Sermon 31, THE KING FEASTING IN HIS GARDEN (Song of Solomon 5:1), was preached at the Metropolitan Tabernacle, Newington, on Lord's Day morning, March 6th, 1870.

Sermon 32, LOVE JOYING IN LOVE (Song of Solomon 5:1) was a short address to a few friends at Mentone at the breaking of bread on Lord's Day afternoon, January 9th, 1887.

Sermon 33, ASLEEP AND YET AWAKE – A RIDDLE (Song of Solomon 5:2), was preached at the Metropolitan Tabernacle, Newington, on Lord's Day morning, October 10th, 1880.

Sermon 34, NEARER AND DEARER (Song of Solomon 5:2-8), was preached at the Metropolitan Tabernacle, Newington, on Lord's Day morning, February 2nd, 1868.

Sermon 35, HEAVENLY LOVE-SICKNESS (Song of Solomon 5:8), was preached at the Metropolitan Tabernacle, Newington, on Lord's Day morning, November 8th, 1863.

Sermon 36, THE INCOMPARABLE BRIDEGROOM AND HIS BRIDE (Song of Solomon 5:9), was preached at the Metropolitan Tabernacle, Newington, on Lord's Day evening, June 10th, 1866.

Sermon 37, CHRIST'S PERFECTION AND PRECEDENCE (Song of Solomon 5:10), was preached at the Metropolitan Tabernacle, Newington, on Lord's Day evening, August 1st, 1869.

Sermon 38, SPICES, FLOWERS, LILIES and MYRRH (Song of Solomon 5:13), was preached at the Metropolitan Tabernacle, Newington, on Thursday evening, August 5th, 1880.

Sermon 39, ALTOGETHER LOVELY (Song of Solomon 5:16), was preached at the Metropolitan Tabernacle, Newington, on Lord's Day morning, July 23rd, 1871.

Sermon 40, THE BEST BELOVED (Song of Solomon 5:16), was preached at the Metropolitan Tabernacle, Newington.

Sermon 41, THE CHURCH AS SHE SHOULD BE (Song of Solomon 6:4), was preached at the Metropolitan Tabernacle, Newington.

Sermon 42, OVERCOMING CHRIST (Song of Solomon 6:5), was preached at the Metropolitan Tabernacle, Newington, on Lord's Day evening, October 8th, 1876.

Sermon 43, THE CHARIOTS OF AMMI-NADIB (Song of Solomon 6:12), was preached at the Metropolitan Tabernacle, Newington.

Sermon 44, INWARD CONFLICTS (Song of Solomon 6:13), was preached at the Metropolitan Tabernacle, Newington, on Lord's Day morning, October 9th, 1864.

Sermon 45, 'RETURN, RETURN, O SHULAMITE; RETURN, RETURN!' (Song of Solomon 6:13), was preached at the Metropolitan Tabernacle, Newington, on Lord's Day morning, August 10th, 1884.

Sermon 46, GOOD WORKS IN GOOD COMPANY (Song of Solomon 7:11-13), was preached at the Metropolitan Tabernacle, Newington, on Lord's

Day morning, December 18th, 1864.

Sermon 47, A CALL FOR REVIVAL (Song of Solomon 7:11-13), was preached at the Metropolitan Tabernacle, Newington, on Lord's Day morning, August 18th, 1872.

Sermon 48, LEANING ON OUR BELOVED (Song of Solomon 8:5), was preached at the Metropolitan Tabernacle, Newington, on Lord's Day morning, June 20th, 1869.

Sermon 49, THE SHULAMITE'S CHOICE PRAYER (Song of Solomon 8: 6, 7), was preached at New Park Street Chapel, Southwark, on Lord's Day evening, February 24th, 1861.

Sermon 50, UNPURCHASABLE LOVE (Song of Solomon 8:7), was preached at the Metropolitan Tabernacle, Newington, on Thursday evening, June 6th, 1872.

Sermon 51, THE BRIDEGROOM'S PARTING WORD (Song of Solomon 8:13), was preached at the Metropolitan Tabernacle, Newington, on Lord's Day morning, April 15th, 1883.

Sermon 52, COME, MY BELOVED! (Song of Solomon 8:14), was preached at the Metropolitan Tabernacle, Newington, on Lord's Day evening, March 4th, 1888.

1

BETTER THAN WINE

'Thy love is better than wine'
(Song of Solomon 1:2)

The Scriptural emblem of wine, which is intended to be the symbol of the richest earthly joy, has become desecrated in process of time by the sin of man. I suppose, in the earlier ages when the Word of God was written, it would hardly have been conceivable that there could have existed on the face of the earth such a mass of drunken men and women as now pollute and defile it by their very presence. For man, nowadays, is not content with the wine that God makes, but he manufactures some for himself of which he cannot partake, at least in any abundance, without becoming drunken. Redeem the figure in our text, if you can, and go back from the drinking customs of our own day to more primitive and purer times, when the ordinary meal of a man was very similar to that which is spread upon this communion table – bread and wine – of which men might partake without fear of evil effects; but do not use the metaphor as it would now be understood amongst the mass of mankind, at least in countries like our own.

'Thy love is better than wine.' In considering these words, in the spirit in which the inspired writer used them, I shall, first of all, try to show you that *Christ's love is better than wine because of what it is not*; and, secondly, that *it is better than wine because of what it is*. Next, we will examine the marginal reading of the text, which will teach us something about *Christ's love in the plural*: 'Thy loves are better than wine.' And then, lastly, we will come back to the version we have before us, in which we shall see *Christ's love in the singular*; for the love of Christ, even when it is described in the plural, is always one; though there are many forms of it, it is evermore the same love.

First, then, I want to prove to you that Christ's love is better than wine because of what it is not.

It is so, first, *because it may be taken without question*. There may be, and there always will be in the world, questions about wine. There will be some who will say, and wisely say, 'Let it alone.' There will be others who will exclaim, 'Drink of it abundantly'; while a third company will say, 'Use it moderately.' But there will be no question amongst upright men about partaking to the full of the love of Christ. There will be none of the godly who will say, 'Abstain from it'; and none who will say, 'Use it moderately'; but all true Christians will echo the words of the Heavenly Bridegroom himself, 'Drink, yea, drink abundantly, O beloved.' The wisdom of imbibing freely of the love of Christ shall never be questioned even by the pure spirits in heaven; this is the wine which they themselves quaff in everlasting bowls at the right hand of God, and the Lord of glory himself bids them quaff it to their fill. This is the highest delight of all who know Christ, and have been born again by the regenerating power of the Holy Spirit; this is our greatest joy while here below, and we can never have too much of it. Yea, we may even swim in this sea of bliss, and there shall be none who shall dare to ask any one of us, 'What doest thou there?' Many delightsome things, many earthly joys, many of the pleasures of this world, are very questionable enjoyments. Christians had better keep away from everything about which their consciences are not perfectly clear; but all our consciences are clear concerning the Lord Jesus, and our heart's love to him; so that, in this respect, his love is better than wine.

Christ's love is also better than wine *because it is to be had without money*. Many a man has beggared himself, and squandered his estate, through his love of worldly pleasure, and especially through his fondness for wine; but the love of Christ is to be had without money. What saith the Scripture? 'Come, buy wine and milk without money and without price' (Isaiah 55:1). The love of Christ is unpurchased; and I may add that it is unpurchasable. Solomon says, in the eighth chapter of this Book, 'If a man would give all the substance of his house for love, it would utterly be contemned'; and we may as truly say, 'If a man would give all the substance of his house for the love of Christ, it would be utterly contemned.' The love of Jesus comes to his people freely; not because they deserve it, or ever will deserve it; not because by any merits of their own they have won it, or by any prayers of their own they have secured it: it is spontaneous love; it flows from the heart of Christ because it must come, like the stream that leaps from an ever-flowing fountain. If you ask why Jesus loves his people, we can give no other reason than this: 'Because it seemed good in his sight.' Christ's love is the freest thing in the world – free as the sunbeam, free as the mountain torrent, free as the air. It comes to the child of God without purchase and without merit, and in this respect it is better than wine.

Again, Christ's love is better than wine *because it is to be enjoyed without cloying*. The sweetest matter on earth, which is for a while pleasant to the taste, sooner or later cloys upon the palate. If thou findest honey, thou canst soon eat so much of it that thou wilt no longer relish its sweetness; but the love of Jesus never yet cloyed upon the palate of a newborn soul. He who has had most of Christ's love has cried, 'More! More! More!' If ever there was a man on earth who had Christ's love in him to the full, it was holy Samuel Rutherford; yet you can see in his letters how he laboured for suitable expressions while trying to set forth his hungering and thirsting after the love of Christ. He says he floated upon Christ's love like a ship upon a river, and then he quaintly asks that his vessel may founder, and go to the bottom, till that blessed stream shall flow right over the masthead of his ship. He wanted to be baptised into the love of Christ, to be flung into the ocean of his Saviour's love; and this is what the true Christian ever longs for. No lover of the Lord Jesus has ever said that he has had enough of Christ's love. When Madame Guyon had spent many a day and many a month in the sweet enjoyment of the love of Jesus, she penned most delicious hymns concerning it; but they are all full of craving after more, there is no indication that she wished for any change of affection to her Lord, or any change in the object of her affection. She was satisfied with Christ, and longed to have more and more of his love. Ah, poor drunkard! thou mayest put away the cup of devils because thou art satiated with its deadly draught; but never did he who drinks of the wine of Christ's love become satiated or even content with it; he ever desires more and yet more of it.

Further, Christ's love is better than wine *because it is without lees*. All wine has something in it which renders it imperfect and liable to corruption; there is something that will have to settle, something that must be skimmed off the top, something that needs fining down. So is it with all the joys of earth, there is sure to be something in them that mars their perfection. Men have sought out many inventions of mirth and pleasure, amusement and delight; but they have always found some hitch or flaw somewhere. Solomon gathered to himself all manner of pleasant things that are the delight of kings; he gives us a list of them in the Book of Ecclesiastes 2:4-8: 'I made me great works; I builded me houses; I planted me vineyards: I made me gardens and orchards, and I planted trees in them of all kind of fruits: I made me pools of water, to water therewith the wood that bringeth forth trees: I got me servants and maidens, and had servants born in my house; also I had great possessions of great and small cattle above all that were in Jerusalem before me: I gathered me also silver and gold, and the peculiar treasure of kings and of the provinces: I gat me men singers and women singers, and the delights of the sons of men, as musical instruments, and that of all sorts'; but his verdict concerning all of them was, 'Behold, all was vanity and vexation of spirit' (verse 11). But he who delights himself in the love of Christ will tell you that he finds no vanity and vexation of spirit there; but everything to charm and rejoice and satisfy the heart. There is nothing in the Lord Jesus Christ that we could wish to have taken away from him; there is nothing in his love that is impure, nothing that is unsatisfactory. Our precious Lord is comparable to the most fine gold; there is no alloy in him; nay, there is nothing that can be compared with him, for 'he is altogether lovely', all perfections melted into one perfection, and all beauties combined into one inconceivable beauty. Such is the Lord Jesus, and such is his love to his people, without anything of imperfection needing to be removed.

The love of Christ, too, blessed be his name!, is better than wine *because it will never, as wine will, turn sour*. In certain stages of development, and under certain influences, the sweet ferments, and vinegar is formed instead of wine. Oh, through what fermentations Christ's love might have passed if it had been capable of being acted upon by anything from without! Oh, how often, beloved, have we grieved him! We have been cold and chill towards him when we ought to have been like coals of fire. We have loved the things of this world, we have been unfaithful to our Best-beloved, we have suffered our hearts to wander to other lovers; yet never hath he been soured towards us, and never will he be. Many waters cannot quench his love, neither can the floods drown it. He is the same loving Saviour now as ever he was, and such he always will be, and he will bring us to the rest which remaineth for the people of God. Truly, in all these respects, because there are none of these imperfections in his love, it is better than wine.

Once more, Christ's love is better than wine *because it produces no ill effects*. Many are the mighty men who have fallen down slain by wine. Solomon says, 'Who hath woe? who hath sorrow? who hath contentions? who hath babbling? who hath wounds without cause? who hath redness of eyes? They that tarry long at the wine; they that go to seek mixed wine' (Proverbs 23:29-30). But who was ever slain by the love of Christ? Who was ever made wretched by this love? We have been inebriated with it, for the love of Christ sometimes produces a holy exhilaration that makes men say, 'Whether in the body, or out of the body, I cannot tell' (2 Corinthians 12:3). There is an elevation that lifts the soul above all earthly things, and bears the spirit up beyond where eagles soar, even into the clear atmosphere where God communes with men. There is all that sacred exhilaration about the love of Christ; but there are no evil effects arising from it. He that will may drink from this golden chalice, and he may drink as much as he will, for the more he drinks the stronger and the better shall he be.

Oh, may God grant to us, dear friends, to know the love of Christ, which passeth knowledge! I feel sure that, while I am preaching on such a theme as this, I must seem to some here present to be talking arrant nonsense, for they have never tasted of the love of Jesus; but those who have tasted of it will, perhaps, by my words, have many sweet experiences called to their minds, which will refresh their spirits, and set them longing to have new draughts of this all-precious love which infinitely transcends all the joys of earth.

This, then, is our first point: Christ's love is better than wine because of what it is not.

But, secondly, Christ's love is better than wine because of what it is. Let me remind you of some of the uses of wine in the East. Often, it was employed as a medicine, for *it had certain healing properties.* The good Samaritan, when he found the wounded man, poured into his wounds 'oil and wine' (Luke 10:34). But the love of Christ is better than wine; it may not heal the wounds of the flesh, but it does heal the wounds of the spirit. Do not some of you remember when your poor heart was gashed through and through by the dagger of Moses, when you felt the wounds caused by the law, the deadly wounds that could not be healed by human hands? Then, how sweetly did that wine of Christ's love come streaming into the gaping wounds! There were such healing drops as this, 'Come unto me, all ye that labour, and are heavy laden, and I will give you rest' (Matthew 11:28); or such as this, 'The blood of Jesus Christ his Son cleanseth us from all sin' (1 John 1:7); or this, 'All manner of sin and blasphemy shall be forgiven unto men' (Matthew 12:31); or this, 'He that believeth on him is not condemned' (John 3:18); or this, 'Look unto me, and be ye saved, all the ends of the earth: for I am God, and there is none else' (Isaiah 45:22). I cannot, perhaps, quote the text that dropped like wine and oil into your wounds; but I remember well the text that dropped into mine. The precious vial of wine that healed up all my wounds as in a moment, and made my heart whole, was that text I quoted last, 'Look unto me, and be ye saved, all the ends of the earth.' Wine made by man cannot be medicine to a broken heart, nor can it heal a wounded spirit; but the love of Jesus Christ can do this, and do it to perfection.

Wine, again, was often *associated by men with the giving of strength.* Now, whatever strength wine may give or may not give, certainly the love of Jesus gives strength, and strength mightier than the mightiest earthly force, for when the love of Jesus Christ is shed abroad in a man's heart, he can bear a heavy burden of sorrow. If he could have the load of Atlas piled upon his shoulders, and if he could have all the care of all the world pressing upon his heart, yet if he had the love of Christ in his soul, he would be able to bear the load. The love of Christ helps a man to fight the battles of life; it makes life, with all its cares and troubles, a happy one; it enables a man to do great exploits, and makes him strong for suffering, strong for self-sacrifice, and strong for service. It is wonderful, in reading the history of the saints, to notice what the love of Christ has fitted them to do; I might almost say that it has plucked up mountains, and cast them into the sea, for things impossible to other men have become easy enough to men on fire with the love of Christ. What the Church of Christ wants just now to strengthen her, is more love to her Lord, and her Lord's love more fully enjoyed in the souls of her members; there is no strengthening influence like it.

Wine was also frequently used *as the symbol of joy*; and certainly, in this respect, Christ's love is better than wine. Whatever joy there may be in the world (and it would be folly to deny that there is some sort of joy which even the basest of men know), yet the love of Christ is far superior to it. Human joy derived from earthly sources is a muddy, dirty pool, at which men would not drink did they know there was a stream sweeter, cooler, and far more refreshing. The love of Jesus brings a joy that is fit for angels, a joy that we shall have continued to us even in heaven itself, a joy which makes earth like to heaven; it is therefore far better than wine.

It is better than wine, once more, for *the sacred exhilaration which it gives*. I have already spoken of this; the love of Christ is the grandest stimulant of the renewed nature that can be known. It enables the fainting man to revive from his swooning; it causes the feeble man to leap up from his bed of languishing; and it makes the weary man strong again. Art thou weary, brother, and sick of life? Thou only wantest more of Christ's love shed abroad in thy heart. Art thou, dear brother, ready to faint through unbelief? Thou only wantest more of Christ's love, and all shall be well with thee. I would to God that we were all filled with it to the full, like those believers were on the day of Pentecost, of whom the mockers said that they were full of new wine. Peter truly said that they were not drunken, as men supposed; but that it was the Spirit of God and the love of Christ filling them with unusual power and unusual energy, and therefore men knew not what it was. God grant to us also this great power, and Christ shall have all the glory of it!

But now passing rapidly on, for our time is flying, the marginal reading of our text is in the plural: 'Thy *loves* are better than wine', and this teaches us that Christ's love may be spoken of in the plural, because it manifests itself in so many ways. I ask all renewed hearts that have been won to Jesus, the virgin souls that follow him whithersoever he goeth, to walk with me in imagination over the sacred tracks of the love of the Christ.

Think, beloved, of *Christ's covenant love*, the love he had to us before the world was. Christ is no new lover of his people's souls; but he loved them ere the day-star knew its place, or the planets began their mighty revolutions. Every soul whom Jesus loves now, he loved for ever and ever. What a wondrous love was that – infinite, unbounded, everlasting – which led him to enter into covenant with God that he would bear our sins and suffer our penalties, that he might redeem us from going down into the pit! Oh, the covenant love of Jesus! Some dear souls are afraid to believe this truth; let me persuade them to search the Scriptures till they find it, for, of all the doctrines of Holy Writ, I know of none more full of consolation to the heart when rightly received than the great foundation truths of Divine

Predestination and Personal Election. When we see that we were eternally accepted in the Beloved, and eternally loved by Christ, then shall we say, with holy gratitude, 'Such love as this is better than wines on the lees, well refined.'

Think next, beloved, of *Christ's forbearing love* – the love which looked upon us when we were born, and saw us full of sin, and yet loved us; the love which saw us when we went astray from the womb speaking lies; the love which heard us profanely speak, and wickedly think, and obstinately disobey, yet loved us all the while. Let the thought of it ravish your heart as you sing,

> He saw me ruin'd in the fall,
> Yet loved me, notwithstanding all;
> He saved me from my lost estate,
> His loving-kindness, oh, how great!

Thus were we the subjects of Christ's electing love and forbearing love.

Ay! but the sweetness to us was when we realised *Christ's personal love*, when at last we were brought to the foot of his cross, humbly confessing our sins. May I ask you who can do so to go back to that happy moment? There you lay at the cross-foot, broken in pieces, and you thought there was no hope for you; but you looked up to the crucified Christ, and those blessed wounds of his began to pour out a stream of precious blood upon you, and you saw that he was wounded for *your* transgressions, that he was bruised for *your* iniquities, and the chastisement of *your* peace was upon him, and that with his stripes *you* were healed. That very instant, your sins were all put away; you gave one look of faith to the bleeding Saviour, and every spot and speck and stain of your sins were all removed, and your guilt was for ever pardoned.

When you first felt *Christ's forgiving love*, I will not insult you by asking whether it was not better than wine. Oh, the unutterable joy, the indescribable bliss you felt when Jesus said to you, 'I have borne thy sins in my own body on the tree, I have carried the great load of thy transgressions, I have blotted them out like a cloud, and they are gone from thee for ever!' That was a love that was inconceivably precious; at the very recollection, our heart leaps within us, and our soul doth magnify the Lord.

Since that glad hour, we have been the subjects of *Christ's accepting love*, for we have been 'accepted in the Beloved' (Ephesians 1:6). We have also had *Christ's guiding love*, and *providing love*, and *instructing love*. His love in all manner of ways has come to us, and benefited and enriched us. And, beloved, we have had *sanctifying love*; we have been helped to fight this sin and that, and to overcome them by the blood of the Lamb. The Spirit of God has been given to us, so that we have been enabled to subdue this ruling passion and overcome that evil power. The Lord has also given us *sustaining love* under very sharp troubles. Some of us could tell many a story about the sweet upholding love of Christ – in poverty, or in bodily pain, or in deep depression of spirits, or under cruel slander, or reproach. His left hand has been under our head while his right hand has embraced us. We have almost courted suffering itself by reason of the richness of the consolation which suffering times have always brought with them. He has been such a precious, precious, precious Christ to us, that we do not know how to speak well enough of his dear name.

Then let us reflect with shame upon *Christ's enduring love* to us. Why, even since we have been converted, we have grieved him times without number! As I have already reminded you, we have often been false to him, we have not loved him with the love which he might well claim from us; yet Christ has never cast us away, but still to this moment doth he smile upon us, his own brethren whom he has bought with blood, and to each one he says, 'I have graven thee upon the palms of my hands. I have espoused thee unto myself for ever. I will never leave thee, nor forsake thee.' He uses the most kind and endearing terms towards us to show that his love will never die away. Glory be to his holy name for this! Is not his love better than wine?

There is one word I must not leave out, and that is *Christ's chastening love*. I know that many of you who belong to him have often smarted under his chastening hand, but Christ never smote you in anger yet. Whenever he has laid the cross on your back, it has been because he loved you so much that he could not keep it off. He never took away a joy without meaning thereby to increase your joy, and it was always done for your good. Perhaps we cannot at present say that the Lord's chastising love has always been sweet to us, but we shall say it one day, and I think I must say it now. I bless my dear Master for everything he has done to me, and I can never tell all that I owe to the anvil, and the hammer, and the fire, and the file. Blessed be his name, many of us can say, 'Before I was afflicted I went astray, but now have I kept thy Word' (Psalm 119:67). Therefore will we put in Christ's chastising love among the rest of his loves, and say of it, 'This love also is better than wine.' We would sooner have the chastisements of God than the pleasures of the world; we would rather have God's cup full of gall than the devil's cup full of the sweetest wine he ever made. We prefer to take God's left hand instead of the world's right hand, and would sooner walk with God in the dark than walk with the world in the light. Will not every Christian say that?

Beloved, there are other forms of Christ's love yet to be manifested to you. Do you not sometimes tremble at the thought of dying? Oh, you shall have – and you ought to think of it now – you shall have special revelations of *Christ's love in your dying moments*. Then shall you say, like the governor of the marriage feast at Cana, 'Thou hast kept the good wine until now' (John 2:10). I believe we have hardly any conception of what comfort the Lord pours into his people's souls in their dying moments. We do not need those comforts yet, and we could not bear them now; but they are laid up in store, and when we need them, they will be brought out, and then shall our spirits find that the Lord's promise is fulfilled, 'As thy days, so shall thy strength be' (Deuteronomy 33:25).

And then – but perhaps I had better be silent upon such a theme – when the veil is drawn, and the spirit has left the body, what will be the bliss of *Christ's love to the spirits gathered with him in glory*?

> Oh, for the bliss of flying,
> My risen Lord to meet!
> Oh, for the rest of lying
> For ever at his feet!
>
> Oh, for the hour of seeing
> My Saviour face to face!
> The hope of ever being
> In that sweet meeting-place!

Or, as Dr Watts puts it:

> Millions of years my wondering eyes
> Shall o'er thy beauties rove;
> And endless ages I'll adore
> The glories of thy love.

Then think of *the love of the day of our resurrection*, for Christ loves our bodies as well as our souls; and, arrayed in glory, these mortal bodies shall rise from the tomb. Oh, the bliss of being like our Lord, and being with him, when he comes in all the splendour of the Second Advent, sitting as assessors with him to judge the world, and to judge even the angels! And then to be in his triumphal procession, when he shall ascend to God, and deliver up the kingdom to the Father, and the Mediatorial system shall be ended, and God shall be all in all! And then to be for ever, for ever, for ever, 'for ever with the Lord', with no fear of the soul dying out, with no dread of the false doctrine of annihilation, like a grim spectre, ever crossing our blissful pathway! With a life coeval with the life of God, and an immortality divinely given, we shall outlast the sun; and when the moon grows pale, and wanes for ever, and this old earth and all that is therein shall be burned up, yet still shall we be for ever with him. Truly, his love is better than wine, it is the very essence of heaven, it is better than anything that we can conceive. God grant us foretastes of the loves of heaven in the present realisation of the love of Jesus, which is the selfsame love, and through which heaven itself shall come to us!

Now I must have just a few minutes for my last point, and that is, Christ's love in the singular – a theme which might well suffice for half a dozen sermons at the very least. Look at the text as it stands: 'Thy love is better than wine.'

Think, first, of *the love of Christ in the cluster*. That is where the wine is first. We talk of the grapes of Eshcol; but these are not worthy to be mentioned in comparison with the love of Jesus Christ as it is seen in old eternity, in the purpose of God, in the covenant of grace, and afterwards, in the promises of the Word, and in the various revelations of Christ in the types and symbols of the ceremonial law. There I see the love of Christ in the cluster. When I hear God threatening the serpent that the seed of the woman should bruise his head, and when, later on, I find many prophecies concerning him who is mighty to save, I see the wine in the cluster, the love of Christ that is really there, but not yet enjoyed. What delight it gives us even to look at the love of Christ in the cluster!

Next, look at *the love of Christ in the basket*, for the grapes must be gathered, and cast into the basket, before the wine can be made. I see Jesus Christ living here on earth amongst the sons of men – gathered, as it were, from the sacred vine, and like a cluster thrown into the basket. Oh, the love of Jesus Christ in the manger of Bethlehem, the love of Jesus in the workshop of Nazareth, the love of Jesus in his holy ministry, the love of Jesus in the temptation in the wilderness, the love of Jesus in his miracles, the love of Jesus in his communion with his disciples, the love of Jesus in being so poor that he had not where to lay his head, the love of Jesus in enduring such contradiction of sinners against himself! I cannot hope to enter into this great subject; I can only point it out to you, and pass on.

There is, first, Christ's love in the cluster; and next, there is Christ's love in the basket. Think of it and, as you think of it, say, 'It is better than wine.'

But oh! if your hearts have any tenderness towards him, think of *the love of Christ in the winepress*. See him there, when the cluster in the basket begins to be crushed. Oh, what a crushing was that under the foot of the treader of grapes when Christ sweat as it were great drops of blood, and how terribly did the great press come down again and again when he gave his back to the smiters, and his cheeks to them that plucked off the hair, and hid not his face from shame and spitting! But oh! how the red wine flowed from the winepress, what fountains there were of this precious sweetness, when Jesus was nailed to the cross, suffering in body, depressed in spirit, and forsaken of his God! 'Eloi, Eloi, lama sabachthani?' These are the sounds that issue from the winepress, and how terrible and yet how sweet they are! Stand there, and believe that all your sins were borne by him, and that he suffered what you ought to have suffered, and as your Substitute was crushed for you.

> He bore, that you might never bear,
> His Father's righteous ire.

Yes, beloved, Christ's love in the winepress is better than wine.

Now I want you to think of *the love of Christ in the flagon*, where his precious love is stored up for his people; the love of his promises, given to you; the love of his providence, for he rules for you; the love of his intercession, for he pleads for you; the love of his representation, for he stands at the right hand of the Father as the Representative of his people; the love of his union with his people, for you are one with him, he is the Head, and you are the members of his body; the love of all that he is, and all that he was, and all that he ever shall be, for in every capacity and under all circumstances he loves you, and will love you without end. Think of his rich love, his abundant love towards his people; I call it love in the flagon, this love of his to all the saints which he has stored up for them.

And then, beloved, not only think of but enjoy *the love of Christ in the cup*, by which I mean his love to *you*. I always feel, when I get to this topic, as if I would rather sit down, and ask you to think it over, than try to talk to you about it; this theme seems to silence me. I think, like the poet,

> Come, then, expressive silence, muse his praise.

Love to *me*! Dear child of God, do think of it in this way; let me speak for you. 'He loves *me*! He, a King, loves me! A King? The King of kings, HE loves *me*! God, very God of very God, loves me!' Strange conjunction this between the Infinite and a worm! We have heard and read romantic stories of the loves of emperors to poor village maidens, but what of these? Worms were never raised so high above their meaner fellow-worms as the Lord Jesus is above us. If an angel loved an emmet, there would be no such difference as when Jehovah-Jesus loves us. Yet there is no fact beneath heaven, or in heaven, that is so indisputable as this fact, that he loves us if we are his believing people. For this we have the declaration of inspiration; nay, brethren, we have more even than that to confirm it beyond all question, for we have his own blood, in order that no believer might ever doubt its authenticity. 'Herein is love.' 'Behold what manner of love' there is in the cross! What wondrous love is there! Oh! then, let us have Christ's love in the cup, the love that we may daily drink, the love that we may personally drink just now at this moment, the love which shall be all our own, as if there were no others in the world, and yet a love in which ten thousand times ten thousand have an equal share with ourselves.

God bless you, dear friends, and give you to drink of this wine! And if any here know not the love of Jesus Christ, I pray the Lord to bring them to know it. May he renew their heart, and give them faith in him, for whosoever believeth that Jesus is the Christ is born of God. 'He that believeth and is baptised shall be saved' (Mark 16:16). May the Lord confirm this word by his Spirit, for our Lord Jesus Christ's sake! Amen.

2

REJOICING AND REMEMBERING

'We will be glad and rejoice in thee,
we will remember thy love more than wine'
(Song of Solomon 1:4)

It is a very blessed habit of saints who have grown in grace to enter into actual conversation with the Well-beloved. Our text is not so much speaking *of* him as speaking *to* him: 'We will be glad and rejoice in thee, we will remember thy love more than wine.' Of course, in prayer and in praise, we speak to God; but I suggest that we should seek to have much more of intense and familiar intercourse with the Lord Jesus Christ than the most of us at present enjoy. I find it good sometimes in prayer to say nothing, but to sit or kneel quite still, and to look up to my Lord in adoring silence; and then sometimes to talk to him, not asking anything of him, but just speaking familiarly with Jesus, realising him to be present, and waiting to hear him speak until some precious word of his from Scripture comes into my soul as with living accents newly-spoken by those dear lips which are as lilies dropping sweet-smelling myrrh. The French have a word which they use concerning that conversation which is common among those who love one another, or are on terms of intimate friendship; they call it *tutoyage*, for they say 'thee' and 'thou' to one another, instead of the more formal language used towards strangers. I like that form of expression that is used in our text, and delight to meet with souls that are brought into so rapt a state of fellowship with Christ that they can speak to him in this familiar fashion, 'We will be glad and rejoice in thee, we will remember thy love more than wine.'

If you, dear friends, have not lately conversed with Jesus, do so now in the quietude of your own spirit. Think that his shadow is over you; do not let it be mere imagination, but let it be what is better far than that, a true realising faith, for if he be present where two or three are met together in his name, rest assured that he is not absent where this great assembly of his people has come together to commemorate his passion and his death. Thou art here, blessed Master; we are sure that thou art, and we worship thee, and speak with thee, as really as if we could see thee with that vesture on, woven from the top throughout, as truly as if we saw thee now lifting thy beloved pierced hand, and laying it upon us; and we would say to thee from the bottom of our hearts, 'We will rejoice and be glad in thee, we will remember thy love more than wine.' This text is not so much for me to explain, dear friends, as for you to enjoy. Forget all about the preacher, but take the text, and part it among yourselves; extract as much as you can of its spiritual nourishment, and feed upon it.

As you do so, you will notice, first, that we have here A DOUBLE RESOLVE: 'We will be glad and rejoice in thee, we will remember thy love more than wine.'

I may say of that resolve that it is, first, *a necessary resolve*, for it is not according to human nature to rejoice in Christ, it is not according to the tendency of our poor fallen state to remember his love. There must be an act of the will with regard to this resolve; let us will it now: 'We *will* be glad and rejoice in thee, we *will* remember thy love more than wine.' There are so many things that try to come in between our souls and our Saviour, so many sorrows that would prevent our rejoicing in him, that we must be resolved to be glad in him, whatever our sorrows may be. Down with you, sorrows! Down with you! We have said unto the Lord that we will be glad and rejoice in him, and we mean to prove our words to be true. Then there are so many troublous thoughts that come flying in to mar our full fellowship with our Lord. However tightly windows may be closed and doors may be shut, these thoughts will find an entrance, and we get remembering the sick child at home, or some care that has afflicted us during the week. Oh, but, Lord, we will not remember these things now! We say to thee from our hearts, 'We *will* – we *will* – we *will* remember thy love.' Away with thee, care, sorrow, grief, away with thee! Come to me, O Holy Spirit, and help me now to have a happy time, to be glad and rejoice in my Lord – and to have a holy time, to remember his love, and to remember nought beside! You must will it most intensely, dear friends, or it will not come to pass. It is not sufficient merely to walk into a place of worship, and put ourselves into the posture of devotion, and then to imagine that, doing whatever is proper to the place and the hour, we shall have fellowship with Jesus. Oh, no, beloved; oh, no! We must worship him in spirit and in truth, not in fiction and in sham; not mechanically, as though we could have true fellowship with him without earnest and intense desire. No, there must be these two utterances of our holy resolve, 'We will be glad and rejoice in thee, we will remember thy love more than wine.'

And truly, dear friends, as this resolve is necessary, it is also *a right and proper resolve*. Should we not be glad and rejoice in Christ?

> Why should the children of a King
> Go mourning all their days?

Why should the children of the bride-chamber fast while the Bridegroom is with them? With such a Husband as we have in Christ, should not the spouse rejoice in him? Would it be becoming for a heart that is married to Christ to be in any other condition than that of rejoicing in him? I know you have many things in which you cannot rejoice; well, let them go. But you can rejoice in him – in his person, in his work, in his offices, in his relationships, in his power, in his glory, in his first advent, in his second advent. Surely, these are not things that can be thought of without delightful emotion; it is most proper that we should be glad and rejoice in our Lord. There ought to be a reduplication of our joy; we should joy in him and then rejoice in him, we should 'be glad and rejoice' in him.

It is most proper that we should be glad in the Lord, and what can be more proper than that we should remember him? What a shame it is that we ever forget him! His name should be so deeply engraven on our hearts that we cannot forget him. Let us remember his love, for surely, if there is anything that we ought ever to remember, it is that undying love which is our choicest portion on earth, and which will be the main constituent of our highest bliss in heaven. Then, by the help of God's Spirit, let us make this resolve at this moment. Whatever we may do when we get out of this building, at any rate for the next half-hour, let us resolve to stand to this double declaration, 'We will rejoice, and we will remember.'

Do you not think also that this resolution, if we carry it out, will be *very helpful to ourselves*? What a help it is to a Christian man to be glad in the Lord! I know what it is to be depressed; I do not suppose there is any person in this place who knows what it is to be cast down so low as I sometimes am. Then I feel that there is no help for me, and no hope of my living, and working, except I can get out of that sad condition, and get to be glad in the Lord; and I cry, 'My heart, my heart, what art thou at? Why art thou cast down, O my soul? And why art thou disquieted within me? Hope in God: for I shall yet praise him, who is the health of my countenance, and my God.' There is no way of getting right out of the Styrian bog of the Slough of Despond like rejoicing in the Lord. If you try to rejoice in yourself, you will have a poor reason for joy; but if you rejoice and be glad in the Lord, you have the real, abiding, unchanging source of joy; for he who rejoices in Christ rejoices in him who is 'the same yesterday, and today, and for ever'; and he may always rejoice in him. Come, then, and for your own good hang up the sackbut, and take down the psaltery; put away the ashes. What if men do call this season 'Lent'? We will keep no Lent tonight; this is our Eastertide, our Lord has risen from the dead, and he is among us, and we will rejoice in him. Come, beloved, surely it is time that we did, for a while at least, forget our pain and griefs, and all the worries of this weary world; and for one, I must, I will, be glad and rejoice in my Lord, and I hope many of you will join with me in the happy occupation, which will be helpful to yourselves.

Certainly, it will also be *for the good of others*. I think that believers do much harm if they allow their depressions of spirit to be too conspicuous. There is another meaning besides the first one to that text, 'Thou, when thou fastest, anoint thine head, and wash thy face; that thou appear not unto men to fast' (Matthew 6:17-18). But if you can get right out of your sorrow, and can actually rejoice in the Lord, and if you can so remember him as to be glad and rejoice in him, you will allure many to the fair ways of Christ, which else will be evil spoken of if you go mourning all your days. Come, ye weak ones, come and feast on bread that can make you strong. Come, ye whose eyes are red with weeping, take a handkerchief that shall dry your tears, and make your eyes as bright as diamonds. Remember Christ, and be glad and rejoice in him. Angels round the throne can have no higher joy than this; and they cannot enter so fully into it as you can, for he has not loved even them as he has loved you.

> Never did angels taste above,
> Redeeming grace and dying love.

This, then, is what I earnestly commend to you, this double resolve, that we should all truly say to our Lord, 'We will be glad and rejoice in thee, we will remember thy love more than wine.' But, dear friends, *we cannot carry out that resolve without the help of the Holy Spirit*. Therefore, let us breathe it unto the Lord in prayer; and, as we tell him what we mean to do, let us each one add, 'Draw me, O Lord; then I will run after thee. Help me to come to thee; manifest thyself to me, and then I will be glad and rejoice in thee.'

Now I want to go a step further, and say that I think the resolve of the text is A SUITABLE RESOLVE FOR THIS OCCASION: 'We will be glad and rejoice in thee, we will remember thy love more than wine.'

We are most of us coming to the communion table, to eat of the bread and to drink of the cup in remembrance of our Master's dying love. Surely, now is the hour, if ever in our lives, to be glad and rejoice in him, and to remember him, for the object of this supper is *to commemorate his dying love*. It is idle, and worse than idle, to come to Christ's table if you do not remember him; what good can it do you? The use that it is to the spectator is that you show Christ's death 'till he come'; but if there be not in the spectator any thought of that death, of what use is the sight of the table with its sacred vessels? And if you yourself do not think of Christ, of what avail to you are the emblems of a forgotten or an unknown Lord? No, we are to commemorate his death; so let us in our hearts rejoice in him, and remember him. Well did we sing just now:

> Jesus, when faith with fixed eyes,
> Beholds thy wondrous sacrifice,
> Love rises to an ardent flame,
> And we all other hope disclaim.
>
> Hence, O my soul, a balsam flows
> To heal thy wounds, and cure thy woes;
> Immortal joys come streaming down,
> Joys, like his griefs, immense, unknown.

Recollect, next, that in coming to this communion table, we also *commemorate the results of Christ's death*. One result of our Lord's death is that he gives food to his people; his body broken has become bread for our souls, yea, it is meat indeed. His blood, which was shed for many for the remission of sins, has become drink indeed. By his death, Christ has given us life; and by the completion of his great redeeming work, and by his ever-living intercession, he has given us bread and wine by which that life may be sustained. He has finished it all, and he has gone into the glory to secure the results of his finished work. Sitting around his table, we are reminded of all this; the bread is ready, the cup is filled. We have nothing to do to prepare the feast; all we have to do now is to come and partake of it, and feed even to the full upon heavenly food. So, dear friends, if we come to this table in a right spirit, we must rejoice in our Lord, and we must remember his love.

I think also that there is this further reason why we should rejoice in our Lord, and remember his love, because at this table *the commemoration is made by our Lord to be a feast*. They miss the meaning of the Lord's supper who kneel around what they call an 'altar'. The very point of the supper is that it should be taken while sitting around a table. It is not meant to be an adoration, it is a communion; we come here that we may have fellowship with him who sat at the table with his disciples, and made them to be his companions at his last supper. Joy is becoming at a royal feast. What! will ye come to the King's table with sorrowful countenances? Will ye come sadly to see what he has brought you? Now that he has prepared the bread and wine as a feast for your souls, will you come here hanging your heads like bulrushes? No, but let this be your resolution, 'We will be glad and rejoice in thee, we will remember thy love more than wine.' Do kings make feasts, do they lift high the flowing bowl, are there shouts of joy and exultation at their banquets; and shall it be that this world's poor vine, whose juice is often to men like the wine of Gomorrah, shall bring even the semblance of joy superior to ours when we drink of the wine that comes from the Vine of God, and the clusters that Christ hath trodden in the winepress? Nay; higher far be your joy than ever came to them that have made merry at earthly feasts, more delightful, more intense, more real, more true be your hallowed ecstasies than anything that wine or wealth can ever bring. 'We will be glad and rejoice in thee, we will remember thy love more than wine.' O God, help us to carry out this resolution! It seems to me to be specially right, and proper, and fit, when we come to this high festival of the Church of God, that we should rejoice in the Lord, and remember his love.

Let us also recollect that, when we come to the table of our Lord, *we commemorate a very happy union*. Our text speaks in the plural: '*We* will be glad and rejoice in thee, *we* will remember thy love more than wine.' I do not know how you feel, brethren and sisters, but I should not like to go to heaven alone. If nobody else will go on pilgrimage, Christian must set out by himself, and march alone towards the Celestial City until he finds a suitable fellow-pilgrim; but I like best to go with Christiana, and Mercy, and the children, and all the company together. Though I should enjoy fellowships with my Lord if I were his only loved one, yet it greatly increases my joy as I look at the faces of many of you whom I have known a score of years, and with whom I have lived in such happy union year after year. Many of you who were once 'in the gall of bitterness and in the bond of iniquity' have been plucked, like brands out of the burning, through the preaching of the gospel in this pulpit; and it seems such a happy thing for us to be communing together around the table of our Lord.

Some of you, my dear venerable brothers and sisters, will soon be home; come, we will be glad and rejoice in our Lord, will we not? Before you quite go away from us, join us in another holy song; give us another of your patient, quiet, happy, restful looks. One dear sister went home this morning, at twelve o'clock, while we were worshipping here. I am sure that her spirit is now rejoicing before the throne, and some of you will be going soon; but till you do go, we will rejoice and be glad together, will we not? We will take the cup of blessing still at the Lord's table, whatever our infirmities and sorrows may be; and we will remember him until we drink the new wine in our Father's kingdom above.

And you men and women in the very midst of the battle of life, with all your trials and struggles, we will stand shoulder to shoulder, will we not? We are one in Christ, and there is between us a bond of union that never can be snapped; it binds us for time and for eternity. We came to this communion table to eat and to drink, not each one for himself only, but each one in fellowship with all the rest; and this ought to make us glad. If I am not glad about myself, I will be glad to think that you are glad. If I have a heavy burden to carry, I will be glad that you have not; and if you have a burden, and I have not, try to be glad that I have not one; or, if you have one, and I have another, let us rejoice that we both have the same God to help us to carry them, and let us believe that, as our days, so shall our strength be.

What a joy it adds to this festival when we see the young folk coming among us, the sons and daughters of God's people being brought into the church! Do you not notice how dear Mr William Olney, whenever he prays for a blessing upon our ministry, always breaks out into thanksgiving to God that all his family have been brought to Christ? There are many others of us who can praise the Lord for the same favour, and it is a great joy to us. Yes, Lord, we will remember thy love – husband and wife, sons and daughters, and some of us can say grandchildren, too – we will all come clustering around thy table, and together we will remember thy sweet love to our fathers, and to ourselves, and to our children. We cannot help remembering it, and rejoicing and being glad in it.

I must give you just one more thought upon this point. It does not become us to gather at this communion table with a heavy heart when we recollect that *it is not only a commemoration, but an anticipation*. We are to do this 'till he come'. Did I not try this morning to sound the trumpet of his coming? It would not have startled me if he had come while we were assembled, and I was speaking of 'the glorious appearing of the great God and our Saviour Jesus Christ' (Titus 2:13). Nor should it startle any of you, if, in the dead of this very night, while you are in your beds, you should hear the cry, 'Behold, the Bridegroom cometh' (Matthew 25:6), for he may come at any moment, and he will come 'in such an hour as ye think not' (Matthew 25:44). Let us leap up at the remembrance of this gladsome hope. We are coming to the table, keeping up the memorial of our Lord's first appearing in the fond hope and sure belief of that second appearing when the righteous shall shine forth as the sun in the kingdom of their Father. Wherefore, let us keep the feast with high hope. With joy-notes sound aloud the silver trumpet of the great jubilee; and as ye come to the table, let your hearts be glad in the Lord, whose love you specially remember at this hallowed festival.

I will close in a very few minutes, but I must dwell for a brief space upon what I meant to make my third point concerning this double resolve – LET US CARRY IT OUT. That ought always to be the practical conclusion to every sermon – let us carry it out. We have said to our Lord in the language of the text, 'We will be glad and rejoice in thee, we will remember thy love more than wine'; very well, now let us carry out this resolve.

'We will remember thy love.' Dear Saviour, what we have to remember is *thy love* – thy love in old eternity, or ever the earth was, thy prescient love, which

Saw us ruin'd in the fall,
Yet loved us notwithstanding all.

We remember the love of thine espousals when thou didst espouse thy people unto thyself, and didst resolve that, whatever might be the lot of thine elect, thou wouldst share it with them. The Lord Jesus made up his mind that he would be one with his Church; for this purpose he left his Father that he might be one with his bride. I shall get into great deeps if I go much further in speaking about Christ's love. 'We will remember thy love' – that love which, having once begun, has never wavered, never diminished, never stopped.

Love, so vast that nought can bound;
Love, too deep for thought to sound;
Love, which made the Lord of all
Drink the wormwood and the gall.

Love, which led him to the cross,
Bearing there unutter'd loss;
Love, which brought him to the gloom
Of the cold and darksome tomb.

Love, which will not let him rest
Till his chosen all are blest;
Till they all for whom he died
Live rejoicing by his side.

We remember the love which Jesus bore in his heart right up into the glory at the right hand of the Father; that love which is still as great as when he hung on Calvary to redeem us unto himself.

The wonderful part of all this to me is that it should be the love of such an one as Christ is. That ever so divine a person should set his love on us, is very wonderful. I can understand my mother's love, I can understand my child's love, I can understand my wife's love; but I cannot understand Christ's love. Oh, brothers, we are nothings, we are nobodies; yet this glorious Everybody, this All in All, did actually set his love upon us!

Suppose that all the holy angels had loved us, and that all God's redeemed had loved us; all put together, it would be only so many grains of dust that would not turn the scale, but Christ's love is a mountain, nay, more than all the mountains in the universe. I know of nothing to be compared with it.

That is the first way in which we are to carry out this double resolve, we are to remember and to rejoice in Christ's love.

Next, let each one of us say to Christ, 'I will remember thy love *to me.*' Brothers and sisters, I can believe in Christ's loving you; but there are times when it seems a great mystery that he should ever have loved me. I can truly say that, often, I have felt that if I might sit at the feet of the poorest, meanest, least of God's servants, and serve them, I would count it a heaven to do it if I did but feel sure of Christ's love to my own soul. I see so many beauties in my brethren and my sisters that I can admire the grace of God in them; but often I do see and feel so many imperfections in myself that I can only wonder that ever Christ should have loved me. I suppose that each of you feels the same; I am sure that you do if you are in a right state of heart, for, truth to tell, there is no beauty in any of us that he should desire us, and there is no excellence in any of us that could have made it worth his while to die for us. 'God commendeth his love toward us, in that, while we were yet sinners, Christ died for us' (Romans 5:8). 'When we were yet without strength, in due time Christ died for the ungodly' (Romans 5:6), and died for us as ungodly. Come, then, will you not be glad and rejoice that ever Christ should have loved you? Will you not be glad and rejoice, and yet wonder all the while, that ever it should have been possible for him to draw you 'with cords of a man, with bands of love', and bring you into living, loving, everlasting union with himself?

Still, even that is not all. The text does not merely speak about Christ's love, and Christ's love to me, but it talks about *Christ himself.* 'We will be glad and rejoice in *thee*' – not only in his love, but in himself. Do try, dear friends, to let your thoughts dwell upon Christ, his complex person, God and man, and all the wonders which lie wrapped up in Immanuel, God with us. Thy work, Lord, is fair; but the hand that wrought the work is fairer still. All thy designs of love are full of splendour, but what shall we say of the mind that first gave creation to those designs? The glance, the look of love which thou hast given me, is blessed; but oh, those eyes of thine, those eyes which are brighter than the stars of the morning! The Lord Jesus is better than everything that comes from him; his gifts are infinitely precious, then what must he himself be? Come, then, beloved, and let us be glad and rejoice in him, and let us remember his love more than wine.

The text says, 'we will remember', but some of you cannot remember because you do not know. A man cannot remember what he has never heard of, or seen, or known. But, brothers and sisters, *let us remember what we do know of Christ's love*. I remember the first day I ever tasted of his love consciously to myself. Ah! but I look back, and think of the rivers of love that came streaming down to me when I did not even know that I was receiving them; and I remember that many days have passed since first I could give back the glance of love in return for his love to me; but oh, what his love to me since then has been! His love in sickness, in sorrow, in labour, in backsliding, in prayer, in tears, in unbelief, in faith, in varyings and changings as many as the changes of the moon! Yet, his love has always been the same. What a book some of you could write concerning Christ's love to you if you had but a facile pen! What a story some of you could tell of Christ's love if some guest could be detained while you told out the wondrous story! I sometimes think within myself, that if all the interesting things that are written in all the works of fiction could be put together, I could surpass them all in the literal simple facts of a common life like mine; and I believe that many of God's people here could say the same. A Christian's life is full of interest; last Thursday night, I called the life of a Christian a cluster of Koh-i-noors threaded on a string of divine faithfulness, and I am sure that it is so.

> Wonders of grace to God belong,
> Repeat his mercies in your song.

Repeat his mercies as you remember them, and be glad and rejoice in him even more than in the mercies that come from him.

In conclusion, I would say that I think the people of God, in gathering to the communion table, should try to *be glad and rejoice in their Lord, and in nobody else*, and to *remember him, and nothing else*. Let all be a blank except what Christ has written on your memory, let all be a blank except where that dear face appears:

> The head that once was crown'd with thorns

but –

> Is crown'd with glory now.

Think only of him. Put the glass to your eye, and shut out all the rest of the landscape, and let that glass take nothing within its circle but just the face of the Well-beloved which we soon hope to see without a cloud between.

God bless you, dear friends! I wish that all of you understood this truth of which I have been speaking. Some of you do not; may the Lord lead you to do so, for there is no life like that which is spent at Jesu's feet, and no joy like that which comes from our dear Lord. I wish you knew it. Believe on him, and you shall know it, and shall know it at once. Amen.

3

THE MEMORY OF CHRIST'S LOVE

'We will remember thy love more than wine: the upright love thee' (Song of Solomon 1:4)

I do not think I can preach tonight; I feel so weary, and worn, and ill. Still, I can talk to you a little concerning the great love of Christ. If I were dying, I think I could speak upon that theme; and oh, when we rise again, how we shall talk for ever and ever about Christ's love! This will be our endless theme throughout the eternal ages – His great love wherewith he loved us, even when we were dead in sins.

I have taken for a text the last two sentences in the Song of Solomon, the first chapter, and the fourth verse: 'We will remember thy love more than wine: the upright love thee.'

This is a night for remembering Christ's love. The communion-table spread before us, the sacred feast to which we are about to come, is meant to recall to our minds our Saviour's words: 'This do in remembrance of me. ... This do ye, as oft as ye drink it, in remembrance of me.' But, while we remember Christ, the central thought in our minds shall be that of which Paul wrote, 'who loved me, and gave himself for me'. We will, above all things else tonight, remember his love. Have any of you been forgetting it? Is it long since you had an hour's real enjoyment in meditating upon the love of Christ? Then, beloved, come tonight, and renew your vows; begin again your fellowship; and make this firm resolve, 'We will remember our Lord; we will remember his love tonight!' May the Holy Spirit, who brings everything to remembrance whatsoever Christ has said to us, help us now to remember him! For him to remember us when he comes to his kingdom, will be our heaven. For us to remember him, though he has gone away to his kingdom, shall be a little heaven to us tonight.

As I am able, I will talk with you briefly, first, upon *the preparations for the holy memory* mentioned in our text. We shall find them in the verse in which the text is embedded: 'Draw me, we will run after thee: the king hath brought me into his chambers: we will be glad and rejoice in thee.' When we have considered the preparations for the holy memory here referred to, I will speak upon *the divine subject of this holy memory*: 'We will remember thy love more than wine.' Then, thirdly, we will meditate upon *the divine product of this holy memory*: 'The upright love thee', love thee because they remember thy love.

First, then, dear friends, as I may be helped by the Holy Spirit, I would remind you of THE PREPARATIONS FOR THIS HOLY MEMORY. Here they are.

The first word is, '*Draw me*'. Lord, I would fain come at thee; but, like Mephibosheth, I am lame in both my feet. I would fain fly to thee; but my wings are broken; if, indeed, I ever had any. I cannot come to thee. I lie inert, and dead, and powerless. So the first preparation is, 'Draw me.' It is a sweet, gracious, efficacious exercise of divine power that I need and entreat. I say not, 'Drive me'; but, 'Lord, draw me.' I say not, 'Throw me there, or force me yonder'; but, 'Lord, draw me. Whilst thou dost draw, I shall have liberty left to run: draw me, we will run after thee.'

We do not need to be born again; we who are believers in Christ have had that miracle wrought upon us already. We are not asking now for pardon and justification; as believers in Christ, we have these priceless boons already. What we want is the gentle influence of the Holy Spirt to attract us nearer to Christ; so each one cries to the Lord, 'Draw me.' We are not dead; we are quickened and made alive. Our very pain and anguish, because we are not able to come to Christ as we would, prove that we are alive. I commend this prayer to you, 'Lord, draw me; draw me.' It is the work of Christ to draw: 'I, if I be lifted up from the earth, will draw all men unto me.' It is the work of the Father: 'No man can come to me,' said Christ, 'except the Father which hath sent me draw him.' It is the work of the Spirit of God to draw a soul towards Christ. I pray this for myself, and I trust that you will pray with me, 'Come, Sacred Spirit, and draw us nearer to Christ; enliven our hopes; incline our hearts; arouse our desires; and then help us to yield our whole being to thy gracious influences!'

> If thou hast drawn a thousand times,
> Oh, draw me, Lord, again!

That, then, is the first preparation for the holy memory mentioned in our text – divine drawing: 'Draw me.'

Notice, next, that this verse says, 'Draw me, *we will run after thee*.' I like the change in the pronouns, as though I should pray tonight, 'Lord, draw me; I am the most weighted, the heaviest of all thy children in this congregation; but draw me, we will run after thee. All my brothers and sisters will run at once if thou dost draw me. If thou dost draw the most burdened one towards thyself, all the rest will come to thee at a rapid rate.' Do you not feel, my dear brother or sister, as if you could use this expression: 'Lord, if thou wilt draw me, all my fellow-members will be running with me; yet they will not outstrip me in their eagerness to reach thee, for we will together run after thee. Do, therefore, draw me, my gracious Lord'?

If we would be fully prepared to remember Christ, we must get into this running pace: 'Draw me: we will run after thee.' Be quick, my soul, be quick, about heavenly things! Creep, if thou wilt, about thy worldly business; but run after thy Lord. Oh, that we might every one attain the running pace tonight! Oh, that we might speed along towards our Lord with that strong, impetuous desire which will not let us rest till we are close to him: 'Draw me, we will run after thee.'

Divine drawing is the first preparation for the holy memory, and next comes speedy running.

Now, in the further preparation, if you read the verse through, you will find that an answer comes to the prayer directly it is uttered: *The king hath brought me into his chambers*. 'What I asked for, I have obtained at once; and I have received more than I asked for. I prayed, "Draw me", and he hath carried me bodily: "The king hath brought me into his chambers." I did but pray that I might come a little nearer to my Lord; but he has brought me into his secret places, into his withdrawing rooms. He has brought me where he brings his bride. He has brought me where he receives his courtiers. The King has brought me into his chambers; and now I see how truly royal he is. The King has done it. *The* King, not *a* king; but that King who is King of all kings, the most royal of all monarchs, "the Prince of the kings of the earth", even my Lord Jesus, hath brought me into his chambers.'

How quickly this was done! I want you to believe, beloved, that it could be done just as quickly in your case. Pray, 'Lord, draw me. I feel as if I were coming to the communion-table quite unfit to come.' Is that what you say? Then pray, 'Draw me', and in a moment, before the prayer is uttered, you shall find yourself not only drawn, but actually brought into the secret place of fellowship: 'The king hath brought me into his chambers.' 'Or ever I was aware, my soul made me like the chariots of Ammi-nadib.'

I know, and some of you know, unhappily, what it is to feel very cold and lifeless; but I also know, and some of you know, what it is to become full of life, full of love, full of joy, full of heavenly rapture, in a single moment. You who could only creep begin to run. You who could only sigh begin to sing. I want it to be so with every one of you, dearly beloved, tonight. And you, who think you are forgotten, shall be remembered tonight, at any rate. You who have almost forgotten what a real, hallowed time of communion means, may learn it over again tonight, as you cry, 'Draw me, we will run after thee: the king hath brought me into his chambers.'

Thus we have had three preparations for the holy memory mentioned in our text: drawing, running, and bringing.

There is only one more preparation for remembering Christ, and that is to feel gladness and joy in him: *We will be glad and rejoice in thee*. Come, take these ashes from thy head, thou that art sighing by reason of affliction! Come, unbind that sackcloth and throw it aside, thou that hast lost fellowship with God, and art consequently in the dark! Christ is yours if you believe in him. He has given himself to you, and he loves you. Rejoice in that blessed fact. Remember who he is, and what he is; very God of very God, yet perfect man, God in human nature, Immanuel, God with us, glorified now in the highest heavens, though once, for our sakes, he sank down into the very depths of death and the grave. Bless his dear name. Be glad and rejoice in him.

Now, I pray you, let your mouth be filled with laughter, your tongue with singing, and your heart with holy ecstasy, as you think of who your Well-beloved is, how great he is, and what greatness he puts upon you by virtue of his union with you. We cannot very well remember Christ as we should while we carry about with us a heavy heart. Come, sad spirit, be glad in the Lord! 'Rejoice in the Lord alway: and again I say, Rejoice.' If ever a human soul had reason to rejoice, it must be the soul that believes in Christ. If ever there were any of the sons of Adam who had cause to be glad, and to clap their hands with holy mirth, it is those who have found Christ to be their salvation, and their all in all.

These, then, are the preparations for the holy memory of which our text speaks. If they be well made, you will have no difficulty in remembering Christ's love tonight.

So now, in the second place, as I may be strengthened, I would like to speak about THE DIVINE SUBJECT OF THIS HOLY MEMORY: 'We will remember *thy love*'.

First, we will remember *the fact of Christ's love*. What a wonderful thing it is that the Son of God should love us! I do not wonder so much that he should have any love for you; but I am lost in wonder at the fact that he has any love for me, even for me. Does not each believer feel that the wonder of wonders must ever be that the Lord Jesus Christ loves him? He was in glory, wanting nothing. He was in his Father's bosom, enjoying ineffable delight. If he wanted to cast his eyes of love on any of his creatures, there were myriads of bright spirits before the throne. But, no, he must look down, down, down, to earth's dunghills, and find out us who were utterly unworthy of his regard. Then he might have pitied us, and left us in our lost estate; but it could not be so with one who has such a heart as our dear Saviour has; he must needs love us. What it is for God to love, God only knows. We faintly guess, by the love that burns in our bosom towards the objects of our affection, what the love of God must be. The love of God must be a mighty passion. I use the word because I know no better; I am conscious that it is not the right one, for human language is too feeble to describe divine love.

Stronger his love than death or hell;
Its riches are unsearchable:
The first-born sons of light
Desire in vain its depths to see;
They cannot reach the mystery,
The length, and breadth, and height.

Oh, the love of Christ! It must ever be the wonder of wonders that Jesus Christ, the darling of the heavens, should have set the eyes of his affection upon men of mortal mould, on sinful men, on me! That, to me, is the climax.

We will remember the fact of Christ's love. But we will remember, also, *the character of Christ's love*. What a love it was! He loved us before the foundation of the world. With the telescope of his prescience, he foresaw our existence, and he loved us when we had no being. Then he struck hands with the great Father, and entered into covenant on our behalf, and engaged that he would stand sponsor for us, and redeem us from the ruin of our sin. Oh, the love, the love, the everlasting love of Christ! He has never left off loving us from the very first. All through the ages before the world was, and through the centuries in which the world has existed, he has loved his chosen every moment, and loved them to the full. Can you drink in the sweetness of that thought? Oh, I pray you, remember the antiquity and the constancy of the love of Christ to his people! 'We will remember thy love.'

It was unmerited love, which had no reason in us for it to light upon.

What was there in you that could merit esteem,
Or give the Creator delight?
''Twas even so, Father,' you ever must sing,
'Because it seem'd good in thy sight.'

He loved us because he would love us. It was the sovereignty of his love that made him love those whom he chose to love. He loved them freely, without anything in them, or that would ever be done by them, to deserve his love. But he loved fully as well as freely; he loved intensely, divinely, immeasurably. Thou knowest thy love to thy child; it is but a feeble spark compared to the great sun of Christ's love to thee. Thou knowest thy love to thy husband; it is a tiny rill compared with the ocean of Christ's love to his people. Beloved, turn over the wondrous qualities of the love of Christ to you, and say, as you sit at the communion-table tonight, 'We will remember thy love, for we cannot forget it. We will remember thy love, for the joyous theme forces itself upon us. We will remember thy love more than wine.'

We will also remember *the deeds of Christ's love*. It is a grand story; I cannot stay to tell it to you tonight. You know how, in the fulness of time, the Son of God came out of the glory, and alighted on a stall where the horned oxen fed. He who had made all worlds was hanging at a woman's breast, for he was made flesh that he might save us from our sins. 'Herein is love!'

See him living a laborious life, going about doing good, despised, maligned, yet ever ready to give still greater grace and mercy to the unworthy. You know his life, the wondrous life of Christ. 'Herein is love.'

At last, he gave himself up in agony, even to a bloody sweat. He gave his back to the smiters, and his cheeks to them that plucked off the hair; he hid not his face from shame and spitting. And then he gave himself, his hands to the nails, his feet to the cross and the cruel iron, his side to the lance, his body to the tomb, his soul to depart to his Father. 'Herein is love.'

I wish I could preach upon this theme as it deserves to be proclaimed. Oh, that I knew how to speak of the dying love of Christ! The angels desire to look into the mystery of the love of Jesus; but even they cannot compass its immeasurable height, and depth, and length, and breadth. Will not each of us, who are the objects of it, remember his dying love?

> When to the cross I turn mine eyes,
> And rest on Calvary,
> O Lamb of God! my sacrifice!
> I must remember thee.
>
> Remember thee, and all thy pains,
> And all thy love to me;
> Yea, while a breath, a pulse remains,
> Will I remember thee!

But Jesus rose from the grave. He rose with the same love; he ascended with the same love; he lives with the same love, pleading for us. He loves us now; and he will come for us in love. Love shall give him wings to fly down to earth again. He will reign here; but not without his people. 'The Lord of hosts shall reign in mount Zion, and in Jerusalem, and before his ancients gloriously.' He will reign for ever in love. Evermore, throughout the life to come, and the ages that shall never end, Christ will rest in his love, he will rejoice over his people with joy, he will joy over them with singing. He will also give them to share his glory, and to sit upon his throne, and to reign with him for ever and ever.

Oh, what a theme is this, the deeds of Christ's love! In trying to talk of it, I feel like a poor schoolboy standing here, speaking on a subject he loves. Oh, that there were a Milton, or some one of Miltonic calibre, to tell out the story of this great love of Christ! Yet, mayhap, the theme is better with my poor description than it would be with the loftiest words of men, because you are more likely to forget the description, and to remember the love that cannot be described; whereas, had my discourse been filled with lofty and worthy diction, you might have forgotten the theme, and remembered the speaker.

I would like you, brothers and sisters, tonight, to remember *the proofs of Christ's love*. You were far off, but he sought you, and brought you back. You were deaf, but he called you, and opened your ear to hear his loving call. You came trembling, and afraid, but he cheered you; and in a moment he took your burden from you, and set you free. Do you remember it?

> Dost mind the place, the spot of ground,
> Where Jesus did thee meet?

I remember, tonight, the place where first I saw the Lord; I know it to a yard. Some of you cannot speak as definitely as that, and you need not blush because you cannot. Did Jesus come to you? Did he forgive your sins? Did he comfort you with his love? Then remember it tonight. Never mind about dates and places; but remember his love.

Since Jesus first came to you, and saved you, many a time you have been in trouble, and he has comforted you. You have been in labour; and he has sustained you. You have been in disrepute; but he has honoured you. Alas, you have proved yourself unworthy of his love; but he has forgiven your backslidings. You have wandered from him; but he has restored you. Remember his great love.

No word of mine will, I fear, help you much; but let your memory begin to run over the pages of your diary. Turn over the leaves that record your Lord's favour to you. Are there not some pages with great crosses upon them, which you made in the day of trouble, and other crosses, which you made in the hour of your deliverance when Jesus came to your relief? Oh, remember his love, remember his love more than wine!

I will not detain you on this point any longer; although there was much more I wanted to say. Only, brothers and sisters, if I cannot talk to you, do the thing that we are thinking about. Do remember Christ and his great love. Do now, before you partake of the emblems of his broken body and his shed blood, get to him. You may forget everything else if you like; but I charge you remember Christ's love. There, fling overboard every other recollection, however precious! Let the golden ingots go; but hold you fast to the true lading of the ship, her real cargo, the love wherewith Christ hath loved us. Do remember that, and sit still, and enjoy the blessed memory.

Before I come to the last division of my subject, I should like to ask whether there are any here who cannot remember Christ's love because they never knew it. Is that your case, my dear friend, over yonder? Let me remind you of the lepers of whom we have been reading, and then let me recall to your minds God's ancient law concerning the man suffering from leprosy.

When he was brought for the high priest to examine him, the high priest looked him up and down, from the crown of his head to the sole of his foot, and he said to the leper, 'Here is a place still on thy breast where thy flesh is perfectly clean'; and the leper said, 'Yes, I am pleased to see that it is so.' But the high priest replied, 'You are unclean, you must not go into the house of the Lord, or associate with the people.'

Then there came another, and he searched him all over, and said, 'Here, upon this part of your leg, there is a sound place still.' 'Yes,' said the other, 'I have often thought what a good sign it was.' 'You also are unclean,' said the high priest, 'Go to your separate house and abide there.'

Then there came one poor man who was white all over, and the high priest said to him, 'Have you any clean places?' 'No, my lord, not one; examine me, and see'; and the high priest looked, and there was not a clean spot on him where you could have put a pin's point; but the leprosy was all over him, he was saturated all through with the deadly virus, and foul with the loathsome disease; and there he stood, and cowered and trembled before the high priest. Then the high priest said to him, 'Behold, thou art clean; when thou hast performed the ceremony required by the law, thou mayest go home to thy house, and to the house of thy God, for thou art clean.'

There was a medical reason, I suppose, for this law; the mischief had thrown itself out, it had come out to the skin, the disease was fully developed, and would soon be removed. But, whatever may have been the medical reason, such was the law; and if I am addressing anybody here who feels, 'There is nothing good about me; I am unclean, unclean, unclean, from the crown of my head to the sole of my foot, and the lowest place in hell is my desert', my friend, the grace of God has begun to work in you. Now that you are emptied, God will begin to fill you. Trust you in the atoning sacrifice of his dear Son, and you shall have the assurance that you also are the subject of his saving grace; his love shall be shed abroad in your heart by the Holy Ghost; and you shall join with us in remembering that great love wherewith he hath loved us.

The last thing upon which I have to speak to you is this, THE DIVINE PRODUCT OF THIS HOLY MEMORY: 'The upright love thee.'

So it seems, then, that if we remember Christ, *we shall have a respect for his people*. His people are the upright; and she, who speaks in the sacred Canticle, here looks round upon them, and says, 'The upright love thee.' 'That commends thee to me; for if they who are of a chaste spirit love thee, much more should I.' I think, if you feel as I do sometimes, you would be glad to be sure that you were even the least in God's house. We know the upright love Christ, and we love the upright because they do so; and we esteem Christ because, the better men are, the more they think of him. Is it not so? But sometimes we are afraid we are not among the number of the chosen ones. 'The upright love thee.' Lord, am I one of the upright? Our hymn puts it, even concerning heaven:

> There ye that love my Saviour sit,
> There I would fain have place,
> Among your thrones, or at your feet,
> So I might see his face.

Would we not gladly sit at the feet of the very least of his people if we might but love Christ? They love him. I know how you look about you tonight, and you say, 'There sits Brother So-and-so, he loves Christ; there is Mistress So-and-so, who is so busy in the service of her Lord, she loves Christ. And that dear man (Mr William Olney), whose death we still commemorate by these sad memorials around the pulpit, he loved Christ.' 'Ah, well!' you say, 'I wish I loved him, too, and that I were among the upright in character, who truly admire him.'

Seek that blessing, dear friends, for it is to be had if you seek it aright. Seek it, for the love of Christ will make you love the upright, and foster in you an esteem for them. I do not like to hear Christian people speak ill of one another; and I do not like to hear Christian people speak ill of the Church. If Christ loves her, and is married to her, woe to you if you find fault with my Master's bride! He loves not those who love not his chosen. Have a great love for the people of God, even the poorest of them. Count them to be the aristocrats of the world, the blood-royal of the universe, the men and women who have angels to be their servants, and who are made kings and priests unto God. If you remember Christ, you will remember his people. If you remember his love, you will feel a love towards them. God grant that you may do so!

One thing more, and I have done. In remembering Christ's love as the upright do, *we shall grow upright.* I believe that God blesses trouble to our sanctification, and that he can bless joy to the same end; but I am sure of this, that the greatest instrument of sanctification is the love of Jesus.

One asked what he should think of to make him holy, and his friend answered, 'Think of death.' It is wise to talk with the grave, the mattock, and the shroud; but the living love of Christ has a sanctifying power that even thoughts of death have not.

One has said, 'If thou would'st grow holy, think of the punishment of sin, the pit that God has digged for the wicked. It will make thee tremble at the thought of sin, and cause thee to flee from it as from an arch-destroyer.' This is true; but still, if thou wouldst grow in grace fast, and become holy rapidly, this is the best theme for thy meditation, 'We will remember thy love.'

If you will remember Christ's love, you will be lifted up from your crookedness, and made straight, and put among the upright, who love the Lord.

Come, then, let us join tonight in sweet thoughts of love to Christ. The sermon is short, but the subject is long; and you have now an opportunity for coming to the communion-table, and thinking out that theme which I have started for you, 'The love of Christ to me, the love of Christ to me.' Then follow it up with this, 'Oh, my poor love to Christ!'

Think dear friends, if you remember your own love to Christ, what a small thing it is to remember. His great love is like the sun in the heavens. Your love – well, you have to put on your spectacles before you can see it; it is so small a thing. God grant it may grow tonight; and, at the communion-table, may you have such a visitation from Christ, such delightful fellowship with him, that you may be able to sing again the hymn that you were singing when I was obliged to retire for a while from the platform:

My Jesus, I love thee, I know thou art mine,
For thee all the follies of sin I resign;
My gracious Redeemer, my Saviour, art thou,
If ever I loved thee, my Jesus, 'tis now.

I will love thee in life, I will love thee in death,
And praise thee as long as thou lendest me breath;
And say when the death-dew lies cold on my brow,
'If ever I loved thee, my Jesus, 'tis now.'

May you sing it now, and be able to sing it when the death-dew lies cold on your brow! The Lord be with you, for Jesus' sake. Amen.

4

SELF-HUMBLING AND SELF-SEARCHING

'Look not upon me, because I am black, because the sun hath looked upon me: my mother's children were angry with me; they made me the keeper of the vineyards; but mine own vineyard have I not kept' (Song of Solomon 1:6)

Whence do I draw my text but from the very fountain of love? And to whom shall I address my discourse but to the friends of the bridegroom? Ye must have warm hearts, quick sensibilities, lively emotions, to interpret the sayings and sympathise with the tender notes of this most sacred song.

I suppose that the history of the statues in St Paul's Cathedral, from year to year, would not be remarkably interesting. They are placed upon their pedestals; they stand there quietly; and unless some terrible convulsion should occur, probably that will be the whole of their history for many years to come, as it has been for many years past. During the time in which any one of those statues has stood there, however, the history of any one human person has been checkered with all sorts of incidents, happy and sorrowful. Aches and pains, joys and rejoicings, depressions and exultations, have alternated in the living; but in the cold marble there has been no such change. Many of you in this house know little of what are the experiences of God's people. If you hear of their anxieties and encouragements, their temptations and deliverances, their inward conflicts and spiritual triumphs, their gloomy depressions and cheerful exultations – all those things seem to you as an idle tale. The living, the living, shall know the secret; but unto the mere professor this thing is not revealed.

My subject, which will be mainly addressed to God's working people – to such as are really serving him – will appear to have very little bearing upon any here present who do not understand the spiritual life, and they will probably think that the evening to them is wasted. Just this word on the outset, however, I would drop in your ears. If you do not know anything of spiritual life, what will you do in the end of your natural life? If there be no work of God's Spirit upon your soul, and you are a stranger to the living experience of God's children, what will be your portion for ever? It must be divided to you with the unbelievers. Are you prepared to receive it? Are you willing that this should be your eternal destiny? Are you not, rather, alarmed? Are you not made anxious and desirous if by any means you may pass into that better, truer, state of life? Considering its boundless interests, notwithstanding all the present struggles and sorrows it may entail on you, do you not wish to know and prove what spiritual life means? I pray God you may. Let me remind you that the gospel preached to you is still available for your quickening; and whosoever believeth in Christ Jesus is born of God, and *is* possessor of that spiritual life.

Now, in conducting the people of God to a special survey of our text, 'Look not upon me, because I am black', our first remark shall be this: *the fairest Christians are the most shamefaced with regard to themselves*. The person who says, 'Look not upon me, because I am black', is described by someone else in the eighth verse as the 'fairest among women'. Others, who thought her the fairest of the fair, spoke no less than the truth when they affirmed it; but in her own esteem she felt herself to be so little fair, and so much uncomely, that she besought them not even to look upon her. Why is it that the best Christians depreciate themselves the most?

Is it not because they are most accustomed to look within? They keep their books in a better condition than those unsafe tradesmen, the counterpart of mere professors, who think themselves 'rich and increased in goods', when they are on the very verge of bankruptcy. The Christian in his right state tests himself to see whether he be in the faith. He values too much his own soul to go on blindly. He knows that *Heedless* and *Toobold* are always bad pilots, so he sets *Caution* and *Self-examination* at the helm. He cries to God, 'Search me, and know my heart.' He is accustomed to examine his actions and his motives – to pass his words and his thoughts in review. He does not live the life of one who goes recklessly on; but he stops and considers his ways; and looks well to the state of everything within him 'to have always a conscience void of offence toward God and toward men'. Solomon says, 'The wise man looks to the state of his flocks and his herds'; and it is no marvel if any one suffer loss who neglects the counsel. But he also says, 'Keep thy heart with all diligence, for out of it are the issues of life'; and it is quite certain that he who fails in this exercise is liable to every kind of moral disorder. In his anxiety to be pure from evil, the godly man will be eager to notice and quick to detect the least particle of defilement; and for this reason he discovers more of his blackness than any other man is likely to see. He is no blacker, but he looks more narrowly, and therefore he sees more distinctly the spots on his own character.

The genuine Christian, also, tries himself by a higher standard. The professor, if he be as good as another professor, is well content. He estimates himself by a comparison with his neighbours. He has no standard but that of ordinary commonplace Christianity. Far otherwise is it with the believer who walks near to God; he asks himself, 'What manner of persons ought we to be, in all holy conversation and godliness?' He knows the law to be spiritual, and therefore he judges many things to be sinful which others wink at; and he counts some things to be important duties which others regard as trifles. The genuine Christian sets up no lower standard than perfection. He does not judge himself by others, but by the exact measure of the divine requirements, by the law of God, and especially by the example of his Lord and Master; and when he thus sets the brightness of the Saviour's character side by side with his own, then it is that he cries out, 'Look not upon me, for I am black'. The mere professor never does this: he neither scrutinises himself nor observes his Master with close heed and strained attention, desiring to ascertain the truth; but he flatters himself in his own eyes, and goes on presumptuously. Not so the genuine Christian; he hides his face, sighs in secret, and cries before God, because he is not what he wants to be; not what his Lord was; not fully conformed to Christ in all things; and just because these shortcomings grieve and vex his righteous soul, he cries, 'Look not upon me, for I am black.' All the while he may be of the highest type of Christian, yet he is not so in his own esteem. He may be a star to others, but he is a blot, as he thinks, to himself. In God's esteem he is 'accepted in the Beloved', but in his own esteem he seems to himself to be full of all manner of evil, and he cries out against it before his Lord.

Another reason why the fairest Christians are generally those that think themselves the blackest, is that they have more light. A person may seem to be very fair in the dark, very fair in the twilight; but when the light gets strong, and the eye is strengthened to perceive, then it is that spots that were not noticed before are soon discovered. You have, perhaps, a handkerchief that has looked to you extremely white; so it has been in comparison with other linen: but one day, when there has been a fall of snow, you have laid your handkerchief side by side with the snow, and you have seen that it was very far from the whiteness which you imagined. When the light of God comes into the soul, and we see what purity really is, what holiness really is, then it is the contrast strikes us. Though we might have thought we were somewhat clean before, when we see God in his light we see light, and we abhor ourselves in dust and ashes. Our defects so appal our own heart, that we marvel they do not exhaust his patience.

The better Christian a man is, the more abashed he always feels; because to him sin is so exceedingly hateful, that what sin he sees in himself he loathes himself for far more than others do. The ungodly man would condone very great sin in himself; though he might know it to be there, it would not disturb him; but the Christian being another sort, having a love for holiness and a hatred for sin, cannot bear to see the smallest speck of sin upon himself. He knows what it is. There are persons living before the public eye, and jealous of popularity, who appear quite indifferent to the good opinion of the sovereign in whose kingdom they dwell; there are other persons favourites at court, who would lie awake at night tossed to and fro in fear if they thought that something had been reported to the sovereign's ear that was disloyal. A man who fears not God, will break all his laws with an easy conscience; but one who is the favourite of heaven, who has been indulged to sit at royal banquets, who knows the eternal love of God to him, cannot bear that there should be any evil way in him that might grieve the Spirit and bring dishonour to the name of Christ. A very little sin, as the world calls it, is a very great sin to a truly awakened Christian.

I will ask you now, dear hearers, (most of you are members of this or of other churches), do you know what it is to fret because you have spoken an unadvised word? Do you know what it is to smite upon your breast, because you were angry? Justly provoked, perhaps, but still, being angry, you spoke unadvisedly. Have you ever gone to a sleepless couch, because in business you have let fall a word, or have done an action which, upon mature deliberation, you could not justify? Does the tear never come from your eye because you are not like your Lord, and have failed where you hoped to succeed? I would give little for your godliness, if you know nothing of this. Repentance is as much a mark of a Christian as faith itself. Do not think we have done with repenting when we come to Christ and receive the remission of our sins by the blood that did once atone. No; we shall repent as long as we sin, and as long as we need the precious blood for cleansing. While there is sin, or a proneness to any kind of sin, lurking in us, the grace of God will make us loathe the sin and humble ourselves before the Most High on account of it.

Now, I think our text seems to say just this: there were some that admired the church. They said she was fair. She seemed to say, 'Don't say it; you don't know what I am, or you would not praise me.' Oh, there is nothing that brings a blush to a genuine Christian's face like praising him; for he feels – 'Praise such a heap of dirt as I am? Give any credit to such a worthless worm as I am? No; do not cast admiring glances at me! Do not say, "That man has many virtues and many excellences!" "Look not upon me, for I am black." ' Are there not some who will imitate any Christian – and be very right in so doing – any Christian who is eminently godly and holy? There will be many who will follow in his footsteps. I think I see such a man turn round to his followers, and say, 'Do not look at me; do not copy me. I am black. Copy a better model; even Jesus. If I follow in his footsteps, follow me; but inasmuch as I have gone astray like a lost sheep, follow the shepherd; do not follow my example.'

Every Christian, in proportion as he lives near to God, will feel this self-abasement, this lowliness of heart; and if others talk of admiring or of imitating him, he will say, 'Look not upon me, for I am black.' And as he thus, in deep humility, begs that he be not exalted, he will often desire others that they would not despise him. It will come into his mind, 'Such-and-such a man of God is a Christian indeed; as he sees my weakness, he will contemn me. Such-and-such a disciple of Christ is strong; he will never be able to bear with my weakness. Such-and-such a Christian woman does, indeed, adorn the doctrine of God her Saviour; but as for me, alas! I am not what I ought to be, nor what I would be. Children of God, do not look upon me with scorn. I will not say that you have motes in your own eyes. I have a beam in mine. Look not upon me too severely. Judge me not harshly. If you do look at me, look to Christ for me, and pray that I may be helped; 'for I am black, because the sun hath looked upon me.'

Still I would have you beware of affecting aught that you do not feel. Humility itself may be counterfeited with much ostentation. Wherever there is anything like cant, as it is practised by some people who depreciate themselves but do not mean it, it is loathsome to the last degree. I recollect a very proud man, certain twice as proud as he was high, who used to pray for himself as 'God's poor dust'. There was nothing, I am sure, about his conduct and conversation that entitled him to use any such expression. I have heard of a monk who said he was full of sin – he was as bad as Judas; and when somebody said, 'That is true', he turned round, and said, 'What did I ever do that *you* should say so?' The effrontery of the arrogant is not more odious than the servility of the sycophant. There is a great deal of self-abnegation which is not genuine; it is the offspring of self-conceit, and not of self-knowledge. Much that we say of ourselves would mightily offend our vainglory if anybody else said the same of us. Oh, let us beware of mock humility! At the same time, the more of the genuine article we have the better, and the more truthfully we can cry out to God's people, 'Look not upon me, because I am black', the more clear will it be that we are, after all, amongst the fairest.

But I pass on. The most diligent Christian – let this stand for the second observation – *the most diligent Christian will be the man most afraid of the evils connected with his work*. 'Evils connected with his work!' says one. 'Does work for God have evils contingent upon it?' Yes; but for every evil connected with the work of God, there are ten evils connected with idleness. Nay, all you professors who are doing nothing, are wearing yourselves out faster by rust than you could have done by honest wear. But, you see, in the case of our text, there was evil connected with work. She had been made a keeper of the vineyards, and having to trim the vines, the sun had shone upon her; and she says, 'Look not upon me, because I am black, because the sun hath looked upon me.' The blackness that she confessed was a blackness occasioned by her having to bear the burden and heat of the day.

And now I speak to such as live in active service, doing the work of God. Dear brethren, there are certain evils connected with our lifework, coming of the sun that looks upon us, which we should confess before our heavenly Father. I speak now only to the workers. I have known some whom the sun has looked upon in this respect; their zeal has grown cold through non-success. You went out, first of all, as a Christian, full of fire and life. You intended to push the church before you, and drag the world after you. Peradventure you thought that you were going to work a Reformation almost as great as that of Luther. Well, much of that was of the flesh, though beneath the surface there was earnest zeal for God which was eating you up. But you have been mixed up with Christians for some years of a very cool sort. Use the thermometer tonight. Has not the spiritual temperature gone down in your own soul? Perhaps you have not seen many conversions under your ministry? Or in the class which you conduct you have not seen many children brought to Jesus? Do you feel you are getting cool? Then wrap your face in your mantle tonight, and say: 'Look not upon me, for in losing my zeal I am black, for the sun hath looked upon me.'

Perhaps it has affected you in another way, for the sun does not bring freckles out on all faces in the same place. Perhaps it is your temper that is grown sour? When you joined the church you felt all love, and you expected, as you had a right to do, that everybody would reciprocate the same feeling; it may be that since then you have had to do battle against contentions. You have been in a part of the church where there has been a strife, not altogether for the faith once delivered to the saints, but something of a party feeling was mixed with it, and you have had to take some share in it. And perhaps you have gradually acquired a carping, critical habit, so that where you used to enjoy the word, you are now all for judging the preacher. You are not so much a feeder upon the word, as a mere taster of the dishes, to see if you cannot find some fault with their flavour. Wrap your face again, I beseech you, in your mantle. Again, bow before God, and say, 'Look not upon me, because I am black; the sun hath looked upon me. In my service for God I have been impaired.'

Perhaps, dear friend, you have suffered in another way! I sometimes suffer in this respect very materially. The Christian's walk ought to be calm, peaceful, quiet, unruffled. Leaving everything with the Lord, and waiting his will, our peace should be like a river. But you know that, when there is much to be done in God's service, there is a very strong temptation to want to push this and that thing forward with undue haste. Or if it does not move quickly at the rate you would wish, there is a temptation to be sad, careful and anxious; to be, in fact, like Martha, cumbered with much service. When you get into that condition it is an injury to yourself and really prejudicial to your own work; for they serve Christ best who commune with him most, and broken fellowship means broken strength. Yet this is often our trouble; our energies are exhausted by worry more than by work. Part of our duty is neglected through unexpected cares that have distracted our thoughts.

Pardon me, if I transfer the thing to myself in a figure. Say that this Tabernacle wants all my vigilance concentrated upon its welfare. Then there is another matter that wants instant attention at the same time. Here is a soul seeking Christ; here is another backsliding; here is a brother falling to ears with a brother. Innumerable things crowd upon one's view and clamour for immediate investigation till one gets disturbed and troubled. 'Look not upon me, because I am black; because the sun hath looked upon me. The work I have engaged in for thee hath brought me into the sun, and burnt my face.' It ought to be bright and fair with fellowship; it is soiled and begrimed with service.

Sometimes this evil of sun-burning will come in the shape of joy taken away from the heart by weariness. I do not think, dear brethren, any of us are weary of God's work. If so, we never were called to it. But we may get weary *in* it. You recollect, some of you here – I speak to such as often preach the gospel – how happy you were when first you were permitted to open your mouth for Christ! Oh, what a joy it was! What a pleasure! How you threw your whole soul into it! There was no sleepiness and dulness in your sermon then. But now, year after year, year after year, your brain gets weary, and though the spirit is willing, the flesh is weak; the joy you once had in the service was your strength, and it has somewhat gone from you. The toil is more irksome when the spirits are less buoyant. Well, I would advise you to confess this before God, and ask for a medicine to heal you. You had need get your joy back, but first you must acknowledge that you have lost it. Say, 'I am black, because the sun hath looked upon me'.

On the other hand, it is a bad result of a good work when our humility is injured thereby. Place a Christian man in a position where he has to do much for Christ, and is much thought of and set by; let him have great success, and the tendency will be for him to compliment himself as though he were some great one. You cannot reap great sheaves for the Master without this temptation coming over your soul. What a glorious workman you are, and what a great reward will your soul have for having done so well! It is the sun looking upon you; taking away the fairness of your humility, freckling and blackening your face with a pride that is obnoxious to God. This ought to be confessed at once and heartily repented of.

I do not think I shall attempt to go through the list of all the matters that might come out of Christian service. It will suffice me to say, I am afraid that in many cases our motives get mixed. Pure and simple at first in our service, we may get at last to serve Christ only because it is our office to do so. Woe to the man that preaches only because he is a minister, and does not preach because he loves Christ! We may get also to be self-reliant. It is a great mercy for God's ministers when they tremble on going into the pulpit, even though they have been accustomed to preach for twenty years. Martin Luther declares that he never feared the face of man; and all who knew him could bear witness that it was even so; yet he said he never went up the stairs of the pulpit at Wittenburg but he felt his knees knock together with fear lest he should not be faithful to God and his truth. When we begin to rely upon ourselves, and think we can do it, and our experience and our practice will suffice to bear us safely through the next discourse without help from on high, then the sun has looked upon us, and blackened our face indeed, and the time of our usefulness draws to a close. Come, Christian people, brethren and sisters, thankful though I am that I can address so large a number who are engaged in the Master's work, I beseech you, let us go together to the footstool of the heavenly grace, confess there our blackness, and own that much of it has come upon us even while we were engaged in the service of God.

In the third place, *the most watchful Christian is conscious of the danger of self-neglect*. That is the next part of our text. 'They made me the keeper of the vineyards; but mine own vineyard have I not kept.'

Solemnly, let me speak again to my brethren who are seeking to glorify Christ by their lives. I met some time ago with a sermon by that famous divine, Mr Henry Melvill, which consists all through of one solitary thought, and only one image well worked out. I will give you the pith of what took some eight pages to get through. He supposes a man to be a guide in Switzerland. It is his duty to conduct travellers in that country through the sublime passes, and to point out to them the glories of the scenery, and the beauties of the lakes and streams and glaciers and hills. This man, as he continues in his office, almost inevitably gets to repeat his descriptions as a matter of course; and everybody knows how a guide at last comes to 'talk book', and just iterate words which do not awaken any corresponding feeling in his own mind. Yet when he began, perhaps it was a sincere love of the sublime and the beautiful that led him to take up the vocation of a guide; and at first it really was to him a luxury to impart to others what he had felt amidst the glories of nature; but as, year after year, to hundreds of different parties, he had to repeat much the same descriptions, call attention to the same sublimities, and indicate the same beauties, it is almost impossible but that he should get to be at last a mere machine. Through the hardening tendency of custom, and the debasing influence of gain, his aptest descriptions and most exquisite eulogies come to be of no greater account than the mere language of a hireling.

This thought I will not work out *in extenso* as that famous preacher has done, but I give it to you as a cutting, which may germinate if planted in the garden of your heart. Every worker for Christ is deeply concerned in the application of this parable; because the peril of self-complacency increases in precisely the same ratio as the zeal of proselytising. When counselling others, you think yourself wise. When warning others, you feel yourself safe. When judging others, you suppose yourself above suspicion. You began the work with a flush of ardour; it may be with a fever of enthusiasm; a sacred instinct prompted, a glowing passion moved you. How will you continue it? Here is the danger – the fearful danger – lest you do it mechanically, fall into a monotony, continue in the same train, and use holy words to others with no corresponding feeling in your own soul. May we not stir others up to devout emotions, and yet our own hearts fail to burn with the sacred fire? Oh, may it not be easy for one to stand as a signpost on the road to heaven, and never stir himself? Every preacher who judges himself aright knows that this is the risk he incurs; and I believe the same danger in a measure threatens Christians in every form of work in which they occupy themselves for Christ.

Dear friends, beware of reading the Bible for other people. Get your own text – your own morsel of marrow and fatness – out of Scripture; and do not be satisfied to be sermon-making or lesson-making for your class in the Sunday-school. Feed on the word yourselves, or else your vineyard will not be kept. When you are on your knees in prayer, pray for others by all means; but, oh, let private prayer be kept up with a view to your own edification and your own growth in grace as well. Preach not the Saviour's blood, and yet be without the blood mark on yourselves. Tell not of the fountain, and yet go unwashed. Do not point to heaven, and then turn your back to it and go down to hell. Fellow-workers, look to yourselves, lest after having preached to others ye yourselves should be cast away. Your neighbours certainly, but yourselves also; the children in your class certainly, your own children at home certainly, but look to yourselves also, ye that are workers in God's house, lest ye keep the vineyards of others and your own vineyards be not kept.

It is very possible for a man to get to dislike the very religion which he feels bound still by force of custom to go on teaching to others. 'Is that possible?' says one. Alas! that it is. Have you never heard of the flower-girl in the streets? What is her occupation? I dare say some girls like her have passed by and seen her with a great basket of violets, and said, 'What a delightful occupation, to have that fragrant smell for ever near to one!' Yes, but there was one girl who sold them, and said she hated the smell of violets. She had got to loathe them, and to think that there was no smell in the world so offensive, because they were always under her nostrils all day, and taken home to her little scanty room at night, and having nothing but violets around her, she hated them altogether. And I do believe that there are persons without the grace of Christ in their hearts who keep on talking about grace, and mercy, and practising prayer, and yet in their heart of hearts they hate the very fragrance of the name of Jesus, and need that there should come upon them an awakening out of their sleep of presumption and hypocrisy, to make them know that though they thought they were the friends of God, they were, after all, his enemies. They were mere keepers of other men's vineyards, but their own vineyards had gone to ruin.

Our last reflection is of the deepest importance. *The most conscientious Christian will be the first to enquire for the antidote, and to use the cure.*

What is the cure? The cure is found in the verse next to my text. 'Look not upon me, because I am black, because the sun hath looked upon me. They made me the keeper of the vineyards; but mine own vineyards have I not kept.' What next? 'Tell me, O thou whom my soul loveth, where thou feedest, where thou makest thy flock to rest at noon: for why should I be as one that turneth aside by the flocks of thy companions?' See, then, you workers, if you want to keep up your freshness, and not to get blackened by the sun under which you labour, go to your Lord again – go and talk to him. Address him again by that dear name, 'Thou whom my soul loveth'. Ask to have your first love rekindled; strive after the love of your espousals. There are men in married life who seem to have forgotten that they ever loved their wives; but there are others concerning whom the hymn is true:

> And as year rolls after year,
> Each to other still more dear.

So there are some Christians who seem to forget that they ever loved the Saviour; but I trow there are others in whom that love deepens and becomes more fervent as each year passes over their heads. If any of you are at fault in this, do not give sleep to your eyelids tonight till you have renewed your espousal love. Thy Lord recollects it, if thou dost not, for he says, 'I remember thee, the kindness of thy youth, the love of thine espousals, when thou wentest after me in the wilderness, in a land that was not sown'. You did some wild things in those early days. You were a great deal more zealous than wise; but, though you look back upon that with censure, Christ regards it with delight. He wishes you were now as you were then.

Perhaps today you are not quite cold to him. Do not flatter yourself on that account; for he has said, 'I would thou wert cold or hot'. It is just lukewarmness that he loathes most of all, and he has threatened to spew the lukewarm out of his mouth. Oh, to be always full of love to him! You will never get any hurt by working for him then; your work will do you good. The sweat of labour will even make your face the fairer. The more you do for souls, the purer, and the holier, and the more Christlike will you be, if you do it with him.

Keep up the habit of sitting at his feet, like Mary, as well as serving him with Martha. You can keep the two together; they will balance each other, and you shall not be barren or unfruitful, neither shall you fall into the blackness which the sun is apt to breed. O for more nearness to Christ, more love to Christ, and closer communion with him! Did you notice what the spouse said? 'Tell me, O thou whom my soul loveth, where thou feedest?' I suppose her object was to go and feed with him. Look to the feeding of your own soul, Christian. When a man says, 'I have a hard day's work to do, I shall have no time to eat', you know full well that he is losing time where he thinks he gains it; for if he does not keep himself in good repair he will sicken by-and-by, and in the long run he will do less than if he gave himself due pause. So is it with your soul. You cannot give out a vital energy which you have not got in you healthy and vigorous; and if you have not got power from God in your own soul, power cannot come out of you, for it is not there. Do, therefore, feed upon Christ.

Or do you feel yourself like that guide of whom we spoke just now? Has the routine of service blunted your sensibilities, till you gaze unmoved on those objects of beauty and marvel that should awaken every passion and thrill every nerve of your being? Ask then in what way he might keep up his interest in the lakes and the mountains? Would it not be well for him, occasionally, at any rate, to take a lonely journey to find out new features in the gorgeous scenery, or to stand in solitude, and see the hills in a fresh light, or mark the forest trees in different states of the weather; so that he might again renew his own sensations of admiration, and of gratitude to God for having created such sublimities? Then I can readily believe his enthusiasm would increase rather than abate by an increasing familiarity with the landscape. And you, worker for God, you must go to God alone; feed on precious truth for yourself; dig into the deep things of God and enrich your own spirit. Thus you may serve God as much as ever you will; you will get no hurt therefrom.

Did you notice that she also asked, 'Tell me where thou makest thy flock to rest at noon?' Rest is what the worker wants. Where is the rest of Christ's flock but in his own dear bosom? Where is there repose, but in his own fidelity, in the two immutable things wherein it is impossible for God to lie – the oath and the promise? Oh, never turn away from that rest! Turn into it again, tonight, beloved. As for me, I feel I want my Saviour more than ever I did. Though I have preached his gospel now these five-and-twenty years and more, I need still to come and cling to his cross as a guilty sinner, and find 'life for a look at the crucified One', just as I did at first. O that God's grace may ever keep the most ardent among us always faithful with our own soul, abiding in the Lord, and rejoicing in him!

I have done. This is my word to workers. Let me only say to you for whom there has seemed nothing in the sermon, if you are not workers for Christ, you are workers against him. 'He that is not with me is against me; and he that gathereth not with me scattereth abroad.' O souls, why should you stand out against the Saviour? Why should you resist him? Bleeding out his life for his enemies, the mirror of disinterested love, what is there in him that can make you fight against him? Drop your weapons, man! Drop them tonight, I charge you by the living God! And come now, ask pardon through the precious blood, and it shall be given you. Seek a new heart, and a right spirit. The Holy Ghost will work it. From this night be a worker for Christ. The church wants you. The armies of Christ need recruiting. Take the proffered blessing, and become a soldier of the cross; and may the Lord build up his Zion by many of you who were not his people aforetime, but of whom it is said, 'They were not my people, but they shall be the people of the living God.'

5

THE UNKEPT VINEYARD; OR, PERSONAL WORK NEGLECTED

'They made me the keeper of the vineyards;
but mine own vineyard have I not kept'
(Song of Solomon 1:6)

The text is spoken in the first person singular; 'They made me.' Therefore let the preaching tonight be personal to you, dear friends: personal to the preacher first, and then to each one of this mixed multitude. May we at this hour think less of others than of ourselves! May the sermon be of practical value to our own hearts! I do not suppose that it will be a pleasing sermon: on the other hand, it may be a saddening one. I may bring unhappy memories before you; but let us not be afraid of that holy sorrow which is health to the soul. Since the spouse in this text speaketh of herself, 'They made me the keeper of the vineyards; but mine own vineyard have I not kept', let each one of us copy her example, and think of our own selves.

The text is the language of complaint. We are all pretty ready at complaining, especially of other people. Not much good comes of picking holes in other men's characters; and yet many spend hours in that unprofitable occupation. It will be well for us, at this time, to let our complaint, like that of the text, deal with ourselves. If there is something wrong at home, let the father blame himself; if there is something ill with the children, let the mother look to her own personal conduct as their instructor. Do not let us lend out our ears, but let us keep them at home for our own use. Let us clear out an open passage to the heart, so that everything that is said shall go down into the spirit, and purify our inner man. Let us from the heart make the confession – 'They made me the keeper of the vineyards; but mine own vineyard have I not kept.'

Let us make the text practical. Do not let us be satisfied to have uttered the language of complaint; but let us get rid of the evils which we deplore. If we have been wrong, let us labour to be right. If we have neglected our own vineyard, let us confess it with due humiliation; but let us not continue to neglect it. Let us ask of God that holy results may flow out of our self-lamentations, so that before many days we may begin to keep our own vineyards carefully by the grace of God; and then we shall better carry out the office of keeper of the vineyards of others, if we are called to such an employment.

There are two things upon which I am going to dwell at this time. The first is, that there are many Christian people – I hope they are Christian people – who will be compelled to confess that the greater part of their life is spent in labour which is not of the highest kind, and is not properly their own. I shall find out *the worker who has forgotten his heavenly calling*. And when I have done with this case – and I am afraid that there will be much about it that may touch many of us – I shall then take a more general view, and deal with *any who are undertaking other works, and neglecting their own proper vocation*.

First, then, let me begin with THE CHRISTIAN MAN WHO HAS FORGOTTEN HIS HIGH AND HEAVENLY CALLING. In the day when you and I were born again, my brethren, we were born for God. In the day when we saw that Christ died for us, we were bound henceforth to be dead to the world. In the day when we were quickened by the Holy Ghost into newness of life, that life was bound to be a consecrated one. For a thousand reasons it is true that, 'Ye are not your own: ye are bought with a price.' The ideal Christian is one who has been made alive with a life which he lives for God. He has risen out of the dominion of the world, the flesh, and the devil. He reckons that 'if one died for all, then were all dead: and that he died for all, that they which live should not henceforth live unto themselves, but unto him which died for them, and rose again'. This you will not deny. Christian friends, you admit that you have a high, holy and heavenly calling!

Now let us look back. *We have not spent our life idly*: we have been forced to be keepers of the vineyards. I hope I am not addressing anybody here who has tried to live without employment and labour of some kind. No, we have worked, and we have worked hard. Most men speak of their wages as 'hard-earned', and I believe that in many cases they speak the bare truth. Many hours in the day have to be spent upon our occupations. We wake up in the morning, and think of what we have to do. We go to bed wearied at night by what we have done. This is as it should be, for God did not make us that we might sport and play, like leviathan in the deep. Even in Paradise man was bidden to dress the garden. There is something to be done by each man, and specially by each Christian man.

Come back to what I began with. In the day when we were born again, as many of us as are new creatures in Christ Jesus, we began to live to God, and not to ourselves. Have we carried out that life? We have worked, we have even worked hard; but the questions come to us: What have we worked for? Who has been our master? With what object have we toiled? Of course, if I have been true to my profession as a Christian, I have lived and worked for God, for Christ, for the kingdom of heaven. But has it been so? And is it so now?

Many are working very hard for wealth, which means, of course, for self, that they may be enriched. Some are working simply for a competence, which means, if it goes no farther, still for self. Others work for their families, a motive good enough in its way, but still only an enlargement, after all, of self. To the Christian there must always be a far higher, deeper, purer, truer motive than self in its widest sense; or else, the day must come when he will look back upon his life, and say, 'They made me the keeper of the vineyards; but mine own vineyard' – that is, the service of Christ, the glory of him that bought me with his blood – 'have I not kept'.

It seems to me to be a terrible calamity to have to look back on twenty years, and say, 'What have I done in all those twenty years for Christ? How much of my energy has been spent in striving to glorify *him*? I have had talents: how many of those talents have been used for him who gave them to me? I have had wealth, or I have had influence. How much of that money have I spent distinctly for my Lord? How much of that influence have I used for the promotion of his kingdom?'

You have been busy with this notion, and that motive, and the other endeavour; but have you lived as you will wish to have lived when you stand at his right hand amidst his glories? Have you so acted that you will then judge yourself to have well lived when your Lord and Master shall come to call you to account? Ask yourself, 'Am I an earnest labourer together with God, or am I, after all, only a laborious trifler, an industrious doer of nothing, working hard to accomplish no purpose of the sort for which I ought to work, since I ought to live unto my Lord alone?'

I invite all my fellow-servants to take a retrospect, and just to see whether they have kept their own vineyards. I suppose that they have worked hard. I only put the questions: Have they kept their own vineyards? Have they served the Lord in all things?

I am half afraid to go a step farther. To a very large degree we have not been true to our own professions: *our highest work has been neglected*, we have not kept our own vineyards. In looking back, how little time has been spent by us in communion with God! How little a part of our thoughts has been occupied with meditation, contemplation, adoration, and other acts of devotion! How little have we surveyed the beauties of Christ, his person, his work, his sufferings, his glory! We say that it is 'heaven below' to commune with Christ; but do we do it? We profess that there is no place like the mercy-seat. How much are we at that mercy-seat?

We often say that the Word of God is precious – that every page of it glows with a heavenly light. Do we study it? Friends, how much time do you spend upon it? I venture to say that the bulk of Christians spend more time in reading the newspaper than they do in reading the Word of God. I trust that I am too severe in this statement, but I am afraid, greatly afraid, that I am not. The last new book, perhaps the last sentimental story, will win attentive reading, when the divine, mysterious, unutterable depths of heavenly knowledge are disregarded by us. Our Puritan forefathers were strong men, because they lived on the Scriptures. None stood against them in their day, for they fed on good meat, whereas their degenerate children are far too fond of unwholesome food. The chaff of fiction, and the bran of the Quarterlies, are poor substitutes for the old corn of Scripture, the fine flour of spiritual truth. Alas, my brethren, too many eat the unripe fruit of the vineyards of Satan, and the fruits of the Lord's vines they utterly despise!

Think of our neglect of our God, and see whether it is not true that we have treated him very ill. We have been in the shop, we have been on the exchange, we have been at the markets, we have been in the fields, we have been in the public libraries, we have been in the lecture-room, we have been in the forum of debate; but our own closets and studies, our walk with God, and our fellowship with Jesus, we have far too much neglected.

Moreover, the vineyard of holy service for God we have too much left to go to ruin. I would ask you: How about the work your God has called you to do? Men are dying; are you saving them? This great city is like a seething cauldron, boiling and bubbling up with infamous iniquity; are we doing anything by way of antidote to the hell-broth concocted in that cauldron? Are we indeed a power working towards righteousness? How much good have we done? What have I done to pluck brands from the burning? What have I done to find the lost sheep for whom my Saviour laid down his life? Come, put the questions, and answer them honestly!

Nay, do not back out, and say, 'I have no ability'. I fear you have more ability than you will give an account of with joy at the last great day. I remember a young man who complained that the little church over which he presided was so small. He said, 'I cannot do much good. I have not above two hundred hearers.' An older man replied, 'Two hundred hearers are a great many to have to give an account of at the last great day.' As I came in at yonder door this evening, and looked into these thousands of faces, I could not help trembling. How shall I answer for this solemn charge, for this enormous flock, in that last great day?

You have all a flock of some kind, larger or smaller. You have all, as Christian people, somebody for whom you will have to answer. Have you done your Master's work in reference to those entrusted to you? O men and women, have you sought to save others from going down into the pit? You have the divine remedy: have you handed it out to these sick and dying ones? You have the heavenly word which can deliver them from destruction: have you spoken it in their ears, praying all the while that God might bless it to their souls. Might not many a man among you say to himself, 'I have been a tailor' or 'I have been a shopkeeper' or 'I have been a mechanic' or 'I have been a merchant or 'I have been a physician, and I have attended to these callings; but mine own vineyard, which was my Master's, which I was bound to look to first of all, I have not kept'?

Well, now, *what is the remedy for this*? We need not talk of our fault any more; let us make each one his own personal confession, and then seek amendment. I believe the remedy is a very sweet one. It is not often that medicine is pleasant, but at this time I prescribe for you a charming potion. It is that you follow up the next verse to my text. Read it: 'Mine own vineyard have I not kept. Tell me, O thou whom my soul loveth, where thou feedest, where thou makest thy flock to rest at noon; for why should I be as one that turneth aside by the flocks of thy companions?' Get to your Lord, and in him you will find recovery from your neglects. Ask him where he feeds his flock, and go with him. They have warm hearts who commune with Christ. They are prompt in duty who enjoy his fellowship.

I cannot help reminding you of what I have often spoken of, namely, our Lord's language to the church at Laodicea. That church had come to be so bad that he said, 'I will spew thee out of my mouth.' And yet what was the remedy for that church? 'Behold, I stand at the door, and knock: if any man hear my voice, and open the door, I will come in to him, and will sup with him, and he with me.' After supping with Christ you will not be lukewarm. Nobody can say, 'I am neither cold nor hot' when they have been in his company. Rather they will enquire, 'Did not our heart burn within us, while he talked with us by the way?' If there be an angel, as Milton sings, whose name is Uriel, who lives in the sun, I will warrant you he is never cold; so he that lives in Christ, and walks with him, is never chill, nor slow in the divine service. Away to your Lord, then!

Hasten to your Lord, and you will soon begin to keep your vineyard; for in the Song you will see *a happy change effected*. The spouse began to keep her vineyard directly, and to do it in the best fashion. Within a very short time you find her saying, 'Take us the foxes, the little foxes, that spoil the vines.' See, she is hunting out her sins and her follies. Farther on you find her with her Lord in the vineyard, crying: 'Awake, O north wind; and come, thou south; blow upon my garden, that the spices thereof may flow out!' She is evidently keeping her garden, and asking for heavenly influences to make the spices and flowers yield their perfume. She went down to see whether the vines flourished, and the pomegranates budded. Anon, with her beloved, she rises early to go to the vineyard, and serve your Lord. Come and sit at his feet; lean on his bosom; rest on his arm; and make him to be the joy of your spirit. The Lord grant, dear brethren, that this gentle word, which I have spoken as much to myself as to you, may be blessed to us all!

Now I turn to the congregation in general, and speak with THE MAN WHO IN ANY PLACE HAS TAKEN OTHER WORK, AND NE-

GLECTED HIS OWN. He can use the words of the text: 'They made me the keeper of the vineyards; but mine own vineyard have I not kept.'

We know many persons who are always doing a great deal, and yet do nothing; fussy people, people to the front in every movement, persons who could set the whole world right, but are not right themselves. Just before a general election there is a manifestation of most remarkable men – generally persons who know everything, and a few things besides, who, if they could but be sent to Parliament, would turn the whole world upside down, and put even Pandemonium to rights. They would pay the National Debt within six months, and do any other trifle that might occur to them. Very eminent men are these! I have come across impossibly great men. None could be so great as these feel themselves to be. They are an order of very superior persons: reformers, or philosophers, who know what nobody else knows; only, happily, they have not patented the secret, but are prepared to tell it out to others, and thereby illuminate us all.

I suggest to our highly-gifted friends that it is possible to be looking after a great many things, and yet to be neglecting your own vineyard. There is a vineyard that a great many neglect, and that is *their own heart*. It is well to have talent; it is well to have influence; but it is better to be right within yourself. It is well for a man to see to his cattle, and look well to his flocks and to his herds; but let him not forget to cultivate that little patch of ground that lies in the centre of his being. Let him educate his head, and intermeddle with all knowledge; but let him not forget that there is another plot of ground called the heart, the character, which is more important still. Right principles are spiritual gold, and he that hath them, and is ruled by them, is the man who truly lives. He hath not life, whatever else he hath, who hath not his heart cultivated, and made right and pure.

Have you ever thought about your heart yet? Oh, I do not mean whether you have palpitations! I am no doctor. I am speaking now about the heart in its moral and spiritual aspect. What is your character, and do you seek to cultivate it? Do you ever use the hoe upon those weeds which are so plentiful in us all? Do you water those tiny plants of goodness which have begun to grow? Do you watch them to keep away the little foxes which would destroy them? Are you hopeful that yet there may be a harvest in your character which God may look upon with approval? I pray that we may all look to our hearts. 'Keep your heart with all diligence; for out of it are the issues of life.' Pray daily, 'Create in me a clean heart, O God; and renew a right spirit within me'; for if not, you will go up and down in the world, and do a great deal, and when it comes to the end you will have neglected your noblest nature, and your poor starved soul will die that second death, which is the more dreadful because it is everlasting death. How terrible for a soul to die of neglect! How can we escape who neglect this great salvation? If we pay every attention to our bodies, but none to our immortal souls, how shall we justify our folly? God save us from suicide by neglect! May we not have to moan out eternally: 'They made me the keeper of the vineyard; but mine own vineyard have I not kept'!

Now, pass over that point, and think of another vineyard. Are not some people neglecting *their families*? Next to our hearts, our households are the vineyards which we are most bound to cultivate. I shall never forget a man whom I knew in my youth, who used to accompany me at times in my walks to the villages to preach. He was always willing to go with me any evening; but I did not need to ask him, for he asked himself, until I purposely put him off from it. He liked also to preach himself much better than others liked to hear him; but he was a man who was sure to be somewhere to the front if he could. Even if you snuffed him out, he had a way of lighting himself up again. He was good-natured and irrepressible. He was, I believe, sincerely earnest in doing good. But two boys of his were well known to me, and they would swear horribly. They were ready for every vice, and were under no restraint. One of them drank himself into a dying state with brandy, though he was a mere boy. I do not believe his father had ever spoken to him about the habit of intoxication, though he certainly was sober and virtuous himself. I had no fault to find with him except this grave fault – that he was seldom at home, was not master of the house, and could not control his children. Neither husband nor wife occupied any place of influence in the household; they were simply the slaves of their children: their children made themselves vile, and they restrained them not! This brother would pray for his children at the prayer-meeting, but I do not think he ever practised family prayer.

It is shocking to find men and women speaking fluently about religion, and yet their houses are a disgrace to Christianity. I suppose that none of you are as bad as that; but, if it be so, please spell this text over: 'They made me the keeper of the vineyards; but mine own vineyard have I not kept.'

The most careful and prayerful father cannot be held accountable for having wicked sons, if he has done his best to instruct them. The most anxious and tearful mother cannot be blamed if her daughter dishonours the family, provided her mother has done her best to train her up in the right way. But if the parents cannot say that they have done their best, and their children go astray, then they are blameworthy. If any of them have come to the Tabernacle tonight, and their boys and girls are they do not know where, let them go home quickly, and look them up. If any of my hearers exercise no parental discipline, nor seek to bring their children to Christ, I do implore them to give up every kind of public work till they have first done their work at home.

Has anybody made you a minister, and you are not trying to save your own children? I tell you, sir, I do not believe that God made you a minister; for if he had, he would have begun with making you a minister to your own family. '*They* made me the keeper of the vineyards.' 'They' ought to have known better, and you ought to have known better than to accept the call. How can you be a steward in the great household of the Lord when you cannot even rule your own house?

A Sunday-school teacher, teaching other people's children, and never praying with her own! Is not this a sad business? A teacher of a large class of youths who never has taken a class of his own sons and daughters! Why, what will he do when he lives to see his children plunged into vice and sin, and remembers that he has utterly neglected them?

This is plain dealing; but I never wear gloves when I preach. I know not where this knife may cut; but if it wounds, I pray you do not blunt its edge. Do you say that this is 'very personal'? It is meant to be personal; and if anybody is offended by it, let him be offended with himself, and mend his ways. No longer let it be true of any of us, 'They made me the keeper of the vineyards; but mine own vineyard have I not kept.'

Besides that, every man who knows the Lord should feel that his vineyard lies also *round about his own house*. If God has saved your children, then, dear friend, try to do something for your neighbours, for your work-people, for those with whom you associate in daily labour. God has appointed you to take care of those nearest home. They say the cobbler's wife goes barefooted. Do not let it be true. Begin at home, and go on with those nearest home. Manifest Christian love to your neighbours. It is a great pity that yonder Christian man, living in a very dark part of London, comes to the Tabernacle, and does good in our societies but never speaks a word for Jesus in the court where he lives.

Poor stuff, poor stuff, is that salt which is only salt when it is in the salt-box! Throw that bit of salt away. We want a kind of salt that begins to bite into any bit of meat it touches. Put it where you like, if it is good salt, it begins to operate upon that which is nearest to it. Some people are capital salt *in the box*: they are also good in the cake, they are beautifully white to look at, and you can cut them into ornamental shapes; but they are never used; they are merely kept for show. If salt does not preserve anything, throw it away. Ask the farmer whether he would like it for his fields. 'No,' he says, 'there is no goodness in it.' Salt that has no saltness in it is of no use. You can make the garden path of it. It is good to be trodden under foot of men; but that is all the use to which you can put it.

O my beloved fellow Christians, do not let it be said that you reside in a place to which you do no good whatever. I am sure if there were individual, personal work on the part of Christians in the localities where they reside, God the Holy Ghost would bless the unanimous action of his earnest, quickened church, and London would soon know that God has a people in the midst of it. If we keep away from the masses – if we cannot think of labouring in a district because it is too low or too poor – we shall have missed our vocation, and at the last we shall have to lament, 'They made me the keeper of the vineyards; but mine own vineyard have I not kept.'

You and I must cry mightily to the Holy Spirit to help us to live really and truly the lives which our professions demand of us. A day will come when all church-goings, and chapel-goings, and preachings, and singings, and sacraments, will seem fluff and useless stuff, if there has not been the substance of real living for Christ in all our religiousness. Oh that we would rouse ourselves to something like a divine earnestness! Oh that we felt the grandeur of our heavenly surroundings! We are no common men! We are loved with no common love! Jesus died for us! He died for us! He died for us! And is this poor life of ours, so often dull and worldly, our sole return? Behold that piece of land! He that bought it paid his life for it, watered it with bloody sweat, and sowed in it a divine seed. And what is the harvest? We naturally expect great things. Is the poor starveling life of many a professor a fit harvest for Christ's sowing his heart's blood? God the Father, God the Son, and God the Holy Ghost, all in action – what is the result? Omnipotence linking hands with love, and working out a miracle of grace! What comes of it? A half-hearted professor of religion. Is this all the result? O Lord, was there ever so small an effect from so great a cause? You might almost need a microscope to discover the result of the work of grace in some people's lives. Ought it to be so? Shall it be so? In the name of him that liveth and was dead, dare you let it be so? Help us, O God, to begin to live, and keep the vineyard which thou thyself hast given to us to keep, that we may render in our account at last with joy, and not with grief! Amen.

6

LOVE TO JESUS

'O thou whom my soul loveth'
(Song of Solomon 1:7)

If the life of a Christian may be compared to a sacrifice, then *humility* digs the foundation for the altar; *prayer* brings the unhewn stones and piles them one upon the other; *penitence* fills the trench round about the altar with water; *obedience* lays the wood in order; *faith* pleads the Jehovah-jireh, and places the victim upon the altar; but the sacrifice even then is incomplete, for where is the fire? *Love*, love alone can consummate the sacrifice by supplying the needful fire from heaven. Whatever we lack in our piety, as it is indispensable that we should have faith in Christ, so is it absolutely necessary that we should have love to him. That heart which is devoid of an earnest love to Jesus, is surely still dead in trespasses and sins. And if any man should venture to affirm that he had faith in Christ, but had no love to him, we would at once also venture to affirm as positively, that his religion was vain. Perhaps the great want of the religion of the times is love. Sometimes as I look upon the world at large, and the Church which lieth too much in its bosom, I am apt to think that the Church hath light, but lacketh fire; that she hath some degree of true faith, clear knowledge, and much beside which is precious, but that she lacketh to a great extent, that flaming love with which she once, as a chaste virgin, walked with Christ through the fires of martyrdom; when she showed to him her undefiled, unquenchable love in the catacomb of the city, and the caves of the rock; when the snows of the Alps might testify to the virgin purity of the love of the saints, by the purple stain which marked the shedding of blood in defence of our bleeding Lord – blood which had been shed in defence of him whom, though they had not seen his face, 'unceasing they adore'.

It is my pleasant task this morning to stir up your pure minds, that you, as part of Christ's Church, may feel somewhat in your hearts today of love to him, and may be able to address him not only under the title, 'Thou in whom my soul trusteth', but 'Thou whom my soul loveth'. Last Sabbath day, if you remember, we devoted to simple faith, and tried to preach the gospel to the ungodly; the present hour we devote to the pure, Spirit-born, godlike, flame of love.

On looking at my text, I shall come to regard it thus: First, we shall listen to the *rhetoric of the lip* as we here read it in these words, 'O thou whom my soul loveth.' We shall then observe *the logic of the heart*, which would justify us in giving such a title as this to Christ; and then come in the third place to something which even surpasses rhetoric or logic, the *absolute demonstration of the daily life*; and I pray that we may be able to prove constantly by our acts, that Jesus Christ is *he* whom our soul loveth.

First, then, the loving title of our text is to be considered as expressing RHETORIC OF THE LIP. The text calleth Christ, 'Thou whom my soul loveth.' Let us take this title and dissect it a little.

One of the first things which will strike us when we come to look upon it is the *reality* of the love which is here expressed. Reality, I say; understanding the term 'real', not in contradistinction to that which is lying and fictitious, but in contrast to that which is shadowy and indistinct. Do you not notice that the spouse here speaks of Christ as of one whom she knew actually to exist, not as an abstraction, but as a person. She speaks of him as a real person, 'Thou whom my soul loveth.' Why, these seem to be the words of one who is pressing him to her bosom, who sees him with her eyes, who tracks him with her feet, who knows that he is, and that he will reward the love which diligently seeketh him. Brethren and sisters, there often is a great deficiency in our love to Jesus. We do not realise the person of Christ. We think about Christ, and then we love the conception that we have formed of him. But oh, how few Christians view their Lord as being as real a person as we are ourselves – very man – a man that could suffer, a man that could die, substantial flesh and blood – very God as real as if he were not invisible, and as truly existent as though we could compass him in our minds. We want to have a real Christ more fully preached, and more fully loved by the Church. We fail in our love, because Christ is not real to us as he was to the early Church. The early Church did not preach much doctrine; they preached Christ. They had little to say of truths about Christ; it was Christ himself, his hands, his feet, his side, his eyes, his head, his crown of thorns, the sponge, the vinegar, the nails. Oh for the Christ of Mary Magdalene, rather than the Christ of the critical theologian; give me *the wounded body of divinity* rather than the soundest system of theology. Let me show you what I mean.

Suppose an infant taken away from its mother, and you should seek to foster in it a love to the parent by constantly picturing before it the idea of a mother – and attempting to give it the thought of a mother's relation to the child. Indeed, my friends, I think you would have a difficult task to fix in that child the true and real love which it ought to bear towards her who bore it. But give that child a mother; let it hang upon that mother's real breast; let it derive its nourishment from her very heart; let it see that mother; feel that mother; put its little arms about that mother's real neck and you have no hard task to make it love its mother. So is it with the Christian. We want Christ – not an abstract, doctrinal, pictured Christ – but a real Christ. I may preach to you many a year, and try to infuse into your souls a love of Christ; but until you can feel that he is a real man and a real person, really present with you, and that you may speak to him, talk to him, and tell him of your wants, you will not readily attain to a love like that of the text, so that you can call him, 'Thou whom my soul loveth.' I want you to feel, Christian, that your love to Christ is not a mere pious affection; but that as you love your wife, as you love your child, as you love your parent, so you love Christ; that though your love to him is of a finer cast, and a higher mould, yet it is just as real as the more earthly passion.

Let me suggest another figure. A war is raging in Italy for liberty. The very thought of liberty nerves a soldier. The thought of a hero makes a man a hero. Let me go and stand in the midst of the army and preach to them what heroes should be, and what brave men they should be who fight for liberty. My dear friends, the most earnest eloquence might have but little power. But put into the midst of these men Garibaldi – heroism incarnate; place before their eyes that dignified man – who seems like some old Roman newly arisen from his tomb – they see before them what liberty means, and what daring is, what courage can attempt, and what heroism can perform; for there he is, and, fired by his actual presence, their arms are strong, their swords are sharp, and they dash to the battle at once; his presence ensuring victory, because they realise in his presence the thought which makes men brave and strong. So the Church needs to feel and see a real Christ in her midst. It is not the *idea* of disinterestedness; it is not the idea of devotion; it is not the idea of self-consecration that will ever make the Church mighty: it must be that idea incarnate, consolidated, personified in the actual existence of a realised Christ in the camp of the Lord's host. I do pray for you, and pray you for me, that we may each one of us have a love which realises Christ, and which can address him as 'Thou whom my soul loveth'.

But again, look at the text and you will perceive another thing very clearly. The Church, in the expression which she uses concerning Christ, speaks not only with a realisation of his presence, but with a firm *assurance* of her own love. Many of you, who do really love Christ, can seldom get further than to say, 'O thou whom my soul desires to love! O thou whom I hope I love!' But this sentence saith not so at all. This title hath not the shadow of a doubt or a fear upon it: 'O thou whom my soul loveth!' Is it not a happy thing for a child of God when he knows that he loves Christ? When he can speak of it as a matter of consciousness? A thing out of which he is not to be turned by all the reasonings of Satan? A thing concerning which he can put his hand upon his heart, and appeal to Jesus and say, 'Lord, thou knowest all things, thou knowest that I love thee?' I say, is not this a delightful frame of mind? Or, rather, I reverse the question, Is not that a sad miserable state of heart in which we have to speak of Jesus otherwise than with assured affection? Ah, my brethren and sisters, there may be times when the most loving heart may, from the very fact that it loves intensely and loves sincerely, doubt whether it does love at all. But then such times will be times of distress, seasons of great soul-searching, nights of anguish. He who truly loves Christ will never give sleep to his eyes, nor slumber to his eyelids, when he is in doubt about his heart belonging to Jesus. 'No,' saith he, 'this is a matter too precious for me to question as to whether I am the possessor of it or no; this is a thing so vital that I cannot let it be with a "perhaps", as a matter of haphazard. No, I must know whether I love my Lord or no, whether I am his or not.'

If I am addressing any this morning who fear they do not love Christ, and yet hope they do, let me beg you, my dear friend, not to rest contented in your present state of mind; never be satisfied till you know that you are standing on the rock and until you are quite certain that you really do love Christ. Imagine for a moment, one of the apostles telling Christ that he *thought* he loved him. Fancy for a moment your own spouse telling you that she hoped she loved you. Fancy your child upon your knee saying, 'Father, I sometimes trust I love you.' What a stinging thing to say to you! You would almost as soon he said, 'I hate you.' Because, what is it? Shall he, over whom I watch with care, merely think he loves me? Shall she who lieth in my bosom, doubt, and make it a matter of conjecture, as to whether her heart is mine or no? O God, forbid we should ever dream of such a thing in our ordinary relations of life! Then how is it that we indulge in it in our piety? Is it not sickly and maudlin piety? Is it not a diseased state of heart that ever puts us in such a place at all? Is it not even a deadly state of heart that would let us rest contented there? No, let us not be satisfied till, by the full work of the Holy Spirit, we are made sure and certain, and can say with unstammering tongue, 'O thou whom my soul loveth.'

Now, notice something else equally worthy of our attention. The Church, the spouse, in this speaking of her Lord, thus directs our thoughts not merely to her confidence of love, but to the *unity* of her affections with regard to Christ. She hath not two lovers, she hath but one. She doth not say, '*O ye* on whom my heart is set!' but '*O thou*!' She hath but one after whom her heart is panting. She has gathered her affections into one bundle, she hath made them but one affection, and then she hath cast that bundle of myrrh and spices upon the breast of Christ. He is to her the 'Altogether Lovely', the gathering up of all the loves which once strayed abroad. She has put before the sun of her heart a burning-glass, which has brought all her love to a focus, and it is all concentrated with all its heat and vehemence upon Christ Jesus himself. Her heart, which once seemed like a fountain sending forth many streams, has now become as a fountain which hath but one channel for its waters. She hath stopped up all the other issues, she hath cut away the other pipes, and now the whole stream in one strong current runs toward him, and him alone. The Church, in the text here, is not a worshipper of God and of Baal too; she is no time-server, who hath a heart for all comers. She is not as she seeth none but Christ, and she knoweth none whom her soul desireth, saving her crucified Lord. The wife of a noble Persian having been invited to be present at the wedding feast of King Cyrus, her husband asked her merrily upon her return whether she did not think the bridegroom-monarch a most noble man. Her answer was, 'I know not whether he be noble or not; my husband was so before my eye that I saw none beside him; I have seen no beauty but in him.' So if you ask the Christian in our text, 'Is not Such-an-one fair and lovely?' 'No,' she replieth, 'my eyes are fully fixed on Christ, my heart is so taken up with him that I cannot tell if there be beauty anywhere else; I know that all beauty and all loveliness is summed up in him.' Sir Walter Raleigh used to say, 'That if all the histories of tyrants, the cruelty, the blood, the lust, the infamy, were all forgotten, yet all these histories might be rewritten out of the life of Henry VIII.' And I may say by way of contrast, 'If all the goodness, all the love, all the gentleness, all the faithfulness that ever existed could be blotted out, they could all be rewritten out of the history of Christ.' To the Christian, Christ is the only one she loveth; she hath no divided aims, no two adored ones; but she speaketh of him as of one to whom she has given her whole heart, and none have aught beside. 'O thou whom my soul loveth.'

Come, brethren and sisters, do we love Christ after this fashion? Do we love him so that we can say, 'Compared with our love to Jesus, all other loves are but as nothing.' We have those sweet loves which make earth dear to us; we do love those who are our kindred according to the flesh, we were indeed beneath the beasts if we did not. But some of us can say, 'We do love Christ better than husband or wife, or brother or sister.' Sometimes we think we could say with St Jerome, 'If Christ should bid me go this way, and my mother did hang about my neck to draw me another; and my father were in my way, bowing at my knees with tears entreating me not to go; and my children plucking at my skirts should seek to pull me the other way, I must unclasp my mother, I must push to the very ground my father, and put aside my children, for I must follow Christ.' We cannot tell which we love the most till they have come into collision. But when we come to see that the love of mortals requires us to do this, and the love of Christ to do the reverse, then shall we see which we love best. Oh, those were hard times with the martyrs; with that good man for instance, Mr Nicholas Ferrer, who was the father of some twelve children, all of them but little ones. On the road to the stake his enemies had contrived that his wife should meet him with all the little ones, and she had set them in a row kneeling down by the roadside. His enemies expected that surely now he would recant, and for the sake of those dear babes would certainly seek to save his life. But no! no! He had given them all up to God, and he could trust them with his heavenly Father; but he could not do a wrong thing even for the felicity of covering these little birds with his wings and cherishing them beneath his feathers. He took them one by one to his bosom, and looked, and looked again; and it pleased God to put into the mouth of his wife and of his children words which encouraged him instead of discouraging him, and ere he went from them his very babes had bidden the father play the man and die boldly for Christ Jesus. Ay, soul, we must have a love like this which cannot be rivalled, which cannot be shared; which is like a flood tide – other tides may come up very high upon the shore, but this cometh up to the very rocks and beats there – filling our soul to the very brim. I pray God we may know what such a love to Christ as this may mean.

Furthermore, I want to pluck you one more flower. If you will look at the title before us, you will have to learn not only its reality, its assurance, its unity; but you will have to notice its *constancy*, 'O thou whom my soul loveth'. Not, 'did love yesterday'; or 'may begin to love tomorrow'; but 'thou whom my soul *loveth*' – 'thou whom I have loved ever since I knew thee, and to love whom has become as necessary to me as my vital breath or my native air.' The true Christian is one who loves Christ for evermore. He doth not play fast and loose with Jesus; pressing him today to his bosom, and then turning aside and seeking after any Delilah who may with her witcheries pollute him. No, he feels that he is a Nazarite unto the Lord; he cannot and he will not pollute himself with sin at any time or in any place. Love to Christ in the faithful heart is as the love of the dove to its mate; she, if her mate should die, can never be tempted to be married unto another, but she sitteth still upon her perch and sigheth out her mournful soul until she dieth too. So were it with the Christian; if he had no Christ to love he must e'en die, for his heart has become Christ's. And so if Christ were gone, love could not be; then his heart would be gone, too, and a man without a heart were dead. The heart, is it not the vital principle of the body? And love, is it not the vital principle of the soul? Yet, there are some who profess to love the Master, but only walk with him by fits, and then go abroad like Dinah into the tents of the Shechemites. Oh, take heed, ye professors, who seek to have two husbands; my Master will never be a part-husband. He is not such a one as to have half of your heart. My Master, though he be full of compassion and very tender, hath too noble a spirit to allow himself to be half-proprietor of any kingdom. Canute, the Danish king, might divide England with Edmund the Ironside, because he could not win the whole country, but my Lord will have every inch of thee, or none. He will reign in thee from one end of the isle of man to the other, or else he will not put a foot upon the soil of thy heart. He was never part-proprietor in a heart, and he will not stoop to such a thing now. What saith the old Puritan? 'A heart is so little a thing, that it is scarce enough for a kite's breakfast, and ye say it be too great a thing for Christ to have it all?' No, give him the whole. It is but little when thou weighest his merit, and very small when measured with his loveliness. Give him all. Let thy united heart, thy undivided affection be constantly, every hour, given up to him.

'Can ye cleave to your Lord? can ye cleave to your Lord,
When the many turn aside?
Can ye witness he hath the living Word,
And none upon earth beside?

And can ye endure with the Virgin band,
The lowly and pure in heart,
Who, whithersoever their Lamb doth lead,
From his footsteps ne'er depart?

Do ye answer, 'We can'? Do ye answer, 'We can,
Through his love's constraining power!'
But ah remember the flesh is weak,
And will shrink in the trial-hour.
Yet yield to his love, who round you now,
The bands of a man would cast;
The cords of his love, who was given for you,
To the altar binding you fast.'

May that be your lot, constant, still to abide in him who has loved you.

I will make but one more remark, lest I weary you in thus trying to anatomise the rhetoric of love. In our text you will clearly perceive *a vehemence of affection*. The spouse saith of Christ, 'O thou whom my soul loveth.' She means not that she loves him a little, that she loves him with an ordinary passion, but that she loves him in all the deep sense of that word. Oh, Christian men and women, I do protest unto you I fear there are thousands of professors who never knew the meaning of this word 'love' as to Christ. They have known it when it referred to mortals; they have felt its flame, they have seen how every power of the body and of the soul are carried away with it; but they have not felt it with regard to Christ. I know you can *preach* about him, but do you love him? I know you can *pray* to him, but do you love him? I know you trust him – you think you do – but do you love him? Oh! is there a love to Jesus in your heart like that of the spouse when she could say, 'Let him kiss me with the kisses of his lips, for his love is better than wine.' 'No,' say you, 'that is too familiar for me.' Then I fear you do not love him, for love is always familiar. Faith may stand at a distance for her look is saving; but Love comes near, for she must kiss, she must embrace. Why, beloved, sometimes the Christian so loves his Lord, that his language becomes unmeaning to the ears of others who have never been in his state. Love hath a celestial tongue of her own, and I have sometimes heard her speak so that the lips of worldlings have mocked, and men have said, 'That man rants and raves – he knoweth not what he saith.' Hence it is that Love often becomes a Mystic, and speaks in mystic language, into which the stranger intrudeth not. Oh! you should see Love when she hath her heart full of her Saviour's presence, when she cometh out of her chamber! Indeed, she is like a giant refreshed with new wine. I have seen her dash down difficulties, tread upon hot irons of affliction and her feet have not been scorched; I have seen her lift up her spear against ten thousand, and she has slain them at one time. I have known her give up all she had, even to the stripping of herself, for Christ; and yet she seemed to grow richer, and to be decked with ornaments as she unarrayed herself, that she might cast her all upon her Lord, and give up all to him. Do you know this love, Christian brethren and sisters? Some of you do, I know, for I have seen you evince it in your lives. As for the rest of you, may you learn it, and get above the low standing of the mass of Christ's Church at the present day. Get up from the bogs and fens and damp morasses of lukewarm Laodiceanism, and come ye up, come ye up higher, up to the mountain top, where ye shall stand bathing your foreheads in the sunlight, seeing earth beneath you, its very tempests under your feet, its clouds and darkness rolling down below in the valley, while you talking with Christ, who speaks to you out of the cloud, are almost caught up into the third heaven to dwell there with him.

Thus have I tried to explain the rhetoric of my text, 'Thou whom my soul loveth'

2. **Now let me come to THE LOGIC OF THE HEART, which lies at the bottom of the text**. My heart, why shouldst thou love Christ? With what argument wilt thou justify thyself? Strangers stand and hear me tell of Christ, and they say, 'Why shouldst thou love thy Saviour so?' My heart, thou canst not answer them so as to make them see his loveliness, for they are blind, but thou canst at least be justified in the ears of those who have understandings; for doubtless the virgins will love him, if thou wilt tell to them why thou lovest him.

Our hearts give for their reason why they love him, first, this: We love him for *his infinite loveliness*. If there were no other reason, if Christ had not bought *us* with his blood, yet sometimes we feel if we had renewed hearts, we must love him for having died for others. I have sometimes felt in my own soul, that setting aside the benefit I received from his dear cross, and his most precious passion, which, of course, must ever be the deepest motive of love, 'for we love him because he first loved us'; yet setting aside that, there is such beauty in Christ's character, such loveliness in his passion, such a glory in that self-sacrifice, that one must love him. Can I look into thy eyes and not be smitten with thy love? Can I gaze upon thy thorn-crowned head, and shall not my heart feel the thorn within it? Can I see thee in the fever of death, and shall not my soul be in a fever of passionate love to thee? It is impossible to see Christ and not to love him; you cannot be in his company without at once feeling that you are welded to him. Go and kneel by his side in Gethsemane's garden, and I am persuaded that the drops of gore as they fall upon the ground, shall each one of them be irresistible reasons why you should love him. Hear him as he cries, 'My God, my God, why hast thou forsaken me?' Remember that he endures this out of love to others, and you must love him. If you ever read the history of Moses you believe him to be the grandest of men, and you admire him, and look up to him as to some huge colossus, some mighty giant of the olden times. But you never feel a particle of love in your hearts towards Moses; you could not; his is an unloveable character; there is something to admire, but nothing to win attachment. When you see Christ you look up, but you do more, you feel drawn up; you do not admire so much as love; you do not adore so much as embrace; his character enchants, subdues, o'erwhelms, and with the irresistible impulse of its own sacred attraction, it draws your spirit right up to him. Well did Dr Watts say:

> His worth, if all the nations knew,
> Sure the whole earth would love him too.

But still, love hath another argument why she loveth Christ, namely, *Christ's love* to her. Didst thou love me Jesus, King of heaven, Lord of angels, Master of all worlds, didst thou set thy heart on me? What, didst thou love me from of old, and in eternity choose me to thyself? Didst thou continue to love me as the ages rolled on? Didst thou come from heaven to earth that thou mightest win me to be thy spouse, and dost thou love me so that thou dost not leave me alone in this poor desert world; and art thou this very day preparing a house for me where I shall dwell with thee for ever? A very wretch, Lord, I should prove had I no love to thee. I must love thee, it is impossible for me to resist it; that thought that thou lovest me hath compelled my soul to love thee. Me! me! what was there in me; couldst thou see beauties in me? I see none in myself; my eyes are red with weeping, because of my blackness and deformity; I have said even to the sons of men, 'Look not upon me, for I am black, because the sun hath looked upon me.' And dost *thou* see beauties in *me*? What a quick eye must thou have, nay, rather it must be that thou hast made my eyes to be thy looking-glass, and so thou seest thyself in me, and it is thy image that thou lovest; sure thou couldst not love me. That ravishing text in the Canticles, where Jesus saith to the spouse, 'Thou art all fair my love, there is no spot in thee', can you imagine Christ saying that to you? And yet he has said it, 'Thou art all fair my love, there is no spot in thee', he hath put away thy blackness, and thou standest in his sight as perfect as though thou hadst never sinned, and as full of loveliness as though thou wert what thou shalt be when made like unto him at last.

Oh brothers and sisters, some of you can say with emphasis, 'Did he love me, then I must love him.' I run my eye along your ranks, there sits a brother who loveth Christ who not many months ago cursed him. There sits a drunkard, there another who was in prison for crimes; and he loved *you*, even you; and you could abuse the wife of your bosom, because she loved the dear name, you were never happier than when you were violating his day, and showing your disrespect to his ministers, and your hatred to his cause, yet he loved you. And *me*! even me! forgetful of a mother's prayers, regardless of a father's tears, having much light, and yet sinning much, he loved me, and has proved his love. I charge thee, O my heart, by the roes and by the hinds of the field, that thou givest thyself wholly up to my Beloved, and that thou spend and be spent for him. Is that your charge to your heart this morning? Oh! it must be if you know Jesus, and then know that Jesus loves you.

One more reason does love give us yet more powerful still. Love feels that she must give herself to Christ, because of *Christ's suffering for her*.

Can I Gethsemane forget?
Or there thy conflict see,
Thine agony and bloody sweat,
And not remember thee?

When to the cross I turn mine eyes,
And rest on Calvary,
O Lamb of God! my sacrifice!
I must remember thee.

My life when it shall ebb out may cause me to lose many mental powers, but memory will love no other name than is recorded there. The agonies of Christ have burnt his name into our hearts; you cannot stand and see him mocked by Herod's men of war, you cannot behold him made nothing of, and spit upon by menial lips, you cannot see him with the nails pierced through his hands and through his feet, you cannot mark him in the extreme agonies of his awful passion without saying: 'And didst thou suffer all this for me, then I must love thee, Jesus. My heart feels that no other can have such a claim upon it as thou hast, for none others have spent themselves for me as thou hast done. Others may have sought to buy my love with the silver of earthly affection, and with the gold of a zealous and affectionate character, but thou hast bought it with thy precious blood, and thou hast the richest claim to it, thine shall it be, and that for ever.'

This is love's logic. I may well stand here and defend the believer's love to his Lord. I wish I had more to defend than I have. I dare stand here and defend the utmost extravagancies of speech, and the wildest fanaticisms of action, when they have been done for love to Christ. I say again, I only wish I had more to defend in these degenerate times. Has a man given up all for

Christ? I will prove him wise if he has given up for such an one as Christ is. Has a man died for Christ? I write over his epitaph that he surely was no fool who had but the wisdom to give up his heart for one who had his heart pierced for him. Let the Church try to be extravagant for once; let her break the narrow bounds of her conventional prudence, and for once arise and dare to do wonders – let the age of miracles return to us – let the Church make bare her arm, and roll up from her the sleeves of her formality, let her go forth with some mighty thought within her, at which the worldling shall laugh and scoff, and I will stand here and before the bar of a scoffing world, dare to defend her. O Church of God, thou canst do no extravagance for Christ. Ye may bring out your Marys and they may break their alabaster boxes, but he deserves the breaking well. Thou mayst shed thy perfume, and give to him rivers of oil, and ten thousands of the fat of fed beasts, but he deserves it well.

I see the Church as she was in the first centuries, like an army storming a city – a city that was surrounded with a vast moat, and there was no means of reaching the ramparts except by filling up the moat with the dead bodies of the Church's own martyrs and confessors. Do you see them? A bishop has just now fallen in; his head has been smitten off with the sword. The next day at the tribunal there are twenty wishing to die that they may follow him; and on the next day twenty more; and the stream pours on till the huge moat is filled. Then, those who follow after, scale the walls and plant the blood-red standard of the cross, the trophy of their victory upon the top thereof. Should the world say, 'Why this expense of blood?' I answer, 'He is worthy for whom it was shed.' The world says, 'Why this waste of suffering? Why this pouring out of an energy in a cause that at best is but fanatical?' I reply, 'He is worthy, he is worthy, though the whole world were put into the censer, and all men's blood were the frankincense, he is worthy to have it all sacrificed before him. Though the whole Church should be a slaughtered hecatomb, he is worthy upon whose altar it should be sacrificed. Though every one of us should lie and rot in a dungeon, though the moss should grow upon our eyelids, though our bodies should be given to the kites and the carrion crows, he is worthy to claim the sacrifice; and it were all too mean a gift for such an one as he is.' O Master, restore unto the Church the strength of love which can hear such language, and feel it to be true.

3. **Now I come to my last point, upon which I must dwell but briefly. Rhetoric is good, logic is better, but A POSITIVE DEMONSTRATION is the best**.

I sought to give you rhetoric when I expounded the words of the text. I have tried to give you logic now that I have given you the reasons for the love in the text. And now I want you to give – *I* cannot give it – I want *you* to give, each for himself, the demonstration of your love for Christ in your daily lives. Let the world see that this is not a mere label to you – a label for something that does not exist, but that Christ really is to you 'him whom your soul loves'. You ask me how you shall do it, and I reply thus: I do not ask you to shave your crown and become a monk, or to cloister yourself, my sister, alone, and become a nun. Such a thing might even show your love to yourself rather than your love to Christ. But I ask you to go home now, and during the days of the week engage in your ordinary business; go with the men of the world as you are called to do, and take the calling which Christ has given to you, and see if you cannot honour him in your calling. I, as a minister of course, must find it to some degree less honourable work to serve Christ than you do, because my calling doth as it were supply me with gold; and for me to make a golden image of Christ out of that is but small work, though God wotteth I find it more than my poor strength could do apart from his grace. But for you to work out the image of Christ in the iron, or clay, or common metal of your ordinary conversation – oh, this will be glorious indeed! And I think you may honour Christ in your sphere as much as I can in mine; perhaps more, for some of you may know more trouble, you may have more poverty, you may have more temptation, more enemies; and therefore you, by loving Christ under all these trials, may demonstrate more fully than ever I can, how true your love is to him, and how soul-inspiring is his love to you. Away, I say, and look out on the morrow, and the next day, for opportunities of doing something for Christ. Speak up for his dear name if there be any that abuse him; and if you find him wounded in his members, be you as Eleanor, Queen of England's king, suck the poison out of his wounds. Be ready to have *your* name abused rather than he should be dishonoured; stand up always for him, and be his champion. Let him not lack a friend, for he stood thy friend when you had none beside. If thou meet with any of his poor people, show them love for his sake, as David did Mephibosheth out of love to Saul. If thou knowest any of them to be hungry, set meat before them; thou hadst as good set the dish before Jesus Christ himself. If thou seest them naked, clothe them; thou dost clothe Christ when thou clothest his people.

Nay, do thou not only seek to do this good temporally to his children, but seek thou evermore to be a Christ to those who are not his children as yet. Go among the wicked and among the lost, and the abandoned; tell them words of him; tell them Jesus Christ came into the world to save sinners; go after his lost sheep; be thou shepherd as he was a shepherd, so wilt thou show thy love. Give what thou canst to him; when thou diest, make him heir of some of thy estate; I should not think I loved my friend, if I did not sometimes make him a present; I should not think I love Christ if I did not give him somewhat, some sweet cane with money, some fat of my burnt sacrifices. I heard the other day a question asked concerning an old man, who had long professed to be a Christian. They were saying he left so much and so much, and one said, 'But did he leave Christ anything in his will?' Some one laughed and thought it ridiculous. Ah! so it would be, because men do not think of Christ as being a person; but if we had this love it would be but natural to us to give to him, to live for him, and perhaps if we had ought at last to let him have it – that so even dying we might give our friend in our dying testament a proof that we remembered him, even as he remembered us in his last testament and will.

Oh brothers and sisters – what we want more of in the Church is, more extravagant love to Christ. I want each of you to show your love to Jesus, sometimes by doing something the like of which you have never done before. I remember saying one Sabbath morning that the Church ought to be the place of invention as much as the world. We do not know what machine is to be discovered yet by the world, but every man's wit is at work to find out something new. So ought the wits of the Church to be at work to find out some new plan of serving Christ. Robert Raikes found out Sabbath-schools; John Pounds the Ragged-school; but are we to be content with carrying on their inventions? No; we want something new. It was in the Surrey Hall, through that sermon, that our brethren first thought of the midnight meetings that were held – an invention suggested by the sermon I preached upon the woman with the alabaster box. But we have not come to the end yet. Is there no man that can invent some new deed for Christ? Is there no brother that can do something more for him than has been done today, or yesterday, or during the last month? Is there no man that will dare to be strange and singular and wild, and in the world's eye to be fanatical – for that is no love which is not fanatical in the eye of man. Depend upon it, that is no love that only confines itself to propriety. I would the Lord would put into thy heart some thought of giving an unwonted thank-offering to him, or of doing an unusual service, that so Christ might be honoured with the best of thy lambs, and that the fat of thy bullocks might be exceeding glorified by your proof of love to him.

God bless you as a congregation. I can only invoke his blessing, for O these lips refuse to speak of love which I trust my heart knows, and which I desire to feel more and more. Sinner, trust Christ before thou seek to love him, and trusting Christ thou art saved.

7

THE CHURCH'S LOVE TO HER LOVING LORD

'Tell me, O thou whom my soul loveth, where thou feedest, where thou makest thy flock to rest at noon: for why should I be as one that turneth aside by the flocks of thy companions?' (Canticles 1:7)

We shall need to lift up our hearts to God and ask to be quickened in grace, or the precious truths in our text will not prove to us 'as honey out of the rock', nor the 'feast of fat things, of wine and marrow, of wine on the lees well refined'. We cannot appreciate the spirituality of this book, unless God's Spirit shall help us. Many read these words and only see a proof of the imaginative power of an eastern mind. Some read to scoff and blaspheme, and others, even good people, neglect to read this book altogether, being unable to drink in its spirit because of their want of that higher life of communion with the Beloved, which is here so beautifully laid open to our view. Now I am persuaded better things of you beloved. I am sure that you believe that every word of God is precious, and most certainly we say of this book, 'it is more to be desired than gold, yea than much fine gold, sweeter also than honey, or the droppings of the honey-comb'. This book of the Canticles is most precious to us, it is the inner court of the temple of truth. It seems to us to belong to the secret place of the tabernacle of the Most High. We see our Saviour's face in almost every page of the Bible, but here we see his heart and feel his love to us. We shall hope this morning to speak of our own experience, as well as of the Church who is here speaking. You will perceive that she begins with a title, she expresses a desire, she enforces it with an argument: 'Tell me, O thou whom my soul loveth, where thou feedest, where thou makest thy flock to rest at noon: for why should I be as one that turneth aside by the flocks of thy companions?'

1. We commence with the title: 'O thou whom my soul loveth.'

It is well to be able to call the Lord Jesus Christ by this name without an 'if', or a 'but'. A very large proportion of Christian people can only say of Christ that they *hope* they love him; they *trust* they love him; but this is a very poor and shallow experience which is content to stay here. It seems to me that no one ought to give any rest to his spirit till he feels quite sure about a matter of such vital importance. We are not content to have a hope of the love of our parents, or of our spouse, or of our children; we feel we must be certain there; and we ought not to be satisfied with a hope that Christ loves us, and with a bare trust that we love him. The old saints did not generally speak with buts, and ifs, and hopes, and trusts, but they spoke positively and plainly. 'I know whom I have believed,' saith Paul. 'I know that my Redeemer liveth,' saith Job. 'He whom my soul loveth,' saith Solomon, in the song as we have it here. Learn, dear friends, to get that positive knowledge of your love to Jesus, and be not satisfied till you can talk about your interest in him as a reality, which you have made infallibly sure by having received the witness of the Holy Spirit, and his seal upon your soul by faith, that you are born of God, and belong to Christ.

Speaking then of this title which rings the great bell of love to Jesus, let us notice first the *cause*, and secondly the *effect* of that love. If we can look into the face of him who once sweat great drops of blood, and call him, 'O thou whom my soul loveth', it is interesting to consider what is the cause of our love. And here our reply is very quick. The *efficient cause* of our love is *the Holy Spirit of God.* We should never have had a spark of love to Jesus if it had not been bestowed upon us by the divine Worker. Well said John, 'Love is of God'. Certain it is so. Our love to Christ is one beam from himself, the Sun. Certainly a man can no more naturally love Christ than a horse can fly. I grant you there is no physical disability, but there is a moral and spiritual disability which effectually disqualifies him from the high and lofty emotion of love to Jesus. Into that dead corpse the living spirit must be breathed; for those who are dead in trespasses and sins cannot love Christ. That heart of stone must be transformed into a heart of flesh, for stones may be hurled at the Saviour, but they can never love him. That lion must become a lamb, or it can never claim Christ as its Shepherd. That raven must be turned into a dove, or it will never fly to Christ as its ark. 'Except a man be born again,' we may say he cannot see this precious sparkling jewel of the kingdom of God, love to Christ. Search yourselves then, brethren, do you love him or not, for if you love him, you have been born again; and if you do not love him, then you are still in darkness, and are not his.

> Can you pronounce his charming name,
> His acts of kindness tell;
> And while you dwell upon the theme,
> No sweet emotion feel?

I think some of us would have to answer

> A very wretch, Lord, I should prove,
> Had I no love to thee;
> Sooner than not my Saviour love,
> Oh, may I cease to be!

This, then, is the efficient cause – the Holy Spirit. The *rational cause*, the logical reason why we love Jesus lies in himself – in his looks, in his present working, and in his person, besides many other little founts, which all tend to swell the river – the growing, deepening river of our love to him.

Why do we love Jesus? We have the best of answers – *because he first loved us*. Hearken, ye strangers who inquire why we should love the Saviour so. We will give you such reasons that we will satisfy you and set your mouths watering to be partakers of the same reasons, that you may come to love him too. Why do we love him? Because or ever this round earth was fashioned between the palms of the great Creator, before he had painted the rainbow, or hung out the lights of the sun and moon, Christ's delights were with us. He foresaw us through the glass of his prescience; he knew what we should be – looked into the book in which all his 'members were written, which in continuance were fashioned, when as yet there were none of them'; and as he looked upon us, the glance was love. He delighted to sit upon the throne of glory, and to remember his dear ones who were yet to be born. It was the great prospect which his mighty and infinite Spirit had – a joy that was set before him, that he should see a multitude that no man could number who should be his beloved for ever.

> Lov'd of my Christ, for him again,
> With love intense I'll burn;
> Chosen of Thee ere time began,
> I choose Thee in return.

Oh, could you know that Jesus had loved you from before all worlds, you must love him. At least you will grant there cannot be a better reason for love than love. Love demands; nay, it does not demand, it takes by almighty force, by irresistible energy, that heart captive upon whom it thus sets itself.

This Jesus loved us for no reason whatever in ourselves. We were black as the tents of Kedar; we had much deformity but no beauty, and yet he loved us; and our deformity was of such a kind that it might meritoriously have made him hate us. We kicked against him and despised him. Our language naturally was, 'We will not have this man to reign over us', and when we heard of his loving us, we sneered at it. He was despised and rejected of men; we hid as it were, our faces from him. He was despised and we esteemed him not. We thought his love an empty tale, a paltry trifle, and yet he loved us. Nay, we were his enemies. We slew him; we confess with sorrow that we were the murderers of the Prince of Life and Glory. Our hands were stained with his gore and our garments dyed with his blood, and yet he saw all this and loved us still. Shall we not love him? Sure our heart is harder than adamant, because we do not love him more. But it were hell-hardened steel if it did not love at all.

Our Saviour so loved us that he stripped himself of his robes of radiance.

Listen, ye children of God, it is the old story over again, but it is always new to you. He stripped himself of his bright array, laid aside his sceptre and his crown, and became an infant in Bethlehem's manger amongst the horned oxen. Thirty years of poverty and shame the King of heaven spent among the sons of men, and all out of love to us. Jesus the heavenly lover, panting to redeem his people, was content to abide here without a place whereon to rest his head, that he might rescue you. See him yonder in the garden in his agony, his soul exceeding sorrowful even unto death; his forehead, nay his head, his hair, his garments red with the bloody sweat. See him giving his back to the smiters, and his cheeks to them that pluck off the hair. See him as he hides not his face from shame and spitting, dumb like a sheep before her shearers, and like a lamb that is brought to the slaughter, so he opened not his mouth, but patiently bore it all on our behalf. See him with the cross upon his mangled shoulders, staggering through Jerusalem's streets, unwept, unpitied, except by poor feeble women! See him, ye that love him, and love him more as he stretches out his hands to the nail, and gives his feet to the iron. See him, as with power to deliver himself he is made captive. Behold him as they lift up the cross with him upon it and dash it down into its place and dislocate his bones. Hear that cry, 'I am poured out like water: all my bones are out of joint. Thou hast brought me into the dust of death.' Stand, if ye can, and view that face so full of dolour. Look till a sword shall go through your own heart as it went through his virgin mother's very soul. Oh, see him as he thirsts and has that thirst mocked with vinegar. Hear him, as he prays and has that prayer parodied, 'He cries for Elias, let Elias come and take him down.' See him, as they who love him come and kiss his feet and bathe them with their tears. Will you not love him who did all that friend could do for friend; who gave his life for us? Beloved, here are a thousand crimson cords that tie us to the Saviour, and I hope we feel their constraining power. It is his vast love, the old eternal bond, the love which redeemed, which suffered in our stead, the love which pleaded our cause before the eternal throne; it is this which we give as a sufficient reason why we should love the Saviour, if needs be, even unto death.

Moreover, we have another reason. I trust many here can say that they love the Saviour *because of his present dealings towards them*. What has he not done for us this very day? Some of you came here this morning heavy and you went away rejoicing; perhaps you have had answers to prayer this very week. You have passed through the furnace and not a smell of fire has passed upon you. You have had many sins this week, but you have felt the efficacy of his blood again and again. Some of us have known what it is during the past six days to have the ravishing delights of private commun-ion with him. He has made us glad; our spirits have leaped for very joy, for he hath turned again the captivity of our soul. You have drunk of him as of 'the brook by the way', and you have therefore lifted up your head. Beloved, if there were nothing else which Christ had done for my soul, that which I have tasted and handled of him within the last few months would make me love him for ever, and I know that you can say the same.

Nor is this all. We love the Saviour because of *the excellency of his person*. We are not blind to excellence anywhere, but still we can see no excellence like his.

> Jesus thou fairest, dearest one,
> What beauties thee adorn!
> Far brighter than the noonday sun,
> Or start that gilds the morn.
>
> Here let me fix my wandering eyes,
> And all thy glories trace;
> Till, in the world of endless joys,
> I rise to thine embrace.

When Tigranes and his wife were both taken prisoners by Cyrus, Cyrus turning to Tigranes said, 'What will you give for the liberation of your wife?' and the King answered, 'I love my wife so that I would cheerfully give up my life if she might be delivered from servitude'; whereupon Cyrus said, 'That if there was such love as that between them they might both go free.' So when they were away and many were talking about the beauty and generosity of Cyrus, and especially about the beauty of his person, Tigranes, turning to his wife, asked her what she thought of Cyrus, and she answered that she saw nothing anywhere but in the face of the man who had said that he would die if she might only be released from servitude. 'The beauty of that man,' she said, 'makes me forget all others.' And verily we would say the same of Jesus. We would not decry the angels, nor think ill of the saints, but the beauties of that man who gave his life for us are so great that they have eclipsed all others, and our soul only wishes to see him and not another; for, as the stars hide their heads in the presence of the sun, so may ye all begone, ye delights, ye excellencies, when Christ Jesus, the chief delight, the chief excellency, maketh his appearance. Dr Watts saith:

> His worth, if all the nations knew,
> Sure the whole earth would love him too.

And so it seems to us. Could you see him, you must love him. It was said of Henry VIII, that if all the portraits of tyrants, and murderers and thieves were out of existence, they might all be painted from the one face of Harry VIII; and turning that round another way, we will say, that if all the excellencies, beauties, and perfections of the human race were blotted out, they might all be painted again from the face of the Lord Jesus.

All over glorious is my Lord;
Must be beloved, and yet adored.

These are some of the reasons why our heart loves Jesus. Before I leave those reasons, I should like to put a few questions round amongst this great crowd. O friends, would you not love Jesus if you knew something of this love as shed abroad in your hearts, something of this love as being yours? Now, remember, there is a very great promise that Christ has made, and it is this, 'Him that cometh to me I will in no wise cast out.' Now what does that refer to? Why to any 'him' in all the world, that cometh to Christ. Whoever you may be, if you come to Jesus – and you know that means just trusting him, leaning upon him – if you come to him, he will not cast you out; and when he has received you to his bosom, you will then know (but you cannot know till then) how much he loves you, and then, methinks, you will say with us, 'Yes, his name is "Thou whom my soul loveth".'

I shall now for a short time speak on the *effects* of this love, as we have dwelt on the cause of it. When a man has true love to Christ, it is sure to lead him to *dedication*. There is a natural desire to give something to the person whom we love, and true love to Jesus compels us to give ourselves to him. One of the earliest acts of the Christian's life is to take ourselves, and lay body, soul and spirit upon the altar of consecration, saying, 'Here am I; I give myself to thee.' When the pupils of Socrates had nearly all of them given him a present, there was one of the best scholars who was extremely poor, and he said to Socrates, 'I have none of these things which the others have presented to thee; but, O Socrates, I give thee myself;' whereupon Socrates said it was the best present he had had that day. 'My son, give me thy heart' – this is what Jesus asks for. If you love him, you must give him this.

True love next shows itself in *obedience*. If I love Jesus, I shall do as he bids me. He is my husband, my Lord – I call him 'Master'. 'If ye love me,' saith he, 'keep my commandments.' This is his chosen proof of my love, and I am sure, if I love him, I shall keep his commandments. And yet there are some who profess to love Christ who very seldom think of keeping some of his commandments. 'This do ye in remembrance of me,' he says, and yet some of you never come to his table. May I gently ask you, how you make this disobedience consort with genuine affection for him? 'If ye love me, keep my commandments.'

'Tis love that makes our willing feet
In swift obedience move.

We can do anything for those we love, and, if we love Jesus, no burden will be heavy, no difficulty will be great; we should rather wish to do more than he asks of us, and only desire that he were a little more exacting that we might have a better opportunity of showing forth our affection.

True love, again, is always *considerate* and afraid lest it should give offence. It walks very daintily. If I love Jesus, I shall watch my eye, my heart, my tongue, my hand, being so fearful lest I should wake my beloved, or make him stir until he please; and I shall be sure not to take in those bad guests, those ill-favoured guests of pride and sloth, and love of the world. I shall tell them to be packing, for I have a dear one within who will not tarry long if he sees me giving sidling glances to these wicked ones. My heart shall be wholly his. He shall sit at the head of the table, he shall have the best dish thereon, nay, I will send all others away that I may have him all to myself, and that he may have my whole heart, all that I am, and all that I have.

Again, true love to Christ will make us *very jealous* of his honour. As Queen Eleanor went down upon her knees to suck the poison from her husband's wound, so we shall put our lips to the wound of Christ when he has been stabbed with the dagger of calumny, or inconsistency, being willing sooner to take the poison ourselves, and to be ourselves diseased and despised than that his name, *his cross!* should suffer ill. Oh, what matters it what becomes of us, if the King reigneth? I will go home to my bed, and die in peace, if the King sits on the throne. Let me see King David once again installed in Zion's sacred halls; and my soul, in poverty and shame, shall still rejoice if the banished King Jesus shall once again come back, and have his own, and take his sceptre, and wear his crown. Beloved, I trust we can say we would not mind if Christ would make a mat of us, if he would wipe his Church's filthy sandals on us, if we might but help to make her pure; we would hold the stirrup for him to mount any day, ay, and be his horsing-block that he might mount his glorious charger and ride forth conquering and to conquer. Say, what mattereth it what we are, or where we are, if the King have his own?

If we love Christ, again, we shall be *desiring to promote his cause*, and we shall be desiring to promote it ourselves. We shall wish to see the strength of the mighty turned at the gate, that King Jesus may return triumphant; we shall not wish to sit still while our brethren go to war, but we shall want to take our portion in the fray, that like soldiers that love their monarch, we may prove by our wounds and by our sufferings that our love is real. The apostle says, 'Let us not love in word only but in deed and in truth.' Actions speak louder than words, and we shall always be anxious to tell our love in deeds as well as by our lips. The true disciple asks continually, 'Lord what wilt thou have me to do?' He esteems it his highest honour to serve the Lord. 'I would rather be a doorkeeper in the house of my God than dwell in the tents of wickedness.'

There's not a lamb in all the flock,
I would disdain to feed;
There's not a foe before whose face
I fear thy cause to plead.

Would not my ardent spirit vie
With angels round thy throne,
To execute thy sacred will
And make thy glory known?

Yes, indeed, we thus can sing, and mean, I trust, every word; yea, will go forth into the whole world and preach the gospel to every creature. We will tell of this love to all, and labour to win for the Master's honour a multitude which no man can number out of every nation and kindred and tribe and tongue and people. I believe in an active love, a love which has hands to labour and feet to run, as well as a heart to feel, eyes to glance, and ears to listen. A mother's love is of the purest and intensest sort in the world, and it is the most practical. It shows itself in deeds of untiring devotion both night and day. So also should it be with us; we should let our affections prompt us to lifelong labour. The love of Christ should constrain us to live, and if needs be die to serve him. Heaven is the place of purest, holiest attachment to Christ; then we shall understand most about his love to us, and of all he has done to prove it, and the consequence will be that his servants shall serve him day and night in his holy temple. We are expecting a home in glory not of idleness, but of continual activity. It is written, 'His servants shall serve him', and we are taught to pray now that we may do his will on earth as it is done in heaven. Let us, therefore, each one, be busily engaged in the great harvest-field. The harvest is great and the labourers are few. There is room for all, and each man's place is waiting to receive him. If we truly love our Lord, we shall at once press to the front and begin the 'work of faith and labour of love'. Has not the Master been wont to show his love to us in deeds? Look to Bethlehem, to Gabbatha, to Gethsemane, to Golgotha; yea, look to his whole life as he 'went about doing good', and see if all this will not stir you up to service. Listen to the life-story of the Lord, and you will hear a voice from each one of his deeds of love saying to you, 'Go thou and do likewise.'

And, once again, if we love Jesus we shall be *willing to suffer for him*. Pain will become light; we shall sing with Madame Guyon:

To me 'tis equal whether love ordain my life or death,
Appoint me ease, or pain.

It is a high attainment to come to, but love can make us think ourselves of so small import that if Christ can serve himself of us, we shall make no choice as to what, or where we may be. We can sing once more:

> Would not my heart pour forth its blood
> In honour of thy name,
> And challenge the cold hand of death
> To damp this immortal flame?

Our hearts are, I trust, so full of real devotion to Christ, that we can give him everything, and endure all things for his sake. Cannot we say:

> For him I count as gain each loss,
> Disgrace for him renown,
> Well may I glory in his cross,
> While he prepares my crown.

Darkness is light about us if we can serve him there. The bitter is sweet if the cup is put to our lips in order that we may share in his sufferings, and prove ourselves to be his followers. When Ignatius was led to his martyrdom, as he contemplated the nearness of his death and suffering, he said, 'Now I begin to be a Christian'; he felt that all that he had done and suffered before was not enough to entitle him to be called a follower of Christ, but now as the Master's bloody baptism was before him, he realised the truth so dear to every right-minded Christian, that he was to be 'like unto his Lord'. Here we can all prove our love, we can *suffer his will* calmly if we are not able to *do it publicly*.

> Weak as I am, yet through thy love,
> I all things can perform;
> And, smiling, triumph in thy name
> Amid the raging storm.

I pray God we may have such a love moreover as thirsts after Jesus, which cannot be satisfied without present communion with him.

2. This brings me to the thought, which I shall only touch upon as the swallow skims the brook with his wing, and then up and away, lest I weary you; the second point of consideration is the DESIRE OF THE CHURCH AFTER CHRIST JESUS OUR LORD: having called him by his title, she now expresses her longing to be with him. 'Tell me, O thou whom my soul loveth, where thou feedest, where thou makest thy flock to rest at noon.'

The desire of a renewed soul is to find out Christ and to be with him. Stale meats left over from yesterday are very well when there is nothing else, but who does not like hot food fresh from the fire? And past communion with Christ is very well. 'I remember thee from the land of the Hermonites and the hill Mizar'; but these are only stale meats, and a loving soul wants fresh food every day from the table of Christ, and you that have once had the kisses of his mouth, though you remember the past kisses with delight, yet want daily fresh tokens of his love. He that drinks of this water will never thirst again, it is true, except for this water, and he *will* so thirst for *it*, that he will be like Samuel Rutherford, who began to be out of heart with the buckets and to want to get right to the well-head that he might lie down and drink, and then, if he could have his fill, he would drink the well quite dry. But there is no hope of that, or rather no fear of it: the well can never be empty, for it rises as we drink.

A true loving soul, then, wants present communion with Christ; so the question is, 'Tell me where thou feedest? Where dost thou get thy comfort from, O Jesus? I will go there. Where do thy thoughts go? To thy cross? Dost thou look back to that? Then I will go there. Where thou feedest, there will I feed.'

Or does this mean actively, instead of being in the passive or the neuter? Where doest thou feed thy flock? In *thy house*? I will go there, if I may find thee there. In private *prayer*? Then I will not be slack in that. In the *Word*? Then I will read it night and day. Tell me where thou feedest, for wherever thou standest as the shepherd, there will I be, for I want thee. I cannot be satisfied to be apart from thee. My soul hungers and thirsts to be with thee. She puts it again, 'Where dost thou make thy flock to rest at noon', for there is only rest in one place, where thou causest thy flock to rest at noon. That must be a grace-given rest, and only to be found in some one chosen place. Where is the shadow of that rock? It is very hot just now here in the middle of summer, when the sun is pouring down his glorious rays like bright but sharp arrows upon us, and we, that are condemned to live in this great wilderness of brown bricks and mortar, often recollect those glades where the woods grow thick, and where the waters leap from crag to crag down the hill side, and where the birds are singing among the birks. We delight to think of those leafy bowers where the sun cannot dart his rays, where, on some mossy bank, we may stretch ourselves to rest, or lave our weary limbs in some limpid stream; and this is just what the spouse is after. She feels the heat of the world's sun, and she longs to be away from its cares and troubles that have furrowed and made brown her face till she looked as if she had been a busy keeper of the vineyards. She wants to get away to hold quiet communion with her Lord, for he is the brook where the weary may lave their wearied limbs; he is that sheltered nook, that shadow of the great rock in the weary land where his people may lie down and be at peace.

Jesus, the very thought of thee,
With sweetness fills my breast;
But sweeter far thy face to see,
And in thy presence rest.

For those who find thee, find a bliss,
Nor tongue, nor pen can show,
The love of Jesus, what it is,
None but his loved ones know.

Now do you not want this tonight? Do not your souls want Christ tonight? My brothers, my sisters, there is something wrong with us if we can do without Christ. If we love him, we must want him. Our hearts ever say,

Abide with me from morn till eve,
For without thee I cannot live;
Abide with me when night is nigh,
For without thee I dare not die.

Yes, we cannot do without Christ; we must have him. 'Give me Christ, or else I die', is the cry of our souls. No wonder Mary Magdalene wept when she thought they had taken away her Lord, and she knew not where they had laid him. As the body suffers without food, so should we without Christ. As the fish perish out of water, so should we apart from Christ. I must quote another verse of a hymn, for really the sweet songsters of Israel have lavished all their best poesy, and very rightly so, to tell for us our love-tale concerning our Beloved. I am sure that our heart's inner voice can set to sweetest music the words:

Oh that I could for ever sit
With Mary at the Master's feet:
Be this my happy choice,
My only care, delight, and bliss,
My joy, my heaven on earth be this,
To hear the Bridegroom's voice.

Yes! to be with Jesus is heaven; anywhere on earth, or in the skies, all else is wilderness and desert. It is paradise to be with him; and heaven without Christ would be no heaven to me. My heart cannot rest away from him. To have no Christ would be a punishment greater than I could bear; I should wander, like another Cain, over the earth a fugitive and a vagabond. Verily there would be no peace for my soul. I am sure that the true wife, if her husband is called to go upon a journey, longeth ardently for his return. If he is gone to the wars, she dreads lest he should fall. How each letter comes perfumed to her when it tells of his love and constancy, and how she watches for the day when she shall clasp him in her arms once more. Oh, ye know that when ye were children, if ye were sent to school, how ye counted till the holidays came on. I had a little almanack, and marked out every day the night before, and so counted one day less till the time I should get home again, and so may you.

> May not a captive long his own dear land to see?
> May not the pris'ner seek release from bondage to be free?

Of course he may, and so may you, beloved, pant and sigh, as the hart panteth for the waterbrooks – for the comfortable enjoyment of the Lord Jesus Christ's presence.

3. THE ARGUMENT USED BY THE CHURCH

Here is the desire. Now, to close, she backs that up with an argument. She says, 'Why should I be as one that turneth aside by the flocks of thy companions?' Thou hast plenty of companions, why should I be turned aside? Why should I not be one? Let us talk it over. Why should I lose my Lord's presence? But the devil tells me I am a great sinner. Ah! but it is all washed away, and gone for ever. That cannot separate me, for it does not exist. My sin is buried.

> Plung'd as in a shoreless sea –
> Lost as in immensity.

The devil tells me I am unworthy, and that is a reason. But I always was unworthy, and yet it was no reason why he should not love me at first, and therefore cannot be a reason why I should not have fellowship with him now. Why should *I* be left out? Now I am going to speak for the poorest here – I do not know where he is. I want to speak for you that have got the least faith; you that think yourselves the smallest in all Israel; you Mephibosheths that are lame in your feet, and yet sit at the king's table; you poor despised Mordecais that sit at the king's gate, yet cannot get inside the palace, I have this to say to you – Why should you be left there? Just try and reason. Why should I be left out in the cold, when the night comes on? No, there is a cot for the little one, as well as a bed for his bigger brother. Why should *I* be turned aside? I am equally bought with a price. I cost him, in order to save me, as much as the noblest of the saints: he bought them with blood; he could not buy me with less. I must have been loved as much, or else, seeing that I am of so little worth, I should not have been redeemed at all. If there be any difference, perhaps I am loved somewhat better. Is there not greater, better love shown in the choice of me than of some who are more worthy than I am? Why, then, should I be left out? I know if I have a child that is deformed and decrepit, I love it all the more: it seems as if I had a tenderer care for it. Then why should my heavenly Father be less kind to me than I should be to my offspring? Why should *I* be turned aside? He chose me: he cannot change in his choice. Why, then, should he cast me off? He knew what I was when he chose me; he cannot therefore find out any fresh reason for turning me aside. He foresaw I should misbehave myself, and yet he selected me. Well, then, there cannot be a reason why I should be left to fall away.

Again, I ask, Why should I turn aside? I have a promise all to myself. Has he not said, 'I will not quench the smoking flax, nor break the bruised reed'? Has he not said, 'The Lord taketh pleasure in them that fear him; in them that *hope* in his mercy'? If I cannot do more, I can do that. I do hope in his mercy; then why should I be turned aside? If any should think of doing so, it should not be I, for I want to be near him; I am such a poor plant that I ought to be kept in the sun: I shall never do in the shade. My big brother, perhaps, may manage for a little time without comfort, but *I* cannot, for I am one of the Ready-to-Halts. I recollect how the shepherds of Mount Clear said, 'Come in, Mr Little Faith; come in, Mr Feeble Mind; come in, Mr Ready-to-halt; come in, Mary'; but they did not say, 'Come in, Father Faithful; come in, Matthew; come in, Valiant-for-Truth.' No, they said these might do as they liked; they were quite sure to take their own part; but they looked first to the feeblest. Then why should I be turned aside? I am the feeblest, and want his person most. I may use my very feebleness and proneness to fall as the reason why I should come to him.

Why should I be turned aside? I may fall into sin. My heart may grow cold without his glorious presence; and then, what if I should perish! Why, here let me bethink myself. If I am the meanest lamb in his flock I cannot perish without doing the God of heaven a damage. Let me say it again with reverence. If I, the least of his children, perish, I shall do his Son dishonour, for what will the arch-fiend say? 'Aha,' saith he, 'thou Surety of the Covenant, thou couldst keep the strong, but thou couldst not keep the weak: I have this lamb here in the pit whom thou couldst not preserve. Here is one of thy crown-jewels,' saith he, 'and though it be none of the brightest, though it be not the most sparkling ruby in thy coronet, yet it is one of thy jewels, and I have it here. Thou hast no perfect regalia: I have a part of it here.' Shall that ever be, after Christ has said, 'They shall never perish, neither shall any pluck them out of my hand'? Shall this be, when the strong arm of God is engaged for my succour, and he has said to me, 'The Eternal God is thy refuge; and underneath are the everlasting arms'? Jesus, turn me not aside, lest by my fall I grieve thy Spirit, and lest by my fall I bring disgrace upon thy name.

Why should I turn aside? There is no reason why I should. Come my soul, there are a thousand reasons why thou shouldest not. Jesus beckons thee to come. Ye wounded saints, ye that have slipped to your falling, you that are grieved, sorrowing and distressed, come to his cross, come to his throne again. Backsliders, if ye have been such, return! return! return! A husband's heart has no door to keep out his spouse, and Jesus' heart has no power to keep out his people. Return! return! There is no divorce sued out against you, for the Lord, the God of Jacob saith, 'He hateth putting away.' Return! return! Let us go to our chambers, let us seek renewed fellowship; and, oh, you that have never had it, and have never seen Christ, may you thirst after him tonight, and if you do, remember the text I gave you, 'Him that cometh to me I will in nowise cast out.' Whosoever thou mayest be, if thou wilt come to Jesus, he will not cast thee out.

Come, and welcome sinner, come.
God bring thee for Jesus' sake. Amen.

8

THE GOOD SHEPHERDESS

'Tell me, O thou whom my soul loveth, where thou feedest, where thou makest thy flock to rest at noon: for why should I be as one that turneth aside by the flocks of thy companions? If thou know not, O thou fairest among women, go thy way forth by the footsteps of the flock, and feed thy kids beside the shepherds' tents' (Song of Solomon 1:7, 8)

The bride was most unhappy and ashamed because her personal beauty had been sorely marred by the heat of the sun. The fairest among women had become swarthy as a sunburnt slave. Spiritually it is so full often with a chosen soul. The Lord's grace has made her fair to look upon, even as the lily; but she has been so busy about earthly things that the sun of worldliness has injured her beauty. The bride with holy shamefacedness exclaims, 'Look not upon me, for I am black, because the sun hath looked upon me.' She dreads alike the curiosity, the admiration, the pity, and the scorn of men, and turns herself alone to her Beloved, whose gaze she knows to be so full of love that her swarthiness will not cause her pain when most beneath his eye. This is one index of a gracious soul – that whereas the ungodly rush to and fro, and know not where to look for consolation, the believing heart naturally flies to its Well-beloved Saviour, knowing that in him is its only rest.

It would appear from the preceding verse that the bride was also in trouble about a certain charge which had been given to her, which burdened her, and in the discharge of which she had become negligent of herself. She says, 'They made me the keeper of the vineyards', and she would wish to have kept them well, but she felt she had not done so, and that, moreover, she had failed in a more immediate duty – 'Mine own vineyard have I not kept.' Under this sense of double unworthiness and failure, feeling her omissions and her commissions to be weighing her down, she turned round to her Beloved and asked instruction at his hands. This was well. Had she not loved her Lord she would have shunned him when her comeliness was faded, but the instincts of her affectionate heart suggested to her that he would not discard her because of her imperfections. She was, moreover, wise thus to appeal to her Lord against herself. Beloved, never let sin part you from Jesus. Under a sense of sin do not fly from him; that were foolishness. Sin may drive you *from* Sinai; it ought to draw you *to* Calvary. To the fountain we should fly with all the greater alacrity when we feel that we are foul; and to the dear wounds of Jesus, whence all our life and healing must come, we should resort with the greater earnestness when we feel our soul to be sick, even though we fear that sickness to be unto death. The bride, in the present case, takes to Jesus her troubles, her distress about herself, and her confession concerning her work. She brings before him her double charge, the keeping of her own vineyard, and the keeping of the vineyards of others.

I know that I shall be speaking to many this morning who are busy in serving their Lord; and it may be that they feel great anxiety because they cannot keep their own hearts near to Jesus: they do not feel themselves warm and lively in the divine service; they plod on, but they are very much in the condition of those who are described as 'faint, yet pursuing'. When Jesus is present labour for him is joy, but in his absence his servants feel like workers underground, bereft of the light of the sun. They cannot give up working for Jesus; they love him too well for that, but they pine to have his company while they are working for him, and like the young prophets who went to the wood to cut down every man a beam for their new house, they say to their master, 'Be content, we pray thee, and go with thy servants.' Our most earnest desire is that we may enjoy sweet communion with Jesus while we are actively engaged in his cause. Indeed, beloved, this is most important to all of us. I do not know of any point which Christian workers need more often to think upon than the subject of keeping their work and themselves near to the Master's hand.

Our text will help us to this, under three heads. We have here, first, *a question asked*: 'Tell me, O thou whom my soul loveth, where thou feedest, where thou makest thy flock to rest at noon?' Secondly, *an argument used*: 'Why should I be as one that turneth aside by the flocks of thy companions?' And, thirdly, we have *an answer obtained*: 'If thou know not, O thou fairest among women, go thy way forth by the footsteps of the flock, and feed thy kids beside the shepherds' tents.'

1. Here is A QUESTION ASKED. Every word of the enquiry is worthy of our careful meditation. You will observe, first, concerning it, that it is *asked in love*. She calls him to whom she speaks by the endearing title, 'O thou whom my soul loveth.' Whatever she may feel herself to be, she knows that she loves *him*. She is black, and ashamed to have her face gazed upon, but still she loves her Bridegroom. She has not kept her own vineyard as she ought to have done, but still she loves him; that she is sure of, and therefore boldly declares it. She loves him as she loves none other in all the world. He only can be called 'Him whom my soul loveth'. She knows none at all worthy to be compared with him, none who can rival him. He is her bosom's Lord, sole prince and monarch of all her affections. She feels also that she loves him intensely – from her inmost *soul* she loves him. The life of her existence is bound up with him: if there be any force and power and vitality in her, it is but as fuel to the great flame of her love, which burns alone for him.

Mark well that it is not 'O thou whom my soul believes in'. That would be true, but she has passed further. It is not 'O thou whom my soul honours'. That is true too, but she has passed beyond that stage. Nor is it merely 'O thou whom my soul trusts and obeys'. She is doing that, but she has reached something warmer, more tender, more full of fire and enthusiasm, and it is 'O thou whom my soul *loveth*'. Now, beloved, I trust many of us can speak so to Jesus. He is to us the Well-beloved, 'the chief amongst a myriad'; 'his mouth is every sweetness, yea, all of him is loveliness', and our soul is wrapt up in him, our heart is altogether taken up with him. We shall never serve him aright unless it be so. Before our Lord said to Peter, 'Feed my lambs', and 'Feed my sheep', he put the question, 'Simon son of Jonas lovest thou me?' and this he repeated three times; for until that question is settled we are unfit for his service. So the bride here, having both herself and her little flock to care for, avows that she loves the spouse as if she felt that she would not dare to have a part of his flock to look after if she did not love himself; as if she saw that her right to be a shepherdess at all depended upon her love *to* the Great Shepherd. She could not expect his help in her work, much less his fellowship in the work, unless there was first in her that all-essential fitness of love to his person. The question therefore becomes instructive to us, because it is addressed to Christ under a most endearing title; and I ask every worker here to take care that he always does his work in a spirit of love, and always regards the Lord Jesus not as a taskmaster, not as one who has given us work to do from which we would fain escape, but as our dear Lord, whom to serve is bliss, and for whom to die is gain.

'O thou whom my soul loveth' is the right name by which a worker for Jesus should address his Lord.

Now note that the question, as it is asked in love, is also *asked of him*: 'Tell me, O thou whom my soul loveth, where thou feedest.' She asked him to tell her, as if she feared that none but himself would give her the correct answer; others might be mistaken, but he could not be. She asked of him because she was quite sure that he would give her the kindest answer. Others might be indifferent, and might scarcely take the trouble to reply; but if Jesus would tell her himself, with his own lips, he would mingle love with every word, and so console her as well as instruct her. Perhaps she felt that nobody else could tell her as he could, for others speak to the ear, but he speaks to the heart; others speak with lower degrees of influence, we hear their speech but are not moved thereby; but Jesus speaks and the Spirit goes with every word he utters, and therefore we hear to profit when he converses with us. I do not know how it may be with you, my brethren, but I feel this morning that if I could get half a word from Christ it would satisfy my soul for many a day. I love to hear the gospel, and to read it, and to preach it; but to hear it fresh from himself, applied by the energy of the Holy Spirit! Oh, this were refreshment! This were energy and power! Therefore, Saviour, when thy workers desire to know where thou feedest, tell them thyself, speak to their hearts by thine own Spirit, and let them feel as though it were a new revelation to their inmost nature. 'Tell me, O thou whom my soul loveth.' It is asked in love: it is asked of him.

Now, observe what the question is. She wishes to know how Jesus does his work, and where he does it. It appears, from the eighth verse, that she herself has a flock of kids to tend. She is a shepherdess, and would fain feed her flock; hence her question, 'Tell me where thou feedest?' She desires those little ones of hers to obtain rest as well as food, and she is troubled about them; therefore she says, 'Tell me where thou makest thy flock to rest', for if she can see how Jesus does his work, and where he does it, and in what way, then she will be satisfied that she is doing it in the right way, if she closely imitates him and abides in fellowship with him. The question seems to be just this: 'Lord, tell me what are the truths with which thou dost feed thy people's souls; tell me what are the doctrines which make the strong ones weak and the sad ones glad; tell me what is that precious meat which thou art wont to give to hungry and fainting spirits, to revive them and keep them alive; for if thou tell me, then I will give my flock the same food. Tell me where the pasture is wherein thou dost feed thy sheep, and straightway I will lead mine to the selfsame happy fields. Then tell me how thou makest thy people to rest. What are those promises which thou dost apply to the consolation of their spirit, so that their cares and doubts and fears and agitations all subside? Thou hast sweet meadows where thou makest thy beloved flock to lie calmly down and slumber, tell me where those meadows are that I may go and fetch the flock committed to my charge, the mourners whom I ought to comfort, the distressed ones whom I am bound to relieve, the desponding whom I have endeavoured to encourage; tell me, Lord, where thou makest thy flock to lie down, for then, under thy help, I will go and make my flock to lie down too. It is for myself, but yet far more for others, that I ask the question, 'Tell me where thou feedest, where thou makest them to rest at noon.' I have no doubt that the spouse did desire information for herself and for her own good, and I believe Dr Watts had caught some of the spirit of the passage when he sang

> Fain would I feed among thy sheep,
> Among them rest, among them sleep.

But it does not strike me that this is all the meaning of the passage by a very long way. The bride says, 'Tell me where thou feedest thy flock', as if she would wish to feed with the flock; 'where thou makest thy flock to rest', as if she wanted to rest there too: but it strikes me the very gist of the thing is this, that she wished to bring her flock to feed where Christ's flock feeds, and to lead her kids to lie down where Christ's little lambs were reposing; she desired, in fact, to do her work in his company; she wanted to mix up her flock with the Lord's flock, her work with his work, and to feel that what she was doing she was doing for him, yea, and with him and through him. She had evidently met with a great many difficulties in what she had tried to do. She wished to feed her flock of kids, but could not find them pasture. Perhaps when she began her work as a shepherdess she thought herself quite equal to the task but now the same sun which had bronzed her face had dried up the pasture, and so she says, 'O thou that knowest all the pastures, tell me where thou feedest, for I cannot find grass for my flock'; and suffering herself from the noontide heat, she finds her little flock suffering too; and she enquires 'Where dost thou make thy flock to rest at noon? Where are cool shadows of great rocks which screen off the sultry rays when the sun is in its zenith and pours down torrents of heat? For I cannot shade my poor flock and give them comfort in their many trials and troubles. I wish I could. O Lord, tell me the secret art of consolation; then will I try to console my own charge by the selfsame means.' We would know the groves of promise and the cool streams of peace, that we may lead others into rest. If we can follow Jesus we can guide others, and so both we and they will find comfort and peace. That is the meaning of the request before us.

Note well that she said most particularly, 'Tell *me*.' 'O Master, do not merely tell thy sheep where thou feedest, though they want to know; but tell me where thou feedest, for I would fain instruct others.' She would fain know many things, but chiefly she says, 'Tell me *where thou feedest*', for she wished to feed others. We want practical knowledge, for our desire is to be helped to bring others into rest; to be the means of speaking peace to the consciences of others, as the Lord hast spoken peace to ours. Therefore the prayer is, 'Tell me.' 'Thou art my model, O Great Shepherd; thou art my wisdom. If I be a shepherd to thy sheep, yet am I also a sheep beneath thy Shepherdry, therefore teach thou me, that I may teach others.'

I do not know whether I make myself plain to you, but I wish to put it very simply. I am preaching to myself, perhaps a great deal more than to you. I am preaching to my own heart. I feel I have to come, Sabbath after Sabbath and weekday after weekday, and tell you a great many precious things about Christ, and sometimes I enjoy them myself; and if nobody else gets blessed by them, I do, and I go home and praise the Lord for it; but my daily fear is lest I should be a handler of texts for you, and a preacher of good things for others, and yet remain unprofited in my own heart. My prayer is that the Lord Jesus will show me where he feeds his people, and let me feed with them, that then I may conduct you to the pastures where he is, and be with him myself at the same time that I bring you to him. You Sabbath-school teachers and evangelists, and others, my dear, earnest comrades, for whom I thank God at every remembrance, I feel that the main point you have to watch about is that you do not lose your own spirituality while trying to make others spiritual. The great point is to live near to God. It would be a dreadful thing for you to be very busy about other men's souls and neglect your own. Appeal to the Well-beloved, and entreat him to let you feed your flock where he is feeding his people, that he would let you sit at his feet, like Mary, even while you are working in the house, like Martha. Do not do less, but rather more; but ask to do it in such communion with him that your work shall be melted into his work, and what you are doing shall be really only his working in you, and you rejoicing to pour out to others what he pours into your own soul. God grant it may be so with you all, my brethren.

Secondly, here is AN ARGUMENT USED. The bride says, 'Why should I be as one that turneth aside by the flocks of thy companions?' If she should lead her flock into distant meadows, far away from the place where Jesus is feeding his flock, it would not be well. As a shepherdess would naturally be rather dependent, and would need to associate herself for protection with others, suppose she should turn aside with other shepherds, and leave her Bridegroom, would it be right? She speaks of it as a thing most abhorrent to her mind, and well might it be.

For, first, would it not look very unseemly that the bride should be associating with others than the Bridegroom? They have each a flock: there is he with his great flock, and here is she with her little one. Shall they seek pastures far off from one another? Will there not be talk about this? Will not onlookers say, 'This is not seemly: there must be some lack of love here, or else these two would not be so divided'? Stress may be put, if you like, upon that little word, 'I'. Why should *I*, thy blood-bought spouse; I, betrothed unto thee, or ever the earth was; I, whom thou hast loved – why should I turn after others and forget thee? Beloved, you had better put the emphasis in your own reading of it just there. Why should *I*, whom the Lord has pardoned, whom the Lord has loved, whom the Lord has favoured so much – I, who have enjoyed fellowship with him for many years – I who know that his love is better than wine – I who have aforetime been inebriated with his sweetness – why should I turn aside? Let others do so if they will, but it would be uncomely and unseemly for me. I pray you, brother and sister, try to feel that – that for you to work apart from Christ would have a bad look about it; that for your work to take you away from fellowship with Jesus would have a very ugly appearance; it would not be among the things that are honest and of good repute.

For the bride to feed her flock in other company would look like unfaithfulness to her husband. What, shall the bride of Christ forsake her Beloved? Shall she be unchaste towards her Lord? Yet it would seem so if she makes companions of others and forgets her Beloved? Our hearts may grow unchaste to Christ even while they are zealous in Christian work. I dread very much the tendency to do Christ's work in a cold, mechanical spirit; but above even that I tremble lest I should be able to have warmth for Christ's work and yet should be cold towards the Lord himself. I fear that such a condition of heart is possible – that we may burn great bonfires in the streets for public display, and scarcely keep a live coal upon our hearth for Jesus to warm his hands at. When we meet in the great assembly the good company helps to warm our hearts, and when we are working for the Lord with others they stimulate us and cause us to put forth all our energy and strength, and then we think, 'Surely my heart is in a healthy condition towards God.' But, beloved, such excitement may be a poor index of our real state. I love that quiet, holy fire which will glow in the closet and flame forth in the chamber when I am alone, and that is the point I am more fearful about than anything else, both for myself and for you, lest we should be doing Christ's work without Christ; having much to do but not thinking much of *him*; cumbered about much serving and forgetting him. Why, that would soon grow into making a Christ out of our own service, an Antichrist out of our own labours. Beware of that! Love your work, but love your Master better; love your flock, but love the great Shepherd better still, and ever keep close to him, for it will be a token of unfaithfulness if you do not.

And mark again, 'Why should I be as one that turneth aside by the flocks of thy companions?' We may read this as meaning, 'Why should I be so unhappy as to have to work for thee, and yet be out of communion with thee?' It is a very unhappy thing to lose fellowship with Jesus, and yet to have to go on with religious exercises. If the wheels are taken off your chariot it is no great matter if nobody wants to ride, but how if you are called upon to drive on? When a man's foot is lamed he may not so much regret it if he can sit still, but if he be bound to run a race he is greatly to be pitied. It made the spouse doubly unhappy even to suppose that she, with her flock to feed and herself needing feeding too, should have to turn aside by the flocks of others and miss the presence of her Lord. In fact, the question seems to be put in this shape: 'What reason is there why I should leave my Lord? What apology could I make, what excuse could I offer for so doing? Is there any reason why I should not abide in constant fellowship with him? Why should I be as one that turneth aside? Perhaps it may be said that others turn aside, but why should *I* be as one of them? There may be excuses for such an act in others, but there can be none for me: thy rich love, thy free love, thy undeserved love, thy special love to me, hath bound me hand and foot: how can I turn aside? There may be some professors who owe thee little, but I, once the chief of sinners, owe thee so much, how can I turn aside? There may be some with whom thou hast dealt hardly who may turn aside, but thou hast been so tender, so kind to me, how can I forget thee? There may be some who know but little of thee, whose experience of thee is so slender that their turning aside is not to be wondered at; but how can I turn aside when thou hast showed me thy love, and revealed thy heart to me? Oh, by the banqueting house where I have feasted with thee, by the Hermonites and the hill Mizar, where thou hast manifested thy love, by the place where deep called to deep, and then mercy called to mercy; by those mighty storms and sweeping hurricanes in which thou wast the shelter of my head, by ten thousand thousand mercies past which have been my blessed portion, why should *I* be as one that turneth aside by the flocks of thy companions?'

Let me address the members of this church, and say to you, if all the churches in Christendom were to go aside from the gospel, why should you? If in every other place the gospel should be neglected, and an uncertain sound should be given forth; if Ritualism should swallow up half the churches and Rationalism the rest, yet why should *you* turn aside? You have been peculiarly a people of prayer; you have also followed the Lord fully in doctrine and in ordinance; and consequently you have enjoyed the divine presence, and have prospered beyond measure. We have cast ourselves upon the Holy Ghost for strength, and have not relied upon human eloquence, music, or beauties of colour, or architecture. Our only weapon has been the simple, plain, full gospel, and why should we turn aside? Have we not been favoured for these many years with unexampled success? Has not the Lord added unto our numbers so abundantly that we have not had room enough to receive them? Has he not multiplied the people, and increased the joy? Hold fast to your first love, and let no man take your crown. I thank God there are churches still, a few in England and yet more in Scotland, which hold fast the doctrines of the gospel and will not let them go. To them I would say, why should ye turn aside? Should not your history, both in its troublous and its joyous chapters, teach you to hold fast the form of sound words?

Above all, should we not try to live as a church, and individually, also, in abiding fellowship with Jesus; for if we turn aside from him we shall rob the truth of its aroma, yea, of its essential fragrance. If we lose fellowship with Jesus we shall have the standard, but where will be the standard-bearer? We may retain the candlestick, but where shall be the light? We shall be shorn of our strength, our joy, our comfort, our all, if we miss fellowship with him. God grant, therefore, that we may never be as those who turn aside.

Thirdly, we have here AN ANSWER GIVEN by the Bridegroom to his beloved. She asked him where he fed, where he made his flock to rest, and he answered her. Observe carefully that this answer is *given in tenderness to her infirmity*; not ignoring her ignorance, but dealing very gently with it. 'If thou know not' – a hint that she ought to have known, but such a hint as kind lovers give when they would fain forbear to chide. Our Lord is very tender to our ignorance. There are many things which we do not know, but ought to have known. We are children when we should be men, and have to be spoken to as unto carnal – as unto babes in Christ – when we should have become fathers. Is there one among us who can say, 'I am not faulty in my knowledge?' I am afraid the most of us must confess that if we had done the Lord's will better we should have known his doctrine better; if we had lived more closely to him we should have known more of him. Still, how very gentle the rebuke is. The Lord forgives our ignorance, and condescends to instruct it.

Note next that the answer is *given in great love*. He says, 'O thou fairest among women.' That is a blessed cordial for her distress. She said, 'I am black'; but he says, 'O thou fairest among women.' I would rather trust Christ's eyes than mine. If my eyes tell me I am black I will weep, but if he assures me I am fair, I will believe him and rejoice. Some saints are more apt to remember their sinfulness, and grieve over it, than to believe in their righteousness in Christ, and triumph in it. Remember, beloved, it is quite as true today that you are all fair and without spot as that you are black, because the sun hath looked upon you. It must be true, because Jesus says so. Let me give you one of the sayings of the Bridegroom to his bride: 'Thou art all fair, my love; there is no spot in thee.' 'Ah, that is a figure,' say you. Well, I will give you one that is not a figure. The Lord Jesus, after he had washed his disciples' feet, said, 'He that is washed needeth not except to wash his feet for he is clean every whit'; and then he added, 'And ye are clean.' If you desire an apostolic word to the same effect, let me give you this: 'Who shall lay anything to the charge of God's elect?' – *anything* – any little thing or any great thing either. Jesus has washed his people so clean that there is no spot, nor wrinkle, nor any such thing upon them in the matter of justification before God.

In thy Surety thou art free,
His dear hands were pierced for thee;
With his spotless vesture on,
Holy as the Holy One.

How glorious is this. Jesus does not exaggerate when he thus commands his church. He speaks plain, sober truth. 'O thou fairest among women,' saith he. My soul, dost thou not feel love to Christ when thou rememberest that he thinks thee beautiful? I cannot see anything in myself to love, but he does, and calls me 'all fair'. I think it must be that he looks into our eyes and sees, himself, or else this, that he knows what we are going to be, and judges us on that scale. As the artist, looking on the block of marble, sees in the stone the statue which he means to fetch out of it with matchless skill, so the Lord Jesus sees the perfect image of himself in us, from which he means to chip away the imperfections and the sins until it stands out in all its splendour. But still it is gracious condescension which makes him say, 'Thou art fairest among women', to one who mourned her own sunburnt countenance.

The answer contains much sacred wisdom. The bride is directed where to go that she may find her beloved and lead her flock to him. 'Go thy way forth by the footprints of the flock.' If thou wilt find Jesus, thou wilt find him in the way the holy prophets went, in the way of the patriarchs and the way of the apostles. And if thou dost desire to find thy flock, and to make them lie down, very well, go thou and feed as other shepherds have done – Christ's own shepherds whom he has sent in other days to feed his chosen. I feel very glad, in speaking from this text, that the Lord does not give to his bride in answer to her question some singular directions of great difficulty, some novel prescriptions singular and remarkable. Just as the gospel itself is simple and homely, so is this exhortation and direction for the renewal of communion. It is easy, it is plain. You want to get to Jesus, and you want to bring those under your charge to him. Very well, then, do not seek out a new road, but simply go the way which all other saints have gone. If you want to walk with Jesus, walk where other saints have walked;

and if you want to lead others into communion with him, lead them by your example where others have gone. What is that?

If you want to be with Jesus, go where Abraham went in the path of separation. See how he lived as a pilgrim and a sojourner with his God. If you would see Jesus, 'Come ye out from among them, be ye separate, touch not the unclean thing.' You shall find Jesus when you have left the world.

If you would walk with Jesus, follow the path of obedience. Saints have never had fellowship with Jesus when they have disobeyed him. Keep his statutes and observe his testimonies, be jealous over your conduct and character; for the path of obedience is the path of communion.

Be sure that you do follow the ancient ways with regard to the Christian ordinances: do not alter them, but keep to the good old paths. Stand and enquire what apostles did, and do the same. Jesus will not bless you in using fanciful ceremonies of human invention. Keep to those which he commands, which his Spirit sanctions, and which his apostles practised.

Above all, if you would walk with Jesus, continue in the way of holiness: persevere in the way of grace. Make the Lord Jesus your model and example; and by treading where the footprints of the flock are to be seen, you will both save yourself and them that hear you; you shall find Jesus, and they shall find Jesus too.

We might have supposed that the Lord would have said, 'If you want to lead your flock aright, array yourself in sumptuous apparel, or go get your music and fine anthems; by these fair things you will fascinate the Saviour into your sanctuaries;' but it is not so. The incense which will please the Lord Jesus is that of holy prayer and praise, and the only Ritualism which is acceptable with him is this: 'pure religion, and undefiled before God and the Father is this, to visit the fatherless and the widow, and to keep oneself unspotted from the world.' This is all he wants. Follow that, and you shall both go right and lead others right.

Then the Spouse added, 'Feed thy kids beside the shepherds' tents.' Now, who are these shepherds? There be many in these days who set up for shepherds, who feed their sheep in poisonous pastures. Keep away from them; but there are others whom it is safe to follow. Let me take you to the twelve principal shepherds who came after the great Shepherd of all. You want to bless your children, to save their souls, and have fellowship with Christ in the doing of it; then teach them the truths which the apostles taught. And what were they?

Take Paul as an example: 'I determined not to know anything among you save Jesus Christ, and him crucified.' That is feeding the kids beside the shepherds' tents, when you teach your children Christ, much of Christ, all of Christ, and nothing else but Christ. Mind you stick to that blessed subject. And when you are teaching them Christ, teach them all about his life, his death, his resurrection; teach them his Godhead and his manhood. You will never enjoy Christ's company if you doubt his divinity. Take care that you feed your flock upon the doctrine of the atonement. Christ will have no fellowship with a worker unless he represents him fairly, and you cannot represent Christ truthfully unless you see the ruddy hue of his atoning blood as well as the lily purity of his life.

'Feed thy kids beside the shepherds' tents', then wilt thou teach them the atoning sacrifice, and justification by faith, and imputed righteousness, and union with the risen Head, and the coming of the great One, wherein we shall receive the adoption, to wit, the redemption of the body from the grave. I speak the truth and lie not when I say that if we want to teach a congregation so as to bless them, and keep in fellowship with Christ at the same time ourselves, we must be very particular to teach nothing but the truth – not a part of it, but all of it.

Preach that blessed doctrine of election. Oh, the deeps of divine love which are contained in that blessed truth! Do not shirk it, or keep it in the background. You cannot expect Christ's presence if you do. Teach the doctrine of man's depravity. Lay the sinner low. God will not bless a ministry which exalts men. Preach the doctrine of the Holy Spirit's effectual calling, for if we do not magnify the Spirit of God, we cannot expect that he will make our work to stand. Preach regeneration. Let it be seen how thorough the change is, that we may glorify God's work. Preach the final perseverance of the saints. Teach that the Lord is not changeable – casting away his people, loving them today and hating them tomorrow.

Preach, in fact, the doctrines of grace as you find them in the Book. Feed them beside the shepherds' tents.

Ay, and feed the kids there -– the little children. I begin to feel more and more that it is a mistake to divide the children from the congregation. I believe in special services for children, but I would also have them worship with us. If our preaching does not teach children, it lacks some element which it ought to possess. The kind of preaching which is best of all for grown-up people is that in which children also will take delight. I like to see the congregation made up not all of the young, nor all of the old; not all of the mature, nor all of the inexperienced, but some of all sorts gathered together. If we are teaching children salvation by works, and grown-up people salvation by grace, we are pulling down in the school-room what we build up in the church, and that will never do. Feed the kids with the same gospel as the grown-up sheep, though not exactly in the same terms; let your language be appropriate to them, but let it be the same truth. God forbid that we should have our Sunday-schools the hot-beds of Arminianism, while our churches are gardens of Calvinism. We shall soon have a division in the camp if that be so. The same truth for all; and you cannot expect Christ to be with you in feeding your little flocks unless you feed them where Christ feeds us. Where does he feed us but where the truth grows?

Oh, when I read some sermons, they remind me of a piece of common by the roadside, after a hungry horde of sheep have devoured every green thing; but when I read a solid gospel sermon of the Puritans, it reminds me of a field kept for hay, which a farmer is at last obliged to give up to the sheep. The grass has grown almost as high as themselves, and so they lie down in it, eating and resting too. Give me the doctrines of grace, and I am in clover. If you have to feed others, take them there. Do not conduct them to the starved pastures of modern thought and culture.

Preachers are starving God's people nowadays. Oh, but they set out such beautiful China plates, such wonderful knives and forks, such marvellous vases and damask tablecloths! But as for food, the plates look as if they had been smeared with a feather, there is so little on them. The real gospel teaching is little enough. They give us nothing to learn, nothing to digest, nothing to feed upon; it is all slops, and nothing substantial. Oh for the good old corn of the kingdom; we want that, and I am persuaded that when the churches get back to the old food again, when they begin to feed their flocks beside the shepherds' tents, and when in practical living, Christians – the saints – get back to the old Puritanic method, and follow once again the tracks of the sheep, and the sheep follow the tracks of Christ, then we shall get the church into fellowship with Jesus, and Jesus will do wonders in our midst. But to get that, each individual must aim at winning it for himself; and if the Lord shall grant it to each one of us, then it will be granted to the whole, and the good times which we desire will certainly have come. My beloved, do you desire to work with Christ? Do you want to feel that Jesus is at your right hand? Then go and work in his way. Teach what he would have you teach, not what you would like to teach. Go and work for him, as he would have you work, not as your prejudices might prescribe to you. Be obedient. Follow the footsteps of the flock. Be diligent also to keep hard by the shepherds' tents, and the Lord bless you more and more, you and your children, and his shall be the glory.

I have spoken only to God's people: I would there had been time to speak to the unconverted too, but to them I can only say this: may God grant you grace to know the beauties of Jesus, for then you will love him too. May he also show you the deformities of yourselves.

And remember, if any one of you wants Christ, *he* wants *you*; and if you long for him, he longs for you. If you seek him, he is seeking you. If you will now cry to him, he is already crying after you. 'Whosoever will, let him come and take of the water of life freely.' The Lord save you for his name's sake. Amen.

9

A BUNDLE OF MYRRH

'A bundle of myrrh is my well-beloved unto me; he shall lie all night betwixt my breasts' (Canticles 1:13)

Certain divines have doubted the inspiration of Solomon's Song; others have conceived it to be nothing more than a specimen of ancient love-songs, and some have been afraid to preach from it because of its highly poetical character. The true reason for all this avoidance of one of the most heavenly portions of God's Word lies in the fact that the spirit of this Song is not easily attained. Its music belongs to the higher spiritual life, and has no charm in it for unspiritual ears. The Song occupies a sacred enclosure into which none may enter unprepared. 'Put off thy shoes from off thy feet, for the place whereon thou standest is holy ground' is the warning voice from its secret tabernacles. The historical books I may compare to the outer courts of the Temple; the Gospels, the Epistles, and the Psalms, bring us into the holy place or the Court of the priests; but the Song of Solomon is *the most holy place*: the holy of holies, before which the veil still hangs to many an untaught believer. It is not all the saints who can enter here, for they have not yet attained unto the holy confidence of faith, and that exceeding familiarity of love which will permit them to commune in conjugal love with the great Bridegroom.

We are told that the Jews did not permit the young student to read the Canticles; that years of full maturity were thought necessary before the man could rightly profit by this mysterious Song of loves; possibly they were wise, at any rate the prohibition foreshadowed a great truth. The Song is, in truth, a book for full-grown Christians. Babes in grace may find their carnal and sensuous affections stirred up by it towards Jesus, whom they know rather 'after the flesh' than in the spirit; but it needs a man of fuller growth, who has leaned his head upon the bosom of his Master, and been baptised with his baptism, to ascend the lofty mountains of love on which the spouse standeth with her beloved. The Song, from the first verse to the last, will be clear to those who have received an unction from the Holy One, and know all things (1 John 2:20).

You are aware, dear friends, that there are very few commentaries upon the Epistles of John. Where we find commentaries upon any book of St Paul, you will hardly find one upon John. Why is that? Is the book too difficult? The words are very simple; there is hardly a word of four syllables anywhere in John's Epistles. Ah! but they are so saturated through and through with the spirit of love, which also perfumes this Book of Solomon, that those who are not taught in the school of communion, cry out, 'We cannot read it, for it is sealed.' The Song is a golden casket, of which love is the key rather than learning. Those who have not attained unto heights of affection, those who have not been educated by familiar intercourse with Jesus, cannot come near to this mine of treasure, 'seeing it is hid from the eyes of all living, and kept close from the fowls of heaven'. O for the soaring eagle wing of John, and the farseeing dove's eyes of Solomon; but the most of us are blind and cannot see afar off. May God be pleased to make us grow in grace, and give us so much of the Holy Spirit that with feet like hind's feet we may stand upon the high places of Scripture, and this morning have some near and dear intercourse with Christ Jesus.

Concerning our text, let us talk very simply, remarking first, that *Christ is very precious to believers*; secondly, that *there is good reason why he should be*; thirdly, that *mingled with this sense of preciousness, there is a joyous consciousness of possession of him*; and that therefore, fourthly, *there is an earnest desire for perpetual fellowship with him*. If you look at the text again, you will see all these matters in it.

1. CHRIST JESUS IS UNUTTERABLY PRECIOUS TO BELIEVERS. The words manifestly imply this: 'A bundle of myrrh is *my well-beloved* unto me.' She calls him her 'well-beloved', and so expresses her love most emphatically; it is not merely *beloved*, but *well-beloved*. Then she looks abroad about her, to find a substance which shall be at once valuable in itself, and useful in its properties, and lighting upon myrrh, she saith, 'A bundle of myrrh is my well-beloved unto me.' Without looking into the figure just now, we keep to the statement that Christ is precious to the believer.

Observe first, that *nothing gives the believer so much joy as fellowship with Christ*. Ask yourselves, you who have eaten at his table and have been made to drink of his cup, where can such sweetness be found as you have tasted in communion with Jesus? The Christian has joy as other men have in the common mercies of life. For him there are charms in music, excellence in painting, and beauty in sculpture; for him the hills have sermons of majesty, the rocks hymns of sublimity, and the valleys lessons of love. He can look upon all things with an eye as clear and joyous as another man's; he can be glad both in God's gifts and God's works. He is not dead to the happiness of the household: around his hearth he finds happy associations, without which life were drear indeed. His children fill his home with glee, his wife is his solace and delight, his friends are his comfort and refreshment. He accepts the comforts which soul and body can yield him according as God seeth it wise to afford them unto him; but he will tell you that in all these separately, yea, and in all of them added together, he doth not find such substantial delight as he doth in the person of his Lord Jesus.

Brethren, there is a wine which no vineyard on earth ever yielded; there is a bread which even the cornfields of Egypt could never bring forth. You and I have said, when we have beheld others finding their god in earthly comforts, 'You may boast in gold, and silver, and raiment, but I will rejoice in the God of my salvation.' In our esteem, the joys of earth are little better than husks for swine compared with Jesus the heavenly manna. I would rather have one mouthful of Christ's love, and a sip of his fellowship, than a whole world full of carnal delights. What is the chaff to the wheat? What is the sparkling paste to the true diamond? What is a dream to the glorious reality? What is time's mirth in its best trim compared to our Lord Jesus in his most despised estate? If you know anything of the inner life, you will all of you confess that our highest, purest and most enduring joys must be the fruit of the tree of life which is in the midst of the Paradise of God. No spring yields such sweet water as that well of God which was digged with the soldier's spear. As for the house of feasting, the joy of harvest, the mirth of marriage, the sports of youth, the recreations of maturer age, they are all as the small dust of the balance compared with the joy of Immanuel our best beloved. As the Preacher said, so say we, 'I said of laughter, It is mad: and of mirth, What doeth it?' 'Vanity of vanities; all is vanity.' All earthly bliss is of the earth earthy, but the comforts of Christ's presence are like himself, heavenly. We can review our communion with Jesus, and find no regrets or emptiness therein; there are no dregs in this wine; no dead flies in this ointment. The joy of the Lord is solid and enduring. Vanity hath not looked upon it, but discretion and prudence testify that it abideth the test of years, and is in time and in eternity worthy to be called *the only true delight*.

What is the world with all its store?
'Tis but a bitter sweet;
When I attempt to pluck the rose,
A pricking thorn I meet.
Here perfect bliss can ne'er be found,
The honey's mix'd with gall;
'Midst changing scenes and dying friends,
Be thou my All in All.

We may plainly see that Christ is very precious to the believer, because *to him there is nothing good without Christ*. Believer, have you not found in the midst of plenty a dire and sore famine if your Lord has been absent? The sun was shining, but Christ had hidden himself, and all the world was black to you; or it was a night of tempest, and there were many stars, but since the bright and morning star was gone on that dreary main, where you were tossed with doubts and fears, no other star could shed so much as a ray of light. O, what a howling wilderness is this world without my Lord!

If once he groweth angry and doth, though it be for a moment, hide himself from me, withered are the flowers of my garden; my pleasant fruits decay; the birds suspend their songs, and black night lowers over all my hopes. Nothing can compensate for the company of the Saviour: all earth's candles cannot make delight if the Sun of Righteousness be gone.

On the other hand, *when all earthly comforts have failed you, have you not found quite enough in your Lord*? Your very worst times have been your best times? You must almost cry to go back to your bed of sickness, for Jesus made it as a royal throne, whereon you reigned with him. Those dark nights – ah! they were not dark, your bright days since then have been darker far. Do you remember when you were poor? Oh! how near Christ was to you, and how rich he made you! You were despised and rejected of men, and no man gave you a good word! Ah! sweet was his fellowship then, and how delightful to hear him say, 'Fear thou not; for I am with thee: be not dismayed; for I am thy God!' As afflictions abound, even so do consolations abound by Christ Jesus. The devil, like Nebuchadnezzar, heated the furnace seven times hotter, but who would have it less furiously blazing? No wise believer; for the more terrible the heat the greater the glory in the fact that we were made to tread those glowing coals, and not a hair of our head was singed, nor so much as the smell of fire passed upon us, because the Son of God walked those glowing coals in our company. Yes, we can look with resignation upon penury, disease, and even death; for if all comforts be taken from us, we should still be blest, so long as we enjoy the presence of the Lord our Saviour.

Nor should I be straining the truth if I say that *the Christian would sooner give up anything than forsake his Master*. I have known some who have been afraid to look that text in the face which saith, 'He that loveth son or daughter more than me is not worthy of me', or that 'Except a man hate (or love less) his father and mother, and wife and children, he cannot be my disciple.' Yet I have found that those have frequently proved to be the most sincere lovers of Jesus who have been most afraid that he had not the best place in their hearts. Perhaps the best way is not to sit down calmly to weigh our love, for it is not a thing to be measured with cool judgment, but put your love to some practical test. Now, if it came to this, that you must deny Christ, or give up the dearest thing you have, would you deliberate? The Lord knoweth I speak what I feel in my own soul – when it comes to that, I could not hesitate a second. If there were a stake and burning faggots, I might flinch from the fire, but so mighty is divine love that it would doubtless drive me to the flames sooner than let me leave Jesus. But if it comes to this, 'Wilt thou lose thine eyes or give up Christ?' I would cheerfully be blind. Or if it were asked, 'Wilt thou have thy right arm withered from its socket or give up Christ?' Ay; let both arms go; let them both drop from the shoulder blades. Or if it should be, 'Wilt thou be from this day dumb and never speak before the multitude?' Oh! better to be dumb than lose him. Indeed, when I talk of this it seems to be an insult to my Master to put hands and eyes and tongue in comparison with him.

> Nor to my eyes is light so dear
> Nor friendship half so sweet.

If you compare life itself with Jesus, it is not to be named in the same day. If it should be said, 'Will you live without Christ or die with Christ?' you could not deliberate, for to die with Christ is to live with Christ for ever; but to live without Christ is to die the second death, the terrible death of the soul's eternal perdition. No, there is no choice there. I think we could go further, dear friends, and say, not only could we give up everything, but I think, when love is fervent, and the flesh is kept under, *we could suffer anything with Christ.* I met, in one of Samuel Rutherford's letters, an extraordinary expression, where he speaks of the coals of divine wrath all falling upon the head of Christ so that not one might fall upon his people. 'And yet,' saith he, 'if one of those coals should drop from his head upon mine and did utterly consume me, yet if I felt it was a part of the coals that fell on him, and I was bearing it for his sake, and in communion with him, I would choose it for my heaven.' That is a strong thing to say, that to suffer with Christ would be his heaven, if he assuredly knew that it was for and with Christ, that he was suffering. Oh! there is indeed a heavenliness about suffering for Jesus. His cross hath such a majesty and mystery of delight in it, that the more heavy it becometh, the more lightly doth it sit upon the believer's shoulders.

One thing I know proveth, beloved, that you esteem Christ to be very precious, namely, that *you want others to know him too*. Do you not feel a pining in your souls till others' hearts be filled with the love of Christ? My eyes could weep themselves out of their sockets for some of you who are ignorant of my Master's love. Poor souls! ye are sitting outside the feast when the door is wide open, and the king himself is within. Ye choose to be out in the highways and under the hedges sooner than come to this wedding-feast, where the oxen and fatlings are killed, and all things are ready. Oh! did you know *him*, did you know *him*, you would never be able to live without him. If your eyes had ever seen him once, or if your heart had ever known the charm of his presence, you would think it to be a hell to be for a moment without Christ. O poor blind eyes which cannot see him, and deaf ears which cannot hear him, and hard stony hearts which cannot melt before him, and hell-besotted souls which cannot appreciate the majesty of his love, God help you! God help you! and bring you yet to know and rejoice in him. The more your love grows, beloved, the more insatiable will be your desire that others should love him, till it will come to this that you will be, like Paul, 'in labours more abundant', spending and being spent that you may bring the rest of Christ's elect body into union with their glorious head.

But, secondly, THE SOUL CLINGETH TO CHRIST, AND SHE HATH GOOD REASON FOR SO DOING, for her own words are, '*A bundle of myrrh* is my well-beloved unto me'. We will take the myrrh first, and then consider the bundle next.

(a) *Jesus Christ is like myrrh.* Myrrh may be well the type of Christ for its *preciousness*. It was an exceedingly expensive drug. We know that Jacob sent some of it down into Egypt as being one of the choice products of the land. It is always spoken of in Scripture as being a rich, rare and costly substance. But no myrrh could ever compare with him, for Jesus Christ is so precious, that if heaven and earth were put together they could not buy another Saviour. When God gave to the world his Son, he gave the best that heaven had. Take Christ out of heaven, and there is nothing for God to give. Christ was God's all, for is it not written, 'In him dwelleth all the fulness of the Godhead bodily'? Oh! precious gift of the whole of deity in the person of Christ! How inestimably precious is that body of his which he took of the substance of the virgin! Well might angels herald the coming of this immaculate Saviour, well might they watch over his holy life, for he is precious in his birth, and precious in all his actions. How precious is he, dear friends, as myrrh in the offering of his great atonement! What a costly sacrifice was that! At what a price were ye redeemed! Not with silver and gold, but with the precious blood of Christ. How precious is he too, in his resurrection! He justifies all his people at one stroke – rising from the dead – that glorious sun scatters all the nights of all his people by one rising. How precious among men! And how precious today in those incessant pleadings of his through which the mercies of God come down like the angels upon Jacob's ladder to our needy souls! Yes, he is to the believer in every aspect like myrrh for rarity and excellence.

Myrrh, again, was *pleasant*. It was a pleasant thing to be in a chamber perfumed with myrrh. Through the nostrils myrrh conveys delight to the human mind; but Christ gives delight to his people, not through one channel but through every avenue. It is true that all his garments smell of myrrh and aloes and cassia, but he hath not spiritual smell alone, the taste shall be gratified too, for we eat his flesh and drink his blood. Nay, our feeling is ravished, when his left hand is under us, and his right hand doth embrace us. As for his voice it is most sweet, and our soul's ear is charmed with its melody. Let God give him to our sight, and what can our eyes want more?

Yea, he is altogether lovely. Thus every gate of the soul hath commerce with Christ Jesus in the richest and rarest commodities. There is no way by which a human spirit can have communion with Jesus which doth not yield unto that spirit fresh and varied delights. O beloved, we cannot compare him merely to myrrh. He is to everything which is good to look upon, or to taste, or to handle, or to smell – all put together in one, the quintessence of all delights. As all the rivers run into the sea, so all delights centre into Christ. The sea is not full, but Jesus is full to the very brim.

Moreover, myrrh is *perfuming*. It is used to give a sweet smell to other things. It was mingled with the sacrifice, so that it was not only the smoke of the fat of kidneys of rams, and the flesh of fat beasts, but there was a sweet fragrance of myrrh, which went up with the sacrifice to heaven. And surely, beloved, Jesus Christ is very perfuming to his people. Doth not he perfume their prayers, so that the Lord smelleth a sweet savour? Doth he not perfume their songs, so that they become like vials full of odour sweet? Doth he not perfume our ministry, for is it not written, 'He causeth us to triumph in Christ, and maketh manifest the savour of his knowledge by us in every place. For we are unto God a sweet savour of Christ, in them that are saved, and in them that perish.' Our persons are perfumed with Christ. Whence get we our spikenard but from him? Whither shall we go to gather camphire which shall make our persons and presence acceptable before God but to him? 'For we are accepted in the beloved.' 'Ye are complete in him' – 'perfect in Christ Jesus' – 'for he hath made us kings and priests unto our God, and we shall reign for ever and ever.'

Myrrh has *preserving* qualities. The Egyptians used it in embalming the dead: and we find Nicodemus and the holy women bringing myrrh and aloes in which to wrap the dead body of the Saviour. It was used to prevent corruption. What is there which can preserve the soul but Christ Jesus? What is the myrrh which keeps our works, which in themselves are dead and corrupt and rotten – what, I say, keeps them from becoming a foul stench in the nostrils of God, but that Christ is in them? What we have done out of love to Christ, what we have offered through his mediation, what has been perfumed by faith in his person, becomes acceptable. God looketh upon anything we say, or anything we do, and if he seeth Christ in it, he accepteth it; but if there be no Christ, he putteth it away as a foul thing. See to it then, beloved, that you never pray a prayer which is not sweetened with Christ. I would never preach a sermon – the Lord forgive me if I do – which is not full to overflowing with my Master. I know one who said I was always on the old string, and he would come and hear me no more; but if I preached a sermon without Christ in it, he could come. Ah! he will never come, while this tongue moves, for a sermon without Christ in it – a Christless sermon! A brook without water; a cloud without rain; a well which mocks the traveller; a tree twice dead, plucked up by the root; a sky without a sun; a night without a star. It were a realm of death – a place of mourning for angels and laughter for devils. O Christian, we must have Christ! Do see to it that every day when you wake you have a fresh savour of Christ upon you by contemplating his person. Live all the day, trying as much as lieth in you, to season your hearts with him, and then at night, lie down with him upon your tongue. It is said of Samuel Rutherford, that he often did fall asleep talking about Christ, and was often heard in his dreams, saying sweet things about his Saviour. There is nothing which can preserve us and keep us from sin, and make our works holy and pure, like this 'bundle of myrrh'.

Myrrh, again, was used as a *disinfectant*. When the fever is abroad, we know people who wear little bags of camphor about their necks. They may be very good; I do not know. But the Orientals believed that in times of pest and plague, a little bag of myrrh worn between the breasts would be of essential service to whoever might carry it. And there doubtless is some power in myrrh to preserve from infectious disease. Well, brethren, certain I am it is so with Christ. You have to go into the world which is like a great lazar-house; but if you carry Christ with you, you will never catch the world's disease. A man may be worth never so much money, he will never get worldly if he keepeth Christ on his heart. A man may have to tug and toil for his livelihood, and be very poor, he will never be discontented and murmuring if he lives close to Christ. O you who have to handle the world, see to it that you handle the Master more than the world. Some of you have to work with drunken and swearing men; others are cast into the midst of frivolities – O take my Master with you! and sin's plagues can have no influence upon your moral nature.

But myrrh was believed by the ancient physicians to do more than this: it was *a cure* – it did not merely prevent, but it healed. I do not know how many diseases are said to be healed by the use of myrrh, nor do I altogether suppose that these Oriental physicians spoke from facts, for they were too much given to ascribe qualities to drugs, which those drugs did not possess; however even modern physicians believe myrrh to have many valuable medical properties. Certain is it that your Christ is the best medicine for the soul. His name is Jehovah Rophi – 'I am the LORD that healeth them.' When we see Luke called 'the beloved physician', we almost grudge him the name. I will take it from him and give it to my Master, for he deserves it far more than Luke. The beloved physician! He touched the leper, and he was made whole. He did but look upon those who were lame, and they leaped as a hart. His voice startled the silence of Hades, and brought back the soul to the body. What cannot Christ do? He can heal anything. You who are sick this morning, sick with doubts and fears, you who are sick with temptation, you who struggle with an angry temper, or with the deathlike sleep of sloth, get Christ, and you are healed. Here all things meet, and in all these things we may say, 'A bundle of myrrh is my well-beloved unto me.'

I have not done yet, for myrrh was used in the East as a *beautifier*. We read of Esther, that before she was introduced to Ahasuerus, she and the virgins were bidden to prepare themselves, and among other things, they used myrrh. The belief of Oriental women was that it removed wrinkles and stains from the face, and they used it constantly for the perfecting of their charms. I do not know how that may be, but I know that nothing makes the believer so beautiful as being with Christ. He is beautiful in the eyes of God, of holy angels, and of his fellow-men. I know some Christians whom it is a great mercy to speak to: if they come into your cottage, they leave behind them tokens of remembrance, in the choice words they utter. To get them into the Church is a thousand mercies, and if they join the Sunday School, of what value they are! Let me tell you that the best gauge of a Christian's usefulness will be found in the degree in which he has been with Jesus and learned of him. Do not tell me it is the scholar, do not say to me it is the man of eloquence, do not say it is the man of substance – well we would have all these consecrate what they have to Christ – but it is the man of God who is the strong man; it is the man who has been with Jesus who is the pillar of the Church, and a light to the world. O brethren, may the beauty of the Lord be upon us through being much with Christ.

And I must not close this point without saying that myrrh might well be used as an emblem of our Lord from *its connection with sacrifice*. It was one of the precious drugs used in making the holy oil with which the priests were anointed and the frankincense which burned perpetually before God. It is this, the sacrificial character of Christ, which is at the root and bottom of all that Christ is most precious to his people. O Lamb of God our sacrifice, we must remember thee.

(b) Now there has been enough, surely, said about the myrrh. Have patience while we just notice that he is called a *bundle* of myrrh, or as some translate it, a bag of myrrh, or a box of myrrh.

There were three sorts of myrrh: there was the myrrh in sprigs, which being burnt made a sweet smell; then there was myrrh, a dried spice; and then thirdly, there was myrrh a flowing oil. We do not know to which there is reference here. But why is it said, 'a *bundle* of myrrh'? First, for *the plenty of it*. He is not a drop of it, he is a casket full. He is not a sprig or flower of it, but a whole bundle full. There is enough in Christ for my necessities. There is more in Christ than I shall ever know – perhaps more than I shall understand even in heaven.

A bundle again, for *variety*; for there is in Christ not only the one thing needful, but 'ye are complete in him'; there is everything needful. Take

Christ in his different characters, and you will see a marvellous variety – prophet, priest, king, husband, friend, shepherd. Take him in his life, death, resurrection, ascension, second advent; take him in his virtue, gentleness, courage, self-denial, love, faithfulness, truth, righteousness – everywhere it is a bundle. Some of God's judgments are manifold, but all God's mercies are manifold, and Christ being the sum of God's mercies, hath in fold upon fold of goodness. He is 'a bundle of myrrh' for variety.

He is a bundle of myrrh again, for *presentation* – not loose myrrh to be dropped on the floor or trodden on, but myrrh tied up, as though God bound up all virtues and excellencies in his Son: not myrrh spilt on the ground, but myrrh in a box – myrrh kept in a casket. Such is Christ. The virtue and excellence which goeth out of Christ is quite as strong today as in the day when the woman touched the hem of his garment and was healed. 'Able to save unto the uttermost them that come unto God through him', is he still unto this hour.

A bundle of myrrh again, to show *how diligently we should take care of it.* We must bind him up, we must keep our thoughts of him and knowledge of him as under lock and key, lest the devil should steal anything from us. We must treasure up his words, prize his ordinances, obey his precepts, tie him up and keep him ever with us as a precious bundle of myrrh.

And yet again, a bundle of myrrh *for speciality*, as if he were not common myrrh for everybody. No, no, no; there is distinguishing discriminating grace – a bundle tied up for his people and labelled with their names from before the foundation of the world. No doubt there is an allusion here to the scent bottle used in every land. Jesus Christ is a bottle of myrrh, and he doth not give forth his smell to everybody but to those who know how to draw forth the stopper, who understand how to get into communion with him, to have close dealings with him. He is not myrrh for all who are in the house but for those who know how to put the bottle to their nostrils and receive the sweet perfume. Oh! blessed people whom the Lord hath admitted into his secrets! Oh! choice and happy people who are thus made to say 'A bottle of myrrh is my well-beloved unto me'.

But I am afraid I tire you, especially those of you who do not know anything about my subject. There are some such here who know no more about what I am talking of than if they were Mohammedans. They are listening to a new kind of religion now. The religion of Christ is as high above them as is the path of the eagle above that of the fish, and as much hidden from them as the way of the serpent on the rock from the eye of man. This is a path which the eagle's eye hath not seen, nor hath the lion's whelp trodden it; but I trust there are some here who know it.

Our third remark was to be - that with a sense of Christ's preciousness is combined A CONSCIOUSNESS OF POSSESSION. It is '*my* well-beloved'. My dear hearer, is Christ *your* well-beloved? *A* Saviour – that is well; but *my* Saviour – that is the best of the best. What is the use of bread if it is not mine? I may die of hunger. Of what value is gold, if it be not mine? I may yet die in a workhouse. I want this preciousness to be *mine*. '*My* well-beloved.' Have you ever laid hold on Christ by the hand of faith?

Will you take him again this morning, brethren in Jesus? I know you will. Would that those who never did take him, would take him now and say, '*My* Saviour.' There stands his atonement, freely offered to you; may you have the grace to take it, and say, 'My Saviour, my Saviour', this morning. Has your heart taken him? It is well for us to use both hands, not only the hand of faith, but the hand of love, for this is the true embrace when both arms meet around our beloved. Do you love him? O souls, do you LOVE Christ, with an emphasis upon the word. Do not talk to me about a religion which dwells in the head and never gets into the heart. Get rid of it as quickly as you can; it will never bring you to heaven. It is not 'I believe this and that' merely, but 'I love'. Ah! some who have been great fools in doctrine have been very wise in love. We tell our children to learn things 'by heart'. I think you can, you love Jesus, and if you cannot you must confess as I do:

> A very wretch, Lord, I should prove,
> Had I no love to thee;
> Sooner than not my Saviour love,
> O may I cease to be.

But that is not the only word. 'A bundle of myrrh is my well-beloved *unto me*.' That is not a redundant expression, 'unto *me*'. He is not so to many. Ah! my Lord is a root out of a dry ground to multitudes. A three-volume novel suits them better than his Book. They would sooner go to a play or a dance than they would have any fellowship with him. They can see the beauties upon the cheeks of this Jezebel world, but they cannot see the perfections of my Lord and Master. Well! well! well! Let them say what they will, and let them think as they please, every creature hath its own joy, but 'a bundle of myrrh is my well-beloved unto *me*' – unto *me* – unto *me*, and if there is not another who finds him so, yet 'a bundle of myrrh is my well-beloved unto *me*'.

I would it were not with others as it is – I would that others did think so also of him; but let them say what they will, they shall not drive me out of my knowledge of this – 'a bundle of myrrh is my well-beloved *unto me*.' The infidel saith, 'There is no God.' The atheist would altogether laugh me to scorn. They shall say what they will, but 'a bundle of myrrh is my well-beloved *unto me*'. Even bishops have been found who will take away a part of his Book, and so rend his garments, and rob him; and there be some who say his religion is out of date, and grace has lost its power; and they go after philosophy and vain conceit, and I know not what, but 'a bundle of myrrh is my well-beloved *unto me*'. They may have no nostril for him, they may have no desire after him; so let it be, but 'a bundle of myrrh is my well-beloved *unto me*'. I know there are some who say they have tried him and not found him sweet, and who have turned away from him and gone back to the beggarly elements of the world because they see nothing in Christ that they should desire him; but 'a bundle of myrrh is my well-beloved *unto me*'.

Ah! Christian, this is what you want, a personal experience, a positive experience; you want to know for *yourself*, for there is no religion which is worth a button which is not burnt into you by personal experience, a positive experience; and there is no religion worth a straw which does not spring from your soul, which does lay not hold upon the very vitals of your spirit. Yes, you must say – I hope you can say as you go down those steps this morning, and enter again tomorrow into that busy, giddy world – you must say, 'Let the whole world go astray, "a bundle of myrrh is my well-beloved unto *me*".'

4. **Now the practical point closes it. A SENSE OF POSSESSION AND A SENSE OF ENJOYMENT WILL ALWAYS LEAD THE CHRISTIAN TO DESIRE CONSTANT FELLOWSHIP**. 'He' or rather 'it shall lie all night betwixt my breasts'. The Church does not say, 'I will put this bundle of myrrh on my shoulders' – Christ is no burden to a Christian. She does not say, 'I will put this bundle of myrrh on my back' – the Church does not want to have Christ concealed from her face. She desires to have him where she can see him, and near to her heart. The bundle of myrrh shall lie all night upon my heart. The words 'all night' are not in the original; I do not know how they got into the translation. He is to be always there, not only all night but all day. It would be always night if he were not there, and it cannot be night when he is there, for

> Midst darkest shade, if he appear,
> My dawning has begun.

He shall always be upon our heart. I think that expression just means these three things. It is an expression of *desire* – her desire that she may have the consciousness of Christ's love continually. Do not you feel the same desire? O Christian, if thou hast ever been made like the chariots of Amminadib, it will be ill for thee if thou canst be content to be otherwise. If thou hast but once tasted Christ, thou wilt want to feed upon him all day and all night, and as long as thou livest. My desire is that Jesus may abide with me from morn till even, in the world, and in the Church, when I awake, when I sleep, when I go abroad, and when I come home into the bosom of my family. Is not that your desire that he may be always with you?

But then, it is not only her desire, but it is also her *confidence*. She seems to say, 'He will be with me thus.' You may have a suspension of visible fellowship with Christ, but Christ will never go away from his people really. He will be all night betwixt your breasts; he will at all times abide faithful to you. He may close his eyes and hide his face from you, but his heart never can depart from you. He has set you as a seal upon his heart, and increasingly will make you sensible of it. Recollect there is no suspension of Christ's union with his people, and no suspension of those saving influences which always make his people to stand complete in him.

To conclude, this is also *a resolve*. She desires, she believes, and she resolves it. Lord, thou shalt be with me, thou shalt be with me always. I appeal to you, brethren, will you not make this resolve in God's strength this morning to cling close to Christ? Do not go talking, as you go home, about all sorts of nonsense; do not spend this afternoon in communion with folly and vanity, but throughout this day let your soul keep to Christ, to nothing but Christ. This evening we shall come to his table to eat bread and drink wine in remembrance of him; let us try if we can, that nothing shall make us give up Christ all this day. Have you got him? Hold him and do not let him go till you bring him to your mother's house, to the chamber of her who bare you. Then there will be the family prayer at night. Oh, seek to keep him till you put your head upon the pillow. And then, on Monday morning, some of you have to go to work, and as soon as you get into the workshop or the factory, you say, 'Now I must lose my Master.' No, do not lose him. Hold him fast when your hand plies the hammer, and when your fingers hold the needle, still cling to him, in the market or in the exchange, on board ship, or in the field, do not let him go. You *may have him with you all day*. The Mahometan usually wears a piece of the Koran round his neck, and one, when converted to Christianity, put his New Testament in a little silken bag and always wore it there. We need not such outward signs, but let us always have the Saviour there; let us hang him about our neck as a charm against all evil; seek his blessed company, place him as a star upon your breast to be your honour and joy.

Well, I have done, but I must have a word with the unconverted. There are some who can say, 'I will have Christ always *on my tongue*.' Away with tongue religion. You must have him on your heart. Ah! there are some who say, '*I hope* I shall have Christ on my heart *in all eternity*.' You cannot have Christ in eternity if you do not have him in time. If you despise him today in this life, he will reject you tomorrow in the world to come; and if *he* call and you refuse, one day *you* will call and he refuse. *Do not put up with desires merely*, dear friends – some of you have desires, and nothing more. Do not only desire Christ, but get him. Do not stop short with saying, 'I should like to have him in my heart'; give no sleep to your eyes nor slumber to your eyelids, till by humble faith you have taken Christ to be your all in all. May the Lord bless these poor words, for Jesus' sake. Amen.

10

THE ROSE AND THE LILY

'I am the rose of Sharon, and the lily of the valleys'
(Song of Solomon 2:1)

Here are sweet flowers blooming serenely amid this wintry weather. In the garden of the soul you may gather fragrant flowerets at all seasons of the year; and although the soul's garden, like every other, has its winter, yet, strange to say, no sooner do the roses and the lilies mentioned in the text begin to bloom, than the winter flies and the summer smiles. Outside in your garden, the summer brings the roses; but within the enclosure of the heart, the roses and lilies create the summer. I trust that we this morning may have grace to walk abroad in the fields of heavenly contemplation, to admire the matchless charms of him whose cheeks are as a bed of spices, as sweet flowers, whose lips are like lilies dropping sweet-smelling myrrh. May our hearts interpret the language of our text, and sing

Is he a rose? Not Sharon yields
Such fragrancy in all her fields;
Or, if the lily he assume,
The valleys bless the rich perfume.

It is our Lord who speaks: 'I am the rose of Sharon.' How is it that he utters his own commendation, for it is an old and true adage, that 'self praise is no recommendation'? None but vain creatures ever praise themselves, and yet Jesus often praises himself. He saith, 'I am the Good Shepherd'; 'I am the Bread of Life'; 'I am meek and lowly of heart'; and in divers speeches he is frequently declaring his own excellencies, yet Jesus is not vain! Scorned be the thought! Yet I said if any *creature* praised itself it must be vain, and that, too, is true. How then shall we solve the riddle? Is not this the answer, that he is no creature at all, and therefore comes not beneath the rule? For the creature to praise itself is vanity, but for the Creator to praise himself, for the Lord God to manifest and show forth his own glory, is becoming and proper. Hear how he extols his own wisdom and power in the end of the book of Job, and see if it is not most seemly, as the Lord himself proclaims it! Is not God constantly ruling both providence and grace for the manifestation of his own glory, and do we not all freely consent that no motive short of this would be worthy of the divine mind? So, then, because Christ talks thus of himself, since no man dare call him vainglorious, I gather an indirect proof of his deity, and bow down before him, and bless him that he gives me this incidental evidence of his being no creature, but the uncreated one himself. An old Scots woman once said, 'He is never so bonnie as when he is commending himself;' and we all feel it so: no words appear more suitable out of his own lips than these, 'I am the rose of Sharon, and the lily of the valleys.'

Our Lord, when he thus praises himself, doubtless does so for an excellent reason, namely, that no one can possibly reveal him to the sons of men but himself. No lips can tell the love of Christ to the heart till Jesus himself shall speak within. Descriptions all fall flat and tame unless the Holy Ghost fills them with life and power; till our Immanuel reveals himself within the recesses of the heart, the soul sees him not. If you would see the sun, would you light your candles! Would you gather together the common means of illumination, and seek in that way to behold the orb of day? No, the wise man knoweth that the sun must reveal itself, and only by its own blaze can that mighty lamp be seen. It is so with Christ. Unless he so manifest himself to us, as he doth not unto the world, we cannot behold him. He must say to us, 'I am the rose of Sharon', or else all the declarations of man that he is the rose of Sharon will fall short of the mark. 'Blessed art thou, Simon Bar-jona,' said he to Peter, 'for flesh and blood hath not revealed this unto thee.' Purify flesh and blood by any educational process you may select, elevate mental faculties to the highest degree of intellectual power, yet none of these can reveal Christ. The Spirit of God must come with power, and overshadow the man with his wings, and then in that mystic Holy of Holies the Lord Jesus must display himself to the sanctified eye, as he doth not unto the purblind sons of men. Christ must be his own mirror; as the diamond alone can cut the diamond, so he alone can display himself.

Is it not clear enough to us all, that Jesus being God, befittingly praises himself, and we being frail creatures, he must necessarily commend himself, or we should never be able to perceive his beauty at all? Each reason is sufficient, both are overwhelming; it is most suitable that Jesus should preach Jesus, that love should teach us love. Beloved, happy are those men to whom our Lord familiarly unveils his beauties. He is the rose, but it is not given unto all men to perceive his fragrance. He is the fairest of lilies, but few are the eyes which have gazed upon his matchless purity. He stands before the world without form or comeliness, a root out of the dry ground, rejected by the vain, and despised by the proud. The great mass of this blear-eyed world can see nothing of the ineffable glories of Immanuel. Only where the Spirit has touched the eye with eye-salve, quickened the heart with divine life, and educated the soul to a heavenly taste, only there is that love-word of my text heard and understood, 'I am the rose of Sharon, and the lily of the valleys.' 'To you that believe he is precious'; to you he is the corner stone; to you he is the rock of your salvation, your all in all; but to others he is 'a stone of stumbling, and a rock of offence, even to them which stumble at the word, being disobedient'.

Let it be our prayer before we advance a single foot further, that our Redeemer would now reveal himself to his own chosen people, and favour each one of us with at least a glimpse of his all conquering charms. May the King himself draw near unto his guests this morning, and as of old, when it was winter he walked in the temple in Solomon's porch, so may he walk in the midst of this waiting assembly.

First, this morning, I shall speak with you a little, as I may be helped by the Holy Ghost, upon THE MOTIVES OF OUR LORD IN THUS COMMENDING HIMSELF.

I take it that he has designs of love in this speech. He would have all his people rich in high and happy thoughts concerning his blessed person. Jesus is not content that his brethren should think meanly of him; it is his pleasure that his espoused ones should be delighted with his beauty, and that he should be the King and Lord of their spirits: he would have us possess an adoring admiration for him, joined with most cheerful and happy thoughts towards him. We are not to count him as a bare necessary, like to bread and water, but we are to regard him as a luxurious delicacy, as rare and ravishing delight, comparable to the rose and the lily. Our Lord, you observe, expresses himself here poetically: 'I am the rose of Sharon.' Dr Watts, when he had written his delightful hymns, was the subject of Dr Johnson's criticism, and that excellent lexicographer, who wrote with such authority upon all literary matters, entirely missed his mark when he said that the themes of religion were so few and so prosaic that they were not adapted for the poet, they were not such as could allow of the flight of wing which poetry required. Alas, Dr Johnson! how little couldst thou have entered into the spirit of these things, for if there be any place where poetry may indulge itself to the uttermost, it is in the realm of the infinite. Jordan's streams are as pure as Helicon, and Siloa's brook as inspiring as the Castalian fount. Heathen Parnassus has not half the elevation of the Christian's Tabor, let critics judge as they may. This book of Solomon's Song is poetry of the very highest kind to the spiritual mind, and throughout Scripture the sublime and beautiful are as much at home as the eagles in their eyries of rock. Surely our Lord adopts that form of speech in this song in order to show us that the highest degree of poetical faculty may be consecrated to him, and that lofty thoughts and soaring conceptions concerning himself are no intruders, but are bound to pay homage at his cross. Jesus would have us enjoy the highest thoughts of him that the sublimest poesy can possibly convey to us; and his motives I shall labour to lay before you.

Doubtless, he commends himself because *high thoughts of Christ will enable us to act consistently with our relations towards him*. The saved soul is espoused to Christ. Now, in the marriage estate, it is a great assistance to happiness if the wife has high ideas of her husband. In the marriage union between the soul and Christ, this is exceedingly necessary. Listen to the words of the Psalm, 'He is thy Lord; and worship thou him.' Jesus is our husband, and is no more to be named Baal, that is, thy master, but to be called Ishi, thy man, thy husband; yet at the same time he is our Lord: 'For the husband is the head of the wife, even as Christ is the head of the church: and he is the saviour of the body.' When the wife despises her husband, and looks down upon him, then the order of nature is broken, and the household is out of joint; and if our soul should ever come to despise Christ, then it can no longer stand in its true relation to him; but the more loftily we see Christ enthroned, and the more lowly we are when bowing before the foot of the throne, the more truly shall we be prepared to act our part in the economy of grace towards our Lord Jesus. Brethren, your Lord Christ desires you to think well of him, that you may submit cheerfully to his authority, and so be a better spouse to this best of husbands.

Moreover, our Master knows that *high thoughts of him increase our love*. Men will not readily love that which they do not highly esteem. Love and esteem go together. There is a love of pity, but that would be far out of place in reference to our exalted Head. If we are to love him at all, it must be with the love of admiration; and the higher that admiration shall rise, the more vehemently will our love flame forth. My brethren and sisters in Christ, I beseech you think much of your Master's excellencies. Study him in his primeval glory, before he took upon himself your nature! Think of the mighty love which drew him from his starry throne to die upon the cross of shame! Consider well the omnipotent affection which made him stretch his hands to the nails, and yield his heart to the spear! Admire him as you see him conquering in his weakness over all the powers of hell, and by his sufferings overthrowing all the hosts of your sins, so that they cannot rise against you any more for ever! See him now risen, no more to die; crowned, no more to be dishonoured; glorified, no more to suffer! Bow before him, hail him in the halls of your inner nature as the Wonderful, the Counsellor, the mighty God within your spirits, for only thus will your love to him be what it should.

A high esteem of Christ, moreover, as he well knoweth, *is very necessary to our comfort.* Beloved, when you esteem Christ very highly, the things of this world become of small account with you, and their loss is not so heavily felt. If you feel your losses and crosses to be such ponderous weights, that the wings of Christ's love cannot lift you up from the dust, surely you have made too much of the world and too little of him. I see a pair of balances. I see in this one the death of a child, or the loss of a beloved relative; but I perceive in the other scale the great love of Christ; now we shall see which will weigh the most with the man: if Jesus throws the light affliction up aloft, it is well, but if the trouble outweighs Jesus, then it is ill with us indeed. If you are so depressed by your trials that you can by no means rejoice, even though you know that your name is written in heaven, then methinks you cannot love Jesus as you should. Get but delightful thoughts of him, and you will be like a man who has lost a pebble but has preserved his diamond; like the man who has seen a few cast clouts and rotten rags consumed in the flames, but has saved his children from the conflagration. You will rejoice in your deepest distress because Christ is yours if you have a high sense of the preciousness of your Master. Talk not of plaisters that will draw out all pain from a wound! Speak not of medicines which will extirpate diseases! The sweet love of Christ once clapped on to the deepest wound which the soul can ever know, would heal it at once. A drop of the precious medicine of Jesus' love tasted in the soul would chase away all heart pains for ever. Jesus, Jesus, Jesus, be thou within us, and we make no choice of situations: put us in Nebuchadnezzar's furnace, if thou wilt walk the glowing coals as our companion, we will fear no evil.

Further, *our Lord would have us entertain great thoughts of himself, because this will quicken all the powers of our soul.* I spoke to you just now of love receiving force from an esteem of Jesus, I might say the like of faith, or patience, or humility. Wherever Christ is highly esteemed, all the faculties of the spiritual man exercise themselves with energy. I will judge of your piety by this barometer: does Christ stand high or low with you? If you have thought little of Christ, if you have been content to live without his presence, if you have cared little for his honour, if you have been neglectful of his laws, then I know that your soul is sick – God grant that it may not be sick unto death! But if the first thought of your spirit has been, how can I honour Jesus? If the daily desire of your soul has been, Oh that I knew where I might find him! I tell you that you may have a thousand infirmities, and may even scarcely know whether you are a child of God at all, and yet I am persuaded, beyond a doubt, that you are safe, since Jesus is great in your esteem. I care not for thy rags, what thinkest thou of *his* royal apparel? I care not for thy wounds, though they bleed in torrents, what thinkest thou of *his* wounds? Are they like glittering rubies in thine esteem?

I think nothing the less of thee, though thou liest like Lazarus on the dunghill, and the dogs do lick thee; I judge thee not by thy poverty: what thinkest thou of the King in his beauty? Has he a glorious high throne in thy heart? Wouldst thou set him higher if thou couldst? Wouldst thou be willing to die if thou couldst but add another trumpet to the strain which proclaims his praise? Ah! then, it is well with thee. Whatever thou mayest think of thyself, if Christ be great to thee, thou shalt be with him ere long.

High thoughts of Jesus will set us upon high attempts for his honour. What will not men do when they are possessed with the passion of love! When once some master thought gets hold of the mind, others who have never felt the power of it, think the man to be insane; they laugh at him and ridicule him. When the grand thought of love to God has gained full possession of the soul, men have been able to actually accomplish what other men have not even thought of doing. Love has laughed at impossibilities, and proved that she is not to be quenched by many waters, nor drowned by floods. Impassable woods have nevertheless been made a footway for the Christian missionary; through the dense jungle, steaming with malaria, men have passed, bearing the message of truth; into the midst of hostile and savage tribes, weak and trembling women even have forced their way to tell of Jesus; no sea has been so stormy, no mountains have been so elevated that they could shut out the earnest spirit; no long nights of winter in Labrador or in Iceland have been able to freeze up the love of the heir of heaven to be overcome, though all the elements have combined with the cruelty of wicked men, and with the malice of hell itself. Christ's people have been more than conquerors through him that hath loved them, when his love has been shed abroad in their hearts by the Holy Spirit, and they have had elevated thoughts of their Lord.

I wish it were in my power to put this matter more forcibly, but I am persuaded, brethren, that our Lord in commending himself to us, this morning, in the words of our text, does so with this as his motive, that by the power of his Spirit we may be led to esteem him very highly in the inmost secret of our heart. And shall he speak to us in vain? Shall he stand in this pulpit, this morning, as he does in spirit, and shall he say, 'I am the rose of Sharon'? And shall we reply, 'But we see not thy beauty'? Shall he add a double commendation, 'I am the lily of the valley'? And shall our cold hearts reply, 'But we admire not thy spotless purity'? I trust we are not so utterly abandoned to spiritual blindness and ingratitude. Far rather, although we confess before him that we do not admire him as we should, we will add humbly, and with the tear of repentance in our eye

> Yet we love thee and adore
> O for grace to love thee more.

Whatever may be the commendable motive for any statement, yet it must not be made if it be not accurate, and therefore, in the second place, I come to observe OUR LORD'S JUSTIFICATION FOR THIS COMMENDATION, which is abundantly satisfactory to all who know him.

What our Lord says of himself is strictly true. It falls short of the mark, it is no exaggeration. Observe each one of the words. He begins, '*I am*'. Those two little words I would not insist upon, but it is no straining of language to say that even here we have a great deep. What creature can, with exact truthfulness, say, 'I am'? As for man, whose breath is in his nostrils he may rather say, 'I am not', than 'I am'. We are so short a time here, and so quickly gone, that the ephemera, which is born and dies under the light of one day's sun, is our brother. Poor short-lived creatures, we change with every moon, and are inconstant as the wave, frail as the dust, feeble as a worm, and fickle as the wind. Jesus saith, 'I am', and blessed be his name, he can fairly claim the attributes of self-existence, and immutability. He said, 'I am', in the days of his flesh, he saith, 'I am', at this hour: whatever he was he is, whatever he has been to any of his saints at any time, he is to us this day. Come, my soul, rejoice in thine unchangeable Christ, and if thou gettest no further than the first two words of the text, yet thou hast a meal to stay thine hunger, like Elijah's cakes, in the strength of which he went for forty days. 'I am' hath revealed himself unto thee in a more glorious manner than he did unto Moses at the burning bush, the great 'I AM' in human flesh has become thy Saviour and thy Lord.

'I am *the rose*.' We understand from this that Christ is lovely. He selects one of the most charming of flowers to set forth himself. All the beauties of all the creatures are to be found in Christ in greater perfection than in the creatures themselves.

> 'White and ruddy is my Beloved,
> All his heavenly beauties shine;
> Nature can't produce an object,
> Nor so glorious, so divine;
> He hath wholly
> Won my soul to realms above.'

'Whatsoever things are true, whatsoever things are honest, whatsoever things are just, whatsoever things are pure, whatsoever things are lovely, whatsoever things are of good report', all are to be found stored up in our Well-beloved. Whatever there may be of beauty in the material world, Jesus Christ possesses all that in the spiritual world, only in a tenfold multiplication. He is infinitely more beautiful in the garden of the soul, and in the paradise of God, than the rose can be in the gardens of earth, though it be the universally-acknowledged queen of flowers.

But the Spouse adds, 'I am the rose *of Sharon.*' This was the best and rarest of roses. Jesus is not 'the rose' alone, but 'the rose of Sharon' just as he calls his righteousness 'gold', and then adds, 'the gold of Ophir' – the best of the best. Jesus, then, is not only positively lovely, but superlatively the loveliest

> None among the sons of men,
> None among the heavenly train,
> Can with Sharon's rose compare,
> None so sweet and none so fair.

The Son of David takes the first place as the fairest among ten thousand. He is the sun, and all others are the stars; in his presence all the feebler lights are hidden, for they are nothing, and he is all in all. Blush for your deformities, ye beauties of earth, when his perfections eclipse you! Away, ye pageants, and ye pompous triumphs of men, the King in his beauty transcends you all! Black are the heavens and dark is the day in comparison with him. Oh, to see him face to face! This would be a vision for which life would be a glad exchange. For a vision of his face we could fain be blind for ever to all joys beside.

Our Lord adds, '*I am* the lily', thus giving himself a double commendation. Indeed, Jesus Christ deserves not to be praised doubly, but sevenfold, ay, and unto seven times seven. Heap up all the metaphors that express loveliness, bring together all the adjectives which describe delight, and all human speech and all earth-born things shall fail to tell of him. The rose with all its redness is not complete till the lily adds its purity, and the two together are dim reflections of our glorious Lord. I learn from the text that in Christ Jesus you have a combination of contrasted excellencies. If he be red with the flush of courageous zeal, or red with triumph as he returns from Edom, he is the rose; but he is a warrior without sinful anger or cruel vengeance, he is as pure and spotless as the timid virgin who toys with the dove – he is therefore our snow-white lily. I see him red as the rose in his sacrifice, as

> from his head, his hands, his feet,
> Sorrow and love flow mingled down,

but I see him white as the lily as he ascends on high in his perfect righteousness, clothed in his white robe of victory, to receive gifts for men. Our Beloved is a mingling of all perfections to make up one perfection, and of all manner of sweetness to compose one complete sweetness. Earth's choicest charms commingled, feebly picture his abounding preciousness.

He is the 'lily *of the valleys*'. Does he intend by that to hint to us that he is a lily in his lowliest estate, a lily of the valley? The carpenter's son, living in poverty, wearing the common garb of the poor, is he the lily of the valleys? Yes; he is a lily to you and to me, poor dwellers in the lowlands. Up yonder he is a lily on the hilltops, where all celestial eyes admire him; down here, in these valleys of fears and cares, he is a lily still as fair as in heaven. Our eyes can see his beauty, can see his beauty now, a lily to us this very day. Though we have not seen the King in his beauty, yet I say unto you, that Solomon in all his glory was not arrayed like Jesus Christ in our eyes, as we see him by faith in a glass darkly.

The words, having been opened up one by one, teach us that *Christ is lovely to all our spiritual senses*. The rose is delightful to the eye, but it is also refreshing to the nostril, and the lily the same. So is Jesus. All the senses of the soul are ravished and satisfied with him, whether it be the taste or feeling, the hearing, the sight, or the spiritual smell, all charms are in Jesus. Often when we have not seen the Anointed, we have perceived his presence. Travelling on the Lake Lugano, one morning, we heard the swell of the song of the nightingale, and the oars were stilled on the blue lake as we listened to the silver sounds. We could not see a single bird, nor do I know that we wished to see – we were so content with the sweetness of the music: even so it is with our Lord; we may enter a house where he is loved, and we may hear nothing concerning Christ, and yet we may perceive clearly enough that he is there, a holy influence streaming through their actions pervades the household; so that if Jesus be unseen, it is clear that he is not unknown. Go anywhere where Jesus is, and though you do not actually hear his name, yet the sweet influence which flows from his love will be plainly enough discernible.

Our Lord is so lovely, that *even the recollection of his love is sweet*. Take the rose of Sharon, and pull it leaf from leaf, and lay by the leaves in the jar of memory, and you shall find each leaf most fragrant long afterwards, filling the house with perfume; and this very day we remember times of refreshing enjoyed at the Lord's table still delightful as we reflect upon them.

Jesus is lovely in the bud as well as when full blown. You admire the rose quite as much when it is but a bud as when it bursts forth into perfect development: and methinks, Christ to you, my beloved, in the first blush of your piety, was not one whit less sweet than he is now. Jesus full blown, in our riper experience, has lost none of his excellence. When we shall see him fully blown in the garden of paradise, shall we not count it to be our highest heaven to gaze upon him for ever?

Christ is so lovely that he needs no beautifying. When I hear men trying to speak of him with polished sentences, which have been revised and re-revised upon their manuscripts, I would ask them why they need to paint the rose of Sharon, and what they can be at in seeking to enamel the lily of the valleys? Hold up Christ crucified, and he himself is beautiful enough without our paint and tinsel. Let the roughest tongue speak sincerely of him in the most broken but honest accents, and Jesus himself is such a radiant jewel that the setting will be of small consequence, he is so glorious that he is 'Most adorned when unadorned the most'. May we ever feel thus concerning him, and if we are tempted to display our powers of oratory when we have to speak of him, let us say, 'Down, busy pride, and let Christ rule, and let Christ be seen.' He needs no help from thee.

He is so lovely, again, that he satisfies the highest taste of the most educated spirit to the very full. The greatest amateur in perfumes is quite satisfied with the rose, and I should think that no man of taste will ever be able to criticise the lily, and cavil at its form. Now, when the soul has arrived at her highest pitch of true taste, she shall still be content with Christ, nay, she shall be the better able to appreciate him. In the world's history, we are supposed to have arrived at an age of taste, when colour and form are much regarded. I must confess I think it a gaudy, tasteless age, and the fashion of the day is staring, vulgar, childish and depraved. Bright and glittering colours and antique grotesque forms are much run after; and men must need introduce their chosen fineries and fopperies into their worship, supposing that it is comely to worship God with silks, and laces, and ribbons, and gilt, and tinsel, and I know not what of trumpery besides. Just as the harlot of Babylon arrayed herself in pearls, and fine linen, and purple, and silk, and scarlet, even so do her imitators adorn themselves. As for us, my brethren, the beauty of Christ is such that if we go into a barn to worship, we are quite as satisfied as though it were a cathedral, with groined arches and glowing windows; such is the beauty of Christ in our eyes, that we are quite content to hear of him without the pealing organ and the swell of Gregorian chants; and we are even satisfied though there should be no display of taste, nothing sensuous and scenic, nothing to please the eye or charm the ear. Jesus alone affords our mind all that delight in architecture, poetry and music could profess to give, and when our soul getteth near to him, she looketh upon all outward adornments as mere child's toys, fit to amuse the rattle-brains of this poor idiot world, but vain gewgaws to men in Christ Jesus, who by reason of use have had their senses exercised, and learned to delight in nobler things than those in which the swine of this earth delight themselves. God give you to know that if you want beauty, Jesus is Sharon's rose; if you want spotless charms to delight your true taste, he is the lily of the valleys.

Dwelling for another minute on this subject, let me remark that our Lord Jesus Christ deserves all that he has said of himself. First, *in his divine glory*. The glory of Christ as God, who shall write upon it? The first born sons of light desire to gaze into this vision, but feel that their eyes are unable to endure the excess of light. He is God over all, blessed for ever. Concerning Christ, I may say, that the heavens are not pure in his sight, and he charged his angels with folly. Nothing is great, nothing is excellent but God, and Christ is God. O roses and lilies, where are ye now?

Our Lord deserves these praises, again, *in his perfection of manhood.* He is like ourselves, but in him was no sin. 'The prince of this world cometh, but hath nothing in me.' Throughout the whole of his biography, there is not a faulty line. Let us write as carefully as we will after the copy, we still blot and blur the pages, but in him there is no mistake. His life is so wonderfully perfect that even those who have denied his deity have been astounded at it, and they have bowed down before the majesty of his holiness. Ye roses of ardent love, and ye lilies of purest holiness, where are ye now when we compare you with this perfect man?

He deserves this commendation, too, *in his mediatorial qualifications.* Since his blood has washed us from all our sins, we talk no more of the red roses, for what can they do to purify the soul? Since his righteousness has made us accepted in the Beloved, we will speak no more of spotless lilies, for what are these?

He deserves all this praise, too, *in his reigning glory.* He has a glory which his Father has given him as a reward, in the power of which he sits down at the right hand of God for ever and ever, and shall soon come to judge the world in righteousness, and the people with equity. Beloved, when I think of the pompous appearance when he shall descend a second time in splendour upon the earth, I say again, ye roses, your radiant beauties are utterly eclipsed, and ye lilies, your snow-white purity is forgotten, I can scarce discern ye; O fair flowers of earth, ye are lost in the blaze of the great white throne, and in the flames of fire that shall go before the Judge of all to prepare his way.

View the Lord Jesus in any way you please, all that he himself can say concerning himself he richly deserves, and therefore glory be unto his name for ever and ever, and let the whole earth say, Amen.

I shall now conduct you to a third consideration, namely, THE INFLUENCE OF THIS COMMENDATION UPON US.

Christ desires our loftiest thoughts of himself, and his desires are for our good. O my beloved, I wish time would stay its wing a moment or two, that I might urge upon you, with all your hearts, to second the endeavours of Christ, to labour after holy elevated thoughts concerning himself, since he desires them for you. And if ye ask me how you are to attain unto them, let me aid you a minute.

Think of the ruin of this world till Christ came into it! Methinks I see in vision a howling wilderness, a great and terrible desert, like to the Sahara.

I perceive nothing in it to relieve the eye, all around I am wearied with a vision of hot and arid sand, strewn with ten thousand bleaching skeletons of wretched men who have expired in anguish, having lost their way in the pitiless waste. O God, what a sight! How horrible! a sea of sand without a bound, and without an oasis, a cheerless graveyard for a race forlorn! But what is that I see? Upon a sudden, upspringing from the scorching sand I see a root, a branch, a plant of renown; and as it grows it buds, the bud expands – it is a rose, and at its side a lily bows its modest head; and miracle of miracles! as the fragrance of those flowers is diffused in the desert air, I perceive that wilderness is transformed into a fruitful field, and all around it blossoms exceedingly, the glory of Lebanon is given unto it, the excellency of Carmel and Sharon. Call it not Sahara, call it Paradise. Speak not of it any longer as the valley of deathshade, for where I saw the skeletons bleaching in the sun, I see a resurrection and up spring the dead, a mighty army, full of life immortal – you can understand the vision. Christ is the rose which has changed the scene.

If you would have great thoughts of Christ think of *your own ruin*. Yonder I behold you cast out an infant, unswathed, unwashed, defiled with your own blood, too foul to be looked upon except by beasts of prey. And what is this that has been cast into your bosom and which lying there has suddenly made you fair and lovely? A rose has been thrown into your bosom by a divine hand, and for its sake you have been pitied and cared for by a divine providence, you are washed and cleaned from your defilement, you are adopted into heaven's family, the fair seal of love is upon your forehead, and the ring of faithfulness is on your hand – a prince unto God – though just now you were an orphan, cast away. O prize the rose, the putting of which into your bosom has made you what you are!

Consider your daily need of this rose. You live in the pestilential air of this earth: take Christ away, you die. Christ is the daily food of your spirit. You know, believer, that you are utterly powerless without your Lord. O prize him then in proportion to the necessities you have for him! As you cannot even pray or think an acceptable thought apart from his presence, I beseech you press him to your bosom as the beloved of your soul. You are like a branch cut off and withered, thrown outside the garden gate to be burnt as are the noxious weeds, apart from him; but when you are near him you bring forth fruit unto the glory of God. Praise Christ I say then, after the rate of the necessity that you have for him.

Think, beloved, of *the estimation that Christ is had in beyond the skies*, in the land where things are measured by the right standard, where men are no longer deceived by the delusions of earth. Think how God esteems the only begotten, his unspeakable gift to us. Consider what the angels think of him, as they count it their highest honour to veil their faces at his feet.

Consider what the blood-washed think of him, as day without night they sing his well-deserved praises with gladdest voices. Remember how you yourself have sometimes esteemed him. There have been happy hours when you would freely have given your eyes, and felt you cared no longer for the light of earth's brightest days, for your soul's eyes would serve you well enough if you could for ever be favoured with the same clear sight of Christ. Have there not been moments when the chariots of Amminadib seemed but poor dragging things, compared with the wheels of your soul, when Jesus ravished your heart with his celestial embrace? Estimate him today as you did then, for *he* is the same, though *you* are not.

Think of him today as you will think of him in the hour of death, and in the day of judgment, when none but Jesus can avail to keep your soul alive. The great King has made a banquet, and he has proclaimed to all the world that none shall enter but those who bring with them the fairest flower that blooms. The spirits of men advance to the gate by thousands, and they bring each one the flower which he has thought the best; but in crowds they are driven from his presence, and enter not into the banquet. Some bear in their hand the deadly nightshade of superstition, or carry the flaunting poppies of Rome, but these are not dear to the King, the bearers are shut out of the pearly gates. My soul, hast thou gathered the rose of Sharon? Dost thou wear the lily of the valley in thy bosom constantly? If so, when thou comest up to the gates of heaven thou wilt know its value, for thou hast only to show this, and the porter of the gate will open; not for a moment will he deny the admission, for to that rose the porter openeth ever. Thou shalt find thy way with this rose in thy hand up to the throne of God himself, for heaven itself possesses nothing which excels the rose of Sharon, and of all the flowers that bloom in paradise there is none that can rival the lily of the valleys. Get Calvary's blood-red rose into thy hand by faith, wear it; by communion preserve it; by daily watchfulness make it your all in all, and you shall be blessed beyond all bliss, happy beyond a dream. So be it yours for ever.

Lastly, I shall close by asking you to make CONFESSIONS SUGGESTED BY MY TEXT.

I will not make them for you, and therefore need not detain you from your homes. I will utter my own lamentation and leave you every one apart to do the like. I stand before this text of mine to blush, this morning, and to weep while I acknowledge my ungrateful behaviour. 'My Lord, I am truly ashamed to think that I have not gazed more upon thee. I know, and in my heart believe, that thou art the sum total of all beauty, yet must I sorrowfully lament that my eyes have been gadding abroad to look after other beauties; my thoughts have been deluded with imaginary excellencies in the creatures, and I have meditated but little upon thyself. Alas! my

Lord, I confess still further that I have not possessed and enjoyed thee as I ought. When I might have been with thee all the day and all the night, I have been roving hither and thither, and forgetting my resting place. I have not been careful to welcome my Beloved and to retain his company. I have stirred him up by my sins, and have driven him away by my lukewarmness. I have given him cold lodgings, and slender hospitality within the chambers of my heart. I have not held him fast, neither have I pressed him to abide with me as I ought to have done. All this I must confess, and mourn that I am not more ashamed while confessing it. Moreover, my good Lord, although I know thy great sacrifice for me might well have chained my heart for ever to thine altar (and oh that thou hadst done so!) I must acknowledge that I have not been a living sacrifice as I should have been. I have not been so fascinated by the lustre of thy beauty as I should have been. Oh that all my heart's rooms had been occupied by thee, and by thee alone! Would God my soul were as the coals in the furnace, all on flame, and not a single particle of me left unconsumed by the delightful flames of thy love. I must also confess, my Lord, that I have not spoken of thee as I should have done. Albeit I have had many opportunities, yet I have not praised thee at the rate which thou deservest. I have given thee at best but a poor, stammering, chilly tongue, when I should have spoken with the fiery zeal of a seraph.'

These are my confessions. Brethren and sisters, what are yours? If you have none to make, if you can justly claim to have done all that you should have done to your Beloved, I envy you; but methinks there is not a man here who will dare to say this. I am sure you have all had falls, and slips, and shortcomings, with regard to him. Well, then, come humbly to Jesus at once. He will forgive you readily, for he does not soon take offence at his spouse. He may sometimes speak sharp words to her, because he loves her, but his heart is always true and faithful and tender. He will forgive the past, he will receive you at this moment; ay, this moment he will display himself to you. If you will but open the door to him, he will enter into immediate fellowship with you, for he saith, 'Behold, I stand at the door and knock: if any man hear my voice, and open the door, I will come in to him, and sup with him, and he with me.' O Christ, our Lord, our heart is open, come in, and go out no more for ever. 'Whosoever believeth on the Son hath everlasting life.' Sinner, believe and live.

11

THE BEST OF THE BEST

'I am the rose of Sharon, and the lily of the valleys'
(Song of Solomon 2:1)

The time of flowers has come, and as they are in some faint degree emblems of our Lord, it is well, when God thus calls, that we should seek to learn what he desires to teach us by them. If nature now spreads out her roses and her lilies, or prepares to do so, let us try, not only to see them, but to see Christ as he is shadowed forth in them.

'I am the rose of Sharon, and the lily of the valleys.' If these are the words of the Well-beloved – and I have no doubt that they are – then it may be suggested by some that here we have the Saviour praising himself; and it is true; but in no unworthy sense, for well may he praise himself since no one else can do it as it should be done. There is no human language that can ever set forth his beauties as they deserve to be told. As good John Berridge says:

> Living tongues are dumb at best,
> We must die to speak of Christ

as he should be spoken of. He will never fully be described unless he shall describe himself. For certain, we should never have known God if he had not revealed himself; and every good thing that you or I know of him, he himself has told us. We make no discoveries of God except as God discovers himself to us. If, then, any cavillers were to find fault with the Christ of God because he did commend himself, I would answer, Does not God commend himself, and must not his well-beloved Son do the same? Who else is there that can possibly reveal him to us unless he unveils his own face to our admiring gaze?

Moreover, be it always remembered that human self-praise is evil because of the motive which underlies it. We praise ourselves – and, alas! that we should be so foolish as to do so – we do it out of pride; but when Christ praises himself, he does it out of humility. 'Oh!' say you, 'how can you prove that to be true?' Why, thus; he praises himself that he may win our love; but what condescension it is on his part that he should care about the love of such insignificant and undeserving persons as we are! It is a wonderful stoop that the Christ of God should speak about having a bride, and that he should come to seek his bride among the sons of men. If princes were to look for consorts among beggars, that would be after all but a small stoop, for God hath made of one blood all nations of men that dwell upon the face of the earth; but for Christ to forsake the thrones and glories of heaven, and the splendours of his Father's courts above, to come down to win a well-beloved here, and for her sake to take upon himself her nature, and in her nature to bear the shame of death, even the death of the cross, this is stupendous condescension of which only God himself is capable; and this praising of himself is a part of that condescension, a necessary means of winning the love of the heart that he has chosen. So that this is a matchless instance, not of pride, but of humility, that those dear lips of the heavenly Bridegroom should have to speak to his own commendation, and that he should say, 'I am the rose of Sharon, and the lily of the valleys.' O human lips, why are ye so hard that ye will never feel until Christ himself shall address you? O human eyes, why are ye so blind that ye shall never see till Christ shows himself in his own superlative light and loveliness? I think I need not defend my Master, though he used these sweet emblems to set forth himself; for this is an instance, not of his pride, but of his humility.

It is also an instance of the Master's wisdom, for as it is his design to win hearts to himself, he uses the best means of winning them. How are hearts won? Very often, by the exhibition of beauty. Love at first sight has been begotten by the vision of a lovely countenance. Men and women, too, are struck with affection through the eye when they perceive some beauty which charms and pleases them; so, the Saviour lifts the corner of the veil that conceals his glories, and lets us see some glimpse of his beauty, in order that he may win our hearts. There are some who seem to think that they can bully men to Christ; but that is a great mistake. It is very seldom that sinners can be driven to the Saviour; his way is to draw them. He himself said, 'I, if I be lifted up from the earth, will draw all men unto me. This he said, signifying what death he should die.' And the drawings of Christ are not, as it were, with a cart rope, but with silken bonds, ay, with invisible chains, for his beauty is of such a character that it creates love, his beauty is so attractive that it draws the heart. So, in infinite wisdom, our Lord Jesus Christ sets forth his own beauties that thereby he may win our hearts. I do believe that there is no preaching like the exaltation of Christ crucified. There is nothing so likely to win the sons of men as a sight of him; and if God the Holy Ghost will but help all his ministers, and help all his people, to set forth the beauties of Christ, I shall not doubt that the same Spirit will incline men's hearts to love him and to trust him. Note, then, the condescension and also the wisdom which are perceptible in this self-commendation on the part of Christ: 'I am the rose of Sharon, and the lily of the valleys.'

I think that our Lord also speaks thus as an encouragement to timid souls; his tender familiarity in praising himself to us is one of the most effectual proofs of his lowliness. Does Christ commend himself to us? Does he say to us, for instance, 'I am meek and lowly in heart'? What is his object in speaking thus but that we may take his yoke upon us, and may learn of him, and that we may find rest unto our souls? And if he says, 'I am the rose of Sharon', what does he mean but that we may pluck him, and take him for our own? If he says, 'I am the lily of the valleys', why does he take the trouble to tell us that but because he wants us to take him, and to have him for our very own? I think that it is so sweet of Christ to praise himself in order to show that he longs for us to come to him. He declares himself to be a fountain of living water; yet why is he a fountain but that we may come unto him, and drink? He tells us, 'I am the bread which came down from heaven'; but why does he speak of himself as bread, whereof if a man eat, he shall never hunger? Why, because he wants us to partake of him! You need not, therefore, be afraid that he will refuse you when you come to him. If a man praises his wares, it is that he may sell them. If a doctor advertises his cures, it is that other sick folk may be induced to try his medicine; and when our Lord Jesus Christ praises himself, it is a kind of holy advertisement by which he would tempt us to 'come, buy wine and milk without money and without price'. If he praises himself, it is that we may fall in love with him; and we need not be afraid to come and lay our poor hearts at his feet, and ask him to accept us, for he would not have wooed us by unveiling his beauties if he had meant, after all, to trample on our hearts, and say, 'I care nothing for such poor love as yours.'

I feel most grateful, then, that I have not at this time so much to praise my Master as to let him speak his own praises, for 'never man spake like this Man'. When he commends himself, what would have been folly in others is wisdom in him; and whereas we say to our fellow-man, 'Let another man praise thee, and not thine own mouth', I would say to Christ, 'My Master, praise thyself, for thou alone canst do it as it ought to be done. As for thy poor servant, he would try to be the echo of thy voice, and that will be infinitely better than anything he can say of himself.'

I think, also, that there is good reason for our Lord to praise himself in the fashion that he does in our text, because, after all, it is not praise. 'What!' say you, 'and yet you have been talking all this while as if it was praise.' Well, so it is in one sense, to us, but it is not so to Christ. Suppose the sun were to compare itself with a glow-worm, would that be praise? Suppose an angel were to compare himself with an emmet, would that be praise? And when my Lord and Master, whose eyes outshine the sun, and who is infinitely higher than the mightiest of the angels, compares himself to a rose and a lily, is that praise? Well, it is so to you and to me, but it certainly cannot be so to him. It is a marvellous stoop for Christ, who is 'God over all, blessed for ever' and the Light of the universe to say, 'I am a rose; I am a lily.' O my blessed Lord, this is a sort of incarnation, as when the Eternal God did take upon himself an infant's form! So here, the Everlasting God says, 'I am' – and what comes next? – a 'rose and a lily'. It is an amazing stoop, I know not how to set it forth to you by human language; it is a sort of verbal rehearsal of what he did afterwards when, though he counted it not robbery to be equal with God, 'he took upon himself the form of a servant, and was made in the likeness of sinful flesh, and became obedient unto death, even the death of the cross.' 'I am God, yet,' saith he, 'I am the rose of Sharon, and the lily of the valleys.'

What does our text mean? I think it means that our Lord Jesus Christ is exceedingly delightful, so, let us speak, first, of *the exceeding delightfulness of our Lord*; and then, inasmuch as he uses two emblems, first the rose, and then the lily, surely this is to express *the sweet variety of his delightfulness*; and, inasmuch as he speaks of himself as the rose of Sharon, and the lily of the valleys, I shall have to show you, in the last place, that this hints to us *the exceeding freeness of his delightfulness*.

First, then, the text sets forth THE EXCEEDING DELIGHTFULNESS OF OUR LORD.

He compares himself here, not as in other places to needful bread and refreshing water, but to lovely flowers, to roses and lilies. What is the use of roses and lilies? I know what the use of corn is; I must eat it, it is necessary to me for food. I know why barley and rye and all sorts of roots and fruits are created; they are the necessary food of man or beast. But what do we want with roses? What do we want with lilies? They are of no use at all except for joy and delight. With their sweet form, their charming colour, and their delicious fragrance, we are comforted and pleased and delighted; but they are not necessaries of life. A man can live without roses; there are millions of people, I have no doubt, who live without possessing lilies of the valley. There are all too few roses and lilies in this smoky Babylon of ours; but, when we do get them, what are their uses? Why, they are things of beauty, if not 'a joy for ever'. Jesus is all that and more; he is far more than 'a thing of beauty', and to all who trust him he will be a 'joy for ever'. To you who are Christ's people, he is your bread, for you feed on him, and he makes you live; you could not do without him as the sustenance of your soul. He is the living water, and your soul would pine and perish of a burning thirst if you did not drink of him. But that is not all that Jesus is to you; God has never intended to save his people on the scale of the workhouse, to give you just as much as you absolutely need, and nothing more. No, no, no; he means you to have joy as well as to have life, to look upon beauty as well as to be in safety, and to have not only a healthy atmosphere, but an atmosphere that is laden with the odour of sweet flowers. You are to find in Christ roses and lilies, as well as bread and water; you have not yet seen all his beauties, and you do not yet know all his excellence.

The exceeding delightfulness of Christ is suggested to our mind by his declaration, 'I am the rose, and I am the lily.' And first, *he is in himself the delight of men*. He speaks not of offices, gifts, works, possession; but of himself: 'I am'. Our Lord Jesus is the best of all beings; the dearest, sweetest, fairest and most charming of all beings that we can think of is the Son of God, our Saviour. Come hither, ye poets who dream of beauty, and then try to sing its praises; but your imagination could never reach up to the matchless perfection of his person, neither could your sweetest music ever attain to the full measure of his praise. Think of him as the God-man, God incarnate in human nature, and absolutely perfect; I was going to say something more than that, for there is not only in him all that there ought to be, but there is more than your thoughts or wishes have ever compassed. Eyes need to be trained to see beauty. No man seeth half or a thousandth part of the beauty even of this poor, natural world; but the painter's eye – the eye of Turner, for instance – can see much more than you or I ever saw. 'Oh!' said one, when he looked on one of Turner's landscapes, 'I have seen that view every day, but I never saw as much as that in it.' 'No,' replied Turner, 'don't you wish you could?' And, when the Spirit of God trains and tutors the eye, it sees in Christ what it never saw before. But, even then, as Turner's eye was not able to see all the mystery of God's beauty in nature, so neither is the most trained and educated Christian able to perceive all the matchless beauty that there is in Christ.

I do not think, brethren, that there is anything about Christ but what should make his people glad. There are dark truths concerning him, such as his bearing our sin; but what a joy it is to us that he did bear it, and put it away for ever! It makes us weep to look at Jesus dying on the cross, but there is more real joy in the tears of repentance than there is in the smiles of worldly mirth. I would choose my heaven to be a heaven of everlasting weeping for sin, sooner than have a heaven – if such a heaven could be – consisting of perpetual laughing at the mirth of fools. There is more true pleasure in mourning before God than in dancing before the devil. Christ, is, then, all beauty; even the dark parts in him are light, and the bitter parts are sweet. He has only to be seen by you, and you must perceive that, whether it be his Godhead or his manhood, whether it be his priesthood, his royalty, or his prophetic office, whether it be on the cross or on the throne, whether it be on earth, or in heaven, or in the glory of his second coming, every way,

> All over glorious is my Lord,
> Must be beloved, and yet ador'd;
> His worth if all the nations knew,
> Sure the whole earth would love him too.

But, next, our Lord is *exceedingly delightful to the eye of faith*. He not only tells us of what delight is in himself – 'I am the rose, and I am the lily' – but he thereby tells us that there is something to see in him, for the rose is very pleasing to look upon. Is there a more beautiful sight than a rose that is in bud, or even one that is full-blown? And the lily – what a charming thing it is! It seems to be more a flower of heaven than of earth. Well now, Christ is delightful to the eye of faith. I remember the first time I ever saw him; I shall never forget that sight, and I have seen him many a time since, and my grief is that I ever take my eyes from him, for it is to look away from the sun into blackness; it is to look away from bliss into misery. To you who look at Christ by faith, a sight of him brings such peace, such rest, such hope, as no other sight can ever afford; it so sweetens everything, so entirely takes away the bitterness of life, and brings us to anticipate the glory of the life to come, that I am sure you say, 'Yes, yes the figure in the text is quite correct; there is a beauty in Jesus to the eye of faith, he is indeed red as the rose and white as the lily'.

And, next, the Lord Jesus Christ is *delightful in the savour which comes from him to us*. In him is a delicious, varied, abiding fragrance which is very delightful to the spiritual nostril. Smell is, I suppose, a kind of delicate feeling; minute particles of certain substances touch sensitive membranes, and we call the sensation that is produced smelling. It is a mysterious sense; you can understand sight and hearing better than you can understand smelling. There is a spiritual way of perceiving the savour of Christ; I cannot explain it to you, but there is an ineffable sweetness that proceeds from him which touches the spiritual senses, and affords supreme delight; and as the body has its nose, and its tender nerves that can appreciate sweet odours, so the soul has its spiritual nostril by which, though Christ be at a distance, it yet can perceive the fragrant emanations that come from him, and is delighted therewith.

What is there that comes from Christ, from day to day, but his truth, his Spirit, his influence, his promises, his doctrines, his words of cheer? All these have a heavenly sweetness, and make us, with the psalmist, say to our Lord: 'All thy garments smell of myrrh, and aloes, and cassia, out of the ivory palaces, whereby they have made thee glad.' Whenever these sweet odours are wafted down to us, they make us also glad; anything that has the savour of Christ in it is sweet to a Christian. If Christ has touched it, let me put it in my bosom, and keep it there as a sweet forget-me-not, until I see his face in glory. Ay, the very stones he trod on, I was about to say, the very mountains at which he looked, have become dear to us. We have no idolatrous or superstitious reverence for Palestine, or even for the garden in which he sweat great drops of blood; but for spiritual things with which he has to do, we have a never ceasing reverence and affection. Everything that comes from him is wondrous as the songs of the angels must have been to the shepherds of Bethlehem, and sweet to the taste as the manna that dropped from the skies around Israel's desert camp. Yes, brethren and sisters, there is a sweet savour about the Lord Jesus Christ; do you all perceive it?

Once more, *in all that he is, Christ is the choicest of the choice*. You notice, the Bridegroom says, 'I am the rose.' Yes, but there were some particularly beautiful roses that grew in the valley of Sharon; 'I am that rose,' said he. And there were some delightful lilies in Palestine; it is a land of lilies, there are so many of them that nobody knows which lily Christ meant, and it does not really matter, for almost all lilies are wondrously beautiful. 'But,' said he, 'I am the lily of the valleys', the choicest kind of lily that grew where the soil was fat and damp with the overflow of mountain streams. 'I am the lily of the valleys': that is to say, Christ is not only good, but he is the best; and he is not only the best, but he is the best of the best. He is a flower; ay, but he is a rose, that is the queen of flowers; ay, but then he is the best rose there is, he is the rose of Sharon. He is a Saviour, and a great one; yea, the only Saviour. He is a Husband; but what a Husband! Was there ever such a Bridegroom as Christ Jesus the Lord? He is the Head; but Father Adam was a poor head compared with him. He is inexpressibly, unutterably, indescribably lovely; I might as well leave off talking about him, for I cannot hope to set him forth as he deserves. If you could but see him, I would leave off, for I am sure I should be only hanging a veil before him with the choicest words that I could possibly use.

Suppose you had a dear son or husband or friend, far away, and that I was a painter who could carry pictures in my mind's eye, and then draw them to the very life. If I stood here, trying to paint your well-beloved friend, laying on my colours with all the skill I possessed, and doing my best to reproduce his features; suppose while I was at work, that the door at the back was opened, and he came in, I should cry out, 'Oh, stop, stop, stop! Let me put away my canvas, let me pack up my brushes and my paints. Here is the loved one himself; look at him! Look at him, not at my portrait of him!' And you would rise from your seat, and say, 'It is he! It is he! You may talk as long as you like, dear sir, when he is away; but when he is himself here, your talk seems but mere chatter.'

Well, I shall be quite content that you should think so, I shall be even glad if you do, provided that the reason shall be that you can say, 'We have seen the Lord. He has manifested himself to us as he does not unto the world.' 'I am the rose of Sharon, and the lily of the valleys.' The best of the best, the fairest of the fair, the sweetest of the sweet, is Jesus Christ to you and to me if we are indeed his people. I cannot say more about the exceeding delightfulness of my Lord; I wish I could.

I must pass on, next, to notice THE SWEET VARIETY OF CHRIST'S DELIGHTFULNESS. He is not only full of joy, and pleasure, and delight to our hearts, but he is full of all sorts of joy, and all sorts of pleasure, and all sorts of delights to us.

> Nature, to make his beauties known,
> Must mingle colours not her own.

The rose is not enough, you must have the lily also, and the two together fall far short of the glories of Christ, the true 'Plant of renown'.

'I am the rose.' That is *the emblem of majesty*. The rose is the very queen of flowers; in the judgment of all who know what to admire it is enthroned above all the rest of the beauties of the garden. But the lily – what is that? That is *the emblem of love*. The psalmist hints at this in the title of the forty-fifth Psalm, 'Upon Shoshannim, a Song of love'. Shoshannim signifies lilies, so the lily-psalm is the love-song, for the lilies, with their beauty, their purity, their delicacy, are a very choice emblem of love. Are you not delighted when you put these two things together, majesty and love? A King upon a throne of love, a Prince, whose very eyes beam with love to those who put their trust in him, a real Head, united by living bonds of love to all his members; such is our dear Lord and Saviour. A rose and yet a lily; I do not know in which of the two I take the greater delight, I prefer to have the two together. When I think that my Saviour is King of kings and Lord of lords, I shout, 'Hallelujah!' But when I remember that he loved me, and gave himself for me, and that still he loves me, and that he will keep on loving me for ever and ever, there is such a charm in this thought that nothing can excel it. Look at the lily, and sing:

> Jesus, lover of my soul,
> Let me to thy bosom fly,
> While the nearer waters roll,
> While the tempest still is high!
> Hide me, O my Saviour, hide,
> Till the storm of life be past;
> Safe into the haven guide;
> Oh receive my soul at last.

Then look at the rose, and sing:

> All hail the power of Jesus' name!
> Let angels prostrate fall;
> Bring forth the royal diadem,
> And crown him Lord of all,

then put the rose and the lily together, and let them remind you of Christ's majesty and love.

The combination of these sweet flowers also suggests our Lord's *suffering and purity.*

> White is his soul, from blemish free,
> Red with the blood he shed for me.

The rose, with its thorn, reminds us of his suffering, his bleeding love to us, his death on our behalf, his bearing of the thorns which our sin created. Christ is a royal rose beset with thorns; but the lily shows that

> For sins not his own,
> He died to atone.

Jesus, when on earth, could say, 'The prince of this world cometh, and hath nothing in me.' The devil himself could not see a spot or speck in that lovely lily. Jesus Christ is perfection itself, he is all purity; so you must put the two together, the rose and the lily, to show Christ's suffering and perfection, the infinitely pure infinitely suffering. In which of the two do you take the greater delight? Surely, in neither, but in the combination of both; what would be the value of Christ's sufferings if he were not perfect? And of what avail would his perfections be if he had not died, the Just for the unjust, to bring us to God? But the two together, the rose and the lily, suffering and purity, fill us with delight.

Of both of these there is a great variety. I wonder how many different sorts of roses there are, I should not like to have to tell you; they vary exceedingly, perhaps there are as many kinds as there are days in the year. How many varieties of lilies are there? Possibly there are as many sorts of lilies as there are of roses, for both of them are wonderfully diversified; but the joys that flow from our Lord Jesus Christ are as abundant, and as varied as the roses and the lilies. Bring me which rose you please, and I will tell you that it smells sweet; bring which lily you choose, and I will say, 'Yes, that also has a delicate perfume that will do, with the rose, to serve as an emblem of Christ.' Our Lord Jesus possesses every kind of beauty and fragrance. 'He is all my salvation, and all my desire.' All good things meet in Christ; in him all the lines of beauty are focused. Blessed are they who truly know him.

Further, *Christ is the very essence of the sweetness both of the rose and of the lily.* When he says, 'I am the rose', he means, not only that he is like the rose, but that he made all the sweetness there is in the rose, and it is still in him; and all the sweetness there is in any creature comes to us from Christ, or else it is not sweetness such as we ought to love. I like to look upon the bread I eat as his gift to me, and to bless his providential hand that bestows it. I like to look upon all the landscape on such a fair day as this has been, and to say, 'Christ is in all this, giving this charming view to such a poor, unworthy creature as I am.' He is in all there is that is good, he is the goodness of all the good there is. He is the very soul of the universe, whatever there is in the universe that is worthy of our soul's love. All good for our soul comes from him, whether it be pardon of sin, or justification, or the sanctification that makes us fit for glory hereafter, Christ is the source of it all; and in the infinite variety of delights that we get from him, he is himself the essence of it all. We can become tired of most things, I suppose that we can become tired of everything earthly; but we shall never tire of Christ. I remember one who, when near his death-hour, forgot even his wife, and she was greatly grieved that he did not recognise her. They whispered in his ear the name of his favourite child; but he shook his head. His oldest friend, who had known him from his boyhood, was not recognised. At last they asked him, 'Do you know Jesus Christ?' Then he said, 'Ah, yes! and I am going to him.' The ruling passion was strong in death; Christ was nearer and dearer to him than those he loved best here. All flowers will fade, even roses and lilies among them; but not this blessed Rose of Sharon, and Lily of the valleys. Christ does not say, 'I was a rose, and I was a lily'; but '*I am* the rose, and *I am* the lily'. He is now all that he ever was, and he will be in life, in death, and throughout all eternity, to the soul that knows him, an infinite variety of everything that is delightful.

I must now very briefly take up the last head of my discourse, which is, THE EXCEEDING FREENESS OF OUR LORD'S DELIGHTFULNESS.

It is not very pleasant or satisfying for hungry people to stand in the street, and hear someone praising a good meal, of which they cannot get even a taste. I have often noticed boys standing outside a shop window, in which there have been all sorts of dainties; they have flattened their noses against the windowpane, but they have not been able to get anything to eat.

I have been talking about my Master, and I want to show you that *he is accessible*, he is meant to be plucked and enjoyed as roses and lilies are. He says in the text, 'I am the rose of Sharon.' What was Sharon? It was an open plain where anybody might wander, and where even cattle roamed at their own sweet will. Jesus is not like a rose in Solomon's garden, shut up within high walls, with broken glass all along the top. Oh, no! he says, 'I am the rose of Sharon', everybody's rose, the flower for the common people to come and gather. 'I am the lily.' What lily? The lily of the palace of Shushan, enclosed and guarded from all approach? No: but, 'I am the lily of the valleys', found in this glen, or the other ravine, growing here, there, and everywhere: 'I am the lily of the valleys.'

Then *Christ is as abundant as a common flower*. Whatever kind of rose it was, it was a common rose; whatever kind of lily it was, it was a well-known lily that grew freely in the valleys of that land. Oh, blessed be my Master's name, he has brought us a common salvation, and he is the common people's Christ! Men in general do not love him enough, or else they would have hedged him in with all sorts of restrictions; they would have made a franchise for him, and nobody would have been able to be saved except those who paid I know not how much a year in taxes. But they do not love our Lord enough to shut him in, and I am glad they have never tried to do so. There he stands, at the four-cross roads, so that everybody who comes by, and wants him, may have him. He is a fountain, bearing this inscription, 'Let him that is athirst come. And whosoever will, let him take the water of life freely.' 'I am the rose of Sharon, and the lily of the valleys.' Why do roses grow in Sharon? Why do lilies grow in the valleys? Why, to be plucked, of course! I like to see the children go down into the meadow when it is decked in grass, and adorned with flowers, gilded with butter-cups, or white with the day's-eyes; I love to see the children pluck the flowers, and fill their pinafores with them, or make garlands, and twist them round their necks, or put them on their heads. 'O children, children!' somebody might cry, 'do not spoil those beautiful flowers, do not go and pick them.' Oh, but they may! Nobody says they may not; they may not go into our gardens, and steal the geraniums and the fuchsias; but they may get away into the meadows, or into the open fields, and pluck these common flowers to their heart's content. And now, poor soul, if you would like an apronful of roses, come and have them. If you would like to carry away a big handful of the lilies of the valleys, come and take them, as many as you will. May the Lord give you the will! That is, after all, what is wanted; if there be that grace-given will, the Rose of Sharon and the Lily of the valleys will soon be yours. They are common flowers, growing in a common place, and there are plenty of them; will you not take them?

Even to those who do not pluck any, there is one strange thing that must not be forgotten. A man passes by a rose-bush, and says, 'I cannot stop to think about roses', but as he goes along he exclaims, 'Dear, dear, what a delicious perfume!' A man journeying in the East goes through a field that is full of lilies; he is in a great hurry, but, for all that, he cannot help seeing and smelling the lilies as he rushes through the field. And, do you know, the perfume of Christ has life in it? He is 'a savour of life unto life'. What does that mean but that the smell of him will save? Ah! if you do but glance at him, though you were so busy that you could not come in till the sermon had begun, yet a glance at this Lily will bring you joy and peace, for he is so free that, often, even when men are not asking for him, he comes to them. 'What?' say you, 'is it so?' Yes, that it is; such is the freeness of Christ's grace that it is written, 'I am found of them that sought me not.' He sends his sweet perfume into nostrils that never sniffed after it. He puts himself in the way of eyes that never looked for him. How I wish that some man who has never sought for Christ, might find him even now!

You remember the story that Christ tells of the man that was ploughing the field; he was only thinking of the field, and how much corn it would take to sow it; and he was ploughing up and down, when suddenly, his ploughshare hit upon something hard. He stopped the oxen, and took his spade and dug, and there was an old crock, and it was full of gold. Somebody had hidden it away, and left it. This man had never looked for it, for he did not even know it was there, but he had stumbled on it, as men say, by accident. What did he do? He did not tell anybody, but he went off to the man who was the owner of the field, and he said, 'What will you take for that field?' 'Can you buy it?' 'Yes, I want it, what will you take for it?' The price was so high that he had to sell the house he lived in, and his oxen, and his very clothes off his back; but he did not care about that, he bought the field, and he bought the treasure, and then he was able to buy back his clothes, his house, and his oxen, and everything else.

If you find Christ, and if you have to sell the coat off your back in order to get him, if you have to give up everything you have that you may find him, you will have such a treasure in him that, for the joy of finding him, you would count all the riches of Egypt to be less than nothing and vanity; but you need not sell the coat off your back, Christ is to be had for nothing, only you must give him yourself. If he gives himself to you, and he becomes your Saviour, you must give yourself to him and become his servant. Trust him, I beseech you, the Lord help you to do so, for Jesus' sake! Amen.

12

THE LILY AMONG THORNS

'As the lily among thorns, so is my love among the daughters'
(Song of Solomon 2:2)

We shall not enter into any profitless discussion this morning. We take it for granted that the Song of Solomon is a sacred marriage song between Christ and his Church, and that it is the Lord Jesus who is here speaking of his Church, and indeed of each individual member, saying, 'As the lily among thorns, so is my love among the daughters.' I will not even enter into any disquisition as to what particular flower is here intended by the word translated 'lily', for it would be very difficult to select a plant from the Holy Land about which travellers and botanists would agree. The lily, which we should most naturally fix upon, is, as I have gathered from books of travel, not at present found in that country, though we may not therefore be sure that it was never there, or may not yet be discovered. Several other fair and beautiful forms, according to the fancies of various travellers, have been preferred to occupy the place of the plant intended by the original Hebrew, but none of them quite come up to the ideal suggested to an English reader by our translation. I will for once take the liberty to clothe the Scripture in a western dress, if need be, and venture to do what Solomon would surely have done if his Song of songs had been written in England. I shall assume that he means one of our own lilies: either the lily of the valley, or one of those more stately beauties, matchless for whiteness, which so gloriously adorn our gardens. Either will do, and serve our turn this morning. 'As the lily among thorns, so is my love among the daughters.' It is of small moment to be precise in botany so long as we get the spirit of the text. We seek practical usefulness and personal consolation, and proceed at once in the pursuit, in the hope that it may be with us as with the great Bridegroom himself, of whom the golden canticle saith, 'He feedeth among the lilies.'

Many are taking root among us now, newly transported from the world, and it is well that they should be rooted in a knowledge of their calling by grace and what it includes. They ought to know at the very commencement what a Christian is when he is truly a Christian, what he is expected to be, what the Lord means him to be, and what the Lord Jesus regards him as really being; so that they may make no mistakes, but may count the cost, and know what it is that they have ventured upon. Thinking over this subject carefully, and anxiously desiring to warn our new converts without alarming them, I could not think of any text from which I should be able, in the exposition of it, better to set forth the position, condition and character of a genuine Christian. Jesus himself knows best what his own bride is like, let us hear him as he speaks in this matchless song. He knows best what his followers should be, and well may we be content to take the words out of his own mouth when in sweetest poetry he tells us, 'As the lily among thorns, so is my love among the daughters.' Join me, then, my brethren, at this time in considering our Lord's lilies, how they grow.

Concerning the Church of God, there are two points upon which I will enlarge: first, *her relation to her Lord*; secondly, *her relation to the world.*

First I think my text very beautifully sets forth THE RELATION OF THE CHURCH AND OF EVERY INDIVIDUAL TO CHRIST. He styles her, 'my love'. An exquisitely sweet name; as if his love had all gone forth of him, and had become embodied in her. The first point then of her relation to Christ is that *she has his love*. Think of it, and let the blessed truth dwell long and sweetly in your meditations. The Lord of life and glory, the

Prince of the kings of the earth, has such a loving heart that he must have an object upon which to spend his affection; and his people, chosen from among men, whom he calls his Church, these are they who are his 'love', the object of his supreme delight. 'Christ loved the church, and gave himself for it.' He looked on his people and he exclaimed, 'As the Father hath loved me, even so have I loved you.' Every believer, separated from mankind, and called unto the fellowship of Christ, is also the peculiar object of his love. Not in name only, but in deed and in truth, does Jesus love each one of us who have believed on him. You may each one of you say with the apostle, 'He loved me'; you may read it in any tense you please: He loved me; he loveth me; he will love me, for he gave himself for me. This shall be your song in heaven: 'Unto him that loved us, and washed us from our sins in his own blood, to him be glory.' Let your hearts saturate themselves with this honied thought; heaven lies hid within it, it is the quintessence of bliss – Jesus loves me. It is not in the power of words to set forth the charming nature of this fact; it is a very simple proposition, but the heights and depths, the lengths and breadths of it surpass our knowledge. That such a poor, insignificant, unworthy being as I am should be the object of the eternal affection of the Son of God is an amazing wonder; yet wonderful as it is, it is a fact! To each one of his people he saith this morning by the Holy Spirit, 'I have loved thee with an everlasting love, therefore with lovingkindness have I drawn thee.' Each one of us may rejoice in the title under which our Lord addresses us – 'my love'.

This love is distinguishing love, for in its light one special object shines as a lily, and the rest, 'the daughters', are as thorns. Love has fixed on its chosen object, and compared with the favoured one all others are as nothing. There is a love of Jesus which goeth forth to all mankind, for 'the Lord is good to all, and his tender mercies are over all his works'; but there is a special and peculiar love which he beareth to his own. As a man loveth his neighbours but still he hath a special affection for his own wife, so is the Church Christ's bride, beloved above all the rest of mankind, and every individual believer is the favoured one of heaven. The saint is united to Christ by a mystical union, a spiritual marriage bond, and above all others Christ loves the souls espoused to him. He said once, 'I pray for them. I pray not for the world, but for them which thou hast given me'; thus indicating that there is a speciality about his intercession. We rejoice in the largeness and the width of Jesus' love, but we do not therefore doubt its speciality. The sun shines on all things, but when it is focused upon one point, ah, then there is a heat about it of which you little dreamed! The love of Jesus is focused on those whom the Father hath given him. Upon you, my brother or sister, if indeed you are a believer in Jesus Christ, the Lord's heart is set and he speaks of you in the words of the text as 'my love', loved above all the daughters, precious in his sight and honourable, so that he will give men for you and people for your life.

Observe that this is a love which he openly avows. The bridegroom speaks and says before all men, 'As a lily among thorns, so is my love among the daughters.' He puts it upon record in that book which is more widely scattered than any other, for he is not ashamed to have it published on the housetops. The love of Christ was at first hidden in his heart, but it soon revealed itself, for even of old his delights were with the sons of men, and he bent his steps downward to this world in divers forms or ever Bethlehem's song was sung. And now, since the incarnate God has loved, and lived, and died, he has unveiled his love in the most open form, and astonished heaven and earth thereby. On Calvary he set up an open proclamation, writ in his own heart's blood, that he loved his own even unto the end. He bids his ministers proclaim it to the world's end, that many waters could not quench his love, neither could the floods drown it; and that neither life, nor death, nor things present, nor things to come, nor height, nor depth, nor any other creature, shall be able to separate us from the love of God which is in Christ Jesus our Lord. He would have it known, for he is not ashamed to call his people 'the bride, the Lamb's wife'. He declares it that his adversaries may know it, that he hath a people in whom his heart delights, and these he will have and hold as his own when heaven and earth shall pass away.

This love, wherever it has been revealed to its object, is reciprocated. If the Lord has really spoken home to your soul and said, 'I have loved thee', your soul has gladly answered, 'This is my Beloved, and this is my Friend; yea, he is altogether lovely.' For what saith the spouse in another place? 'My Beloved is mine, and I am his.' I am his beloved, but he is my beloved too. By this, dear hearer, shall you know whether this text belongs to you or not. What sayest thou when Jesus asks of thee, 'Lovest thou me?' Is your heart warmed at the very mention of his name? If you can truly say with Peter, 'Lord, thou knowest all things; thou knowest that I love thee', then rest assured you love him because he first loved you. Doubt not the fact, but be well assured of it, that love in your heart towards Jesus is the certain and infallible pledge of his infinite, eternal and immutable love to you. If his name is on *your* heart, then be sure of this, that your name is on *his* breast, and written on the palms of his hands. You are espoused unto him, and the bands of the mystical wedlock shall never be snapped. This is the first point of the relation of the Church to her Lord: she is the object of his love.

Next, *she bears his likeness*. Notice the first verse of the chapter, wherein the bridegroom speaks: 'I am the rose of Sharon, and the lily of the valleys.' He is the lily, but his beloved is like him; for he applies his own chosen emblem to her: 'As the lily among thorns, so is my love among the daughters.' Notice that he *is* the lily, she is *as* the lily, that is to say, *he* has the beauty and *she* reflects it; she is comely in his comeliness, which he puts upon her. If any soul hath any such beauty as is described here Christ has dowered that beloved soul with all its wealth of charms, for in ourselves we are deformed and defiled. What is the confession of this very spouse in the previous chapter? She says, 'I am black' – that is the opposite of a lily; if she adds, 'but comely', it is because her Lord has made her comely. There is no grace but what grace has given, and if we are graceful it is because Christ has made us full of grace. There is no beauty in any one of us but what our Lord has wrought in us.

Note, too, that he who gave the beauty is the first to see it. While they are unknown in the world, Jesus knows his own. Long before anybody else sees any virtue or any praise in us, Jesus descries it, and is pleased therewith. He is quick to say, 'Behold, he prayeth', or 'Behold, he repenteth'. He is the first to say, 'I have surely heard Ephraim bemoaning himself.' Love's eyes are quick, and her ears are open. Love covers a multitude of faults, but it discovers a multitude of beauties. Can it be so, O my soul, can it be so that Christ hath made thee comely in his comeliness? Hath he shed a beauty upon thee, and does he himself look complacently upon it? He whose taste is exquisite, and whose voice is the truth, who never calls that beautiful which is not beautiful, can he see a beauty in thy sighs and tears, in thy desires after holiness, in thy poor attempts to aid his cause, in thy prayers and in thy songs, and in thy heart's love towards him – can he see a beauty in these? Yes, assuredly he can, or he would not speak as he does in this text. Let his condescending discernment have all honour for this generous appreciation of us. Let us bless and love him because he deigns to think so highly of us who owe everything to him. 'Thou art,' saith he, 'my love, as the lily.'

It is evident that the Lord Jesus takes delight in this beauty, which he has put upon his people. He values it at so great a rate that he counts all rival beauties to be but as thorns. He looks upon the court of an earthly monarch, and sees my lords and ladies, but makes small account of them compared with his poor saints. If in that court he spies out one that loves him, one who wears a coronet and prays, he marks that one, and counts him or her 'as the lily among thorns'. There is a wealthy household, honoured and favoured among the old county families, but in it there is no lover of the Saviour except one, and she perhaps is a little maid whose service is among the pots, yet shall she be as the wings of a dove covered with silver. 'As the lily among thorns' shall she be. All the kingdoms of the earth are but thornbrakes to the Lord Jesus compared with his Church. Be they Roman, German, French or English, all empires, with all their splendours, are mere gorse and furze upon the common, bramble-bushes and thorn coverts, the haunts of wild and noxious creatures in the view of the King of kings; but his Church, and those that make up the body of the faithful, are as lilies in his discerning eyes. He delights in them, he finds a sweet content in gazing on them.

So you see the Lord has given to his people his likeness, and that likeness he looks upon and loves.

Bringing out still further the relationship between Christ and his Church, I want you to notice that *her position has drawn out his love*. 'As the lily,' saith he, '*among thorns*, so is my love.' He spied her out among the thorns. She was at the first no better than a thorn herself; his grace alone made her to differ from the briars about her; but as soon as ever he had put his life and his grace into her, though she dwelt among the ungodly, she became as the lily, and he spied her out. The thornbrake could not hide his beloved. Christ's eye towards his people is so quick because it is cleared by love. There may at this time be in a Popish convent one truly seeking Jesus in spirit and in truth. He spies out the believer among the trusters in themselves, and calls her his love among thorns. There may be at this moment in the most godless haunt in London, a poor, trembling heart that loves Jesus in secret: the Lord knows that heart, and it is to him as a lily among thorns. You, perhaps, are the only serious working man in the shop in which you earn your daily bread, and the whole band hold you in derision. You may hardly know yourself whether you are really a Christian, for you are sometimes staggered about your own condition; and yet the enemies of Christ have made up their minds as to whose you are, and treat you as one of the disciples of the Nazarene. Be of good courage, your Lord discerns you and knows you better than you know yourself. Such is the quickness of his eye that your difficult and perilous position only quickens his discernment, and he regards you with the more attention. The thorns cannot hide you, thickly as they cluster around you: in your loneliness you are not alone, for the Crucified is with you.

'As the lily among thorns' wears also another meaning. Dr Thompson writes of a certain lily, 'It grows among thorns, and I have sadly lacerated my hand in extricating it from them. Nothing can be in higher contrast than the luxuriant, velvet softness of this lily and the withered, tangled hedge of thorns about it.' Ah, beloved, you know who it was that in gathering your soul and mine, lacerated not his hand only, but his feet, and his head, and his side, and his heart, yea, and his inmost soul. He spied us out and said, 'Yonder lily is mine, and I will have it.' But the thorns were a terrible barrier; our sins had gathered round about us, and the wrath of God most sharply stopped the way. Jesus pressed through all that we might be his, and now when he takes us to himself he does not forget the thorns which girded his brow, and tore his flesh, for our sakes. This then is a part of our relationship to Christ, that we cost him very dear. He saw us where we were, and he came to our deliverance; and now, even as Pharaoh's daughter called the young child's name 'Moses' 'because,' said she, 'I drew him out of the water', so doth Jesus call his chosen, 'the lily among thorns', because such she was when he came to her rescue. Never will he forget Calvary and its thorns, nor should his saints allow the memory thereof to fade.

Yet once more, I think many a child of God may regard himself as still being a lily among thorns, because of his afflictions. Certainly the Church is so, and *she is thereby kept for Christ's own.* If thorns made it hard for him to reach us for our salvation, there is another kind of thorn which makes it hard for any enemy to come at us for our hurt. Our trials and tribulations, which we would fain escape from, often act as a spiritual protection: they hedge us about and ward off many a devouring foe. Sharp as they are, they serve as a fence and a defence. Many a time, dear child of God, you would have been an exposed lily, to be plucked by any ruthless hand, if it had not been that God had placed you in such circumstances that you were shut up unto himself. Sick saints and poor saints and persecuted saints are fair lilies enclosed by their pains, and wants and bonds that they may be for Christ alone. I look on John Bunyan in prison writing his *Pilgrim's Progress*, and I cannot help feeling that it was a great blessing for us all that such a lily was shut up among the thorns, that it might shed its fragrance in that famous book, and thereby perfume the church for ages. You that are kept from roaming by sickness or by family trials need not regret these things, for perhaps they are the means of making you more completely your Lord's. How charmingly Madame Guyon wrote when she was immured in a dungeon. Her wing was closely bound, but her song was full of liberty, for she felt that the bolts and bars only shut her in with her Beloved, and what is that but liberty? She sang:

A little bird I am,
Shut from the fields of air;
And in my cage I sit and sing
To him who placed me there;
Well pleased a prisoner to be,
Because, my God, it pleaseth thee.

Nought have I else to do,
I sing the whole day long;
And he whom most I love to please
Doth listen to my song;
He caught and bound my wandering wing,
But still he bends to hear me sing.

'As the lily among thorns' she lived in prison shut in with her Lord, and since the world was quite shut out, she was in that respect a gainer. Oh to have one's heart made as 'a garden enclosed, a spring shut up, a fountain sealed'. So let my soul be, ay, so let it be even if the enclosure can only be accomplished by a dense growth of trials and griefs. May every pain that comes and casts us on our bed, and lays us aside from public usefulness; may every sorrow which arises out of our business, and weans us from the world; may every adversary that assails us with bitter, taunting words only thicken the thorn hedge which encases us from all the world, and constrains us to be chaste lilies set apart for the Well-beloved.

Enough upon this point I think; only do let me entreat all of you who have lately come to know the Lord to think much of your relationship *to him*. It is the way by which you will be supported under the responsibilities of your relationship to the world. If you know that you are his, and that he loves you, you will be strong to bear all burdens; nothing will daunt you if you are sure that he is for you, that his whole heart is true to you, that he loves you specially, and has set you apart unto himself, that you may be one with him for ever. Dwell much, in your meditations, upon what this text and other Scriptures teach of the relationship of the renewed heart to Christ, and know him of whom you are so well known. May the Holy Spirit teach us all this lesson so that it may be learned by our hearts.

But now, secondly, our text is full of instruction as to THE RELATIONSHIP OF THE CHURCH, AND EACH INDIVIDUAL BELIEVER, TO THE WORLD – 'The lily among thorns'.

First, then, *she has incomparable beauty*. As compared and contrasted with all else she is as the lily to the thornbrake. Did not our Lord say of the natural lilies: 'Solomon in all his glory was not arrayed like one of these'? And when I think of Christ's lilies, adorned in his own righteousness, and bearing his own image, I feel that I may repeat my Master's words and say with emphasis, 'Solomon in all his glory was not arrayed like one of these!' In Christ's esteem his Church bears the bell for beauty; she is the fairest among women. She is not to be compared, she has to be contrasted with the rest of mankind. Our Lord means that if you take worldlings at their best and in their bravest attire, in their pomp and glory and parade, they are but as thorns in contrast with his Church. Though the Church may seem to be little and poor, and despised, yet is she better than all the princes and kingdoms and glories of the earth. He means that true Christians are infinitely superior to ungodly men. These ungodly men may make a fair show of virtue, and they may have much prudence and wit, and count themselves wise and great, but Jesus calls all unconverted ones 'thorns', while his own believing ones he compares to 'lilies'. The thorns are worthless, they flourish, and spread, and cumber the ground, but they yield no fruit, and only grow to be cut down for the oven. Alas, such is man by nature, at his best. As for the lily, it is a thing of beauty and a joy for ever; it lives shedding sweet perfume, and when it is gathered its loveliness adorns the chamber to which it is taken. So does the saint bless his generation while here, and when he is taken away he is regarded with pleasure even in heaven above as one of the flowers of God. He will ere long be transplanted from among the thorns to the garden enclosed beyond the river, where the King delights to dwell, for such a flower is far too fair to be left for ever amid tangled briars.

There are among worldly people some who are very fair to look upon in many respects: philanthropic, kind and upright, they have many virtues; but since these virtues have no bearings towards God, and no reference to Christ, he counts the bearers of them to be but thorns. What virtue can there be in him whose principle in life is disregard of his Maker, and disbelief in his Saviour? He is an avowed rebel, and yet would be commended by the Lord whom he rejects. How can it be? Acts done from other motives than those of obedience to God or love to Christ are poor things. There may be a great inward difference between actions which outwardly are the same. The apple of nature hath never the flavour of the pomegranate of grace. It may seem even to excel the fruit of grace, but it is not so. Two babes before us may appear alike as they seem to sleep side by side, but the child of nature, however finely dressed, is not the living child, and the Lord will not own the dead thing as belonging to his family. Ah, you that are struggling after holiness for Christ's sake, you that are seeking after virtue in the power of the Holy Ghost, you have the beauty of the lily, while all else are still to Christ but as a thicket of thorns.

Ay, and let me say, what I am sorry to add – a real Christian is as superior even to a professing Christian as a lily is to thorns. I know churches in which there are many who make a profession, but, ah me, it is a pity that they should, for their life does not adorn their doctrine, their temper is not consistent with the indwelling of the Holy Spirit. They live like worldlings, to amass money, or to carry on business, or to enjoy good eating and drinking, or to dress and go to parties; they are as much for this world as if they were never renewed, and it is to be feared they never were. It will often grieve those who really love the Lord to see how mere professors pretend to do what saints labour to perform. Saints are mimicked, I had almost said mocked and mimicked, by empty professors, and this is a standing source of sorrow. Their cold words often vex the zealous heart and pierce it as with thorns. When you are full of zeal their want of consecration almost kindles indignation in the minds of those who are willing to give their last penny, ay, and their last breath, for their Master's honour. Do not, however, be at all astonished, for it must be so; he who is full of the grace of God will always be as the lily among thorns, even in the professing Church. Do not marvel, young brother, if older professors damp your ardour, and count your warm love to be a mere fanaticism. God give you grace to keep up your first love, and even to advance upon it, though the thorny ones wound and hinder you. May you be distinguished above your fellow professors, for I fear that unless it be so your life will be a poor one.

This then is the relationship of the Church to the world, and of Christians to the world, that they are as much superior to the unregenerate in moral and spiritual beauty as the lily is to the thorns among which it finds itself.

Secondly, in the comparison of the saint to the lily we remark that *he has, like the lily, a surpassing excellence*. I point not to its beauty just now, but to its intrinsic excellence. The thorn is a fruit of the curse: it springs up because of sin. 'Thorns also and thistles shall it bring forth to thee.' Not so the lily: it is a fair type of the blessing which maketh rich without the sorrow of carking care. The thorn is the mark of wrath and the lily is the symbol of divine providence. A true believer is a blessing, a tree whose leaves heal and whose fruit feeds. A genuine Christian is a living gospel, an embodiment of goodwill towards men. Did not the old covenant blessing run, 'In thee and in thy seed shall all the nations of the earth be blessed'? I cannot refrain from quoting a metrical meditation of one who loved the Song of Solomon, and drank into its spirit. He says of the Church, she is

> A radiant thing, where all is gloomy else,
> Florescent where all else is barrenness;
> A blossom in the desert, that proclaims
> Man is no friendless outcast, hopeless doomed
> To traverse scenes of wickedness and grief,
> But, pilgrim as he is, has One who plans
> Not only to protect but cheer his way.
> Oh, ever testifying desert flower,
> Still holding forth the story of God's love,
> How wonderful it is that busy throngs
> Pause not to look on thee! That few reflect
> On the strange fact of thine existence still,
> A lily among thorns – a life in death,
> Distinct from, yet in contact with, the world;
> Burning, yet unconsumed; though cumbered, free
> With glorious liberty!

Yes, the Church is a blessing, a blessing abiding and scattering its delights in the midst of the curse; and each particular believer is in his measure a blessing too, 'as the lily among thorns'.

A true Christian knows not how to harm his fellow men. He is like the lily which stings no one, and yet he lives among those who are full of sharpness. He aims to please, and not to provoke, and yet he lives among those whose existence is a standing menace. The thorn tears and lacerates: it is all armed from its root to its topmost branch, defying all comers. But there stands the lily, smiling, not defying: charming, and not harming. Such is the real Christian, holy, harmless, full of love and gentleness and tenderness. Therein lieth his excellence. The thorn pierces, but the lily soothes: the very sight of it gives pleasure. Who would not stop and turn aside to see a lily among thorns, and think he read a promise from his God to comfort him amid distress? Such is a true Christian: he is a consolation in his family, a comfort in his neighbourhood, an ornament to his profession, and a benediction to his age. He is all tenderness and gentleness, and yet it may be he lives among the envious, the malicious, and the profane, a lily among thorns. The thorn saith, 'Keep away; no one shall touch me with impunity.' The lily cries, 'I come to you, I shed my soul abroad to please you.'

The sweet odours of the lily of the valley are well known; perhaps no plant has so strong a savour about it of intense and exquisite sweetness as that lily of the valley which is found in Palestine. Such is the sanctified believer. There is a secret something about him, a hallowed savour which goeth out from his life, so that his graciousness is discovered; for grace, like its Lord, 'cannot be hid'. Even if the regenerate man be not known as a professor, yet doth he discover himself by the holiness of his life, 'his speech betrayeth him'. When I was resting in the south, I wandered by the side of a flowing stream, gathering handfuls of maiden-hair fern from the verdant bank – and as I walked along I was conscious of a most delicious fragrance up from among the grass at my feet. The violets had hidden themselves from sight, but they had betrayed themselves by their delicious scent. So doth a Christian reveal his hidden life; his tone and temper and manners bespeak his royal lineage, if indeed the Spirit of God be in him. Such are the people of God; they court no observation, but are like that modest flower of which the poet says:

> She ne'er affects
> The public walk, nor gaze of midday sun;
> She to no state nor dignity aspires,
> But silent and alone puts on her suit,
> And sheds a lasting perfume, but for which
> We had not known there was a thing so sweet
> Hid in the gloomy shade.

I want you, dear Christian people, to be just like this: to have about you a surpassing wealth of blessing, and unrivalled sweetness of influence by which you shall be known of all men. Is it so with you, or are you as rough, and stern, and repellent as a thorn bush? Are you as selfish and as quarrelsome as the unregenerate? Or do you shed yourself away in sweet odours of self-denying kindness in your families and among your neighbours? If you do so, then doth Jesus say of you, 'As the lily among thorns, so is my love among the daughters.'

The last point with regard to our relationship to the world is that the Church and many individual Christians are called to endure *singular trials*, which make them feel 'as the lily among thorns'. That lovely flower seems out of place in such company, does it not? Christ said, 'Behold, I send you forth as sheep among *sheep*' – no, no, that is my mistake, 'as sheep among *wolves*'. It is a very blessed thing to be as sheep among sheep: to lie down with them under the shadow of the great rock, and feed with them in green pastures under the Shepherd's eye. This is our privilege, and we ought to value it greatly, and unite with the Church and frequent its ordinances; but even then we shall, some of us, have to go home to an ungodly family, or to go out into the world to win our bread, and then we shall be as sheep among wolves. Grow in the Church and you will be lilies in the garden; still, you cannot always live in the Tabernacle, and so you will have to go back to the ungodly world, and there you will be lilies among thorns.

The lily startles you if you find it in such a position. Often you come upon one of God's elect ones in a most unexpected manner, and are as much amazed as if an angel crossed your path. This is the wonder of the lily among thorns. You are making your way over a wild heath and come to a tangled thornbrake through which you must force your way. As you are driving through the dense mass, rending and tearing your garments, suddenly you stand still as one who has seen a vision of angels, for there among the most rugged brambles a lily lifts its lovely form and smiles upon you. You feel like Moses at the back of the desert when he saw the bush which burned with fire and yet was not consumed. So have you met in a back slum, where blasphemy abounded, a beauteous child of God, whom all recognised as such, and you have felt amazed. So have you in a wealthy family full of worldliness and vanity come upon a humble man or patient woman living unto Christ, and you have asked, how came this grace to this house? So, too, in a foreign land, where all bowed down to crucifix and image, you have casually met with a confessor who has stood his ground among idolaters, protesting for his God, not by his speech so much as by his holy walk. The surprise has been great. Expect many such surprises. The Lord has a people where you look not for them. Think not that all his lilies are in his garden, there are lilies among thorns, and he knows their whereabouts.

Many saints reside in families where they will never be appreciated any more than the lily is appreciated by the thorns. This is painful, for the sympathy of our fellows is a great comfort. Lilies of the valley love to grow in clusters, and saints love holy company, and yet in some cases it must not be; they must live alone. Nor need we think that this loneliness is unrelieved, for God goeth out of the track of men, and he visits those whom his own servants are passing by. The poet saith:

> Full many a flower is born to blush unseen,
> And waste its sweetness on the desert air.

But the poet forgot that God is in the wilderness and the solitary place, and the sweetness of lonely flowers is his. He who planted the lily among thorns sees its beauty. It is God's flower, and does it waste its sweetness because no human nostril smells thereat? It were blasphemous to count that wasted which is reserved for the great King. The Lord understandeth the incense of nature better than we do, and as he walks abroad he rejoices in his works. Grace struggling in loneliness is very choice in God's esteem. If man sees thee not, O lonely believer, thou mayest nevertheless sing, 'Thou God seest me.' The flower which blooms for God alone has a special honour put upon it, and so hath the saint whose quiet life is all for Jesus. If you are unappreciated by those around you, do not therefore be distressed, for you are honourable in the sight of God.

The lily is altogether unassisted too by its surroundings – 'the lily among thorns' borrows nothing from the growth which gathers about it. A genuine Christian is quite unhelped by ungodly men; what is worse, he is cumbered by them. Yet through divine grace he lives and grows. You know how the good seed could not grow because of the thorns which sprang up and choked it, but here is a good seed, a choice bulb, which flourishes where you could not have looked for it to do so. God can make his people live and blossom even among the thorns, where the ungodly by their evil influences would choke and destroy them. Happy it is when the gracious one can overtop the thorn-thicket, which would check his growth, and make his influence to be known and felt above the grossness of surrounding sin.

We should not do justice to this text if we failed to see in it a reminder of the persecution to which many of the best of God's people are subjected. They live all their lives long like the lily among thorns. Some of you, dear friends, are in this condition. You can hardly speak a word but what it is picked up and made mischief of; you cannot perform an action but what it is twisted and motives imputed to you which you know not of. Nowadays persecutors cannot drag men to the stake, but the old trial of cruel mockings is still continued; in some cases it rages even more fiercely than ever. God's people have been a persecuted people in all times, and you only fare as they fare. Bear well the burden common to all the chosen! Make no great wonder of it; this bitter trial has happened to many more before; and you may well rejoice that you are now in fellowship with apostles and prophets and honourable men of all ages. The lily among thorns should rejoice that it is a lily and not a thorn, and when it is wounded it should consider it a matter of course, and bloom on.

But why doth the Lord put his lilies among thorns? It is because he works transformations, singular transformations, by their means. He can make a lily grow among thorns till the thorns grow into lilies. Remember how it is written, 'The wilderness and the solitary place shall be glad for them; and the desert shall rejoice, and blossom as the rose.' He can set a Christian in a godless family till first one and then another shall feel the divine power, and shall say, 'We will go with you, for we perceive that God is with you.' It cannot happen in nature, but it does happen in grace perpetually, that the sweet perfume of the lily believer, shed abroad upon the thornbrake of the ungodly, turns it into a lily garden. Such holy work among ungodly people is the truest and best 'FLOWER MISSION'. They do well who give flowers to cheer the poor in their dreary habitations, but they do better still who are themselves flowers in the places where they live. Be lilies, my dear brethren, preach by your actions, preach by your kindness, and by your love; and I feel quite sure that all your influence will be a power for good. If the Holy Spirit helps all of you to stand among your associates as lilies among the thorns, the day will come when thorns will die out, and lilies will spring up on every side: sin will be banished and grace will abound. An Australian gentleman told me yesterday that in his colony the arum lily abounds as much as weeds do with us. When will this happen spiritually on our side of the globe? Ah, when! Blessed Lord, when wilt thou remove the curse? When wilt thou bring the better days? These are ill times, wherein the thorns grow thicker and more sharp than ever; protect thy lilies, increase their number, preserve their snowy whiteness, and delight thyself in them; for Jesus' sake, Amen.

13

THE APPLE TREE IN THE WOOD

'As the apple tree among the trees of the wood,
so is my beloved among the sons' (Song of Solomon 2:3)

By the apple tree would probably be intended by the oriental writer either the citron, or the pomegranate, or the orange. I suppose he did not refer to the apple tree of our gardens, for it would scarcely be known to him. The word would not, however, be properly rendered if we confined it to any of the three fruit trees we have mentioned, or if we excluded our own apple from it, for the term 'apple' comprehends all large round fruit not enclosed in a shell; and so we may, without making any mistake, think of the apple tree of our own English orchards, and yet the metaphor will stand good, except that the shadow of our apple tree at home is hardly so excellent a retreat from the sun as the shadow of the other trees included under the term. Our own apple tree will suffice us, however, and we shall not need to enter into any minute distinctions, or to carry you away to Palestine; we can sit at home in England, and can say with great propriety, if we love the Lord Jesus Christ, 'As the apple tree among the trees of the wood, so is my beloved among the sons.'

The point of the metaphor is this. There are many trees of the forest, and they all have their uses, but when one is hungry and faint and thirsty, the forest trees yield no succour, and we must look elsewhere; they yield shelter, but not refreshing nutriment. If, however, in the midst of the wood one discovers an apple tree, he there finds the refreshment which he needs; his thirst is alleviated, and his hunger removed. Even so the Church here means to say that there are many things in the world which yield us a kind of satisfaction – many men, many truths, many institutions, many earthly comforts – but there are none which yield us the full solace which the soul requires; none which can give to the heart the spiritual food for which it hungers; Jesus Christ alone supplies the needs of the sons of men. As the apple tree is the exception to the forest trees in bearing its fruit, as it stands on that account in contrast to the trees of the wood, so does Jesus our Beloved contrast with all others, and transcendently excel them:

> An apple tree in simple beauty stands,
> And waves its juicy treasure gracefully,
> Among the barren trees which crowd the wood,
> Of lofty form, but destitute of fruit:
> So Jesus, 'midst the failing sons of men
> Bears for my use the fruits of covenant love,
> And fills my heart with rare delight and rest.

Wandering, as I have been during the last few days, up and down in the New Forest, the only real forest of our country, and finding rest in its vast solitudes, often has this text occurred to me, and therefore I can do no other than speak of it to you: 'As the apple tree among the trees of the wood, so is my beloved among the sons'.

We shall at the outset speak of *the tree which the fainting soul most desires*. We shall then remark that *it is no small wonder that the needy one finds an apple tree in so singular a position*. And, thirdly, we shall note *her very natural conduct when she found so desirable a tree in such a position* – she sat down under its shadow with great delight, and feasted upon the delicious fruit.

First, then, our text speaks of THE TREE WHICH THE FAINTING SOUL MOST DESIRES. Imagine yourself, upon some sultry day in autumn, as a wanderer in the leafy lanes of a great forest, where the grand cathedral aisles reach before you to lengths immeasurable, or huge domes of foliage rise above you like a second sky. Imagine yourself roaming amidst the ferns and brakes, trampling on the briars and hollies, or sitting down on mossy banks and knolls soft with layers of sere leaves. Suppose also that you are hungry and thirsty, and that no rippling streams offer their cooling floods, while you are so far away from human call that, hungry though you might be even to death, there would be no eye to see you, and consequently no hand outstretched for your help. In such a plight it needs no imagination to conceive you as glancing to the trees, your only companions, and silently appealing to them for aid. Some of them look as if their bowing branches would sympathise if they could, others grotesquely grin at you, and the most of them sternly refuse you succour by their solemn silence. You will ask in vain of oak, or ash, or elm.

Suppose you appeal to yonder stately tree which is *the* greatest of them all, the king of the forest, unequalled in greatness or girth; admire its stupendous limbs, its gnarled roots, its mossy bark, the vast area beneath its boughs. You look up at it and think what a puny creature you are, and how brief has been your life compared with its duration. You try to contemplate the storms which have swept over it, and the suns which have shone upon it. Great, however, as it is, it cannot help you: if it were a thousand times higher, and its topmost boughs swept the stars, yet it could minister no aid to you. This is a fit picture of the attempt to find consolation in systems of religion which are recommended to you because they are greatly followed. Here is a religion which has been patronised by kings and nobles for centuries, a religion which has the support of the great and fashionable at the present hour, will not this content you? Is it not enough to belong to the same religion as the majority, especially when that majority includes the aristocrats of the land? Is not the voice of the people the voice of God? What more do you want? Why should you be singular? Alas, the great tree is not the fruit-bearing tree.

The true Christian, believing in Jesus Christ with all his heart, counts it no desirable thing to be found in the broad road where the many go, for he remembers that his Master spake of it as leading to destruction; majorities are nothing to him, for he remembers that 'strait is the gate and narrow is the way which leadeth unto life, and few there be that find it'. He does not reckon that the greatness of the company will make right wrong, or overawe the Judge of all, or make eternal punishment one whit the less intolerable.

We desire not the way of the multitude; the way of the Crucified we delight to follow. It is not the mightiest tree of the forest that we look to with hope, but to the Lord Jesus, our Beloved, who is the apple tree among the trees of the wood; his fruit is sweet to our taste. He is the way, the truth, and the life to us; his person is most dear unto us, and his teachings are the fruit of our spirits. Happy are ye who dare to be singular with Christ. Blessed are ye who have found the narrow way which leadeth unto life eternal. Blessed are ye because ye are not carried away with the strong current and fashion of the age, but have heard the voice that saith, 'Be not conformed to this world, but be ye transformed by the renewing of your minds.' Wisdom tells the hungry man to prefer the solitary apple tree to whole groves of the hugest oaks or beeches; and wisdom given from above has brought you, O believer in Jesus, to prefer your Redeemer to all the great ones of the earth.

Suppose that in your wanderings to and fro you come upon another tree which is said to be *the oldest* in the forest. We all of us have a veneration for age. Antiquity has many charms. I scarcely know, if antiquity and novelty should run a race for popular favour, which might win. Nowadays we are pestered by a class of men who would fain fascinate our nation to error by the charms of antiquity. They will tell us that a certain ceremony, though no trace of it is to be found in Scripture, must be venerable because practised in the fourth century; and they imagine that worship in buildings which were founded by Saxons and garnished by Normans, must be peculiarly acceptable with God. To be ancient is it not a great advantage? As cleanliness is next to godliness, surely antiquity must be next to orthodoxy. Yet if there be no Scripture to warrant it an ancient ceremony, it is only an ancient farce. There are some things which are so old as to be rotten, wormeaten, and fit only to be put away. Many things called ancient are but clever counterfeits, or wherein they are true they are but the bones and carcases of that which once was good when life filled it with energy and power. There is an 'old way which wicked men have trodden', as well as a good old way in which the righteous walk. We cannot be certain that a thing is right because it is old, for Satan is old, and sin is old, and death is old, and hell is old; yet none of these things is right and desirable on that account. No; Jesus Christ our Lord, since the day in which we have known him by faith, has quieted our conscience, has calmed our fears, has given us joy and peace through believing and we are not to be seduced from him by all the antiquated falsehoods which may weave their spells around us. Old even to decay may be the trees in which other travellers delight, but as for us, we choose the tree of heavenly fruit – the apple tree is our choice, Jesus is our Beloved. Ritualists may glory in their fourth century doctrines, their fathers, their councils, and their ancient customs; the Bible is primitive enough for us, the cross of our Lord Jesus Christ is venerable enough for us; we are content with him and want no more. To us the main thing is to find food for our souls, the bread that never perishes, the fruit which will quench our desperate thirst. We have found it in the Saviour, and from the Saviour we will not depart.

It may be that in the midst of the forest while you are hungry and thirsty, you come upon a strangely *beautiful tree*: its proportions are exact, and as you gaze upon it from a distance you exclaim: 'How wonderful are the works of God!' and you begin to think of those trees of the Lord which are full of sap, the cedars of Lebanon, which he hath planted. You stand under it and look up among the majestic boughs and the spreading branches, and you again admire the beauty of nature as it comes from the hand of the Most High. But beauty can never satisfy hunger, and when a man is dying of thirst it is vain to talk to him of symmetry and taste. He wants food. This reminds us that nowadays there be some who try to satisfy the souls of men with beauty. Look at their processions: who would not be charmed with their varied costumes, their spangled banners, their gilded crosses, and their melodious hymns? Listen to their choir; is not the singing perfection? If you want a concert on the Sabbath day, and do not like to attend a theatre, you can find it in the cathedral, and in many a parish church, and please the Lord almost as well; if you want to have your senses gratified and cannot conscientiously attend an opera on Sunday, you can have ear and eye gratified at church, ay, and the nose as well in some places; and these amusements they mistake for religious exercises. Compared with the plainness of worship which we follow – our casting out of everything like symbol, our abhorrence of everything that would take away the mind from God himself and fix it upon secondary objects – compared with all this their worship is enchanting indeed to the carnal mind, and we do not wonder that those who are led by taste should follow after it. But oh, if a man once hungers after the bread of heaven, his taste for finery will be reduced to a very secondary position as a governing power of his mind. If once the soul craves after God, after peace, pardon, truth, reconciliation, holiness, it will seek the Lord Jesus, the apple tree, and forget the other trees, however shapely they may be. 'These bear no fruit for me,' says the hungry soul. The awakened conscience listens to the chant as it is echoed among the massive pillars, and watches the smoke as it rises like a cloud among the arches of the roof, and he cries, 'What are the chanting and smoke to me? I want a Saviour.' He sees the procession, and after he has gazed upon it he says, 'What are these mummeries to me? I want washing in the blood of Christ.'

As the incense smokes to heaven he says to himself, 'Oh for the incense of the Saviour's merit; what are these gums of Araby to me if they should burn all day long?' He turns away, sick and faint at heart, from all the gew-gaws and outward trappings of modern Popery, and he cries, 'O God, thou art a Spirit, and they that worship thee must worship thee in spirit and in truth. I want thee, O my God; I want spiritual life within myself, that I may commune with thee, and where can I find it but in my Saviour? He gives it to me; he is the only fruit-bearing tree amongst the trees of the wood.'

We will pursue our investigations in the forest, and while we are doing so we shall come upon some very *wonderful* trees. I have seen just lately instances in which branches are curiously interlaced with one another; the beech sends forth a long drooping bough, and lest it should not be able to support itself, another bough strikes up from below to buttress it, or descends from above and clasps it, and the boughs actually grow into one another. Strange things may be observed in the undisturbed woods, which are not to be seen in our hedgerow trees, or discerned in our gardens; trees have odd habits of their own, and grow marvellously if left to their own sweet wills. I have stood under them and said, 'How can this be? This is singular indeed! How could they grow like this? What wondrous interlacings, and intertwinings, and gnarlings, and knottings!' Yes, but if a man is hungry and thirsty, he would not be satisfied with curiosities.

So it is with some preaching that I know of. If you regard it from the standpoint of literary excellence you confess that it is wonderful. There are great orators and deep thinkers to be found to whom I would not presume to hold a candle, whose performances are really wonderful; I have felt, after I have heard their essays, like the Primitive Methodist who went to dinner with the squire, and then pronounced the blessing afterwards: 'Lord, we thank thee that we do not have such a good dinner as this every day for it is too rich to agree with us.' I have felt just like that after hearing the fine oration, though, mark you, I did not remember a bit of it after it was over, and my heart was none the better. How many sermons are published nowadays, as well as preached, which are full of what is called thought. By the cant word 'thought' is generally meant contradicting the plain meaning of scripture and starting new notions. A man who preaches plainly what God reveals is said to be an echo of the Puritans, a dealer in platitudes, a repeater at second-hand of exploded dogmas; but to find out some new lie every week to tell your people, to shake their faith in inspiration every time you open your mouth, and make them believe that there is nothing certain, but that everything is a mere matter of opinion – that is 'thought and culture' in these days. And there are in certain dissenting pulpits the most miserable specimens of this school, and in the pews a number of their silly admirers. Brethren, some of us are too old-fashioned ever to be led astray in that way, and what is more, we have such an awful appetite, we are possessed of such a dreadful hunger, and such insatiable thirst, that we dare not go away from the apple tree, because we want to be always eating; we dare not go away from Jesus Christ, because we are always wanting pardon, always wanting fresh life, and provided we can retain our hold on Jesus we are not particular about the way in which some of these marvellous trees twist their boughs. We do not feel concerned about the marvels of modern thought, or the resurrections of ancient errors.

Should all the forms that men devise,
Assault my soul with treach'rous art,
I'd call them vanities and lies,
And bind the gospel to my heart.

For if we search the globe around,
Yea, search from Brighton to Japan,
There shall be no religion found,
So just to God, so safe to man.

But as we are wandering in the forest and are still hungry, I hear some one saying, 'Ah, here is the place for food; you need not boast of your apple tree: the ground is covered with meat beneath this noble tree.' I look up, it is autumn time, and I see a huge tree loaded with beech nuts which fall from it like rain. 'Here is the place for food.' Was that a human voice I heard? No, it was the gruntings of a herd of the mast as it falls from the tree. Yonder is a grove of oaks, all shedding their acorns, and how delighted the swine are! How they fatten upon the spoil! 'Will you not come here?' they seem to say, as they munch in comfort; 'will you not come here? Do not tell us about trees which bear no fruit: there is fruit enough here surely.' Even thus I hear a voice from the Exchange: 'Here are the trees which bear us golden apples, come hither and be filled.' I hear it from those who cater for public amusements: 'Here are the fruits which can delight the soul. Here is the place to spend a happy day.' And so I hear it from the gay followers of vice: 'This dalliance, this dance, this flowing bow, this sweet-sounding viol, these are real joys.' Yes, to you, to you who choose them. Beech nuts and acorns are good enough for swine. To you who can find comfort, solid comfort, in the gain of merchandise, or in the pleasures of sin, or in the delights of pomp, these things are good enough; but a *man*, a God-made man, a man into whom God has put a new heart – not a swine's heart, but a man's heart – wants apples, not acorns, wants spiritual food, food for an immortal nature, and there is no such food to be found short of the Lord Jesus Christ, for he, and he only, is the apple tree among the trees of the wood.

I might enlarge, but I will not. I will simply say what every child of God here knows, that the Lord Jesus Christ has given to us, ever since we found him, everything we have wanted. When we came to him we were worn out with faintness, we were hungry to get rid of our sins, but we are now rid of them, every one of them. We went up to his cross, and as we saw him hanging on it, the strings which bound our burden to our shoulders began to crack, our load rolled off into his sepulchre, and we have never seen it since. We have half fancied we have felt it again, but we never have, for if our sins be searched for they cannot be found, yea, they shall not be, saith the Lord. You remember when you first came to that precious tree whereon the Saviour died, and found that your sin was blotted out, and that you were accepted in the Beloved, and were made to be henceforth an heir of heaven. Oh, the lusciousness of the fruit which you gathered then! Oh, the delightful quiet of that shadow under which you sat that day; blessed be his name! You had searched among the other trees, but you found no fruit there: you tried to rest in the shadow of other boughs, but you never rested till on that bloodstained tree of the cross you saw your sin put away and your salvation secured, and then you rested and were satisfied.

But the Lord Jesus Christ has not only satisfied us as to the past, see what he has done for us as to the present! My dear hearers, there are some of you who have never known yet what it is to be perfectly happy. I do not call it being perfectly happy to be full of excitement, and laughter, and apparent joy, and then to go home in the evening and sit down and feel disgusted with it all. That is the froth of fancy, and not the true wine of joy. But to be perfectly happy is to be able to think about all things on earth, and all things in heaven, and yet to say, 'I lack nothing; there is nothing I desire, nothing I pine after; I am saved; I am a child of God; the eternal God is my own Father. I am on my way to his own glorious house; if death should strike me it will make no difference to me, for all is well, and could not be better. If there are crosses in my lot, they are God-sent crosses; if I have troubles they work my lasting good; if I lose, I am a gainer by my losses; if I have all things, I see God in all things; and if I have nothing, yet I see all things in my God: nothing more can I desire. Christ is all, and Christ is mine, and therefore I have all things.' Now, that is the position of the Christian this day. He sits down under the shadow of Christ, and Christ's fruit is sweet to him. Let me ask you, can you imagine any other place where such peace of mind or such happiness can be enjoyed? Why, I know sick people who are far more happy in their sickness than worldlings are in their health; and I know poor men who are infinitely more at peace, and more contented, than rich men who have not the Saviour. Jesus Christ alone satisfies us for the past and delights us for the present.

And then as to the future. The man who has found Christ looks forward to it not merely with complacency, not simply without a dread, but with a joyous expectancy and hope. Those things which make others tremble make us glad. There is such a thing as dying: thank God, there is. Who wants to live here always? That narrow stream which separates this country from the better land must be forded by each of us. Who would have it otherwise? Instead of being afraid to cross it, we have sometimes said

> O Lord of hosts, the waves divide,
> And land us now in heaven.

The judgment? The Christian quails not at the thought. Who shall lay anything to his charge? The coming of the Lord? The believer fears it not; nay, it is his grandest hope. Eternity, and its never-ending cycles? He dreads it not, for it is to him the climax of his joy that it is to be everlasting. O happy people who have Christ; happy souls who rest in Jesus. They may say what none others can – 'As the apple tree among the trees of the wood, so is my Beloved among the sons.' Dear hearer, is he your Beloved? Can you claim him as your own? If you can, then I am sure you will bear witness, as the text does, to the satisfying power of the Saviour, and declare with Ralph Erskine:

> What fool soever disagrees,
> My sweet experience proves
> That Jesus is the tree of trees
> Among a thousand groves.

2. **The spouse spoke of the tree which she most desired: THE WONDER WAS THAT SHE FOUND IT**. It was an apple tree, but it was not in a garden, a fruit tree but not in a vineyard; it was 'among the trees of the wood'. Who would know of so great a rarity as an apple tree in a wood if he were not first told of it? So Jesus Christ at this present day is not known to all mankind. It is a most unhappy thought that probably the majority of the human race have not heard of the Saviour at all, and a very large proportion have never heard of him except through misrepresentations. Only a small minority of our fellow men know anything about the Saviour.

> What millions never knew the Lord!
> What millions hate him when he's known.

Even in our own country you will not find it a difficult thing to meet with persons who are totally ignorant of Christ. Try it, and you shall find in country towns and in hamlets men grown up who could not give you an answer to this question, 'How is it that the death of Jesus saves the soul?' Nay, who do not even know the fact that Jesus Christ came into the world to save sinners. 'Well,' say you, 'we know the rural districts are ignorant.' Yes, but they are far superior in light to parts of London. You can readily find children in our streets, and what is worse, artisans in our workshops, to whom the bare name of Jesus may be known, but anything like the doctrine of his substitutionary atonement is a thing of which they have not heard. Living in the light they abide in darkness, amid a thousand lamps they see not. One of the problems which may most surprise us is the existence of such dense ignorance in persons who live in intimate connection with instructed people. If you want the grossest ignorance, probably you would not find it in Peking or Timbuctoo, but in London or New York. Where the greatest light is, there the shadows are deepest. Men nearest to the church are often furthest from God.

You cannot easily find an apple tree in a great forest. If you were put down in the middle of a forest and told there was an apple tree there, you might wander for many a day before you discovered it, and often go over your own footsteps, lost in endless mazes, but you would not find the object of your search; and so, though there be a Saviour, men have not found the Saviour, and there may even be souls here present who long for that which Jesus is able to give, and yet have not discovered him. You know all about him in the letter of his word, but you cannot find him spiritually, and I hear you cry, 'Oh, that I knew where I might find him.' I know I am speaking to some such. You have been going up and down for months with your prayers, and your tears, and your good works; you have been trying to do all you can to save yourselves, but you find your own actions to be barren trees, and you know that there is an apple tree somewhere, but you cannot find it. Ah, poor soul, you are like the Ethiopian eunuch, when he was asked if he understood what he read, he gave the answer, 'How can I unless some man should guide me?' Do you not wonder that the spouse found her apple tree among the trees of the wood?

The fact is, none ever find it except they are led there, and none can lead a soul to that apple tree but the eternal Spirit of God. He can make use of his ministers, and he does; and therefore, brethren in the ministry, let us always be preaching about this apple tree; let us preach up Jesus Christ, let us make tracks to the tree of life. Whatever we do not preach, let us preach Jesus Christ. I have found, wherever I have been during the last month, that though there might not be a road to this place or that, there was sure to be a London road. Now, if your sermon does not happen to have the doctrine of election, or the doctrine of final perseverance in it, let it always have Christ in it. Have a road to London, a road to Christ, in every sermon. Still, the plainest preaching will require the Spirit of God to go with it, or else the soul will hear about this glorious tree, and about the sweetness of the fruit, but will never find the shadow, and will never eat the dainty apples. Have you come to Christ, dear brother and sister? Then give God the glory of it. Jesus led you, his Spirit guided you; praise and bless his holy name.

Now, is it not a strange place for an apple tree to be found in – in a wood? We seldom hear of such a thing; an apple tree should grow in a garden. How should it be found in a forest? And is it not a strange thing that a Saviour should be found for us among men – not among angels? Ye shall search for a Saviour amongst 'the helmed cherubim and sworded seraphim' as long as you will, but there is none there. The Saviour is found in a manger at Bethlehem, in a carpenter's shop at Nazareth; amongst the poor and needy is he seen while he sojourns amongst the sons of men. As I was turning this text over in my mind I thought, 'Ah, and what strange trees this tree grew among, for there it stands with a gallows tree on either side, and two thieves hanging upon them. "He was numbered with the transgressors." Not among you, O ye cedars, not among you, O mighty oaks, but amongst the bushes of the desert, amongst the trees accursed was Jesus found: "He made his grave with the wicked." '

> As in some sere and unproductive wood
> One lovely, fruit-producing apple-tree,
> Bright contrast to the ruin'd thousands round;
> So in this populous but vicious world
> O thou Desire of nations, didst thou stand.

Now, there is something very sweet about this, because a wood is the very place where we most love to find Christ growing. If I had come the other day upon an apple tree in the forest, and it had happened to be the time of ripe fruit, I should have felt no compunction of conscience in taking whatsoever I was able to reach, for a tree growing in the forest is free to all comers. Should there be a hungry one beneath its bough, he need not say, 'May I?' when his mouth waters at the golden fruit: he need not say, 'It would be stealing; I am unfit to take it; I am unworthy of it.' Man, if there be an apple tree in the forest, no man can keep it for himself or deny your right to it, for each wanderer has a right to what fruit he can gather. The animals have rights of pasturage, and the birds have rights of nesting, and you have rights of feeding. Pluck away, man, and eat to thy full. The shadows and the fruits of forest trees are free to all who need them. This ought to delight any seeking soul here this morning. Jesus Christ is not hedged about in the Scriptures, as some theologians would fain guard him from coming souls; the Lord has planted no protection of thorns and hollies by saying, 'You must bring with you preparations for grace, you must feel that, and feel the other, and only then may you dare to come to Christ.' It is a gross error to tell a man to do something and be something before he believes in Jesus. No; there he stands with no hedge about him, and whosoever will may partake freely. If you hear the gospel call, your reply to it should be

> Just as I am, thy love unknown
> Has broken every barrier down;
> Now to rely on thee alone,
> O Lamb of God, I come.

Christ has no barriers around him to keep you from him. If there be any they are of your own making.

> None are excluded hence but those
> Who do themselves exclude;
> Welcome the learned and polite,
> The ignorant and rude.

Whoever shall come shall be welcome to this priceless apple tree. There is some comfort, therefore, in thinking that he grows among the trees of the wood.

3. It was little wonder that when the spouse, all hungry and faint, did come upon this apple tree in the forest SHE ACTED AS SHE DID. Straightway she sat down under its shadow, with great delight, and its fruit was sweet unto her taste. She looked up at it; that was the first thing she did, and she perceived that it met her double want. The sun was hot, there was the shadow: she was faint, there was the fruit. Now, see how Jesus meets all the wants of all who come to him. God's anger, like the hot noonday sun, falls on me, how can I escape it? There is no escape from the anger of God except by an interposer. What is a shadow? Is it not caused by the interposition of the bough, or the rock, or whatever it may be, which comes between us and the sun? If we sit under a tree in the shadow, it is because the tree receives the heat, and so we escape from it. Jesus Christ's great office is the Interposer, the Mediator, the Substitute, the Atonement, the Sacrifice, and when we hide beneath him we are screened. God's wrath cannot come on us, because it has come upon him on our behalf.

> When Christ my screen is interposed
> Between the sun and me,
> My joyful heart and lips unclosed,
> Adore the glorious tree.

That is a beautiful picture in Solomon's Song where the king is said to ride in his chariot of love. He takes his spouse with him, and they ride together in his palanquin, and it has over it a canopy. Did you ever notice what it is made of? It is said, 'The covering thereof was of purple'; for truly the only interposition between us and the sun of God's wrath is the purple canopy of the atoning blood. Is it not delightful to sit down beneath the scarlet canopy of the Saviour's blood, and feel, 'God cannot smite me: he has smitten his Son; payment he cannot demand the second time: if Jesus suffered in my stead, how can God make me suffer again for sin? Where were the justice of the Most High to punish an immaculate Substitute, and then punish men for whom that Substitute endured his wrath?' This is the cool, calm, holy shadow under which we abide.

But then, the spouse also found that she herself was thirsty, and that the fruit of the tree exactly met her case. Our inner life wants sustenance and food; now, in the Lord Jesus is life, and the bread of life. He is that bread which came down from heaven, whereof if a man eat he shall live for ever. Oh, to get a heartful of Christ, to get a whole Christ into one's inmost soul, to have him to abide in you; this is bliss. Then your soul feels, 'It is enough: I have all things, for I have Jesus.' Let us therefore seek at this time, and especially this afternoon, in our meditations, and when we come to the communion table this evening, to abide under the shadow of Jesus, and there to be found abundantly eating of his fruit.

One thing more is to be noted: the spouse, when she had begun to enjoy the provision and the shade, and had sat down under it as if she intended to say, 'I never mean to leave this place; in this delicious shadow I mean to repose for ever', then she also began to tell of it to others. In the text she describes Christ as the apple tree, and gives her reason for so calling him: 'I sat down under his shadow with great delight, and his fruit was sweet to my taste.' Experience must be the ground upon which we found our descriptions. If a preacher wants to preach with power, let him tell what he has felt, and tasted, and handled. It is of little use to say Christ is precious, unless you can add, 'I have found him so.' Therefore the Church brings in her own experience: 'Sweet shade! I there sat down as one at home, and there regaled my soul with most delicious fare.' She could not hold her tongue about her Beloved. She must speak; she could not retain the secret of this apple tree, and say to herself, 'Others may go to it, and so perhaps when I go another time there may be nothing left for myself;' but she spread the news. She set it down in black and white in the inspired volume for an everlasting testimony that there is an apple tree among the trees of the wood, of which she had eaten, so that others might eat of it too and enjoy the same sweetness for themselves.

This morning every renewed heart desires that every other heart should know the Saviour. I can speak well of my Lord and Master. I do not know that I can say anything better of him than most of his people can, for the experience of the saints is much alike; but I can say this, if there be happiness beneath the sky, Jesus can give it you; if there be peace and rest to a jaded soul, Jesus can give it you; if there be a delight, a brimming delight, an overflowing delight, if there be that which can make the eyes to sparkle, and the pulse to beat right merrily, and the blood to leap in the veins, it is when Jesus Christ is consciously ours, and we are resting in him. I am sure, if there were an apple tree in any forest, and it were once found out, everybody would be taken to see it, it would be such an attraction; there would be many paths to it, and everybody who had been in the forest and seen it would tell his neighbours. Now, I beseech you who have found the Saviour to be telling others what you know about him, and try to lead others to look at him. You cannot make them feed upon him, but God can, and if you can lead them to the tree, who knows but God will give them spiritual hunger, and will lead them to feed as you have fed.

O you silent Christians, you silent Christians, who neither by your tongue, nor your pen, nor by any other way, ever tell about Christ, I do not know what to make of you. I wonder the seats you sit on do not push you off and speak instead of you, and that the stones of the street do not cry out against you as you pass over them. Why, what can you be made of, to be saved from going down to hell, and not want others to be saved too! Shame on you! Shame on me also whenever I am silent about such a blessed salvation, such a divine redemption. I would fain set your tongues going about this blessed apple tree among the trees of the wood. There is nothing about which you can speak so freely, without fear of exaggeration.

All the world has been talking about the Shah of Persia; I wish they would talk half as much about the Christ of God. All the good you will ever get out of the Shah you may see with your eyes shut, but the benefit that will come from the King of heaven to your own souls, and ten thousands of other souls, is unlimited. Cry the Saviour up, beloved. Set him on a high throne; give him the best of your thoughts, the best of your words, the best of your actions: give him of your time and your substance. He deserves to have honour above all the sons of men, for he is the best of all. As the apple tree to the hungry man excels all other trees, so does Jesus excel all other loves. Let us give him today our hearts' warmest love, and praise him for ever and for ever.

God grant it, for his name's sake.

14

THE ROES AND THE HINDS

'By the roes, and by the hinds of the fields' (Song of Solomon 2:7)[1]

The spouse was in the full enjoyment of fellowship with her Beloved. Her joy was so great as almost to overpower her, and yet, so nearly does fear tread upon the heels of joy, she was filled with dread lest her bliss should come to an end. She feared lest others should disturb her Lord, for if he were grieved she would be grieved also, and if he departed the banquet her delight would be over. She was afraid even of her friends, the daughters of Jerusalem; she knew that the best can interrupt fellowship as well as the worst, and therefore she adjured even Zion's daughters not to sin against Zion's King. Had they aroused her Beloved and broken his sacred peace she would not have found a recompense in their company, but would rather have regarded them with aversion, for having robbed her of her chief delight. The adjuration which she used is a choice specimen of oriental poetry: she charges them, not as we should prosaically do, by everything that is sacred and true, but 'by the roes, and by the hinds of the field'. So far as we understand her meaning we will endeavour to profit by it during our brief meditation. It touches one of the most mysterious points of the secret life of the believer, and we shall much need the guidance of the Holy Spirit while we endeavour to open up its meaning.

'The roes and the hinds of the field' are creatures of great *beauty*. Who can gaze upon them as they wander among the bracken without an inward admiration? Now, since nothing can be more lovely than communion with Jesus, the spouse exhorts the daughters of Jerusalem by all the loveliest objects in nature to refrain from disturbing it. No one would wish to drive away the gazelle, but would feast his eyes upon it, and yet its graceful elegance can never be compared with that beauty of holiness, that comeliness of grace which are to be seen in fellowship with Jesus. It is beautiful from both sides; it is a lovely display of condescension for our beloved Lord to reveal himself to us, and on the other hand it is a charming manifestation of every admirable virtue for a believer to enter into fellowship with his Lord. He who would disturb such mutual intercourse must be devoid of spiritual taste, and blind to all which is most worthy of admiration.

As one delights to see the red deer in the open glades of the forest, and counts them the finest ornaments of the scene, so do men whose eyes are opened rejoice in the saints whose high communion with heaven renders them beings of superior mould to common mortals. A soul in converse with its God is the admiration of angels. Was ever a lovelier sight seen than Jesus sitting at the table with the beloved disciple leaning on his bosom? Is not Mary sitting at the Master's feet a picture worthy of the choicest art? Do nothing, then, O ye who joy in things of beauty, to mar the fellowship in which the rarest beauty dwells. Neither by worldly care, nor sin, nor trifling make even the slightest stir which might break the Beloved's repose. His restful presence is heaven below, and the best antepast of heaven above; in it we find everything that is pure and lovely and of good report. It is good, and only good. Why, then, O daughters of Jerusalem, should ye stir up our Beloved, and cause his adorable excellency to be hidden from us? Rather join with us in preserving a joy so fair, a bliss so comely.

The next thought suggested 'by the roes, and by the hinds of the field' is that of *tender innocence*. These gentle creatures are so harmless, so defenceless, so timid, that he must have a soul-less soul who would do them harm or cause them fright. By all, then, that is tender the spouse beseeches her friends not to disturb her Beloved. He is so good, so kind, so holy, harmless, and undefiled, that the most indifferent ought to be ashamed to molest his rest. About him there is nothing to provoke offence, and everything to forbid it. He is a man of sorrows and acquainted with grief; he gave his back to the smiters, and his cheeks to them that plucked off the hair, he hid not his face from shame and spitting. Being reviled he reviled not again, but in his death agonies he prayed for his enemies. Who, then, could find cause for offence in him? Do not his wounds ward off the blows which might be challenged had he been of another character? Who will wish to vex the Lamb of God? Go elsewhere, ye hunters! 'The hind of the morning' has already sweated great drops of blood falling to the ground. When dogs compassed him and the assembly of the wicked enclosed him he felt the full of grief – will ye afflict him yet again?

In fellowship with Jesus there is a tenderness which ought to disarm all opposition, and even command respectful deference. The world may rise against the proselytising zeal, or defiant controversy, or ostentatious ceremonialism, for these have prominence and power, and are fair game for martial spirits; but fellowship is quiet, retiring, unobtrusive, harmless. The saints who most abound in it are of a tender spirit, fearful to offend, non-resistant, and patient – surely it would be a superfluity of cruelty to wish to deprive them of their unselfish happiness, which deprives no heart of a drop of pleasure, and costs no eye a tear. Rather let even those who are most indifferent to religion pay a generous respect to those who find their delight in it. Though the worldling may care nothing for the love which overpowers the believer's ravished spirit, let him tread with reverent care when he passes the closet of devotion, or hears a stray note from the song of meditative gratitude. Rough men have paused when they have suddenly come upon a fair gazelle grazing in a secluded spot: charmed at the sight of such tender loveliness they have scarce dared to move a foot lest they should alarm the gentle roe; and some such feeling may well forbid the harsh criticism or the vulgar laugh when even the infidel beholds a sincere heart in converse with its Lord. As for those of us who know the blessedness of fellowship with Jesus, it behoves us to be doubly jealous of our words and deeds, lest in a single instance we offend one of the Redeemer's little ones, and cause him to lose even for an hour his delight in the Lord. How often are Christians careless about this; till at the sight of some professors the more spiritual may well take alarm, and cry out in anguish, 'I charge *you*, O ye daughters of Jerusalem, by the roes, and by the hinds of the field, that ye stir not up, nor awake my love, till he please.'

A third thought most certainly had place in the mind of the anxious spouse; she meant to adjure and persuade her friends to silence by everything which sets forth *love*. The lilies and the roes have always been sacred to love. The poet of the Canticles had elsewhere used the symbol of the text to set forth married love. 'Let her be as the loving hind and pleasant roe' (Proverbs 5:19). If ever there was true love in all this selfish world, it is the love of Jesus first, and next the love of his people. As for his love, it passeth the love of women, many waters cannot quench it, neither can the floods drown it; and as for the love of the church, he who best knows it says, 'How fair is thy love, my sister, my spouse! How much better is thy love than wine! and the smell of thine ointment than all spices!' If love, therefore, may plead immunity from war, and ask to have its quietude respected, the spouse used a good argument when she pleaded 'by the roes and by the hinds of the fields', that her royal Bridegroom's rest of love might not be invaded. If you love, or are loved, or wish to be loved, have a reverent regard for those who commune with Jesus, for their souls take their fill of love, and to drive them from their bliss would be inexcusable barbarity. O ye who have any hearts to feel for others, do not cause the bitterest of sorrow by depriving a sanctified soul of the sweetest of delights. Draw not nigh hither with idle tale, or wanton speech, or empty mirth: the place whereon thou standest is holy ground, for surely God is in that place where a heart enamoured of the altogether Lovely One delights itself in the Lord.

O that all believers were so anxious to retain the enjoyment of divine love that they would warn off every intruder, whoever he might be. The daughters of Jerusalem were welcome to visit the spouse at fitting times, she even on another occasion bade them carry a message for her to her Beloved One, and gave them a full description of his surpassing charms, but when her Lord was with her at the banquet, she only asked of them that they would not come between her and the sunshine of his presence. Nor do we wonder at her jealous fear, for we have had a sip of those sweets which she had tasted, and we would sooner lose all else than lose the luxury of love divine. It is such joy as cannot be imagined by those who have never partaken of it, such joy as can never be rivalled even in the paradise above, if in that place there be any other joy than that which springs from divine love. Let none, then, deprive us of its continued enjoyment. By the sanctities of true love, let every friendly mind assist us to preserve the hallowed quiet so essential to communion with our Lord.

Once more, upon the very surface of the figure lies the idea of *delicate sensitiveness*. The roes and the hinds of the field are soon away if anything occurs to disturb them. In this respect they set forth to the life the speediness with which the Beloved departs when he is annoyed by sin. He is as a roe or a young hart, for this quality among many others that while 'he comes leaping upon the mountains, skipping upon the hills', he also soon withdraws himself and is gone. Ah, then his spouse bewails his absence, saying, 'I sought him, but I could not find him; I called him, but he gave me no answer.' The Lord our God is a jealous God. In proportion to the fire of love is the heat of jealousy, and therefore our Lord Jesus will not brook a wandering affection in those greatly beloved ones to whom he manifests himself. It needs constant watchfulness to maintain constant fellowship. Hence the spouse entreats and beseeches those who came near her not to give umbrage to her Lord. They might do this unwittingly, hence she warns them; they might do it in wanton carelessness, hence she 'charges' them. She would have them speak softly and move gently, lest he should be disturbed. Should we not feel a like anxiety that nothing in our families, or in any of our relations or connections should be tolerated by us so as to envelope us in the wrong, and grieve our Lord? Should we not specially watch every thought of our mind, desire of our heart, word of our tongue, and deed of our hand, lest any of these should give him umbrage, and break our rapturous intercourse? If we would be favoured above others we must be more on our guard than others are. He who becomes 'a man greatly beloved' must needs keep his heart with sevenfold diligence, for to whom much is given, of him much will be required. Kings will bear from common subjects behaviour which could not be endured in favourites; that which might cause but slight pain from an enemy will sorely wound if it come from a friend. Therefore the favoured spouse may well use in her entreaty the name of the most tenderly susceptible of love's favourites, and plead 'by the roes and by the hinds of the field'.

Dear friend, do you know what intercourse with Jesus means? If so, imitate the spouse whenever you are in the enjoyment of it. Be jealous of yourself and all around you, that the Well-beloved may not be vexed. Aim at the maintenance of life-long communion. Remember how for centuries Enoch walked with God: our lives are but a span compared with his, why should we not always come up from the wilderness leaning on our

Beloved? The Holy Ghost has almighty power. Let us ask and receive that our joy may be full.

If you do not understand this precious secret, may the Lord reveal it to you even now. You must first receive the Lord Jesus as your Saviour, or you can never know him as your Bridegroom. Faith must trust him before love can embrace him. You must be brought to be washed, or you can never be brought to be banqueted. Pant after the Redeemer as the hart panteth after the water brooks, and when you have drunk of the water of life then shall you be as a hind let loose: then, too, your feet shall be like hinds' feet, and you shall be set upon your high places. When this shall have been made your own by experience you shall understand the text, and shall also breathe the prayer of another verse of the same song – 'Make haste, my beloved, and be thou like to a roe or to a young hart upon the mountains of spices.'

15

A SERMON FOR SPRING

'My beloved spake, and said unto me, Rise up, my love, my fair one, and come away. For, lo, the winter is past, the rain is over and gone; the flowers appear on the earth; the time of the singing of birds is come, and the voice of the turtle is heard in our land; the fig tree putteth forth her green figs, and the vines with the tender grape give a good smell. Arise, my love, my fair one, and come away' (Song of Solomon 2:10-13).

The things which are seen are types of the things which are not seen. The works of creation are pictures to the children of God of the secret mysteries of grace. God's truths are the apples of gold, and the visible creatures are the baskets of silver. The very seasons of the year find their parallel in the little world of man within. We have our winter – dreary howling winter – when the north wind of the law rusheth forth against us, when every hope is nipped, when all the seeds of joy lie buried beneath the dark clods of despair, when our soul is fast fettered like a river bound with ice, without waves of joy, or flowings of thanksgivings. Thanks be unto God, the soft south wind breathes upon our soul, and at once the waters of desire are set free, the spring of love cometh on, flowers of hope appear in our hearts, the trees of faith put forth their young shoots, the time of the singing of birds cometh in our hearts, and we have joy and peace in believing through the Lord Jesus Christ. That happy springtide is followed in the believer by a rich summer, when his graces, like fragrant flowers, are in full bloom, loading the air with perfume; and fruits of the Spirit like citrons and pomegranates swell into their full proportion in the genial warmth of the Sun of Righteousness. Then cometh the believer's autumn, when his fruits grow ripe, and his fields are ready for the harvest; the time has come when his Lord shall gather together his 'pleasant fruits', and store them in heaven; the feast of ingathering is at hand – the time when the year shall begin anew, an unchanging year, like the years of the right hand of the Most High in heaven.

Now, beloved, each particular season has its duty. The husbandman finds that there is a time to plough, a time to sow, a time to reap; there is a season for vintage, and a period for the pruning of the vine; there is a month for the planting of herbs, and for the ingathering of seeds. To everything there is a time and a purpose, and every season has its special labour. It seems from the text, that whenever it is springtide in our hearts, then Christ's voice may be heard saying, 'Arise, my love, my fair one, and come away.' Whenever we have been delivered from a dreary winter of temptation or affliction, or tribulation – whenever the fair spring of hope cometh upon us, and our joys begin to multiply, then we should hear the Master bidding us seek after something higher and better, and we should go forth in his strength to love him more, and serve him more diligently than aforetime. This I take to be the truth taught in the text, and it shall be the subject of this morning's discourse; and to any with whom the time of the singing of birds is come, in whom the flowers appear – to any such I hope the Master may speak till their souls shall say, '*My* beloved spake, and said unto *me*, Rise up, my love, my fair one, and come away.' I shall have to use the general principle in illustration of four or five different cases.

1. First, with regard to THE UNIVERSAL CHURCH OF CHRIST. In looking upon her history, with half an eye you can plainly perceive that she has had her ebbs and flows. Often it seemed as if her tide retired; ungodliness, heresy, error, prevailed; but she has had her flood tide when once again the glorious waves have rolled in, covering with their triumphant righteousness the sands of ignorance and evil. The history of Christ's Church is a varied year of many seasons. She has had her high and noble processions of victory; she has had her sorrowful congregations of mourners during times of disasters and apparent defeat. Commencing with the life of Christ, what a smiling spring it was for the world when the Holy Spirit was poured out in *Pentecost*. Then might the saints sing with sweet accord:

> The Jewish wintry state is gone,
> The mists are fled, the spring comes on;
> The sacred turtle dove we hear,
> Proclaim the new, the joyful year;
> The immortal vine of heavenly root,
> Blossoms and buds and gives her fruit;

Lo, we are come to taste the wine,
Our souls rejoice and bless the vine.

The winter was over and past – that long season in which the Jewish state lay dead, when the frosts of Phariseeism had bound up all spiritual life. The rain was over and gone, the black clouds of wrath had emptied themselves upon the Saviour's head; thunder and tempest and storm, all dark and terrible things were gone for ever. The flowers appeared on the earth; three thousand in one day blossomed forth, baptised in the name of the Lord Jesus Christ. Fair promises created for beauty and delight sprang up and with their blest fulfilment clothed the earth in a royal garment of many colours. The time of the singing birds was come, for they praised God day and night, eating their bread with joy and singleness of heart. The voice of the turtle was heard, for the Spirit – that hallowed dove from heaven – descended with tongues of fire upon the apostles, and the gospel was preached in every land. Then had earth one of her joyous Sabbaths; the fig tree put forth her green figs; in every land there were some converts; the dwellers in Mesopotamia, Medes, Parthians, Elamites – some of all – had been converted to God, and the tender grapes of new born piety and zeal gave forth a sweet smell before God. Then it was that Christ spake in words which made the heart of his Church to burn like coals of juniper:

My Fellow-friende, my Beautiful,
Arise and come thy way.

The bride arose, charmed by the heavenly voice of her spouse, she girt on her beautiful garments and for some hundred years or more, she did come away; she came away from her narrowness of spirit, and she preached to the Gentiles the unsearchable riches of Christ: she came away from her attachment to the State, and she dared to confess that Christ's kingdom was not of this world: she came away from her earthly hopes and comforts, for 'they counted not their lives dear unto them that they might win Christ and be found in him': she came away from all ease and rest of body, for they laboured more and more abundantly, making themselves sacrifices for Christ. Her apostles landed on every shore; her confessors were found among people of every tongue; her martyrs kindled a light in the midst of lands afflicted with the midnight of heathen darkness. No place trodden by foot of man was left unvisited by the heralds of God, the heroic sons of the Church. 'Go ye forth into all the world and preach the gospel to every creature', was ringing in their ears like a clarion sounding the war charge, and they obeyed it like soldiers who had been men of war from their youth. Those were brave days of old when with a word the saints of God could overcome a thousand foes, that word the faithful promise of a gracious God.

Alas, alas, that season passed away, the Church grew dull and sleepy; she left her Lord, she turned aside, she leaned upon an arm of flesh, courting the endowments of earthly kingdoms, then there came a long and dreary winter, the dark ages of the world, the darker ages of the Church. At last the time of love returned, when God again visited his people and raised up for them new apostles, new martyrs, new confessors. Switzerland and France, and Germany, and Bohemia, and the Low Countries, and England and Scotland had all their men of God, who spoke with tongues as the Spirit gave them utterance. The time of Luther and Calvin, and Melancthon, and of Knox was come – heaven's sunny days when once again the frost should give way to approaching summer. Then it was that men could say once again, 'The winter is passed', priestcraft has lost its power, the rain is over and gone; false doctrines shall no more be as tempests to the Church; the flowers appear on the earth – little Churches; plants of God's right hand planting, are springing up everywhere.

The time of the singing of birds was come; Luther's hymns were sung by ploughmen in every field; the Psalms translated were scattered among all people – carried on the wings of angels, and the Church sang aloud unto God, her strength, and entered into his courts with the voice of thanksgiving, in such sort as she had not hoped for during her long and weary winter's night. In every cottage and under every roof-tree, from the peasant's hut to the prince's palace, the singing of birds was come. Then peace came to the people and joy in the Lord, for the voice of the turtle was heard delighting hill and valley, grove and field, with the love-notes of gospel grace. Then fruits of righteousness were brought forth, the Church was 'an orchard of pomegranates, with pleasant fruits', camphire with spikenard, spikenard and saffron; calamus and cinnamon, with all trees of frankincense; myrrh and aloes, with all the chief spices; and a sweet savour of faith and love went up to heaven, and God rejoiced therein. Then the Master sweetly cried:

> 'Rise up, my love, my fair one; come away,
> Soar on the wings of thy victorious faith
> Above the realms of darkness and of sin!'

But she did not hear the voice, or she heard it but partially. Satan and his wiles prevailed; the little foxes spoiled the vines and devoured the tender grapes. Corruption, like a strong man armed, held the spouse, and she came not forth at her beloved's call. In England she would not come away; she hugged the arm of flesh; she laid hold upon the protection of the State; she would not venture upon the bare promise of her Lord. O that she had left dignities and endowments and laws to worldly corporations, and had rested on her Husband's love alone. Alas for our divisions at this time, what are they but the bitter result of the departure of our fathers from the chastity of simple dependence such as Jesus' loves? In other lands she confined herself too much within her own limits, sent forth few missionaries, laboured not for the conversion of the outcasts of Israel; she would not come away, and so the reformation never took place. It commenced but it ceased, and the Churches, many of them, remain to this day half reformed, in a transition state, somewhere between truth and error, like the Lutheran Church and the Established Church of England at the present day - too good to be rejected, too evil to be wholly received, having such a savour of godliness therein that they are Christ's, but having such a mixture of Popery therein that their garments are not clean. Oh! would to God that the Church could *then* have heard her Master's voice, 'Rise up, my love, my fair one, and come away.'

And now, brethren, in these days we have had another season of refreshing. God has been pleased to pour out his Spirit upon men again. Perhaps the late revivals have almost rivalled Pentecost – certainly in the number of souls ingathered, they may bear rigid comparison with that feast of firstfruits. I suppose that in the north of Ireland, in Wales, in America, and in many parts of our own country, there have been wrought more conversions than took place at the descent of the Holy Spirit. The Lord's people are alive and in earnest, and all our agencies are quickened with new energy. The time of the singing of birds is come, though there are some harsh croaking ravens still left. The flowers do appear on the earth though much unmelted snow still covers the pastures. Thank God, the winter is over and passed to a great extent, though there are some pulpits and churches as frost-bound as ever. We thank God that the rain is over and gone, though there are still some who laugh at the people of God and would destroy all true doctrine. We live in happier times than those which have passed. We may speak of these times as the good old times wherein time is older than ever it was, and, I think, better than it has been for many a day.

And what now? Why, Jesus says, 'Rise up my love, my fair one, and come away.' To each denomination of his Church he sends this message, 'Come away.' He seems to speak to Episcopacy and say, 'Come away; cut out of the liturgy that which is not according to my mind, leave the State, be free.' He speaks to the Calvinist and says, 'Come away: be no more dead and cold as thou hast been; let not thy sons hold the truth in unrighteousness.' He speaks to each denomination according to its need, but to the same import, 'Rise and come away; leave deadness and coldness and wrong-doing and hardness and harshness, and bitterness of spirit; leave idleness and slothfulness and lukewarmness; rise up and come away. Come away to preach the gospel among the heathen; come away to reform the masses of this wicked city; come away from your little heartedness; from your coldness of spirit, come away: the land is before you; go up and possess it.' Come away, your Master waits to aid you: strike! he will strike with you;

build! he will be the great master builder: plough! he himself shall break the clods; arise and thresh the mountains, for he shall make you a sharp threshing instrument having teeth, and the mountains shall be beaten small until the wind shall scatter them like chaff, and you shall rejoice in the Lord. Rise up, people of God, in this season of revival, and come away! 'Why sleep ye? arise and pray, lest ye enter into temptation.'

2. Methinks the text has a very SPECIAL VOICE TO US AS A CHURCH. We must use the Scripture widely, but yet personally. While we know its reference to the universal Church, we must not forget its special application to ourselves. We, too, have had a season of refreshing from the presence of the Lord.

The day was with this Church in the olden times when we were minished and brought low through oppression, affliction, and sorrow; when we could not meet more than twenty in a place, and sometimes not more than five, without fine and persecution. Then the Church had its elders, who could meet the few in private houses – and cheer their hearts, bidding them abide in patience, waiting till better times might come. Then God sent them a pastor after his own heart, Benjamin Rider, who fed them with knowledge and understanding, and gathered together the scattered sheep during the times of peace.

Then there followed him a man worthy to be pastor of this Church, one who had sat in the stocks at Aylesbury, had seen his books burned by the common hangman before his face, and who counted not even his life dear unto him that he might win Christ, that man was Benjamin Keach, the opener of the parables, and expositor of metaphors. On old Horselydown, then a great common, a large house was built where he preached the word, and his hearers were very many. The flowers then appeared on the earth, and the time of the singing of birds was come to this Church.

He passed away and slept with his fathers, and was followed by Dr Gill, the laborious commentator; and for some time during his sound and solid ministry it was a good and profitable season, and the Church was multiplied and built up. But again, even under his ministry the ranks were thinned, and the host grew small. There was doctrine in perfection, but more power from high was needed.

Then after a space of fifty years or more of Dr Gill's ministry, God sent Dr Rippon, and once more the flowers appeared upon the earth, and the Church multiplied exceedingly, bringing forth fruit unto God; and out of her there went many preachers who testified of the truth that was in Jesus and were the parents of Churches which still flourish. Then the good old man, full of years and of good works, was carried to his home: and there came others who taught the Church, and ingathered many souls, but they were not to the full extent successors of the men who went before them, for they tarried but a little season. Much good they did, but they were not such builders as those were who had gone before.

Then came a time of utter deadness; the officers mourned; there was strife and division; they looked upon empty pews where once there had been full congregations; they looked about them to find one who might fill the place and bring together the scattered multitude; but they looked and looked in vain, and despondency and despair fell upon some hearts with regard to this Church; but the Lord had mercy on them, and in a very short space, through his providence and grace, the winter was passed, and the rain was over and gone. The time of singing of birds had come; there were multitudes to sing God's praises. The voice of the turtle was heard in our land; all was peace and unity, and affection and love. Then came the first ripe fruits. Many were added to the Church. Then the vines gave forth a sweet smell. Converts came, till we have often said, 'Who are these that fly as a cloud, and as doves to their windows?'

Often has this Church asked the question, 'Who has begotten me these?' And now these eight years we have had a season, not of spasmodic revival, but of constant progress. A glad period of abundant increase in which there has been as many converts as we could receive, till every officer of the Church has had his hands full in seeing enquirers, and we have only had time to stop now and then and take breath, and say, 'What hath God wrought?' The time came when we erected this house, because no other place was large enough for us; and still God continues with us, till our Church-meetings are not sufficient for the reception of converts; and we know not how large a proportion of this assembly are believers in Christ, because time fails to hear the cases of conversion.

Well, what ought we to do? I hear the Master saying, 'Rise up, my love, my fair one, and come away'. I hear Jesus speaking to this Church, and saying, 'Where much is given, there much shall be required.' Serve not the Lord as other Churches, but yet more abundantly. As he has given you showers of love, so give him your fertile fields. Let us rejoice with thanksgiving; let this Church feel that she ought to be more dedicated to Christ than others; that her members should be more holy, loving, living nearer to God; that they should be more devoted, filled with more zeal, more fervency, doing more for Christ, praying more for sinners, labouring more for the conversion of the world; and let us be asking ourselves what can we do, as a Church, that shall be more than we have ever thought of doing: inasmuch as he feeds us with the bread of heaven, multiplies our numbers, keeps us in perfect concord and makes us a happy people; let us be a peculiar people, zealous for good works, showing forth his glory among the sons of men.

It is a solemn responsibility to rest on any man's mind to be the pastor of such a Church as this, numbering very nearly two thousand in Church fellowship. I suppose such a Baptist Church has never existed before. If we be found craven in this day of battle, woe unto us! If we be unfaithful to our charge and trust, woe unto us! If we sleep when we might do so much, surely will the Master say, 'I will take the candlestick out of its place, and quench their light in darkness. Laodicea is neither cold nor hot, but lukewarm, I will spue her out of my mouth.' And there shall come a dark day to us, with Ichabod on the forefront of our house of prayer, and with darkness in our souls, and bitterness and remorse in our spirits, because we served not Christ while we might. I will cry aloud to you and spare not to admonish and encourage you, my brethren and comrades, in the conflict for truth. Men, brethren, and fathers; young men, maidens, and mothers in Israel, shall any of us draw back *now*? O Lord, after thou hast so richly blessed us, shall we be ungrateful and become indifferent towards thy good cause and work? Who knoweth but thou hast brought us to the kingdom for such a time as this? Oh! we beseech thee, send down thy holy fire on every heart, and the tongue of flame on every head, that every one of us may be missionaries for Christ, earnest teachers of the truth as it is in Jesus!

I leave these thoughts with you. You can feel them better than I can express them; and I can better feel their might than I can make you feel it. O God! do thou teach us what our responsibility is, and give us grace that we may discharge our duty in thy sight.

3. When the time of the bridal of the soul has arrived to each convinced sinner, then also there are special duties.

Can you not remember, dearly beloved, that day of days, that best and brightest of hours, when first you saw the Lord, lost your burden, received the roll of promise, rejoiced in full salvation, and went on your way in peace? My soul can never forget that day. Dying, all but dead, diseased, pained, chained, scourged, bound in fetters of iron, in darkness and the shadow of death, Jesus appeared unto me. My eyes looked to him; the disease was healed, the pains removed, chains were snapped, prison doors were opened, darkness gave place to light. What delight filled my soul, what mirth, what ecstasy, what sound of music and dancing, what soarings towards heaven, what height and depths of ineffable delight! Scarce since then have we known joys which surpassed the rapture of that first hour. Oh! do you not remember it, dear brethren, and was it not a spring time to you? The winter was passed. It had been so long, so dreary – those months of unanswered prayer, those nights of weeping, those days of watching. The rain was over and gone; the mutterings of Sinai's thunders were hushed; the flashings of its lightnings were no more perceived; God was beheld as reconciled unto you; the law threatened no vengeance, justice demanded no punishment. Then the flowers appeared in our heart; hope, love, peace, patience sprung up from the sod; the snowdrop of pure holiness, the crocus of perfect faith, the daffodil lily of love, all decked the garden of the soul. The time of the singing birds was come, all that is within us magnified the holy name of our forgiving God. Our soul's exclamation was:

> I will praise thee every day,
> Now thine anger's turned away;
> Comfortable thoughts arise,
> From the bleeding sacrifice.
>
> Jesus is become at length,
> My salvation and my strength;
> And his praises shall prolong,
> While I live my pleasant song.

Every meal seemed now to be a sacrament; our clothes were vestments; the common utensils of our trade were 'holiness to the Lord'. We went out abroad into the world to see everywhere tokens for good. We went forth with joy and were led forth with praise; the mountains and the hills brake forth before us into singing, and all the trees of the fields did clap their hands. It was, indeed, a happy, a bright and a glorious season.

Do I speak to some who are passing through that spring-tide now? Young convert, young believer, in the dawn of thy piety, Jesus says, 'Rise up, my love, my fair one, and come away.' He asks thee to come out from the world and make a profession of thy faith in him *now*: put it not off; it is the best time to profess thy faith whilst thou art young, while as yet to thee the days come not, nor the days draw nigh, when thou shalt say, 'I have no pleasure in them.' Make haste and delay not to keep his commandments. Arise, and be not the unclean thing; follow Christ in this perverse generation, that you may hear him say at the last, 'Of you I am not ashamed, for you were not ashamed of me. In the day when I was despised and rejected of men.'

In this your early time, subscribe it with your hand, yet draw it up in your heart and subscribe it with your soul: 'Lord, I am thine – wholly thine: all I am, and all I have, I would devote to thee. Thou hast bought me with thy blood. Lord, take me into thy service: thou hast put away all thy wrath and given my spirit rest. Let me spend myself and be spent - in life and in death let me be consecrated to thee.' Make no reserves. Come altogether away from selfishness – from aught which would divide your chaste and pure love to Christ, your soul's husband. Rise up and come away.

In this the beginning of your spiritual life, the young dawn of marvellous light, come away from your old habits; avoid the very appearance of evil; come away from old friendships which may tempt you back to the fleshpots of Egypt. Leave all these things. Come away to higher flights of spirituality than your fathers as yet have known. Come away to private communion. Be much alone in prayer. Come away: be diligent in the study of God's Word. Come away, shut the doors of your chamber, and talk with your Lord Jesus, and have close and intimate dealing with him.

I know I speak to some young babes in grace, beginners in our Israel. Oh! take care that you begin aright by coming right away from the world, by being strictly obedient to every divine command, by making your dedication perfect, complete, unreserved, sincere, spotless.

> While from your newly-sprouted vines
> Whose grapes are young and tender, choice and rich,
> The flavour cometh forth.—Beloved one, rise!
> Rise from this visible engrossing scene,
> And with affections linked to things above,
> Where Christ, thy treasure is, be soaring still!

4. But in the next place our text deserves to be used in another light. It may be that you and I have had winters of dark trouble, succeeded by soft *springs of deliverance.*

We will not enlarge much on our sorrows, but some of us have been to the gates of death, and, as we thought then, into the very jaws of hell. We have had our Gethsemanes, when our souls have been exceeding sorrowful: nothing could comfort us, we were like the fool who abhorred all manner of meat; nothing came with any consolation to our aching hearts. At last the Comforter came to us, and all our troubles were dissipated. A new season came, the time of the singing of birds was once more in our hearts. We did not chatter any more like the swallow or the crane, but we began to sing like the nightingale, even with the thorn in our breast; we learned to mount to heaven like the lark, singing all the way. The great temporal affliction which had crushed us was suddenly removed, and the strong temptation of Satan was taken off from us. The deep depression of spirit which had threatened to drive us to insanity was on a sudden lifted off, and we became elastic in heart, and once again like David danced before the ark, singing songs of deliverance.

I address some who this morning are looking back to such seasons. You have just reached the realm of sunlight, and you can look back upon long leagues of shadow and cloud through which you have had to march; the valley of the shadow of death you have just traversed, you can well remember the horrible pit and the miry clay, and hark! We can hear still the rushing as of the wings and feet of crowded miseries, and still we can remember the terrible shadow of confusion; but we have come through it – through it all: the winter is past, the rain is over and gone, and we can rejoice now in covenant faithfulness, and renewed lovingkindness. Now, have we our assurance back again; and Christ is near to us, and we have fellowship with the Father, and with his Son Jesus Christ. Well, then, what are we to do? Why, the Master says to us, 'Rise up, and come away.' Now is the time when we should mount up to be nearer to himself. Now that the day dawns and the shadows flee away, let us seek our beloved amid the beds of spices, and by the lilies where he feeds.

I would we had more in the Church – more in this Church – like Madame Guyon, who loved the Lord as that woman did who had much forgiven, or like Mrs Rowe, who in England was what Madame Guyon was in France; or like Dr Hawker, or like Samuel Rutherford, who could pant, and long, and sigh, for nearer fellowship with Christ. If there is ever a season when we ought to follow hard after the Lord, and not be content until we have embraced him, it is when we have come up from the wilderness, leaning upon our Beloved. Then should the chaste virgins sing with joyous heart concerning him to whom they are espoused:

> What is this vain, this visionary scene
> Of mortal things to me? My thoughts aspire
> Beyond the narrow bounds of rolling spheres.
> The world is crucified and dead to me,
> And I am dead to all its empty shows.
> But, oh! *for thee* unbounded wishes warm
> My panting soul, and call forth all her powers.
> Whate'er can raise desire or give delight,
> Or with full joy replenish every wish,
> Is found *in thee*, thou infinite abyss of ecstasy and life!

Each believer should be thirsting for God, for the living God, and longing to put his lip to the well-head of eternal life - to follow the Saviour and say, 'Oh, that thou wert as my brother, that sucked the breasts of my mother, when I should find thee without, I would kiss thee; yea, I should not be despised. I would lead thee, and bring thee into my mother's house, who would instruct me: I would cause thee to drink of spiced wine of the juice of my pomegranate. His left hand would be under my head, and his right hand should embrace me. I charge you, O daughters of Jerusalem, that ye stir not up, nor awake my love, until he please. Who is this that cometh up from the wilderness, leaning upon her beloved? I raised thee up under the apple tree: there thy mother brought thee forth; there she brought thee forth that bare thee.'

Oh that the believer would never be content with having drops and sips of love, but long for the full feast. Oh that my soul thirsteth to drink deep of that cup which never can be drained and to eat of all the dainties of that table which boundless love has furnished. I am persuaded that you and I are content to live on pence when we might live on pounds; that we eat dry crusts when we might taste the ambrosial meat of angels; that we are content to wear rags when we might put on king's robes; that we go out with tears upon our faces when we might anoint them with fresh oil. Satisfied I am that many a believer lives in the cottage of doubt when he might live in the mansion of faith. We are poor starveling things when we might be fed; we are weak when we might be mighty, feeble when we might be as the giants before God, and all because we will not hear the Master say, 'Rise up, my love, my fair one, and come away.'

Now, brethren, is the time with you, after your season of trouble, to renew your dedication vow to God. Now, beloved, you should rise up from worldliness and come away from sloth, from the love of this world, from unbelief. What enchants you to make you sit still where you are? What delights you to make you as you now are? Come away! There is a higher life; there are better things to live for, and better ways of seeking them. Aspire! Let thy high ambition be unsatisfied with what thou hast already learned and known; not as though thou hadst already attained, either wert already perfect; this one thing do thou – press forward to the things that are before. Rise, thou soul, greatly beloved, and enter into thy Master's rest.

I cannot get my words this morning as I would have them; but if these lips had language I would seek by every motive of gratitude for the mercies you are enjoying, by every sensation of thankfulness which your heart can experience for grace received, to make you now say, 'Jesus, I give up myself to thee this day, to be filled with thy love; and I renounce all other desire but the desire to be used in thy service, that I may glorify thee.' Then, methinks, there may go out of this place this morning many young men and old men too, many youths and maidens, determined to be doing something for Christ.

I well remember preaching a sermon one Sabbath morning which stirred up some brethren to the midnight meeting movement, and much good was done thereby. What if some new thought should pass through some newly quickened spirit, and you should think of some fresh invention for glorifying Christ at this good hour! Is there no Mary here who has an alabaster box at home unbroken yet? Will she not today break it over the Master's head? Is there no Zaccheus here who will today receive Christ into his house, constrained by love divine?

Oh! by the darkness that has gone, and by the brightness that has come, live lovingly towards Christ. Oh! by the fears that have been hushed, by the pains that have been removed, by the joy you now experience and by the delights which he has vouchsafed to you, I beseech you cling to him and seek to serve him. Go into the world to bring in his lost sheep, to look after his hidden ones, to restore to him that lost piece of money for which he has lit the candle and desires you to sweep the house.

O Christian men and brethren, it is an angel's work I have attempted now, and mortal lips fail; but I conjure you if there be any bowels of mercy, if there be any consolation in Christ Jesus, 'if ye then be risen with Christ, seek those things which are above, where Christ sitteth at the right hand of God.' Lay not up your treasure upon earth, where thieves break through and steal; but lay up your treasure in heaven: for where your treasure is there shall your heart be also. If you love my Master, serve him; if you do not, if you owe him nothing, oh if you owe him nothing, and have had no favour from him, then I conjure you to seek mercy; but if you have found it; if ye do know it, oh, for his love's sake *love him*! This dying world needs your help; this wicked sinful world needs your aid. Up, and be doing! The battle is raging furiously. Multitudes, multitudes in the valley of decision! Guards, up and at them! Do you sleep, sirs – sleep when now the shots are flying thick as hail, and the foemen are rallying for the last charge in the world's mighty Armageddon? Up! for the defiant standard of hell waves proudly in the breeze. Do you say you are feeble? He is your strength. Do you say you are few? It is not by many nor by few that God worketh. Dost thou say, 'I am obscure'? God wanteth not the notoriety and fame of men. Up, men, women and children in Christ! Up! be no more at ease in Zion, but serve God while it is called today, for the war needs every hand, and the conflict calls for every heart, and night cometh when no man can fight or work.

5. And now, last of all, the time is coming to us all, when we shall lie upon our dying beds. Oh, long-expected day, hasten and come! The best thing a Christian can do is to die and be with Christ which is far better. Well, when we shall lie upon our beds panting out our life we shall remember that then the winter is past for ever. No more now of this world's trials and troubles. 'The rain is over and gone'; no more stormy doubts, no more dark days of affliction. 'The flowers appear on the earth.' Christ is giving to the dying saint some of the foretastes of heaven; the angels are throwing over the walls some of the flowers of Paradise. We have come to the land Beulah, we sit down in beds of spices, and can almost see the celestial city on the hill tops, on the other side of the narrow stream of death. 'The time of the singing of the birds is come'; angelic songs are heard in the sick-chamber. The heart sings too, and midnight melodies cheer the quiet entrance of the grave. 'Though I walk through the valley of the shadow of death I will fear no evil, for thou art with me.' Those are sweet birds which sing in the groves by the side of the river Jordan. Now it is that 'the voice of the turtle is heard in our land'; calm, peaceful, and quiet, the soul rests in the consciousness that there is no condemnation to him that is in Christ Jesus. Now does 'the fig tree put forth her green figs'; the first fruits of heaven are plucked and eaten while we are on earth. Now do the very vines of heaven give forth a smell that can be perceived by love. Look forward to your death, ye that are believers in Christ, with great joy. Expect it as your spring tide of life, the time when your real summer shall come, and your winter shall be over for ever.

> One distant glimpse my eager passion fires!
> Jesus! to thee my longing soul aspires!
> When shall I hear thy voice divinely say,
> 'Rise up my love, my fair one come away.
> Come meet thy Saviour bright and glorious
> O'er sin and death and hell victorious.

May God grant that the people who fear his name may be stirred up this morning, if not by my words, yet by the words of my text, and by the influences of God's Spirit, and may you who have never had sweet seasons from the presence of God, seek Christ and he will be found of you, and may we all meet in the land where winters of sin and sorrow shall be all unknown.

16

THE TENDER GRAPES

'The vines with the tender grape give a good smell'
(Song of Solomon 2:13).

The vine is of all trees the most useless unless it bears fruit. You cannot make hardly anything of it; you would scarcely be able to cut enough wood out of a vine to hang a pot upon; you cannot turn it into furniture, and barely could you use it in the least degree for building purposes. It must either bear fruit, or else it must be consumed in the fire. The branches of the vine that bear no fruit are necessarily cut off, and they are used, as I have seen them used in the South of France many a time, in little twisted bundles for kindling the fire. They burn very rapidly, so there is soon an end to them, and then they are gone.

The vine is constantly used in Scripture as a picture of the nominal Church of Christ; so, like the vine, we must either bring forth fruit or we shall be accounted as good for nothing. Dear friends, we must serve God, we must bring forth from our very soul, love to God and service to him as the fruit of our renewed nature, or else we are useless, worthless, and shall only abide our time, and then we shall be cut down to be burned. Our end must be destruction if our life be not fruitful. This gives a very solemn importance to our lives, and it should make each of us seriously ask, 'Am I bringing forth fruit unto God? Have I brought forth fruit meet for repentance? For if not, I must, by-and-by, feel the keen edge of the Vine-dresser's knife, and I shall be taken away from any sort of union that I now have with the Church which is Christ's vine, and be flung over the wall as a useless thing whose end is to be burned.'

Beloved, you all know that there is no possibility of bringing forth any fruit except we are in Christ, and except we abide in Christ. We must bear fruit, or we shall certainly perish; and we cannot have fruit unless we have Christ, we must be knit to Christ, vitally one with him, just as a branch is really, after a living fashion, one with the stem. It would be no use to tie a branch to the stem of the vine; that would not cause it to bring forth fruit. It must be joined to it in a living union, so must you and I be livingly joined to Christ. Do you know, by experience, what that expression means? For, if you do not know it by experience, you do not know it at all. No man knoweth what life is but the one who is himself alive, and no man knoweth what union to Christ is but he who is himself united to Christ. We must become one with Christ by an act of faith; we must be inserted into him as the graft is placed in the incision made in the tree into which it is to be grafted. Then there must be a knitting of the two together, a vital unction, a union of life, and a flowing of the sap, or else there cannot be any bearing of fruit. Again, I say, what a serious thing this makes our life to be! How earnest should be our questioning of ourselves! 'For the divisions of Reuben there were great searchings of heart'; and so may there be about this matter. Let each one of us ask, 'Am I bearing fruit? I am not unless I am vitally united to Christ. I have openly professed that I am in Christ, but am I bringing forth fruit unto his honour and glory?'

I think I hear someone say, 'I hope I have begun to bring forth some fruit, but it is very little in quantity, and it is of very poor quality; and I do not suppose that the Lord Jesus will hardly stoop to notice it.' Well, now, listen to what the text says; it is the Heavenly Bridegroom, it is Christ himself, who, in this Song, speaks to his spouse, and bids her come into the vineyard, and look about her. For, saith he, 'The vines with the tender grape give a good smell.' So, you see, there was some fruit, though it could only be spoken of as 'the tender grape'. Some read the passage, 'The vines in blossom give forth fragrance'; others think it refers to the grape just as it begins to form. It was a poor little thing, but the Lord of the vineyard was the first to spy it out; and if there is any little fruit unto God upon anyone here present, our Lord Jesus Christ can see it. Though the berry be scarcely formed, though it be only like a flower which has just begun to knit, he can see the fruit, and he delights in that fruit.

I want, as the Holy Spirit shall help me, to speak about those early fruits – those tender grapes – that are being brought forth by some who have but lately come to know the Lord; and first, we will enquire, *what are these tender grapes?* Secondly, *what is the Lord's estimate of them?* and thirdly, *what is the danger to these tender grapes?* You will learn what that is from the 15th verse: 'Take us the foxes, the little foxes, that spoil the vines; for our vines have tender grapes.'

First, then, WHAT ARE THESE TENDER GRAPES? What are these firstfruits of the Spirit of God of which our text says, 'The vines with the tender grape give a good smell'? While I am preaching I shall be going over my own experience and the experience of many of God's people; and though I shall not be specially speaking to them, it will do them good to recollect what they passed through in the early days of their Christian life.

One of the first tender grapes that we spy out on living branches of the true Vine is *a secret mourning for sin*, and very often, an open mourning, too. The man is no longer the mirthful, jovial, light-headed, dare-devil sort of fellow that he was. He has found out that his life has not been right in the sight of God; he has become conscious that he has done much that is altogether wrong, and that he has left undone a thousand things which he ought to have done, and he feels heavy of heart, and sad in spirit. His old companions notice that there is a change in him; he does not tell them much because they would only laugh at him, but he has a wound somewhere within his heart, an arrow has pierced his conscience, and his soul bleeds inwardly. The pleasure which he once took in sin is all gone now; and what is more, he grieves to think that he ever should have taken any pleasure in it. He hopes that God will forgive him, but he feels that he never will forgive himself. He smites upon his breast, and wishes he could smite so hard as to kill the sin which is there; but he discovers that when he would do good, evil is present with him, and that makes him cry, 'O wretched man that I am! who shall deliver me from the body of this death?' He used to think that to believe in Christ was a very easy thing, and that to be a Christian was almost as simple a matter as kissing his hand; but he finds it quite another thing now. He has a heavy burden to carry, and it is crushing him to the ground; he is fighting with himself, and cannot get the victory. Whenever he sees his sin, it grieves him; and he is grieved because he does not grieve his sin, it grieves him; and he is grieved because he does not grieve more than he does. He wishes his heart would become softer, and that by some means he could weep for sin more thoroughly, for he really does hate it with all his soul. Well now, this is one of the tender grapes; and if any of you are brought into that condition, I thank God for it. This is a crop that will ripen and sweeten before long. Surely, never was there a truly gracious soul who did not put forth this as one of the firstfruits of the Spirit, a secret mourning for sin.

Another tender grape is *a humble faith in Jesus Christ*. The man, perhaps, has got no farther than to say, 'Lord, I believe, help thou mine unbelief! I do trust myself with thee, and thou hast said I am saved if I do that, and therefore I conclude that I am saved; but, oh, that I had more faith! Oh, that I could trust thee without a doubt! But, Lord, thou knowest all things; thou knowest that, humbly, tremblingly, I do accept thee as my Saviour, and I am hopeful to be numbered among thy people, though meanest of them all. Though my faith be but as a grain of mustard seed, I bless thee that I have even that grain; and I know that it will grow, for it has within it the life thou didst impart.' That little trembling faith, like a freshly-lighted candle which is easily blown out, is, nevertheless, one of the tender grapes. It will grow, it will come to perfection in due time, for the least true faith has everlasting life in it. All the devils in hell could not quench a single spark of God-given faith, for it is a living thing, and it cannot be destroyed. This faith possesses immortality, it shall defy death itself; yet, while it is so little, it is like the tender grape which gives a good smell.

Then there comes another tender grape, and that is *a genuine change of life*. The man has evidently turned right about; he is not looking the way he used to look, and he is not living as he used to live. At first he fails, and perhaps fails a good many times, like a child who is learning to walk, and has many a tumble; but it will never walk if it does not tumble a bit. So, when men begin to live the new life, they have many slips. They thought that ugly temper of theirs would never rise again, but it does, and it grieves them very much; and some old habit, from which they thought they had clean escaped, entangles them unawares, and they say, 'Surely I cannot be a child of God if I do these things again'; and there is great sorrow, and brokenness of spirit, and soul-humbling. Well, that very soul-humbling is a tender grape. That effort to do better – not in your own strength, because you have none, and you are sure to fail utterly if you attempt such a task alone; but the effort to do better in the strength of God, yet with the full consciousness of your own weakness – all that indicates a real change. I know that there are some men who have been so long steeped in evil that to get their old habits down is a very hard task. 'Can the Ethiopian change his skin, or the leopard his spots? then may ye also do good, that are accustomed to do evil.' Nothing but almighty power could get the blackness out of the Ethiopian's skin, or the spots out of the leopard. God can do it, and he can reverse the whole current of our lives; yet, nevertheless, while it is being done, there is often much of painful contrition and of brokenness of heart before him. See what a change it is that the Lord works in a man when he converts him from the error of his ways. There is Niagara, see the mighty flood come roaring down; what a sight it is! But can that Niagara be made to flow up hill? Yes, God can accomplish that marvellous feat; but while it is being done, think of the twists, and twirls, and whirlpools, and sheets of spray that there will be. The vast mass of water has to stop, and then to rush up again. What roaring of waves and shaking of rocks there will be even while God is performing this great operation! So is it when there is a change of heart in one who has long been steeped in evil, one who has been an open sinner; there is a great deal of distress of heart while the work is being done. Yet, if there be a radical change in the man, it is like the tender grape, which is a sure sign of life in the vine which brings it forth.

Another very blessed fruit of spiritual life in the soul is *secret devotion*. The man never prayed before; he went sometimes to a place of worship, but he did not care much about it. Now, you can see that he tries to get alone for private prayer as often as he can. He may not have the privilege of a room to himself, but he climbs up into a hay-loft, or goes down into a saw-pit, or retires behind a hedge; or, in order to be quite alone, perhaps he walks the streets of London. It is very easy to be alone in a crowded street; in busy Cheapside, there is many a man who is utterly lonely, for he does not know anybody in all the throng that rushes past him. It is a really awful loneliness that a man may have in the midst of a dense crowd, and his heart may then be talking with God as well as if he were shut up in some private room. A soul must get alone if it is really born again, it cannot live without private prayer. I like also to see the young beginners in the divine life carrying a pocket Testament, so that they may just read a short portion whenever they can get a few spare moments – two or three verses to lie in their memory, like a lozenge under the tongue, to melt there, and dissolve into their inmost being. It is a grand thing to keep a man right, and it is one of the tender grapes on the vine when there is a love for the Word of God, and a love for private prayer; I am sure that it is one of the tokens by which we are not very often deceived. 'Behold, he prayeth' is an indication that God has renewed his heart.

Another of these tender grapes is *an eager desire for more grace*, a longing for more of the good things of the covenant. Why, those who are just brought to know the Lord would like us to preach seven sermons a day, and they would like to hear them all! I know that, when I was first brought to Christ, I was ravenous after the gospel. I felt like the great beast mentioned in the Book of Job, that 'drinketh up a river, and trusteth that he can draw up Jordan into his mouth', so thirsty did I seem to be after the river of the water of life. I do not think that the seats felt hard to me then, or that standing in the aisle was too tiresome so long as it was but the gospel that was preached to me, for there was an eager desire after it in my soul. If anyone can tell the poor seeking one, who has just a little light, where he can get ten times the grace he has, I warrant you that he will make the journey if he may but find it, that his feeble faith may grow to full assurance, that his repentance may be deeper, that his love to God may be more intense. If his whole soul is set on attaining this object, it is manifest that these are the tender grapes that grow out of the life that is within the branches of the Vine.

There is also, in such persons, another very precious sign of grace, and that is *a simple love to Jesus*. The heart knows little, but it loves much; the understanding is not yet fully enlightened, but the affections are all on fire. 'Thy first love' is mentioned with special commendation in the Book of the Revelation; and I think that some of us, who have known the Lord for thirty years or more, can look back upon our first love with something of regret. I hope that we love Christ better now than we did then, but there was a vividness about our first love which we do not always realise in our more matured experience. It was then very much as it is when your servant lights a fire; at the first, the shavings, or the paper, or whatever it may be at the bottom of the kindling, makes a great deal more of a blaze than appears afterwards, and the fire is at its best when it all gets into one great steady ruby glow. It is to this state that the ardent love of Christians should come; but still, there is something very pleasing about that first blaze, and I could almost wish that we always blazed away as we did in the fervour of our first love. That first flame was one of the sure tokens that the fire was there, just as the tender grapes prove that the life is in the Vine-branches. If, dear friends, you are now full of love to Christ, do not let anybody quench it, or even damp it down; but may it burn more and more, like coals of juniper, which have a most vehement flame! God grant that this love, and all the other tender grapes that I have mentioned, may be seen in everyone who has newly sought and found the Lord!

Now I must try to answer our second question: WHAT IS THE LORD'S ESTIMATE OF THESE TENDER GRAPES? What does he think of that sorrow for sin, that little faith, that humble trust in his atoning sacrifice, that earnest attempt to live a changed life, that weariness of frivolity, that private prayer and study of the Scriptures, that eager desire for more grace, and that childlike love? What does the Lord think of all this?

Well, first, he thinks so much of it that *he calls his Church to come and look at it*. Look at the verses that precede our text: 'My beloved spake, and said unto me, Rise up, my love, my fair one, and come away. For, lo, the winter is past, the rain is over and gone; the flowers appear on the earth; the time of the singing of birds is come, and the voice of the turtle is heard in our land; the fig tree putteth forth her green figs, and the vines with the tender grape give a good smell'. We do not usually call our friends to look at things which we do not ourselves admire; so here the Bridegroom calls his spouse to share in his joy in these tokens of the heavenly life of the Church of God. Be always on the look out for the tender grapes.

I think I know some Christians who do not appreciate these early fruits as they ought. When dear children are brought to know the Lord, we cannot expect that such little shoots as they are should at first bring forth anything but tender grapes. There are some who do not take that view of the matter. 'Ah!' they say, 'there is no flavour in those grapes.' Did you expect that there would be? 'Oh!' they cry, 'they are tart and sour.' Of course they are; while they are tender grapes, they must be so. You cannot get the ripeness or the sweetness of maturity in that which is just beginning to grow. Our Lord would not have us find fault with the fruit of young converts, but rather go and look at it, and admire it and bless God that there is at least some, and that it is as good as it is. 'Ah!' says one, 'that young man does not know much.' Does he know that one thing, whereas he was blind, now he can see? Then, be thankful that he knows as much as that. 'Oh!' you exclaim, 'but he has not much prudence.' No, my dear friend, do you suppose that this young man is to have as much prudence as you might have at your age, and you are perhaps sixty or seventy? I might possibly say with truth that you have not quite so much zeal as you might have to go with your prudence. 'Oh, but!' you say, 'we want the young man to be more mature.' Give him time, and he will get as mature as you are; but while the grapes are still tender, your Master and his, calls you to look at them, and to thank him for them, for there is something very cheering in the sight of the first weak, faint tokens of the working of the Holy Spirit in the soul of a young believer.

What is Christ's estimate of these tender grapes? Why, next, *he calls them tender*. He does not call them mature, he does not speak of them as ripe; he calls them 'tender'. Do you know how he might have described them? He might have called them sour, but he does not; he calls them 'tender'. He likes to use a sweet word, you see, the softest and best word that he can use; so, when you describe a young convert, my dear brother, do not at once point out his immaturity, but call him 'tender'. Do not speak about his want of discretion but call him 'tender'. Do not say, 'Oh well, I question whether he can be a child of God or not!' He is one of God's little ones. A little child is just as much its mother's bairn as the biggest one in the family is; and no doubt that little one whose voice we heard just now is as much beloved of the mother as any of her older sons and daughters. So it should be with those who are the little children in God's great family of love; therefore, imitate your Lord, and call them 'tender'.

Then he says something more: 'The vines with the tender grape give a good smell'. Of what do they smell.

Well, first, they smell of *sincerity*. You say, 'That young man does not know much, but he is very sincere.' How many do I see, who come to make a confession of their faith in Christ, who do not know this doctrine, or have not had that experience, but they are very sincere! I can tell that they are genuine by the way they speak; they often make such dreadful blunders, theologically, that I know they have not learnt it by rote, as they might get up a lesson. They talk straight out of their loving but ignorant hearts, and I like that they should do so, for it shows how true they are in what they say; and our Lord Jesus always loves sincerity. There is no smell so hateful as the smell of hypocrisy; a religious experience that is made to order, religious talk such as some indulge in, which is all cant, is a stench in the nostrils of God. The Lord save us from it! But these vines with the tender grape give forth the sweet smell of sincerity.

Next, there is about these young believers a sweet smell of *heartiness*. Oh, how hearty they generally are, how earnest, how lively! By-and-by, some of the older folks talk about the things of God as if they were worn threadbare, and there was nothing of special interest in them; but it is not so with these new-born souls, everything is bright and fresh, they are lively, and full of earnestness, and Jesus loves that kind of spirit. He said to the angel of the church of the Laodiceans, 'I would thou wert cold or hot.' It is lukewarmness that he cannot bear, but he approves of warm, simple heartiness; it is to him like the smell of the vines that bear the tender grapes.

There is sure to be also about these young Christians the sweet smell of *zeal*; and, whatever may be said against zeal, I will take up the cudgels for it as long as I live. In the work of God, we cannot do without fire. We Baptists like water because our Master has ordained the use of it; but we must also have fire, fire from heaven, the fire of the Holy Ghost. When I see our young men and young women full of zeal for God's glory, I say, 'God bless them! Let them go ahead.' Some of the old folk want to put a bit in the mouths of these fiery young steeds, and to hold them in; but I trust that I shall ever be on their side, and say, 'No, let them go as fast as they like. If they have zeal without knowledge, it is a deal better than having knowledge without zeal; only wait a bit, and they will get all the knowledge they need.'

These young believers have another sweet smell: they are *teachable*, ready to learn, willing to be taught from the Scriptures and from those whose instructions God blesses to their souls. There is also another delicious smell about them, and that is, they are generally *very joyful*. While they are singing, some dear old brother, who has known the Lord for fifty years, is groaning; what is the matter with the good man? I wish that he could catch the sweet contagion of the early joy of those who have just found the Saviour. There is something delightful in all joy when it is joy in the Lord, but there is a special brightness about the delight of those who are newly-converted.

You see that Christ forms a correct, condescending, wise estimate of these vines with the tender grape. He calls his Church to look at them, he calls them tender, he says that they have a sweet smell, and then he shows that he cares very much about them, for he says, 'Take us the foxes, the little foxes, that spoil the vines: for our vines have tender grapes'. He does not want even the tender grapes to be spoiled.

Some people seem to think that none but advanced Christians are worth looking after, but our Lord is not of that opinion. 'Oh, it was only a lot of girls that joined the church,' said somebody. 'A lot of girls?' That is not the way our Lord Jesus Christ speaks about his children. He calls them King's daughters; and let them be called so. 'They were only a pack of boys and young men.' Yes, but they are the material of which old men are made; and boys and young men, after all, are of such account in the Master's esteem. May we always have many such in this church!

So I come to my third and closing question: WHAT IS THE DANGER TO THESE TENDER GRAPES? The 15th verse says that they are in danger from foxes, and gives the command, 'Take us the foxes, the little foxes, that spoil the vines: for our vines have tender grapes.'

Dear young friends who have lately found Christ, there are foxes about. We try all we can to stop the gaps in the hedge, that we may keep the foxes out; but they are very crafty, and they manage to get in sometimes. The foxes in the East are much smaller than ours, and they seem to be even more cunning and more ferocious than those we have in this country, and they do much mischief to the vines.

In the spiritual vineyard there are foxes of many kinds. There is, first, *the hard censurer*. He will spoil the vines if he can, and especially the vines that have the tender grapes. He finds fault with everything that he can see in you who are but young believers. You know that you are simply depending upon Christ for salvation; but this censurer says, 'You are no child of God, for you are far from being perfect.' If God had no children but those who are perfect, he would have none under heaven. These censorious people will find fault with this and that and the other in your life and character, and you know well enough that you have all too many imperfections, and if they look for them, they can soon spy them out. Then they say, 'We do not believe that there is any grace at all in you,' though you know that by the grace of God you are what you are. It may be that there is a fault in you which they have discovered, perhaps you were taken by surprise, and suddenly overcome. Possibly, they even set a trap for you, and allured you into it, provoking you to anger, and then turning round upon you, said, 'You have made a profession, have you? That is your religion, is it?' and so on. May God deliver you from these cruel foxes! He will often do so by enabling you not to mind them. After all, this is only the way in which all Christians have been tried, there is nothing strange in your experience from these censurers; and they are not your judges, you will not be condemned because they condemn you. Go and do your best in the service of your Lord; trust in Christ, and do not mind what they say; and you will be delivered from that kind of fox.

A worse fox even than that one, however, is *the flatterer*. He comes to you smiling and smirking, and he begins to express his approval of your religion, and very likely tells you what a fine fellow you are. Indeed, you are so good that he thinks you are rather too precise, you have gone a little over the line! He believes in religion, he says, fully; though, if you watch his life, you will not think so; but he says that he does not want people to be righteous overmuch; he knows that there is a line to be drawn, and he draws it. I never could see where he drew it; but still he says he does, and he thinks that you draw the line a little too near the cross. He says, 'You might be a little more worldly, you cannot get through life in your way; if you get out of society, you may as well get out of the world at once. Why do you make yourself appear so singular?' I know what he is after; he wants to get you back among the ungodly. Satan misses you, and he wants to have you again, and he is sending Mr Flatterer to wheedle you back, if possible, into your former bondage to himself. Get away from that fox at once. The man who tells you that you are too precise ought to be precisely told that you do not want his company. There never lived a man yet who was too holy, and there never will live a man who will imitate Christ too closely, or avoid sin too rigidly. Whenever a man says that you are too Puritanical, you may always smell one of these foxes. It would be better if we were all more Puritanical and precise. Has not our Father said to us, 'Be ye holy; for I am holy'? Did not our Lord Jesus say to his disciples, 'Be ye therefore perfect, even as your Father which is in heaven is perfect'?

Then there comes another foul fox, *Mr Worldly-wiseman*. He says, 'You are a Christian, but do not be a fool. Carry your religion as far as you can make it pay; but if it comes to losing anything by it, well then, don't you do it. You see, this practice is the custom of the trade; it is not right, I know, but still, other people do it, and you ought to do it. If you do not, you will never get on in business.' Mr Worldly-wiseman further says, 'Never mind if you tell a lie or two, make your advertisements say what is not true; everybody else does it as a matter of course, and why should not you? Then try whether you cannot get a slice out of your customer here and a slice there when he does not know it, it is the custom of the trade; it is the way other people do, and, as it is the custom, of course you must do it.' To all such talk I reply that there is another custom, a custom that God has, of turning all liars into hell; mind that you do not come under that divine rule and law.

There is another custom that God has, namely, of cutting down as hypocrites those who do not walk honestly and uprightly towards their fellow-men. The plea of custom will not stand for a moment at the judgment-seat of Christ; and it ought to have no weight with us here. I know that there are many young people who, unless they are watchful and careful at the very beginning of their spiritual life, will get lamed, and never walk as they ought to do, because this fox has bitten them.

There is another ugly fox about, and that is, *a doubting fox*. He comes and says, 'You seem very happy, and very joyful; but is it true? You appear to have become quite a different person from what you used to be; but is there, after all, such a thing as conversion?' This fox begins nibbling at every doctrine, he even nibbles at your Bible, and tries to steal from you this chapter and that verse. God save you young people from all these foxes!

There are some foxes of *evil doctrine*, and they generally try to spoil our young people. I do not think anybody ever attempts now to convert me from my belief; the other day, when a man was arguing with another, I asked him, 'Why don't you try me?' 'Oh!' he said, 'I have given you up as a bad case, there is no use trying to do anything with you.' It is so when we get to be thoroughly confirmed in our convictions of the truth; they give us up, and they generally say that we are such fools that we cannot learn their wisdom, which is quite correct; and so we intend to be as long as ever we live. But with some of the younger folk, they manage it thus. They say, 'Now, you are a person of considerable breadth of thought, you have an enlarged mind, you are a man of culture; it is a pity that you should cling to those old-fashioned beliefs, which really are not consistent with modern progress'; and the foolish young fellow thinks that he is a wonder, and so is puffed up with conceit. When a man has to talk about his own culture, and to glory in his own advancement, it is time that we suspected the truth about him. When a man can despise others who are doing vastly more good than he ever dreamed of doing, and call such people antiquated and old-fashioned, it is time that he should get rebuked for his impudence, for that is what it really is. These clever men, as far as I know them, are simply veneered with a little learning, not the sixteen-thousandth of an inch thick. There is nothing in the most of them but mere pretence and bluster; but there are some who hold firmly to the old gospel, who have read as much as they are ever likely to do, and are fully their equals in learning, though they do not care to boast of their acquirements. Do not any of you young people be carried away with the notion that all the learned men are heretics; it is very largely the reverse, and it is your sham, shallow philosopher who goes running after heresy. Get out of the way of that fox, or else he will do much mischief to the tender grapes.

So, brethren, I close with this remark. If you have any sign of spiritual life, if you have any tender grapes upon your branches, the devil and his foxes will be sure to be at you; therefore, endeavour to get as close as ever you can to two persons who are mentioned hard by my text, namely, the King and his spouse. First, keep close to Christ, for this is your life; and next, keep close to his Church, for this is your comfort. Get among elderly Christian people, seek to catch up with those who have long known the Lord, those who are farther on the heavenly road than you are. Pilgrims to Zion should go to heaven in company, and often, when they go in company, and they can get a Mr Greatheart to go before them, it saves them from many a Giant Slaygood and many a Giant Grim, and they get a safe and happy journey to the Celestial City where else they might have been buffeted and worried. Keep close to God's people, whoever they may be; they are the best company for you, young believers. Some Christians may, like Bunyan's pilgrim, start on the road to heaven alone; but they miss much comfort which they might have with companions of a kindred spirit. As for Christiana and her children, and the younger folk especially, they will do well to keep in company with some one of the Lord's champions, and with the rest of the army with banners who are marching towards the Celestial City. God bless and comfort all of you who know his name, henceforth and for ever! Amen.

17

THE INTEREST OF CHRIST AND HIS PEOPLE IN EACH OTHER

'My beloved is mine, and I am his' (Song of Solomon 2:16)

The Church says concerning her Lord, 'My beloved *is* mine and I *am* his.' No 'ifs', no 'buts'. The two sentences are solemn assertions. Not 'I hope, I trust, I think'; but, 'my beloved *is* mine, and I *am* his'. 'Yes,' but you will say, 'the Church must then have been gazing upon her husband's face; it must have been a season of peculiar enjoyment with him, when she could speak thus.' Nay, brethren, nay; the Church, when she thus spake, was in darkness; for in the very next verse she cries: 'Until the day break, and the shadows flee away, turn, my beloved, and be thou like a roe or a young hart upon the mountains of Bether.' I say, brethren, this solemn certainty, this double assertion of her interest in Christ and Christ's interest in her, is the utterance of the Church even in her darkness, in the cheerless season of his absence. So, then, you and I, if we believe in Christ, ought, even when we do not see his face, still to cultivate full assurance of faith, and never be satisfied unless we can say, 'My beloved is mine, and I am his.' When thou canst not say this, my hearer, give no sleep to thine eyes, nor slumber to thine eyelids. Be not happy; take no solace; find no comfort, as long as there is any doubt about thy union with the beloved – his possession of thee and thy possession of him.

We will now, having thus prefaced the text, come at once to it. There are two members, you perceive, to the sentence, 'My beloved is mine, and I am his.' These two things come in a strange order, you will say, 'Surely we are first Christ's, before Christ is ours.' A right thought of yours. We shall take the text then, this evening two ways: we shall first speak of it *as it would be in the order of time*. 'I am my beloved's, and my beloved is mine'; we shall afterwards speak *in the order of the text, which is the order of experience*. The words as Solomon penned them are not the order of fact as far as God is concerned, but the order in which *we* find out God's great doings.

You know God's first things are our second things, and our second things are God's first things. 'Make your calling and election sure.' Calling is your first thing; election is the second. But election is God's first thing, and calling is the next. You are not elected because you are called; and yet, at the same time, you shall never know your election until first you have made your calling and election sure. The order of the text is the order of experience. We shall take the members of the sentence as they would be if they spoke in the order of fact.

To begin, then. I AM MY BELOVED'S, AND MY BELOVED IS THEREFORE MINE.

(1) '*I am my beloved's.*' Glorious assertion! I am his *by the Father's gift*. Long ere suns and moons were made, and stars twinkled in the midnight darkness, God the eternal Father had given the chosen to Christ, to be his heritage and marriage dowry. If God, then, hath given my soul to Christ, I am my Beloved's. Who shall dispute the right of God to give, or who shall take from Christ that which his Father has given to be his heritage? Fiends of hell! legions of the pit! when God gives, can you take back the gift? If he puts the souls of the chosen into the hands of Christ, can ye pluck them thence? If *he* makes them Christ's sheep, can ye pluck them out of his fold, and make them your own? God forbid we should indulge the blasphemous thought that any can dispute the property which God has in his people, derived from his Father's gift.

But I am my Beloved's, if I be a believer, because *of Jesus Christ's purchase* of me. We were 'bought not with corruptible things, as with silver and gold but with the precious blood of Christ'. Christ has an absolute right to all that he bought with blood. I do not believe in that dreamy atonement, by which Christ redeems and purchases, and yet the purchase is a fiction, and the redemption a metaphor. All that Christ bought with blood he will have. If a man buy with gold and silver of an honest man, he gets his own, nor will he be content until he do; but when Christ ransoms with blood, and buys of God himself, and redeems his own people, it is not possible that he should be frustrated of his purpose, or denied the object of his death. I am my Beloved's then, because he has paid the full price for me, counted down the purple drops, and positively and surely hath as much bought me with his money as ever Abraham of old bought flocks of sheep and oxen, or as ever of old Jacob served for Rachel and for Leah. No title deeds ever made estate more truly the property of the purchaser, than did the resurrection guarantee the rights of Christ in the 'purchased possession'. 'I am my Beloved's', by a double tie – by the Father's gift, and by the Son's divine purchase. These two things are not easily reconcilable in some minds, but let it be carried in your hearts as a matter of fact, that there is as much grace in the Father's giving the elect to Christ as if no price were paid, and secondly, that there was as full and true a price paid to the Father as though the Father had been justice only, and not love. The grace of God and his justice are both of them full-orbed; they are never eclipsed; they are never made to shine with both of them full-orbed; they are never eclipsed; they are never made to shine with divided lustre; he is as gracious as though he were not just; he is as awfully severe as though there were no grace in his nature.

But more than this, 'I am my Beloved's', for I am his *by conquest*. He fought for me, and he won me, let him possess me. He went alone to that great battle. He defied all the hosts which had made me their prey, encountered first my sins, and slew them with his blood, encountered next Satan himself, and bruised the serpent's head, encountered death, and slew him by 'destroying him that had the power of death, that is, the devil'. O Christ! thou deservedst to have those for whom thou didst wrestle and agonize even unto blood, and who by thy strong hand thou broughtest out of the land of their captivity. Never could conqueror claim a subject so justly as Christ claims his people. They were not only his, eternally his, by the purchase of his blood, but they are his because he has taken them by overwhelming might, having delivered them out of the hand of him who was stronger than they. That sword which he girds upon this thigh is both the right by which he claims and the might by which he keeps his ransomed.

Besides this, every true believer can add, 'I am my Beloved's', by *a gracious surrender*. 'With full consent I give myself to thee.' This is your language, brothers and sisters. It is mine. 'I am my Beloved's.' If I was never his before, I do desire to give myself up to him now. His love shall be the fetters in which I, a happy captive, will walk at his triumphant chariot wheels. His grace shall bind me with its golden chains, so that I will be free, and yet his bondman for ever. The mercies of each hour shall be fresh links, and the benefits of each day and night shall be new rivets to the chain. No Christian man would like to be his own. To be one's own is to be lost; but to be Christ's is to be saved. To be one's own is to be a wandering sheep; to be Christ's is to return to the great bishop and shepherd of our souls. Do you not remember, many of you, the night when you first surrendered to Christ? He stood at the door and knocked; the door was overgrown with brambles; the hinges had rusted from long disuse; the key was lost; the wards of the lock were welded together with filth and rust; nay, from within, the door was bolted fast. He knocked, at first a gentle knock, enough to let you know who it was. You laughed. He knocked again; you heeded not. You heard his voice as he cried, 'Open to me, open to me; my hair is wet with dew, and my locks with the drops of the night.' But you had a thousand frivolous excuses, and you would not open to him. Oh! do you remember when at last he put in his hand by the hole of the lock, and your bowels were moved for him. 'Jesus, Saviour! I yield, I yield; I can hold out no longer; my heart melts; my cruel soul relents. Come in! Come in! and pardon me that I have kept thee out so long, resisted so long the wooings of thy heavenly love.' Well, *you* will say tonight, and set your solemn hand and seal to it, that you are Christ's because you do once again, voluntarily and freely, surrender yourself to him.

I think tonight would be a very proper occasion for each of us to renew our dedication vows. We are many of us believers; let us go to our chamber and say thus: 'O God! thou hast heard our prayers as a Church; we have entered into thy house; we have seen it filled to the full. By this, the answer which thou hast given to our prayers we re-dedicate ourselves to thee, desiring to say with the house more fully than heretofore, "I am my Beloved's".'

Let us pause here an instant. We have seen how we came to be our Beloved's. Let us enquire in what sense we are so now.

We are his, first of all, by *a near affinity* that can never be sundered. Christ is the head; we are his members. There is nothing which my head possesses so truly as my hand and my heart. Your head could not say that its helmet and plume are so truly its own as the neck, the sinews, the veins, which are joined thereunto. The head manifestly has a distinct and peculiar property in every member. 'I am my Beloved's', then, even as my hand and foot are mine. 'I am my Beloved's'; if he lose me, he will be mutilated. 'I am my Beloved's', if I be cut away, or even wounded, *he* will feel the pain. The head *must* suffer when the members are tempted and tried. There is nothing so true and real, in the sense of property, as this. I would that you who doubt the perseverance of the saints would take these few words to heart. If once Christ should lose his people, he would be a head without a body; that were a ghastly sight. Nay, if he lost one of his people he would be the head of a mutilated body, that were not a glorious sight. If you imagine the loss of one mystical member of Christ, you must suppose an imperfect Christ – one whose fullness is not full, whose glory is not glorious, whose completeness is not complete. Now, I am sure you would scout that idea, and it will be joy for you to say, 'As the members belong to the head, so am I my Beloved's.'

Further than this; we are our Beloved's by a most *affectionate relationship*. He is the husband, believers are the spouse. There is nothing that a man has that is so much his property as his own wife, except it be his very life. A man's wealth may melt by losses; a man's estate may be sold to pay his debts; but a man's wife, as long as she liveth, is his absolute property. She can say, 'He is mine'; he can say, 'She is mine'. Now Christ saith of all his people, 'Ye are mine, I am married unto you; I have taken you unto myself, and betrothed you unto me in faithfulness.' What say you! Will you deny the celestial marriagebond? God forbid. Will you not say to your Lord tonight, 'Yes, I am my Beloved's'? Ah! there is no divorce court in heaven, there is no division, no separation bill possible, for he 'hateth putting away'. If chosen, he will not reject, if once embraced, he will never cast out; his she is, and his she shall be evermore. In this sense, then, 'I am my Beloved's.'

Yet once more: 'I am my Beloved's' by an *indissoluble connexion*, just as a child is the property of his father. The father calls his child his own. Who denies it? What law is so inhuman as to allow another to rend away the offspring of his bowels from the parent? There is no such law among civilised men. Among the aboriginal savages such a thing may exist; but among civilised men there never can be any dispute but that the father's right to his child is supreme, and that no master and no owner can override the rights of the parent to his son. Come, then; even so are we his, 'He shall see *his* seed.' 'He shall see of the travail of his soul.' If he could lose his glories, if he could be driven from his kingdom, if he could be despoiled of his crown, if his throne could totter, if all his might could melt away as the snow-wreath melts before the summer's sun, yet at least his seed would be his own. No law, human or divine, could unchild the believing child, or unfather Christ, the everlasting Father. So then, it is a great joy to know that each believer may say, in the highest sense: '"I am my Beloved's". I am his child, and he is my parent.' I half wish that instead of my preaching now, we could stand up, each of us who feel the force of this sweet sentiment, and say, ''Tis true, great God; by eternal donation, by complete purchase, by a full surrender, by a mighty conquest, I am my Beloved's. He is my Head, my Husband, my Father, and my All.'

(2) The second sentence in order of time is '*My Beloved is mine*'. Ah! you very poor men and women, you who could not call one foot of land your own, and probably never will till you get the space where you lie down to

sleep the sleep of death! If you can say, 'My Beloved is mine', you have greater wealth than Croesus ever knew, or than a miser ever dreamed. If my soul can claim Christ, the eternal God and the perfect man, as being my own personal property, then my soul is rich to all the intents of bliss, should the body walk in rags, or should the lips know hunger, or the mouth be parched with thirst.

But how is my Beloved mine? He is mine, because *he gave himself to me of old.* Long ere I knew it, or had a being, he covenanted to bestow himself on me – on all his chosen. When he said, 'Lo, I come; in the volume of the Book it is written of me, I delight to do thy will, O God', he did in fact become my substitute, giving himself to do my work and bear my sorrow. Mine he is because *that covenant has been fulfilled* in the *actual* gift. For me (I speak in the first person, because I want you each to speak in the first person too), for thee, my soul, he laid aside his robes of glory to become a man; for thee he was swaddled in the weakness of infancy, and lay in the poverty of the manger; for thee, my soul, he bore the infant body, the childish form, and the human flesh and blood; for thee the poverty which made him cry, 'Foxes have holes, and the birds of the air have nests, but I, the Son of Man, have not where to lay mine head.' For thee, my soul, for thee that shame and spitting, that agony and bloody sweat, that cross, that crown of thorns, those expiring agonies, that dying groan. 'My Beloved', in all this, 'is mine'. Nay, thine the burial; thine the resurrection and its mystic meaning; thine the ascension and its triumphant shouts; thine the session at the right hand of God; yes, and by holy daring we avow it, he who sits today, 'God over all, blessed for ever', is ours in the splendour of his majesty, in the invincibility of his might, in the omnipresence of his power, in all the glory of his future advent. Our beloved is ours, because he has given himself to us, just as he is.

But besides that, our beloved is not only ours by his own gift, which is the bottom of all, but he is ours by *a graciously completed union.* What a wonderful thing is the doctrine of union with Christ. 'We are members of his body, of his flesh, and of his bones. For this cause shall a man leave his father and mother, and shall cleave unto his wife, and they twain shall become one flesh. This is a great mystery, but I speak concerning Christ and the Church.' Christ and his Church are one – one, as the stones are one with the foundation; one, as the branches are one with the vine; one, as the wife is one with the husband; one, as the members are one with the head; one, as the soul is one with the body; nay, if there can be conceived a union closer still, and there is but one, we are one with Christ, even as Christ is one with his Father. 'I in them, and thou in me'; for thus the union stands. Now, as soon as ever we are one with Christ, you see at once that Christ must be ours. There is a common property between Christ and his people. All theirs belongs to him; his belongs to them. They have not two stocks, they have but one. He has cast in his wealth, they have cast in their poverty; from that day they have common funds; they have but one purse, they have all things in common. All he is and all he has is theirs, and all they are or can be belongs to him.

I might add, but this is a high point, and needs to be experienced rather than preached upon, Christ is ours *by his indwelling*. Ignatius used to call himself the God-bearer, and when some wondered at the title he said: 'I carry God about within me; our bodies are the temples of the Holy Ghost.' That is an awful text, awful in the splendour of its meaning. Does the Holy Ghost dwell in a man? Ay, that he does. Not in this temple, 'not in the tabernacles made with hands'; that is to say of man's building, but within this soul, and in your soul, and in the souls of all his called ones, he dwells. 'Abide in me,' said he, 'and I in you.' Christ must be in you, the hope of glory; Christ must be formed in you, as he was in Mary, or you have not come yet to know to the full the divine meaning of the spouse when she said: 'My Beloved is mine, and I am his.'

Now, tonight, I wish that we could get practical good, to our comfort, out of the thought that Christ is ours, if we be believers. Hear me, then, a moment or two, while I dilate upon that thought. Christ is *surely* yours. It is not a questionable property, a matter to be put into dispute with Heaven's chancery; beyond question Christ *is* the property – the rightful heritage – of every elect and called one.

Again: Christ is ours *personally*. We sometimes speak of severally and jointly. Well then, Christ is ours jointly; but, blessed be his name, he is ours severally too. Christ is as much yours tonight, however mean you may be, as though he did not belong to another man living. The whole of Christ is yours; he is not part mine, and part thine, and part another man's. He is all mine, all yours; personally mine, personally yours. Oh that we could realise this fact!

And then, again, Christ is *always* ours. He is never more ours at one time, and less ours at another. The moment we believe in him we may know our perfect and invariable right to Christ – a right which depends not upon the changes of the hour, or upon the temperature of our frames and feelings, but upon those two immutable things wherein it is impossible for God to lie. Christ is ours tonight; and, glory be to his name for it, if we believe he is ours for ever:

This sacred bond shall never break,
  Though earth's old columns bow;
The strong, the feeble, and the weak
  Can claim their Saviour now.

And this they shall do, perhaps with greater joy, but not with greater right, when they stand before the throne of God.

I cannot, tonight, in a place to which I am so little accustomed, bring all my thoughts together as I would; but, methinks if I could but put this truth before you, or rather, if the Spirit of God would put it so that you could *feel* Christ to be yours, it would make you spring from your pew with ecstasy. Why, it is enough to thrill every chord in a man; and if a man may be compared to a harp, make every string in him pour forth an ocean of music. Christ mine – myself Christ's; there cannot be a gladder and more heavenly theme beneath the skies.

I have thus completed the first work of this evening, taking the sentences of the text in the order of time. I shall now take the text **IN THE ORDER IN WHICH IT IS GIVEN TO US, WHICH IS THE ORDER OF OUR EXPERIENCE.**

Do you not see, that to a man's experience God's order is reversed? We begin thus: 'My Beloved is mine'. I go to him, take him up in the arms of my faith, as Simeon took up the little child in the temple, and pressing him to my heart, I say: 'Jesus, thou art mine. All unholy and unclean, I nevertheless obey thy command; I believe thee; I take thee at thy word; I touch the hem of thy garment; I trust my soul wholly with thee; thou art mine, and my soul can never part with thee.' What next? Why then the soul afterwards says: 'Now I am thine, tell me what thou wouldst have me to do. Jesus, let me abide with thee. Lord, I would follow thee whithersoever thou goest; put me on any service; dictate to me any commandment; tell me what thou wouldst have me to do to glorify thee?'

Through floods, through flames, if Jesus lead,
I'll follow where he goes.

For I am his. Christ is mine – this is faith. I am his – this is good works. Christ is mine: that is the simple way in which the soul is saved. I am Christ's: that is the equally simple method by which salvation displays itself in its practical fruits. I am afraid some of you have never carried out the last sentence, 'I am Christ's.' I know some, for instance, who believe (mark, I am not speaking to those who do not) who believe it to be the duty of every Christian to profess his faith in baptism, and are nevertheless not baptised. They say they are Baptists in principle. They are Baptists without any principle at all. They are men who know their Master's will, and do it not; and they shall surely be beaten with many stripes. In other men it becomes a sin of ignorance; but with such men it is wilful. They reply, 'It is a non-essential.' Things non-essential to salvation are nevertheless essential to obedience. As I said a few Sabbaths ago, you would not like a servant who only did what he liked to do, and told you that some of your commands were non-essential. I am quite certain that if a soldier did not load his gun, or stand in rank, or shoulder arms at the word of command, the court-martial would never listen for an instant to the plea of non-essential. God's commands require obedience, and it is essential that every servant be found faithful. I say, it is exceedingly essential to a Christian to do what he is told to do. Whatever Jesus bids us do, if it save us not from anything else, at any rate the fulfilment of it will save us from the sin of being disobedient to him.

Now will you try, my dear friends, not in the one command only, which lies at the threshold of the house, but in all others, to feel that you are not your own? 'Ah!' says one man, 'I am not my own, I have so much to do for my family'; another, 'I am not my own, I belong to a political party'; another, 'I am not my own, I belong to a firm'. Just so: all these are ways in which men are kept from saying, 'I am my Beloved's, and my Beloved is mine.' Oh that we could, by any means whatever, feel that we were all Christ's! If I thought I had a drop of blood in my veins that was not his, I would seek to have it let out; and if there were a single power I have, mental, physical, or spiritual, which could not and would not serve God, though it might impair my comfort, I would devoutly pray that this Jonah might be thrown into the sea, this Achan stoned with stones, this Haman hanged on the gallows. This cankered thing, this deadly thing, this damnable thing must be cut away once for all, for 'better to enter into heaven halt and maimed, than having two eyes and two arms to be cast into hell-fire'. We must have a single eye; we must feel that we are all Christ's, and live as if we were all Christ's; for we have no right to say, 'My Beloved is mine', unless we can add, 'And I am his'. Why look, sirs, look at the great multitude of professors. How few there are that ever live as if they belonged to Christ! They act independently of *him*; they buy, they sell, on their own account; that they are stewards never penetrates their thick brain; that all they have is not their own, but his, never seems to have come into their heart, though they have sung it with their lips:

And if I might make some reserve,
  And duty did not call,
I love my God with zeal so great,
  That I would give him all.

Many a man has sung that, with his thumb-nail going round a coin in his purse, to find out whether it was a fourpenny or a threepenny bit. He says he would give Christ all; but then he means that the bill is to be drawn at the very last credit, and he will pay when he dies: he will give up what he cannot take away with him, and when he leaves his rotten carcase he will leave his rotten wealth. Oh that we could all feel that we were all Christ's!

Why, the Church of God would not be penned and shut up within the narrow bounds of England and America long, if once we felt we were Christ's. At this very moment China is opened to Christian enterprise. The leader of the so-called 'rebels' turns out to be, after all, a man who is exceedingly enlightened in the things of God. He has said to Mr Roberts, the missionary, 'I open today eighteen chapels in Nankin; write to your friends, and tell them to come over and preach, and we will be glad to hear them. I give you a passport, that no man may touch you, and any man who will preach Christ's gospel shall go unharmed through my dominions'; and he actually issued, but a few days before the coming of the last mail, a proclamation by which all idolatry is abolished throughout his dominions, and witchcraft and fortune-telling are made crimes, and he invites and prays his brethren in England especially to send over the Word of life, that they may have it among the people.

Now, I do honestly avow, if this place had not been built, and I had had nothing beyond the narrow bounds of the place in which I have lately preached, I should have felt in my conscience bound to go to learn the language and preach the Word there; but I now know what to do. I *must* here abide, for this is *my* place; but I would to God some were found in the Church, some in London, who have not such a gracious tie as this to keep them in their own land, to say, 'Here am I, send me; I am Christ's man; there is Christ's field; let me go and reap it, for the harvest is ripe; help me, O God, and I will seek to ingather it for thine honour.' 'My Beloved is mine and I am his.' That last 'I am his' would make life cheap, and blood like water and heroism a common thing, and daring but an everyday duty, and self-sacrifice the very spirit of the Christian life. Learn well, then, the meaning of that sentence, '*I am his.*'

But will you please to notice once again – (I fear lest I shall weary you, and therefore will be brief) 'My Beloved is mine' – that is my calling. He calls me to him. He gives himself to me; he is mine. I am his – that is my election. I was his before I knew him to be mine; but I learned my calling first, and my election afterwards. We have scores of people who will not come to Christ, because they cannot understand election. Meet a boy in the street, and invite him to go to a two-penny school. 'No,' says the boy, 'I don't feel fit to go to a national school to learn to read and write; for, to tell you the truth, I don't understand the Hebrew language.' You would reply, 'But, my good lad, you will learn Hebrew afterwards, if you can; but that is no reason, at any rate, why you should not learn English first. Come first to the little school; you shall go afterwards to the grammar school; if you get on, you shall go to the University, take your BA degree, and perhaps come out as a Master of Arts.' But here we have poor souls that want to be MAs before they have gone to the penny school. They want to read the tomes before they will read the horn-book. They are not content to spell ABC – 'I am a sinner, Christ is a saviour' – but they long to turn over the book of decrees, and find out the deep things of God. You shall find them out afterwards; you shall go step by step, while the master shall say to you, each time, 'Friend, come up higher.' But if you begin with election, you will have to come down again: for there will be a more honourable man than you, who will come in, and you will begin with shame to take the lowest room. I have seen plenty of high-flying Christians, who began at the top of the tree; they were *the* men; wisdom would die with them; the judges, the dictators, the very consuls, the cardinals, the popes; they knew everything; and whenever such men are gracious men, the Lord always puts the lancet into them, and makes them grow smaller, and smaller, and smaller, till at last they say, 'Woe is me, for I am undone'; and they cry, 'My soul is even as a weaned child.' Begin at the bottom, and grow up; but do not begin at the top and come down. That is hard work; but going up is pleasant work, joyous work. Begin by saying, 'My Beloved is mine'; you shall come to know your election bye-and-bye, and say, 'I am his.'

And now I do not think I will preach any longer about my text, but just come down upon my hearers for a few minutes, with all my might. How many among us can dare to say this tonight? Hundreds of you can; thousands of you can. If this were the day of judgment – if tonight you stood, fresh risen from your graves – if now you heard the trumpet sound – if now you saw the King in his beauty sitting upon the great white throne, I know that many of you would say, 'My beloved is mine, and I am his'. If this day the millenial reign of Christ had begun – if the vials had been opened, the plagues poured out, and if now Christ were come, that the wicked might be driven out and that his saints might reign – I am sure there are many of you who would say, 'Welcome, welcome, Son of God; my Beloved is mine, and I am his'; and there are many of you, too, who if the angel of death should pass the pew, and flap his black wing into your face, and the cold air of death should smite you, would say, ''Tis well, for my Beloved is mine, and I am his.' You could shut your eyes and your ears to the joys and to the music of earth, and you could open them to the splendours and melodies of heaven. To be fearless of death should always be the mark of the Christian. Sometimes a sudden alarm may rob us of our presence of mind; but no believer is in a healthy state, if he be not ready to meet death at any hour and at any moment. To walk bravely into the jaws of the dragon – to go through the iron gates, and to feel no terror – to be ready to shake hand with the skeleton king, to look on him as a friend, and no more a foe – this should be the habitual spirit and the constant practice of the heir of heaven. Oh! if this be written on my soul, 'My Beloved is mine, and I am his', come, welcome death!

Come, death, and some celestial band,
I'll gladly go with you.

But – and a solemn – 'but' – pass the question round these galleries, and in this area, and how many among you must say, 'I never thought of that. I never thought whether I was Christ's, or Christ mine.' I will not rebuke you tonight. I will not thunder at you. God's grace to me forbids that *this* should be a day of thunder. Let it be a day of feasting to every one, and of sorrow to none. What shall I say to you, then, but this? O that Christ *may* be yours. When he was here on earth he chose to go among sinners – sinners of the blackest hue; and now he is in heaven, up yonder he loves sinners as much as ever he did. He is as willing to receive you tonight, as to receive the thief. It will give as much joy to his heart to hear your cry tonight, as when he thanked God that these things were revealed unto babes. It is to his honour that you should be his; it is to his joy that he should be yours. Sinner! if thou wilt have Christ – if now the Spirit of God makes thee willing – there is no bar on God's part, when the bar is taken away on thine. If thou art willing, he is more willing than thou art. If the gate of thy heart be on the latch, the gate of heaven is wide open. If thy soul do but yearn after Christ, his bowels have long yearned after you. If you have but a spark of love to Christ, he has a furnace of love to you. And if you have none at all – no love, no faith – oh! may you have it now! 'Believe in the Lord Jesus Christ, and you shall be saved.' *You*; *yes*, *you*!

Did you come here out of curiosity? Zaccheus heard Christ out of curiosity; but he was saved. Did you come for worse purpose? God bless you, anyhow, for whatever you came; and may he bring you to himself tonight! Trust Christ now and you are saved. My life for yours; if you perish trusting in Christ I will perish too. Even should I have an ear listening to me which belongs to a harlot, to a thief, to a murderer, yet 'he that believeth in the Lord Jesus Christ shall be saved'; and if you believe in him, and you are lost, I will be lost with you; and the whole Church of Christ must be lost too; for there is the same way to heaven for the best as for the worst – for the vilest as for the most righteous. 'No man cometh unto the Father but by Christ.' Nothing can damn a man but his own righteousness; nothing can save him but the righteousness of Christ. All your sin – your past sin – shall not destroy you; if you now believe in Jesus, it shall be cast into the sea for ever, and you shall begin again as though you had never sinned; his grace shall keep you for the future, and you shall hold on your way, an honour to Christ's grace, and a joy to your own soul. But if ye be disobedient, and will not eat of the good of the land, then will I say, as Esaias said of old, 'I am found of them that sought me not, but all day long have I stretched out my hands to an ungodly and gainsaying generation.' God *has* stretched out his hands. Oh that ye were wise, and would run into his arms tonight!

I know I am speaking to some self-righteous men – some who say, 'It is a shame to tell men they are depraved. *I* am not.' Well, we think, if their lives were written it might be proved they were. 'It is a shame,' they say, 'to tell men that they cannot get to heaven by their good works, because then they will be wicked.' It is an odd thing, though, that the more this truth is preached, the better people are. Preaching good works as the way to heaven always makes drunkards and thieves; but preaching faith in Christ always produces the best effects. Dr Chalmers, who was no fanatic, says, 'When I preached mere morality, I preached sobriety till they were all drunkards; I preached chastity till it was not known any where; I preached honesty till men grew to be thieves'; but, he says, 'as soon as ever I preached Christ there was such a change in the village as never was known.' Well, we believe that self-righteousness will destroy you, my friend, and we therefore tell you, honestly and plainly, that you might as well hope to get to heaven by flying up in a balloon, as to get there by your own good works. You may as soon sail to India in a sieve as get to glory by your own goodness. You might as well go to court in cobwebs as seek to go to heaven in your own righteousness. Away with your rags, your filthy, rotten rags. They are only a harbour for the parasites of unbelief and pride. Away with your rotten righteousness, your counterfeit gold, your forged wealth. It is of nothing worth whatever in the sight of God. Come to him, empty, poor, naked! It grates on your proud ear, does it? Better, I say, to lose your pride, than to lose your soul! Why be damned for pride's sake? Why carry your head so high that it must needs be cut off? Why feed your pride on your soul's blood? Surely there is cheaper stuff than that for pride to drink? Why let it suck the very marrow out of your bones? Be wise! Bow, stoop, stoop to be saved. And now, in the name of Jesus of Nazareth, the man, the God, I do command you, as his messenger and his servant, and at your peril reject the command – 'Believe, repent, and be baptized, every one of you.' 'Believe in the Lord Jesus Christ, and you shall be saved'; 'for he that believeth and is baptized shall be saved; he that believeth not shall be damned.'

God add his blessing, for his name's sake. Amen.

18

A SONG AMONG THE LILIES

'My beloved is mine, and I am his: he feedeth among the lilies' (Song of Solomon 2:16).

Last Sabbath, in our morning's sermon,[1] we began at the beginning and described the turning point in which the sinner sets his face towards his God, and for the first time gives practical evidence of spiritual life in his soul. He bestirs himself, he goes to his Father's house, and speedily is pressed to his Father's bosom, forgiven, accepted, and rejoiced over. This morning we are going far beyond that stage, to a position which I may call the very crown and summit of the spiritual life. We would conduct you from the door-step to the innermost chamber, from the outer court to the Holy of Holies; and we pray the Holy Spirit to enable each one of us who have entered in by Christ Jesus, the door, to pass boldly into the secret place of the tabernacles of the Most High, and sing with joyful heart the words of our text, 'My beloved is mine, and I am his.'

For he is mine and I am his,
The God whom I adore;
My Father, Saviour, Comforter,
Now and for evermore.

This passage describes a high state of grace, and it is worthy of note that the description is full of Christ. This is instructive, for this is not an exceptional case, it is only one fulfilment of a general rule. Our estimate of Christ is the best gauge of our spiritual condition; as the thermometer rises in proportion to the increased warmth of the air, so does our estimate of Jesus rise as our spiritual life increases in vigour and fervency. Tell me what you think of Jesus and I will tell you what to think of yourself. Christ is all to us, yea, more than all when we are thoroughly sanctified and filled with the Holy Ghost. When pride of self fills up the soul, there is little room for Jesus; but when Jesus is fully loved, self is subdued, and sin driven out of the throne. If we think little of the Lord Jesus we have very great cause to account ourselves spiritually blind, and naked, and poor, and miserable. The rebel despises his lawful sovereign, but the favoured courtier is enthusiastic in his praise. Christ crucified is the revealer of many hearts, the touchstone by which the pure gold and the counterfeit metal are discerned; his very name is as a refiner's fire and like fuller's soap; false professors cannot endure it, but true believers triumph therein. We are growing in grace when we grow in the knowledge of our Lord and Saviour Jesus

Christ. Let everything else be gone and let Christ fill up the entire space of our soul, then, and only then, are we rising out of the vanity of the flesh into the real life of God.

Beloved, the grandest facts in all the world to a truly spiritual man are not the rise and fall of empires, the marches of victory, or the desolations of defeat; he cares neither for crowns nor mitres, swords nor shields; his admiring gaze is wholly fixed upon Christ and his cross and cause. To him Jesus is the centre of history, the soul and core of providence. He desires no knowledge so much as that which concerns his Redeemer and Lord; his science deals with what Jesus is and what he is to be, what he has done, what he is doing, and what he will do. The believer is mainly anxious as to how Jesus can be glorified and how sinners can be brought to know him. That which concerns the honour of Jesus is our chief concern from day to day; as for other matters let the Lord do as he wills with them, only let Jesus Christ be magnified, and all the rest of the world's story has small significance for us. The Beloved is the head and front, the heart and soul of the Christian's delight when his heart is in its best state. Our text is the portrait of a heavenly-minded child of God, or rather, it is the music of his well stringed harp when love as minstrel touches the tenderest chords: 'My beloved is mine, and I am his; he feedeth among the lilies.'

We shall note then, first, that here is *a delighting to have Christ*; secondly, *a delighting to belong to Christ*; and thirdly, *a delighting at the very thought of Christ.*

First, here is A DELIGHTING TO HAVE CHRIST. *'My beloved is mine.'* The spouse makes this the first of her joy notes, the cornerstone of her peace, the fountain of her bliss, the crown of her glory. Observe here that where such an expression is truthfully used the existence *of the Beloved is a matter of fact.* Scepticism and questioning have no place with those who thus sing. There are dreamers nowadays who cast doubt on everything; taking to themselves the name of philosophers, and professing to know something of science, they make statements worthy only of idiots, and demand for the self-evidently false assertions the assent of rational men. The word 'philosopher' will soon come to mean a lover of ignorance, and the term 'a scientific man' will be understood as meaning a fool, who has said in his heart there is no God. Such attacks upon the eternal verities of our holy faith can have no effect upon hearts enamoured of the Son of God, for, dwelling in his immediate presence, they have passed the stage of doubt, left the region of questioning far behind, and in this matter have entered into rest. The power of love has convinced us; to entertain a doubt as to the reality and glory of our Well-beloved would be torment to us, and therefore love has cast it out. We use no perhapses, buts, or ifs concerning our Beloved, but we say positively that he is, and that he is ours. We believe that we have better evidence of his being, power, Godhead, and love to us than can be given for any other fact. So far from being abashed by the cavils of sceptics, or quailing beneath the question, 'Is there such a Beloved?', we are not careful to answer in this matter, for we know that there is; our love laughs at the question, and does not condescend to answer it save by bidding those who seriously inquire to 'come and see' for themselves.

We have ever found, beloved, that when a time of chilling doubt has come over us – and such ague fits will come – we have only to return to meditations upon Jesus and he becomes his own evidence by making our hearts burn within us with love of his character and person, and then doubt is doomed. We do not slay our unbelief by reason, but we annihilate it by affection. The influence of love to Jesus upon the soul is so magical – I wish I had a better word – so elevating, so ravishing, so transporting, it gives such a peace, and withal inspires such holy and lofty aspirations, that the effect proves the cause. That which is holy is true, and that which is true cannot rise out of that which is false. We may safely judge a tree by its fruit, and a doctrine by its result: that which produces in us self-denial, purity, righteousness, and truth cannot itself be false, and yet the love of Jesus does this beyond everything else. There must be truth for a cause where truth is the effect; and thus love, by the savour which it spreads over the soul by contemplation of Christ, puts its foot upon the neck of doubt and triumphantly utters bold, confident declarations, which reveal the full assurance of faith. New-born love to Jesus, while yet in its cradle, like a young Hercules, takes the serpents of doubt and strangles them. He who can say from his heart 'My Beloved' is the man who is in the way to confirmed faith. Love cannot, will not doubt; it casts away the crutches of argument and flies on the wings of conscious enjoyment, singing her nuptial hymn, 'My Beloved is mine, and I *am* his.'

In the case before us *the love of the heavenly-minded one is perceived and acknowledged by herself.* '*My* beloved,' saith she; it is no latent affection, she knows that she loves him, and solemnly avows it. She does not whisper, 'I hope I love the peerless one', but she sings, '*My* beloved.' There is no doubt in her soul about her passion for the altogether lovely one. Ah, dear friends, when you feel the flame of love within your soul, and give it practical expression, you will no longer inquire, 'Do I love the Lord or no?' Then your inner consciousness will dispense with evidences. Those are dark days when we require evidences; well may we then fast, for the Bridegroom is not with us; but when he abides with us, enjoyment of his fellowship supersedes all evidences. I want no evidence to prove that food is sweet when it is still in my mouth; I want no evidence of the existence of the sun when I am basking in his beams, and enjoying his light, and even so we need no evidence that Jesus is precious to us when, like a bundle of myrrh, he perfumes our bosom. We are anxious doubters as to our safety, and questioners of our own condition, because we are not living with Jesus as we ought to be; but when he brings us to his banqueting house, and we walk in the light as he is in the light, we have fellowship with him and with the Father, and then we believe and are sure, and our love to Jesus is indisputable, because it burns within too fervently to be denied. Why, when a Christian is in a right state, his love to Jesus is the mightiest force in his nature, it is an affection which, like Aaron's rod, swallows up all other rods; it is the mainspring of his action, and sways his whole body, soul, and spirit. As the wind sweeps over all the strings of the Æolian harp, and causes them to vibrate, so does the love of Jesus move every power and passion of our soul, and we feel in our entire being that our Beloved is indeed ours, and that we love him with all our hearts. Here, then, is the Beloved realised, and our love realised too.

But the pith of the text lies here, *our possession of him is proven*, we know it, and we know it on good evidence – 'My beloved *is mine.*' You know it is not a very easy thing to reach this point. Have you ever thought of the fact that to claim the Lord and call him 'my God', is a very wonderful thing? Who was the first man in the Old Testament who is recorded as saying 'My God'? Was it not Jacob, when he slept at Bethel, and saw the ladder which reached to heaven? Even after that heavenly vision it took him much effort to reach to 'My God'. He said, 'If God will be with me and will keep me in the way that I go, and will give me bread to eat and raiment to put on, so that I come again to my father's house in peace, then shall the LORD be my God.' Only after long experience of divine goodness could he climb up to the height of saying 'My God'. And who is the first man in the New Testament that calls Jesus 'My Lord and my God'? It was Thomas, and he must needs have abundant proofs before he can speak thus: 'Except I see in his hands the print of the nails, and put my finger into the print of the nails, and thrust my hand into his side, I will not believe.' Only when he had received such proofs could he exclaim 'My Lord and my God'. Blessed are they who reach it by simpler faith, who have not seen and yet have believed.

'*My* Beloved' is a strong expression. 'Beloved' is sweet, but 'MY Beloved' is sweetest of all. If you think of it, it is no little thing to claim God as ours, to claim Jesus the Beloved as ours, yea, to put in the singular and call him *mine*; and yet, when the believer's heart is in the right condition, he makes the claim, and is warranted in so doing; for Jesus Christ is the portion of all believers. His Father gave him to us, and he has given himself to us. Jesus was made over to every believing soul, as his personal possession, in the eternal covenant ordered in all things and sure; Jesus actually gave himself for us in his incarnation, becoming bone of our bone and flesh of our flesh; he has made himself ours by his passion and death, loving us and giving himself for us, to save us from our sins; he has also given us power to appropriate him by the gracious gift of faith, by which we are in very deed married to him, and are enabled to call him the husband of our souls, who is ours to have and to hold, for better for worse, for life and for death, by a bond of marriage union which neither death nor hell, time nor eternity, can break. Jesus is ours by the promise, the covenant, and oath of God; a thousand assurances and pledges, bonds and seals, secure him to us as our portion and everlasting heritage.

This precious possession becomes to the believer his sole treasure. 'My beloved is mine,' saith he, and in that sentence he has summed up all his wealth. He does not say, 'My wife, my children, my home, my earthly comforts are mine'; he is almost afraid to say so, because while he is yet speaking, they may cease to be his: the beloved wife may sicken before his eyes, the child may need a tiny coffin, the friend may prove a traitor, and the riches may take to themselves wings; therefore the wise man does not care to say too positively that anything here below is his; indeed, he feels that in very truth they are not his, but only lent to him 'to be returned anon'; but the Beloved is his own, and his possession of him is most firm. Neither doth the believer when his soul is in the best state so much rejoice even in his spiritual privileges as in the Lord from whom they come. He has righteousness, wisdom, sanctification and redemption; he has both grace and glory secured to him, but he prefers rather to claim the fountain than the streams. He clearly sees that these choice mercies are only his because they are Christ's, and only his because Christ is his. Oh, what would all the treasures of the covenant be to us if it were possible to have them without Christ? Their very sap and sweetness would be gone. Having our Beloved to be ours, we have all things in him, and therefore our main treasure, yea, our sole treasure, is our Beloved. O ye saints of God, was there ever possession like this? You have your beloveds, ye daughters of earth, but what are your beloveds compared with ours? He is the Son of God and the Son of Man! The darling of heaven and the delight of earth! The lily of the valley and the rose of Sharon! Perfect in his character, powerful in his atoning death, mighty in his living plea! He is such a lover that all earthly loves put together are not worthy to touch the hem of his garment, or loose the latchet of his shoes. He is so dear, so precious, that words cannot describe him nor pencil depict him, but this we will say of him, he is 'the chief among ten thousand, and the altogether lovely', and he is ours. Do you wonder that we glory in this fact, and count this the crowning delight of our lives, 'My beloved is mine'?

The very tenure upon which we hold this priceless possession is a matter to glory in. O worldlings, you cannot hold your treasures as we hold ours.

If you knew all, you would never say of anything, 'It is mine', for your holding is too precarious to constitute possession. It is yours till that frail thread of life shall snap, or that bubble of time shall burst. You have only a leasehold of your treasures, terminable at the end of one frail life; whereas ours is an eternal freehold, an everlasting entail. 'My beloved is mine' – I cannot lose him, nor can he be taken from me; he is mine for ever, for 'who shall separate us from the love of God which is in Christ Jesus our Lord'? So that, while the possession is rare, the tenure is rare also, and it is the life of our life, and the light of our delight that we can sing:

Yea, thou art mine, my blessèd Lord,
O my Belovèd, thou art mine!
And, purchased with thy precious blood,
My God and Saviour, I am thine.

My Christ! Oh, sing it in the heavens,
Let every angel lift his voice;
Sound with ten thousand harps his praise,
With me, ye heavenly hosts, rejoice.

The gift unspeakable is given,
The grace of God has made him mine;
And, now, before both earth and heaven,
Lord, I will own that I am thine.

Now, beloved friends, I cannot talk about this as I feel, I can only give you hints of that which fills me to the full with joy. I beg you to contemplate for a single moment the delight which is stored up in this fact, that the blessed Son of God, the 'brightness of the Father's glory', is all our own. Whatever else we may have, or may not have, he is ours. I may not exhibit in my character all the grace I could wish, but 'My beloved is mine'; I may have only one talent, but 'My beloved is mine'; I may be very poor and very obscure, but 'My beloved is mine'; I may have neither health nor wealth, but 'My beloved is mine'; I may not be what I want to be, but 'My beloved is mine'. Yea, he is altogether mine, his Godhead and his manhood, his life, his death, his attributes, and prerogatives, yea, all he is, all he was, all he ever will be, all he has done, and all he ever will do, is mine. I possess not a portion in Christ, but the whole of him. All his saints own him, but I own him as much as if there were never another saint to claim him. Child of God, do you see this? In other inheritances, if there are many heirs, there is so much the less for each, but in this great possession every one who has Christ has a whole Christ all to himself, from the head of much fine gold, down to his legs, which are as pillars of marble. The whole of his boundless heart of love, his whole arm of infinite might, and his whole head of matchless wisdom – all is for thee, beloved. Whoever thou mayst be, if thou dost indeed trust in Jesus, he is all thine own.

My beloved is all mine, and absolutely mine; not mine to look at and talk about merely, but mine to trust in, to speak to, to depend upon, to fly to in every troublous hour, yea, mine to feed upon, for his flesh is meat indeed, and his blood is drink indeed. Our beloved is not ours only to use in certain ways, but ours outright, without restriction. I may draw what I will from him, and both what I take and what I leave are mine. He himself in his ever glorious person is mine, and mine always. Mine when I know it, and mine when I do not know it; mine when I am sure of it, and mine when I doubt it; mine by day, and mine by night; mine when I walk in holiness, ay, and mine when I sin, for 'if any man sin we have an advocate with the Father, Jesus Christ the righteous'. He is mine on the hill Mizar, and mine in the swellings of Jordan; mine by the grave where I bury those I love, mine when I shall be buried there myself, mine when I rise again; mine in judgment, and mine in glory; for ever mine.

Note well that it is written, 'My beloved is *mine*', in the singular. He is yours, I am glad of it; but still to me it is most sweet that he is mine. It is well to bless God that others have a possession in Christ, but what would that avail if we were strangers to him ourselves? The marrow and the fatness lie in the personal pronoun singular, '*My* beloved is *mine.*' 'I am so glad that Jesus loves *me.*' Oh for a blessed grip with both hands on such a Christ as this! Observe well that he is ours *as our Beloved*, so that he is ours as whatever our love makes of him. Our love can never praise him enough, or speak well enough of him, she thinks all descriptions fall short of his deservings; well, then, Jesus is ours at his best; if we think him so glorious, he is ours in all that glory. Our love says that he is a fair, lovely, sweet, and precious Christ, and let us be sure that, however lovely, sweet, and precious he is, he is all ours. Our love says there is none like him, he is King of kings and Lord of lords, he is the ever blessed; well, as the King of kings and Lord of lords he is yours. You cannot think too much of him, but when you think your best he is yours at that best. He has not a glory so high that it is not yours, nor a lustre so brilliant that it is not yours. He is my beloved, and I would fain extol him, but never can I get beyond this golden circle, when I most extol him he is still mine.

Here, then, is the basis of Christian life, the foundation on which it rests: to know that most surely Christ is altogether ours is the beginning of wisdom, the source of strength, the star of hope, the dawn of heaven.

The second portion of the text deals with DELIGHTING TO BELONG TO CHRIST. '*I am his.*' This is as sweet as the former sentence. I would venture to put a question to each loving wife here present – when you were married which was the sweetest thought to you, that you were your husband's, or that he was yours? Why, you feel that neither sentence would be sweet alone: they are necessary to each other. Ask any fond, loving heart which of these declarations could best be parted with, and they will tell you that neither can be given up. Christ is mine, but if I were not his it would be a sorry case, and if I were his and he were not mine it would be a wretched business. These two things are joined together with diamond rivets – 'My beloved is mine, and I am his.' Put the two together, and you have reached the summit of delight.

That we are his is a fact that may be proven – yea, it should need no proving, but be manifest to all that 'I am *his*'. Certainly we are his by creation: he who made us should have us. We are his because his Father gave us to him, and we are his because he chose us. Creation, donation, election are his triple hold upon us. We are his because he bought us with his blood, his because he called us by his grace, his because he is married to us, and we are his spouse. We are his, moreover, to our consciousness, because we have heartily, from the inmost depths of our being, given ourselves up to him, bound by love to him for ever. We feel we must have Christ, and be Christ's, or die – 'For me to live is Christ.' Brethren and sisters, mind you attend to this clause; I am sure you will if the former one is true to you. If you can say, 'My beloved is mine', you will be sure to add, 'I am his, I must be his, I will be his: I live not unless I am his, for I count that wherein I am not his I am dead, and I only live wherein I live to him.' My very soul is conscious that I am his.

Now this puts very great honour upon us. I have known the time when I could say, 'My beloved is mine' in a very humble trembling manner, but I did not dare to add 'I am his' because I did not think I was worth his having. I dared not hope that 'I am his' would ever be written in the same book side by side with 'My beloved is mine'. Poor sinner, first lay hold on Jesus, and then you will discover that Jesus values you. You will prize him first, and then you will find out that he prizes you, and that though you do not feel worthy to be flung on a dunghill, yet Jesus has put a value upon you, saying, 'Since thou wert precious in my sight thou hast been honourable, and I have loved thee.' It is no small joy to know that we poor sinners are worth Christ's having, and that he has even said, 'They shall be mine in the day when I make up my jewels.'

This second part of the text is true as *absolutely* as the first. 'I am his' – not my goods only, nor my time, nor my talents, nor what I can spare, but '*I* am his'. I fear that some Christians have never understood this. They give the Lord a little of their surplus, which they never miss. The poor widow who gave all her living, had the true idea of her relation to her Lord. She would have put herself into the treasury if she could, for she felt 'I am his'.

As for myself, I wish I could be dropped bodily through the little slit of Christ's treasure box, and be in his casket for ever, never to be heard of any more as my own, but to be wholly my Lord's. Paul desired to spend and be spent. It is not easy to do those two things distinctly with money, for when you spend a thing it is spent at one and the same time, but the apostle meant that he would spend himself by activity, and then when he could do no more, he would be glad to be spent by passive endurance for Christ's sake. The believer feels that he belongs to Jesus absolutely; let the Lord employ him as he may, or try him as he pleases; let him take away all earthly friends from him or surround him with comforts; let him either depress him or exalt him, let him use him for little things or great things, or not use him at all, but lay him on the shelf; it is enough that the Lord does it, and the true heart is content, for it truthfully confesses, 'I am his. I have not mortgage or lien upon myself, so that I can call a part of my being my own, but I am absolutely and unreservedly my Lord's sole property.' Do you feel this, brethren and sisters? I pray God you may.

Blessed be God, this is true *evermore* – 'I am his'; his today, in the house of worship, and his tomorrow in the house of business; his as a singer in the sanctuary, and his as a toiler in the workshop; his when I am preaching, and equally his when I am walking the streets; his while I live, his when I die; his when my soul ascends and my body lies mouldering in the grave; the whole personality of my manhood is altogether his for ever and ever.

This belonging to the Well-beloved is a matter of fact and practice, not a thing to be talked about only, but really to be acted on. I am treading on tender ground now, but I would to God that every Christian could really say this without lying: 'I do live unto Christ in all things, for I am his. When I rise in the morning I wake up as his, when I sit down to a meal I eat as his, and drink as his. I eat, and drink, and sleep unto the Lord, in everything giving thanks unto him.' It is blessed even to sleep as the Lord's beloved, to dream as his Abrahams and Jacobs do, to awake at night and sing like David, and then drop off to 'sleep in Jesus'. 'It is a high condition,' say you. I grant it, but it is where we ought to abide. The whole of our time and energy should be consecrated by this great master principle, '*I am his*.' Can you say it? Never rest till you can. And if you can, beloved, it involves great privilege. 'I am his', then am I honoured by having such an owner. If a horse or a sheep is said to belong to the Queen, everybody thinks much of it: now you are not the Queen's, but you are the Lord's, and that is far more. Through belonging to Christ you are safe, for he will surely keep his own. He will not lose his own sheep, he paid too dear a price for them to lose them. Against all the powers of earth and hell the Redeemer will hold his own and keep them to the end. If you are his he will provide for you. A good husband careth for his spouse, and even thus the Lord Jesus Christ cares for those who are betrothed unto him. You will be perfected too, for whatever Christ has he will make worthy of himself and bring it to glory. It is because we are his that we shall get to heaven, for he has said, 'Father, I will that they also whom thou hast given me be with me where I am.' Because they are his he would have them with him.

Now, give your thoughts licence to wonder that any one of us should be able to say, 'I am his.' 'I who used to be so giddy and thoughtless, so sceptical, and perhaps profane, I am his.' Ay, and some of you can say, 'I who used to be passionate and proud, I who was a drunkard, I whose lips were black with blasphemy, I am his.' Glory be unto thee, O Jesus Christ, for this, that thou hast taken up such worthless things as we are and made us thine. No longer do we belong to this present evil world, we live for the world to come. We do not even belong to the church, so as to make it our master; we are part of the flock, but like all the rest we belong to the Great Shepherd. We will not give ourselves up to any party, or become the slave of any denomination, for we belong to Christ. We do not belong to sin, or self, or Satan; we belong entirely, exclusively, and irrevocably to the Lord Jesus Christ. Another master waits upon us and asks us to give our energies to his services, but our answer is, 'I am already engaged.' 'How is that?' 'I bear in my body the marks of the Lord Jesus, and therefore from henceforth trouble me no more.' 'But can you not serve me in part?' 'No, sir, I cannot serve two masters; I am not like a man who can do as he pleases, I have no time to call my own.' 'How is that?' 'I belong to Christ, I am wholly his. If there is anything to be done for him I am his man to the best of my ability; I decline no service to which he calls me, but I can serve no other Lord.' Lord Jesus, help each one of us now to say:

I am thine, and thine alone,
This I gladly, fully own;
And in all my works and ways,
Only now would seek thy praise.

To conclude: the saint feels DELIGHT IN THE VERY THOUGHT OF CHRIST. '*He feedeth among the lilies*.' When we love any persons, and we are away from home, we delight to think of them, and to remember what they are doing. You are a husband travelling in a foreign land; this morning you said to yourself, 'At this time they are just getting up at home.' Perhaps the time is different, for you are in another longitude, and you say to yourself, 'Ah, now the dear children are just getting ready to go to the Sabbath-school'; and by-and-by you think they are at dinner. So delight in the thought of Christ made the church say, 'He feedeth among the lilies.' She was pleased to think of where he was and what he was doing.

Now, where is Jesus? What are these lilies? Do not these lilies represent the pure in heart, with whom Jesus dwells? The spouse used the imagery which her Lord had put into her mouth. He said, 'As the lily among thorns, so is my love among the daughters', and she appropriates the symbol to all the saints. A preacher who is great at spiritualising has well said on this verse, 'The straight stalk, standing up erect from the earth, its flowers as high from the ground as possible, do they not tell us of heavenly-mindedness? Do they not seem to say, "Set your affection on things above, not on things on the earth"? And if the spotless snow of the leaves teaches us of grace, then the gold of the anthers tells us of that crown which shall be the reward of grace.' The violet and the primrose in spring nestle close to the earth, as if in sympathy with her chill condition, but the lily lifts up itself towards heaven in sympathy with the summer's light and splendour. The lily is frail, and such are the saints of God; were not Jesus among them to protect them the wild beast would soon tread them down. Frail as they are, they are surpassing lovely, and their beauty is not that which is made with hands. It is a beauty put upon them by the Lord, for 'they toil not, neither do they spin, yet Solomon in all his glory was not arrayed like one of these.' The saints work not for life, and spin no righteousness of their own, and yet the royal righteousness which adorns them far surpasses all that wisdom could devise or wealth procure.

Where, then, is my Lord today? He is up and away, among the lilies of Paradise. In imagination I see those stately rows of milk-white lilies growing no longer among thorns: lilies which are never soiled with the dust of earth, which for ever glisten with the eternal dews of fellowship, while their roots drink in unfading life from the river of the water of life which waters the garden of the Lord. There is Jesus! Can you see him? He is fairer even than the lilies which bow their heads around him. But he is here too where we are, like lilies which have scarce opened yet, lily buds as yet, but still watered by the same river, and yielding in our measure the same perfume. O ye lilies of Christ's own planting, he is among you; Jesus is in this house today, the unction which has made his garments so fragrant is discerned among us.

But *what is he doing* among the lilies? It is said, 'He feedeth among the lilies.' He is feeding himself, not *on* the lilies, but *among* them. Our Lord finds solace among his people. His delights are with the sons of men; he joys to see the graces of his people, to receive their love, and to discern his own image in their faces. As he said to the woman of Samaria, 'Give me to drink', so does he say to each one of his people, 'Give me to drink', and he is refreshed by their loving fellowship. But the text means that he is feeding his people. He feedeth that part of his flock redeemed by blood of which we read that 'the Lamb which is in the midst of the throne shall feed them and shall lead them into living fountains of waters'. Nor does he forget that part of his flock which is in the low lands of earth, but he gives them also their portion of food. He has fed us this morning, for he is the good Shepherd, and leaves none of his sheep to famish.

Then *what shall I do*? Well, I will abide among the lilies. His saints shall be my companions. Where they flourish I will try to grow. I will be often in their assemblies. Ay, and I will be a lily too. By faith I will neither toil nor spin in a legal fashion, but I will live by faith upon the Son of God, rooted in him. I would be pure in life, and I would have the golden anther of looking to the recompense of the reward. I would lift up my soul aloft towards heaven as the lily lifts up its flower. Jesus will come and feed by my side if I am a lily, and even I may yield him some pleasure by my humble gratitude.

Beloved, this is a choice subject, but it is more sweet as a matter of fact than mere hearing can make it. 'He feedeth among the lilies.' This is our joy, that Christ is in his church, and the point of all I want to say is this: never think of yourself or of the church apart from Jesus. The spouse says, 'My beloved is mine, and I am his'; she weaves the two into one. The cause of the church is the cause of Christ; the work of God will never be accomplished by the church apart from Christ, her power lies in his being in her midst. He feedeth among the lilies, and therefore those lilies shall never be destroyed, but their sweetness shall make fragrant all the earth. The church of Christ, working with her Lord, must conquer, but never if she tries to stand alone or to compass any end apart from him.

As for each one of us personally, let us not think of ourselves apart from Christ, nor of Christ apart from us. Let George Herbert's prayer be ours:

> Oh, be mine still, still make me thine,
> Or rather make nor mine nor thine.

Let *mine* melt into *thine*. Oh, to have joint stock with Christ, and to trade under one name; to be married to Christ and lose our old name, and wear his name, and say, 'I live, yet not I, but Christ liveth in me.' As the wife is lost in the husband, and the stone in the building, and the branch in the vine, and the member in the head, we would be so amalgamated with Christ, and have such fellowship with him that there shall be no more mine nor thine.

Last of all, poor sinner, you will say, 'There is nothing in all this for me', and I should not like to send you away without a word. You are saying, 'This is a day of good tidings, but it is only for God's own people.' I beg you to read through the first and second chapters of the Song, and see who it was that said, 'My beloved is mine', because I should not wonder but what you are very like her. She was one who confessed, 'I am black', and so are you. Perhaps grace will, one of these days, help you to say, 'I am comely.' She was one with whom her mother's children were angry –

perhaps you, too, are a speckled bird. She had done servile work, for they made her a keeper of the vineyards. I should not wonder but what you are doing servile work, too, trying to save yourself instead of accepting the salvation which Jesus has already wrought out for sinners. So it came to pass that she became very sorrowful and passed through a winter of rain and cold. Perhaps you are there; and yet you know she came out of it, her winter was past, and the birds began to sing. She had been hidden in the secret places of the stairs, as you are now; but she was called out from the dust and cobwebs to see the face of her Lord.

One thing I wish to whisper in your ears – she was in the clefts of the rock. O soul, if thou canst but get there, if thou canst shelter in the riven side of our Beloved, that deep gash of the spear from which flowed blood and water, 'to be of sin the double cure'; if thou canst get there, I say, though thou be black and grimed with sin, and an accursed sinner, only fit to be a firebrand in hell, yet shalt thou, even thou, be able to sing with all the rapture of the liveliest saint on earth, and one day with all the transport of the brightest ones above, 'My beloved is mine, and I am his: he feedeth among the lilies.' There, go your way with those silver bells ringing in your ears; they ring a marriage peal to saints, but they ring also a cheery invitation to sinners, and this is the tune they are set to – Come and welcome! Come and welcome! Come and welcome! Sinner, come! God bless you, for Jesus' sake. Amen.

19

LOVED AND LOVING

'My beloved is mine, and I am his: he feedeth among the lilies'
(Song of Solomon 2:16)

'MY BELOVED' – this is a sweet name which our love takes liberty to apply to the Lord Jesus. His inexpressible beauty has won our affection, and we cannot help loving him whatever may come of it: whether he be ours or not, and whether he smiles upon us or frowns, we love him and cannot do otherwise. We are carried away by the torrent of his goodness, and have no longer the control of our affections. As long as we live we must and will love the altogether lovely One. Yes, he is, and must be to me, 'My Beloved'.

BUT SUPPOSE – suppose for a moment that we loved and had no right to love. Many a heart that has cried '*My beloved*', has been wounded even unto death, because it could not come at its choice, but was doomed never to exclaim, 'My beloved is mine.' The beloved was longed for, but could not be grasped. This is often so in earthly love, since such love may be unlawful, or unwise, and in every case it is the source of grievous misery. Thank God, this is not the case with the soul enamoured of Christ Jesus; for he freely presents himself in the gospel as the object of our confidence and love. Though he be infinitely above us, yet he delights to be one with all his loving ones, and of his own will he gives himself to us. A polluted sinner may love the perfect Saviour, for there is no word in Scripture to forbid. Ay, if a sinner would be wedded to the Lord of glory there is none to forbid the banns.

Suppose that our possession of Jesus were a matter of doubt, as, alas! it is with far too many: that would be a door of sorrow indeed. Life would be unhappy if it were soured by a question as to whether our Well-beloved is ours or no. To an awakened and instructed mind it is anguish to be dubious of our hold of Christ; about this we must needs be sure, or be unhappy. All else may be in jeopardy, but, O most blessed Lord, never allow our possession of thyself to be in dispute! It would be a poor thing to say, 'My beloved may be mine', or even 'he was mine', or 'perhaps he is mine': we cannot bear any verb but one in the indicative mood, present tense – 'My beloved *is* mine'.

Suppose yet once again that, though we loved, and rightly loved, and actually possessed the beloved object, yet our affection was not returned. Ah, misery! to love and not be loved! Blessed be God, we can not only sing, 'My Beloved is mine', but also, 'I am his.' He values me, he delights in me, he loves me! It is very wonderful that Jesus should think us worth the having; but since he does so, we find a matchless solace in the fact. Which is the greater miracle – that he should be mine, or that I should be his? Certainly, the second is the surer ground of safety, for I cannot keep my treasures, since I am feebleness itself; but Jesus is able to preserve his own, and none can pluck them out of his hand. The truth that Jesus calls me his is enough to make a man dance and sing all the way between here and heaven. Realize the fact that we are dear to the heart of our incarnate God, and amid the sands of this wilderness a fountain of overflowing joy is open before us.

BUT THE TEXT IS FREE FROM ALL SUPPOSITION: it is the language of indisputable possession, the exclamation of a confidence which has made its assurance doubly sure. There are two positive verbs in the present tense, and not the smell of a doubt has passed upon them. Here is a brave positiveness which fears no controversy, 'my beloved is mine and I am his', doubt it who may; nay, if you must needs doubt it, ask himself. There he is, for 'he feedeth among the lilies'. The spouse sees him of whom she speaks; he may be a mere myth to others but he is a substantial, loveable, lovely, and actually beloved person to her. He stands before her, and she perceives his character so clearly that she has a comparison ready for him, and likens him to a gazelle feeding on the tender grass among the lilies. This is a very delightful state of heart. Some of us know what it is to enjoy it from year to year. Christ is ours, and we know it. Jesus is present, and by faith we see him. Our marriage union with husband or wife cannot be more clear, more sure, more matter of fact, than our oneness with Christ and our enjoyment of that oneness. Joy! Joy! Joy! He whom we love is ours! We can also see the other side of the golden shield, for he whom we prize beyond all the world also prizes us, and we are his. Nothing in the universe besides deserves for an instant to be compared in value with this inestimable blessing. We would not change with the cherubim: their chief places in the choirs of heaven are poor as compared with the glory which excelleth – the glory of knowing that I my best Beloved's am and he is mine. A place in Christ's heart is more sweet, more honourable, more dear to us than a throne among the angels. Not even the delights of Paradise can produce a rival to this ecstatic joy – 'My Beloved is mine, and I am his.'

YET HAS THE TEXT A NOTE OF CAUTION. The condition of fully assured love is as tender as it is delightful. The spouse in the seventh verse had charged her companions by all things of gentleness, delicacy, and timidity – 'by the roes, and by the hinds of the field' – to refrain from offending her beloved while he deigned to abide with her; she had also compared him to a roe or a young hart, rather hiding than revealing himself; and here she likens him to the same roe, quietly pasturing in the gardens, so gently moving that he does not break or even bruise a lily, but softly insinuates himself among their delicate beauties, as one of the same dainty mould. This hints in poetic imagery at the solemn and sacred truth that the dearest fellowship with Jesus can never be known by the rough and the coarse, the hard and the restless, but remains the priceless heritage of the lowly and meek; and these can only retain it by a studious care which cherishes love, and guards it from even the least intrusion. A gazelle among the lilies would start at the bark of a fox, and be gone at the voice of a stranger; and therefore soft whispers of inward love must say, 'Take us the foxes, the little foxes', and nimble hands with noiseless fingers must draw up the lattice that kindly eyes may look forth at the windows, and may be seen of him who delights in love.

The evident intent of the language is to set forth the delicacy of the highest form of holy fellowship. The Lord our God is a jealous God, and that jealousy is most seen where most his love is displayed. The least sin, wilfully indulged in, will grieve the Holy Spirit; slights, forgetfulness and neglects will cause him to turn away. If we would remain positively and joyously assured that the Beloved is ours and that we are his, we must use the utmost circumspection and holy vigilance. No man gains full assurance by accident, or retains it by chance. As the gentle hind wanders in lovely spots where grow the pure white lilies, and as he shuns the places profaned by strife, and foul with rank weeds and nettles, so does the Lord Jesus come to holy minds perfumed with devotion and consecrated to the Lord, and there in sacred quiet he finds solace and abides with his saints.

May the Lord preserve us from pride, from self-seeking, from carnality, and wrath, for these things will chase away our delights even as dogs drive off the hind of the morning. Both our inward and outward walk must be eagerly watched, lest anything should vex the Bridegroom. A word, a glance, a thought may break the spell, and end the happy rest of the heart, and long may it be ere the blessing be regained. We have some of us learned by bitter experience that it is hard to establish a settled peace, and easy enough to destroy it. The costly vase, the product of a thousand laborious processes, may be broken in a moment; and so the supreme delight of communion with the Lord Jesus, the flower of ten thousand eminent delights, may be shattered by a few moments' negligence. Hence the one lesson of our little sermon is – 'I charge you, O ye daughters of Jerusalem, by the roes, and by the hinds of the field, that ye stir not up, nor awake my love, till he please.'

For I am jealous of my heart
Lest it should once from him depart;
Then should I lose my best delight
Should my Beloved take to flight.

20

'MY BELOVED *IS* MINE'

'My beloved is mine, and I am his' (Song of Solomon 2:16)

This is a versicle from the Song of Songs, and I do not hesitate to say that it is the soul and heart of that divine composition. The bride dressed in her richest poesy wears no jewel more precious than this diamond of full assured possession. There is poetry here which none of the sons of music can excel. It is the heart's minstrelsy at its very best. This little sonnet might be sung in heaven, and the golden harps would be well employed if every string went with the accompaniment. How I wish you could each one sing it now with a clear sweet voice!

Now I my best Beloved's am,
And he is mine.

Alas! many of the Lord's own chosen and called ones are afraid to take up this chorus and join with us. I do not condemn them, but I am eager to comfort them. What would they give – say, rather, what would they not give – if they could but say 'Christ is mine'? Yet they hesitate: the desire is strong, but the doubt is killing, and they dare not sing with us. It seems too good, too great, too glorious a claim to come from their lips. They sometimes hope, but they as often fear. They make a dash for it now and then, and trust that Christ is theirs; and then they subside into their former questioning. They are humble, modest, retiring; I fear I must add they are, at least in a measure, unbelieving. I want to lead these true hearts up to the table that they may feast upon the dainties provided for faith. I know that even now, as they hear the text, 'My Beloved is mine, and I am his', they are saying, 'Happy people that can speak thus, but I cannot. I am afraid it would be presumption, and perhaps hypocrisy, on my part, if I were to use such language.' And yet, dear heart, it is very possible that you have a perfect right to put in your claim; yes, and that you ought to be among the most confident and the most fully assured. What a pity it is that you should be losing so much joy! Yet some of the truest children of God walk in darkness at times, and we have provision made for them under the circumstances. 'Who is among you that feareth the LORD, that obeyeth the voice of his servant, that walketh in darkness, and hath no light? let him trust in the name of the LORD, and stay upon his God' (Isaiah 50:10). Oh, that I might be the means of enabling some of you to trust more bravely, and hold to your Lord in the darkness, for soon that darkness would be over!

Did I hear one mourn his faults, and lament his temptations? This need not be a hindrance. She who first sang this priceless stanza was herself warring against enemies. Read the previous verse: 'Take us the foxes, the little foxes, that spoil the vines: for our vines have tender grapes.' Instead of letting go her Lord to hunt the foxes, she clung the more to him, and joined him with herself in the effort to take them. 'Foxes or no foxes,' saith she, 'my Beloved is mine.' Jesus belongs to us in our imperfect condition, while yet we are beset with many mischievous and cunning foes. The Song before us is found in our own Bible, which is a Book to be used on earth rather than in heaven. While yet the foxes prowl around us we may sing, 'My Beloved is mine, and I am his.' Indeed, it is by strength derived from such a cheering confidence that we are enabled to kill these foxes, and preserve the tender clusters till they are ripe for our Lord. Come, brethren, let us not do ourselves the serious hurt of refusing the greatest of blessings for reasons which are not valid. Let us mourn our faults, but let us not therefore forego our privileges. I will not let my Lord go because I see a fox. Nay, rather, I will cling to him the more closely. If that fox should hurt my vine, yet I have a better Vine in my Lord, and one which no fox can touch. Away, ye beasts of the field, ye sins, and doubts, and fears, for my heart dares to sing, 'My Beloved is mine, and I am his.'

I feel that I am a bearer of a tenfold portion to the Benjamin of the family. Joseph - I mean, Jesus – has sent it, and I am eager to deliver it fresh from his dear hand. O trembling believer, it is all for thee! Receive it, and eat abundantly thereof. I am under the impression that my Master has bidden me remember that there is a Ruth here who only desires to glean, and trembles while she gathers a few scanty ears. She has not the courage to take a sheaf herself, but my Lord has said, 'Let fall handfuls on purpose for her', and I would try to do so; but I pray that timid Ruth may have courage enough to take up what I shall gladly let fall for her, for the good Boaz, in whose field I serve, has his eye upon her, and means more kindness to her than I can tell.

What I have to do tonight is to mention a few things which may help some timid one to say, 'My Beloved is mine', and then to do the same with regard to the second sentence in the text, 'I am his.'

Thou askest, perhaps, 'May I say, "My Beloved is mine"?' You know who that Beloved is; I have no need to tell you that. He is the chief among ten thousand, and the altogether lovely. You believe that it is he who is the ever-blessed Son of God, who became man for our sake, and, as the God-man, made atonement for our sin; and, having died, has risen from the dead, and gone into his Father's glory within the veil, where he ever maketh intercession for us. It is that Christ who is the light of heaven, the joy of everlasting bliss, the adored of angels. It certainly does seem a great thing to call him the adored of angels. It certainly does seem a great thing to call him mine; to think that he should ever be mine, and that all he is, and all he has, and all he says, and all he does, and all he ever will be, is all mine. When a wife takes a husband to be hers, he becomes all hers, and she reckons that she has no divided possession in him; and it certainly is so with thee, dear heart, if Christ be thine. He is still thine, and altogether thine, even if it does look as though you were opening your mouth very wide to be able to say it. Some of you were brought up in a school which is full of the law, and you are afraid to say what the gospel permits you to say, you have not dared yet to avail yourselves of your privileges. Some of God's heirs are often kept in the back kitchen when they have a right to sit in the parlour, and to eat of the dainties of their Lord. Some are kept from the joys to which they have a fair claim, so I am going to ask you a few questions to see whether you are one of them.

First, *hast thou taken hold of Christ by faith*? Faith is the hand with which we grasp the Lord Jesus Christ. Hast thou believed that Jesus is the Christ, and that God hath raised him from the dead? Dost thou trust thyself wholly to him? I say, 'wholly' – with no other secret confidence. Dost thou lean thy whole weight on him? He that hangs on two boughs, one of which is rotten, will go down. Thou hadst best trust thy whole self with Christ, and let him be the top and bottom of thy confidence. If thou dost that, then he is thine; this faith makes him thine to thy joyful experience. Listen to his own words: 'God so loved the world, that he gave his only begotten Son, that whosoever believeth in him should not perish, but have everlasting life.' If thou believest in Christ, thou hast Christ to be thine everlasting life, and thou mayest say, 'My Beloved is mine.'

I should hope that this is not a very difficult question for you to answer; you either are trusting in Christ, or you are not. If you are not trusting in Christ, God forbid that I should exhort you to say what would be presumptuous! But if you are resting on him who lived, and loved, and died, that he might wash us from our sins in his blood – I say, if he be all thy salvation and all thy desire, then hesitate not to say, 'My Beloved is mine.' There is no surer claim in the world than the claim of faith. God has given Christ to every believing sinner – be he who he may – God has given Christ to him by a covenant of salt, and Christ is his, and shall be his for ever. Poor trembler, if thou believest on him, even thou mayst say, 'My Beloved is mine.'

Let me ask thee another helpful question. *Is he truly thy Beloved, the Beloved of thy soul*? I remember well a dear Christian woman, who frequently said to me, 'I do love Jesus, I know I do; but does he love me?' Her question used to make me smile. 'Well,' I said, 'that is a question that I never did put to myself – "If I love him, does he love me?" No, the question that used to puzzle me was, "Do I love him?" When I could once settle that point, I was never again the victim of your form of doubt.' If thou lovest Christ, Christ loves thee for certain, for thy love to Christ is nothing more nor less than a beam out of the great sun of his love; and the grace that has created that love in thy heart towards him, if thou dost indeed love him, proves that he loves thee. Is it not so: 'We love him because he first loved us'? Did love ever get into the heart by any other door than that? I am sure that it never did; so that, if thou lovest him, thou canst say, 'My Beloved is mine.' There are many who may love on earth, and never obtain the object of their affection; but if thou lovest Christ, raise thou no question about his love to thee; he is thine, and thou art his. That test may help someone who, perhaps, is standing trembling behind the door, full of blushes, and afraid to come in amongst God's people. To thee, poor timid soul, we say, 'Come in, thou blessed of the Lord, wherefore standest thou without? If thou lovest him, thou art welcome to all he has.'

Next, I would help thee with a third question. *Is Jesus dear to thee above all thy possessions*? Perhaps thou hast a great deal of this world's goods. Dost thou set small store by all that thou hast as compared with Jesus? Wouldst thou see it all burn away, or melt away, or be stolen, infinitely rather than lose Christ? If thou canst say, 'Ay', to that question, then he is thine. Perhaps thou hast very little indeed, few earthly comforts, a narrow room, and a scant pittance to live upon; but wouldst thou sooner have Christ than all the riches of the world, or wouldst thou be willing to sell Christ in order to rise in the world? Wouldst thou sell him that thou mightest be made rich, and great, and famous? Thou who art sick, which wouldst thou sooner have, thy sickness and Christ, or go without Christ to be made healthy and strong? According to thy answer to these enquiries will be my answer to the other questions, 'Art thou Christ's, and is Christ thine?' I hope that many of you can say, 'O sir, we would give all that we have, we would suffer all that might be suffered, we would part with the very light and our eyes, too, if we could but be sure that we might each one truly say, "My Beloved is mine".' Well, if thou lovest Christ beyond all earthly things, rest assured that he is thine.

Further, *dost thou love him beyond all earthly companions*? Couldst thou part with your dearest ones for his sake? Say, art thou sure of this? Oh, then, he is assuredly thine! *Dost thou love him beyond all earthly objects*? Ay, beyond the desire of learning, or honour, or position, or comfort – wouldst thou let all go for his dear sake? Many of his saints have had to do it, and they have done it very cheerfully, and said with the apostle, 'Yea doubtless, and I count all things but loss for the excellency of the knowledge of Christ Jesus my Lord: for whom I have suffered the loss of all things, and do count them but dung, that I may win Christ, and be found in him.' Canst thou go that length? If thou canst, then surely he is thine.

Let me further help thee by another question. *Is Jesus so fully thy hope and thy trust that thou hast no other*? I have often led persons into liberty through that question. They have said, 'I am afraid that I do not trust Christ.' I have then asked, 'Well, where do you trust? Every man has a reliance of some sort; where are you trusting?' When I have pressed them closely, they have said, 'Oh, we have no other trust! God forbid that we ever should have!' When I have mentioned their good works, they have said, 'Good works! Why, we should be foolish indeed to talk of them!' When I have mentioned trusting in a priest, or in sacraments, they have scorned the thought, it has been loathsome to them. Then I have said, 'If thou hast no other trust but Christ, and thou art sure that thou hast a trust somewhere, then thy trust is in Christ, and though thou mayest question it, and doubt it, yet if thou dost so trust in him as to trust nowhere else, he is thine, and thou art his.'

There is many a good and true believer who, nevertheless, is afraid that he is not a believer. When you are once on board ship, even if the vessel is tossed to and fro, and you yourself are ill, perhaps sadly sea-sick, yet as long as that ship does not go down, you will not go down, for your safety now does not depend upon your health and strength, but upon the ship into which you have entered. So, if thou hast fled to Christ away from everything else, then, though thou mayest sigh, and cry, and fear, and tremble – for all of which I am sorry, for I would have every man on board ship to be well and strong, and able to handle the ropes – still, if thou canst not touch a rope, and if thou canst not even eat thy meals in thy cabin, yet, if thou art aboard the ship, and if that ship gets safe to land, so wilt thou. Wherefore, be of good cheer. O poor heart, if thou art clean divorced from every confidence but Christ, then I believe that thou art married unto Christ, notwithstanding that thou tremblest sometimes, and askest whether it be so or not. Let that thought also help thee.

I would further help you in this way. *If Christ is yours, your thoughts go after him*. You cannot say that you love a person if you never think of him. You could not, I am sure, let another person fill your heart as Christ must fill his people's hearts, and yet never let that person occupy your thoughts. He to whom Christ belongs, often thinks of him. 'Well,' says one, 'I am so busy during the day that often my mind is taken up with my business, and I do not think of Christ.' Do you know where those crows live that are feeding on that ploughed field? They are going up and down the furrows, picking up all the worms they can find; and as you look at them, you cannot tell where their home is, can you? No; but wait till the evening, when the day's feeding is over; then you will see which way the crows fly, and you will find out where their nests are. Do you see how quickly they are winging their way to yonder rookery? So is it with us; while we are busy in the world, picking up the worms, as it were, we have to think about those things; we cannot do our business properly without our thoughts going that way; but when the business is over, when the evening comes, which way do you go then? Then you have an opportunity for thought, when your mind is going to its resting-place, which way do your thoughts fly? That shall be the true test; and if, when your thoughts are set free, they fly away to Jesus, rest assured that he is yours. That thought may help some of you poor trembling ones. We read of the apostles, 'Being let go, they went to their own company'. Just so. I heard a working-man, who was expounding that chapter very well; he said, 'If some fellows were put in prison, and they were let out, they would go to the first public-house they see, for that is where they would find their company.' Just so; 'birds of a feather flock together.' Now, when you are let go, when your mind gets out of the prison of your daily business, do you go to the world for your pleasure? Do you go to carnal things for your mirth, or do you fly to Christ? If you can answer, 'My thoughts go naturally to Christ', then you can truly say, 'My Beloved is mine.'

Again, do you do more than this? *Do you long for Christ's company*? If 'my Beloved' is indeed mine, I shall want to see him; I shall want to speak with him; I shall want him to abide with me. How is it with you? There is a great deal of religion in the world which only consists of shells, or husks; the kernels are not there at all. A man goes upstairs, and kneels down for a quarter of an hour, and he says that he is praying; yet possibly he has not really prayed at all. Another opens his Bible, and he reads a chapter, and he says that he has been studying the Scriptures. Perhaps it has been a mere mechanical act, and there has been no heart and soul in it. John Bradford, the famous martyr, used to say, 'I have made a point of this, that I will never go from a duty till I have had communion with Christ in it.' Hence, when he prayed, he prayed till he did really pray. When he praised, he praised till he did truly praise. If he was bowing in humiliation before God, he humbled himself till he was actually humbled. If he was seeking communion with Christ, he would not go away with the pleasure of merely having sought, but he kept on seeking until he found, for he felt that he had done nothing aright till he had come into communion with God, and into touch with Christ.

And, once more, *if thy Beloved is thine, thou wilt own it to be so*. Coming unto this Tabernacle, or going down to the communion table, or gathering round the family altar, what is all that if Christ be not there? It should be with you as it is with a wife whose husband is far away across the sea. 'Oh!' she cries, 'that I could hear the music of his footstep! The rooms seem all empty now that he is away. There is his portrait on the wall, but it only makes me sigh the more for my beloved. The very dog as he comes in seems to know that his master is away, and he makes me think of him.' Is it so with you in regard to Christ? In every duty do you sigh for him, and long for him? Holy Bernard was wont to say, and I believe that he could say it truly (it was in Latin but I will give you the English of it), 'O my Jesus, I never went from thee without thee!' He meant that he never left his knees, and left Christ behind him; he never went out of the house of God, and left Christ behind him; but he went through the outward act of devotion with a consciousness of the presence of Christ. Now, if this be your habit to keep up or to labour to keep up continued communion with Christ, and if you are longing for more and more of that communion, then, dear friends, you are his, and he is yours.

Further, let me help you with a still closer question. *Have you ever enjoyed that communion with Christ*? Didst thou ever speak with him? Hast thou ever heard his voice? I think I see you turning over the leaves of your diary; I hope you have not to go far back to read the record of your fellowship with your Lord. I hope that this morning was one instance of it, and that this evening may be another. But are there not some special days, red-letter days, in your history? I recollect that Rutherford sent this message to one of his friends who was in great sorrow, 'Tell him to remember Torwood.' Nobody knew what was meant except the two who had been to Torwood, where they had enjoyed such fellowship with Christ that they could never forget it all their days. That is what David meant when he said, 'Therefore will I remember thee from the land of Jordan, and of the Hermonites, and the hill Mizar.' Those were some choice spots that he recollected where the Lord had met with him. How can Christ be thine if thou knowest nothing about communion with him? Art thou married to him if he has never shown thee his face, and thou hast never heard his voice, and never spoken with him? But if thou hast had Christ's company, he has manifested himself to thee as he does not unto the world. He would never have shown thee such things as these if thou wert not his. Ah! hast thou not, sometimes, crept out of the very dungeon of despair, and seen thy Lord's blessed face, and in a moment thou hast been dancing for joy? Hast thou not lain on the bed of sickness, 'weary, and worn, and sad', till his presence has made the chamber of affliction bright with the light of heaven? Hast thou not, sometimes, at dead of night, been weary in watching for sleep that would not come, and thy Lord hast come to thee, and then thou hast been afraid to go to sleep lest thou shouldst lose the joy of his presence, and wake up without him? Oh! some of us know what that experience means – when earth has been the vestibule of heaven, and when, even in our sickness and sadness, we have been on the very verge of Jordan, and we have smelt the fragrance of the spices that was wafted by the breath of the Spirit from the golden gardens on the other side of the stream. If thou knowest anything experimentally about this matter, then thou mayest conclude that thy Beloved is indeed thine.

But supposing that thou art not enjoying Christ's presence, I am going to put another question to thee. *Art thou cast down when he is away*? If thou hast grieved his Spirit, art thou grieved? If Christ be gone, dost thou feel as if the sun itself had ceased to shine, and the candle of thy existence had been snuffed out in utter darkness? Do you cry when he is away,

> What peaceful hours I then enjoyed!
> How sweet their memory still!
> But now I find an aching void
> The world can never fill?

Oh, then he is thine! If thou canst not bear his absence, he is thine. Last Thursday night, I preached a sermon which was intended to be a very searching one, and I hope that it was. It was upon the text, 'Now if any man have not the Spirit of Christ, he is none of his.' Now see the difficulty of a poor minister. If I preach very comforting sermons, there are sure to be hypocrites who suck them down, and say, 'How delightful!' But when I preach a soul-searching sermon, some dear child of God, who is as precious to her Lord as gold tried in the furnace, takes everything to herself, and begins to be very sorrowful, and to say, 'That sharp knife is meant for me, for I am not one of the Lord's people'. Well, after last Thursday night's sermon, a dear woman came to my vestry, broken-hearted, crying and sobbing. I hope that the discourse will be a blessing to her in the long run;

but I protest that I never meant to preach to her at all, I was not aiming at her or at the sort of people to whom she belongs; it was a very different class whom I was addressing.

If the preacher says anything about hypocrites, very often the hypocrites will not take it to heart, but the most sincere saint in the congregation very likely says, 'Oh, I am afraid that I am a hypocrite!' If you are, you are an odd sort of hypocrite, for I never knew of a hypocrite who was afraid that he was one. He has not grace enough for that kind of fear, but just goes on in the self-conceit that all is right with him.

I, for my part, feel more confidence in the broken-hearted tremblers than I do in the boasters who never have a question about their being all right, but set it down as an undisputed fact that they are in the covenant of grace. O beloved, I am glad if sometimes thou dost moan like a dove, and cry in the bitterness of thy spirit, 'Oh, that I knew where I might find him!' It may seem to be a spot on your character, but this spot is the spot of God's children, and I am not sorry to see it upon you. If the Prince Immanuel has left the town of Mansoul, then there can be no marriage bells or joyous music there until he comes back again. We must invite him and entreat him to return, we must clothe ourselves in sackcloth till he does come back; if we do not act thus, then he is not ours. If you *can* do without Christ, you *shall* do without Christ; but if you cannot do without him, if you cry, 'Give me Christ, or else I die', then he shall be yours. Stretch out the hand of faith, and take him, and then say without hesitation, 'My Beloved is mine.' I am not going on to the rest of the text; but I want to say just this – if there is any man or woman here (and I know there are many) who can sit down in the pew, and quietly say, 'Yes, weighing everything the preacher has said, and judging myself as severely as I can, yet I dare take Christ to be mine, and to say, "My Beloved is mine".' If that is your case, dear friend, then you shall get confirmatory evidence of this fact by *the witness of the Spirit within your soul*, which will very likely come to you in the form of perfect contentment of spirit, perfect rest of heart.

When I can say, "My God is mine",
When I can feel thy glories shine;
I tread the world beneath my feet,
And all that earth calls good or great.

'There,' says the believer, 'now that my Beloved is mine, I have no other wish or want.' Now will he be like Simeon when he took that blessed Babe into his arms. 'Lord,' said he, 'now lettest thou thy servant depart in peace, according to thy Word.' 'Have you nothing more to live for, Simeon?' 'No,' replies the good old man, 'what more can there be?' 'Don't you think that, if you lived a little longer, you might have a heavy purse of gold in your hands?' 'Yes,' he answers, 'possibly I might; but it would be a cumbrous burden. This dear Child is better than all the gold and silver in the world. If he is mine, I have enough, yea, I have all.' That blessed rest of soul, which comes of a sure possession of Christ, is not to be imitated, but it is greatly to be desired.

I know that some good people, who I believe will be saved, nevertheless do not attain to this sweet rest. They keep on thinking that it is something that they may get when they are very old, or when they are about to die, but they look upon the full assurance of faith, and the personal grasping of Christ, and saying, 'My Beloved *is* mine', as something very dangerous. I began my Christian life in this happy fashion as a boy fifteen years of age; I believed fully and without hesitation in the Lord Jesus Christ; and when I went to see a good Christian woman, I was simpleton enough to tell her that I believed in Christ, that he was mine, and that he had saved me. She said to me, 'Ah! I don't like such assurance as that.' And then she added, 'I trust you are believing in Christ – I hope so – but I have never got beyond a hope, or a trust, and I am an old woman.' Bless the old woman, she was no example for us who know whom we have believed; we are to rise infinitely beyond that grovelling kind of life. The man who begins right, and the boy who begins right, and the girl who begins right, will begin by saying, 'God hath said it: "He that believeth on him is not condemned". I believe on him, therefore I am not condemned; Christ is mine.'

O dear friends, do not always keep on with that miserable hoping, and hoping, and hopping! Walk on both your feet, and get a good firm standing on the Rock of Ages, and say without boasting, but without doubting, 'My Beloved *is* mine.' This will bring you into the condition of the psalmist when he said, 'He maketh me to lie down in green pastures: he leadeth me beside the still waters.' David would never have said that if he had not begun the Psalm with 'The Lord *is* my Shepherd'. If he had begun by saying, 'Perhaps the Lord is my Shepherd', he would have gone on to say, 'Perhaps there may be green pastures, possibly there may be still waters; but as yet my soul is in a dry and thirsty land where no water is, and not a blade of grass either.' Ah! David was not so stupid as that; he had his times of depression, but when he was singing that Psalm, he was in a positive, certain frame of mind. 'The Lord is my Shepherd.' He used the indicative mood, not the subjunctive or conditional. The Lord help you to do the same! And you may. If Christ is a satisfaction to your spirit, so that your soul is satisfied with marrow and fatness, then do not hesitate to say, and to emphasise the utterance, 'My Beloved *is* mine'. He either is, or he is not; which is it? Do not go to sleep tonight till you know. If Christ is yours, heaven is yours. If Christ is not yours, you are neither fit to live, nor fit to die. Remember that awful verse, 'If any man love not the Lord Jesus Christ, let him be Anathema Maranatha' – 'let him be accursed, the Lord cometh!' Take heed unto yourselves, therefore; if Christ is not yours, you are in terrible poverty; but if Christ is yours, you are eternally rich to all the intents of bliss. Oh, that he might be yours now by your stretching out the hand of faith, and taking him to yourself!

'I dare not take him,' says one. Well, you are a strange person; *I* dare not let him alone, and I challenge you to shape that 'dare' into any other proper form. If he bids you take him, and trust him, how dare you refuse him? Take him now and be safe and happy for ever. God bless you, for Jesu's sake! Amen.

21

DARKNESS BEFORE THE DAWN

'Until the day break, and the shadows flee away, turn, my beloved, and be thou like a roe or a young hart upon the mountains of Bether' (Song of Solomon 2:17).

The spouse sings, 'Until the day break, and the shadows flee away', indicating that the beloved of the Lord may be in the dark. It may be night with her who has a place in the heart of the Well-beloved. A child of God, who is a child of light, may be for a while in darkness; first, darkness comparatively, as compared with the light he has sometimes enjoyed, for days are not always equally bright. Some days are bright with a clear sunshine, other days may be overcast. So the child of God may one day walk, with full assurance of faith, in close fellowship with the Father and with his Son Jesus Christ; and at another time he may be questioning his interest in the covenant of grace, and may be rather sighing than singing, rather mourning than rejoicing. The child of God may be, then, in comparative darkness.

Yes, and he may be in positive darkness. It may be very black with him, and he may be obliged to cry, 'I see no signs of returning day.' Sometimes, neither sun nor moon appears for a long season to cheer the believer in the dark. This may arise partly through sickness of body. There are sicknesses of the body which in a very peculiar way touch the soul; exquisite pain may yet be attended with great brightness and joy, but there are certain other illnesses which influence us in another way. Terrible depressions come over us; we walk in darkness, and see no light. I should not like to guess how heavy a true heart may sometimes become; there is a needs-be that we be in heaviness through manifold trials. There is not only a needs-be for the trials, but also for the heaviness which comes out of them. It is not always that a man can gather himself together, and defy the fierce blasts, and walk through fire and through water with heavenly equanimity. No, brethren, 'a wounded spirit who can bear?', and that wounded spirit may be the portion of some of the very fairest of the sons of God; indeed, the Lord has some weakly, sickly sons who, nevertheless, are the very pick of his family. It is not always the strong ones by whom he sets the most store; but, sometimes, those that seem to be driven into a corner, whose days are spent in mourning, are among the most precious in his sight. Yes, the darkness of the child of God may be comparative darkness, and it may to a great extent be positive darkness.

But yet it can only be temporary darkness. The same text which suggests night promises dawn: 'Until the day break, and the shadows flee away,' says the song of the spouse. Perhaps no text is more frequently upon my lips than is this one; I do not think that any passage of Scripture more often recurs to my heart when I am alone, for just now I feel that there is a gathering gloom over the church and over the world. It seems as if night were coming on, and such a night as makes one sigh and cry, 'Until the day break, and the shadows flee away.'

I am going to speak upon three things which are in our text. The first will be *our prospect*. We have a prospect that the day will break, and the shadows flee away. Secondly, *our posture*: 'until the day break, and the shadows flee away'. Thirdly, *our petition*: 'Turn, my Beloved, and be thou like a roe or a young hart upon the mountains of division'. We are content to wait if he will come to us; if gladdened with his presence, the night shall seem short, and we can well endure all that it brings. Let the prayer of our text be put up by any of you who are waiting in the darkness, and may it be speedily answered in your happy experience!

First of all, let us consider OUR PROSPECT. Our prospect is, that the day will break, and that the shadows will flee away. We may read this passage in many ways, and apply it to different cases.

Think, first, of *the child of God who is full of doubt*. He is afraid that, after all, his supposed conversion was not a true one, and that he has proved it to be false by his own misbehaviour. He is afraid, I scarcely know of what, for so many fears crowd in upon him. He is crying to God to remove his doubts, and to let him once again:

> Read his title clear
> To mansions in the skies.

His eyes are looking toward the cross, and somehow, he has a hope, if not quite a persuasion, that he will find light in Christ, where so many others have found it. I would encourage that hope till it becomes a firm conviction and a full expectation. The day will break for you, dear mourner, the shadows will yet flee away. While I say that, I feel able to speak with great confidence, for my eye, as it looks round on this congregation, detects many brothers and sisters with whom I have conversed in the cloudy and dark day. We have prayed together, dear friends, have we not? I have repeated in your hearing those precious promises which are the pillows of our hope; yet, at the time, it seemed as if you would never be cheered or comforted. Friends who lived with you grieved much to see you so sad; they could not understand how such as you, who have lived so scrupulously as you believed to be right, should, nevertheless, come into sadness and despondency. Well, you have come out of that state, have you not? I can almost catch the bright expression in your eye as you flash back the response, 'It is so, sir; we can sing among the loudest now, we can leap as a hart, and the tongue that once was dumb can now sing praises unto the Lord who delivered us.' The reason of this great change is that you did still cling to Christ even when it seemed to be no use to cling. You had a venturesome faith; when it seemed a risky thing even to believe, you did believe, and you kept on believing, and now the day has dawned for you, and the shadows have fled away. Well, so shall it be to all who are in like case if they will but trust in the Lord, and stay themselves upon our God. Though they walk in darkness, and see no light, yet by-and-by the day shall break for them also.

This expression is equally applicable when we come into some *personal sorrow not exactly of a spiritual kind.* I know that God's children are not long without tribulation. As long as the wheat is on the threshing-floor, it must expect to feel the flail. Perhaps you have had a bereavement, or you may have had losses in business, or crosses in your family, or you have been sorely afflicted in your own body, and now you are crying to God for deliverance out of your temporal trouble. That deliverance will surely come. 'Trust in the Lord, and do good; so shalt thou dwell in the land, and verily thou shalt be fed.' 'I have been young,' said David, 'and now am old; yet have I not seen the righteous forsaken.' The Lord will yet light your candle, and surround your path with brightness. Only patiently hope and quietly wait, and you shall yet see the salvation of the Lord. 'Many are the afflictions of the righteous.' Mark that; you know that part of the verse is true, and so is the rest of it: 'but the Lord delivereth him out of them all.' Clutch at that, for it is equally true. 'In the world ye shall have tribulation.' You know that is true. 'Be of good cheer,' says Christ, 'I have overcome the world.' Therefore, expect that you also will overcome it through your conquering Lord. Yes, in the darkest of all human sorrows, there is the glad prospect that the day will break, and the shadows will flee away.

This is the case again, I believe, on a grander scale with reference to *the depression of religion at the present time*. Some of us are obliged to go sorrowing when we look upon the state of the church and the world. We are not accustomed to take gloomy views of things, but we cannot help grieving over what we see. More and more it forces itself upon us that the old-fashioned gospel is being either neglected or trampled in the dust. The old spirit, the old fire that once burned in the midst of the saints of God, is there still, but it burns very low at present. We want – I cannot say how much we want a revival of pure and undefiled religion in this our day. Will it come? Why should it not come? If we long for it, if we pray for it, if we believe for it, if we work for it, and prepare for it, it will certainly come. The day will break, and the shadows flee away. The mockers think that they have buried our Lord Jesus Christ. So, perhaps, they have; but he will have a resurrection. The cry is, 'Who will roll us away the stone?' The stone shall be rolled away, and he, even the Christ in whom our fathers trusted, the Christ of Luther and of Calvin, of Whitefield and of Wesley, that same Christ shall be among us yet in the fulness and the glory of his power by the working of the Holy Ghost upon the hearts of myriads of men. Let us never despair; but, on the contrary, let us brush the tears from our eyes, and begin to look for the light of the morning, for 'the morning cometh', and the day will break, and the shadows will flee away.

Let me encourage any friends who have been labouring for Christ in any district which has seemed strikingly barren, where the stones of the field have seemed to break the ploughshare. Still believe on, beloved; that soil which appears most unfruitful will perhaps repay us after a while with a hundred-fold harvest. The prospect may be dark; perhaps, dear friends, it is to be darker yet with us. We may have worked, and seemed to work in vain; possibly the vanity of all our working is yet to appear still more; but for all that, 'the morning cometh'. 'They that sow in tears shall reap in joy.' We must not be in the least afraid even in the densest darkness; but, on the contrary, look for the coming blessing.

I believe that this is to be the case also *in this whole world*. It is still the time of darkness, it is still the hour of shadows. I am no prophet, nor the son of a prophet, and I cannot foretell what is yet to happen in the earth; it may be that the darkness will deepen still more, and that the shadows will multiply and increase; but the Lord will come. When he went up from Olivet, he sent two of his angels down to say, 'Ye men of Galilee, why stand ye gazing up into heaven? This same Jesus, which is taken up from you into heaven, shall so come in like manner as ye have seen him go into heaven.' He is surely coming; and though the date of his return is hidden from our sight, all the signs of the times look as if he might come very speedily. I was reading, the other day, what old Master William Bridge says on this subject: 'If our Lord is coming at midnight, he certainly will come very soon, for it cannot be darker than it now is.' That was written two hundred years ago, but our Lord has not come yet, and I might say the same as Master Bridge did. Do not doubt as to Christ's coming because it is delayed. A person lies dying, and the report concerning him is, 'Well, it does not look as if he could live many hours.' You call again, and they say, 'Well, he still survives, but it seems as if he would scarcely get through the night.' Do you go away and say, 'Oh, he will not die; for I have expected, for several days, to hear that he has passed away'? Oh, no! but each time you hear the report, you feel, 'Well, it is so much nearer the end.' And so is our Master's coming; it is getting nearer every hour, so let us keep on expecting it. That glorious advent shall end our weary waiting days, it shall end our conflicts with infidelity and priestcraft, it shall put an end to all our futile endeavours; and when the great Shepherd shall appear in his glory, then shall every faithful under-shepherd and all his flock appear with him, and then shall the day break, and the shadows flee away.

As to the shadows fleeing; what are those shadows that are to fly at his approach? The types and shadows of the ceremonial law were all finished when Christ appeared the first time; but many shadows still remain: the shadows of our doubts; the grim mysterious shadows of our fears; the shadows of sin, so black, so dense; the shadows of abounding unbelief; ten thousand shadows. When he cometh, these shall all flee away; and with them shall go heaven and earth – the heaven and earth that now are – for what are these but shadows? All things that are unsubstantial shall pass away when he appeareth; when the day breaks, then shall everything but that which is eternal and invisible pass away. We are glad that it shall be so; and we pray that soon the day may break, and the shadows flee away. This, then, is our prospect.

Now I want to occupy a few minutes of your time in considering OUR POSTURE: 'until the day break, and the shadows flee away.' We are here, like soldiers on guard, waiting for the dawn. It is night, and the night is deepening; how shall we occupy ourselves until the day break, and the shadows flee away?

Well, first, we will wait in the darkness with *patient endurance* as long as God appoints it. Whatever of shadow is yet to come, whatever of cold damp air and dews of the night is yet to fall upon us, we will bear it. Soldiers of the cross, you must not wish to avoid these shadows; he who has called you to this service knew that it would be night time, and he called you to night duty; and being put upon the night watch, keep at your post. It is not for any of us to say, 'We will desert because it is so dark.' Has not the thought sometimes crossed your mind, 'I am not succeeding; I will run away'? Have you not often felt, like Jonah, that you would go to Tarshish that you might escape from delivering your Master's message? Oh, do not so! The day will break, and the shadows flee away; and until then, watch through the night, and fear not the shadows. Play the man, remembering through what a sevenfold night your Master passed, when, in Gethsemane, he endured even to a bloody sweat for you. When, on the cross, even his mid-day was midnight, what must have been the darkness over his spirit? He bore it; then bear you it. Let no thought of fear pass over your mind; or, if it does, let not your heart be troubled, but rise above your fear until the day break, and the shadows flee away. Be of good courage, soldiers of Christ, and still wait on in patient endurance.

What next are we to do until the day break? Why, let there be *hopeful watching*. Keep your eyes towards the East, and look for the first grey sign of the coming morning. 'Watch!' Oh, how little is done of this kind of work! We scarcely watch as we ought against the devil; but how little do we watch for the coming of our Master! Look for every sign of his appearing, and be ever listening for the sound of his chariot wheels. Keep the candle burning in the window, to let him see that you are awake; keep the door on the latch, that when he cometh you may quickly open unto him. Hopefully watch until the day break, and the shadows flee away.

Then, further, dear friends, while we maintain patient endurance and hopeful watching, let us give each other *mutual encouragement*. Men who have been shipwrecked will give each other a hand, and say, 'Brother, mayhap we shall escape after all.' Now that it is midnight all around, let every Christian give his fellow-soldier a grip of his hand. Courage, brothers; the Lord has not forgotten us. We are in the dark, and cannot see him; but he can see us, and he knows all about us, and maybe he will come, walking on the stormy waters in the middle watch of the night when our little bark seems ready to be sunk beneath the waves by the boisterous wind. I seem just now as though I were a soldier in this great guard-room, and as if we were sitting in these shadows, and perhaps in the darkness, and seemed very much dispirited; and I would say to you my comrades, 'Come, brothers, let us cheer up. The Lord hath appeared to one and another of us. He hath given to some of us the light of his countenance, and he is coming back to welcome us all unto himself. Let us not be dismayed; our glorious Leader forgets not the weakest and feeblest of us, neither is any part of the battlefield beyond the reach of the great Captain's eye. He sees which way the struggle is going, and he has innumerable reserves, which he will bring up at the right time. I seem to hear the music of his horse's hoofs even now. He is coming who shall turn the scale in the worst moment of the conflict, for the battle is the Lord's, and he will deliver the enemy into our hands. Let no man's heart fail him because of yonder Goliath; the God who has raised up men to slay the lion and the bear, will yet find a David and a smooth stone to kill this mighty giant. Wherefore, brothers, be of good courage.'

What further should we do in the dark? Well, one of the best things to do in the dark is to *stand still and keep our place*. 'Until the day break and the shadows flee away', let us keep our place, and firmly maintain our position. A brother who sat the back of me, twenty years ago, dropped in again recently to hear me preach; and he said to me, after the service, that he had been back in America, and come over here again after twenty years, and he added, 'It is the same old story, Spurgeon, as when I was here before; you are sticking to the same old gospel.' I replied, 'Yes, and if you will come in twenty years' time, if God spares me, I shall still be sticking to the same old gospel, for I have nailed my colours to the mast, and I do not mean to have anything to do with this new-fangled progressive theology.' To me, the gospel came to perfection long ago in the person of the Lord Jesus Christ, and it can never go beyond that perfection. We preach nothing but that gospel which has saved our own souls, and saved the souls of the myriads who have gone to their eternal rest, and we do not intend preaching anything else until somebody can find us something better, and that will not be tomorrow, nor the day after, nor as long as the world stands. It is dark, very dark, so we just stop where we are, in steadfast confidence in the Lord who has placed us where we are. We are not going to plunge on in a reckless manner, we mean to look before we leap; and as it is too dark to look, we will not leap, but will just abide here hard by the cross, battling with every adversary of the truth as long as we have a right hand to move in the name of Almighty God, 'until the day break, and the shadows flee away'.

What else ought we to do? Keep up a *careful separateness* from the works of darkness that are going on all around us. If it seems dark to you, gather up your skirts, and gird up your loins. The more sin abounds in the world, the more ought the Church of God to seek after the strictest holiness. If ever there was an age that wanted back again the sternest form of Puritanism, it is this age. If ever there was a time when we needed the old original stamp of Methodists, we need them now – a people separated unto God, a people that have nothing to do but to please God and to save souls, a people that will not in any way bow themselves to the fashions of the time. For my part, I would like to see a George Fox come back among us, ay, Quaker as he was, to bear such a testimony as he did bear in the power of the Spirit of God against the evils of his time. God make us to feel that now, in the dark, we cannot be even as lenient as we might have been in brighter days towards the sin that surrounds us!

Are any of you tempted into 'society' so-called, and into the ways of that society? Every now and then, those who read the papers get some little idea of what is going on in 'society'. The stench that comes from 'society' tells us what it must be like, and makes us wish to keep clear of it. The awful revelations that were once before made, which caused us to be sick with shame and sorrow, might be made again; for there is just the same foulness and filthiness beneath the surface of the supposed greater decency. O

Christian people, if you could but know, as the most of you ought not to know, how bad this world is, you would not begin to talk about its wonderful improvements, or to question the doctrine of human depravity.

We are going on, according to some teachers, by 'evolution' into something; if I might prognosticate what it is, I should say that it is into devils that many men are being evolved. They are going down, down, down, save where eternal grace is begetting in the heart of men a higher and better and nobler nature, which must bear its protest against the ignorance or hypocrisy which this day talks about the improvements of our civilization, and the progress that we are making towards God. 'Until the day break, and the shadows flee away', keep yourselves to your Lord, and hear you this voice sounding through the darkness, the voice of a wisdom that sees more than you see, 'Come out from among them, and be ye separate, saith the Lord, and touch not the unclean thing; and I will receive you, and will be a father unto you, and ye shall be my sons and daughters, saith the Lord Almighty.' 'Until the day break, and the shadows flee away', lift your hands to heaven, and pledge yourselves to walk a separated pilgrim life, until he cometh before whose face heaven and earth shall flee away.

3. Now I close by noticing OUR PETITION: 'Until the day break, and the shadows flee away, turn, my Beloved, and be thou like a roe or a young hart upon the mountains of Bether.'

I am not going to preach upon that part of our text, but only just to urge you to turn it into prayer. We have to wait, brothers and sisters; we have to wait in the darkness, cheered here and there with the light from a golden lamp that glows with the light of God. The world lieth in darkness, but we are of God, little children, therefore this must be our prayer to our Well-beloved, '*Come unto us.*' 'Turn to me, O my Beloved, for thou hast turned away from me, or from thy Church. Turn again, I beseech thee. Pardon my lukewarmness, forgive my indifference. Turn to me again, my Beloved. O thou Husband of my soul, if I have grieved thee, and thou hast hidden thy face from me, turn again unto me! Smile thou, for then shall the day break, and the shadow flee away. Come to me, my Lord, visit me once again.' Put up that prayer, beloved.

The prayer of the spouse is in this poetic form: '*Come over the mountains of division.*' As we look out into the darkness, what little light there is appears to reveal to us Alp upon Alp, mountain upon mountain, and our Beloved seems divided from us by all these hills. Now our prayer is, that he would come over the top of them; we cannot go over the top of them to him, but he can come over the top of them to us, if he think fit to do so. Like the hinds' feet, this blessed Hind of the morning can come skipping over the hills with utmost speed to visit and to deliver us. Make this your prayer, 'Great

Master, sweetly-beloved One, come over the mountains of division, and come quickly, like a roe or a young hart. Come easily, come unexpectedly; as roes and harts let no man know when they will come, so come thou unto me.'

I wish that, even while we are sitting here, our Divine Lord would come to our spirits with all his ravishing charms, so that we might cry, 'Or ever I was aware, my soul made me like the chariots of Ammi-nadib.' Have you never felt an influence steal over you which has lifted you out of yourself, and made you go as on burning wheels with axles hot with speed, where before you had been sluggish and dull? Our Well-beloved can come and visit us, all on a sudden, without any trouble to himself. It cost him his life's blood to come to earth to save us; it will cost him nothing to come just now to bless us. Remember what he has already done; for, having done so much, he will not deny you the lesser blessing of coming to you. Are you saved by his grace? Then do not think that he will refuse you fellowship with himself. Pray for it now. Before we come to the communion table, pray for it, and while you are sitting there, let this be your cry, 'Come to me, my Beloved, over the hills of division; come as a roe or a young hart'; and he will come to you. Put up your prayers in the sweet words we sang just now,

> When wilt thou come unto me, Lord?
> O come, my Lord most dear!
> Come near, come nearer, nearer still,
> I'm blest when thou art near.
> When wilt thou come unto me, Lord?
> Until thou dost appear,
> I count each moment for a day,
> Each minute for a year.

Oh, that this might be one of those happy seasons when you shall not be fed by the preacher's talk but by the Master revealing himself to you! May God graciously grant it!

I may be addressing some who long to find the Saviour. This morning, I got, from a friend who came in to see me, an illustration which I will give to you. He told me – and oh, how he made my heart rejoice! – that, six years ago, he was, as the apostle says, 'going about to establish his own righteousness'. He is a man of reputation, and when a friend sent him some of my sermons to read, he thought to himself, 'What do I want these sermons for? I am as good as any man can be.' But he did read them, and the friend asked him, 'Have you read those sermons of Mr Spurgeon's that I sent you?' 'Yes,' he replied, 'I have; but I have got no good out of them.' 'Why not?' 'Why,' he said, 'he has spoiled me; he has dashed my hopes to the ground, he has taken away my comfort and my joy; I thought myself as good as anybody living, and he has made me feel as if I were rotten right through.' 'Oh!' said his friend, 'that medicine is working well, you must take some more of it.' But the more of the sermons he read, the more unhappy he became, the more he saw the hollowness of all his former hopes; and he came into a great darkness, and the day did not break, and the shadows did not flee away. But, on a sudden, he was brought out into the light. As he told me the story this morning, his eyes were wet, and so were mine.

This is how the Lord led him into peace; I wish the telling of it might bring the same blessing to some of you. He said, 'I went with my friend to fish for salmon in Loch Awe. I threw a fly, and as I threw it, a fish leaped up, and took it in a moment.' 'There,' said the friend to him, 'that is what you have to do with Christ, what that fish did with your fly. I am sure I do not know whether the fly took the fish, or the fish took the fly; it was both, the bait took the fish, and the fish took the bait. Do just so with Christ, and do not ask any question. Leap up at him, take him in, lay hold of him.'

The man did so, and at once he was saved; I wish that somebody else would do the same. I never ask you to answer the question whether it is Christ who takes you or you who take Christ, for both things will happen at the same moment. Will you have him? Will you have him? If you will have him, he has you. If you are willing to have Christ, Christ has already made you willing in the day of his power. Throw yourself upon Christ, as the salmon opened his mouth, and took in the bait; so do you take Christ into your very soul. Writing to the Romans, Paul says, 'The word is nigh thee, even in thy mouth.' What is the thing to do with that which is in your mouth when you want to keep it? Why, swallow it, of course! Do so with Christ, let him go right down into your soul. Accept him, receive him, and he is yours directly. Then shall the day break, and the shadows flee away, and your Beloved shall have come to you over the mountains of division, never to leave you again, but to abide with you for ever. God bless you! Amen.

22

LOVE'S VIGILANCE REWARDED

> 'It was but a little that I passed from them, but I found him whom my soul loveth: I held him, and would not let him go, until I had brought him into my mother's house, and into the chamber of her that conceived me' (Song of Solomon 3:4).

When I look upon this great assembly of people, I think to myself there will be many here to whom these chapters that we have read out of Solomon's Song will seem very strange. Of course they will; for they are meant for the inner circle of believers in the Lord Jesus Christ. This sacred Canticle is almost the central Book of the Bible; it seems to stand like the tree of life in the midst of the garden of Eden, in the very centre of the Paradise of God. You must know Christ, and love Christ, or else many of the expressions in this Book will seem to you but as an idle tale.

The subject on which I am about to speak will be very much of the same character. Outsiders will not be able to follow me; but then we are coming to the communion table, so I must for a while forget the unsaved among my hearers, and think only of those who do know the secret of the Lord which is with them that fear him. To my mind, it is a very melancholy thought that there should be any who do not know the sweetest thing in all the world, the best and happiest thing beneath the stars, the joy of having Christ in their heart as the hope of glory. While I may seem to forget you, dear friends, for a while, I cannot really help remembering you all the time; and it is the earnest desire of my heart that while I am speaking of some of those delights which are enjoyed only by the people of God, you may begin to long for them; and I remind you that, when you truly long for them, you may rest assured that you may have them. Around the garden of the Lord there is no wall so high as to keep out one real seeking and trusting soul; and in the wall itself there is a gate that ever stands ajar, nay, that is ever wide open to the earnest seeker.

I am not going to try so much to preach a sermon as to talk out freely from my heart some of those delightful experiences which belong to the children of God. I want this service to be a time, not of carving meat, but of eating it; not of spreading tables, but of sitting at them, and feasting to the full on the bounteous provisions that our Lord has prepared for us.

First, before we actually come to our text, we may notice **THREE PRELIMINARY STEPS IN THE SPOUSE'S PROGRESS.**

The first one is implied in the words, '*I love him.*' She refers to her Beloved under the title of 'him whom my soul loveth.' Can you, dear friend, give to the Lord Jesus that title? If he were to come here just now as he came to the Lake of Galilee and pass along these crowded ranks, and say to each one of us, 'Lovest thou me?' what would be your answer? I am glad that I speak to many whose answer would be, 'Lord, thou knowest all things; thou knowest that I love thee.' I can at this moment think of many reasons why I should love the Christ of Calvary, but I cannot think of one reason why I should not love him. If I turn to what I read about him in this blessed Book, it all makes me love him. If I recall what I have experienced of his grace in my heart, it all makes me love him. When I think of what he is, and what he did, and what he is doing, and what he will yet do, it all makes me love him. I am inclined to say to my heart, 'Never beat again if thou dost not beat true to him.' It were better for me that I had never been born, than that I should not love one who is in himself so inconceivably lovely, who is, indeed, perfection's self.

Yet there is one reason that rises above all others why you and I should love the Lord Jesus Christ; it is this, 'He loved me, and gave himself for me.' It used to be said by the old metaphysicians that it was impossible for love not to be returned, in some measure or other. I do not think that statement is universally true; but I hope it is true concerning our Lord's love to us and our heart's love to him. If he has loved us with an everlasting love, if he loved us even when we were his enemies, and loved us so as to take upon himself our nature – if this dear Son of God loved us so that he became man for our sakes, and, being found in fashion as a man, humbled himself, and became obedient unto death, even the death of the cross – oh! then, we must love him in return. We should be worse than the beasts that perish if, conscious of such love as this, we did not feel love to him alone! Can you stand at the cross-foot, and not kiss the feet of him who was wounded for our transgressions? Can you see him dead, and taken down from the cross, and not wish to wrap him in your fine linen, and bring your sweet spices to embalm his precious body? Can you see him risen from the grave, and not call him 'Rabboni', and long, as Mary did, to hold him by the feet? Can you, by faith, see him in our assemblies, saying, 'Peace be unto you', and not feel that you delight in him in your inmost soul? It cannot be; surely, it cannot be. We must and will say, and we feel that we may appeal to the Searcher of all hearts while we say it, 'I love him, I do love him because he first loved me.'

Then, in the spouse's progress, there came another step, '*I sought him.*' Notice how the chapter begins: 'By night on my bed I sought him whom my soul loveth', for love cannot bear to be a distance from the loved one, love longs for communion, love will do anything to get at the object of its affection. Where there is true love to Jesus Christ, we cannot bear to be away from him; and since we must be so in personal presence for a while, till the day break, and the shadows flee away, we long to be with him in heart, and to feel that he also is with us in spirit according to his promise, 'Lo, I am with you alway, even unto the end of the world.'

'I sought him.' Can you put your finger on that sentence, and say, 'That is true, too'? Have you been seeking him this Sabbath day? Are you coming to his table tonight seeking him? Were you at the Saturday night prayer-meeting, or at this morning's early gathering, seeking him with his people? Or, in your private devotions, did you make a point of crying, 'Lord, let me meet with thee, let me find thee'? If not, begin now; seek him with your whole heart, let your soul breathe out its burning desires after him.

'I sought him.' He is not far from any one of us. You sought him once, when you were burdened with your sin, and then you found him. He cast that sin of yours into the depths of the sea; come and seek him again, and your fears, your doubts, your distresses of mind, shall be buried in the same deep grave.

So the spouse sings of her Beloved, 'I sought him.'

Then comes in a little minor or mournful music, for the next clause is, 'I sought him, *but I found him not*.' The spouse is so sad about it that she tells out her woe twice, 'I sought him, but I found him not.' Do you know that experience? I hope you are not realizing it at this time; but many of us have known what it is. If we have been indulging in any sin, of course we could not find him then. If we have been cold-hearted, like the spouse who sought him on her bed, like her we have not found him. We have had to rise, we have had to stir up ourselves to lay hold of him, or else we have not found him. You have known what it is to go to the public service of the sanctuary, where others have been fed, yet you have had to come away, and say, 'There has not been a morsel for me.' Have you not even turned to the Bible, and to private prayer, and still you have had to say, 'I sought him, but I found him not'? This is a very sad experience; but if it makes you sad, it will be good for you. Our Lord Jesus Christ would not have us think little of his company; and, sometimes, it is only as we miss it that we begin to appreciate the sweetness of it. If we always had high days and holidays, we might not be so thankful when our gala days come round.

I have even known some of Christ's people get so pleased with the joy of his company that they have almost forgotten himself in the joy. If a husband gave his wife gold rings and ornaments, and she was so gratified with the presents that she took but little note of him, but only prized the jewels that he gave her, I can well understand what would be the jealousy of his heart. It may be that this is why your Lord hides his face, for you never know his value so much as when the darkness deepens, and the Star of Bethlehem shines not. When real soul-hunger comes on, and the Bread of heaven is not there, when you feel the pangs of the thirst of the spirit, and you are like Hagar in the wilderness, and cannot find the well of water, then will your Lord teach you his true value; and when you really know him, and know him better than you formerly knew him, then you shall no longer have to sigh, 'I sought him, but I found him not', but you shall change your dolorous ditty for the cheerful language of the text, 'It was but a little that I passed from them, but I found him whom my soul loveth.'

So I have brought you back to the text; these are the three steps by which we have ascended to the holy gate: first, 'I love him'; next, 'I sought him'; and then, 'I found him not'.

Secondly, inside the text, there are **THREE FURTHER STEPS**: 'I found him', 'I held him', 'I brought him into my mother's house, and into the chamber of her who conceived me'.

This is the first of the second series of steps, '*I found him*'. I do not wish to stand here, and speak for myself alone; but I want, beloved, that you should each one of you also say, 'I love him', 'I sought him', and now, 'I have found him'. Notice what the spouse said, 'I found *him*'. She was not satisfied with finding anything else: 'I found him'. If she had found her nearest and dearest friend, if the mother of whom she speaks had met her, it would not have sufficed. She had said, 'I love him, I sought him', and she must be able to add, 'I found him'. Nothing but Christ consciously enjoyed can satisfy the craving of a loving heart which once sets out to seek the King in his beauty.

The city watchmen found the spouse, and she spoke to them; she enquired of them, 'Saw ye him whom my soul loveth?' She did not sit down, and say to any one of them, 'O watchman of the night, thy company cheers me! The streets are lonely and dangerous; but if thou art near, I feel perfectly safe, and I will be content to stay awhile with thee.' Nay, but she leaves the watchmen, and still goes along the streets until she finds *him* whom her soul loveth. I have known some who love the Lord to be very happy while the preacher is proclaiming the truth to them; but they have stopped with the preacher, and have gone no further. This will never do, dear friends; do not be content to abide with us, who are only watchmen, but go beyond us, and seek till you find our Master. I should groan in heart, indeed, if any of you believed simply because of my word, as if it were my word alone that led you to believe, or if you should look merely to me for anything you need for your soul. In myself, I am nothing, and I have nothing; I only watch that, if I can, I may lead you to my Lord, whose shoe-latchets I am not worthy to unloose. O you who love Christ, go beyond the means of grace! Go beyond ordinances, go beyond preachers, go beyond even the Bible itself, into an actual possession of the living Christ; labour after a conscious enjoyment of Jesus himself, till you can say with the spouse, 'I found him whom my soul loveth.' It is good to find sound doctrine, for it is very scarce nowadays. It is good to learn the practical precepts of the gospel, it is good to be in the society of the saints; but if you put any of these in the place of communion with your Lord himself, you do ill. Never be content till you can say, 'I found *him*.' Dear souls, did you ever find him? Have you yet found him? If you have not, keep on seeking, keep on praying, till at last you can say, 'Eureka! I have found him whom my soul loveth. Jesus is indeed mine.'

What is meant by the words, 'I found him'? Well, I think a soul may say 'I found him' in the sense employed in the text, when first of all it has a clear view of his person. My Beloved is divine and human, the Son of God and yet the Son of man. My Beloved died, yet he is alive again. My Beloved was on earth, but he is now in heaven, and he will shortly come again. I want thus to find him myself, and I want each one of you to do the same. Picture him on Calvary, see him risen from the dead. Try, if you can, not so much by imagination as by faith, to behold him as he now sits at the right hand of the Majesty on high, where harps unnumbered tune his praise. Yet even there he bears the wounds he received for us here below. How resplendent shine the nail-prints! The marks of his death on earth are the glory of his person above.

> This is the Man, th'exalted Man,
> Whom we unseen adore;
> But when our eyes behold his face,
> Our hearts shall love him more.

Let your soul picture him so plainly that you can seem to see him, for this will be a part of your finding him.

But that will not be enough; you must then get to know that he is present with you. We cannot see him, but yet he that walketh amidst the golden candlesticks is, in spirit, in this house of prayer at this moment. My Master, thou art here. There is no empty seat at the table left to be filled by thee, nor do we expect to see thee walking among us, in thy calm majesty, clothed with thy seamless garment down to thy feet; and we do not want to see thee. Our faith realizes thee quite as well as sight could do, and we bless thee that thou hearest us as we speak to thee. Thou art invisible, yet assuredly present; thou art looking into our faces, thou art delighting in us as objects of thy redeeming love. Thou dost especially remember that thou didst die for us; and, as a mother gazes upon the babe for whom she has endured so much, or as a shepherd looks upon the sheep that he has brought back from its long wanderings, so art thou now looking upon each one of thy loved ones. If, dear friends, you can get that thought fully into your minds, that Christ is really here in our midst, you can then each one begin to say, 'I have found him.'

But you want more than that, namely, to feel that he loves you, loves you as if there were nobody else for him to love, loves you even as the Father loves him. That is a daring thing to say, and I should never have said it if he had not first uttered it; but he says, 'As the Father hath loved me, so have I loved you.' Can you comprehend how each one of the blessed Trinity loves each of the others, and especially how the Father loves the Son? Even so does Jesus Christ love you, my believing brother, my believing sister. Note that he *loves* you; it is not only that he did love you, and died for you, but he still loves you. He says to you, individually, 'I have graven thee upon the palms of my hands.' Look at the nail-print, that is his memorial, his forget-me-not, and by it he says to thee:

> Forget thee I will not, I cannot, thy name
> Engraved on my heart doth for ever remain:

The palms of my hands whilst I look on I see
The wounds I received when suffering for thee.

Now have you not found him? If you have pictured him to your mind's eye, if you are certain of his presence with you, and then, above all, if you are fully assured of his love, you can say, 'I have found him.'

If you can in truth say that, I hope there will come with it this one other thing, namely, *an exceeding great joy*. I cannot speak to you as I would wish; my words cannot express the joy of heart which I feel in knowing that I have found him, that he is with me, and that he has loved me with an everlasting love. I shall never understand, even in heaven, why the Lord Jesus should ever have loved me. I can say to Jesus what David said in his lamentation over Jonathan, 'Thy love to me was wonderful, passing the love of women.' There is no love like it, and why was it fixed upon me? Have you never felt that you could go in, like David, and sit before the Lord, and say, 'Who am I, O Lord God? and what is my house, that thou hast brought me hitherto?' Yet wonderful as it is, it is true; Jesus loves you, loves you now at this very moment. Do you not rejoice in it? I assure you that in the least drop of the love of Christ when it is consciously realized, there is more sweetness than there would be in all heaven without it. Talk of bursting barns, overflowing wine-vats, and riches treasured up; these give but a poor solace to the heart. But the love of Jesus, this is another word for heaven; and it is a marvel that even while we are here below we should be permitted to enjoy a bliss beyond what the angels know, for

Never did angels taste above
Redeeming grace and dying love,

but that joy is ours if we can truly say, 'I have found him.'

If you have come as far as that – and if you have not, may God help you to this point right speedily – come to the table of your Lord. You are indeed his children, so you have a right to come. Hear the King's invitation, 'Eat, O friends; drink, yea, drink abundantly O beloved.' These joys are not merely for some of the Lord's people but for all his saints; then, stand not back, but come and feast on the rich provision of love divine.

Now we come to the second step. The spouse says, '*I held him*.' This is a deeper experience than the former one; 'I held him' means more than 'I found him'. Sometimes, Jesus comes to his children and manifests himself very sweetly to them; but they behave to him in an unseemly manner, and soon he is gone. I have known him reveal himself to his people, most delightfully, but they have grown cold and wayward and foolish, and he has been obliged to go away from them. When you get to the top of the mountain, it needs great grace to keep there. I do not find it difficult to get into communion with Christ, but I confess that I do not find it so easy to maintain that communion. So that, if you have found him, do as the spouse says that she did, 'I held him.'

How are we to hold Christ? Well, first, let us hold him by our heart's resolve. If now we have him near us, let us lovingly look him in the face and say, 'My Lord, my sweet, blessed Lord, how can I let thee go? My all in all, my heart's Lord and King, how can I let thee go? Abide with me, go not from me.' Hold him by your love's resolve, and it shall be as chains of gold to fasten him to you. Say to him, 'My Lord, wilt thou go away from me? See how happy thou hast made me; a glimpse of thy love has made me so blest that I do not envy the angels before thy throne; wilt thou take that joy away from me by taking thyself away? Why didst thou give me a taste of thy love if thou dost not mean to give me more? This little has but made me out of liking for all things else; thou hast spoilt me now for all my former joy. O tarry with me, my Master, else am I unhappy indeed!' Further say to him, 'Lord, if thou go, thy chosen one will be unsafe. There is a wolf prowling about; what will thy poor lamb do without thee, O mighty Shepherd? There are cruel adversaries all around seeking my hurt; how can I live without thee? Wilt thou deliver thy turtle-dove over to the cruel fowler who seeks to slay her? Be that far from thee, O Lord! Therefore, abide with me.' Tell him how you will sorrow if he goes away.

> 'Tis paradise if thou art here,
> If thou depart, 'tis hell.

'Nothing can revive my spirit if thou be gone from me. Oh, stay with me, stay with me, I beseech thee, most blessed Lord!' As long as you can find arguments for his staying, Christ does not want to go from you. His delights are with the sons of men, and he is happy in the society of those whom he has purchased with his precious blood. Keep on giving your reasons why he should remain with you, and so hold him; be bold enough even to say to him, 'I will not let thee go.' Get you to Jacob's boldness when he said to the Angel of the covenant, 'I will not let thee go except thou bless me'; but go even beyond that, do not put in any 'except' at all, but say, 'I will not let thee go, for I cannot be blest if thou art gone from me.'

Further, brethren, hold him by making him your all in all. He will never go away if you treat him as he should be treated. Yield up everything to him, be obedient to him, be willing to suffer for him, grieve not his Holy Spirit, crown him, extol him, magnify him, keep on singing his praises, for so will you hold him. Renounce all else for him; for he sees that you truly love him when you count all things but dross for his dear sake. He says, 'I remember thee, the kindness of thy youth, the love of thine espousals, when thou wentest after me in the wilderness.' Those were the days when some of you could brook a father's frown for the sake of Christ's love, when you could have given up your situation and all your prospects in life to follow Jesus, it was then that he delighted in you; and in proportion as you break your idols, put away your sins, and keep your heart chaste and pure for him alone, you shall abide in his love. Yea, and you shall get deeper and deeper into it till what was a stream up to your ankles shall soon be breast-deep, and, by-and-by, shall be waters to swim in. Christ and you cannot fully agree unless you walk as he would have you walk, in careful holiness and earnest service for him. 'Can two walk together, except they be agreed?' And is there anything in this vile world that is fit to stand in rivalry with him? Is there any gain, is there any joy, is there any beauty, that can be compared with his gain, his joy, his beauty? Let each of us cry, 'Christ for me. Go, harlot-world; come not near even the outside of my door. Go thou, for my heart is with my Lord, and he is my soul's chief treasure.' If you will talk like that, you will hold him fast till you have your heart's desire, and bring him to your mother's house.

Hold him, too, by a simple faith. That is a wonderful hold-fast. Say to him, 'My Lord, I have found thee now, and I rejoice in thee; but still, if thou hidest thy face from me, I will still believe in thee. If I never see a smile from thee again till I see thee on thy throne, yet will I not doubt thee, for my heart is fixed, not so much upon the realization of thy presence, as upon thyself, and thy finished work. Though thou slay me, yet will I trust in thee.' Ah! then he will not go away from you; you can hold him in that way; but if you begin to put your trust in enjoyments of his presence instead of in himself alone, it may be that he will take himself away from you in order to bring you back to your old moorings, so that, as a sinner, you may trust the sinner's Saviour, and trust in him alone.

One word more before we leave this point. The only way to hold Christ is to hold him by his own power. I smiled to myself as I read my text, and tried to make it all my own: 'I held him, and would not let him go.' I thought to myself, the spouse said of her Bridegroom that she would not let him go; and shall I ever say to my Lord that I will not let him go? He is the King of kings, the omnipotent Jehovah; can I hold him? He is the mighty God, and yet a poor puny worm like myself says, 'I would not let him go.' Can it be really so? Well, the Holy Ghost says that it is, for he guided the pen of the writer of this Song when he wrote, 'I held him, and would not let him go.' Think of poor Jacob, who, when the angel did but touch him, felt his sinews shrink directly, yet he said, 'I will not let thee go.' And I, a poor trembling creature, may hold the Omnipotent himself, and say to him, 'I will not let thee go.' How is that wonder to be accomplished? I will tell you. If Omnipotence helps you to hold Omnipotence, why, then, the deed is done! If Christ, and not you alone, holds Christ, then Christ is held indeed, for shall he vanquish his own self? No, Master, thou couldst slay death, and break the old serpent's head, but thou canst not conquer thine own self; and if thou art in me, I can hold thee, for it is not I, but Christ in me, that holdeth Christ, and will not let him go. This is the power which enables us, with the apostle, to say, 'I am persuaded that neither death, nor life, nor angels, nor principalities, nor powers, nor things present, nor things to come, nor height, nor depth, nor any other creature, shall be able to separate us from the love of God, which is in Christ Jesus our Lord.'

The next step is described in the words, '*I brought him.*' With this we finish: 'I brought him into my mother's house, and into the chamber of her that conceived me.' And where, I pray you, beloved, is our mother's house? I do not believe in any reverence for mere material buildings; but I have great reverence for the true Church of the Living God. The Church is the house of God, and the mother of our souls. It was under the ministry of the Word that most of us were born to God, it was in the assembly of the saints that we heard the message which first of all quickened us into newness of life, and we may well be content to call the Church of Christ our mother, since our elder Brother – you know his name – when one said to him, 'Behold, thy mother and thy brethren stand without, desiring to speak with thee', pointing to his disciples answered, 'Behold, my mother, and my brethren. For whosoever shall do the will of my Father which is in heaven, the same is my brother, and sister, and mother.' Surely, where Jesus chooses to call the assembly of the faithful by the sacred name of mother, we may rightly do the same.

And we love the Church, which is our mother. I do hope that all the members of this church love the whole Church of God, and also have a special affection for that particular part of it in which they were born for God. It would be unnatural – and grace is never unnatural, though it is supernatural – it would be unnatural not to love the place where we were born into the heavenly family. I do not know, and never shall know on earth the man who was the means of my conversion, I may know him when I get to heaven; but if he is still living anywhere in this world, God bless him! And I know that many of you would say the same of the outward instrumentality which was used as the means of blessing to you; and you will say the same, will you not, of all the brotherhood of which some of us are but the spokesmen and representatives? We love the Church of God. Well, then, whenever we find our Beloved, we have to hold him, and not let him go, and then to bring him down to the house of our mother, and to the chamber of her that conceived us.

How can you bring Christ to his Church? Partly, you can bring him by your spirit. There is a wonderful power about a man's spirit, even though he does not speak a word. Silent worshippers can contribute very greatly to the communion of saints. I know some brethren – I will not say that any of them are here now – but I have known some brethren whose very faces dispirit and discourage one, whose every movement seems to make one feel anything but spiritual. But I know others of whom I can truly say that it is always pleasant to me to get a shake of their hands, and to have a look from their eyes. I know that they have been with Jesus, for there is the very air of saintliness about them; I do not mean sanctimoniousness, that is a very different thing. In the old pictures, the painters used to put a halo round the head of a saint – a most absurd idea; but I do believe that there is a real spiritual halo continually surrounding the man who walks with God.

If you, dear friend, have really found Christ, and bring him with you into the assembly, you will not be the man who will criticize, and find fault, and quarrel with your neighbour because he does not give you enough room in the pew. You will not be the person to pick holes in other people's coats; but you will be very considerate of others. As for yourself, anything will do for you, and anywhere will do for you, for you have seen the Beloved. You want other people to get as much good as they can; you are no longer selfish; how can you be, when you have found him whom your soul loveth? And now your poor brother need not be very choice in the selection of his words: if he will only talk about Jesus, you will be quite satisfied; if his accents should be a little broken, you will not mind that. So long as you feel that he wishes to extol your Lord, that will be enough for you.

So, in this manner, you will in spirit bring the Beloved to your mother's house, to the chamber of her that conceived you.

But, dear friend, it will also be a happy thing if you are able to talk about your Lord, for then you can bring him to the Church with your words. Those of us who are called to preach the Word have often to cry unto the Lord to help us to bring Christ into the assembly by our words – though, indeed, the words of any human language are but a poor conveyance for the Christ of God. Oh, let the King, my blessed Master, ride in the chariot of angelic song, and not in the lumbering waggon of my poor sermons! I long to see him flying on the wings of the wind, and not in the car of my feeble language; yet has he come to you many a time that way, and you have been glad. Let him come as he will, if he will but come, it is our delight to bring him into our mother's house, into the chamber of her that conceived us. Therefore, dear friends, each one of you in turn, as you are able, talk to your brother and to your sister, and say, 'I have found him whom my soul loveth.' You know that, when Samson killed the lion, he said nothing about it; it would have been a great feat for anyone else to boast of, but Samson could kill a lion any day, so he did not think much of doing that; but when he afterwards found a swarm of bees and honey in the carcase of the lion, he took some of it and began to eat, and carried a portion of it to his father and mother. So, if ever you find sweetness and preciousness in Christ, the true strong One, be sure that you carry a handful of the honey to your friends, and give portions to those for whom otherwise nothing might be prepared.

Thus hold Christ fast, and bring him to your mother's house by your spirit and by your words.

But if, alas! You feel that you cannot speak for Christ, then, beloved, bring him by your prayers. Do pray, especially at these communion seasons, that the King himself will come near, and feast his saints today. Ask him not only to bless you, but to bless all his saints, for you are persuaded that they all love him better than you do, and that they all want him as much as you do, and that they will all praise him even more than you do if he will but come and manifest himself to them. In this way, each one of you, as you come to the house of prayer, and to the place of fellowship, will be a real accession to our spiritual force, and we shall seem to get nearer and nearer to our Master as the house fills with loving worshippers who have found him, and held him, and brought him here.

Now may we find all this to be especially true as we gather around the table! The Lord be with you all, for his dear name's sake! Amen.

23

THE REAL PRESENCE, THE GREAT WANT OF THE CHURCH

'It was but a little that I passed from them, but I found him whom my soul loveth: I held him, and would not let him go, until I had brought him into my mother's house, and into the chamber of her that conceived me. I charge you, O ye daughters of Jerusalem, by the roes, and by the hinds of the field, that ye stir not up, nor awake my love, till he please' (Song of Solomon 3:4, 5).

Is it necessary to say that the Lord Jesus Christ is no longer corporeally present in his church? It ought not to be needful to assert so evident a truth; and yet it is important to do so, since there are some who teach that in what they are pleased to call 'the Holy Sacrament' Christ is actually present in his flesh and blood. Such persons unwittingly deny the real humanity of our Lord Jesus Christ, for if he has indeed assumed our humanity, and is in all points made like unto his brethren, his flesh and blood cannot be in two places at one time. Our bodily humanity could not be present in more places than one at one time, and if Christ's humanity be like ours it cannot be in an unlimited number of places at once; in fact, it can only be in one place. Where that place is we know from Scripture, for he sitteth at the right hand of God, expecting till his enemies be made his footstool. Unless you are to suppose that the humanity of Christ is something altogether different from ours, it cannot be here and there and everywhere; but to suppose that it is a different humanity from ours is to deny that he is incarnate in our nature. Our Lord Jesus told his disciples that he would go away, and he has gone away. He ascended into heaven, bearing humanity up to the throne of God. 'He is not here, for he is risen.'

Remember, also, that because the Lord Jesus is absent corporeally, the Holy Spirit the Comforter is with us, for he especially said, 'If I go not away, the Comforter will not come unto you: but if I depart, I will send him unto you.' Those who believe that Christ's flesh and blood are or can be present on earth, deny the presence of the Holy Spirit; for the Scripture is plain enough upon that point – that the bodily absence of our Lord is the cause and condition of the presence of the Comforter. If Jesus dwells still corporeally upon the earth, then the Spirit of God is not upon the earth. Many other most serious errors follow from the supposition that the humanity of the Redeemer is present anywhere except at the right hand of God, even the Father; yet it is an imagination which lies at the basis of the sacramental system, and thousands are greatly enamoured of it.

No word of mine this morning is intended to have the remotest connection with any sacramental presence of the corporeal nature of our Lord; our mind has a far other matter before it. Let us, therefore, having guarded ourselves so as not to be misunderstood, proceed to speak of another presence of our blessed Lord. The fact is that Christ Jesus the Lord, is present in his church by the Holy Spirit. The Holy Spirit is this day the representative of Christ in the midst of the church, and it is in the power and the energy of the Holy Ghost that Christ is with us always, and will be even to the end of the world. As God, Jesus is everywhere; as man, he is only in heaven; as God and man in one person, Mediator and Head of the Church, he is present with us by the Holy Ghost, the Comforter, whom the Father has sent in his name. It is by the working of the Spirit of God that Christ's presence in the church is manifested; and we are to expect no other presence than that. We have the spiritual divine presence of the second person of the blessed Trinity, and the presence of Christ Jesus also in the power of his representative on earth, the Holy Ghost.

This presence, not a bodily but a spiritual presence, is the glory of the church of God. When she is without it she is shorn of her strength; when she possesses it all good things ensue. Brethren, if a church be without the Spirit of God in it, it may have a name to live, but it is dead, and, you know, that after death there follows corruption, corruption which breeds foulness and disease. Hence, those churches which have turned aside unto error, have not only lost all power to do good, but they have become obnoxious and the causes of great evil in the midst of the world. If any professing church abides not in Christ it is cast forth as a branch and is withered; and while it is decaying, it is injurious, and there is need for the world's welfare that it be utterly destroyed. We must have Christ in the church, or the body which was meant to be the medium of the greatest good becomes the source of the grossest evil.

Let the Spirit of God be in the church, then there is power given to all her ministries; whether they be ministries of public testimony in the preaching of the Word, or ministries of holy love amongst the brethren, or ministries of individual earnestness to the outside world, they will all be clothed with energy, in the fulness of the power of the Lord Jesus. Then her ordinances become truly profitable, then baptism is burial with the Lord, and the sacred supper is a feast of love; then the communion of the brethren in their solemn prayer and praise becomes deep and joyful, and their whole life and walk are bright with the glow of heaven. In the presence of the Lord the graces of the saints are developed; the church grows rich in all spiritual gifts; her warfare becomes victorious, and her continual worship sweet as the incense of the golden censer. What the moon is to the night, or the sun to the day, or the Nile to Egypt, or the dew to the tender herb, or the soul to the human frame, that is the presence of Jesus to his church.

Give us the Spirit of God and we will ask no endowments from the State, nor sigh for the prestige of princely patronage. Endow us, O God, with the Holy Ghost, and we have all we need. The poverty of the members, their want of learning, their want of rank, all these shall be as nothing. The Holy Ghost can make amends for all deficiencies, and clothe his poor and obscure people with an energy at which the world shall tremble. This made the apostolic church mighty, she had the Holy Ghost outpoured upon her; the lack of this made the medieval ages dark as midnight, for men contended about words and letters, but forgot the Spirit; the return of this inestimable blessing has given us every true revival; the working of the eternal Spirit, the presence of Christ in the midst of his people is the Sun of Righteousness arising with healing beneath his wings. This has been our confidence, as a church, these eighteen years, and if we are yet to see greater and better things, we must still rely on this same strength, the divine presence of Jesus Christ by the wonder-working Spirit. 'Not by might, nor by power, but by my Spirit, saith the Lord.'

It becomes then the great desire of every earnest Christian who loves the church of God, that Christ should be in the church, and that by his Spirit he should work wonders there, and I have selected this text with the view of stirring up the spiritual-minded among you to seek so great a blessing. Let me endeavour, in opening up this blessed text, to show the means and the course of action necessary if we would see the church revived by her Lord's presence.

And first, we learn from the text that before ever we can bring the Well-Beloved into our mother's house, the church, **WE MUST FIND HIM PERSONALLY FOR OURSELVES.**

We begin with that. 'It was but a little that I passed from them, but I found him whom my soul loveth.' How can we bring into the chamber of the church him whom we have not yet met with ourselves? How can we communicate grace to others instrumentally, unless, first of all, we have received it into our own hearts? I am not now about to speak of the need of conversion; we all know that no spiritual act can be performed until we become spiritual men; but I am now speaking about something higher than bare conversion. If we would bless the church, we must ourselves occupy a higher platform than that of being merely saved; we must be believers, walking in fellowship with Christ, and having, in that respect, found him whom our soul loveth.

There are many believers who have only just enough grace to enable us to hope that they are alive; they have no strength with which to work for God's cause; they have not an arm to lend to the help of others, neither can they even see that which would comfort others, for they are blind, and cannot see afar off, they want all their sight, and all their strength, for themselves. Those who are to bring the Well-Beloved into our mother's house, must be of another kind. They must get beyond the feebleness which is full of doubting and fearing, into the assurance which grasps the Saviour, and the fellowship which lives in daily communion with him.

I know there are some such in this church, and I would single them out, and speak to them thus: 'Brother, if thou wouldst bring Christ into the church which thou lovest, then, first of all, *thine inmost soul must so love Christ, that thou canst not live without his company.* This must be thy cry: 'Saw ye him whom my soul loveth?' and this must be the goal of thine aspirations: 'I have found him whom my soul loveth.' It must not be talk, it must be soul-love; it must not be a profession of affection for Jesus, but the inmost bowels of our being must be moved by his name.

The words are very strong, 'him whom my soul loveth'; as if though the spouse might love the daughters of Jerusalem, might love the watchmen of the city, might love them all in their place, yet her soul's love, the essence of her love, her deepest, fondest, purest, and most real love was all for him. Are there not such hearts here, virgin minds in whom Christ is first, last, midst, chief, and all in all? Oh, if there be, ye are the men, ye are the women, who, finding your Beloved, can bring him into the church. May God multiply your number, and may each of you have compassion on the languishing church of this chill age, and labour to restore to her the glory which has faded from her brow. Pray ye for Laodicea in her lukewarmness, and Sardis in her spiritual death; but you will only prevail in proportion as your inmost soul loves the Redeemer and abides in his love.

These ardent lovers of Jesus *must diligently seek him*. The chapter before us says that the spouse sought him, sought him on her bed, sought him in the streets, sought him in the broadways, sought him at last at the lips of the watchmen, sought him everywhere where he was likely to be found. We *must* enjoy the perpetual fellowship of Jesus. We who love him in our souls cannot rest until we know that he is with us. I fear that with some of us our sins have grieved him, and he has betaken himself to the far-off 'mountains of myrrh and hills of frankincense'. It may be our lax living, our neglect of prayer, or some other fault, has taken from us the light of his countenance. Let us resolve this morning that there shall be no rest unto our souls until once again he has returned unto us in the fulness of his manifested love, to abide in our hearts. Seek him, brother, seek him, sister. He is not far from any of you, but do seek him with an intense longing for him, for until thou dost thou art not the man to bring him into the assembly of the brethren. Labour to bring Jesus into the chambers of the church, but first be sure that thou hast him thyself, or thy zeal will be hypocrisy.

In seeking our Lord we must *use all ministries*. The spouse enquired of the watchmen. We are not to despise God's servants, for he is usually pleased to bless us through them, and it would be ungrateful both to him and to them to pass them by as useless. But, while we use the ministries, *we must go beyond them*. The spouse did not find her Lord through the watchmen; but she says, 'it was but a little that I passed from them, that I found him whom my soul loveth.' I charge you, my dear hearers, never rest content with listening to me. Do not imagine that hearing the truth preached simply and earnestly will of itself be a blessing to your souls. Far, far beyond the servant, pass to the Master. Be this the longing of each heart, each Sabbath-day, 'Lord, give me fellowship with thyself.' True, we are led to see Jesus sometimes, and I hope often, through listening to the truth proclaimed, but, O Lord, it is no outer court worship that will satisfy us; we want to come into the holy of holies and stand at the mercy-seat itself. It is no seeing thee afar off and hearing about thee that will content our spirits, we must draw nigh unto thee, and behold thee as the world cannot. Like Simeon, we must take thee into our arms or we cannot say that we have seen God's salvation: like John, we must lean our heads upon thy bosom or we cannot rest. Thine apostles are well enough, thy prophets well enough, thy evangelists well enough; but oh, we feel constrained to go beyond them all, for we thirst after fellowship with thee, our Saviour. Those who feel thus will bless the church, but only such.

Note, that we must *search to the very utmost* till we find our Beloved. The Christian must leave no stone unturned till he gets back his fellowship with Christ. If any sin obstructs the way, it must be rigorously given up; if there be any neglected duty, it must be earnestly discharged; if there be any higher walk of grace, which is necessary to continuous fellowship, we must ascend it, fearing no hill of difficulty. We must not say, 'there is a lion in the way' – if there be lions we must slay them; if the way be rough we must tread it; we must go on hands and knees if we cannot run; but we must reach to fellowship with Jesus; we must have Christ or pine till we do. Sacrifices we must make and penalties we must endure, but to Christ we must come, for we are feeble when we are absent from him, and quite incapable of rendering any great service to the church, till once for all we can say, 'I found him, I held him, and I would not let him go.' O dear brethren and sisters, I know there are some of you who can enter into what I mean; but I would to God there were many more to whom the first thought of life was Christ Jesus. Oh, for more Enochs, men who walk with God, whose habitual spirit is that of close communion with Jesus, meditating upon him, yea, more than that, sympathising with him, drinking into his spirit, changed into his likeness, living over again his life, because he is in them the monarch of their souls. O that we had a chosen band of elect spirits of this race, for surely the whole church would be revived through their influence; God, even our own God, would bless us; and we should see bright, halcyon days dawning for the bride of Christ. Here, then, is the first point: we must find the Lord Jesus for ourselves, or we cannot bring him into our mother's house.

I would beg every believer here to ask himself a few questions, such as these: 'Am I walking in constant fellowship with Christ? If I am not, why not? Is it that I am worldly? Is it that I am proud, or indolent, or envious, or careless? Am I indulging myself in any sin? Is there anything whatever that divides me from Christ my Lord?' Let this be the resolution of every one of the Lord's people: 'From this time forth I will seek unto the Lord my Saviour, and I will not be satisfied until I can say, "I am coming up from the wilderness leaning upon the Beloved." '

This brings us to the second point of the subject. If we would be a blessing to the church, and have already found Christ, **WE MUST TAKE CARE TO RETAIN HIM**. 'I found him whom my soul loveth; I held him, and I would not let him go.' From this I learn that in order to be of great use to the church of God, it is needful for those who commune with Christ to continue in that communion. How comparatively easy it is to climb to the top of Pisgah! It needs but a little effort; many bold and gracious spirits are fully equal to it. But to keep there, to abide in that mountain, this is the difficulty. To come to Christ, and to sit down at his feet, is a simple thing enough for believers, and many of us have attained to it; but to sit day after day at the Master's feet is quite another matter. Oh, could I always be as I sometimes am! Could I not only rise above but remain there! But, alas, our spiritual nature is too much like this weather – it is balmy today, one would think that spring or summer had come; but, perhaps, tonight we may be chilled with frost and tomorrow drenched with rain. Ah, how fickle are our spirits. We are walking with Christ, rejoicing, leaping for joy; and anon the cold frosts of worldliness come over us, and we depart from him. Ye will never be strong to impart great blessings to others till you cease to wander, and learn the meaning of that text: 'Abide in me.' Note well, it is not 'Look at me'; nor 'Come near to me, and then go away from me', but 'Abide in me.' The branch does not leave the vine and then leap back again to the stock; you never saw a living branch of the vine roaming into the corners of the vineyard, or rambling over the wall; it abides in connection with the parent stem at all times, and even so should it be with the Christian.

Mark, that according to the text, it is very apparent that *Jesus will go away if he be not held.* 'I held him and I would not let him go'; as if he would have gone if he had not been firmly retained. When he met with Jacob that night at the Jabbok, he said, 'Let me go.' He would not go without Jacob's letting him, but he would have gone if Jacob had loosed his hold. The patriarch replied, 'I will not let thee go, except thou bless me.' This is one of Christ's ways and manners; it is one of the peculiarities of his character. When he walked to Emmaus with the two disciples, 'he made as if he would have gone further'; they might have known it was none other than the Angel of the Covenant by that very habit. He would have gone further, but they constrained him, saying, 'Abide with us for the day is far spent.' If you are willing to lose Christ's company, he is never intrusive, he will go away from you, and leave you till you know his value and begin to pine for him. 'I will go,' says he, 'and return to my place, till they acknowledge their offence, and seek my face: in their affliction they will seek me early.' He will go unless you hold him.

But note, next, *he is very willing to be held.* Who could hold him if he were not? He is the omnipotent Saviour, and if he willed to withdraw he could do so: let us hold him as we might. But, mark his condescension. When his spouse said, 'I held him, and I would not let him go', he did not go, he could not go, for his love held him as well as her hands. Christ is willing to be held. He loves that sacred violence which takes him by force, that holy diligence which leaves not a gap open by which he may escape, but shuts every door, bars every bolt, and saith, 'I have thee now and I will take care that if I lose thee it shall be through no fault of mine.' Jesus is willing enough to be retained by hearts which are full of his love.

And, brethren, whenever you have Christ, please to remember that *you are able to hold him.* She who held him in the Song was no stronger than you are; she was but a feeble woman, poorly fed under the Old Testament dispensation; you have drunk the new wine of the new covenant, and you are stronger than she. You can hold him, and he will not be able to go from you. 'How,' say you, 'shall I be able to hold him?' Oh, have you grasped him? Is he with you?

Now, then, hold him fast by your faith; trust him implicitly, rest in him for every day's cares, for every moment's ills. Walk by faith and he will walk with you.

Hold him also with the grasp of love. Let your whole heart go out towards him. Embrace him with the arms of mighty affection, enchain him with ardent admiration. Lay hold upon him by faith, and clasp him with love.

Be also much in prayer. Prayer casts a chain about him. He never leaves the heart that prays. There is a sweet perfume about prayer that always attracts the Lord; wherever he perceives it rising up to heaven there will he be.

Hold him, too, by your obedience to him. Never quarrel with him. Let him have his way. He will stop in any house where he can be master; he will stay nowhere where some other will lords it over his. Watch his words; be careful to obey them all. Be very tender in your conduct, so that nothing grieves him. Show to him that you are ready to suffer for his sake.

I believe that where there is a prayerful, careful, holy, loving, believing walk towards Jesus, the fellowship of the saint with his Lord will not be broken, but it may continue for months and years. There is no reason, except in ourselves, why fellowship with Jesus should not continue throughout an entire life; and oh, if it did, it would make earth into heaven, and lift us up to the condition of angels, if not beyond them, and we should be the men who would bring Christ into the church, and through the church into the world. The church would be blest, and God would be glorified, and souls would be saved, if there were some among us who thus held him, and would not let him go.

I want to call your attention to one thought before I leave this, and that is, the spouse says, 'I held *him*.' Now, a great many persons in the world are holding their creed, and if it is a correct one I hope they will hold it; but that is the main business of their religious life; they do nothing else but hold this doctrine or that. Hold it, brother, hold it: it would be a pity you should let it go if it be the truth, but still it is more important to hold your Lord. Certain others are engrossed in holding scriptural ordinances, and saying, 'I hold this and I hold that.' Well, hold it brother; if it is God's ordinance do not let it go. But, after all, if there be anything I hold above all else, I hold *him*. Is not that the best grip a soul ever gets, when she lays hold of Christ? 'I held *him* and I would not him go.' Ah, Lord, I may be mistaken about doctrine, but I am not mistaken about thee. I may, perhaps, be staggered in my belief of some dogma which I thought was truth, but I am not staggered about *thee*. Thou Son of God made flesh for me, thou art all my salvation and all my desire: I rest on thee only, without a shadow of mixture of any other hope, and I love thee supremely, desiring to honour thee and to obey thee in life and until death. I hold thee, thou Covenant Angel, and I will not let thee go.

Dear friends! make this the mark of your life, that you hold him and will not let him go. You will be the kind of men to bless the church by leading the Well-Beloved into her chambers, if you know how to abide in him yourselves.

It appears from the text that, after the spouse had thus found Christ for herself and held him, **SHE BROUGHT HIM INTO THE CHURCH** – 'I brought him to my mother's house.' We ought lovingly to remember the church of God. By the Holy Spirit we were begotten unto newness of life, but it was in the church, and through the preaching of the word there that we were brought into the light of life. We owe our conversion, the most of us, to some earnest teacher of the truth in the church of God, or to some of those godly works which were written by Christian men. Through the church's instrumentality the Bible itself has been preserved to us, and by her the gospel has been preached to every age. She is our mother and we love her. I know that many of you, dear friends, the members of this church, love the church, and you can say, 'If I forget thee, let my right hand forget her cunning.' When you are away from this place, and cannot mix in our solemn assemblies, your heart mourns like one in banishment. Have not I heard you cry, 'Ziona, Ziona, our holy and beautiful house, wherein we have worshipped our God, the house which is built of living stones, among whom Christ himself is the corner-stone, even thy church, O Jesus: would God I were in her midst again, and could once more unite my praises with those that dwell within her.' Yes, and because we love our mother's house and the chamber of her that conceived us, we desire to bring Christ into the church more and more. Did I hear a harsh but honest voice exclaim, 'But I find much fault with the church'? Brother, if thou lovest her, thou wilt go backward and cast a mantle over all. But, suppose thy candour is compelled to see faults in her; then there is so much the more need of her Lord's presence in her to cure those faults. The more sickly she is, the more she wants him to be her strength and her physician. I say, therefore, to thee, dear friend, above all things, seek to bring Christ into an imperfect church, and a weak church, and an erring church, that she may become strong in the Lord and in the power of his might.

I have shown you by whom it must be – by those who have found him, and who hold him; and now we will mention the methods by which our blessed Lord can be brought into his church.

The saints can bring him in by their *testimony*. I hope that often Christ is here when I have borne testimony to you of his power to save, of his atoning blood, of his exaltation in heaven, of the perfection of his character, of his willingness to save. Many a Sabbath day his name has been like ointment poured forth in this place. Is there any subject that so delights you as that which touches upon Christ? Is not that the rarest string in all the harp of scriptural truth? Well, every true minister, by bearing witness for Christ, helps to bring him into the church.

But others can do it by their *prayers*. There is a mysterious efficacy in the prayers of men who dwell near to God. Even if they were compelled to keep their beds, and do nothing but pray, they would pour benedictions upon the church. We want our dear sick friends to get well and come among us at once in full health; but I do not know, I do not know, they may be of more service to the church where they are. 'Ye that make mention of the Lord keep not silence, and give him no rest day or night, till he establish and make Jerusalem a praise in the earth.' Now, if there were not some saints kept awake at night by sickness to pray, we should not so fully realise that word, 'Give him no rest day nor night.' Some of those dear ones, whose faces we miss from among us, keep up the perpetual ministry of intercession. Their incense of prayer goes up at all hours; when the most of us are rightly enough at sleep they are compelled to wake, and therefore are led still to pray.

How many blessings come down upon the church of God through the prayers of his feeble saints it is not possible for us to tell; but I believe if all of us were to set apart a special time for praying and pleading with Christ that he would come into his church, we should not be long before we saw a wonderful effect resulting from those pleadings. Wrestling prayers bring Christ into the innermost chambers of the church of God. Let us try the power of prayer.

And, there is no doubt, dear brethren, that Christ is often brought into the church *by the example of those eminent saints who abide in Christ*. You know what I mean. There is a very manner and air about some Christian men which honours Christ, and benefits his people. They may not be gifted in speech, but their very spirit speaks, they are so gentle, loving, tender, earnest, truthful, upright, gracious. Their paths, like the paths of God himself, drop fatness. They are the anointed of the Lord, and you perceive it. Perhaps you could not say that this virtue or that is very prominent, but it is the altogether; it is their life at home, their life in public, their church life, their private life, their entire conduct makes you see that the Holy Ghost is in them, and when they come into the church they bring the Spirit of God with them, and are thus a great means of blessing to all with whom they associate. I do pray, brethren, that in some way or other, each one of us may try to bring Jesus Christ into the midst of his own people.

I am afraid there are some who on the contrary are driving him away – church members that, instead of blessing the church, are a curse to it. I see a great heap before me – a vast heap that God has gathered through my instrumentality; but the winnowing fan is going, and the chaff is flying. Are you, dear friends, among the chaff or the wheat? Are you seed for the sower, or fuel for the flame unquenchable? Oh! Live near to Christ; live in Christ; may Christ live in you; then will you enrich the church of God; but if you do not, but only make a profession of love with your lips, what shall I say unto you? I mourn over you. Take heed of living a weak life, a life without God in it, a life without Christ in it, a life which a Pharisee might live. Seek to live the life of a true-born child of God, lest you hinder the church's usefulness, and deprive her of her Lord's presence.

This leads me to the last point, which is this, to **CHARGE THE CHURCH THAT SHE BE CAREFUL NOT TO DISTURB THE LORD'S REPOSE**, if we have been enabled by divine grace to bring the Lord into the chambers of our mother's house. 'I charge you, O ye daughters of Jerusalem, by the roes and by the hinds of the field, that ye stir not up, nor awake my love, till he please.'

Observe, then, that *the Lord Jesus in this church is not indifferent to the conduct of his people*. We are not to suppose that because the sin of all God's elect is pardoned, therefore it is of small consequence how they live. By no manner of means. The Master of this great house is not blind nor deaf, neither is he a person who is utterly careless as to how the house is managed; on the contrary, as God is a jealous God, so is Christ a jealous husband to his church. He will not tolerate in her what he would tolerate in the world. She lies near his heart, and she must be chaste to him.

What a solemn work the Lord did in the early church. That story of Ananias and Sapphira – it is often used most properly to illustrate the danger of lying; but that is not the point of the narrative. Ananias and Sapphira were members of the church at Jerusalem, and they lied not unto men, which would have been sin enough, but in lying to the church officers they lied unto God, and the result was their sudden death. Now, you are not to suppose that this was a solitary case. Wherever there is a true church of God, the judgments of God are always going on in it. I speak now not only what I have read, but what I have known and seen with mine eyes; what I am as sure of as I am sure of any fact in history.

The apostle Paul, speaking of the same in his day, said that in a certain church there was so much sin that many were weak and sickly among them, and many slept; that is to say, there was great sickness in the church, and many died. Judgments are begun in the house of God and are always going on there. I have seen men in the church who have walked at a distance from God, who have been visited with severe chastisements; others who have been of hot and proud spirit, have been terribly humbled; and some who have arrogantly touched God's ark, and the doom of Uzzah has befallen them. I have seen it and do know it. And so it always will be.

The Lord Jesus Christ looking around his church, if he sees anything evil in it, will do one of two things; either he will go right away from his church because the evil is tolerated there, and he will leave that church to be like Laodicea, to go on from bad to worse, till it becomes no church at all; or else he will come and he will trim the lamp, or to use the figure of the fifteenth of John, he will prune the vine-branch, and with his knife will cut off this member, and the other, and cast them into the fire; while, as for the rest, he will cut them till they bleed again, because they are fruit-bearing members, but they have too much wood, and he wants them to bring forth more fruit. It is not a trifling matter to be in the church of God. God's fire is in Zion, and his furnace in Jerusalem. 'His fan is in his hand, and he shall thoroughly purge' – what? The world. O no, 'his floor', the church. And then, again, 'he shall sit as a refiner and purifier of silver, and he shall purify' – what? The heathen nations. No, 'the sons of Levi' – his own people. So that Christ is not indifferent to what is going on in the church, and it is needful that when he comes to the church to take his repose, and solace himself there, we should not stir him up nor awake him till he please.

But many things will drive our Lord away, and these shall have our closing words. Dear fellow members of this church, may we each one be more watchful lest the Bridegroom should withdraw from us. He will go away if we grow proud. If we are boastful, and say, 'There is some reason why God should bless us', and should begin to speak hectoringly towards weaker brethren, the Lord will let us know that 'not unto us, not unto us, but unto his name shall be all the glory'.

Again, if there be a want of love among us, the Lord of love will be offended. The holy dove loves not scenes of strife; he frequents the calm still waters of brotherly love. There the Lord commanded the blessing, even life for evermore, where brethren dwelt together in unity. If any of you have half a hard thought towards another, get rid of it; if there be the beginnings of anything like jealousy, quench the sparks. 'Leave off strife,' says Solomon, 'before it be meddled with', as if he said, 'End it before you begin it', which, though it seems strangely paradoxical, is most wise advice. 'Little children love one another.' 'Walk in love as Christ also has loved us.' May discord be far from us.

Notice the beautiful imagery of the text. 'I charge you by the roes and the hinds of the field.' In ancient times gazelles were often tamed, and were the favourite companions of Eastern ladies: the gazelle might be standing near its mistress, fixing its loving eyes upon her, but if a stranger clapped his hands it would hasten away. The roes and hinds *of the field* are even yet more jealous things, a sound will startle them, even the breath of the hunter tainting the gale puts them to speedy flight. Even thus it is with Jesus. A little thing, a very little thing, will drive him from us, and it may be many a day before our repentance shall be able to find him again. He has suffered so much from sin that he cannot endure the approach of it. His pure and holy soul abhors the least taint of iniquity.

Let us gather from the text that there are some things in the true church which give our Lord rest. He is represented here as though he slept in the church, 'That ye stir not up nor awake my love till he please.' Wherever he sees true repentance, real faith, holy consecration, purity of life, chastity of love, there Christ rests. I believe he finds no sweeter happiness even in heaven than the happiness of accepting his people's prayers and praises. Our love is very sweet to him; our deeds of gratitude are very precious, the broken alabaster boxes of self-sacrifices done for him are very fair in his esteem. He finds no rest in the world, he never did; but he finds sweet rest on the bosoms of his faithful ones. He loves to come into a pure church, and there to say, 'I am at home, I will declare thy name unto my brethren: in the midst of the congregation will I praise thee.'

Let us be very watchful, too, against all impurity. Anything like uncleanness in a Christian will soon send the Master away from the church. You know what it was that brought the evil upon the house of Eli. It was because his sons made themselves vile even at the tabernacle door. The young people in that case were the immediate cause of the mischief, but it was the fault of the elder ones that they restrained them not. Watch against all evil passions and corrupt desires. Be ye holy even as your Father which is in heaven is holy.

And then, again, a want of prayer will send him away. There are members of some churches who never come to the prayer-meetings and I should be afraid that their private prayers cannot be any too earnest. Of course we speak not of those who have good excuse; but there are some who habitually and wilfully neglect the assembling of themselves together; these are worthy of condemnation. Oh, let us continue a prayerful church as we have hitherto been, otherwise the Master may say, 'They do not value the blessing, for they will not even ask for it; they evidently do not care about my Spirit, for they will not meet together and cry for him.' Do not grieve him by any such negligence of prayer.

So, too, we may grieve the Spirit by worldliness. If any of you who are rich get to imitate the fashions of the world and act as worldlings do, you cannot expect the Lord to bless us. You are Achans in the camp, if such is the case. And if you who are poor get to be envious of others and speak harshly of others to whom God has given more substance than to you, that again will grieve the Lord. You know how the children of Israel in the wilderness provoked him, and their provocation mostly took the form of murmuring; they complained of this and that: if they had the manna they wanted flesh, and if they had water gushing from the rock they must needs have more. I pray you by the bowels of mercies that are in Christ Jesus, by all the compassion he has manifested towards us, by the high love he deserves of us, since he laid down his life for us, by your allegiance to him as your King, by your trust in him as your Saviour, by your love to him as the Bridegroom of your souls, 'stir not up nor awake my love till he please.'

Let me ask you to be more in prayer; let me pray you to live nearer to him; let me entreat you for the church's sake, and for the world's sake, to be more thoroughly Christ's than you ever have been; and may the power of the Holy Spirit enable you in this. I do not fear lest I should lose that which I have wrought, for God will establish the work of our hands upon us; but yet I do put up to him daily the prayer that this church may not be found in years to come to be a building of wood and hay and stubble, that shall be consumed in the fire of heresy or discord, or some other testing flame which God may suffer to come upon it; but oh, may you, my beloved brethren and sisters, be gold and silver and precious stones, that the workman at the last, saved himself, may not have to suffer loss, nor the Master be dishonoured in the eyes of men. May you stand as a sparkling pile of precious gems, inhabited by the eternal Spirit, to the praise and glory of his grace, wherein he hath made us accepted in the Beloved. Amen.

24

THE ROYAL PAIR IN THEIR GLORIOUS CHARIOT

> 'Who is this that cometh out of the wilderness like pillars of smoke, perfumed with myrrh and frankincense, with all powders of the merchants? Behold his bed, which is Solomon's; threescore valiant men are about it, of the valiant of Israel. They all hold swords, being expert in war: every man hath his sword upon his thigh because of fear in the night. King Solomon made himself a chariot of the wood of Lebanon. He made the pillars thereof of silver, the bottom thereof of gold, the covering of it of purple, the midst thereof being paved with love, for the daughters of Jerusalem. Go forth, O ye daughters of Zion, and behold king Solomon with the crown wherewith his mother crowned him in the day of his espousals, and in the day of the gladness of his heart' (Song of Solomon 3:6-11).

Great princes in the east are in the habit of travelling in splendid palanquins, which are at the same time chariots and beds. The person reclines within, screened by curtains from public view; a bodyguard protects the equipage from robbers, and blazing torches light up the path along which the travellers proceed. King Solomon, in this Song, describes the Church of Christ, and Christ himself, as travelling through the world in such a palanquin. The day is coming when both our divine Lord and his chosen bride shall be revealed in glory before the eyes of all men. The present age is the period of concealment – the mystical Solomon and his beloved Solyma are both on earth, but they are unseen of men; like the ark of old they dwell within curtains; only the anointed priests of God can discern their beauties, and even these gaze rather by faith than by sight. 'Lo I am with you alway, even unto the end of the world' is certainly true, for Jesus is here; but equally correct is that word of Peter, 'Whom having not seen, ye love; in whom, though now ye see him not, yet believing, ye rejoice with joy unspeakable and full of glory.' He is here in the reality, power, and influence of his presence, but he is not here as to the visibility of his kingdom and person, for we wait with our loins girt about, and with patience of hope, until the revelation of Jesus Christ.

The portion of the blessed canticle now before us is, we think, descriptive of the progress of the hidden Christ through the world. He has been borne along, in very truth, but he himself has been so little perceived of men, that they even ask the question, 'Who is this that cometh out of the wilderness?' He is not now manifested openly to men. If any should say, 'Lo here!' or 'Lo there! this is Christ!' believe them not, for Christ is not as yet seen. When he doth come he shall be as perceptible as the lightning's flash, which every man's eye discerneth without the need of an instructor. So, also, with his true Church. She also is hidden like her Lord, and though her hand, her foot, or her face may be sometimes seen, yet the whole elect body has never yet been beheld. If any say, 'Lo, here is the Church of Christ!' or 'Lo there!' believe them not, for it is a fact that there is no corporation of men of which we can say exclusively or even universally, 'Lo, this is the Church of Christ.' There are tares growing with wheat in the best guarded field, and on the other hand no one enclosure contains all the wheat. The true Church of God is scattered here and there; it is found amongst all denominations, and there is not one denomination of which you can say, 'This only is the Church of Christ, or all its members belong to the body of Christ's spouse.' Just now the mystical bride is in a certain sense as invisible as her husband. Behold, then, the betrothed ones carried through the world in the sumptuous chariot of which we have to speak this morning.

I must now claim your attention while I notice, first, *the glory of the progress of Christ through the world*, as described in the sixth verse; secondly, *the security of Christ's cause*, as represented in the seventh and eighth; thirdly, *the superlative excellence of it*, as described in the ninth and tenth; and lastly, *our joyful duties with regard to it*, as openly declared in the eleventh.

First, then, THE MAGNIFICENT PROGRESS, THE GLORIOUS ON-GOING OF THE CHURCH AND HER LORD THROUGH THE WORLD.

'Who is this that cometh out of the wilderness like pillars of smoke, perfumed with myrrh and frankincense, with all powders of the merchant?' The equipage excites the attention of the onlooker; his curiosity is raised, and he asks, '*Who is this*?' Now, in the first progress of the Christian Church, in her very earliest days, there were persons who marvelled greatly; and though they set down the wonders of the day of Pentecost to drunkenness, yet, 'they were all amazed, and were in doubt, saying to one another, What meaneth this?' In after years, many a heathen philosopher said, 'What is this new power which is breaking the idols in pieces, changing old customs, making even thrones unsafe – what is this?' Bye-and-bye, in the age of the Reformation, there were cowled monks, cardinals in their red hats, and bishops, and princes, and emperors, who all said, 'What is this? What strange doctrine has come to light?' In the times of the modern reformation, a century ago, when God was pleased to revive his Church through the instrumentality of Whitefield and his brethren, there were many who said, 'What is this new enthusiasm, this Methodism? Whence came it, and what power is this which it wields?' And, doubtless, whenever God shall be pleased to bring forth his Church in power, and to make her mighty among the sons of men, the ignorance of men will be discovered breaking forth in wonder, for they will say, 'Who is this?' Spiritual religion is as much a novelty now as in the day when Grecian sages scoffed at it on Mars' Hill. The true Church of God is a stranger and pilgrim still; an alien and a foreigner in every land; a speckled bird; a dove in the midst of ravens; a lily among thorns.

The ignorance of men concerning spiritual things is not, however, caused by the darkness of the things themselves, for Christ and his Church are *the great lights of the world*. When great personages travelled in their palanquins, and more especially on marriage processions, they were attended by a number of persons who, at night, carried high up in the air burning cressets which gave forth a blaze of light. Sometimes these lights were simply torches carried in the hands of running footmen; at other times they were a sort of iron basket lifted high into the air, upon poles, from which went up a pillar of smoke and flame. Our text says, 'Who is this that cometh out of the wilderness like pillars of smoke?' a beautiful illustration of the fact that wherever Christ and his cause are carried, light is a sure accompaniment. Into whatsoever region the gospel may journey, her every herald is a flash of light, her every minister a flaming fire. God maketh his Churches the golden candlesticks, and saith unto his children, 'Ye are the lights of the world.' As certainly as ever God said, 'Let there be light', and there was light over the old creation, so does he say, whenever his Church advances, 'Let there be light', and there is light. Dens of darkness, where the bats of superstition had folded their wings and hung themselves up for perpetual ease, have been disturbed by the glare of these divine flambeaux; the innermost caverns of superstition and sin, once black with a darkness which might be felt, have been visited with a light above the brightness of the sun. 'The people which sat in darkness have seen a great light, and to them which sat in the region and shadow of death light has sprung up.' Thus saith the Lord unto the nation where his kingdom cometh, 'Arise, shine, for thy light is come, and the glory of the Lord hath risen upon thee!' Bear ye the Church of Christ to the South Seas; carry Christ and his spouse in his palanquin to the Caffre, the Hottentot, or the Esquimaux, and everywhere the night of death is ended, and the morning with its glorious dawn has come. High lift your lamps, ye servants of our Lord. High lift up the cross of the Redeemer; for in him is light, and the light is the life of men.

But you will tell me that our text rather speaks of *pillars of smoke* than of sparkling lamps. Brethren, the smoke is but the effect of the flame, and even the pillar of smoke is luminous. What is the smoke that has attended the Church? What but the deaths of her martyrs, the sufferings of her confessors, the patient endurance of her valiant sons? Wherever she goes, the thick smoke of her suffering goeth up to heaven. 'We are alway delivered unto death,' said the apostle. The cause of truth involves a perpetual sacrifice; her smoke ascendeth for ever. Black smoke I say it is in the eye of man, but unto God it is a sweet-smelling savour. Never did fat of rams, or the fat of kidnies of fed beasts, smell so sweetly before the Most High as the faith, the love, the courage, which has ascended up to heaven from the dauntless heroes of the Church in past ages when at the stake they have been faithful even unto death. Suffering and grief and woe are the lot of the spouse of the despised and rejected Saviour, but all these are as things of nought if thereby she may scatter that terrible blackness which blinds the face of man and makes him a stranger to his God.

It often happens that oriental monarchs of immense possessions are not content with burning common coals in these cressets, but frequently consume sandal-wood and other woods which give forth a delightful smell; or else, if they use ordinary coals, they sprinkle upon them frankincense and myrrh, so that a delicious perfume is spread on all sides. In the olden times, they also went to great expense in obtaining drugs, which the merchants collected from all parts of the earth, and these were carefully compounded into the renowned '*powders of the merchants*', which yielded a delicious variety of delicate perfumes, not to be produced by any one aromatic essence. Our inspired poet describes the travelling procession of the royal pair, and fails not to dwell upon the delightful perfume of myrrh and frankincense, with all the powders of the merchant, 'which make the wilderness smell as a garden of roses'.

Wherever the Church of Christ proceeds, though her pathway is a desert, though she marches through a howling wilderness, she scatters the richest perfume. The page of history were only worthy to be blotted in oblivion were it not for the sweet odours which the Church has left upon it. Look at all past ages, and the track of the Church is still redolent with all the richest fragrance of human virtue and divine grace. Wherever the Church advances she makes manifest the savour of the knowledge of Christ in every place! Men believe in Jesus, and unto the Lord faith has all the fragrance of myrrh. They love Jesus; and love in the esteem of heaven is better than frankincense. Loving Christ they endeavour to be like him, till patience, humility, brotherly-kindness, truthfulness, and all things that are honest, lovely and of good repute, like 'powders of the merchant', are spread abroad throughout the whole earth. Tell me where the Church is not, and I will tell you where sin reigns; tell me where Christ and his Church are carried, and I will tell you where you shall find every virtue that can adorn humanity, and every excellence that can magnify the excellence of the grace of God. If you would find an antidote for the deadly exhalations which lurk among this world's deserts of sin; if you would destroy the foul pestilence which reigns in the darkness of heathenism, of Popery, and of infidelity, cry unto the Mighty One – 'Arise, thou unknown traveller, arise, and bid thy servants carry thee into the midst of all this misery and death! The light of thy flaming torches shall scatter the darkness, and the burning of thy precious perfumes shall say unto evil – "Fold thy wings!" and unto the pestilence of sin – "Get thee back unto thy den!" '

Among the ten wonders which Jewish tradition ascribes to the temple, we find that the rain never extinguished the fire of the wood which was laid in order upon the altar, nor did the wind ever conquer the pillar of smoke so as to disperse or bend it. Verily it is so with the Church of God, as she cometh out of the wilderness: who shall quench her flaming lamp, or stay the incense of her golden censers? Ride on, Great Prince, and bear thy spouse with thee in thy majestic chariot, till thou hast lit the world with thy divine light, and hast made it a temple filled with a cloud of incense of sweet smell to the nostrils of Jehovah!

We have, secondly, to notice THE SECURITY OF CHRIST'S CHURCH AT ALL TIMES.

Of course when travelling through a wilderness, a royal procession was always in danger of attack. Arabs prowled around; wandering Bedouins were always prepared to fall upon the caravan; and more especially was this the case with a marriage procession, because then the robbers might expect to obtain many jewels, or, if not, a heavy ransom for the redemption of the bride or bridegroom by their friends.

What shall I say of the attacks which have been made upon the Church of Christ, and upon Christ himself? They have been incessant. When one form of evil has been routed, another has presented itself. Evil teems with children. The frogs and lice of Egypt were not more numerous than the enemies of the Lord's anointed and his bride. Every day produces new battles. These attacks arise from all quarters; sometimes from the world, and sometimes, alas! from even professed members of the Church. Adversaries lurk everywhere, and until the Church and her Lord shall be revealed in the splendour of the Millennium, having left the wilderness for ever, we must expect to find her molested on every side. My dear brethren, we know that Christ's cause in the world is always safe because of divine protection, and because the legions of God's angels keep watch and ward over the saints. But we have something more tangible than this. Our gracious God has been pleased to commit unto *men* the ministry of Christ. 'Unto the angels hath he not put in subjection the world to come, whereof we speak.' The Lord ordaineth that chosen men should be the protectors of his Church; not that they have any power as of themselves to do anything, but he girdeth the weak with strength and maketh the feeble mighty; so then, men, even the sons of men stand in array around the travelling palanquin of Christ, to guard both the bridegroom and the bride.

Read the 7th and 8th verses carefully, and you will notice that *there are enough swordsmen*. 'Threescore valiant men are about it.' There are always enough men chosen of God to guard the Church. Poor Unbelief holds up her hands and cries – 'Ah! the good men are all dead; Zion is under a cloud; the Lord hath taken away the great men; we have no valiant defenders of the faith, none such as this crisis may require!' Ah! Unbelief, let the Lord say unto thee as he did unto Elias: 'Yet have I left me seven thousand in Israel, all the knees which have not bowed unto Baal.' There shall be just as many warriors as the crisis shall require. We do not know where the men are to come from, but the Lord will provide. There may be sitting in the Sunday school today a child who shall one day shake this nation from one end to the other; there may be even here, unknown, obscure and unobserved, the man whom God will make strong to rebuke the infamous infidelity of our age. We know not where the anointing rests. We, in our folly, would anoint Eliab or Abinadab, but God hath chosen David, the shepherd's boy, and he will bring him forth and teach him how to hurl the stone at Goliath's brow. Tremble not, neither be ye afraid; God who makes man and makes man's mouth, will find the sixty men when the sixty men shall be needed. 'The Lord gave the word, great was the company of them that published it.' The glory of the Lord shall be revealed, and all flesh shall see it together, for the mouth of the Lord hath spoken it.

Observe that these warriors *are men of the right mettle*. 'Yes,' says poor trembling Little-Faith, 'we have hosts of men, but they are not like the greathearts of old; they have not the qualifications which the age requires.' Ah! but remember, about the bed of Solomon there are 'threescore *valiant* men'; and glory be unto my Master, while I may not flatter the ministry, I must not dishonour him by believing that he has left his Church without *valiant* defenders. There are Luthers still living who bid defiance to all adversaries; men who can say, 'We count not our lives dear unto us that we may finish our course with joy, and fulfil the ministry which the Lord hath delivered unto us.' Fear not; you may not at present know the valour of the Lord's bodyguard, but when the Church's battle grows hotter than just now, suddenly there shall be seen a champion stalking to the front of the battle, and men shall say, 'Who is this? How he wields that battleaxe! How he splits the armour of his foes! See how he piles them heaps on heaps, and mounts that hill of slaughtered enemies to smite a greater foe! Who is this?' And the answer shall be, 'This is a man whom God hath found; the world knew not of him, but God has trained him in the camps of Dan, and now the Spirit moveth him to smite the Philistines.'

'Ah!' I think I hear you say, 'but though there may be so many men, and men of the right sort, I am afraid *they are not in the right place*.' Look again at the text. It is written: 'Threescore valiant men are ABOUT IT'; that is, there are some on that side, and some on this, some before, and some behind; they are all round the travelling chariot of Christ. 'I wish there might be one in our parish,' says one. Pray for him, and he who has promised to send you all good things may yet send him to you. 'Pray ye the Lord of the harvest that he may send forth labourers into his harvest.' It is singular how God sometimes raises a mighty man, in this denomination, then in that, and then in the other. Suppose any body of Christians should try to monopolize all the valiant men themselves; why, they could not do it, because every side of the royal bed must be guarded, and in his own place each man is set for the defence of the gospel. The Church is compassed about with mighties, who are under God to do great exploits. If the Lord guides the flight of sparrows, surely he knows how to dispose his ministers; and let the Church be well content to let them occupy their posts until the wilderness is past, and the glory shall be revealed. The Church often makes mistakes, and thinks she can make ministers, or at least choose their position. She can do no such thing. God sends the valiant man; all you can do is to recognise his valour, and accept him as your champion; beyond that you cannot go; this is God's work, not man's. A minister made by men, made valiant by human strength, had better betake himself at once ignominiously to his tent, for his disgrace will be certain. God who sends the men, knows where to put them, so that they may stand around about the bed, and leave no corner unprotected.

Notice that these men *are all well armed.* The text says expressly, 'They all hold swords.' What swords are these? Every valiant man in Christ's Israel holds the sword of the Spirit, which is the Word of God. A man who is a good textuary will usually be a good divine; he who draws from the treasury of the written Word will find his spoken word to be fruitful in profit to the people of God. If we use carnal reason, if we rely upon refinement, argument, eloquence, or any other form of the wisdom of man, we shall soon find our enemies will defeat us; but to ply the Word right and left; to give gospel cuts and strokes such as the devil himself cannot parry, this is to overcome the world through the Word of God. Besides this, and here is an opportunity for you all to carry swords – every valiant man in God's Israel carries the sword of prayer, which is comparable to those huge two-handed swords of the olden time, which the soldier lifted up and brought down with such tremendous force, as to cleave a man in halves: prayer is a weapon which no man can effectually resist. If you know how to use it, bring it down upon your foeman's head, and woe unto him! I would to God that in this Church there were found many of these valiant men of Israel! Indeed, would God all the Lord's servants were prophets, that it might be said of all of you that you hold swords. Your holy lives can be swords with which to smite your enemies. The tongues with which you speak of Christ lovingly, tenderly, persuasively – these may be weapons against our common enemy. Oh that when we hear the muster roll at last, it may be said of every Church-member that he held a sword! Do not tremble, ye timid ones, for the ark of the Lord; neither let your fears promote your unbelief; God knows full well how to give the right weapons to the right men, and his Church shall be secure even to the end.

Further, my brethren, these men are not only well armed, *but they are well trained.* They are all expert in war; men who have endured temptations themselves; men whose souls have been exercised; men who have slain both the lion and the bear, and are men of war from their youth. Christian ministers especially should be no novices, but both in the school of temptation, and in some school of the prophets, they should be disciplined for fight. May there be such found here! I look out daily for such among you as are taught of God, and much of my time is spent with our young soldiers to make them expert in war. O that the Lord would hear my prayers and bless our college with men, and means, and above all with his Spirit. Fools are not the men for this age. We want a sound knowledge of doctrine, practical power in preaching, and a thorough insight into the human heart; and where these by earnest prayer can be found in a man and further developed by careful teaching, we are bound to give our aid. Such men should be looked after, and no pains should be spared to bring them forth; in fact, dear friends, you ought to think it a high honour to be allowed to help in putting such men into working order. Oh! how I groan to get my friends to feel the importance of sending out trained young ministers. I give my time and my substance cheerfully, but when will the Christian Church help in this matter as it should?

Further, these men were not only well-trained, but you will see *that they were always ready*. Each man has his sword upon his thigh, ready to be drawn forth. I know some nominal ministers who seem to me to carry no sword at all. They keep a sheath, a very handsome sheath, with a hilt at the top and a stick inside. What is the good of such men? We want men to have *swords* in their sheaths, men who can speak with power, and have the demonstration of the Spirit and the power thereof resting upon them. Such men should wear their swords where they are to be got at, so that when the adversary comes they may dash at him at once. Rejoice, O daughter of Zion, thy Lord hath not left thee, even at this day, without some such men!

Observe also that these men were *watchful*, for 'they had their sword on their thigh because of fear *in the night*'. They never sleep, but watch always for the Church's interest. Pray ye that the Lord may raise up many such, who night and day with tears shall watch for the souls of men, and against the enemies of our Israel.

Dear friends, some of you may at times be alarmed when you hear of attacks made upon the Bible. At one time it was thought that ethnology would prove that the human race could not be one; and Moses was terribly abused by some who said it was not possible that all of us could have come of one pair. That battle was fought, and you hear nothing of it now; it is over; learning and argument in the hand of God has routed those antagonists. Then they pelted us with shells, and bones of lizards. Geology threatened to dig our graves; but we have lived all through that struggle, and we have found geology to be a great blessing, for it has shed a new light on the first chapter of Genesis, and made us understand a great deal better what it meant. Another Amalekite advanced to combat; this time it is with figures and numbers; we are to be speared with arithmetic, and slain with algebra! And what will be the result of it? Why, it will do the Bible a world of good, for we shall understand it better. I thank God whenever the Bible is attacked; for all those who know the times and the seasons begin to study just that part of Scripture more carefully, and then we get a clearer light shed upon it, and we find ourselves more confirmed than ever that this is the very truth, and that God hath revealed it to us. 'Well, but who will take this matter up?' I do not know, and I do not particularly care, but I know my Master has his threescore valiant men round about his bed, and that each man has his sword upon this thigh because of fear in the night, and never mind what the battle will be, the end of it will be for God's glory, and there shall be progress with the chariot of Christ through that which seemed as if it must overthrow it. Cast aside your fears; rejoice, and be glad, O daughter of Zion! Thy Lord is with thee in the travelling chariot, and the threescore valiant men are watching against thy foes.

Meanwhile, reposing in peace, let us notice THE EXCELLENCY OF THIS CHARIOT IN WHICH JESUS RIDES.

It is not difficult to convey to persons the most unacquainted with Eastern manners and customs, an idea of what this palanquin is. It is a sort of large sedan in which one or two persons may recline with ease. Of course, this palanquin could not be made of gold or silver, because then it would be too heavy for carriage; it must be made of wood; hence King Solomon made a bed, or chariot, or palanquin, of the wood of Lebanon. Then there needs to be four pillars supporting the covering and the curtains; the pillars thereof are of silver. The bottom of it should be something massive, in order to sustain the weight of the person; the bottom thereof is of gold. The canopy on the top, is a covering of purple. Since to lie on gold would be very unpleasant, it is covered with delicate, daintily wrought carpets; and so we have the bottom thereof paved, or rather carpeted with love for the daughters of Jerusalem. Some delicate devices of needlework adorn the bottom of this bed-chariot in which the king and his spouse recline during their journey.

The doctrines of the gospel are comparable, for their antiquity, for their sweet fragrance, for their incorruptibility, to the wood of Lebanon. The gospel of Christ never decays; Jesus Christ the same yesterday, today, and for ever. Not one single truth bears any sign of rot. And to those souls that are enlightened from above, the gospel gives forth a fragrance far richer than the wood of Lebanon.

> No beams of cedar or of fir,
> Can with thy precious truth compare.

I rejoice to know concerning you as a Church that the more you understand the doctrines of grace the better you love them. You are confirmed in the present faith, and well you may be, for our doctrine is worthy of your confidence. We are not afraid that any truth which Christ has uttered should be tried by the most stringent criticism, for not one single stone of all the bulwarks of gospel doctrine can ever be removed out of its place. When cedars of Lebanon have yielded to the worm, even then shall the truth as it is in Jesus remain the same.

As for the silver pillars which bear up the canopy, to what should I liken them but to *the attributes of God* which support and guarantee the efficiency of the great atonement of Christ beneath which we are sheltered. There is the silver pillar of God's *justice*. He cannot, he will not smite the soul that hides beneath the cross of Christ. If Christ hath paid the debt, how is it possible that God should visit again a second time the iniquity of his people, first on their Surety, and then again on themselves? Then stands the next, the solid pillar of his *power*. 'They shall never perish, neither shall any pluck them out of my hand; my Father which gave them me is greater than all, and none is able to pluck them out of my Father's hand.' Then on the other side is the pillar of his *love*, a silver pillar indeed, bright and sparkling to the eye; love unchanging and eternal, strong as the power and fast as the justice which bear up the canopy on the other side. And here on this side stands *immutability*, another column upon which the atonement rests. If God could change, then might he cast away his blood-bought; but 'because I am God and change not, therefore ye sons of Jacob rejoice'. As for *the covering of the chariot*, it is of purple. I need not tell you where it was dyed. No Tyrian hues are mingled here. Look up, Christian, and delight thyself in that blood-red canopy which shelters thee from the sun by day and from the moon by night! From hell and heaven, from time and from eternity, art thou secured by this covering which is of purple. Oh! tempting theme to dilate upon the precious and glorious doctrine of atonement! Whenever our adversaries assail the Church, whatever may be the apparent object of their animosity, their real one is always the same, a desperate hatred to the great truth that God was in Christ reconciling the world unto himself, not imputing their trespasses unto them. Well, as *they* hate it, let *us* love it; and under it let us take our greatest delight.

As for the *bottom of this palanquin*, which is of gold – may not this represent the eternal purpose and counsel of God, that purpose which he formed in himself or ever the earth was? Pure was the decree of God, holy, wise, just, for his own glory, and most true; and as the precious things of the temple were all of gold, well may the basis of eternal love, an immutable and unchangeable decree, be compared to much fine gold. I do not know brethren, how it is with you, but I find it most pleasant to have as the basis of my hope, the firm decree of God. Atonement covers me, I know, but still on this I must rest, Jehovah wills it; God decrees it; he hath said it, and it must be done; he hath commanded and it standeth fast. Oh! that golden sovereignty, whereon is written: 'I will have mercy on whom I will have mercy; it is not of him that willeth, nor of him that runneth.' Dear brethren, the Apostle plainly tells us that this is the basis on which even the silver pillars rest, 'for he hath blessed us with all spiritual blessings in Christ Jesus, according as he hath chosen us in him from before the foundation of the world.'

Then, to make all this soft and pleasant to recline upon, here is pavement of needlework. Soft cushions of love on which to rest. There is a double meaning here, for both the bride and bridegroom find rest in love. Our Lord finds rest in the love of his people. 'Here will I dwell for ever.' They do, as it were, make these carpets of needlework in their love and affection for him, and in their trust and confidence in him; and here he rests. On the other hand, our Beloved spent his life to work for us our bed of rest, so that we must translate it, 'love *of*,' as well as love *for* the 'daughters of Jerusalem'. *We* rest in Christ's love; *he* rests in our love. Come, I need not explain further, brothers and sisters. Take your rest now to the full. You are married unto Christ; you are one with him; betrothed unto him in faithfulness, embraced in the arms of his affection. Fear not the noise of the archers; the 'three-score valiant men' protect you, and the king himself embraces you; now solace yourself with him; take your full of his sweet society, and say unto him from the bottom of your heart, 'Let him kiss me with the kisses of his mouth, for his love is better than wine.' Leave fighting for the evidences to the valiant men who can do it; as for you, ye daughters of Jerusalem, rest upon your Lord's bosom; leave conflict to the men ordained to fight, the men expert in war; as for you, be you expert in communion; understand the motions of Jesus' heart; look unto the lustre of his loving eyes; behold his beauties; be ravished with his divine affection to you; and now let your soul be satisfied with favour, and be full of the lovingkindness of the Lord!

We close, then, by noticing THE DUTY OF EVERY BELIEVING HEART in connection with the subject.

Let every believer, while he recognises himself as part of the Church inside the palanquin, yet look upon himself personally as one of the daughters of Zion, and let us each *go forth* this morning to meet King Solomon. It is not King David; King David is the type of Christ up to the time of his crucifixion – 'despised and rejected of men, a man of sorrows and acquainted with grief', and yet King of the Jews. King Solomon is the type of Christ ever since the day when

> They brought his chariot from above,
> To bear him to his throne

and, with sound of trumpet, conducted him to his Father's presence chamber above. Now it is King Solomon; King Solomon for wealth, for wisdom, for dignity, for honour, for peace. He is the Wonderful, the Counsellor, the Mighty God, the Everlasting Father, the Prince of Peace, and therefore is he King Solomon going forth. Get up from your beds of sloth; rise from your chambers of ease; go forth, go forth to pray, to labour, to suffer; go forth to live in purity, leaving Babylon behind; go forth to walk with him alone, leaving even your kinsfolk and acquaintance if they will not follow with you. Wherefore tarriest thou at home when the King is abroad? 'Behold the Bridegroom cometh, come ye forth to meet him', *and behold King Solomon.* Today let your eye rest upon him. Let your eye behold the head that today is crowned with glory, wearing many crowns. Behold ye, too, his hands which once were pierced, but are now grasping the sceptre. Look to his girdle where swing the keys of heaven, and death, and hell. Look to his feet, once pierced with iron, but now set upon the dragon's head. Behold his legs, like fine brass, as if they glowed in a furnace. Look at his heart, that bosom which heaves with love to you, and when you have surveyed him from head to foot exclaim, 'Yea, he is the chief among ten thousand, and altogether lovely'. Does sin prevail? Behold King Solomon. Have doubts and fears arisen? Behold King Jesus. Are you troubled, and does your enemy annoy you? Look up to him, behold king Solomon.

I pray you remember the light in which you are to behold him. Do not think that Christ has lost his former power. Behold him as he was at Pentecost, *with the crown wherewith his mother crowned him in the day of his espousals.* Oh! how glorious was our Lord when the Church crowned him with her zeal, and the arrows went abroad, and three thousand fell slain by his right hand to be made alive by the breath of his mouth! Oh, how these early saints crowned him, when they brought their substance and laid it at the apostle's feet, neither did any man count that ought he had was his own. They crowned him with their heart's purest love; the Church had on her brow her bridal-wreath, and her husband wore his nuptial crown. Behold him today as wearing that crown still, for he is the same Christ, and do you go forth to meet him, and labour for him, and love him as the first saints did.

Forget not that his mother is to crown him soon in the day of his espousals. He is our brother as well as our husband, and the Church is *his* mother as well as ours. Oh! she is to crown him soon! The day of his espousals draweth nigh. Hark! I hear the trumpet sound! Jesus comes, and his feet stand upon Mount Olivet; kings and princes lick the dust before him; he gathers sheaves of sceptres beneath his arm even as the mower gathereth wheat with the sickle. He treadeth on principalities and powers, the young lion and the dragon doth he trample under foot. And now his saints cry, 'Hosanna, blessed is he that cometh in the name of the Lord.' The long-expected one is come, and his mother crowns him in the day of his espousals! Courage, poor heart, courage! Go forth and see King Solomon today as he is to be, and remember,

> It doth not yet appear
> How great we shall be made;
> But when we see our Saviour here,
> We shall be like our Head.

When we look on Him; let us rejoice that this is to be our glory. We are to put off this sackcloth and put on scarlet and fine linen. The dust is to be wiped from our brow and the sweat from our face; the shackles are to be taken from our wrist, and the gyves from our legs; and we are to be emancipated, ennobled, glorified, made partners with Christ in all his splendour, and taught to reign with him world without end.

But there are some here that I can hardly call the daughters of Jerusalem, yet they are always round about Zion's gate. Oh, there are many of you who are always listening to our voice, and joining in our hymns, and yet you have not seen our Master yet! Go forth; leave your sinful pleasures, and leave your self-righteousness too; go forth and behold King Solomon. Look to Jesus, sinner, bleeding on the cross, and as thou lookest, love and trust; and I know that as soon as thou hast seen him and trusted him, thou wilt have a crown to put upon his head. It will be the day of thine espousal unto him, and thou wilt crown him with such a crown. Thou wilt decorate that crown with jewels dug from the secret mine of thy deepest heart, and having made this crown, thou wilt put it on his head, and fall down before him and sing:

> All hail the power of Jesus' name,
> Let angels prostrate fall;
> Bring forth the royal diadem,
> And crown him Lord of all.

Well, then, we will lay aside every fear, and continue all the day gazing upon our matchless Christ, adoring him, exalting him, and having fellowship with him; for all is well; his travelling chariot is always safe, and soon will he step out of it with his bride at his right hand, and the world shall be astonished to behold the beauties of the royal pair when he shall be exalted, and they that are with him, before the presence of his Father and all the holy angels!

25

PAVED WITH LOVE

'The midst thereof being paved with love, for the daughters of Jerusalem' (Canticles 3:10)

This portion of the Song describes the royal bridegroom as travelling up from the wilderness in an eastern palanquin, attended by his bodyguard, and by those who bear torches and burn perfumes. We have a description of the sumptuous chariot-bed in which this great monarch travelled, describing it as being made of cedar-wood, with pillars of silver, a basis of gold, curtains of purple, and then within it a tesselated floor, with pavement, not of precious stones, but of priceless love. Metaphor is suddenly dropped in this last item, and the result is a complicated, but very expressive form of speech. Some regard the expression as signifying a pavement of stone, engraved with hieroglyphic emblems of love, which made up the floor of this travelling chariot; but this would surely be very uncomfortable and unusual, and therefore others have explained the passage as referring to choice embroidery and dainty carpets, woven with cost and care, with which the interior of the travelling-chair was lined. Into such embroidery sentences of love-poetry may have been worked. Needlework was probably the material of which it was composed; skilful fingers would therein set forth emblems and symbols of love. As the spouse in the second chapter sings, 'His banner over me was love', probably alluding to some love-word upon the banner; so, probably, tokens of love were carved or embroidered, as the case may have been, upon the interior of the chariot, so that 'the midst thereof was paved with love, for the daughters of Jerusalem'. We need not, however, tarry long over the metaphor, but endeavour to profit by its teaching.

This palanquin or travelling chariot in which the king is carried, represents the covenant of grace, the plan of salvation, and, in fact, the whole system by which the Lord Jesus comes down in mercy among men, and by which he bears his people along with himself through the wilderness of this world, onward to the rest which he hath prepared for them. It is, in a word, the mediatorial work of Jesus. The ark was carried through the wilderness preceded by the pillar of cloud and fire, as the symbol of the divine presence in mercy, and here we have a somewhat similar representation of the great King of grace, borne in regal splendour through the world, and bearing his elect spouse with him. May it be ours to be made to ride like Jeshurun, upon the high places of the earth in happy fellowship with him whose goings forth were of old, even from everlasting.

I shall beg you to notice, first, this morning, THE GROWTH WHICH IS INDICATED HERE AS TO OUR VIEWS OF THE COVENANT OF GRACE. The description advances step by step, each sentence mentioning an additional and far-enhanced preciousness. Thus do those who study the work of salvation prize it more and more. At the first glance the sweet singer who speaks in this song perceived that the chariot was made of cedar, a costly wood; a closer view revealed 'the silver pillars, beauteous to behold'; a further observation showed 'the basis all of burnished gold'. From cedar to silver, and from silver to gold, we have a clear advance as to precious material. On looking again, the observer remarks 'the top of princely purple' which is yet more precious as the type of imperial dignity, and the token of that effectual atonement which was wrought out by the ensanguined stream of Calvary. The blood which dyed that purple canopy is much more precious than gold that perisheth, though it be tried with fire. And then, though one would think there could be no advance beyond the precious blood, the song proceeds yet one step further, for we find that 'the midst thereof was paved with love, for the daughters of Jerusalem'.

Beloved, the whole way of salvation was devised by the Lord Jesus Christ. It is all his own planning, and all his own carrying out. Hence the Song says, 'King Solomon made himself a chariot of the wood of Lebanon.' Jesus is the sole author and finisher of our faith; salvation is his from first to last; every part of the covenant reveals his master hand. This is the glory of the whole, and this the believing eye perceives at the very first glance, and is thereby made glad; but further knowledge reveals other bright and glorious facts; and as the matter is considered, wonder and gratitude increase. Let us, then, take a brief survey of this glorious gospel chariot, that wondrous thing – Jehovah's covenant of grace.

The first item is, that it is made of the 'wood of Lebanon'. The finest wood upon the earth was that of the cedar, and the finest cedars were those which grew upon the Lebanon range. The Lebanon cedars, indeed, appear to have possessed qualities not found in the common cedar with which we are acquainted. That which was reckoned the best wood is used as the token of the super-excellence of the covenant of grace. Cedar, moreover, was not only the most costly wood, and most esteemed, but it is one of the most lasting. Loudon says that it is particularly valued for its durability; fit type of that 'covenant ordered in all things and sure', of which not one jot or tittle shall ever fail. Heaven and earth shall pass away, but the word on which we trust shall abide for ever.

In addition to its other excellencies cedar-wood exhales a sweet perfume, so that a chariot of cedar would not only be very lasting but very delightful to ride in, even as at this day we joy in God's salvation, and are filled with peace through believing. When we look at the covenant of salvation, at the very first glimpse of it we see that there is none like it: many schemes have been imagined and preached up as ways of salvation, but not one of them can be likened to the method of atonement by blood, reconciliation through a substitutionary sacrifice, redemption by the incarnate God, salvation all of grace from first to last. When this is compared to a chariot, no timber less noble than the sweet-scented fir, cut from the monarch of Israel's royal forest, could worthily set it forth. Lies and vanity make up all other plans, but this is royal truth. Other ways of salvation have been tried, but they have soon proved to be failures; the worm of human depravity has eaten into the choicest wood that was ever felled in the forests of human merit; decay has seized upon all the goodly oaks of unaided human endeavours; and rottenness has devoured all carnal boastings, but the cedar-wood of our hope in Jesus has shown no sign of crumbling to decay, and it never will. There is in the atonement made by Christ a perpetuity of prevalence; it has availed for sin and will avail to the very end of time, so that whosoever confides in it has a hope which will not deceive him.

I dare await the test of a long and afflicted life, or of a sudden and painful death, for the ground of my hope is undisturbed by outward circumstances; like the cedar, it is adapted to abide all weathers. As surely as the body of the Lord saw no corruption, so surely shall my hope never turn to despair, and even if it be buried it shall rise again. What consolation such a hope affords us! And for this reason, as perfume comes forth from cedar-wood, so do fragrant comforts come pouring forth from the salvation which Jesus Christ has wrought out for us. It is a pleasant as well as a safe thing to rest in what Christ has done. Our joy is greatest when our faith in him is most simple; the bare cedar-wood is most fragrant. We derive from every part of his work some joy, every part of it smells most sweetly; he is all happiness, all consolation, all bliss to us; and when our spirit casts itself in perfect simplicity upon him it breathes a perfumed atmosphere, delicious and reviving. If such be the first and lowest item in the description of the chariot, what will the richer portions be?

We will now look more closely at the royal chariot, and note well the four pillars which support the canopy; and as we gaze we find that they are of silver – something more precious than cedar-wood, for the salvation of Jesus grows upon us, and unto us who believe he is more and more precious. There are some pictures so well painted that you may examine them with a magnifying glass, and instead of detecting defects you will perceive yet greater beauties; so may you examine the work of our blessed Lord microscopically, if you choose; and the more you look the more will you marvel, he is so really glorious, so intrinsically precious, so infinitely to be admired. And what are these pillars, think you, which support the canopy and add such beauty to the chariot? What are they but divine holiness, and infinite purity?

Silver is constantly used in Scripture as the type of that which is precious and pure: 'As silver tried in a furnace of earth, purified seven times.' And O beloved, how holy the gospel is; the Lord's word is very pure in itself, and very purifying to those who receive it. Wherever the true gospel is preached it promotes holiness, and in so doing acts according to its nature, creating its like. There is not a doctrine of the gospel which is not according to godliness, none of its blessings make provision for the flesh, none of its precepts encourage sin, none of its promises wink at iniquity. The spirit of the gospel is the spirit of holiness always; it wages determined war against the lustings of the flesh, and consequently the gospel is abhorred by the unclean. It lays the axe at the root of sin, and like a fire devours all evil. As for the Lord Jesus Christ himself, is he not immaculate holiness? If you would see holiness embodied, where can you look but to the person of our well-beloved Master? Where are his imperfections? Can you find a flaw either in his language or in his actions, in himself or in the spirit that moved him? Is he not altogether perfect?

Look, then, at the gospel, the way of salvation, and the covenant of grace, and you shall see holiness conspicuous everywhere, but especially when you come to deal with the centre of the gospel, the great atoning sacrifice. Four silver pillars hold up this crimson canopy. The blood red propitiation covers us from the wrath of God, and the holiness of God holds up this interposing medium. He is not unrighteous to forget the blood of the atonement. Because he is a just God he is now the Saviour of those who are sheltered beneath the reconciling blood of Calvary. The Lord could not forgive sin till first the honour of his law had been vindicated; but that being done, the selfsame honour requires that the atonement should be respected and the believing sinner saved. When we see Christ upon the cross we learn how God's inflexible justice, like unbending pillars of pure silver, holds up aloft the crimson shelter of vicarious death, beneath which the saints are secure. Even to save his own elect, Jehovah would not mar his integrity, nor suffer his great white throne to be stained with injustice. He is no respecter of persons, and when sitting on the throne of judgment, even his own chosen, whom he loves with everlasting love, must be treated with the same impartiality as his enemies. This he has effected by accepting his Son in their stead, and exacting from him those penalties which were due from them, but might be justly received at the hands of their federal Head. There is no injustice in the salvation of the believer, there is not even an abatement of the claims of just retribution; all is done openly, and so as to challenge the severest examination. Conspicuously before the eyes of all, the silver pillars of purity upbear the sacred atonement. Is not this a matter for superlative delight?

But we look more closely and discern what would not have been perceived at a distance – 'the bottom' of the chariot-bed 'is of gold', the most precious metal of all. This is to indicate that the foundations of salvation are imperishable, and unchangeably precious. The basis of grace is laid in the immutable purpose and unchanging decree of God, and in the everlasting, undiminished, unchangeable love of God towards his dear Son and to those who are in him. Blessed be God for a salvation which will not yield under pressure, or fail us in our hour of peril. It is not base metal, but gold tried in the fire. I cannot understand those who think that God loves his people one day and hates them the next; that though he knew what they would be, and knew that they would fall into sin, yet he resolved to take them to himself as his children for a little while, and then afterwards to disinherit them. God forbid I should ever understand a doctrine so dishonouring to the Lord, who changes not. My own love to my children makes me feel that they must be my children as long as *they* live and *I* live; and surely God's children must and shall be his children while God himself shall live and his people shall exist. Beloved, the basis on which we rest as saved sinners is not the shifting foundation of our own feelings, doings, prayings and resolvings. If our salvation depended upon our good behaviour, we might as well build on the clouds, and pile up bubbles as our cornerstones: ay, and if it rested upon our own unaided faith, if there were no guarantee of grace to keep that faith alive, but all rested on the exercise of faith by us, it were better never to have had a hope of salvation at all, than to have had such a wretched, unsubstantial mockery, certain to end ere long in fatal disappointment. You and I have not so learned Christ. We have left the miry clay for the solid rock. God has made an eternal purpose concerning his people, and that will never be changed; infinite love ordained their salvation, and will never reverse its decree, though day and night should cease. Infinite power guarantees the fulfilment of the divine purpose, and what can stand against omnipotence? A complete atonement has been already made, and it will never lose its efficacy, and therefore those for whom it was wrought out must be saved. There is, moreover, an indwelling Spirit who has come into God's people, to abide with them for ever, according to the covenant promise, 'I will dwell in them, and I will walk in them. I will be their God, and they shall be my people.' Our spiritual life does not hang on a thread, as it would do if it were in our own keeping, but it depends upon Jesus; for has he not said, 'Because I live ye shall live also'? Nothing can be more secure than the salvation of the soul that believes in Jesus, for it rests in God alone. Of the chariot of salvation, we may say with quaint Ralph Erskine:

> Its bottom is a groundwork sure
>   Of pure and solid gold,
> From bankrupt beggary to secure,
>   From falling through t'uphold.

Let us view the royal canopy of the chariot: 'the covering thereof is of purple'. As the king and his bride travelled they needed to be screened from the sun's baleful rays; lo, over the head of the spouse hangs a regal covering of purple. Look up, my soul, and see what interposes between thy God and thee! He must smite thee, for thou art a sinner; but thou art covered and sheltered, and art living happily. What is it that doth shield thee? What, indeed, but the atoning blood!

> Ah, who can view that purple covering
> And turn away unmoved, insensible?
> Who can discern it, and forget that day
> When impious greetings shouted forth disdain,
> When, crowned with thorns, the Man of sorrows stood
> In *purple* robes of cruel mockery;
> Despised, rejected, yet a king indeed,
> Whom they shall see hereafter on his throne.

The atonement shelters us: never was a soul injured by the rays of God's justice when hidden beneath this purple; and never shall there be. There is no repose for the conscience anywhere else, but there is perfect repose here. I often hear theories about what Christ did which remind me of Dr Duncan's description of Robertson of Brighton: 'Robertson believed that Christ did something or other, which somehow or other had some connection or other with salvation.' This may suit others, but is of no sort of use to me. I feel that if Christ did not actually and literally die as my Substitute, the just for the unjust, I am not saved, and never can be at rest in my heart again. I renounce all preaching whatsoever if substitution be not the leading feature of my theme, for there is nothing worth preaching when that is gone. I regard that doctrine as the fundamental truth of the gospel, which, denied, you have slain the gospel, and which, cast into the background, you have covered the gospel with a cloud. That Jesus Christ was made sin for us, that we might be made the righteousness of God in him; that though he was just, he was created as a sinner, and in our room and place and stead suffered the wrath of God due to us; this is the kernel and vital heart of the gospel. Conscience tells every man that God must punish sin; its voice, more or less loudly, always proclaims that sin must be punished. This is no arbitrary arrangement, it is inevitable; sin and suffering have a natural relationship. If God be just, sin must bring evil consequences upon the man who commits it, and until conscience understands that this evil was borne by Christ, that he suffered what ought to have been suffered by the sinner, and that he was justly a substitute because he was the head and Adam of those for whom he died – until, I say, the conscience knows this, it cannot find rest. Get under the blood-red canopy, and then you are at peace, but not till then.

Hence you find that whenever God revealed himself to his people, the most apparent thing was always the blood. Abel must bring a bleeding lamb, and Noah a slaughtered beast. When the King feasted with his chosen in Egypt, the blood adorned the lintel and the two side-posts of every house wherein he revealed his saving power. When he marched through the wilderness, one of the coverings of his tabernacle was made of rams' skins dyed red; and all within and around the holy courts themselves were perpetual sprinklings of blood, for almost all things were, under the law, purified by blood; the voice of the law always proclaiming what the gospel proclaims too, that 'without shedding of blood there is no remission of sin'. Our Saviour's life must end in blood upon the tree; and ere that closing scene, his last feast of love, his communion with his disciples had for its most conspicuous provision the cup of red wine by which his blood was symbolised. Every time he sets forth visibly his communion with his people here below the wine must be poured forth. God cannot and will not reveal himself to man except through the medium of the perfect satisfaction by the pouring out of the life of the Substitute in the stead of the sinner.

'The covering thereof is of purple.' Oh, it is not for these lips to tell how precious that purple is; it is not possible even for this heart to know how precious is the blood of the Son of God, the vital blood which out of love to us he poured out freely for our redemption. Sit you at your ease, my brethren and sisters, in the chariot of salvation, rejoicing as you look upward, and let no doubts nor fears, mistrusts nor suspicions, vex you, for beneath the blood-red canopy you are secure.

There is yet one more step; we rise from the blood to the love which caused it to flow, and we read of the royal chariot: 'The midst thereof was paved with love, for the daughters of Jerusalem'; not merely the bottom covered with it, but, as in a carriage, the whole vehicle lined with something soft to sit upon, and lean upon; so the whole covenant of grace is, within, garnished and beautified, and made delightful to the believer's soul, by the sweet love of God in Christ. The covenant is love in its secret places, all love, unalloyed love, invisible love, nothing else but love. When one comes to know most of the covenant, and admires the wisdom, the power, the purity, the eternity of all that God has done, yet the most striking characteristic of it to the advanced Christian is the love, the mighty love of God, by which he is brought by Jesus Christ into eternal salvation. 'Thou hast crowned me with lovingkindness; thou hast loved my soul out of the pit; thou hast loved me, and given thyself for me. Thy love has redeemed me with a price most precious; thy love has made me what I am; thy love carries on the work, and thy love will complete it, and present me to thee in its own perfect image; for "the midst of it is paved with love, for the daughters of Jerusalem".'

The point we have proved is this, that everything in the study of the gospel grows upon you. I earnestly exhort you, therefore, to meditate much in the Scriptures, to consider much the person and character of your Lord, to meditate full often upon his beauties, and upon all the work which he has done in your behalf. Do not be satisfied with a superficial survey, as many

Christians are. These are not the days of contemplation as the old Puritan times were, we are too apt to be superficial; but do remember that while there are nuggets of gold upon the very surface of Scripture, yet the most valuable mines of gold are far down, and you must dig into them. Pray God that you may be well taught in the things of Christ. There are some sciences in which you can master all that is worth knowing in a short time, and the further you go in the study the more you perceive that nothing is very certain, and you soon get weary of it; but the science of Christ crucified grows upon you; you get more assured of the facts of it, and more intensely delighted in them. I exhort you, therefore, to sit constantly at the Master's feet with Mary, and I pray that each one of us may know, by following on to know the Lord, what are 'the heights and depths, and to know the love of Christ, which passeth knowledge'.

We shall now NOTE THE POSITION FROM WHICH THE LOVE MENTIONED IN OUR TEXT IS BEST SEEN. 'The midst thereof is paved with love.' It is not, therefore, to be seen from the outside. The mere outsider understands nothing of the love of God to his people as displayed in the covenant of grace. I am certain that there are many of you here present who have heard the gospel for years, and yet no more know the sweetness of it than the floor I am standing upon. A man may pass the door of the London Tavern or the Mansion House for years, and yet have no notion of the banquets within, for these are indoors, and you must enter to partake of them. Savoury vapours floating from the festive board may awaken a transient imagination, but no more. The cock on the dunghill turned over the diamond, and according to the fable, remarked that he cared very little for it, he would sooner have found a grain of barley; so, many hear of the sweetness of true religion, but they have not the taste or the ability to perceive its sweetness. Oh, unregenerate hearer, you never will know how sweet the gospel is, it is impossible you should while you remain in the state you now are in; but I tell you, if you could get half a glimpse of the joy which even the poorest Christian has, you would never rest content until you enjoyed it too. If men have said concerning Naples, 'See Naples and die', because of its beauty, I might say to you, it were worth while dying a thousand deaths to get a glimpse of Christ: when once your faith has perceived his beauty you will wonder how you could have been satisfied to be blinded so long. What must it be to be forgiven all your sins and to know it? What must it be never to be afraid of death, to be able to look forward to departing from this world as a thing to be longed for, and not to be dreaded? What must it be to be able to look up and say, 'God is my Father, and I feel that I am his child'? What must be the joy and bliss of having familiar intercourse with God, so that you are called his friends, as

Abraham was of old? I wish I could set your mouths watering after these things. If you had but a little taste of them you would long for more; but until the Lord shall grant you that taste, all we can say of the love of Christ will have no charm for you. The love which lines the chariot of salvation is not to be known by those who remain outside; 'the secret of the Lord is with them that fear him, and he will show them his covenant.'

And so note next, when the Christian himself stands apart from his Lord, and judges by outward appearances, he cannot perceive, as once he did, the lovingkindness of the Lord. Providence grows dark as a winter's day. The tried believer cries, 'My wife has been taken from me; my property is melting away, my business fades; I am sick in body and weary in soul; I cannot see a trace of the love of God to me in all this.' Brother, the description in the Song does not say that the chariot is plated with love on the outside, but it is paved with love *within*, 'in the midst of it'. Oh that you had faith to believe that the heart and real core of every providence is love. The exterior of it may be as a thorn hedge, but sweet fruit ripens within. 'Oh,' say you, 'but I have looked at the Bible lately, and as I have glanced over its once-cheering promises they appear to smile at me no more. Some of the words grate very harshly on my ear, and almost condemn me.' I do not wonder, for although I can at this moment see love in the very outside of Scripture, yet there are times when I cannot, when I can only feel as if every text thundered at me, and out of God's own mouth came heavy sentences against me. Beloved, it does not say, I repeat it, that the exterior part of this palanquin was adorned with self-apparent love, but that love was in the midst. If you stand examining the exterior of providence, and the mere letter of the Word, and begin to judge and try your God, I should not wonder if little enough of love should be conspicuous to you. Look into the heart of God and read what he has written there. When faith takes a step upward, and mounts to the inside of the chariot of grace, she finds that it is paved with love for the daughters of Jerusalem.

Come and sit side by side with Jesus in his chariot of grace, his bed of rest. Come and recline with him in hallowed friendship. There is room enough for you, and strength enough to bear your weight. Come now and be carried with him who carried all your cross. Sit down with him who on his hands, and on his side, bears the memorials of his dying love to you. What company you have, and what royal accommodation is provided for you! Methinks I sit in the chariot with the Beloved now, and I begin to look around me. I catch a glimpse of the purple above my head, and remember the unspeakable love which bled and died for sinners; I look at the silver pillars which support the covering, and how infinite holiness stands fast, and in love to me secures my perfection; I place my foot on the golden bottom of the chariot, and know that divine power is pledged by love to preserve and bear me through; I see above me, and around me, and beneath me, nothing but love – the free, unbounded love of God.

Now, beloved, indulge yourselves with a glance around you for a minute. Look back to old eternity; let your eye peer through the mists which hide that ancient age before the ages began! What see you there but love, 'according to his eternal purpose which he purposed in Christ Jesus or ever the earth was'? Look a little closer; see the garden of Eden and the fall – what strikes your eye there but love? The seed of the woman shall bruise the serpent's head. Look to the cross, and at God incarnate here below; behold Jesus living in suffering, and dying in shame! Here love comes to her climax, and lays bare all her matchless charms. Look to the time of your own life. Was not love present at your birth, perfuming your first breath? Were you not nursed in love, cradled in love, and swaddled in love? Have you not since then, even in your sinfulness, been loved with an exceeding great and wondrous love? Did not love turn your heart of stone into flesh? Has not love dwelt in you since then even to this day? Have not even your trials been sent in love? Blind unbelief called it severity; look now, as Jesus sits at your side, and say, was it not the wisest form of love that smote you, and made you cry out in bitterness? Oh, I do remember at this day nothing in the dealings of God to me but love. I sat me down last night, as this text charmed my spirit, and tried to think over my whole life, if perhaps I might light upon some unkindness of my God to me; but my solemn witness is that from the first day my life began to beat, from the first hour I knew anything of the Lord whatever, all his dealings have been love, love, love, love, love, love alone – nothing else but love. Of my life I can and must say, 'the midst thereof has been paved with love'.

Look at the tesselated pavement of love beneath your feet for a moment. See you not the Father's love – that golden mass of uncreated love, for the Father himself loveth you: look at Jesus' love, another diamond pavement beneath your foot: Jesus loved you to the death with a love that many waters could not quench, nor floods drown: look at the love of the Spirit, too: equally precious is the tender affection of the loving Comforter. Think how the Holy Ghost has borne with you, has striven with you, and endured your ill manners in the wilderness, and blessed you still. Look at those delightful embroideries from the divine needle – the precious promises. A thousand promises there are, but they are all love. Look down and see how all the attributes of God are engaged for you, but they are all in league with love. Look, then, at all the providences of God towards you, at all the exercises of his grace in your heart, and you will see many and strange colours of varied beauty, all blending in one wondrous pattern of deep, unsearchable love. I cannot talk this morning, my tongue fails me, but I feel the love of Jesus in my own soul, and I pray that you may feel it in yours. This one thing be assured of, that as it was in the beginning, it is now, and ever shall be, love, love, love, right on, for ever and for aye. The Lord who has begun to love you will never cease from doing so. The midst of the covenant of grace is paved with love for the daughters of Jerusalem.

I want you to notice THE PECULIAR POSITION OF THE PAVEMENT OF LOVE DESCRIBED IN THE TEXT. It is 'in the midst' of the chariot, and only from the midst is it to be seen. It is in the midst of it; and therefore Jesus rides upon it, and his espoused ones ride upon it. It is a very simple thought, but it richly deserves to be beaten out a little. Jesus is represented here as the King in the chariot, and as the chariot is lined with love, we are taught that Jesus dwells in love. Where is he now? Among the thrones and principalities above, but he abides still in love. Love brought him down from heaven to earth, love conducted him in all his weary journeys over the acres of Palestine; love led him to the garden, the death-sweat, and the cross; and equally at this hour does love attend him: he loves in heaven as he loved below. Whatever he is doing, whatever he is feeling, whatever he is saying, we know this one thing about him, he dwells in love to us. He is in his chariot, and all around him in that chariot is love.

The chariot was a royal one, and as the king rode along he was reigning, but he was reigning in love, and it is so with Jesus. All things are in his hands, and he governs all things in love to his people. Heavenly principalities serve him, and angels are his willing messengers; but there is no power which Jesus has which he does not wield in love to us. Has his power seemed sometimes to be exercised harshly? It is not so: it cannot be so. He reigns in love. Our Joseph is lord over all Egypt, and since Joseph loves his brethren, the good of all the land of Egypt is theirs. Jesus rules all the world for his people's benefit; all things are theirs, whether things present or things to come, all are theirs. Jesus reigns in love.

And Jesus rests in love. This chariot was a place for the traveller to rest in; he reclined as he was carried along. Nothing gives Jesus such rest as his love for his people. It is his solace and his joy. It is almost inconceivable by us that Jesus should derive joy from the fact that he loves us, but it is so. That text in Zephaniah which we read on Monday evening comes again to our recollection: 'He will rest in his love, he will joy over thee with singing.' It is a joy to Christ to love his people. His own heart finds a joy in their joy, a heaven in their heaven. To see them saved is bliss to him. Oh, how glad we ought to be of this. Jesus rests in love.

But as the traveller rested he also proceeded on his way; the bearers carried the palanquin from place to place, and the traveller made progress, but always with the same surroundings within his curtained bed. So Jesus in all his glorious marchings, in everything he does or is to do, still marches on in love. Read you the Book of Revelation, and think of the trumpets, and the falling stars, and the opened vials full of judgments, and you may well tremble; but then fall back upon the doctrine of the Scriptures, and say, 'These are the goings forth of my Lord the King, but he always rides in a chariot which is paved with love for the daughters of Jerusalem. So let him come: with earthquake and with flame, if so he chooseth, let him come; let him even loose destroying angels to smite the earth, and let the whole world before his coming rock and reel, and all men's hopes depart like visions of the night, I will not fear, for sure am I that he cannot come except in love to me.' No judgment can bear wrath to his people, no overturning can overturn their hopes, no rod of iron can shatter their bliss. This is surely a thought which should make your spirit glad.

Now notice that as Jesus rides in this chariot, so do you, O believer, and at this moment your standing is upon love. You stand up in this palanquin upon love. You are accepted in the Beloved: you are not judged according to the law, but you are judged according to grace: you are not estimated at the judgment seat by what you have done, but according to his abounding mercy. Recline this morning in the love of God. Ah, take your rest in it. As the rich man tries to find solace in his riches, and the strong man in his strength, and the great man in his fame, so stretch yourselves and lie at ease upon this glorious bed of almighty love.

And, beloved, take care that when you labour to make progress, you still make it in the power and energy of his love. Do not strive after virtue and grace by the law, for you will never get them. The chariot in which you rest is also the chariot in which you are to be carried forward towards perfection. Grow in grace, but keep to the cross. Cling still to the love of God in Christ Jesus, for that keeps you always safe. You sleep in it; you wake in it; you eat and you drink in it. Wherever you are, love surrounds you. It is in the atmosphere you breathe; it is to be found in every place, wherever you roam. You are never out of the love which is in the midst of the chariot.

These are things not to be talked of so much as to be thought over. Carry them home, and if you have leisure this afternoon, try to mark, learn, and inwardly digest this precious truth – 'the midst thereof is paved with love for the daughters of Jerusalem.'

To close, DWELL ON THAT LOVE itself just for a moment. Remember it is special love. It is not love for all men. There is some consolation in universal benevolence, but here we go deeper, and rejoice in love for the daughters of Jerusalem. There is an electing, discriminating, distinguishing love, which is settled upon a chosen people – a love which goes forth to none beside, but only to them; and it is this love which is the true resting-place of the saint.

It is love undeserved, for what daughter of Jerusalem ever deserved that our glorious King should fall in love with her? It is a love, therefore, which is a theme for eternal wonder. Why didst thou love me, Redeemer? Why didst thou make a covenant of grace with me, and line that covenant with immutable love?

This love is everlasting and eternal. It never had a beginning, it never will have an end. Simply as I have stated the truth, it is a nut with heaven for its kernel. Thou wast always loved, O believer, and thou always shalt be, come what may.

It is love unrivalled, for never was there such affection as that which Christ has for his chosen; love unexampled, to which none of us shall ever reach. We should seek to love as God has loved us, but to the infinite, the boundless degree, we shall never arrive. There is no love like the love of God in Christ. It is love which to us has become this day our brightest thought, our truest comfort, and our most potent incentive. Law rules the slaves of this world, but loves rules the freemen of the world to come. The ungodly, if they do right after a fashion, do it from fear of punishment or hope of reward; but the true-born children of God find in the love of Christ their sole motive. They are obedient not because they are afraid of being lost – they know they never shall be; not because they hope to get to heaven by their good works – they have heaven already by the works of another, guaranteed to them by the promise of God; but they serve God out of pure gratitude for what they have received, rejoicing as they work in the service of one they love so well.

Beloved, may the love of God be shed abroad in your hearts by the Holy Ghost this morning, and all the days of your lives, and O that many who have never tasted of that love may be made to long for it, that they may be made alive by it, and unto God shall be glory. Amen and Amen.

26

CHRIST'S ESTIMATE OF HIS PEOPLE

'How fair is thy love, my sister, my spouse! how much better is thy love than wine! and the smell of thine ointments than all spices! Thy lips, O my spouse, drop as the honeycomb: honey and milk are under thy tongue; and the smell of thy garments is like the smell of Lebanon' (Song of Solomon 4:10, 11).

I shall not, this evening, attempt to prove that the Song of Solomon has a spiritual meaning. I am sure it has. It has been frequently said, and, I believe, has commonly been thought, that this song was originally written by Solomon upon his marriage with Pharaoh's daughter. Now I am as sure as I am of my own existence, that this is one of the grossest mistakes that ever was committed. There is nothing about Pharaoh's daughter in it.

It is, first of all, improbable that it was written of her; and in the next place I will go further, and affirm that it is impossible that it could have been written by Solomon in honour of her. If you look all through the song you will find that this is so; in the very beginning she is compared to a shepherdess. Now, all shepherds are abominations to the Egyptians; do you think, therefore, that Solomon would compare an Egyptian princess to the very thing which she abominated?

In the next place, all the scenery is in the land of Canaan, none of it in Egypt; and besides that, all the places that Solomon speaks of, such as Engedi, Lebanon, Amana, and Damascus, were all out of the way; not one of them would have been passed in coming out of Egypt into Jerusalem, and very probably the Egyptian princess did not even know there were such places at all, so that if Solomon had wished to praise her he would not have compared her eyes to the fish-ponds of Heshbon, but would have spoken of the sweet waters of the Nile.

Besides, it could not have been Pharaoh's daughter. Did Pharaoh's daughter ever keep sheep? Yet the person who is represented here did. Did the watchmen ever follow her about the streets, and try to take away her veil from her? Solomon would have shown them something if they had; therefore, that is impossible. In one place, Solomon compares her to a company of horses in Pharaoh's chariot. Now, horses were, among the Israelites, common things; and what would Pharaoh's daughter have said, if Solomon had compared her to a company of horses? She might have well looked him in the face and said, 'Have you not some better comparison for me than my father's horses?' It is very unlikely that Solomon perpetrated that folly.

It is improbable, therefore, and we may almost say impossible, that it could be Pharaoh's daughter. She never came from Lebanon and from the top of Amana; most probably she never heard of those places, or, if she heard of them, she could not have come from them, for she came from Egypt. The fact is, that this book has been a puzzle to many men, for the simple reason that it was not written for them at all. Learned men and wise men find this a stone on which they are broken to powder, just because it was not written for them. Men who are disposed to laugh at Scripture find here an opportunity to exercise their profane wit, just because the book is not written for them.

This book was called by the Jews, 'the Holiest of Holies'; they never allowed any one to read it till he was thirty years of age; it was thought to be such a Sacred book. Many a Christian who reads it cannot understand it. And as good Joseph Irons says:

> 'This dwarfish age is not likely to esteem this book as it ought to be esteemed; only those who have lived near to Jesus, have drunk out of his cup, have eaten his flesh and drank his blood, only those who know the fulness of the word "communion", can sit down to this book with delight and pleasure; and to such men these words are as wafers made with honey, manna, angels' food: every sentence is like gold, and every word is like much fine gold.'

The true believer who has lived near to his Master will find this book to be a mass, not of gold merely, for all God's Word is this, but a mass of diamonds sparkling with brightness; and all things thou canst conceive are not to be compared with it for its matchless worth. If I must prefer one book above another, I would prefer some books of the Bible for doctrine, some for experience, some for example, some for teaching, but let me prefer this book above all others for fellowship and communion. When the Christian is nearest to heaven, this is the book he takes with him. There are times when he would leave even the Psalms behind, when standing on the borders of Canaan, when he is in the land of Beulah, and he is just crossing the stream, and can almost see his Beloved through the rifts of the storm-cloud, then it is he can begin to sing Solomon's Song. This is about the only book he could sing in heaven, but for the most part, he could sing this through, there still praising him who is his everlasting lover and friend.

With these preliminary remarks, let us go at once to the text. I have said that this is Jesus speaking to his Church. Now when the Church praises Jesus, you do not wonder, for he deserves all she can say of him, and ten thousand times more. When she uses such large expressions concerning his loveliness, you feel that she falls far short of her mighty theme; that she does but demean him by her comparisons, for she can but compare the greater with the less, and the beautiful and the eternal, with that which is mutable and transient. But to hear Christ turn round upon his Church, and seem to say to her: 'Thou hast praised me, I will praise thee; thou thinkest much of me, I think quite as much of thee; thou usest great expressions to me, I will use just the same to thee. Thou sayest my love is better than wine, so is thine to me; thou tellest me all my garments smell of myrrh, so do thine; thou sayest my word is sweeter than honey to thy lips, so is thine to mine. All that thou canst say of me, I say it back to thee; I see myself in thy eyes, I can see my own beauty in thee; and whatever belongs to me, belongs to thee. Therefore, O my love, I will sing back the song: thou hast sung it to thy beloved, and I will sing it to my beloved, thou hast sung it to thy Ishi, I will sing it to my Hephzibah, thou hast sung it to thy husband, I will sing it to my sister, my spouse.'

Now note how sweetly the Lord Jesus sings to his spouse. First, he praises *her love*: 'How fair is thy love, my sister, my spouse! how much better is thy love than wine!' Next he praises *her graces*: 'The smell of thy ointments, is much better than all spices.' Then he praises *her words*: 'Thy lips, O my spouse, drop as the honeycomb.' Then he praises *her thoughts*, the things that do not come out of her mouth, but lie under her tongue: 'Honey and milk are under thy tongue.' Then he finishes by praising *her works*: 'The smell of thy garments is like the smell of Lebanon.'

Begin at the beginning then, Christ first PRAISES HIS PEOPLE'S LOVE. Dost thou love God, my hearer? Dost thou love Jesus? If not, stand back! These things have nothing to do with thee, for if thou lovest not Christ, thou hast neither part nor lot in the matter. Thou art in the gall of bitterness, and in the bond of iniquity. But canst thou say as Peter did, when his Master asked him thrice: 'Simon, son of Jonas, lovest thou me?' Canst thou say, 'Lord, thou knowest all things, thou knowest that I love thee; and thou knowest, O my Lord! that my grief is that I do not love thee more, I pant to have my little love increased, that my heart may be eaten up with love, that zeal of love to thee may completely consume me?' Hearken then, to what the Lord Jesus says to thee tonight, by his Holy Spirit, from this song! Thy love, poor, feeble, and cold though it be, is very precious unto the Lord Jesus, in fact it is so precious, that he himself cannot tell how precious it is. He does not say how precious, but he says, 'how fair'. This is an expression that men use when they do not know how to describe anything. They lift up their hands, they put in a note of exclamation, and they say, 'How fair! how precious! how much better is thy love than wine!' The fact is that Jesus values our love at such a price, that the Holy Spirit when he dictated this Song of Solomon, could not see any word in all human language that was large enough to set forth Christ's estimation of our love.

Have you never thought of Christ's love to you, till your heart has been melted, while your beloved spake to you, till the tears have run down your eyes, and you have believed you could do as Mary Magdalene did, could kiss his feet, and wash them with your tears, and wipe them with the hairs of your head? Now can you believe it? Just what you think of Christ's love, Christ thinks of yours. You value his love, and you are right in so doing; but I am afraid that still you undervalue it. He even values your love, if I may so speak, he sets a far higher estimate upon it than you do, he thinks very much of little, he estimates it not by its strength, but by its sincerity. 'Ah,' he says, 'he does love me, he does love me, I know he does; he sins, he disobeys me, but still I know he loves me, his heart is true, he does not love me as I deserve, but still he loves me.' Jesus Christ is delighted with the thought that his people love him, this cheers and gladdens him. Just as the thought of his love gladdens us, so the thought of our love gladdens him.

Notice how he puts it, he says, 'How much better is thy love than wine!'

Now wine when used in Scripture, frequently signifies two things: a great luxury and a great refreshment. Wine is a luxury, especially it is so in this country, and even in the East, where there was more of it, good wine was still a dainty thing. Now Jesus Christ looks upon his people's love as being a luxury to him; and I will show you that he does. When he sat at the feast of Simon the Pharisee, I have no doubt there were sparkling wine cups on the table, and many rich dainties were there, but Jesus Christ did not care for the wine, nor for the banquet. What did he care for then? That poor woman's love was much better to him than wine. He could say to Simon the Pharisee, if he had chosen, 'Simon, put away thy wine cups, take away thy dainties; this is my feast, the feast of my people's love.'

I told you also that wine was used as an emblem of refreshment. Now, our Saviour has often been refreshed by his people's love. 'No,' says one, 'that cannot be.' Yes! you remember once he was weary and thirsty, and sat upon the well of Samaria. He needed wine then indeed to refresh him, but he could not get so much as a drop of water. He spoke to a woman whom he had loved from before all worlds, he put new life into her, and she at once desired to give him drink; but she ran away first to tell to the Samaritans what she had heard. Now the Saviour was so delighted at her wishing to do good, that when his disciples came, they expected to find him fainting, for he had walked many a weary mile that day, so they said, 'Whence hath he meat?' and he said, 'I have meat to eat that ye know not of.' It was that woman's love that had fed him. He had broken her heart, he had won her to himself, and when he saw the tear roll from her eye, and knew that her heart was set upon him, his spirits all revived, and his poor flagging strength grew strong. It was this encouraged him.

Nay, I will go farther. When Christ went to his cross there was one thing that cheered him even in the agonies of death, it was the thought of his people's love. Are we not told by the apostle Paul in the Hebrews, that our blessed and divine husband, the Lord Jesus, 'for the joy that was set before him, endured the cross, despising the shame'? What was that joy? Why, the joy that he should see his seed, and that seed should love him, and that he should have his love written in their hearts, in remembrance of his dying pains and agonies. Jesus was cheered, even in his death agonies, by the thought of the love of his people. When the bulls of Bashan roared upon him, and the dogs bayed him, when the sun was put out in darkness, when his Father's hand was heavy upon him, when the legions of hell compassed him, when the pangs of body, and the tortures of spirit all beset him – it was this that cheered him: 'My people they are dear to me; for them I stretch these bleeding hands; for them shall this heart be pierced, and oh, how they will love me, how they will love me on earth! how they will love me spiritually in Paradise!' This was the wine the Saviour had to drink; this was the cup of his delightful joy that made him bear all these pains without a murmuring, and this was the meaning of these words of Jesus – 'How much better is thy love than wine!'

Pause here, my soul, to contemplate a moment, and let thy joy wait awhile. Jesus Christ has banquets in heaven, such as we have never yet tasted, and yet *he* does not feed there. He has wines in heaven richer far than all the grapes of Eshcol could produce, but where does he seek his wine? In our hearts, my friends, in our hearts. Not all the love of angels, nor all the joys of Paradise, are so dear to him as the love of his poor people, sprinkled with sin, and compassed with infirmity. Is not that a thought! I may preach about it, I can only speak it to you; read it, mark it, learn it, and inwardly digest it; and oh, if you saw him standing here tonight, and looking into your eyes, and saying to you personally, 'You love me, I know that you love me, thy love is to me better far than wine'; would you not fall at his feet and say, 'Lord, is my love so sweet to thee? Then shame upon me that I should give thee so little of it.' And then you would break out into the song of *Krishnu*, which we sung this morning,

> O now, my soul, forget no more
> The Lord who all thy misery bore,
> Nor him forget, who left his throne,
> And for thy life gave up his own.

This is the first point: the love of the believer is sweet to Christ.

2. Do not imagine, however, that Christ despises our faith, or our hope, or our patience, or our humility. All these GRACES are precious to him, and they are described in the next sentence under the title of ointment, and the working of these graces, their exercise and development, are compared to the smell of ointment.

Now both wine and ointment were used in the sacrifice of the Jews; sweet smelling myrrh and spices were used in meat offerings and drink offerings before the Lord. 'But,' saith Jesus Christ to his church, 'all these offerings of wine, and all that burning of incense, is nothing to me compared to your graces. Your love is my wine, your virtues are my sweet smelling ointments.'

For now you have a little faith, but oh, how little it is. You seem to have got just faith enough to know how unbelieving you are; you have got love, but somehow you have only got about love enough to let you know how little you love him. You have some humility, but you have only enough humility to discover you are very proud; you have some zeal for Christ, but you have only zeal enough to make you chide yourself that you are so cold; you have some hope, but you have only hope enough to lead you to see how despairing and desponding you often are; you have some patience, but you have only patience enough to teach how often you murmur when you ought not. 'I confess,' say you, 'that all my graces are a stench in my own nostrils, and all the good things I trust I have, I cannot look upon them with any pride or self-congratulation. I must bury myself in dust and ashes; and even those things I can but weep over them, for they are so marred by my own evil nature.'

But now then, the very things that you and I very properly weep over, Christ delights in. He loves all these: the smell may seem to be but very faint and feeble, yet Jesus observes it, Jesus smells it, Jesus loves it, and Jesus approves it. Yes, believer, when you are on your sick bed and are suffering with patience; when you go about your humble way to do good by stealth; when you distribute of your alms to the poor; when you lift up your thankful eye to heaven; when you draw near to God with humble prayer; when you make confession of your sin to him; all these acts are like the smell of ointment to him, the smell of a sweet savour, and he is gratified and pleased. O Jesus, this is condescension indeed, to be pleased with such poor things as we have. Oh this is love; it proves thy love to us, that thou canst make so much out of little, and esteem so highly that which is of such little worth! Have you never known a little child when he feels love in his heart go into the garden or the field and bring you a little flower, it may be but a little buttercup or a daisy, a great thing to him, perhaps, but a trifle to you – worthless in fact – you have taken it, and you have smiled and have felt happy because it was a token of your child's love? So Jesus esteems your graces, they are his gift to you.

Mark, first of all, they are very poor things in themselves; still he esteems them as tokens of your love, and he rejoices in them, and declares they are sweet to him as all the spices of Araby, and all the rich odours of the merchant. This is the second thing.

Now we come to the third. 'Thy lips, O my spouse, drop as the honey-comb.' Christ's people are not a dumb people, they were once but they TALK NOW. I do not believe a Christian can keep the secret that God gives him if he were to try; it would burst his lips open to get out. When God puts grace into your heart, you may try to hide it, but hide it you cannot. It will be like fire in the bones, and will be sure to find its way out. Now the church is a talking church, a preaching church, and a praising church; she has got lips, and every believer will find he must use his lips in the service of Christ. Now it is but poor, poor matter that any of us can speak. When we are most eloquent in our Master's praise, how far our praises fall beneath his worth! When we are most earnest in prayer, how powerless is our wrestling compared with the great blessing that we seek to obtain! When our song is loudest, and it begins to be something akin to the chorus of the angels, even then how marred it is with the discord of our unbelief and of our worldliness! But Jesus Christ does not find any fault in what the Church speaks. He says, 'No, "Thy lips, O my spouse, drop as the honeycomb".' You know the honey that drops out of the honeycomb is the best – it is called the life-honey. So the words that drop from the Christian's lips are the very words of his life, his life-honey, and they ought to be sweet to every one. They are as sweet to the taste of the Lord Jesus as the drops of the honeycomb.

A little caution to some of you that talk too much. Some of you do not let your words drop as the honeycomb, they gush out as a great stream that sweeps everything before it, so that others could not thrust in a word edgeways; no, not if it were squeezed together and sharpened at one end could it be got in. They must talk; their tongue seems set on a hinge, like a pendulum, for ever going on, swing! swing! swing! Now Christ does not admire that. He says of his church in his commendation, her lips 'drop as the honeycomb'. Now a honeycomb, when it drops, does not drop so much even as the drops that fall from the eaves of houses; for the honey is thick, and rich, and therefore it takes some time. One drop hangs for a time; then comes another, and then another, and does not all come in quick succession. Now when people are often talking a great deal, it is poor and thin, and good for nothing; but when they have something good to say, it drops by slow degrees like the honey from the honeycomb. Mark, I do not want you to say one good word less. They are those other words, those awkward ones. Oh that we could leave them out! I am as guilty of this myself, I fear, as many others. If we could talk half as much, it would be, perhaps, twice as good; and if we were to say only a tenth of what we do, perhaps we should be ten times better, for he is a wise man that knows how to speak well, but he is a great deal wiser man that knows how to hold his tongue.

The lips of the true church, the lips of the true believer drop like the honeycomb, with rich words, rich thoughts, rich prayers, rich praises. 'Oh,' says one, 'but I am sure my lips do not drop like that when in prayer. Sometimes even I cannot get on at all, and when I am singing I cannot put my heart into it, and when I am trying to instruct others, I feel I am so ignorant that I know nothing myself.' That is your estimate; I am glad you are so humble as to think that. But Christ does not think so. 'Ah,' he says, 'that man would preach if he could; that man would honour me better if he could.' And he does not measure what we do, but what we want to do; and so it is that he reckons that our lips drop like the honeycomb. What is sweeter in the world than honey from the honeycomb? But whatever may be the sweetest thing to the world, the words of the Christian are the sweetest thing to Christ.

Sometimes believers are privileged to set down together, and they begin to talk about what *he* said, and what *he* suffered for them here below, they begin to speak of his exceeding glories and his boundless and matchless love; they begin to tell to one another what they have tasted and handled of the good word of life, and their hearts begin to burn within them when they speak of these things by the way. Do you know that Jesus is in that room, smiling Jesus is there, and he is saying to his own soul, 'It is good to be here, the lips of these my brethren drop as the honeycomb, and their words are sweet to me.' At another time the Christian is alone in his chamber, and he talks with his God in a few broken words, and with many sighs, many tears, and many groans; and little does he think that Jesus Christ is there, saying to such an one, 'Thy lips, O my beloved, drop with honey like the honeycomb.'

And now Christians will you not talk much about Jesus? Will you not speak often of him? Will you not give your tongue more continually to prayer and praise, and speech that ministers to edifying, when you have such a listener as this, such an auditor who stoops from heaven to hear you, and who values every word you speak for him? Oh, it is a sweet thing to preach when the people listen to catch every word. I would give in if I had to preach to an inattentive audience. And yet I do not know. Plato, we are told, was once listening to an orator, and when all the people had gone away but Plato, the orator went on with all his might. Being asked why he proceeded, he replied, that Plato was sufficient audience for any man. And surely if in preaching, or in praying, all the world should find fault, and all the world should run from it, Jesus is enough to be the bearer for any man. And if he is satisfied, if he says our words are sweeter than the honeycomb, we will not stop; all the devils in hell shall not stop us. We could continue to preach, and praise, and pray, while immortality endures. If this be honey, then the honey shall drop. If Christ prizes it, we set his opinion against all the opinion in the world; he knows better than any others; he is the best judge, for he is the last and final Judge – we will go on talking of him, while he goes on to say, our lips drop as the honeycomb.

'But,' says one, 'if I were to try to talk about Jesus Christ, I do not know what I should say.' If you wanted any honey, and nobody would bring it to you, I suppose the best way, if you were in the country, would be to keep some bees, would it not? It would be very well for you Christian people if you kept bees. 'Well,' says one, 'I suppose our thoughts are to be the bees. We are always to be looking about for good thoughts, and flying on to the flowers where they are to be found; by reading, by meditation, and by prayer, we are to send bees out of the hive.' Certainly, if you do not read your Bibles, you will have no honey, because you have no bees. But when you read your Bibles, and study those precious texts, it is like bees settling on flowers, and sucking the sweetness out of them. There are many other books, though the Bible is the chief one, that you may read with great advantage; over which your thoughts may be busied as bees among flowers. And then you must attend the means of grace continually; you must listen often to the preaching of the Word and if you hear a minister who is a plant of the Lord's right hand planting, and you believe in what you hear, you will be like the bees sucking sweetness out of flowers, and your lips will be like the honeycomb. But some people have nothing in their heads, and they are never likely to have; for they are so wise that they cannot learn, and they are such fools that they will never teach. Some waste the time they have. Now I would have my people read much the Word of God, and study it, and then read such books as shall illustrate it.

I will tell you where I have been sipping a bit just lately, and I have often sipped much from – it is this book of Solomon's Song. It is a favourite book of mine. And there is a sweet little book of Joseph Irons' called *Nymphas*, a blank verse explanation of it. If any of you have that little book, set your bees to work on it, and if you do not suck honey out of it, I am very much mistaken. Then let the bees bring the honey to the hive of your memory, and let it be added to the stores of your mind, and in this way you will get rich in precious things, so that when you speak, the saints will be edified, your prayers will be full of marrow and fatness, and your praises will have something in them, because you have sent your bees well abroad, and therefore your lips will drop as the honeycomb.

4. This brings us to the next topic – 'Honey and milk are under thy tongue'. I find it necessary when I preach to keep a good stock of words under my tongue as well as those that are on it. It is a curious operation of the mind in the man who continually preaches. It sometimes happens while I am speaking to you that I am thinking about what I am going to say at the close of my sermon, and when I am thinking about people down stairs or in the gallery, and how I shall hit Mr So-and-So, I am still talking right on, speaking with all my heart on the subject on which I am addressing you. It is because by continually preaching we get into the habit of keeping words under our tongue as well as those that are on the top, and sometimes we find it necessary to keep those words under our tongue altogether and not to let them come further. Very often I have got a simile just ready to come out, and I have thought, 'Ah, that is one of your laughable similes, take that back.' I am obliged to change it for something else. If I did that a little oftener perhaps it would be better, but I cannot do it. I have sometimes a whole host of them under my tongue, and I am obliged to keep them back. 'Honey and milk are under thy tongue.'

That is not the only meaning. The Christian is to have words ready to come out by-and-by. You know the hypocrite has words upon his tongue. We speak about solemn sounds upon a thoughtless tongue; but the Christian has his words first under the tongue. There they lie. They come from his heart; they do not come from the top of his tongue – they are not superficial surface-work, but they come from under the tongue – deep down -- things that he feels, and matters that he knows. Nor is this the only meaning.

The things that are under the tongue are thoughts that have yet been expressed; they do not get to the top of the tongue, but lie there half formed and are ready to come out; but either because they cannot come out, or we have not time to let them out, there they remain, and never come into actual words. Now Jesus Christ thinks very much even of these; he says, 'Honey and milk are under thy tongue'; and Christian meditation and Christian contemplation are to Christ like honey for sweetness and like milk for nourishment. Honey and milk are two things with which the land of Canaan was said to flow; and so the heart of a Christian flows with milk and honey, like the land which God gave to his ancient people.

'Well,' says one, 'I cannot find that my heart is like that. If I do sit down and think of Jesus, my thoughts turn upon the glories of his person and the excellency of his office; but oh, sir, my thoughts are such dull, cold, useless things; they do not feed me or delight me.' Ah but, you see, Christ does not estimate them as you do; he feeds on them; they are like honey to him, and though you think very little of your own thoughts, and are right in so doing, yet, oh remember, such is the love of Jesus, such is his abundant condescension and compassion, that the very least things that you have he values at a great price. The words you are not speaking, the words you cannot utter, the groans you cannot bring out, these the Holy Spirit utters for you, and these Jesus treasures up as choice and peculiarly precious things – 'honey and milk are under thy tongue.'

5. And then, last of all, 'the smell of thy garments is like the smell of Lebanon'. The odiferous herbs that grew on the side of Lebanon delighted the traveller, and, perhaps, here is an allusion to the peculiarly sweet smell of the cedar wood. Now, the garments of a Christian are two-fold: the garment of imputed righteousness, and the garment of inwrought sanctification. I think the allusion here is to the second. The garments of a Christian are his EVERY DAY ACTIONS – the things that he wears upon him wherever he goes. Now these smell very sweet to the Lord Jesus.

And here let us speak to some of you here present who manifestly are not God's children, for you smell of the garlic of Egypt rather than of the cedar of Lebanon; and there are some professors, and, perhaps, some now present, whose smell is anything but like that of Lebanon. Take heed, ye that do not live up to your profession. You have sad evidences within that you have not possession. If you can dishonour Christ's holy gospel by living in sin, tremble! lest when he shall come in the terror of judgment, he should cry, 'Depart, ye cursed; I never knew you'.

But if you be humble lovers of Christ and really have your hearts set upon him, your daily actions are observed by him, and the smell of it is to him as sweet as the smell of Lebanon. What should you think if Jesus should meet you at the close of the day, and say to you, 'I am pleased with the works of today'? I know you would reply, 'Lord, I have done nothing for thee.' You would say like those at the last day, 'Lord, when saw we thee hungry and fed thee? when saw we thee thirsty and gave thee drink?' You would begin to deny that you had done any good thing. He would say, 'Ah, when thou wast under the fig tree I saw thee; when thou wast at thy bedside in prayer, I heard thee; I saw thee when the tempter came, and thou saidst, "Get thee hence, Satan"; I saw thee give thine alms to one of my poor sick children; I heard thee speak a good word to the little child and teach him the name of Jesus; I heard thee groan when swearing polluted thine ears; I heard thy sigh when thou sawest the iniquity of this great city; I saw thee when thine hands were busy; I saw that thou was not an eye-servant or a man-pleaser, but that in singleness of purpose thou didst serve God in doing thy daily business; I saw thee, when the day was ended, give thyself to God again; I have marked thee mourning over the sins thou hast committed, and I tell thee I am pleased with thee.' 'The smell of thy garments is like the smell of Lebanon.'

And, again, I hear you say, 'Lord, I never knew love like this: I have heard that love covers a multitude of sins, but I never knew a love so broad as to cover all mine. And then to declare that thou canst see no sin in me at all – ah! that is love!' It may melt our heart, and make us seek to be holy, that we might not grieve Christ, make us labour to be diligent in his service, that we might not dishonour him.

I dare say some of you think when ministers preach or go about to do their pastoral duty, that of course Christ is very much pleased with them. 'Ah,' says Mary, 'I am only a poor servant girl; I have to get up in the morning and light the fire, lay out the breakfast things, dust the parlour, make the pies and puddings for dinner, and clear away the things again, and wash them up. I have to do everything there is to do in the house – Christ cannot be pleased with this.' Why Mary, you can serve Christ as much in making beds, as I can in making sermons; and you can be as much a true servant of Christ in dusting a room, as I can in administering discipline in a church. Do not think for a single moment that you cannot serve Christ. Our religion is to be an everyday religion: a religion for the kitchen as well as for the parlour; a religion for the rolling pin, and the jack-towel, quite as much as for the pulpit stairs and the Bible; a religion that we can take with us wherever we go. And there is such a thing as glorifying Christ in all the common actions of life. 'Servants be obedient to your masters, not only to those who are good and gentle, but to the froward.'

You men of business, you need not think that when you are measuring your ribbons, or weighing out your pounds of sugar, or when you are selling, or buying or going to market, and such like, that you cannot be serving Christ. Why a builder can serve Christ in putting his bricks together, and you can serve Christ in whatever you are called to do with your hands, if you do it as unto the Lord, and not unto men. I remember Mr Jay once said, that if a shoeblack were a Christian, he could serve Christ in blacking shoes. He ought to black them, he said, better than anyone else in the parish; and then people would say, 'Ah, this Christian shoeblack, he is conscientious; he won't send the boots away with the heels half done, but will do them thoroughly.' And so ought you. You can say of every article you sell, and of everything else you do, 'I turned that out of my hands in such a manner that it shall defy competition. The man has got his money's worth; he cannot say I am a rogue or a cheat. There are tricks in many trades, but I will not have anything to do with them; many get money fast by adulteration in trade, but I will not do it; I would sooner be poor than do it.' Why, the world says, 'There is a sermon in that grocer's window. Look, you don't see him telling lies to puff his goods: there is a sermon there.' People say as they pass by, 'It is a godly man that keeps that shop, he cannot bring his conscience down to do what others do. If you go there, you will be well treated, and you will come out of his shop and say, I have spent my money well, and I am glad that I have dealt with a Christian man.' Depend upon it, you will be as good preachers in your shops as I shall be in my pulpit, if you do that; depend upon it, there is a way of serving Christ in this manner; and this is to comfort you and cheer you.

Upon all the actions of your daily life the Lord Jesus looks down from heaven and says, 'The smell of thy garments is like the smell of Lebanon.' I know you can hardly believe that Jesus Christ takes notice of such little things as that, but he does. You say, 'Oh, but they are too trifling.' But don't you know, the God that wings an angel guides a sparrow? Don't you know, 'the very hairs of your head are all numbered'? God not only wings the whirlwind, and gives an edge to the lightning flash, but he guides the chaff from the hand of the winnower, and steers the grain of dust in the evening gale. Do not think anything too little for you. He observes the mighty orbs as they whirl through space, but he notices you too, as you go about your business. And those little cups of cold water you give to his people, those little services you do for his church, those self-denials that you make for his honour, and those conscientious scruples which you foster, and which will not allow you to act as the world acts, all these he observes, and he says, 'The smell of thy garments is like the smell of Lebanon.'

And now to conclude, what shall we say to this? I was reading sometime ago, an article in a newspaper, very much in my praise; and you know, it makes me sad, so sad that I could cry, if ever I see anything praising me; it breaks my heart; I feel I do not deserve it; and then I say, 'Now I must try and be better, so that I may deserve it. If the world abuses me, I am a match for that; I begin to like it; it may fire all its big guns at me, I will not return a solitary shot, but just store them up and grow rich upon the old iron. All the abuse it likes to heap upon me I can stand; but when a man praises me, I feel it is a poor thing I have done, and that he praises me for what I do not deserve. This crushes me down, and I say I must set to work and deserve this. I must preach better. I must be more earnest, more diligent in my Master's service.

Now, will not this text produce just the same effect on you? When the Lord comes to you, and begins saying, 'You are not so humble, nor so prayerful, nor so believing as you ought to be,' you say, 'I do not care about this whipping'; but when he comes and begins to praise you, and tells you, 'That your lips drop as the honeycomb, that all your actions smell of myrrh, and that your love is better than wine and milk', what will you say? Oh, Lord, I cannot say thou art mistaken, for thou art infallible; but if I might say such a thing, if I dared to think thou art mistaken, I should say, 'Thou art mistaken in me'; but Lord I cannot think thou art mistaken, it must be true. Still, Lord, I do not deserve it; I am conscious I do not, and I never can deserve it; still if thou wilt help me, I will strive to be worthy of thy praise in some feeble measure. I will seek to live up to those high encomiums which thou hast passed upon me. If thou sayest, 'My love is better than wine'; Lord, I will seek to love thee better, that the wine may be richer and stronger. If thou sayest, 'My graces are like the smell of ointment', Lord, I will try to increase them, so as to have many great pots filled with them, and I will try to make them better, so that thou mayest think more of such honey; and if thou declarest that the thoughts under my tongue are to thee like honey and milk, then, Lord, I will seek to have more of those divine thoughts; and if my daily actions are to thee as the smell of Lebanon, Lord, I will seek to be more holy, to live nearer to thee; I will ask for grace, that my actions may be really what thou sayest they are.

Ye that love not God, I can weep over you, for ye have nothing to do with this text. It is a frightful thing that you should be shut out of such praise as this – may Christ bring you in! You must first be brought to feel you are nothing; you must then be led to feel that Christ is everything, and then, after that, you shall understand this text, and these words will be spoken to you.

27

THE LORD'S OWN VIEW OF HIS CHURCH AND PEOPLE

A garden inclosed is my sister, my spouse; a spring shut up, a fountain sealed' (Song of Solomon 4:12).

We understand this sacred love-song to be a Canticle of Communion between the Lord Jesus Christ and his church. He is the Bridegroom, and she the bride. Solomon furnishes the figure, as some think, and his Solyma is with him; but the type is dimly seen, it is the antitype which shines forth as the sun to the view of all spiritual minds.

At the very outset of the present discourse it is needful, for the sake of the less instructed, to say what the church is. A church is a congregation of the faithful, that is to say, of believers in the Lord Jesus, those in whom the Holy Spirit has created faith in Christ, and the new nature of which faith is the sure index. The one church of Jesus Christ is made up of all believers throughout all time. Just as any one church is made up of faithful persons, so is the one church of Christ made up of all faithful churches in all lands, and of all faithful people in all ages.

The church was viewed as one in the purpose of God before the world was. The Eternal Father chose to himself a people, and gave them over to his Son, that they might be his portion for ever and ever. This is the church of which we read: 'Christ loved the church, and gave himself for it.' This is 'the church of God, which he hath purchased with his own blood'. This is the church with which the marriage supper shall be celebrated when the Well-beloved shall come to take his own unto himself for ever. While we at this time speak of the church as a whole, it will be quite correct for each individual believer to take home to himself any truth, whether doctrinal, experimental, or practical, which we treat of as the heritage of the church. Each saint may say, 'This belongs to me.' That which belongs to the redeemed family belongs to each member of that family. That which is true of light is true of each beam; that which is true of water is true of each drop; and that which is true of the church as a whole is true of each member of that mystical body.

The love of the Lord Jesus is to his church as a body, and it is the same to each believer as a member of that body. That which is true of the whole number is true of the units which make it up. He who invites a company to a feast virtually invites each person of the company. Jesus loves each one of his people with that same love wherewith he loves the whole of his people; insomuch that if you, my brethren, are Christ's beloved, and if you were the only persons that were ever born into the world, and all his love were yours, he would not then love you one atom more than he loves you now. The love of Jesus is dispersed, but not divided; it flows to all with the same force with which it flows to one. To redeem a single soul our Ransom must have laid down his life for each one, as much as if there had not been another to redeem. We shall not be presumptuous if we enjoy all the love of Jesus of which we are capable, enjoying and appropriating the words of love to ourselves as if they were meant for us alone. The invitation of the Bridegroom in this Song gives a permit to the largest faith and to the most daring enjoyment. 'Eat, O friends; yea, drink abundantly, O beloved.'

I shall call your attention to four things, with as much brevity and earnestness as possible. Come, gracious Spirit, and lead us into the sweetness of them!

The first is, THE NEARNESS OF KIN OF THE CHURCH TO CHRIST, AND CHRIST TO THE CHURCH. He calls her in the text, 'My sister, my spouse.' As if he could not express his near and dear relationship to her by any one term, he employs the two. 'My sister' – that is, one by birth, partaker of the same nature. 'My spouse' – that is, one in love, joined by sacred ties of affection that never can be snapped. 'My sister' by birth, 'My spouse' by choice. 'My sister' in communion, 'My spouse' in absolute union with myself. I want you who love the Saviour to get a full hold of this thought of near and dear kinship under this head. Oh, how near akin Christ is to all his people!

But first, *do try to realise the person of Christ*. I am not going to speak to you at this time of a doctrine, or a mere historical fact that has vanished into the dim past. No, we speak of a real person. Jesus Christ *is*. As man and as God in the perfection of his nature he still exists. He dwells at the right hand of God at this moment, and though he cannot be here in his corporeal person, yet he is everywhere by his spiritual presence, which is more real still. Do not spirit him away. Believe that he truly is, and that he truly is here, as much here and as really here as he was at Jerusalem, when he sat at the head of the table, and entertained the twelve at the last supper. Jesus is a real Man, a real Christ – recollect that.

Then let this further truth be equally well realised, that *he has so taken upon himself our human nature that he may correctly call his church his sister*. He has become so truly man in his incarnation, that he is not ashamed to call us brethren. He calls us so because we are so. No: he is not a deified man any more than he is a humanised God. He is perfectly God but he is also perfectly man; and man such as we are, touched with the feeling, not only of our attainments, but of our infirmities; not only trusting in all points as we do, but tempted in all points like as we are, though without sin. He was, when he was here, evidently man and eminently man; and he now so remembers all that he passed through while here below that he remains in perfect sympathy with us at this very moment. Change of place has made no change of heart in him. He in his glory is the same Jesus as in his humiliation.

No man is so fully a man as Jesus Christ. If you speak of any other man, something or other narrows his manhood. You think of Milton as of a poet and an Englishman rather than as a man. You think of Cromwell rather as of a warrior than as a man. Either his office, his work, his nationality, or his peculiar character, strikes you in many a man rather than his manhood; but Jesus is *the* Man, the model Man: in all his deeds and words man to the fulness of manhood, in its purest and truest state. The second Adam is, *par excellence*, man.

We may not think of him as one amongst a vast number who may be distantly akin to us, as all men are akin to one another by descent; but *the Lord comes near to each individual.* He takes each one of his believing people by the hand, and says, 'My brother'. In our text he salutes the whole church as 'My sister'. HE says this with tender emphasis. The love between brothers, if those brothers are what they should be, is very strong and peculiarly disinterested and admirable. A brother is born for adversity. A true brother is one upon whom you can rely in time of need. One heart in two bodies in the realisation of true brotherhood. Such is, emphatically, the relationship of the Redeeming Lord to each believer. He is your brother. 'The man is next of kin unto us.' You may have the joy of saying, 'I know that my near Kinsman liveth, and that he shall stand at the latter day upon the earth: and though after my skin worms destroy this body, yet in my flesh shall I see God.' Happy man who, without presumption, can feel the ties of kinship with the Son of Man, and can sing with the poet of the sanctuary:

> Jesus, our Kinsman and our God,
> Array'd in majesty and blood,
> Thou art our life; our souls in thee
> Possess a full felicity.

As we have already observed, the first term, 'sister', implies kinship of nature; but *the second term, 'my spouse', indicates another kinship, dearer, and, in some respects, nearer*: a kinship undertaken of choice, but once undertaken, irrevocable and everlasting. This kinship amounts to unity, insomuch that the spouse loses her name, loses her identity, and, to a high degree, is merged in the greater personality to which she is united. Such is our union to Christ, if indeed we be his, that nothing can so well set it forth as marriage union. He loves us so much that he has taken us up into himself by the absorption of love. We may henceforth forego our name, for 'this is the name wherewith *she* shall be called, The Lord our righteousness'. Wonderful that the very name which belongs to our Lord Jesus, and one of the most majestic of his names, should yet be used as the name of his church. The Lord Jesus Christ's name is now named upon her, and she is permitted to make use of his name whenever she draws near to the throne of the heavenly grace in prayer. 'In his name' – this is to be her great plea whenever she intercedes with heaven. She speaks in the name which is above every name, the name at which angels bow.

The Bridegroom calls his church 'my sister, my spouse'. Now come, renewed heart, thou that hast learned to trust thy Saviour, see how near, how dear, thou art to him! If he says, 'My sister, my spouse', answer to him, 'My Brother, my Husband.' If he is not strange to thee, oh, be not cold to him! Think not of him as of some great one to whom thou mayest not approach. Have thou in thy memory that great text, 'It shall be at that day, saith the Lord, that thou shalt call me Ishi (my Husband), and shalt call me no more Baali, (my Lord). For I will take away the names of Baalim out of her mouth, and they shall no more be remembered by their name.' We feel no dreadful lordship now. Though he is Master and Lord, yet it is such a loving lordship which he exercises towards us that we rejoice in it. We hear a voice full of music, saying, 'He is thy Lord, and worship thou him'; but his commandments are not grievous. His yoke is easy, and his burden is light. When we bow before him, it is not because we fear with servile trembling, but because we rejoice and love. We rejoice in his rule and reign. Perfect love hath cast out fear. We live in such joyful fellowship with him as a sister has with a brother, or a wife with a husband. Be not backward towards your own Betrothed. Be not stiff and cold. Set not a bound about the mount, for it is not Sinai: there are no bounds to the hill of Zion. Hang not up a curtain, for he has rent the veil. Think not of him as though he were far divided from you, when he is exceeding near to you, and has taken you up unto himself, to be one with him for ever.

Lost in astonishment I see,
Jesus, thy boundless love to me:
With angels I thy grace adore,
And long to love and praise thee more.

Since thou wilt take me for thy bride,
Oh, keep me, Saviour, near thy side!
I fain would give thee all my heart,
Nor ever from my Lord depart.

I do not know how to preach upon this subject. Who can? Is it a subject for exposition in a mixed assembly? If it were, who could compass it? I beg you, O believers, to sit in your pews, and let holy thought occupy you: let this choice subject saturate your willing minds. If you are true believers, if you have been born again, if you are really looking to Christ alone for salvation, he has brought you into a condition of the utmost conceivable nearness with himself: he has participated in *your* nature, and he has made you a partaker of *his* nature, and in so many words he says, 'I will betroth thee unto me for ever; yea, I will betroth thee unto me in righteousness, and in judgment, and in faithfulness: and thou shalt know the Lord'. Can you grasp it? It will make your heart dance for joy if you can. Never did a more joyful thought illuminate a human mind. One with Jesus! By eternal union, one with Jesus! Is not this heavenly? There can be no divorce between Christ and his church, for thus it is written, 'The Lord, the God of Israel, saith that he hateth putting away.' He will have nothing to do with putting away. Having espoused us, he declares the thing done. 'I am married unto you, saith the Lord.' He has taken our nature, and made us 'partakers of the divine nature': and after he has done that, who shall separate us from the love of God which is in Christ Jesus our Lord? Neither height, nor depth, nor angels, nor principalities, nor powers, nor things present, nor things to come, shall ever be able to effect a break up of this most complete, perfect, mystical union between Christ and his people. Again I pray the Holy Ghost to make every believer feel this, and then we shall go home from this house glad in spirit. My heart will be as a wedding-feast, and the joy-bells of my soul will ring out the words:

> White and ruddy is my Belovèd,
>   All his heavenly beauties shine;
> Nature can't produce an object,
>   Nor so glorious, so divine;
>   He hath wholly
> Won my soul to realms above.
>
> Such as find thee find such sweetness
>   Deep, mysterious, and unknown;
> Far above all worldly pleasures,
>   If they were to meet in one;
>   My Belovèd,
> O'er the mountains haste away.

To a second thought I would call your attention. See in the text THE SECURITY OF THE PEOPLE OF GOD IN CONSEQUENCE OF BEING WHAT THEY ARE: 'A garden inclosed is my sister, my spouse; a spring shut up, a fountain sealed.' We are not only like a garden, but a garden enclosed. If the garden were not enclosed, the wild boar out of the wood would bark the vines, and uproot the flowers; but infinite mercy has made the church of God an enclosure, into which no invader may dare to come. 'For I, saith the Lord, will be unto her as a wall of fire round about, and will be the glory in the midst of her.' Is she a spring? Are her secret thoughts, and loves, and desires like cool streams of water? Then the Bridegroom calls her 'a spring shut up'. Otherwise, every beast that passed by might foul her waters, and ever stranger might quaff her streams. She is a spring shut up, a fountain sealed, like some choice cool spring in Solomon's private garden around the house of the forest of Lebanon – a fountain which he reserved for his own drinking, by placing the royal seal upon it, and locking it up by secret means, known only to himself. The legend hath it that there were fountains which none knew of but Solomon, and he had so shut them up that, with his ring he touched a secret spring, a door opened and living waters leaped out to fill his jewelled cup. No one knew but Solomon the secret charm by which he set flowing the pent-up stream, of which no lip drank but his own. Now, God's people are as much shut up, and preserved, and kept from danger by the care of Christ, as the springs in Solomon's garden were reserved expressly for himself.

Beloved, this is a cheering thought for all believers, that the Lord has set apart him that is godly for himself. He has taken measures to preserve all his chosen from all those who would defile and destroy them. He walled them round about with his divine decree of old, saying, 'This people have I chosen for myself.' He then issued his command that none should injure them, saying, 'Touch not mine anointed, and do my prophets no harm.' He sets a hedge about them in providence, so that nothing shall by any means harm them. He has shut them up from the enemy, and sealed them up for perpetual preservation. The wandering Bedouins in the East plunder the open fields; but a king's garden, enclosed and protected, is safe from their ravages. So are the saints enclosed from all invading powers. Specially has the Lord walled them about with grace. While angels keep watch and ward around this sacred garden to drive off the powers of darkness, the invincible grace of God is ever like a wall about the plants of the Lord's right hand planting, so that neither sin nor the world shall be able to uproot them. You are a garden, and a garden is a tender thing, soon destroyed; but the Lord, who planted you, has seen to your protection and provision. A garden in the East is a very needy place. One day's burning sun might suffice to wither all its verdure; but then the Lord has declared of his church, 'The sun shall not smite thee by day, nor the moon by night.' 'I the Lord do keep it; I will water it every moment; lest any hurt it, I will keep it night and day.' A garden is a dependent thing, requiring perpetual care from the husbandman; and that care the church of God shall have, for it is written, 'He careth for you.' Jesus says, 'My Father is the husbandman'; and surely that is enough.

In a garden weeds spring up; and, alas! in the church, and in our hearts, the weeds of sin are plentiful; but there is One who will take care to pluck up evil growths, and cut away all rank shoots, that none of the precious plants may be choked or overgrown. In all ways every single plant, however feeble, shall be tended with all-sufficient skill.

It is very precious to see how the Lord lays himself out to preserve his own beloved. We are too dear to him to let us perish. Yet, O tender plant, thou art often fearful! Didst thou say the other day that he had left thee? How can this be? Dost thou know at what a price he bought thee? Leave thee! Will the husband forget his beloved spouse, and will the Husband of your soul forget you? Let not the thought tarry with you for a moment, for it is dishonouring to your Lord's love. 'Can a woman forget her sucking child, that she should not have compassion on the son of her womb? yea, they may forget, yet will I not forget thee.' You are as safe as Jesus, for on his heart he bears your name. You are as safe as he is, for on the arm of his strength he wears your name, as the high priest wore the names of the tribes upon his shoulder, as well as upon his breastplate. 'I give unto my sheep,' says he, eternal life; and they shall never perish, neither shall any man pluck them out of my hand.' I want you to enjoy a sense of this security. I will not preach upon it much, but I will ask you to believe it, and to rejoice in it. Are you really in Christ? If so, who is to pluck you thence? Are you really trusting him? How can he fail you? Have you been begotten again into the divine family? How can that new life be quenched? Do not let anything drive from your mind a sense of your security in Christ. I hear somebody say that this might lead men to carnal security. Far from it: the security of the Spirit is a deathblow to the security of the flesh. I tell you, sirs, that it is most needful that you should not believe in Jesus Christ half way, as some do who trust the Lord to put away the sin of the past, but cannot trust for the future. I believe in him to put away all my sins that ever shall be, as well as all the sins that have been. To believe in him only to obliterate the years of former sin is but a limping halfway faith. Believe in him for all the years that shall be. What saith he? 'The water that I shall give him shall be in him a well of water springing up into everlasting life.' Do you believe in him to give you life for a little time, so that you venture to take a quarter's ticket of membership? I am glad that you believe even so much; but why limit his power? Believe in the Lord Jesus for the whole of life, yea, for eternity. 'According to your faith be it unto you.' Do you believe in him to give you a sip of the living water to stay your thirst for a while? Believe in him a great deal more than that, and accept him as quenching your thirst for ever. For 'ye are complete in him'. 'He that believeth in him hath everlasting life.'

I look upon this sense of security in a Christian as being the mainspring of unselfish virtue. What is that perpetual anxiety to save yourself? What is that daily hungering and perpetual thirsting? It is only a spiritualised selfishness. Only when a man is saved does he forget self. When I know that I am saved I am able to glorify God. The thought of saving myself by anything that I shall do, or be, or feel, I hurl to the winds, for I am already saved as a believer in Christ. Now is there scope for virtue. Now is there an opportunity to love God, and to love one's fellow-men from a pure, unselfish motive. A man is drowning, the ship is going down from under him; he is not a likely man to be looking after the interests of those about him. Once let him grasp an oar in the lifeboat, and he is the man to be the saviour of others. I want you to be out of the wreck, and in the lifeboat, that you may be a hearty workers for the salvation of the perishing. I want you to get out of that 'if', 'perhaps', 'peradventure', 'may be', into certainty and full assurance, for then your undivided zeal will go for the glory of God. 'We know that we have passed from death unto life,' says the apostle, speaking in the name of the saints in his day; and when you once know this, then you will rejoice to proclaim life to those around you. When you are assured that you are not only a garden, but a garden enclosed, not only a spring, but a spring shut up, and a fountain sealed against all adversaries, then you will give all your strength to him who has thus secured you. A happy and holy security in Christ will put spirit into you, and cause you to do exploits. For the love you bear his name, you will be ready to live to this sole end – to magnify and glorify the Lord Jesus, whose you are, and whom you serve.

I leave the thought, but I pray the Holy Spirit to breathe over his people a delicious sense of perfect security in Christ Jesus.

Thirdly, THE MOST STRIKING IDEA OF THE TEXT IS THAT OF SEPARATION: 'A garden inclosed is my sister, my spouse; a spring shut up, a fountain sealed.' A garden is a plot of ground separated from the common waste for a special purpose: such is the church. The church is a separate and distinct thing from the world. I suppose there is such a thing as 'the Christian world'; but I do not know what it is, or where it can be found. It must be a singular mixture. I know what is meant by a worldly Christian; and I suppose the Christian world must be an aggregate of worldly Christians. But the church of Christ is not of the world. 'Ye are not of the world,' says Christ, 'even as I am not of the world.'

Great attempts have been made of late to make the church receive the world, and wherever it has succeeded it has come to this result, the world has swallowed up the church. It must be so. The greater is sure to swamp the less. They say, 'Do not let us draw any hard and fast lines. A great many good people attend our services who may not be quite decided, but still their opinion should be consulted, and their vote should be taken upon the choice of a minister, and there should be entertainments and amusements, in which they can assist.' The theory seems to be, that it is well to have a broad gangway from the church to the world: if this be carried out, the result will be that the nominal church will use that gangway to go over to the world, but it will not be used in the other direction. It is thought by some that it would perhaps be better to have no distinct church at all. If the world will not come up to the church, let the church go down to the world; that seems to be the theory. Let the Israelites dwell with the Canaanites, and become one happy family. Such a blending does not appear to have been anticipated by our Lord in the chapter which was read just now: I mean the fifteenth of John. Read verses eighteen and nineteen: 'If the world hate you, ye know that it hated me before it hated you. If ye were of the world, the world would love his own: but because ye are not of the world, but I have chosen you out of the world, therefore the world hateth you.' Did he ever say: 'Try to make an alliance with the world, and in all things be conformed to its ways'? Nothing could have been further from our Lord's mind. Oh, that we could see more of holy separation; more dissent from ungodliness, more nonconformity to the world! This is 'the dissidence of Dissent' that I care for, far more than I do for party names and the political strife which is engendered by them.

Let us, however, take heed that our separateness from the world is of the same kind as our Lord's. We are not to adopt a peculiar dress, or a singular mode of speech, or shut ourselves out from society. He did not so; but he was a man of the people, mixing with them for their good. He was seen at a wedding-feast, aiding the festivities: he even ate bread in a Pharisee's house, among captious enemies. He neither wore phylacteries, nor enlarged the borders of his garments, nor sought a secluded cell, nor exhibited any eccentricity of manner. He was separate from sinners only because he was holy and harmless, and they were not. He dwelt among us, for he was of us. No man was more a man than he; and yet, he was not of the world, neither could you count him among them. He was neither Pharisee nor Sadducee nor Scribe; and at the same time, none could justly confound him with publicans and sinners. Those who reviled him for consorting with these last did, by that very reviling, admit that he was a very different person from those with whom he went. We want all members of the church of Christ to be, manifestly and obviously, distinct persons, as much as if they were of a separate race, even when they are seen mingling with the people around them. We are not to cut ourselves off from our neighbours by affectation and contempt. God forbid. Our very avoiding of affectation, our naturalness, simplicity, sincerity and amiability of character should constitute a distinction. Through Christians being what they seem to be, they should become remarkable in an age of pretenders. Their care for the welfare of others, their anxiety to do good, their forgiveness of injuries, their gentleness of manner – all these should distinguish them far more than they could be distinguished by a livery, or by any outward signs. I long to see Christian people become more distinct from the world than ever, because I am persuaded that, until they are so, the church will never become such a power for blessing men as her Lord intended her to be. It is for the world's good that there should be no alliance between the church and the world by way of compromise, even to a shade. See what came to pass when the church and the world became one in Noah's day: when 'the sons of God saw the daughters of men that they were fair', and were joined with them. Then came the deluge. Another deluge, more desolating even than the former, will come, if ever the church forgets her high calling, and enters into confederacy with the world.

The church is to be a garden, walled, taken out of the common, and made a separate and select plot of ground. She is to be a spring shut up, and a fountain sealed, no longer open to the fowl of the air, and the beasts of the field. Saints are to be separate from the rest of men, even as Abraham was when he said to the sons of Heth, 'I am a stranger and a sojourner with you.'

Come now, my dear friends, are you of this sort? Are you foreigners in a country not your own? You are no Christians, remember, if you are not so. 'Come out from among them and be ye separate, saith the Lord, and touch not the unclean thing.' That is the Lord's own word to you. Did not he himself suffer without the gate that you might go forth unto him without the camp? Are you at one with the rest of mankind? Could anybody live with you, and never see that any alteration had taken place in you? Would they think that you were just the same as any other man? Then, by your fruits ye shall be known. If there is no difference of life between you and the world, the text does not address *you* as the 'sister' and the 'spouse' of Christ. Those who are such are enclosed from the world, and shut up for Christ. 'I wish I were more so,' cries one. So do I, my friend, and may you and I practically prove the sincerity of that desire by a growing separateness from the world!

Lastly, I think THE TEXT BEARS EVEN MORE FORCIBLY ANOTHER IDEA, NAMELY, THAT OF RESERVATION. The church of God is 'a garden enclosed'. What for? Why, that nobody may come into that garden, to eat the fruit thereof, but the Lord himself. It is 'a spring shut up', that no one may drink of the stream but the Lord Jesus. I beg you to consider this for a few minutes, and then practically to remember it all your lives.

A church exists only for the Lord Jesus to accomplish his ends and purposes among the sons of men. Never may this be forgotten. May the

Spirit of God daily sanctify us unto the Lord, to be a peculiar people! I am persuaded that if any church desires to be much honoured of the Lord in these days, both as to internal happiness and external usefulness, it will find that the nearest way to its desire is to be wholly consecrated to the Lord. The church is not formed to be a social club, to produce society for itself; not to be a political association, to be a power in politics; nor even to be a religious confederacy, promoting its own opinions: it is a body created of the Lord to answer his own ends and purposes, and it exists for nothing else. The heavenly bridegroom says to his church, 'Forget also thine own people, and thy father's house; so shall the king greatly desire thy beauty: for he is thy Lord; and worship thou him.' Churches which fail of their high vocation shall be cast forth as salt that has lost its savour. If we do not live for the Lord, we are dead while we live. If we do not bring glory to his name we cannot justify our existence. If we are not as a garden enclosed for Jesus, we are mere bits of waste land; if we are not fountains sealed for Jesus, we are mere brooks in the valley, and shall soon run dry.

'But,' cries one, 'are we not to seek the good of our fellow-men?' Assuredly we are to do so for Christ's sake. 'Are we not to seek to help on sanitary, educational and purifying processes, and the like?' Yes, so far as all can be done for his sake. We are to be the Lord's servants for the blessing of the world, and we may do anything which he would have done. In such a garden as the text speaks of, every plant bears flowers for its owner, every tree yields fruit for him. I pray God that this church, whether it carries on its Orphan-houses or its College or its Colportage or whatever else it does, may do it all for Christ. Keep this thought to the front as a church and people. You are not to bear fruit for the markets, but fruit for the Master's table. You are not to do good that you may have honour as an industrious and energetic community, but that glory may be given to Jesus, to whom you belong. 'All for Jesus' is to be our motto. No one among us may dare to live unto himself, even in the refined way in which many are doing it, who even try to win souls that they may have the credit of being zealous and successful. We may so far degenerate as even to attempt to glorify Christ that we may have the credit of glorifying him. It will not do. We must be truly, thoroughly, really living for Jesus: we must be a garden enclosed, reserved, shut up for him. O brother, your life is to be a stream that flows for the refreshment of him who poured out his life for you! You are to let him drink of the deep fountains of your heart, but no one else may rival Jesus there. You are a spring shut up, a fountain sealed for Jesus, for Jesus only, and that altogether and always. Should self come forward, or personal advantage, you are to bid them be gone. They must have no admission here. This garden is strictly private. Trespassers beware! Should the world, the flesh, or the devil leap over the wall, and stoop down to drink of the crystal fountain of your being, you are to chase them away, lest their leprous lips should defile this spring, and prevent the King from drinking thereat again. Our whole being is to be a fountain sealed for Jesus Christ alone. All for Jesus: body for Jesus, mind for Jesus, spirit for Jesus, eyes for Jesus, mouth for Jesus, hands for Jesus, feet for Jesus, all for Jesus. The wall must wholly enclose the garden, for a gap anywhere will admit an intruder everywhere. If one part of our being be left under the dominion of sin, it will show its power everywhere.

The spring must be sealed at the very source, that every drop may be for Jesus throughout the whole of its course. Our first thoughts, desires, and wishes must be his, and then all our words and deeds. WE must be 'wholly reserved for Christ that died, surrendered to the Crucified'. Brethren, do we belong to Jesus? Does he know the walks of our garden and the secret springs of our nature? Here is an evidence by which you may judge whether Jesus fully possesses you. Is there anything, my brethren, that ever stirs you like the name of Jesus? I recollect, some years ago, when I was very weary, faint, and heart-sore, I was vexed with the question as to whether all was right between my Lord and my heart. I went into an obscure country meeting-house, where a brother who preached did me a great service. There was not much in the preaching of itself, but it was all about Jesus Christ, and I found myself within a few minutes weeping freely. The gospel had found out the secret fountains of my being, and set them flowing. The name of Jesus acted on me like a charm. Ay, I thought, my Lord knows how to get at my heart as nobody else does; depend upon it, he must have been there before! I was quite sure that my Lord had the key that could open the sealed fount of my being, for I was stirred to the innermost depth of my soul. Then I knew that he was no stranger to me. There is a secret drawer inside my soul that nobody ever can open except himself. He made that drawer, and knows the secret spring which shuts and opens it. My Lord, and my Lord only, can play upon the strings of my heart as a minstrel on his harp; and therefore I know that I belong to him.

Beloved, I am sure that many of you can thus assure yourselves of your interest in Christ. He holds the clue of the maze of your soul, and can enter the sacred chamber of your spirit. Can he not? Do you ever feel so happy as when he is near? Why, you love the very place where his honour dwelleth. It happens at times that you are sick and sorry, and begin to doubt your interest in Christ; but if anybody begins extolling the Saviour, you are ready to cry out with delight. Oh how I love to hear him praised! It sets my heart a-dancing. I cry with Herbert, 'Oh, for a well-tuned harp!' for I want to make music too. When Jesus is set forth in all his glories and beauties, you can hardly contain yourself; you want to be singing his high praises. No wonder that the Methodist cries, 'Bless the Lord!' You, who are very proper and quiet, half wish that you had courage enough to shout 'Hallelujah!' You may freely do so if you like.

Well now, if the Lord Jesus Christ holds the reins of your soul at that rate, I feel persuaded that you are his. If his name wakes the echoes of your whole being as nothing else does, then it must be because there are certain secrets between you and himself which none else can know. My heart is often like the captive king, who sat pining in a lonely tower, with nothing to relieve his sadness, as he remembered his native land, and his vacant palace, and the malice of the enemy who kept him in exile. Nothing aroused him from his dreamy melancholy. Many were the voices within and without the castle, but they were nothing to him. The serenade of troubadours only locked his misery. But on a day a tender voice thrilled him. He listened to the verse of a song. It was even as life from the dead. None knew the next verse but himself. See what effect that sonnet has had on the monarch! His eyes, how they sparkle! His whole frame, how it is reanimated! He sings in response. With what rapture he pours forth the lay! He is a fine singer, surely! We did not know that the King had such a voice. How charmed he is as a third stanza is sung by the minstrel below! And why? Because it is Blondel, his friend, who has at last found him out, and thus salutes him. They knew, and nobody else in the world knew that song. Even thus, the secret of the Lord is with them that fear him. My Lord knows what it is that can move me, and my heart melts when he speaks. My heart hath a song which it singeth to her Beloved, and he hath a song for me. I feel that I must be his, for nobody stirs my soul as he does.

Dear friends, if you know that this is so, be happy in his love. See to it that you live wholly to him, and for him. As you have a good hope that he is altogether yours, *be* altogether his. Honour him in your families, and honour him in the outside world. Serve the Lord wherever you are, whether you are most found in the kitchen, the parlour, the workshop, the street, or the field. Make it your delight that you are reserved unto him. Acknowledge that the vows of the Lord are upon you. You are his sister and his spouse '– give him love in both forms; find in him brother and bridegroom. You are his garden enclosed, his spring shut up, his fountain sealed; then yield your all to him, both of fruit and flow, of work of hand and warmth of heart. Be yours the honour, the bliss, of being altogether your Lord's.

28

A SECRET AND YET NO SECRET

'A garden enclosed is my sister, my spouse;
a spring shut up, a fountain sealed.'
'A fountain of gardens, a well of living waters,
and streams from Lebanon'
(Song of Solomon 4: 12, 15)

Observe the sweet titles with which Christ the husband addresses his Church the bride. '*My sister*', one near to me by ties of nature, my next of kin, born of the same mother, partaker of the same sympathies. *My spouse*, nearest and dearest, united to me by the tenderest bands of love; my sweet companion, part of my own self. *My sister*, by my Incarnation which makes me bone of thy bone and flesh of thy flesh; *my spouse*, by heavenly betrothal in which I have espoused thee unto myself in righteousness. *My sister*, whom I knew of old and over whom I watched from her earliest infancy; *my spouse*, taken from among the daughters, embraced by arms of love, and affianced unto me for ever. See, my brethren, how true is it that our royal kinsman is not ashamed of us, for he dwells with manifest delight upon this twofold relationship. Be not, O Beloved, slow to return the hallowed flame of his love. We have the word 'my' twice in our version. As if Christ dwelt with rapture on his possession of his Church. 'His delights were with the sons of men', because those sons of men were his. He, the Shepherd, sought the sheep, because they were *his* sheep; he lit the candle and swept the house, because it was *his* money that was lost; he has gone about 'to seek and to save that which was lost', because that which was lost was *his* long before it was lost to itself or lost to him. The Church is the exclusive portion of her Lord; none else may claim a partnership, or pretend to share her love. Jesus, thy Church delights to have it so! Let every believing soul drink solace out of these wells. Soul! Christ is near to thee in ties of relationship; Christ is dear to thee in bonds of marriage union, and thou art dear to him; behold he grasps both of thy hands with both his own, saying, '*My* sister, *my* spouse.' Mark the two sacred holdfasts by which thy Lord gets such a double hold of thee that he neither can nor will ever let thee go. Do thou say in thy heart this morning, 'My brother, my husband?' Seek to be near to him in nature – to be like thy brother, a son of God; and to be near to him in fellowship – to have near and dear intercourse with thy husband, that thou mayest know him and have fellowship with him, being conformable unto his death.

Leaving this porch of cedar, let us enter the palace. Observe the contrast which the two verses present to us. I think that the Spirit of God intends that the verses should be understood, as we intend to use them this morning, but even if we should be mistaken as to the precise interpretation of the passage in its connection, we shall not err in enlisting so beautiful a string of metaphors in the service of the truth. You know, beloved, there are two works of the Holy Spirit within us. The first is when he puts into us the living waters; the next is when he enables us to pour forth streams of the same living waters in our daily life. Our blessed Lord expressed what we mean, when on that great day of the feast he cried, saying, 'If any man thirst let him come unto me and drink. He that believeth on me, as the Scripture hath said, out of his belly shall flow rivers of living water. This spake he of the Spirit, which they that believe on him should receive.' The Spirit of God first implants in us the new nature. This is his work – to regenerate us, to put into us the new principle, the life of God in Christ. Then next, he gives us power to send forth that life in gracious emanations of holiness of life, of devoutness of communion with God, of likeness to Christ, of conformity to his image. The streams are as much of the Holy Spirit as the fountain itself. He digs the well, and he afterwards with heavenly rain fills the pools. He first of all makes the stream in the desert to flow from the flinty rock, and afterwards out of his infinite supplies he feeds the stream and bids it follow us all our days.

I was pleased to meet a quotation the other day, from one of the early fathers, which just contains in it views I have frequently expressed to you: 'The true believer is composed of body, soul, and the Holy Spirit.' After the greatest research, eminent mental philosophers have given up all idea of a third principle which they can discover in man, as man. They can find nothing but the body and the soul. But, rest assured that as there is a certain something in the vegetable which makes vegetable life, as there is a sensitive substance which makes animal life, as there is a mysterious subsistence developed as mental life, so there is some real, substantial, divine principle forming spiritual life. The believer hath three principles, the body, the soul, and the indwelling spirit, which is none other than the Holy Spirit of God, which abideth in the faithful continually. Just such a relationship as the soul bears to the body, does the spirit bear to the soul; for as the body without the soul is dead, so the soul without the spirit is dead in trespasses and sins; as the body without the soul is dead naturally, so the soul without the spirit is dead spiritually. And, contrary to the general teaching of modern theologians, we do insist upon it that the Spirit of God not only renovates the faculties which were there already, but does actually implant a new principle – that he does not merely set to rights a machinery which had before gone awry, but implants a new life which could not have been there. It is not a waking up of dormant faculties – it is the infusion of a supernatural spirit to which the natural heart is an utter stranger. Now, we think the first verse, to a great extent, sets forth the secret and mysterious work of the Holy Spirit in the creation of the new man in the soul. Into this secret no eye of man can look. The inner life in the Christian may well be compared to an enclosed garden – to a spring shut up – to a fountain sealed. But the second verse sets forth the manifest effects of grace, for no sooner is that life given than it begins to show itself. No sooner is the mystery of righteousness in the heart, than, like the mystery of iniquity, it 'doth already work'. It cannot lie still; it cannot be idle; it must not reset; but, as God is ever active, so this Godlike principle is active too; thus you have a picture of the outer life, proceeding from the inner. 'A fountain of gardens, a well of living waters, and streams from Lebanon.' The first is what the Christian is before God; the next is what the Christian will become before men. The first is the blessedness which he receives in himself; the next is the blessedness which he diffuses to others.

We will begin, then, where God the Holy Ghost begins with us, when he enters the recesses of the heart and breathes the secret life.

(1) With regard to the first text; you will clearly perceive that in each of the three metaphors you have very plainly the idea of *secrecy*. There is a garden. A garden is a place where trees have been planted by a skilful hand; where they are nurtured and tended with care, and where fruit is expected by its owner. Such is the Church; such is each renewed soul. But it is a garden *enclosed*, and so enclosed that one cannot see over its walls; so shut out from the world's wilderness, that the passer-by must not enter it; so protected from all intrusion that it is a guarded Paradise; as secret as was that inner place, the holy of holies, within the tabernacle of old.

The Church – and mark, when I say the Church, the same is true of each individual Christian – is set forth next as a *spring*. 'A spring' – the mother of sweet draughts of refreshing water, reaching down into some impenetrable caverns, and bubbling up with perennial supplies from the great deeps. Not a mere cistern, which *contains* only, but a fresh spring, which through an inward principle within, begets, continues, overflows. But then, it is a spring *shut up*: just as there were springs in the East, over which an edifice was built, so that none could reach the springs save those who knew the secret entrance. So is the heart of a believer when it is renewed by grace; there is a mysterious life within which no human skill can touch.

And then, it is said to be a *fountain*; but it is a fountain *sealed*. The outward stones may be discovered, but the door is sealed, so that no man can get into the hidden springs; they are altogether hidden, and hidden too by a royal will and decree of which the seal is the emblem.

I say the idea is very much that of secrecy. Now, such is the inner life of the Christian. It is a secret which no other man knoweth, nay, which the very man who is the possessor of it cannot tell to his neighbour. 'The wind bloweth where it listeth, and thou hearest the sound thereof, but canst not tell whence it cometh or whither it goeth; so is every one that is born of the Spirit.' There are mysteries in nature so profound, that we only label them with some hard name, and leave them, and all the knowledge that we have about them is, that they are beyond the reach of man; but what they are, what are those mysterious impulses which link distant worlds with one another, what the real essence of that power which flashes along the electric wire, what is the very substance of that awful force which rives the oak or splits the spire, we do not know. These are mysteries; but even if we could enter these caverns of knowledge, if we could penetrate the secret chamber of nature, if we could climb the lofty tree of knowledge till we found the nest where the callow principles of nature as yet unfledged are lying, yet even then we could not find out where that hidden life is. It is a something – as certainly a something as the natural life of man. It is a reality – not a dream, not a delusion: it is as real (though far more divine) as that 'vital spark' which we say is 'of heavenly flame'. But though real, it is not in itself perceptible by human senses. It is so hidden from the eyes of men who have it not, that they do not believe in its existence. 'Oh,' say they, 'there is no difference between a Christian and another man. There may sometimes be a little difference in his outward acts, but as to his being the possessor of another life the idea is vain.' As to the regenerate being men of a distinct race of being, as much above man naturally as man is above the brute beasts, that carnal men would scorn to acknowledge. They cannot make this out. How can they? It is a spring shut up; it is a fountain sealed.

Nay, and the Christian himself, though he feels the throbbings of the great life-force within, though he feels the perpetual bubblings up of the ever-living fountain, yet he does not know what it is. It is a mystery to him. He knows it came there once upon a time; perhaps he knows the instrumentality by which it came; but what it was he cannot tell. 'One thing I know, whereas I was blind now I see; whereas I once loved sin I now hate it; whereas I had no thoughts after God and Christ, now my heart is wholly set upon divine things.' This he can say. But how it was he does not know. Only God did it – did it in some mysterious way, by an agency which it is utterly impossible for him to detect.

Nay, there are times when the Christian finds this well so shut up that he cannot see it himself, and he is led to doubt about it. 'Oh!' saith he, 'I question whether the life of God be in me at all.' I know some have scouted the idea of a Christian's being alive and, at the same time, doubting his spiritual existence; but however great a paradox it may seem, it is, nevertheless, a mournful truth in our experience. That spring, I say, is sometimes shut up even to ourselves, and that fountain is so fast sealed, that although it is as really there as when we could drink of it, and the garden is as truly there as when we refreshed ourselves among its spicy beds, yet we cannot find any solace therein. There have been times, when if we could have the world for it, we could not discover a spark of love in our hearts towards God – nay, not a grain of faith. Yet he could see our love when our blind eyes could not, and he could honour our faith even when we feared we had none. There have been moments when, if heaven and hell depended on our possession of full assurance, we certainly must have been lost, for not only had we no full assurance, but we had scarce any faith. Children of light do walk in darkness: there are times when they see not their signs, when for three days neither sun nor moon appears. There are periods when their only cry is, 'My God, my God, why hast thou forsaken me?' There is little wonder about this when we see how secret, how impalpable, how undiscernible by eye or touch or human intellect is the Spirit of God within us. It is little wonder that sometimes flesh and blood should fail to know whether the life of God be in us at all. 'A garden enclosed, a spring shut up, a fountain sealed.'

A second thought is written upon the surface of the text. Here you see not only secrecy, but *separation*. That also runs through the three figures. It is a garden, but it is a garden enclosed – altogether shut out from the surrounding heaths and commons, enclosed with briars and hedged with thorns, which are impassable by the wild beasts. There is a gate through which the great husbandman himself can come; but there is also a gate which shuts out all those who would only rob the keeper of the vineyard of his rightful fruit. There is separation in the spring also. It is not the common spring, of which every passer-by may drink; it is one so kept and preserved distinct from men, that no lip may touch, no eye may even see its secret. It is a something which the stranger intermeddleth not with; it is a life which the world cannot give and cannot take away. All through, you see, there is a separateness, a distinctness. If it be ranged with springs, still it is a spring specially shut up; if it be put with fountains, still it is a fountain bearing a particular mark – a king's royal seal, so that all can perceive that this is not a general fountain, but a fountain that has a proprietor, and stands specially by itself alone.

So is it with the spiritual life. It is a separate thing. The chosen of God, we know, were separated in the eternal decree. Their names were written in a different book from the rest of men; the Book of Life records their names, and none but theirs. They were separated by God in the day of redemption, when Christ redeemed them from among men, out of every kindred, and nation and tribe. They are separated day by day by divine providence, for the fiery pillar gives light to them, while it is darkness to the Egyptians. But their separation, so far as they can most clearly see it, must be a separation caused by the possession of the life which others have not.

I fear there are some professed Christians who have never realised this. They are a garden. One could hardly speak ill of their character, their carriage is excellent, their deportment amiable; their good works commend them before men; but still they are not separate from sinners; in vital essential distinction they have little manifest share. Their speech may be half of Canaan, but the other half is of Ashdod; they may bring unto God thank-offerings, but there is a niche in their house for Baal too. They have not yet heard the cry, 'Come ye out of her, my people, that ye be not partakers of her plagues.' Not yet has the mandate of the prophet rung in their ears, 'Depart ye, depart ye, go ye out from hence; be ye clean that bear the vessels of the Lord.' They are a garden, but they are not a garden walled round. Oh, how many we have in this day of this kind. They can come to the church, they can go to the world; they can talk as God's people talk, and they can murmur as the rebellious murmur; they understand well the gift of prayer, but they understand little of the secret of the inner life of devotion.

Brethren, if you and I have ever received that third, that noble, that divine principle, the life of God, into our souls, it will be utterly impossible for us to feel at home with the men of the world. No, we shall say, 'without the camp' must be my place, bearing his reproach. Sometimes, indeed, we shall not feel at home with the professing Church, we shall be constrained to come even out of her, if we would follow the Lord fully. Ay, and there are sacred seasons when we shall be so enclosed that we shall not be at ease in any society, however select, for our souls will pine for sweet solitude, secret communion, hidden embraces; we shall be compelled to walk alone with Christ. The garden will be shut up even from other gardens, distinct even from other places where Christ walks. Oh, there will be periods with your soul, if it be renewed, when you must be alone, when the face of man will disturb you, and when only the face of Jesus can be company to you. I would not give a farthing for that man's spiritual life who can live altogether with others; if you do not sometimes feel that you must be a garden enclosed, that you must enter into your closet, and shut-to the door; if you do not feel seasons when the society of your dearest friend is an impediment, and when the face of your sweetest relation would but be a cloud between you and Christ, I cannot understand you. Be ye, O ye children of Christ, as chaste virgins kept alone for Christ. Gad thou not abroad, O my heart, but stay at home with Jesus, thy lover, thy Lord, thy all. Shut up thy gates, O my heart, to all company but his. O my sweet wellspring of delights, be shut up to every lip but his, and O thou fountain of the issues of my heart, be thou sealed, only for him, that he may come and drink, and drink again, and take sweet solace in thee, thy soul being his, and his alone.

In the third place, it is worthy of a more distinct remark that you have in the text the idea of *sacredness*. The garden enclosed is walled up that it may be sacred to its owner; the spring shut up is preserved for the use of some special person; and the fountain sealed more eminently still bears the mark of being sacred to some distinguished personage. Travellers have said that they have discovered gardens of Solomon which were of old enclosed where the king privately walked, and they have also found wells of most deliciously cold water, which had been dextrously covered, so that no person unacquainted with the stone in the wall, which might revolve, or might be removed, could have found the entrance to the spring. At the foot of some lofty range of mountains, a reservoir received the cooling streams which flow from melted snows; this reservoir was carefully guarded, and shut out from all common entrance, in order that the king alone might enter there, and might refresh himself during the scorching heats.

Now such is the Christian's heart. It is a spring kept for Christ. Oh, I would that it were always so. Oh, how often do we pollute the Lord's altar! How frequently, my soul, dost thou let in intruders; alas! how common it is for us to be feasting other friends and shutting the door against *him*. How often do we keep him waiting in the street, while we are entertaining some barbarian who is passing by, who offers us his kiss, but is meanwhile stabbing us with his right hand. Christian men and women, I appeal to your experience now. Have you not to mourn frequently, that you are not so much for Christ as you could wish to be? Though you recognise the truth of the text, 'Ye are not your own, but are bought with a price', do you feel its force as you ought to do, in the actions which you perform for Christ? Are they all wholly for him? Could you take for your motto, 'All for Jesus'? Could you feel that, whether you buy or sell, whether you read or pray, whether you go out in the world or come back to your home, that Jesus only is the one object on whom your heart is set, and for whom your life is spent? Blessed are they, those virgin souls, who whithersoever the Lamb doth lead, from his footsteps ne'er depart! Thrice happy are they who wear the white robe unsoiled by contact with the world! Thrice blessed are they who can say, 'Let him kiss me with the kisses of his lips, for his love is better than wine'! Every Christian should feel that he is God's man – that he has God's stamp on him – and he should be able to say with Paul, 'From henceforth let no man trouble me, for I bear in my body the marks of the Lord Jesus.'

But I think there is another idea prominent, and it is that of *security* – security to the inner life. 'A garden enclosed.' 'The wild boar out of the wood shall not break in there, neither shall the little foxes spoil the vines.

'A fountain shut up.' The bulls of Bashan shall not mud her streams with their furious feet; neither shall the wild beast of Lebanon come there to drink. 'A fountain sealed.' No putrid streams shall foul *her* springs; her water shall be kept clear and living; her fountains shall never be filled up with stones. Oh, how sure and safe is the inner life of the believer. Satan does not know where it is, for 'our life is hid with Christ'. The world cannot touch it; it seeks to overthrow it with troubles and trials and persecutions, but we are covered with the Eternal wings, and are safe from fear of evil. How can earthly trials reach the spirit? As well might a man try to strike a soul with a stone, as to destroy a spirit with afflictions. Surely in the floods of great waters they shall not come nigh unto him; he hath placed us in the secret place of the tabernacles of the Most High; in his pavilion hath he hidden us, and in a high rock hath he secured us. As a castle preserves the besieged, and as the ramparts keep those who find refuge behind them, even so munitions of stupendous rock thy dwelling place shall be. 'Who is he that shall harm you', when God is your protector? 'No weapon that is formed against thee shall prosper, and every tongue that riseth against thee in judgment shall thou condemn.' No temptation shall be able to destroy the purity of the life within; no crushing weights of doubt shall be able to take away the vital principle from that new source of strength. If all the powers of earth and hell could combine, and in their uttermost fury assault the spirit in its weakest hour, that immortal principle must still exist – it would boldly defy them all, and triumph over every one of them; for he who gave it pledged his life for its preservation. The Spirit in the Christian is a spark of the Godhead, and till the Godhead dies the Christian's inner life can never expire. We are immortal, even though we be mortal. Within this outward crust that perisheth there is a soul which endures, and within that soul which endures there is a something which might outlast even the soul itself – a part of the being of God, the indwelling Holy One of Israel, who is himself most surely divine. 'God dwelleth in us, and we in him.' We are one with Christ, even as Christ is one with the Father; therefore as imperishable through Christ's life as Christ himself. Truly may we rejoice in the fact that 'because he lives we shall live also'.

Once more only. I think in looking at the text you receive the thought of unity. You notice, it is but one garden – 'a garden enclosed'. '*A* garden.' It is but *one* spring , and that is shut up; it is but *one* fountain. So the inner life of the Christian is but one. There is the old life which still survives – that old death rather, the body of sin and death, struggling against the law of life which God has put into his members, but this has no kinship with the life divine. It is alone, and knows no relationship with earth. There is but one life for all Christians; either we have it, or we are dead. There are degrees of operation, but it is the same God. There are differences of administration, but it is the same Spirit that quickeneth. We may not all of us have 'one Lord, one faith, and one baptism'. I wish we had. I would that the two baptisms would cease, and that once again the Church would recognise and practise the baptism of believers. But we *do* have one Spirit, otherwise we are not Christians.

I may dissent myself as much as I please from another man who is in Christ – I cannot do that, however, without sin; but dissociate myself as I may, I must be one with him, for the life that is in him is in me. The same life which quickens me, if I be in Christ, dwells also in him. When I hear strict communion talked of, it reminds me of a little finger which was washed very clean, and therefore thought the rest of the body too filthy to have fellowship with it, so it took a piece of red tape and bound it tightly round itself, that the lifeblood might not flow from itself into the rest of the body. What think you, brethren? Why, as long as that little finger was itself alive, the pulsations and the motions of the blood went from it to all the rest of the body, and that little piece of red tape there was but a ridiculous sham; it did not affect anything; it had not influence; it only enabled the little finger boastfully to glory, and perhaps to earn for itself the sad distinction: 'These be they that separate themselves'; but the blood flowed on unimpeded, and the nerves and sinews felt the common life-throb still. They forgot, when they denied fellowship in the outward act of eating bread and drinking wine, that the essential spirit of communion was far too spiritual to be thus restrained, it had overleaped their boundary and was gone. The only way in which a Christian can leave off communing with all other Christians is by leaving off being a Christian. Thus can the finger leave off communing with the rest of the body – by rotting away, and no how else, as long as it is alive. Communion is the lifeblood of the soul. The Holy Ghost is the Spirit that quickens the body of the Church, and that Holy Ghost will go into every member, and you may try to check him by Church decrees, or to stop him by your trust-deeds and your ordinances, that such-and-such a Church shall never be loosed from the bands of ancestral bigotry, but the Church's life will beat freely through all the members of the Church's fellowship, and communion *will* go to all who are in Christ. There is but one garden, but one spring, but one sealed fountain; and if you have it in your heart, and I have it in mine, there is a relationship between you and me that is as near as if you and I had the same soul, for you and I have the same Spirit. If you could imagine two bodies quickened by the very same mind, what a close connection would that be! But here are hundreds of bodies, hundreds of souls, quickened by the selfsame Spirit. Brethren, indeed not only ought we to love one another, but the love of Christ constraineth us, so that we cannot resist the impulse; we do love each other in Christ Jesus.

(2) I shall now need your attention, while with brevity I try to open the second text, which presents a decided contrast, because it deals not so much with the inner life as with the active life which goes abroad into all the deeds of the Christian in the world, and is the natural outgoing of the life within.

First, notice that in contradistinction to our first thought of secrecy you have in the text *manifestation*. 'A fountain of gardens.' Everybody can see a fountain which runs streaming through many gardens, making deserts fertile. 'A well of living waters.' Whatever the traveller does not see, when he is riding along on a thirsty day, he is sure to see the fountain; if there be one anywhere he is certain to observe that. 'And streams from Lebanon.' So that any passer-by in the valley, looking up the side of the mountain, will see by the clusters of trees which skirt the stream where the stream is; or, if it be a smaller brook, just as sometimes in Cumberland or Westmoreland, on a rainy day you see the mountain suddenly marked with streaks of silver all adown its brown sides, where the brooks are rippling; so the Christian becomes like the streams leaping adown Lebanon's steep sides clearly perceived even from a distance, manifest to the most casual observer. Now, brethren, this is what you and I ought to be. No man ought to court publicity for his virtue, or notoriety for his zeal; but, at the same time, it is a sin to be always seeking to hide that which God has bestowed upon us for the good of others. A Christian is not to be a city in a valley – he is to be 'a city set upon a hill'; he is not to be a candle put under a bushel, but a candle in a candlestick, giving light to all. Retirement may be lovely in the eyes of some, and the hiding of oneself is doubtless a blessed thing, but the hiding of *Christ* in us can never be justified, and the keeping back of truth which is precious to ourselves is a sin against our kind, and an offence against God.

Those of you who are of a nervous temperament and of retired habits of life must take care that you do not too much indulge your natural propensity, lest you should be useless to the Church. Seek in the name of him who was not ashamed of you to do some little violence to your feelings, and to tell to others what Christ has told to you. Keep not the secret – it is too precious – it too much concerns the vital interests of man. Speak! If thou canst not with trumpet tongue, yet speak with still small voice. If the pulpit must not be thy tribune, if the press may not carry on its wings thy words, yet say, as Peter and John did, 'Silver and gold have I none, but such as I have give I unto thee.' And speak, too, as thou canst – gently to ones, if not loudly to twenties; quietly to twos, if not publicly to scores. By Sychar's well talk to the Samaritan woman, if thou canst not on the mountain preach the sermon; in the house, if not in the temple; in the field, if not upon the exchange; in the midst of thine own household, if thou canst not in the midst of the great family of man. At any rate, hide not thy talent; wrap it not up. 'It is but one,' thou sayest. So much the more reason why thou shouldst make the greater use of that one. Conceal it not; bring it out; trade with it; and so thou shalt multiply the talent, and thou shalt bring in good interest to thy Lord and Master. The inner life is secret – mind that you have this inner mystery; but out of the secret emanates the manifest; the darkness becomes the mother of light; from the dark mines comes the blazing coal. Oh! See to it, that from all that is hidden and secret and mysterious, there comes out the plain and the manifest, that men may see the holiness, truthfulness and zeal of God in thy life.

But clearly enough, again, we have in the second text, in opposition to the separation of the first, *diffusiveness*. The garden was enclosed before; now it is 'a fountain of gardens'; the well was shut up, now it is a well of living waters; before we had the fountain sealed, now we have streams dashing adown the sides of Lebanon. So a Christian is to be separate in his inner life; but in the outer manifestations of that inner life, he is to mingle for good among his fellow-men. It was usual in Romish countries, for women who wished to be specially holy, to make recluses of themselves; and in the Church of St Roche, in Paris, there was a small building erected on the side of the Church. The only opening was a little grating, through which the necessaries of life were passed. Within this narrow cell, there lived for eighty years, and died, I think, at the age of ninety-six, a woman doubtless devout, but certainly superstitious. There she passed her life. The only sound she heard was the tramp of the worshippers upon the Church pavement, and the chant of the daily service; but she lived there, thinking she was serving God by being separate from men.

That is not the separation of the New Testament. We are to be separate from sinners, as Christ was, and who ever went among them more than he did? We are to be healthy, and by that health separate from the leper; we are to be clean, and by that cleanness separate from the filthy. But we are to go among them; we are to visit; we are to distribute ourselves what Christ has given to us. If we keep ourselves altogether apart, we shall be useless to our fellow-men; we shall be like stagnant pools, we shall grow putrid by degrees. WE must let the streams flow abroad; we must seek to give to others what Christ has given to us.

Now, some of you who keep yourselves separate in that sense, may I beg you to see if there be no mission of mercy for you? Go ye out among them as physicians in the midst of the sick, as torchbearers in the midst of darkness. Go ye out as loosers of the bonds among the captives; as openers of prison doors among those that be bound; and he who has given you the true principle within, which is and must be shut up, will bless the outgoings of your zeal, both in the morning and in the evening, and cause that, watering others, your own soul shall be watered too.

Briefly we are obliged to speak on each of these points; but notice, thirdly, that in opposition to the sacredness of the first text we have in the second verse an unlimited *freeness*, especially in that last expression – 'streams from Lebanon'. What can be freer than the brook, which leaps along the mountain side? There the bird wets its wings; there the red deer comes to drink; and even that wild beast of Lebanon, of which we read in the Book of the Kings, comes there, and without let or hindrance slakes its thirst. What can be freer than the rivulet singing with liquid notes adown the glen? It belongs to no one; it is free to all. Whosoever passeth by, be he peer or peasant, may stoop there and refresh himself from the mountain stream. So be it with you, Christian. Carry about with you a piety which you do not wish to keep for yourself. A light loses none of its own lustre when others are lit at its flame. Remember, you shall earn riches by giving riches, and in this sense giving away shall be an increase of your wealth.

I know some who are in an ill sense, like fountains shut up. They love the doctrine of election, but there is one doctrine they love better, and that is, the doctrine of exclusion. They love to think they are shut in, but they feel quite as much delight that others are shut out. Their conversation is always flavoured with the thought of shutting others out. They are told that in such-and-such a Church there has been a large increase. Well, they hope they are genuine; by which they mean that they do not believe they are. A young believer begins to tell them something of his joys. Well, they don't like to be too fast in pronouncing an opinion; by which they mean, they would not like one more to get in than should, and they are half afraid that perhaps some may overstep the bounds of election and get saved who should not be.

Well, brethren, I love the doctrine of election, I love to think that the garden is enclosed, but I do love in my own life to exemplify the equally precious truth of the freeness of the gospel, so that if I speak to any it shall not be to discourage them, but to encourage them, not to say, 'Get you gone!' but 'Come and welcome!' 'Depart, ye cursed' is nothing to do with me; my business is to say 'Come, ye blessed'. I would rather go to the door, and say, 'Come in, thou blessed of the Lord, wherefore standest thou without?' than slam it in a sinner's face with 'What hast thou to do here?' Nay, we must be shut up in the inner life; but let every wall be broken down as to the outer life. We must be hidden springs within, but let us be sweetly flowing rivulets without, giving drink to every passer by.

And not to detain you long, you will notice that, while we had in the other text the idea of security, in connection with that we have here in this text the idea of *approach*. The garden was shut up – that was to keep it. There are no walls here, so that all may come to it. The streams were shut up before; here it is an open well. The fountain was sealed in the first verse; here it is a flowing stream, which is to teach us this: that the way God keeps his people in security is not by shutting out their enemies from attacking them, but while laying them open to temptation and attack, he yet sustains them. It is not much to preserve oneself behind a wall which cannot be scaled, but to stand where arrows are flying thick as hail, where lances are being pushed with fury, where the sword-cuts are falling on every part, to stand, I say, invulnerable, invincible, immortal; this is to wear a divine life which cannot be conquered by human power. Such is the Christian. We *are* to pray, 'Lead us not into temptation'; but indeed, we often are tempted, notwithstanding our prayer. God will put us where we must be tempted – put us where we must be tried, because, if we be not tried, there is no honour to him; and if we be not tempted, then where is the glory to the grace that delivers us out of temptations? The Lord does not put his plants into a hot-house, as some gardeners do; no, he sets them out in the open air, and if the frost is coming, he says, 'Ah! but no frost can kill them, and they will be all the sturdier in the summer for the cold in the winter.' He does not shelter them either from the heat of the sun, or from the cold by night, for in this world we must have tribulation; and we must have much of it too, for it is through much tribulation we inherit the kingdom. But what God does to his people is this. He keeps them *in* tribulation, preserves them in temptation, and brings them joyfully out of all their trials. So, Christian, you may rejoice in your security; but you must not think that you are not to be attacked; you are a stream from Lebanon, to be dashed down many a cascade, to be broken over many a rough rock, to be stopped up with many a huge stone, to be impeded by many a fallen tree; but you are to dash forward with the irresistible force of God, sweeping everything away, till you find at last the place where shall be your perfect rest.

And last of all, in opposition to the unity of which I spake, we have in our second text great *diversity*. You have 'a fountain', not of a garden, but 'of gardens'; you have a well, but it is a well of living waters; you have not a stream, but streams – streams from Lebanon. So a Christian is to do good in all sorts of ways, and his fruits are to be of many kinds; he is to be like the trees of Paradise, which bear twelve manner of fruits. The Christian is to have all sorts of graces. 'Whatsoever things are pure, whatsoever things are lovely, whatsoever things are of good repute'; he is to have all these.

It is an old proverb that a man may have too many irons in the fire; but it depends upon what fire it is; for if it is God's fire, put all the irons in it. A man may attempt too much, they say – but not for Christ. If you should attempt great things, and have great faith, you shall succeed in all that you attempt. There seems to be a fear among some Christian men either of doing too much themselves, or else of letting other people do too much; and I know some to whom that text might *almost* be applied, 'They have the kingdom of heaven, but they neither enter themselves, and they that would they hinder.' Not content to refuse the burden for themselves, they will not even touch it with one of their little fingers; but they are afraid that others shall carry the burden either. Well, we are not afraid as these are. Blessed be God, if there is a trench to be filled up, let us struggle which shall lead the way; if there is a rampart to be climbed, if there is no other man to throw the irons over with the scaling-ladder, let your minister attempt the deed, and lead the van, for he is well assured that there are many here who would jostle with him, and say, 'Let me come first; let me serve my Master; let me live or let me die, if I may but glorify him.' What! bring forth for Christ a little shrivelled cluster upon the topmost bough – a cluster which the very birds of heaven will not deign to touch, because it is too little even for their appetites? No, rather let us have every bough weighed down with clusters, like those of Eshcol, which will take two ordinary men to carry, but which we can bear in rich profusion, because the life of the Spirit of God is in us. We are a race of little doers, of little givers, of little thinkers, of little believers. O God, raise us up again giants in these days; give us again the consecrated men who shall stand upon the sword like the old Roman, and say, 'For God I devote myself; to Christ I give body, soul, and spirit, and if I be offered up upon the sacrifice of your faith, I joy and rejoice with you all.' Oh! if the fountain, the secret fountain, were better seen to, I think there would be more of these outward streams; and if the sealed well were better guarded, we should see more of these rapid streams from Lebanon, which would make glad the people of God, and the world at large.

And now, how many of you have the secret spring within you? If your soul is not renewed by grace you cannot do good. 'Except a man be born again, he cannot *see* the kingdom of God.' No man enters fully into discipleship with Christ, till the water as well as the Spirit has been reverently received: 'Except a man be born of water and of the Spirit ye cannot *enter* the kingdom of heaven.' But these two things being done, being born of water and of the Spirit, go ye forth to show to others the mystery, the *fellowship* of the mystery – to make all men know that God has appeared unto us in Christ Jesus, reconciling the world unto himself, not imputing their iniquities. Preach of Christ when ye know Christ, but not till then. Let the streams flow out when you have the inner fountain, but not till then. Sad reflection! There are some of you that have it not. Oh! if you have it not, you perish. You cannot get it of yourselves, He alone can give it. You are in his hands to give it to you. Oh! may your longings end in groanings today, and may you groan to God, 'Lord! renew me, Lord, cause me to be born again! And those groanings will be proofs that he has begun the good work, and those longings shall be evidence that there is a well in you, though it is a well shut up – a well shut up even from yourself. God grant that you may seek and find through Jesus Christ; and to him be glory, for ever and ever. Amen.

29

GRACE FOR COMMUNION

'Awake, O north wind; and come, thou south; blow upon my garden, that the spices thereof may flow out. Let my beloved come into his garden, and eat his pleasant fruits' (Song of Solomon 4:16).

The soul of the believer is the garden of the Lord. Within it are rare plants such as yield 'spices' and 'pleasant fruits'. Once it was a wilderness, overgrown with thorns and briars; but now it 'a garden enclosed', an 'orchard of pomegranates'.

At times within that garden everything is very still and quiet; indeed, more still than could be wished. Flowers are in bloom, but they seem scentless, for there are no breezes to waft the perfume. Spices abound, but one may walk in the garden, and not perceive them, for no gales bear their fragrance on their wings. I do not know that, in itself, this is an evil condition: it may be that 'So he giveth his beloved sleep'. To those who are worn with labour, rest is sweet. Blessed are they who enjoy a Sabbath of the soul!

The loved one in the text desired the company of her Lord, and felt that an inactive condition was not altogether suitable for his coming. Her prayer is first about her garden, that it may be made ready for her Beloved; and then to the Bridegroom himself, that he would come into his garden, and eat its pleasant fruits. She pleads for *the breath of heaven*, and for *the Lord of heaven*.

First, she cries for THE BREATH OF HEAVEN to break the dead calm which broods over her heart. She cannot unlock the caskets of spice, nor cause the sweet odours to flow forth: her own breath would not avail for such an end. She looks away from herself to an unseen and mysterious power. She breathes this earnest prayer, 'Awake, O north wind; and come, thou south; blow upon my garden!'

In this prayer there is an evident sense of *inward sleep*. She does not mean that the north wind is asleep: it is her poetical way of confessing that she herself needs to be awakened. She has a sense of *absent-mindedness*, too, for she cries, 'Come, thou south.' If the south wind would come, the forgetful perfumes would come to themselves, and sweeten all the air. The fault, whatever it is, cannot lie in the winds; it lies in ourselves.

Her appeal, as we have already said, is to that great Spirit who operates according to his own will, even as the wind bloweth where it listeth. She does not try to 'raise the wind' – that is an earthly expression relating to worldly matters; but, alas, it might fitly be applied to many imitations of spirituality! Have we not heard of 'getting up revivals'? Indeed, we can no more command the Holy Spirit than we can compel the wind to blow east or west. Our strength lies in prayer. The spouse prays, 'Awake, O north wind; and come, thou south!' She thus owns her entire dependence upon the free Spirit. Although she veiled her faith in a divine Worker under the imagery of her song, yet she spoke as to a person. We believe in the personality of the Holy Ghost, so that we ask *him* to 'Awake' and 'Come'. We believe that we may pray to him; and we are impelled to do so.

Notice that the spouse does not mind what form the divine visitation takes so long as she feels its power. 'Awake, O north wind'; though the blast be cold and cutting, it may be that it will effectually fetch forth the perfume of the soul in the form of repentance and self-humiliation. Some precious graces, like rare spices, naturally flow forth in the form of tears; and others are only seen in hours of sorrow, like gums which exude from wounded trees. The rough north wind has done much for some of us in the way of arousing our best graces. Yet it may be that the Lord will send something more tender and cheering; and if so, we would cry, 'Come, thou south.' Divine love warming the heart has a wonderful power to develop the best part of a man's nature. Many of our precious things are brought forth by the sun of holy joy.

Either movement of the Spirit will sufficiently bestir our inner life; but the spouse desires both. Although in nature you cannot have the north wind and the south blowing at the same time; yet in grace you can. The Holy Ghost may be at one and the same time working grief and gladness, causing humiliation and delight. I have often been conscious of the two winds blowing at once; so that, while I have been ready to die to self, I have been made to live unto God. 'Awake, O north wind; and come, thou south.' When all the forms of spiritual energy are felt, no grace will be dormant. No flower can keep asleep when both rough and gentle winds arouse it.

The prayer is – 'blow', and the result is – 'flow'. Lord, if thou blowest, my heart floweth out to thee! 'Draw me, we will run after thee.' We know right well what it is to have grace in our souls, and yet to feel no movement of it. We may have much faith in existence, yet none in exercise, for no occasion summons it into action. WE may have much repentance, yet no conscious repenting; much fire of love, yet no love flaming forth; and much patience in the heart, though at the moment we do not display it. Apart from the occurrences of providence, which arouse our inward emotions one way and another, the only plan by which our graces can be set in active exercise is by the Holy Spirit breathing upon us. He has the power to quicken, arouse and bestir our faculties and graces, so that holy fruits within us become perceptible to ourselves and to others who have spiritual discernment. There are states of the atmosphere in which the fragrance of flowers is much more diffused than at other times. The rose owes much to the zephyr which wafts its perfume. How sweet is even a field of beans after a shower! We may have much spice of piety, and yet yield small fragrance unless the living power of the Holy Spirit moves upon us. In a wood there may be many a partridge or gay pheasant, and yet we may not see so much as one of them until a passing foot tramples down the underwood, and causes the birds to rise upon the wing. The Lord can thus discover our graces by many a messenger; but the more choice and spiritual virtues need an agent as mysterious and all-pervading as the wind – need, in fact, the Spirit of the Lord to arouse them. Holy Spirit, thou canst come to us when we cannot come to thee! From any and every quarter thou canst reach us, taking us on our warm or cold side. Our heart, which is our garden, lies open at every point to thee. The wall which encloses it does not shut thee out. We wait for a visitation. We feel glad at the very thought of it. That gladness is the beginning of the stir; the spices are already flowing forth.

The second half of the prayer expresses our central desire: we long for THE LORD OF HEAVEN to visit us. The bride does not seek that the spices of her garden may become perceptible for her own enjoyment, nor for the delectation of strangers, nor even for the pleasure of the daughters of Jerusalem, but for her Beloved's sake. *He* is to come into his garden, and eat his pleasant fruits. We are a garden for his delight. Our highest wish is that Jesus may have joy in us. I fear that we often come to the table of communion with the idea of enjoying ourselves; or, rather, of enjoying our Lord; but we do not rise to the thought of giving *him* joy. Possibly that might even seem presumptuous. Yet, he says, 'My delights were with the sons of men.' See how joyfully he cries in the next chapter: 'I am come into my garden, my sister, my spouse: I have gathered my myrrh with my spice; I have eaten my honeycomb with my honey; I have drunk my wine with my milk.' Our heavenly Bridegroom rests in his love, he rejoices over us with singing. Often he takes more delight in us than we do in him. We have not even known that he was present, but have been praying him to come; and all the while he has been near us.

Note well the address of the spouse to her Beloved in the words before us. *She calls him hers* – 'My Beloved'. When we are sure that he is ours we desire him to come to us as ours, and to reveal himself as ours. Those words 'My Beloved' are a prose poem: there is more music in them than in all the laureate's sonnets. However slumbering my graces may be, Jesus is mine. It is as mine that he will make me live, and cause me to pour forth my heart's fragrance.

While he is hers she owns that *she is wholly his*, and all that she has belongs to him. In the first clause she says, 'Awake, O north wind; and come, thou south; blow upon *my* garden'; but now she prays, 'Let my beloved come into *his* garden.' She had spoken just before of *her* fruits, but now they are *his* fruits. She was not wrong when she first spoke; but she is more accurate now. We are not our own. We do not bring forth fruit of ourselves. The Lord saith, 'From me is thy fruit found.' The garden is of our Lord's purchasing, enclosing, planting and watering; and all its fruit belongs to him. This is a powerful reason for his visiting us. Should not a man come into his own garden, and eat his own fruits? Oh, that the Holy Spirit may put us into a fit condition to entertain our Lord!

The prayer of the spouse is: '*Let my Beloved come.*' Do we not say, 'Amen, let him come'? If he does not come in the glory of his Second Advent at this moment, as, perhaps, he may not, yet let him come. If not to his judgment-seat, yet let him come into his garden. If he will not come to gather before him all nations, yet let him come to gather the fruit of his redemption in us. Let him come into our little circle; let him come into each heart. 'Let my Beloved come.' Stand back, ye that would hinder him! O my Beloved, let not my sinful, sluggish, wandering thoughts prevent thee from coming! Thou didst visit the disciples, 'the doors being shut'; wilt thou not come where every opened door bespeaks thy welcome? Where shouldst thou come but to thy garden? Surely my heart hath great need of thee. Many a plant within it needs thy care. Welcome, welcome, welcome! Heaven cannot welcome thee more heartily, O my Beloved, than my heart shall now do! Heaven doth not need thee so much as I do. Heaven hath the abiding presence of the Lord God Omnipotent; but if thou dwell not within my soul, it is empty and void and waste. Come, then, to me, I beseech thee, O my Beloved!

The spouse further cries: '*Let him eat his pleasant fruits.*' I have often felt myself overcome with the bare idea that anything I have ever done should give my Lord pleasure. Can it be that any offering I ever gave him should be thought worthy of his acceptance; or that anything I ever felt or said should be a joy to him? Can he perceive any perfume in my spices, or taste any flavour in my fruits? This is a joy worth worlds. It is one of the highest tokens of his condescension. It is wonderful that the King from the far country should come from the glory land, where all choice fruits are at their best, and enter this poor enclosure in the wilderness, and there eat such fruits as ours, and call them pleasant, too! O Lord Jesus, come into our hearts now! O Holy Spirit, blow upon our hearts at this moment! Let faith and love and hope and joy and patience and every grace be now like violets which betray themselves by their perfume, or like roses which load the air with their fragrance!

Though we are not content with ourselves, yet may our Lord be pleased with us! Do come to us, O Lord! That thou art our Beloved is a greater wonder than that thou shouldst come to us. That thou hast made us thy garden is a greater favour than that shouldst eat our fruits. Fulfil to us that gracious promise, 'I will sup with him, and he with me', for we do open to thee. Thou saidst unto the woman of Samaria, 'Give me to drink', and wilt thou not now accept a draught of love from us? She had no husband, but thou art our Husband; wilt thou not drink from the cup which we now hold to thee? Receive our love, our trust, our consecration. Delight thyself also in us, as we now delight ourselves in thee. We are asking a great thing of thee, but thy love warrants large requests. We will now come to thy table, where thou shalt be our meat and drink; but suffer our spices to be the perfume of the feast, and let us each say, 'While the King sitteth at his table my spikenard sendeth forth the smell thereof.' Fulfil this wish of our soul, divine Lord and Master! Amen.

30

'MY GARDEN' – 'HIS GARDEN'

'Awake, O north wind; and come, thou south; blow upon my garden, that the spices thereof may flow out. Let my beloved come into his garden, and eat his pleasant fruits' (Song of Solomon 4:16).

What a difference there is between what the believer was by nature and what the grace of God has made him! Naturally, we were like the waste howling wilderness, like the desert which yields no healthy plant or verdure. It seemed as if we were given over to be like a salt land, which is not inhabited; no good thing was in us, or could spring out of us. But now, as many of us as have known the Lord are transformed into gardens; our wilderness is made like Eden, our desert is changed into the garden of the Lord. 'I will turn unto you,' said the Lord to the mountains of Israel when they were bleak and bare, 'I will turn unto you, and ye shall be tilled and sown'; and this is exactly what he said to the barrenness of our nature. We have been enclosed by grace, we have been tilled and sown, we have experienced all the operations of the divine husbandry. Our Lord Jesus said to his disciples, 'My Father is the husbandman', and he has made us to be fruitful unto his praise, full of sweetness where once there was no fruit, and nothing that could give him delight.

We are a garden, then, and in a garden there are flowers and fruits, and in every Christian's heart you will find the same evidences of culture and care; not in all alike, for even gardens and fields vary in productiveness. In the good ground mentioned by our Lord in the parable of the sower, the good seed did not all bring forth a hundred fold, or even sixty-fold; there were some parts of the field where the harvest was as low as thirty-fold, and I fear that there are some of the Lord's gardens which yield even less than that. Still, there are the fruits and there are the flowers, in a measure; there is a good beginning made wherever the grace of God has undertaken the culture of our nature.

Now, coming to our text, and thinking of Christians as the Lord's garden, I want you to observe, first, that THERE ARE SWEET SPICES IN BELIEVERS.

The text assumes that when it says, 'Blow upon my garden, that the spices thereof may flow out.' There are in the Lord's garden sweet flowers that drip with honey, and all manner of delightful perfumes. There are such sweet spices within the believer's heart; let us think of them for a few minutes, and first, let me remind you of *the names of these sweet spices.*

For instance, there is *faith*; is there anything out of heaven sweeter than faith – the faith which trusts and clings, which believes and hopes, and declares that, though God shall slay it, yet will it trust in him? In the Lord's esteem, faith is full of fragrance. He never delighted in the burning of bulls and the fat of fed beasts, but he always delighted in the faith which brought these things as types of the one great sacrifice for sin. Faith is very dear to him.

Then comes *love*; and again I must ask: Is there to be found anywhere a sweeter spice than this – the love which loves God because he first loved us, the love which flows out to all the brotherhood, the love which knows no circle within which it can be bounded, but which loves the whole race of mankind and seeks to do them good? It is exceedingly pleasing to God to see love growing where once all was hate, and to see faith springing up in that very soul which was formerly choked with the thorns and briers of doubt and unbelief.

And there is also *hope*, which is indeed an excellent grace, a far-seeing grace by which we behold heaven and eternal bliss. There is such a fragrance about a God-given hope that this poor sin-stricken world seems to be cured by it. Wherever this living, lively hope comes, there men lift up their drooping heads, and begin to rejoice in God their Saviour.

You do not need that I should go over all the list of Christian graces, and mention meekness, brotherly kindness, courage, uprightness, or the patience which endures so much from the hand of God; but whatsoever grace I might mention, it would not be difficult at once to convince you that there is a sweetness and a perfume about all grace in the esteem of him who created it, and it delights him that it should flourish where once its opposite alone was found growing in the heart of man. These, then, are some of the saints' sweet spices.

Next notice, that *these sweet spices are delightful to God.* It is very wonderful that we should have within us anything in which God can take delight; yet when we think of all the other wonders of his grace, we need not marvel at all. The God who gave us faith may well be pleased with faith. The God who created love in such unlovely hearts as ours may well be delighted at his own creation. He will not despise the work of his own hands; rather will he be delighted with it, and find sweet complacency therein. What an exaltation it is to us worms of the earth that there should ever be anything in us well-pleasing unto God! Well did the psalmist say, 'What is man, that thou art mindful of him? and the son of man, that thou visitest him?' But God is mindful of us, and he does visit us. Of old, before Christ came into this world in human form, his delights were with the sons of men; much more is it so now that he has taken their nature into heaven itself, and given to those sons of men his own Spirit to dwell within them. Let it ravish your heart with intense delight that, though often you can take no complacency in yourself, but go with your head bowed down like a bulrush and cry, 'Woe is me!' yet in that very cry of yours God hears a note that is sweet and musical to his ears. Blessed is repentance, with her teardrops in her eyes, sparkling like diamonds. God takes delight even in our longings after holiness, and in our loathings of our own imperfections. Just as the father delights to see his child anxious to be on the best and most loving terms with him, so does God delight in us when we are crying after that which we have not yet reached, the perfection which shall make us to be fully like himself. O beloved, I do not know anything that fills my soul with such feelings of joy as does the reflection that I, even I, may yet be and do something that shall give delight to the heart of God himself! He has joy over one sinner that repenteth, though repentance is but an initial grace; and when we go on from that to other graces, and take yet higher steps in the divine life, we may be sure that his joy is in us, and therefore our joy may well be full.

These spices of ours are not only delightful to God, but *they are healthful to man.* Every particle of faith that there is in the world is a sort of purifier; wherever it comes, it has a tendency to kill that which is evil. In the spiritual sanitary arrangements which God made for this poor world, he put men of faith, and the faith of these men, into the midst of all this corruption, to help to keep other men's souls alive, even as our Lord Jesus said to his disciples, 'Ye are the salt of the earth.' The sweet perfumes that flow out from the flowers which God cultivates in the garden of his Church are scattering spiritual health and sanity all around. It is a blessed thing that the Lord has provided these sweet spices to overpower and counteract the unhealthy odours that float on every breeze. Think, then, dear friends, of the importance of being God's fragrant flowers, which may yield perfumes that are delightful to him, and that are blessed and healthful to our fellow-men. A man of faith and love in a church sweetens all his brethren. Give us but a few such in our midst, and there shall be no broken spiritual unity, there shall be no coldness and spiritual death; but all shall go well where these men of God are among us as a mighty influence for good. And as to the ungodly around us, the continued existence in the earth of the Church of Christ is the hope of the world. The world that hates the Church knows not what it does, for it is hating its best friend. The spices with which God is conserving this present evil age, lest his anger should destroy it because of the growing corruption, are to be found in the flowers which he has planted in the garden of his Church.

It sometimes happens that *these sweet odours within God's people lie quiet and still.* There is a stillness in the air, something like that which the poet Coleridge makes 'The Ancient Mariner' speak of in his graphic description of a calm within the tropics. Do you, dear friends, never get into that becalmed condition? I recollect, when I was young, reading an expression – I think of Erskine's – in which he says that he likes a roaring devil better than a sleeping devil. It struck me then that, if I could keep the devil always asleep, it would be the best thing that could possibly happen for me; but now I am not so sure that I was right. At all events, I know this, when the old dog of hell barks very loudly, he keeps me awake; and when he howls at me, he drives me to the mercy-seat for protection; but when he goes to sleep and lies very quiet, I am very apt to go to sleep, too, and then the graces that are within my soul seem to be absolutely hidden. And, mark you, hidden grace, which in no way reveals itself by its blessed odours, is all the same as if there were none, to those that watch from the outside, and sometimes to the believer himself. What is wanted, in order that he may know that he has these sweet perfumes, is something outside himself. You cannot stir your own graces, you cannot make them move, you cannot cause their fragrance to flow forth. True, by prayer, you may help to this end; but then, that very prayer is put into you by the Holy Spirit, and when it has been offered to the Lord, it comes back to you laden with blessings; but often, something more is needed, some movement of God's providence, and much more, some mighty working of his grace, to come and shake the flower-bells in his garden, and make them shed their fragrance on the air. Alas! on a hot and drowsy day, when everything has fallen into a deep slumber, even God's saints, though they be wise virgins, go as soundly asleep as the foolish virgins, and they forget that 'the Bridegroom cometh'. 'While the Bridegroom tarried, they all slumbered and slept'; and, sometimes, you and I must catch ourselves nodding when we ought to be wide awake. We are going through a part of that enchanted ground which John Bunyan describes, and we do not know what to do to keep ourselves awake.

At such times, a Christian is very apt to ask, '*Am I indeed planted in*

God's garden? Am I really a child of God?' Now, I will say what some of you may think a strong thing; but I do not believe that he is a child of God who never raised that question. Cowper truly wrote:

> He has no hope who never had a fear;
> And he who never doubted of his state,
> He may, perhaps – perhaps he may – too late.

I have sung, and I expect that I may have to sing again:

> 'Tis a point I long to know;
> Oft it causes anxious thought;
> Do I love the Lord or no?
> Am I his, or am I not?

I cannot bear to get into that condition, and I cannot bear to keep in it when I am in it, but still, there must be anxious thought about this all-important matter. Because you happened to be excited on a certain occasion, and thought you were converted and were sure of heaven, you had better look well to the evidence on which you are relying. You may be mistaken after all; and while I would not preach up little faith, I would preach down great presumption. No man can have a faith too strong, and no assurance can be too full, if it comes really from God the Holy Spirit; but if it comes merely out of your fancying that it is so, and, therefore, will not examine yourself whether you be in the faith, I begin to make up my mind that it is not so, because you are afraid to look into the matter. 'I know that I am getting rich,' says a merchant, 'I never keep any books, and I do not want any books, but I know that I am getting on well in my business.' If, my dear sir, I do not soon see your name in the *Gazette*, I shall be rather surprised.

Whenever a man is so very good that he does not want to enquire at all into his position before God, I suspect that he is afraid of introspection and self-examination, and that he dare not look into his own heart. This I know; as I watch the many people of God committed to my care here, I see some run on for ten years or more serving God with holy joy, and having no doubt or fear. They are not generally remarkable for any great depth of experience, but when God means to make mighty men of them, he digs about them, and soon they come to me crying, and craving a little comfort, telling me what doubts they have, because they are not what they want to be. I am glad when this is the case, I rejoice because I know that they will be spiritually better off afterwards. They have reached a higher standard than they had previously attained, they have a better knowledge now of what they ought to be. It may be that, before, their ideal was a low one, and they thought that they had reached it. Now, God has revealed to them greater heights, which they have to climb; and they may as well gird up the loins of their mind to do so by divine help. As they get higher, they perhaps think, 'Now we are at the top of the mountain', when they are really only on one of the lower spurs of it. Up they go, climbing again. 'If once I can reach that point, I shall soon be at the summit,' you think. Yes, and when you have at length got there, you see the mountain still towering far above you. How deceptive is the height of the Alps to those who have not seen them before! I said to a friend once, 'It will take you about thirteen hours to get to the top of that mountain.' 'Why,' he replied, 'I can run up in half-an-hour.' I let him have a try and he had not gone far before he had to sit down to pant and rest. So you think of a certain height of grace, 'Oh, I can easily reach that!' Yes, just so; but you do not know how high it is; and those who think that they have reached the top do not know anything about the top; for he who knows how high is the holiness to which the believer can attain will go on clambering and climbing, often on his hands and knees, and when he has reached that point which he thought was the summit, he will sit down and say, 'I thought I had reached the top, but now I find that I have but begun the ascent.' Or he may say with Job, 'I have heard of thee by the hearing of the ear' (and then I did not know much of thee, or of myself either), 'but now mine eye seeth thee. Wherefore I abhor myself, and repent in dust and ashes.'

You see, then, that there are sweet spices lying in Christians, like hidden honey and locked-up perfume within the flowers on a hot day.

What is wanted is that THOSE SWEET ODOURS SHOULD BE DIFFUSED. That is to be our second head. Read the text again: 'Awake, O north wind; and come, thou south; blow upon my garden, that the spices thereof may flow out.'

Observe, first, that *until our graces are diffused, it is the same as if they were not there*. You may go through a wood, and it may be abounding in game, yet you may scarcely see a hare or notice a pheasant anywhere about. There they lie all quiet and undisturbed; but, by-and-by, the beaters go through the wood making a great noise, and away the pheasants fly, and you may see the timid hares run like hinds let loose, because they are disturbed and wakened up. That is what we sometimes need, to be aroused and stirred from slumber. We may not know that we have any faith till there comes a trial, and then our faith starts boldly up. We can hardly know how much we love our Lord till there comes a test of our love, and then we so behave ourselves that we know that we do love him. Oftentimes, as I have already reminded you, something is needed from without to stir the life that lies hidden within. It is so with these sweet flowers in the Beloved's garden, they need either the north wind or the south wind to blow upon them that they may shed abroad their sweet odours.

Notice next, that *it is very painful to a Christian to be in such a condition that his graces are not stirring*. He cannot endure it. We who love the Lord were not born again to waste our time in sinful slumber; our watchword is, 'Let us not sleep, as do others.' We were not born to inaction; every power that God has put within us was meant to be used in working, and striving, and serving the Lord. So, when our graces are slumbering, we ourselves are in an unhappy state. Then we long for any agency that would set those graces moving. The north wind/ Oh, but if it shall blow, then we shall have snow! Well, then, let the snow come, for we must have our graces set in motion, we cannot bear that they should continue to lie quiet and still. 'Awake, O north wind!' – a heavy trial, a bleak adversity, a fierce temptation – anything so long as we do but begin to diffuse our graces. Or if the north wind be dreaded, we say, 'Come, thou south!' Let prosperity be granted to us; let sweet fellowship with our brethren rouse us, and holy meditations, full of delight, stir our souls; let a sense of the divine life, like a soft south wind, come to our spirit. We are not particular which it is, let the Lord send which he pleases, or both together, as the text seems to be imply, only do let us be aroused. 'Quicken thou me, O Lord, according to thy Word' – whichever Word thou shalt choose to apply, only do quicken thy servant, and let not the graces within me be as if they were dead!

Remember, however, that *the best Quickener is always the Holy Spirit*; and that blessed Spirit can come as the north wind, convincing us of sin, and tearing away every rag of our self-confidence; or he may come as the soft south wind, all full of love, revealing Christ, and the covenant of grace, and all the blessings treasured for us therein. Come, Holy Spirit! Come as the Heavenly Dove, or as the rushing mighty wind; but do come! Drop from above, as gently as the dew, or come like rattling hail, but do come, blest Spirit of God! We feel that we must be moved, we must be stirred, our heart's emotions must once again throb, to prove that the life of God is really within us; and if we do not realise this quickening and stirring, we are utterly unhappy.

You see also, dear friends, from this text, that *when a child of God sees that his graces are not diffused abroad, then is the time that he should take to prayer*. Let no one of us ever think of saying, 'I do not feel as if I could pray, and therefore I will not pray.' On the contrary, then is the time when you ought to pray more earnestly than ever. When the heart is disinclined for prayer, take that as a danger signal, and at once go to the Lord with this resolve:

I will approach thee – I will force
My way through obstacles to thee:
To thee for strength will have recourse,
To thee for consolation flee!

When you seem to yourself to have little faith and little love and little joy, then cry unto the Lord all the more, 'cry aloud and spare not'. Say, 'O my Father, I cannot endure this miserable existence! Thou hast made me to be a flower, to shed abroad my perfume, yet I am not doing it. Oh, by some means, stir my flagging spirit, till I shall be full of earnest industry, full of holy anxiety to promote thy glory, O my Lord and Master!' While you are thus crying, you must still believe, however, that God the Holy Spirit can stir your spirit, and make you full of life again. Never permit a doubt about that fact to linger in your bosom, else will you be unnecessarily sad. You, who are the true children of God, cannot ever come into a condition out of which the Holy Spirit cannot uplift you. You know the notable case of Laodicea, which was neither cold nor hot, and therefore so nauseous to the great Lord that he threatened to spue her out of his mouth; yet what is the message to the angel of that church? 'Behold, I stand at the door and knock.' This is not said to sinners, it is addressed to the angel of the church of the Laodiceans: 'Behold, I stand at the door, and knock: if any man hear my voice, and open the door, I will come in to him, and will sup with him, and he with me.' Oh, matchless grace! He is sick of these lukewarm professors, yet he promises to sup with them, and that they shall sup with him. That is the only cure for lukewarmness and decline, to renew heart-fellowship with Christ; and he stands and offers it to all his people now. 'Only do you open the door, and I will sup with you, and you shall sup with me.' O you whose graces are lying so sinfully dormant, who have to mourn and cry because of 'the body of this death' – for death in you seems to have taken to itself a body, and to have become a substantial thing, no mere skeleton now, but a heavy, cumbrous form that bows you down – cry still to him who is able to deliver you from this lukewarm and sinful state! Let every one of us put up the prayer of our text, 'Awake, O north wind; and come, thou south; and blow upon my garden, that the spices thereof may flow out.'

Our third and closing head will help to explain the remaining portion of our text: 'Let my Beloved come into his garden, and eat his pleasant fruits.' **These words speak of THE COMPANY OF CHRIST AND THE ACCEPTANCE OF OUR FRUIT BY CHRIST**.

I want you, dear friends, specially to notice one expression which is used here. While the spouse was, as it were, shut up and frozen, and the spices of the Lord's garden were not flowing out, she cried to the winds, 'Blow upon *my* garden.' She hardly dared to call it her Lord's garden; but now, notice the alteration in the phraseology: 'Let my Beloved come into *his* garden, and eat his pleasant fruits.' The wind has blown through the garden, and made the sweet odours to flow forth; now it is no longer 'my garden' but 'his garden'. It is wonderful how an increase of grace transfers our properties;

while we have but little grace, we cry, '*my*', but when we get great grace, we cry, '*his*'. Wherein you are sinful and infirm, brother, that is yours, you rightly call it '*my*'; but when you become strong, and joyous, and full of faith, that is not yours, brother, and you rightly call it '*his*'. Let him have all the glory of the change while you take all the shame and the confusion of face to yourself that ever you should have been so destitute of grace. So the spouse says, 'Let my Beloved come into his garden. Here are all the sweet perfumes flowing out; he will enjoy them, let him come and feel himself at home amongst them. He planted every flower, and gave to each its fragrance; let him come into his garden, and see what wonders his grace has wrought.'

Do you not feel, beloved, that *the one thing you want to stir your whole soul is that Christ should come into it*? Have you lost his company lately? Oh, do not try to do without it! The true child of God ought not to be willing to bear broken communion for even five minutes; but should be sighing and crying for its renewal. Our business is to seek to 'walk in the light as God is in the light', fully enjoying communion with Christ our Lord; and when that fellowship is broken, then the heart feels that it has cast all its happiness away, and it must robe itself in sackcloth, and sorrowfully fast. If the presence of the Bridegroom shall be taken away from thee, then indeed shalt thou have cause to fast and to be sad. The best condition a heart can be in, if it has lost fellowship with Christ, is to resolve that it will give God no rest till it gets back to communion with him, and to give itself no rest till once more it finds the Well-beloved.

Next observe that, when the Beloved comes into his garden, the heart's humble but earnest entreaty is, '*Let him eat his pleasant fruits.*' Would you keep back anything from Christ? I know you could not if he were to come into his garden. The best things that you have, you would first present to him, and then everything that you have, you would bring to him, and leave all at his dear feet. We do not ask him to come to the garden, that we may lay up our fruits, that we may put them by and store them up for ourselves; we ask him to come and eat them. The greatest joy of a Christian is to give joy to Christ; I do not know whether heaven itself can overmatch this pearl of giving joy to the heart of Jesus Christ on earth. It can match it, but not overmatch it, for it is a superlative joy to give joy to him – the Man of sorrows, who was emptied of joy for our sakes, and who now is filled up again with joy as each one of us shall come and bring his share, and cause to the heart of Christ a new and fresh delight.

Did you ever reclaim a poor girl from the streets? Did you ever rescue a poor thief who had been in prison? Then I know that, as you have heard of the holy chastity of the one or of the sacred honesty of the other of those lives that you have been the means of restoring, you have said, 'Oh, this is delightful! There is no joy equal to it. The effort cost me money, it cost me time, it cost me thought, it cost me prayer, but I am repaid a thousand times.' Then, as you see them growing up so bright, so transparent, so holy, so useful, you say, 'This work is worth living for, it is a delight beyond measure.' Often, persons come to me, and tell me of souls that were saved through my ministry twenty years ago. I heard the other day of one who was brought to Christ by a sermon of mine nearly thirty years ago, and I said to the friend who told me, 'Thank you, thank you; you could not tell me anything that would give my heart such joy as this good news that God has made me the instrument of a soul's conversion.' But what must be the joy of Christ who does all the work of salvation, who redeems us from sin and death and hell, when he sees such creatures as we are, made to be like himself, and knows the divine possibilities of glory and immortality that lie within us?

What are we going to be, brothers and sisters, we who are in Christ? We have not any idea of what holiness and glory and bliss shall yet be ours. 'It doth not yet appear what we shall be.' We may rise even while on earth to great heights of holiness – and the higher the better; but there is something better for us than mortal eye has ever seen or mortal ear has ever heard. There is more grace to be in the saints than we have ever seen in them, the saintliest saint on earth was never such a saint as they are yonder who are before the throne of the Most High; and I know not but that, even when they get there, there shall be a something yet beyond for them, and that through the eternal ages they shall still take for their motto, 'Onward and upward!' In heaven, there will be no '*Finis*'. We shall still continue to develop, and to become something more than we have ever been before; not fuller, but yet capable of holding more, ever growing in the possibility of reflecting Christ, and being filled with his love; and all the while our Lord Jesus Christ will be charmed and delighted with us. As he hears our lofty songs of praise, as he sees the bliss which will ever be flashing from each one of us, as he perceives the divine ecstasy which shall be ours for ever, he will take supreme delight in it all. 'My redeemed,' he will say, 'the sheep of my pasture, the purchase of my blood, borne on my shoulders, my very heart pierced for them, oh, how I delight to see them in the heavenly fold! These my redeemed people are joint heirs with me in the boundless heritage that shall be theirs for ever; oh, how I do delight in them!'

'Wherefore, comfort one another with these words', beloved, and cry mightily that on this church, and on all the churches, God's Spirit may blow, to make the spices flow. Pray, dear friends, all of you, for the churches to which you belong; and if you, my brother, are a pastor, be asking especially for this divine wind to blow through the garden which you have to cultivate, as I also pray for this portion of the garden of the Lord: 'Let my Beloved come into his garden, and eat his pleasant fruits.' The Lord be with each one of you, beloved, for his dear name's sake! Amen.

31

THE KING FEASTING IN HIS GARDEN

'I am come into my garden, my sister, my spouse; I have gathered my myrrh with my spice; I have eaten my honeycomb with my honey; I have drunk my wine with my milk; eat, O friends; drink, yea, drink abundantly, O beloved' (Song of Solomon 5:1).

I believe this text to be appropriate to the spiritual condition of our church. If I am not very sadly mistaken, the Lord of Hosts is with us in a very remarkable manner. Our meetings for prayer have been distinguished by an earnest and fervent spirit; our meetings with enquirers have been remarkably powerful; in a quiet manner, without any outward outcries, souls have been smitten down with conviction of sin, and have been comforted as they have received Christ by faith. We are not a deserted church, we are not left with broken hedges, with the wild boar of the wood committing devastations; but the Lord hath sent a gracious rain, which has quickened the seed, and he hath watered the plants of his garden, and made our souls to rejoice in his presence. Now if the text be appropriate, as I believe it is, the duty to which it especially calls us should have our earnest attention. The workers for Christ must remember that even if they have to care for the garden, their chief business must be to commune with the Lord and Master of that garden, since he himself this morning calls them to do so. 'Eat, O friends; drink, yea, drink abundantly, O beloved.' In happy and auspicious times, when the Spirit of God is working, it is very natural to say, 'We must now work more abundantly than ever', and God forbid that we should hinder such zeal, but the more spiritual privilege is not to be put in the second place. Let us commune as well as work, for therein shall we find strength for service, and our service shall be done the better, and become the more acceptable, and ensure the larger blessing. If while we serve like Martha, we at the same time commune like Mary, we shall not then become cumbered with much serving; we shall serve and not be cumbered, and shall feel no fretfulness against others whose only faculty may be that of sitting at the Master's feet.

The text divides itself readily into three parts. First, we have *the presence of the heavenly Bridegroom* – 'I am come into my garden, my sister, my spouse'; we have, secondly, *the satisfaction which he finds in his church* – 'I have gathered my myrrh with my spice, I have eaten my honeycomb with my honey, I have drunk my wine with my milk'; and, thirdly, we have *the invitation which he gives to his loving people* – 'Eat, O friends; drink, yea, drink abundantly, O beloved.'

1. The voice of the Master himself calls us to consider HIS PRESENCE: 'I am come.'

He tells us he is come. What? Could he come without our perceiving it? Is it not possible? May we be like those whose eyes were holden so that they knew him not? Is it possible for us to be like Magdalene, seeking Christ, while he is standing very near us? Yes, and we may even be like the disciples who, when they saw him walking on the water, were afraid, and thought it was a spirit, and cried out, and had need for him to say, 'It is I, be not afraid', before they knew who it was! Here is our ignorance, but here is his tenderness. He may come and yet we may not recognise him; but here when he cometh, he takes care to advertise us of the blessed fact, and calls us to observe and to consider, and to delight in it. He would, for our own comfort, prevent its being said of us, 'He came unto his own, and his own received him not.'

Let us observe, first, *this coming was in answer to prayer*. Our translators, in dividing the Bible into chapters, seem to have been utterly regardless of the connection or the sense, so that they brought down their guillotine between two verses which must not be divided. The church had said, 'Awake, O north wind; and come, thou south; blow upon my garden'; she had also said, 'Let my beloved come into his garden, and eat his pleasant fruits'. In answer to that prayer the Beloved replies, 'I am come into my garden.' Prayer is always heard, and the prayer of faithful souls finds an echo in Jesus' heart. How quickly the spouse was heard! Scarce had the words died away, 'Let my Beloved come', before she heard him say, 'I am come!' 'Before they call, I will answer; and while they are yet speaking, I will hear.' He is very near unto his people, and hence he very speedily answers their request. And how fully does he answer it too! You will perhaps say, 'But she had asked for the Holy Spirit; she had said, 'Awake, O north wind; and come, thou south'; and yet there is no mention of the heavenly wind as blowing through the garden.' The answer is that the Beloved's coming means all that. His visit brings both north and south wind; all benign influences are sure to follow where *he* leads the way; spices always flow out from the heart when Christ's sweet love flows in, and where he is, Christians have all things in him. There was a full answer to her prayer, and there was more than an answer, for she had but said, 'Let him come and eat', but, lo, he gathers myrrh and spice, and he drinks of wine and milk; he does exceeding abundantly above what she had even asked or even thought, after the right royal manner of the Son of God, who doth not answer us according to the poverty of our expressions and the leanness of our desires, but according to his riches in glory, giving to us grace upon grace out of his own inexhaustible fulness.

Brethren, this church has had a full reward for all her prayers. We have waited upon God often, all the day long there has been prayer in this house, and during this last month there has scarcely been an hour in which supplication has been suspended; and the answer has already come. We are so apt to overlook the answer to prayer. Let it not be so. Let us praise the Lord that prayer has not been a vain service. It has brought down his presence, the chief of all blessings, and that for which we most interceded at his throne. Let us exalt him. We can hear him say now, 'I am come into your meetings, I am blessing you, I am saving souls, I am elevating some of you into nearness of fellowship with myself, I am chastening some of your spirits with sadness to think you have lived in so grovelling an estate; I am with you, I have heard your prayers, I have come to abide with you as a people.'

Now, if this be the case, let us next observe *what an unspeakable blessing this is*! If the voice had said, 'I have sent my angel', that would have been a precious boon; but it is not so spoken; the word is, '*I* am come'. What, doth *he* before whom angels adoringly bow their heads, doth *he* before whom perfect spirits cast their crowns, doth *he* condescend to come into the church? Ay, it is even so. There is a personal presence of Christ in the midst of his people. Where two or three are met together in his name, there is he in the midst of them; his corporeal presence is in heaven, but his spiritual presence, which is all we want – all it is expedient for him as yet to grant – is assuredly in our midst. He is with us truly and really when we meet together in our solemn assemblies, and with us too when we separate and go our own ways in private to fight the battles of the Lord.

Brethren, for us to enjoy his presence as a church is a privilege whose value is only to be measured by the melancholy results of his absence. Where Jesus Christ is not in the garden, the plants wither, and like untimely figs, the fruits fall from the trees. Blossoms come not, or if they appear, they do but disappoint when Jesus is not there to knit and fructify them; but when he comes, even the driest boughs in the garden become like Aaron's rod that budded. Yes, our older brethren in the church remember times of trouble, times when the ministry was not with power, when the gatherings on the Lord's-day were joyless, when the voice of wailing saddened the courts of Zion; but now we do rejoice, yea, and will rejoice. The contrast between the past and the joyous present should increase our gratitude till we praise the Lord on the high-sounding cymbals with jubilant exaltation.

Remember, too, that if he had dealt with us according to our sins, and rewarded us after our iniquities, we should never have heard the footfall of the Beloved traversing the garden. How many have grieved the Holy Spirit by careless living and backsliding! How have most of us followed him afar off instead of keeping step with him in service and fellowship! Alas! my Lord, if thou hadst regarded only the sins of the pastor of the church, thou hadst long ago left this flock; but thou hast not dealt with us severely, but according unto thy love and to thy mercy thou hast blotted out our sins like a cloud, and like a thick cloud our transgressions, and still dost thou condescend to come into thy garden.

If you take each word of this remarkable sentence, you will find a meaning. '*I* am come.' There is the *personal* presence of Christ 'I *am come*'. There is the *certainty* that it is so. It is no delusion, no dream, no supposition. 'I *am* truly come.' Blessed be the name of the Lord, at this present time it is assuredly so. Many of his saints can bear testimony that they have seen his face and have felt the kisses of his lips, and have proved even this day that his love is better than wine. Note the next word, 'I am come *into* my garden.' How near is the approach of Christ to his church! He comes not to the garden door, nor to look over the wall, nor in at the gate and out again, but *into* his garden. Down every walk, midst the green alleys, among the beds of spices he walks, watching each flower, pruning the superfluous foliage of every fruit-bearing plant, and plucking up by the roots such as his heavenly Father hath not planted. His delights are with the sons of men. His intercourse with his chosen is most familiar; so that the spouse may sing, 'My beloved is gone down into his garden, to the beds of spices, to feed in the gardens, and to gather lilies.' Jesus Christ the Lord forgets not his church, but fulfils the promise: 'I the Lord do keep it, I will water it every moment; lest any hurt it, I will keep it night and day.' Brethren, this is a solemn as well as a pleasant fact. You who are members of this church, recollect that Jesus is come into the church, that he is now going his rounds among you, and marking your feelings towards him; he knows today who is in fellowship with him, and who is not; he discerneth between the precious and the vile. He never comes without the winnowing fan when he visits his threshing floor; beware if thou be as chaff. He hath come into his garden. O you that have not enjoyed much of his gracious company, pray him to cast a look towards you, and be you like the sunflower which turns its face to the sun, to refresh itself with his beams. O pant and long for his presence. If you soul is as dark as the dead of night, call out to him, for he heareth the faintest sigh of any of his chosen.

'I am come into my garden,' saith he. Note here the *possession which Christ claims in the church*. If it were not *his* garden, he would not come into it. A church that is not Christ's church shall have none of his presence, and a soul that is not Christ's has no fellowship with him. If he reveal himself at all, it is unto his own people, his blood-bought people, the people that are his by purchase and by power, and by the surrender of themselves to him. When I think of this church as committed to my care, I am overawed, and well may my fellow-officers be cast down under the weight of our responsibility; but after all we may say, 'Master, this garden is not ours; it is *thy* garden. We have not begotten all this people, neither can we carry them in our bosoms; but thou, great Shepherd of the sheep, thou will guard the fold.' Since the garden is his own, he will not suffer even the least plant to perish. My brethren who work for Christ, do not be downcast if certain portions of the work should not seem to succeed. *He* will attend to it. 'The pleasure of the Lord shall prosper in his hand.' It is more his work than ours, and souls are more under his responsibility than ours. So let us hope and be confident, for the Master will surely smile upon his 'vineyard of red wine'.

The next word denotes *cultivation*. 'I am come into my *garden*.' The church is a cultivated spot; it did not spring up by chance, it was arranged by himself, it has been tended by himself, and the fruits belong to himself. Thankful are we if we can truly know that as a church

> We are a garden walled around,
> Chosen and made peculiar ground.

Christ, the Great Cultivator, exercises care and skill in training his people, and he delights to see his own handiwork in them.

And then there are the two choice words at the close, by which he speaks of his church herself rather than of her work. As if he would draw the attention of his people to themselves and to himself, rather than to their work; he says, '*My sister, my spouse*.' There is one name for the garden, but there are two names for herself. The work is his work, the garden is his garden, but see, he wants communion not so much with the work as with the worker, he speaks to the church herself. He calls her, 'My sister, my spouse'. 'Spouse' has something in it of dearness that is not in the first word, for what can be dearer to the husband than the bride? But then there was a time when the spouse was not dear to the bridegroom, there was a period perhaps when he did not know her, when there was no relationship between them twain; though they are made of one flesh by marriage, yet they were of different families; and for this cause he adds the dear name of 'sister', to show an ancient relationship to her, a closeness and a nearness by blood, by birth, as well as by betrothal and wedlock. The two words put together make up a confection of such inexpressible sweetness, that instead of seeking to expound them to you, I will leave them to your meditations, and may he who calls the church 'Sister' and 'Spouse' open up their richness to your souls.

Here, then, is the gist of the whole matter. The Master's presence is in this church in a very remarkable manner. Beloved, I pray that none of you may be like Adam, who fled among the trees to hide himself from God when he walked in the garden. May your business not act like an overshadowing thicket, to conceal you from fellowship. He calls you, O backslider, he calls you as once he called Adam: 'Where art thou?' Come, beloved, come and commune with your Lord; come away from those carking cares and anxieties which, like gloomy groves of cypress, conceal thee from thy Lord, or rather thy Lord from thee. Hearest thou not his call, 'O my dove, that art in the clefts of the rock, in the secret places of the stairs, let me see thy countenance, let me hear thy voice; for sweet is thy voice, and thy countenance is comely.' Let none of us be like the disciples in another garden when their Lord was there, and he was in agony, but they were sleeping. Up, ye sleepers, for Christ has come. If the midnight cry, 'Behold, the Bridegroom cometh', awoke the virgins, shall not 'I am come' awaken you? It is his own voice; it is not 'He cometh', but 'I am come'. Start up, ye slumberers, and now with heart and soul seek fellowship with him. It would be a sad thing if while Christ is with us any should be slumbering, and then should wake up and say, 'Surely God was in this place and I knew it not.' Rather may you invite him to come into your souls, and abide with you until the day break and the shadows flee away, and you behold him face to face.

2. Thus much upon the first point; and **now may his Holy Spirit help us to view OUR LORD'S SATISFACTION IN HIS CHURCH**.

The beautiful expressions of the text are capable of many holy meanings, and it is not possible that any expositions of mine could fully unveil their treasures; but let me observe, first, that Christ is delighted with *the offerings* of his people. He says, 'I have gathered my myrrh with my spice.' We may consider myrrh and spice – sweet perfumes – offered by way of incense to God, as being indicative of the offerings which his people bring to him. What if I say that prayer is like sweet-smelling myrrh, and that the Beloved has been gathering the myrrh of holy prayer, the bitter myrrh of repenting sighs and cries, in the midst of this church, lo, these many months! You perhaps thought that poor wordless prayer of yours was never heard, but Jesus gathered it, and called it spice; and when some brother was praying aloud, and in silence your tears fell thick and fast for perishing sinners, for you could not bear that they should die, nor endure that Christ's name should be blasphemed, the Beloved gathered up the precious drops, and counted them as costly oil of sweetest smell. Was it not said in the Psalm, 'Prayer also shall be made for him continually'? And you did pray for him that his name might be as ointment poured forth, and that he might gird his sword upon his thigh, and ride forth prosperously. Jesus observed, and delighted in your heart's offering. Others knew not that you prayed, perhaps you thought yourself that you scarcely prayed, but he gathered his myrrh with his spice from you. No faithful prayer is lost. The groanings of his people are not forgotten, he gathers them as men gather precious products from a garden which they have tilled with much labour and expense.

And then, may not spice represent our praises? For these, as well as prayer, come up as incense before his throne. Last Thursday night, when my brother spoke to you, if you felt as I did I am sure your heart sent up praise as a smoke of incense from the warm coals of a censer, as he cast on them handfuls of frankincense in the form of various motives for gratitude and reasons for praise. Oh, it was good to sing God's praises as we then did by the hour together. It was delightful, too, to come to his table and make that ordinance in very deed a eucharistical service of praise to God. Praise is pleasant and comely, and most of all so because Jesus accepts it, and says, 'Whosoever offereth praise glorifieth me.'

When the Lord in another place speaks of offering sweet cane bought with money, does he not refer to other offerings which his people bring in addition to their prayers and their praises, when they give to him the first fruits of all their increase, and present thankofferings to his name. He has said, 'None of you shall appear before me empty', and I hope none of you have been content to do so! The contributions given for the spread of his cause, for the feeding of his poor, and clothing of his naked ones, are given by true hearts directly to himself. Though they may be but as two mites that make a farthing, yet offered in his name are they not also included in this word, 'I have gathered my myrrh with my spice'?

The Saviour's satisfaction is found, in the next place, in his people's *love* – 'I have eaten my honeycomb with my honey.' Shall I be wrong if I believe that this sweetness refers to Christian love, for this is the richest of all the graces, and sweetens all the rest. Jesus Christ finds delightful solace in his people's love, both in the inward love which is like the honey, and in the outward manifestation of it, which is like the honeycomb. He rejoices in the love that drips in all its preciousness from the heart, and in the honeycomb of organisation, in which it is for order's sake stored up and put into his hand. Or, what if it should mean that Christ overlooks the imperfections of his people? The honeycomb is not good eating, but he takes that as well as the honey! 'I have eaten my honeycomb with my honey.' As he looks upon his people, and sees what he has done for them, his loving heart rejoices in what his grace has accomplished. As a benevolent man who should have taken a child from the street and educated it, would be pleased to see it growing up, prospering, happy, well-informed, talented, so when Jesus Christ, remembering what his people were, sees in them displays of grace, desires after holiness, self-denials, communion with God, and the like, this is to him like honey. He takes an intense satisfaction in the sweet fruits which he himself has caused us to produce; notwithstanding every imperfection, he accepts our love, and says, 'I have eaten my honeycomb with my honey.'

Turning again to our precious text, we observe that our Lord's satisfaction is compared to drinking as well as eating, and that drinking is of a twofold character. 'I have drunk my wine.' Does he intend by this his *joy* which is fulfilled in us when our joy is full? Does he mean that, as men go to feasts to make glad their hearts with wine, so he comes to his people to see their joy, and is filled with exultation? Meaneth he not so? Surely he doth. And the milk, may not that mean the Christian's common, ordinary *life*? As milk contains all the constituents of nourishment, may he not mean by this the general life of the Christian? Our Lord takes delight in the graces of our lives. One has said that wine may represent those actions resulting from well-considered dedication and deep spiritual thought; for wine must be expressed from the grape with labour and preserved with care, there must be skill, and work, and forethought spent upon it; but milk is a natural production, it flows freely, plentifully, spontaneously; it is a more common and ordinary, yet precious thing. So the Lord delights that his people should give to him those elaborate works which they have to tend with long care and watch over with much anxiety before they are produced. These are the wine; but he would have them give him the simple outgushing of their souls, the ejaculations which flow forth without labour, the little deeds of love which need no forethought, the everyday outgoings of their inner life – these are milk, and are equally acceptable to him. Well, if it be so, certain is it that Christ finds great pleasure in his people, and in their various forms of piety he drinks his wine with his milk.

Permit me now to call your attention to those many great little words, which are yet but one – I refer to the word '*my*'. Observe, that eight or nine times it is repeated. Here is the reason for the solace which the bridegroom finds in his church. Does he walk in the church as men do in a garden for pleasure? Then he says, 'I am come into *my* garden'. Does he talk with his beloved? It is because he calls her '*my* sister, *my* spouse'. Does he love her prayers and praises? It is because they never would be prayed or praised if he had not created these fruits of the lips. He says not, 'I have gathered *your* myrrh with *your* spice.' Oh, no! viewed as ours these are poor things, but viewed as his they are most acceptable, 'I have gathered *my* myrrh with *my* spice.' So if he finds any honey in his people, any true love in them, he first put it there. 'I have eaten *my* honeycomb with *my* honey.' Yes, and if there be any joy and life in them to make his heart glad, he calls it '*my* wine', and '*my* milk'. When I read these words, and thought of our Lord's being fed by us, I could almost have cried out, 'Lord, when saw we thee an hungered, and fed thee? Or thirsty, and gave thee drink? Dost thou find any satisfaction in us? Surely, our goodness extendeth not to thee. Whence should we give thee aught to eat?' Yet he declares it, and we may blushingly believe him, and praise his name, for surely if he found it so, it is because he made it so. If he has gotten anything out of us, he must first have put it in us; if he sees of the travail of his soul, it is because the travail came first.

Note well, ye lovers of Jesus, that our Lord in this heavenly verse is fed first. 'I have eaten,' says he, and then he turns to us, and says, 'Eat, O friends.' If any of you seek friendship with the Well-beloved, you must commence by preparing him a feast. Remember our Lord's own parable: Which of you, having a servant plowing or feeding cattle, will say unto him by-and-by, when he is come from the field, Go and sit down to meat? And will not rather say unto him, Make ready wherewith I may sup, and gird thyself, and serve me, till I have eaten and drunken; and afterward thou shalt eat and drink?' Even if your poverty compels you to say, 'As the Lord liveth, I have not a cake, but a handful of meal in a barrel, and a little oil in a cruse', listen to him as he answers, 'Fear not, make me thereof a little cake first.' Be assured that after you have so done, your barrel of meal shall not waste, neither shall the cruse of oil fail. The way for believers to be fed by Christ is to seek to feed him; look to his being satisfied, and he will assuredly look to you. 'Ye shall eat neither bread, nor parched corn, nor green ears, until the selfsame day that ye have brought an offering unto your God' (Leviticus 23:14). 'Bring ye all the tithes into the storehouse, that there may be meat in mine house, and prove me now herewith, saith the Lord of hosts, if I will not open you the windows of heaven, and pour you out a blessing, that there shall not be room enough to receive it.' See, my brethren, ye must find meat for your Lord, and then, but not till then, there shall be meat for you.

In the feast, it is remarkable how complete the entertainment is. There is the sweetest food, and the most nourishing and exhilarating drink, and then over and above there is the rarest perfume, not counted to be needful in ordinary entertainments, but crowning all and making up a right royal feast. How marvellous that our Beloved should find within his church all that his soul wants! Having given over himself to her, he delights in her, he rests in his love, and rejoices over her with singing. For the joy that was set before him, he endured the cross, despising the shame, and this day he continues to be filled with the selfsame delight.

I would fain linger but time forbids. **We must now remember, in the third place, that the text contains an INVITATION**.

The Beloved says, 'Eat, O friends; drink, yea, drink abundantly, O beloved.' In the invitation we see the character of the invited guests; they are spoken of as *friends*. We were once aliens, we are now brought nigh; we were once enemies, we are made servants, but we have advanced from the grade of service (though servants still) into that of friends, henceforth he calls us not servants, but friends, for the servant knoweth not what his Lord doeth, but all things that he has seen of his Father he has made known unto us. The friendship between Christ and his people is not in name only, but in deed and in truth. Having laid down his life for his friends, having brought them to know his friendship in times of trial and of difficulty, he at all times proves his friendship by telling his secrets to them, and exhibiting an intense sympathy with them in all their secret bitternesses. David and Jonathan were not more closely friends than Christ and the believer, when the believer lives near to his Lord. Never seek the friendship of the world, nor allow your love to the creature to overshadow your friendship with Christ.

He next calls his people *beloved* as well as friends. He multiplieth titles, but all his words do not express the full love of his heart. 'Beloved.' Oh, to have this word addressed to us by Christ! It is music! There is no music in the rarest sounds compared with these three syllables, which drop from the Redeemer's lips like sweet-smelling myrrh. 'Beloved!' If he had addressed but that one word to any one of us, it might create a heaven within our soul, which neither sickness nor death could mar. Let me sound the note again, 'BELOVED!' Doth Jesus love me? Doth he own his love? Doth he seal the fact by declaring it with his own lips? Then I will not stipulate for promises, nor make demands of him. If he loves he must act towards me with lovingkindness; he will not smite his beloved unless love dictates the blow; he will not forsake his chosen, for he never changes. Oh, the inexpressible, the heaped-up blessednesses which belong to the man who feels in his soul that Christ has called him *beloved!*

Here, then, you have the character in the text of those who are invited to commune with Christ; he calls his friends and his beloved. The *provisions* presented to them are of two kinds; they are bidden to *eat* and to *drink*. You, who are spiritual, know what the food is, and what the drink is, for you eat his flesh and drink his blood. The incarnation of the Son of God, and the death of Jesus the Saviour, these are the two sacred viands whereon faith is sustained. To feed upon the very Christ of God is what is needed, nothing but this can satisfy the hunger of the spirit; but he who feeds on him shall know no lack. 'Eat,' saith he, 'and drink.' You ask, 'Where are the provisions?' I answer, they are contained in the first words of the text, 'I am come'. If *he* is come, then eat; if *he* is come, then drink; there is food, there is drink for you in him.

Note that delightful word, *abundantly*. Some dainties satiate, and even nauseate when we have too much of them, but no soul ever had too much of the dear love of Christ, no heart did ever complain that his sweetness cloyed. That can never be. Some things, if you have too much of them, may injure you, they are good to a certain point, beyond that, evil; but even the smallest child of grace shall never over-feast himself with Jesus' love. No, the more ye have the more shall ye enjoy, the more blessed shall ye be, and the more shall ye be like the Lord from whom the love proceeds. O ye that stand shivering in the cold shallows of the river of life, why tarry ye there? Descend into the greater depths, the warmer waves, and let the mighty stream lave you breast-high; yea, go father, plunge where you can find no bottom, for it is blessed and safe swimming in the stream of Christ's everlasting love, and he invites you to it now. When you are at his banquet-table, pick not here and there a crumb. Sip not now and then a drop: he saith, 'eat', and he adds, 'drink abundantly', and the invitation to receive abundantly applies to both refreshments. Your eating and your drinking may be without stint. Ye cannot impoverish the Most High God, possessor of heaven and earth. When ye are satiated with his love, his table shall still be loaded. Your cups may run over, but his flagons will still be brimmed. If you are straitened at all you are not straitened in him, you are straitened in yourselves.

But now let me say to my brethren, and especially to my fellow-workers in the kingdom for Christ, it is for us just now while our Lord is walking in his garden, while he is finding satisfaction in his work and in his people, to beware of taking any satisfaction in the work ourselves, and equally to beware that we do not neglect the appropriate duty of the occasion, namely, that of feasting our souls with our Lord's gracious provisions. You are caring for others, it is well; you are rejoicing over others, it is well; still watch well yourselves, and rejoice in the Lord in your own hearts. What said he to the twelve when they came back glorying that even the devils were subject unto them? Did he not reply, 'Nevertheless rejoice not in this, but rather rejoice that your names are written in heaven'? It is your personal interest in Christ, you being yourself saved, Christ being present with you, that is your main joy. Enjoy the feast for yourselves, or you will not be strong to hand out the living bread to others. See that you are first partakers of the fruit, or you will not labour aright as God's husbandmen. The more of personal enjoyment you allow yourself in connection with your Lord, the more strong will you be for his service and the more out of an experimental sense of his preciousness will you be able to say with true eloquence, 'O taste and see that the Lord is good.' You will tell others what you have tasted and handled; you will say, 'This poor man cried, the Lord heard him, and delivered him from all his fears.' I put this before you with much earnestness, and I pray that none of you may think it safe so to work as to forget to commune, or wise to seek the good of others so as to miss personal fellowship with the Redeemer.

I might now conclude, but it strikes me that there may be some among us who are, in their own apprehensions, outside the garden of Christ's church, and are therefore mourning over this sermon, and saying, 'Alas! that is not for me. Christ is come into his garden, but I am a piece of waste ground. He is fed and satisfied in his church, but he finds nothing in me. Surely I shall perish from the way, when his wrath is kindled but a little!' I know how apt poor hearts are to write bitter things against themselves, even when God has never written a single word against them; so let me see if by turning over this text we may not find thoughts of consolation for the trembling ones. Who knows? There may be a soft breath in the text which may fan the smoking flax, a tender hand that may bind up the bruised reed. I will briefly indicate two or three comfortable thoughts.

Seeking soul, should it not console thee to think that *Jesus is near*? The kingdom of God is come nigh unto you, for he is come into his garden. He was in our last meeting for anxious souls, for many found him there. You are not, then, living in a region where Christ is absent, mayhap when he passeth by he will look on you. Canst thou not put out thy finger and touch the hem of his garment, for Jesus of Nazareth passeth by? Even if thou hast not touched him, yet it should give thee some good cheer to know that he is within reach, and within call. Though thou be like the poor withered lily in the garden, or worse still, like a noxious weed, yet if he be in the garden he may observe thee and have pity on thee.

Notice, too, that although the text speaks of a garden, it never was a garden till he made it so. Men do not find gardens in the wilderness. In the wilds of Australia or the backwoods of America, men never stumble on a garden where human foot hath never been, it is all forest, or prairie, or mountain; so, mark thee, soul, if the church be a garden, Christ made it so. Why cannot he make thee so? Why not, indeed? Has he not said, 'Instead of the thorn shall come up the fir tree, and instead of the brier shall come up the myrtle tree; and it shall be to the Lord for a name, for an everlasting sign that shall not be cut off'? This garden-making gives God a name, Jesus gets honour by ploughing up the wastes, extracting the briers, and planting firs and myrtles there. See, then, there is hope for thee yet, thou barren heart, he may yet come and make thy wilderness like Eden, and thy desert like the garden of the Lord.

Note, too, that the Bridegroom gathered myrrh, and fed on milk, and wine, and honey. Ay, and I know you thought, 'He will find no honey in me, he will find no milk and wine in me.' Ah! but then the text did not say he found them in the church; it is said, 'I have eaten *my* honeycomb with *my* honey; I have drunk *my* wine with *my* milk'; and if he put those things into his church, and then took comfort in them, why not put them into you, and take comfort in you, too? Be of good cheer; arise, he calleth thee, this morning.

Another word perhaps may help you. Did you notice, poor hungry soul, how Jesus said, 'drink *abundantly*'? 'Ah,' say you, 'he did not say that to me.' I know it. He said that to his friends and to his beloved, and you dare not put yourselves among those; but do you not see how generous he is to his friends, and how he stints nothing? He evidently does not mean to lock anything up in the storeroom, for he tells them to eat and drink abundantly. Now, surely, where there is such a festival, though you dare not come and sit at the table with the guests, you might say with the Syrophenician woman, 'Yet the dogs under the table eat of the children's crumbs.' It is good knocking at a door where they are keeping open house, and where the feast reveals a lavish hospitality. Do thou knock now and try it. If it were a poor man's dinner with a dry crust, and a poor herring, or if it were a miser's meal spread most begrudgingly, I would not advise you to knock; but where there is wine and milk in rivers, and the good man of the house bids his guests eat and drink abundantly, I say knock, for God saith it shall be opened.

Another thought. Jesus finds meat and drink in his church, and you are afraid he would find neither in you – I want to tell you a truth which, perhaps, you have forgotten. There was a woman that was a sinner; she had had five husbands, and he with whom she then lived was not her husband, she was an adulteress and a Samaritan; but Christ said, after he had conversed with her, that he had found meat to eat that his disciples knew not of. Where did he get it then? If he had drank that day, he did not get it from Jacob's well; for he had nothing to draw with, and the well was deep. He found his refreshment in that poor woman, to whom he said, 'Give me to drink.' The Samaritan harlot refreshed the soul of Jesus, when she believed in him and owned him as the Christ. Have you never read that word of his, 'My meat and my drink is to do the will of him that sent me, and to finish his work'? And what is the will of him that sent him? Well, I will tell you what it is not. 'It is not the will of your Father, that is in heaven, that one of these little ones should perish.' The will of God and the will of Christ are these, to save sinners; for this purpose was Jesus born and sent into the world; he came into the world to seek and to save that which was lost. See, then, poor lost one, thou wilt look to him and cry to him, and cast thyself upon him, and thou shalt never, as long as thou livest, have any cause for regretting it.

Finally, the text represents the Lord saying, 'I am come into my garden.' It may imply that he is not always in his garden. Sometimes his church grieves him, and his manifest presence departs; but hearken, O sinner, there is a precious thought for thee: he is not always in his garden; but *he is always on the throne of grace*. He does not always say, 'I am come into my garden', but he always says, 'Come unto me, all ye that labour and are heavy-laden, and I will give you rest.' He never leaves the mercy-seat, he never ceases to intercede for sinners. Come, and welcome, then. If you have not seen the Beloved's face, come and bow at his feet. Though you have never heard him say, 'Thy sins are forgiven thee', yet come now with a broken and a contrite heart and seek absolution at his hands. Come, and welcome! Come, and welcome! May the sweet Bridegroom with cords of love draw thee, and may this morning be a time of love; and as he passes by, if he sees thee weltering in thy blood, may he say unto thee, 'Live!'

May the Lord grant it, and on his head shall be many crowns. Amen.

32

LOVE JOYING IN LOVE

'I am come into my garden, my sister, my spouse: I have gathered my myrrh with my spice; I have eaten my honeycomb with my honey; I have drunk my wine with my milk; eat, O friends; drink, yea, drink abundantly, O beloved' (Song of Solomon 5:1).

No sooner does the spouse say, 'Let my Beloved come into his garden', than her Lord answers, 'I am come into my garden.' 'Before they call, I will answer; and while they are yet speaking, I will hear.' When we desire our Lord Jesus to come to us, he has already come in a measure; our desire is the result of his coming. He meets us in all our desires, for he waiteth to be gracious. Our 'come' is no sooner uttered than it is lost in his 'Behold, I come quickly!'

When we perceive that the Bridegroom has come, we perceive also that he has done exactly what he was asked to do. How cheering to find that our mind is in harmony with his mind! Our heart saith, 'Let my Beloved come into his garden, and eat his pleasant fruits.' His heart replies, 'I have gathered my myrrh with my spice; I have eaten my honeycomb with my honey; I have drunk my wine with my milk.' 'Delight thyself also in the Lord; and he shall give thee the desires of thine heart.' The Lord Jesus makes the desires of his saints to be the foreshadowings of his own actions: 'The secret of the Lord is with them that fear him.' His secret counsel is made known in the believing soul by desires inspired of the Holy Ghost.

Note well that the Bridegroom kindly takes to himself as his own all that is in the garden. His spouse spoke of 'his pleasant fruits', and he acknowledges the least and most homely of them to be his own. He repeats the possessive particle – 'my': '*my* myrrh, *my* spice, *my* honeycomb, *my* honey, *my* wine, *my* milk'. He disdains nothing which the garden of his bride produces. He is fond of the notion of joint-heirship, even as in another place he said, 'My Father and your Father, my God and your God'. Let us also value the personal possessive pronouns: the sweetness of the promises lies in them. These are our arms with which we embrace the promises. Beloved brethren in Christ Jesus, is it not charming to see our Lord appropriating us, and all that we are, and all that we have, and all that grows within us, and all the varied forms of his grace, which are the outcome of his own work within our hearts? Within us certain things are bitter, but wholesome; and he saith, 'my myrrh'. Some things are sweet, though homely; and he saith, 'my honey'. Some things are of a rarer sort, and he saith, 'my spice'; while others are commonplace enough, and he saith, 'my milk'. Our Lord taketh no exception to any one of the true growths of the garden, whether it be myrrh or milk; and he asks for nothing more than the garden may be expected to yield; he is content without the butter of kine, or flesh of fed beasts, satisfying himself with honey fresh from the hive.

I note, with much delight, that matters which seem inconsistent with perfection are not refused by the heavenly Bridegroom. As the Lord did not refuse for an offering the leavened cakes of the first-fruits, so in this instance he saith, 'I have eaten my honeycomb with my honey.' The honey would be purer without the comb; but as it is incident thereto, he takes the one with the other. He graciously accepts, not only our heart's desire, but the very mode in which our weakness works towards that desire. It is as if he delighted in the words of our prayers as well as in the essence of our prayers, and prized the notes of our songs as well as the meaning of them. Yes, I believe our Lord puts our tears as well as our sorrows into his bottle, and hears our groanings as well as our desires. The honeycomb which contains the honey is precious to him. After he had risen from the grave, he ate a piece of a honeycomb, and I doubt not that he had a reason for choosing that food: sweet gathered from sweets, yet not without wax. Our Lord accepts our services without nicely noting and critically rejecting the infirmity which goes with them.

I note also that he himself gathers what he enjoys: 'I have gathered my myrrh with my spice.' Many a holy thing, which we have not in detail offered to him in set form, he knows to have been given in the gross; and so he takes with his own hand what he knows we have by a comprehensive covenant made over to him. How sweetly does he fill up our blanks, and believe in our consecration, even when we do not repeat the form of it!

Moreover, he makes mixtures out of our fruits, for he gathers myrrh with balsam, and drinks wine with milk; thus taking the rarer with the more common. He knows how to make holy compounds out of the graces of his people; thus increasing their excellence. He is the best judge of what is admirable, and he is the best fashioner and compounder of character; he is using his skill upon us. Often by our mingled experiences he accomplishes an increase of virtue in us. Some graces are the result of work and wisdom, as wine which must be trodden from the grapes; others are natural, like milk which flows from living fountains without art of man; but the Lord accepts them both, and so combines them that they are pleasant to him to a high degree. Simple faith and experimental prudence make up a sacred milk and wine; and the like may be seen in rapturous love and calm patience, which blend most deliciously. The Lord loves us, and makes the most of us. He is pleased with all that is the true produce of his grace, and finds no faults with it; on the contrary, he says, 'I have eaten my honeycomb with my honey.'

Having made these observations upon the Lord's fulfilling the prayer of the spouse, I should like to deliver the following remarks upon the text:

It is evident that *the Lord Jesus is made happy by us*. These poetical sentences must mean that he values the graces and works of his people. He gathers their myrrh and spice because he values them; he eats and drinks the honey and the milk because they are pleasant to him. It is a wonderful thought that the Lord Jesus Christ has joy of us. We cost him anguish, even unto death, and now he finds a reward in us. This may seem a small thing to an unloving mind, but it may well ravish the heart which adores the Well-beloved. Can it be true that we afford joy to the Son of God, the Prince Emmanuel? The King has been held in the galleries, he has been charmed by us. Our first repentance made him call together his friends and his neighbours; the first gleam of faith he ever saw in us made his heart rejoice; and all that he has seen in us ever since of his own image, wrought by his grace, has caused him to see of the travail of his soul. Never has a husbandman taken such pleasure in the growth of his choice plants as our Lord has taken in us. 'The Lord taketh pleasure in them that fear him, in those that hope in his mercy.' That is a thought to be rolled under the tongue as a sweet morsel. Yes, the Lord's church is his Hephzibah, for, saith he, 'my delight is in her'.

The second thought is that *the Lord Jesus will not and cannot be happy by himself: he will have us share with him*. Note how the words run: 'I have eaten'; 'Eat, O friends!' 'I have drunk'; 'Drink, yea, drink abundantly, O beloved!' His union with his people is so close that his joy is in them, that their joy may be full. He cannot be alone in his joy. That verse of our quaint hymn is always true:

> And this I do find, we two are so joined,
> He'll not be in glory and leave me behind.

He will not be happy anywhere without us. He will not eat without our eating, and he will not drink without our drinking. Does he not say this in other words in the Revelation: 'If any man hear my voice, and open the door, I will come in to him, and will sup with him, and he with me'? The inter-communion is complete: the enjoyment is for both. To make our Lord Jesus happy we must be happy also. How can the Bridegroom rejoice if his bride is sad? How can the Head be content if the members pine? At this table of fellowship his chief concern is that we eat and drink. 'Take, eat,' saith he; and again, 'Drink ye all of it.' I think I hear him now say: 'I have eaten, and I have drunk; and although I will drink no more of the fruit of the vine until that day that I drink it new in the kingdom of God, yet eat ye, O friends: drink, yea, drink abundantly, O beloved!' Thus we have seen, first, that Christ is made happy by us; and, secondly, that he insists upon our sharing his joy with him.

If we have already enjoyed happy fellowship with him, *the Lord Jesus calls upon us to be still more happy*. Though we may say that we have eaten, he will again say, 'Eat, O friends!' He presses you to renew, repeat and increase your participation with him. It is true we have drunk out of the chalice of his love; but he again invites us, saying, 'Drink, yea, drink abundantly, O beloved!' Of other wines it would be ill to say, 'Drink abundantly'; but of this wine the Lord says, with an emphasis, 'Drink abundantly, O beloved!' Oh, for grace to renew all former enjoyments with greater zest and deeper intensity! It has been sweet even to taste and sip; what must it be to eat and drink abundantly?

Must it not mean that, though we know the Lord Jesus, we should try to know more of him, yea, to know all that can be known of that love which passeth knowledge? Should we not labour to realise more of HIM, taking in the whole truth concerning his person and love by meditation, contemplation, understanding and reverent simplicity? Let nothing lie by: let us eat and drink all the stores of the banquet of love.

As the mouth with which we eat is faith, does not the Saviour seem to cry, 'Believe on me. Trust me. Confide in me abundantly'? Eat and drink with large appetite, by receiving into your heart's belief all that can be received. Oh, for grace to appropriate a whole Christ, and all the love, the grace, the glory that is laid up in him!

Does it not also mean – have greater enjoyment of divine things? Partake of them without stint. Do not restrict yourself as though you could go too far in feeding upon the Lord Jesus. Do not be afraid of being too happy in the Lord, or of being too sure of his salvation, or of having too much assurance, or too much devout emotion. Dread not the excitements which come from fellowship with Christ. Do not believe that the love of Jesus can be too powerfully felt in the soul. Permit the full sweep and current of holy joy in the Lord to carry you away: it will be safe to yield to it. 'Rejoice in the Lord alway: and again, I say, Rejoice.'

Beloved, let us now take our fill of Christ. Since we believe, let us believe more unreservedly; if we enjoy, let us enjoy more thoroughly; if we have life, let us have it more abundantly. In this case we may eat and our soul shall live; we may drink, and not only forget our misery, but drink again, and enter into bliss. Our Lord beckons us from the shore to the sea; he calls us from the lower seat to come up higher. He would have us gladder, stronger, fuller, holier. He presses the provisions of his love upon us, like a host whose joy lies in seeing all his guests feasting. Do not hold back. Be not satisfied with little believing, and scant enjoying, and cool feeling; but let us enter fully into the joy of our Lord.

True, we are unworthy, but he invites us. We shall be wise to yield to his loving pressure. We many not have such another feast just yet; and possibly we may have to go for forty days into the wilderness, on the strength of this meal; wherefore let us keep the feast heartily. Our Lord, in his invitation, challenges our friendship and our love. He says: 'Eat, O friends!' Prove yourselves friends by being free at his table. 'Drink, yea, drink abundantly, O beloved!' If this be his way of testing us, let us not be slow in accepting it. Let us show our love by joying in him as he joys in us. Amen.

33

ASLEEP AND YET AWAKE – A RIDDLE

'I sleep, but my heart waketh: it is the voice of
my beloved that knocketh' (Song of Solomon 5:2).

We are glad to perceive in this Song the varied experience of the bride. She was the well-beloved of the heavenly Bridegroom, but she was not without her faults. Though the 'fairest among women', she was human, and, therefore, she had not reached angelical perfection. She was not perfect, to begin with, for at the outset she confessed, 'I am black, because the sun hath looked upon me: they made me the keeper of the vineyards; but mine own vineyard have I not kept.' She was not perfect even in the exhibition of her love to him who had chosen her, for she has to acknowledge, as upon the occasion before us, that she treated him in an unworthy manner. She kept him waiting at her door in the chilly night, and grieved him so that he withdrew. She was not perfect even to the end of the chapter, for she could not hear her Lord's voice so clearly as certain of her companions, and she cried in the last chapter of her song, 'Cause me to hear it.'

Brethren, we shall not be able to claim entire perfection so long as we are this side the hills of division. Till the day break and the shadows flee away our Lord will have to sanctify and cleanse his spouse 'with the washing of water by the word, that he might present it to himself a glorious church, not having spot, or wrinkle, or any such thing'. We are glad, I say, to have the experience of the spouse, that is, of the church as a whole, because we know that as is the church such are the members, and the rule that holds good for the whole will be found in its measure and proportion to be fulfilled in all its parts. We, too, have to say, 'I am black, because the sun hath looked upon me'; and at times we have to ask, 'Why should I be as one that turneth aside by the flocks of thy companions?' We have had mournfully to cry, 'I sought him, but I could not find him; I called him, but he gave me no answer'; while the watchmen have justly smitten us and wounded us for our neglect of our Lord. Let us bless God that in the book of revealed truth he has not merely given us the ideal standard after which we are to seek, but he has also preserved for us the humbler patterns of those who have striven to reach to the utmost height, and who have climbed a good way towards it, but who, nevertheless, have proved that, though they were the best of men, they were men at the best. Thus our Lord has saved us from despair by making us to know that we may be sincere and true and accepted, though we, too, fall short as yet of the holiness which we pant after with our whole hearts.

Nor are we alone favoured with the poetic story of the bride; we have also in the word of God the biographies of the saints, the memoirs of the godly, and these are exceedingly useful to us. I fear we should not, brethren, at certain times, know whether we were God's people at all if we were not able to compare ourselves with others of the family. We may lose our way sometimes as poor sheep have often done, and then though the greatest comfort is derived from seeing the footprints of the Shepherd, yet no small measure of consolation is to be gained through marking the footsteps of the flock. The sight of human footsteps on the sandy waste has caused us to take heart again. We have exclaimed, 'Here one has been who was surely a child of God, and though I am here I may be a child of God too. I have similar failings and weaknesses, and I chide myself for them; but I will not utterly condemn myself and say I cannot be a believer, for I perceive that these spots were on others of God's children too.' The perception of our likeness to others who were truly saints has often afforded us a spark of hope when we were in a maze, and dared scarcely hope that we were right towards God.

Frequently the experience of others will help us to thread our way when it winds and twists, and we cannot see an inch before us. The young man thinks that he understands himself, but no old man does so. Ask the man who is best acquainted with himself, and he will tell you that he is increasingly a riddle, and that his experience becomes an enigma more profound every day. The believer feels that he needs the help of the Divine Teacher to enable him to trace the thread of his spiritual life throughout all the tangle of the skein. It needs a grace-taught man to make himself out, and to comprehend what he is, and where he is, and what is the very truth of his life's paradox. At times I ask myself, 'Am I all sin, or is there yet a spark of grace?' Anon grace shines like the sun, and then I almost dream that sin is extinct. We are driven to read ourselves in others. We look at the saints of Holy Scripture, and as we mark their lives we say, 'I can understand this man better than I can myself; for lookers-on see more than the players; and now by understanding him, I begin also to comprehend my own position. I calculate my latitude and longitude by observing this star; I estimate the contending influences that rage within me by seeing how others drifted, or stemmed the torrent. I see the strange convolutions of my intertwisted soul in others, and, as in a glass, I discern myself.'

But, my brethren, we must take care that we do not wrongly use the memoirs of saints as recorded in Scripture; they are not all for our imitation, but many of them for our warning. You may not do all that a good man has done. If you were to copy certain of the actions of the most gracious men you would soon find yourself more faulty than they; for you would be sure to throw the emphasis upon their errors, but their graces you would probably miss; you would copy their faults and aggravate them. Follow no man where he does not follow Christ. Above all, the lives of the saints may never be used as an excuse for our faults. We shall not be justified in following afar off because Peter did so, nor in calling fire from heaven upon our enemies because James and John wished to do so, nor in quarrelling because Paul and Barnabas fell into sore contention. We may wisely quote David as an encouragement to a penitent, that God will forgive his sin; but not as an apology for ourselves should we be tempted to commit the sin. We must often use even the saints of God rather as beacons than as harbour-lights, as lighthouses set upon rocky coasts to advise us of the dangers into which they fell. Take care that Holy Scripture be used for holy ends, and that holy men are viewed as helps to holiness, and not as excuses for imperfection. Let us learn from their virtues imitation, from their faults warning, and from both instruction. Judgment is profitable to direct. Follow the Lamb whithersoever he goeth; but there is not a sheep of his flock to whom you may do the same. Do whatsoever Jesus does; copy the example of Christ in all its touches, so far as it is imitable, but do not the same even towards the beloved John, though his head be fresh from his Master's bosom; no, nor towards Paul, though he be not a whit behind the very chief of the apostles. Come we, then, dear friends, to use the example of our text, with those due limitations which we have thus set forth.

We have in the text, first, *slumber confessed* – 'I sleep'; but over against this there is *wakefulness claimed* – 'but my heart waketh'. Very soon we have *mystery solved* – how is it that the heart still keeps awake – 'It is the voice of my beloved that knocketh. Before we close we shall try, fourthly, to have *a lesson learned* out of the text. May the Holy Spirit make the whole subject profitable to us, and practically influential upon our lives.

First, then, here is SLUMBER CONFESSED. The spouse laments her state, and sighs out, 'I sleep'.

It strikes us at once that her sleep is *a state recognised.* We are astonished that she should say, 'I sleep', and we conclude that it is not so profound a sleep as it might be; for when a man can say, 'I sleep', he is not altogether steeped in slumber. When children of God perceive their own imperfections and mourn over them, there is evidently a root of virtue in them; when they perceive the decay of their grace there is some grace left undecayed with which they are bemoaning their decline. I would not give you encouragement, dear brother, if you are asleep at all to continue in it; but yet I would say this, that if you mourn over your sluggishness you are not altogether a sluggard, if you feel uneasy in your dulness you are not altogether given over to spiritual stupidity, if you are anxious to be aroused out of your slumber it is certain that you are not given over to sleep yourself into the sepulchre of insensibility. God be thanked that you cannot enjoy pleasant dreams upon the bed of carelessness. You do not sleep as do others; you are evidently not steeped in that fatal slumber of spiritual death in which the dead world is slumbering all around. Infinite mercy has had some dealings with you, and has made you so far to be spiritually awake that you can feel that you sleep, and mournfully confess it.

When a man detects pride within him but has grace enough to long to be humble, when a man feels hardness of heart but groans about it and wishes to be softened, when a man laments the stubbornness of his will and cries to God to give him full submission, when a man mourns a sluggishness of heart and strives after quickening – then he has marks and signs of spiritual life, and of an inward energy which will by God's grace cast out his disease and bring him spiritual health. There is life where there is pain; there is growth where there is a yearning of desire. The holy fire still lingers in the breast, though it be so smothered by the ashes that only a little smoke can be discerned; it will revive again, it will kindle and burn up, for it is of God's creating. He who can mournfully say, 'I sleep', will one day be wide awake. Be very thankful, therefore, when you have a tender conscience. Cultivate a quick perception, and when you are aware of the slightest defalcation or decline, confess at once to God that you begin to sleep.

Further, as this sleep is a matter recognised, so is it *a matter complained of.* The spouse is not pleased to sleep: she says, 'I sleep', but she does not mention it as a matter for congratulation. She is not pleased with her condition. Here again I would remark that it is well for saints, when they perceive that they are in the least degree backsliding, that they should mourn before God, and accuse themselves before him. 'Judge yourselves, that ye be not judged.' Before another person can hint that you are careless, find it out yourself and mourn over it. Before another can complain of your dulness and say, as the shipmen did to Jonah, 'What meanest thou, O sleeper?' complain you of yourself. Act tenderly to others, but severely towards yourselves. So all prudent men will do if God keep them prudent.

This sleepiness is not a thing to be indulged in, but to be abhorred. To say the least of it, *it is a low state of enjoyment*. Sleep is peaceful and quiet, but it cannot enjoy the sweets of the senses, and the delights which the mind can receive thereby. Sleep is cousin unto death, and he that slumbers lies at the door of the sepulchre. The image of death is set upon the sleeper's face, and it is a miracle, and a sort of foretaste of the resurrection, that any man doth wake again after he hath fallen into a deep slumber. It is not, therefore, good spiritually for us to be asleep, for then we cannot taste the honey of the Word, nor enjoy the fragrance of the ordinances, nor see the beauties of Christ, nor will any of the spiritual passions be delighted, nor our spirit be carried away with holy joy. Therefore when we come into God's house, and we hear the old familiar story of the cross, and it does not charm us, let us mournfully say, 'I sleep'. When others are ready to dance before the Lord with exultation while singing the solemn psalm, if we ourselves feel no devout gratitude, let us cry self-complainingly, 'I perceive that I sleep'; and when at the table the chosen emblems of the bread and wine do not bring the Master near to us, and we go away as hungry as we came, because we have not fed on his body and his blood, then let us say again, 'Alas, I sleep, I sleep; for these things would be most sweet and nourishing to me if my spiritual faculties were as they ought to be.' If we fail to enjoy the banquets of our Bridegroom's love it must be because a deadness is stealing over us, and we are not so thoroughly alive and awake as we were in days gone by; and this is a condition to be deplored as soon as it is perceived.

We ought to complain of ourselves if we sleep, because *it is a state of danger*. While men slept the enemy came and sowed tares among the wheat. It is bad, then, to have a drowsy minister and drowsy church officers, for these will not watch the fields for God. He who sleeps is in danger of the thief or the murderer. While Saul lay stretched on the plain, Abishai lifted up his spear and said, 'Let me smite him but this once.' He who sleeps may lose his all, yea, lose himself. Let us, therefore, dread this perilous state; and, if we feel it creeping over us, let us shake ourselves, and say, 'I sleep, but I will not give way to slumber. Lord, arouse me.'

Sleep is *a state of inaction*. A man cannot do his daily business while his eyes are closed in slumber. There is a somnambulism which can do much; but I know of no spiritual somnambulism. You cannot walk the road to heaven asleep, nor preach the gospel as you should, nor serve God and your generation aright, if you are in a spiritual slumber. I know a great many who are so; alive, I hope, but very sleepy. They do very little, they are too sluggish to attempt much. 'The slothful man saith, There is a lion in the way; a lion is in the streets.' This was his argument for keeping in the chimney-corner. In truth the lion is about as real as the monster which has been described of late as prowling over this county of Surrey and devouring women and children all the way from Banstead Downs to Clapham Common. Solomon seems to have been very familiar with this fable of the sluggard's lion, for in another proverb he makes the idler cry, 'There is a lion without. I shall be slain in the streets.' These poor creatures are so dreamy in spirit that they see a lion everywhere, threatening them if they try to do good in any form; they must needs sit quiet and still, and try to enjoy themselves as best their sleep will allow them to do, for they cannot venture out to work because of the lion. They cannot teach a little Sunday-school class, for there is a lion there! Nor go out to speak to a dozen people in a village: a furious lion is roaring there! In fact, they will be devoured if they leave their easy retirement and put their heads out of doors. God help us to escape this lazy condition. May we live while we live. Let not our souls merely act as salt to keep our carcasses from rottenness, but let them be the seed-plot and hotbed of holy actions out of which shall yet spring glory to God and blessing to our fellow men. If you do not feel active and energetic, make it a matter of self-complaint, and utter the shamefaced confession, 'I sleep'.

Yet again: this slumber should be regarded as not only a matter of complaint as an ill to be dreaded, but it should be regarded as *a fault to be ashamed of*. A Christian man should not say, 'I feel dull, careless, and inactive', and make the confession as if he almost deserved to be pitied for a misfortune which was no fault of his. My brother, you may be pitied, but you are also to be blamed, perhaps blamed far more than pitied. An apparent spiritual slumber may creep over us because the body is very weak and sickly, and here pity is allowable, yea, justly due. Certain states and conditions of the flesh no doubt will overcome the spirit, as when even the choicest of the apostles slept in the garden. The Master at first said, 'What, could ye not watch with me one hour?' but afterwards he made a generous excuse for them and said, 'The spirit truly is willing, but the flesh is weak.' Make excuses for others and let your Lord make excuses for you, but do not frame apologies on your own account. David writes in the psalm, 'I said, This is my infirmity.' Quite right, David, I dare say it was so; but the other day I said the same of myself, and ere long I answered to my conscience for it, for conscience asked, 'Is it not your sin as well as your infirmity?' I was compelled to divide the statement, nay, at last to withdraw the first part of it altogether and cry, 'God be merciful to me a sinner.' May we not be too ready to lay the blame of our impatience, our unbelief, or our hastiness upon the body when we ought to take all blame to ourselves. It is always safest to blame ourselves, and it is frequently dangerous to admit an excuse.

Still, sometimes dulness may be an infirmity. When a man is weary with a hard day's work, or with business that has cost him long care, and he kneels by his bedside at a very late hour to pray, and finds himself going to sleep, I do not think that his fault is a very grievous one. It is certainly not that dreadful sin which shall never be forgiven, either in this world or in that which is to come. When a man is brought very low by weakness of body, and he cannot on the Sabbath-day feel himself up to the mark in all respects, I do not think we should hold a church-meeting and turn him out; nor do I think that he should excommunicate himself. When a widowed spirit is broken with bereavement, when the husband is dead, when children or brothers have died, when parents have been snatched away, and the heart is very heavy, if the heart cannot rejoice in the Lord, it is a pity that it cannot, but there is a measure of infirmity as well as fault in the heaviness of the soul. In such cases good people may guardedly say with David, 'This is my infirmity.' May God help us when we feel such infirmities that we may speedily rise above them, being made strong in weakness, and being taught to glory in infirmities because the power of Christ doth rest upon us.

Again, I repeat it, for others we may put in the gentle word even as the Master did for his disciples, 'The spirit truly is willing, but the flesh is weak', but for ourselves we should rather use heart-searching and self-condemnation that we may make the bed of slumber thorny to our idle flesh. Brethren, when a Christian man's soul is heavy with slumber he ought to be ashamed. Think of who it is that loved us, even Jesus, the eternal Son of God. Has *he* loved us and can we ever be cold towards him? Then blush, and let the scarlet abide in the face! Think of what Jesus has done for us and what love he has manifested towards us. O Gethsemane! O Calvary! Are we thus redeemed, and after this does our love decline into slumber? Break, my heart! Break with indignation at thyself that such should be the case! And what is this time in which we live? A time in which all the powers of darkness are on the alert, raging to do evil and mischief. Are we sleeping now, when the adversary is daily making an attack upon us? When men are dying and are perishing by millions can it be that we slumber still? And such as we are, who do little enough when we are wide awake, and have little enough of power and ability; how is it that we can slumber? If we are lethargic should we not bow ourselves in the dust before God, and beseech him to have mercy upon us?

Furthermore, *it was an evil to be fought against*. When a man is obliged to say, 'I sleep', let him not content himself with sleeping on. Now is the time for much prayer: let him wrestle with this deadly foe till he is fully aroused. Falling into indifference on the road to heaven is something like sleeping on the vast plains of snow, where, if a man give away to the natural inclination to slumber which comes on through the intense cold, he may lie down and never rise again. Oh, take care, you that are looking for glory and eternal life, that you yield not to sleep, for your Master cometh, and it may be that within another hour you may hear the midnight cry.

Let us whip ourselves with a strong resolve that we will not sleep. Let us say unto our soul, 'Come, wake up! My spirit, thou shalt not sleep. This cannot be. I must not have it, I will not, I dare not. I will goad thee, I will crucify thee to the cross, for thou shalt not slay thyself with suicidal slumber.' With this resolve let us seek out means of waking ourselves up. Sometimes we may do well to seek for a better ministry than we have attended. Alas, there are ministries which are as cradles to rock babes to sleep in. There are preachers who charm most wisely if their intent be to send the universe to sleep. Beware of preaching which comforts you in idleness and increases your spiritual insensibility. There are certain preachers who mar the gospel, and tell their tale so heartlessly that methinks if all heaven did rock and reel with tempest a man might yet sleep on so long as such soothing voices lulled his ears. We cannot afford to waste our Sabbaths in listening to another gospel, or in hearing lullabies which make us duller than we were. But if you cannot reach a rousing ministry, read good books: turn to solid gospel treatises such as the Puritans bequeathed us. Search the Scriptures, and the works of godly men whose words were all on fire; these thrown upon your soul like burning coals may set it on a blaze. Christian converse, too, is another useful means of keeping us awake. John Bunyan mentions that in going over the Enchanted Ground the pilgrims, to prevent drowsiness, fell into good discourse. Here is his quaint rhyme about it:

> When saints do sleepy grow, let them come hither
> And hear how these two pilgrims talk together:
> Yea, let them learn of them in any wise,
> Thus to keep ope their drowsy, slumb'ring eyes,
> Saints' fellowship, if it be managed well,
> Keeps them awake, and that in spite of hell.

Imitate this example, but if discourse does not avail, get to work for Christ. This is a very effective way of keeping yourself awake, God the Holy Spirit blessing you in it. In looking after the souls of others your own soul will receive a watering. I do not think that soul-slumber so often visits the active as it does those who have little to do in the Master's service. If active service does not suffice, then cry mightily to God, 'I sleep, my Saviour; awake me, I pray thee!' You are half awake already, if you can cry in that fashion. Cry again, 'I sleep, my Lord. Use even a rod upon me to wake me rather than I should slumber.' You are not asleep, brother, you are already awakened: the bitter anguish of the soul in its horror of its own slumber has already been blessed of God to its arousing.

Anyhow, this sleep is *an evil which must be overcome*. Come, make up your minds today, members of this church, that you will not yield to drowsiness. I hope none of you are inclined to say, 'Well, I may get to heaven in this sleepy way, and so what matters it? My fellow members would put me in the ambulance and carry me along like a wounded soldier, and this will be easier than marching at the double day after day.' No, no, my brother, we have enough of the invalided and wounded already. We have as many as we can carry of the non-effectives. We need no more. Ask the blessed Physician to make you strong, that you may tug at the guns with the rest of us, or charge the enemy at bayonet point when the trumpet sounds. I said years ago I would sooner lead a dozen real live earnest Christians than a dozen hundred of the half-and-half sort, and this feeling grows with me. I would almost as soon not be a Christian as be as some Christians are: they have enough religion to make them uncomfortable, but not enough to make them useful. They drink such shallow draughts that they increase their responsibility rather than their energy. Oh for a deep draught of grace which shall fill us with all the fulness of God, and make us men in Christ to the utmost capacity of our sanctified manhood. Cold meat may be pleasant, but cold religion is an ill dish to serve to Christ or to ourselves either. God make us like those creatures that are said to live in the fire. May he fill us with his own Spirit, and make us to burn and blaze with an unquenchable heat of love towards him of whom it is said that the zeal of God's house did eat him up. He poured out his soul unto death that he might redeem us to himself; let us see to it that we are altogether his own. With this I leave the sleeping for another theme.

We reach the point of the paradox; **here is WATCHFULNESS CLAIMED by one who confessed to sleep**. 'My heart waketh,' says the Bride, 'I sleep, but my heart waketh.' It may seem an odd thing to sleep and yet to be awake, but I commenced by saying that the Christian is a great puzzle. Ralph Erskine's *Believer's Riddle* is a remarkable production, but every word of it may be justified by experience and by Scripture. A man is a mass of contradictions, but a man in Christ is far more so. He truly says:

I'm in my own and other's eyes
A labyrinth of mysteries.

We are asleep and awake at the same time. As Erskine rhymes it:

Both sleeping flesh I have, that rests
In sloth unto my shame,
And waking grace, that still protests
Against this lazy frame.

There is an inner life within every Christian which can never die, and there is about him an inward death which can never rise to life. Jesus said, 'The water that I shall give him shall be in him a well of water springing up into everlasting life'; hence this divine life, though it may grow weak and feeble, and slumbering, yet never passes into the condition of absolute death, or even of complete insensibility. Somewhat of heaven is about the man of God when the earth encompasses him most. 'Sin shall not have dominion over you': God has the throne still, even when Satan rages most. This inward life shows itself usually in the *uneasiness* of the declining heart. When a believer feels that he is not what he ought to be, nor what he wants to be, he cannot be happy. He cannot rest and be content. There was a time when such a condition would have satisfied him, but now he is distressed beyond measure, and, like Noah's dove, finds no rest for the sole of his food. Hear him sing in the minor key:

Where is the blessedness I knew
When first I saw the Lord?
Where is the soul-refreshing view
Of Jesus and his Word?

What peaceful hours I then enjoy'd!
How sweet their memory still!
But they have left an aching void
The world can never fill.

He sleeps, but his heart beats, sighs, and palpitates with dire unrest.

The inner life shows itself, too, in *desire*, for the heart is the seat of desire, and it leads the man to say, 'I am not what I would be. I live at a poor dying rate: Christ's love is so great to me, and mine to him so chill. Lord, lift me out of this frozen state. I cannot bear this grave of lethargy. Lord, bring my soul out of prison! Give me more grace; give me to love Jesus better, and to be more like him. Poor as I am, I long to be enriched by thy love and mercy; O visit me with thy salvation!' Such a pleading heart is still awake, though the mind may be dull. The Lord judges us by our earnest desires more than by our accomplishments. An old writer says, if you send a man on horseback for the doctor, if the horse be a sorry jade that cannot move quickly you praise the man when you see him whipping and spurring and doing his best to hasten. You do not blame him for that which is beyond his power. So saith he – oftentimes when our desires do whip and spur our languid spirits God sees what a rate we would go at if we could, and he takes the will for the deed. Often our desires are so aroused that we would harness the lightning and bit the tempest if we could, and spur both to a swifter speed. Desires prove wakefulness; 'I sleep, but my heart waketh.'

The spouse gave another proof of her wakefulness by her *discernment*. She says, 'It is the voice of my beloved, that knocketh.' Even when half sleep she knew her Lord's voice. You may catch a true believer at his worst, but he still knows the gospel from anything else, and can detect another gospel in a moment. You shall come forth with all your eloquence, your poetry and sweet concocted phrases, with a something that is not the gospel of the blessed God, and you shall for a moment please the ear of the Christian, because of the literary excellence of your address, but he soon detects you. It is true of all Christ's sheep, 'A stranger will they not follow, for they know not the voice of strangers.' The awakening believer soon perceives that the most musical voice of a stranger has not the charm in it which is found in the voice of his Lord. Yea, he soon closes his ear to it in disgust and in holy trembling lest he should be deceived. His resolve is, 'I will hear what God the Lord will speak.' He determines to be deaf to other voices, but to his Redeemer he saith, 'Speak, Lord, for thy servant heareth.' Blessed is he who in his dullest state can still discern and discriminate and cry, 'It is the voice of my beloved.'

This wakefulness of heart shows itself often in the soul *chiding* itself. 'I sleep,' saith she. She would not have blamed herself as I have tried to describe her doing if she had not been in some measure awake.

This blessed living wakefulness within the heart will by-and-by display itself in *action*. The heart will wake up all that is within us, and we shall hasten to our Beloved. It is wonderful how a true Christian flies back to his God so soon as the Spirit of the Lord sets him free from the net. 'Whom have I in heaven but thee, and there is none upon earth that I desire beside thee.' Brethren, you and I cannot rest anywhere short of Christ. When we were ravens we could rest on our own wings, or on the carrion of this world, but now that we have been made doves we must seek our Noah and his ark. A friend at the back of this Tabernacle furnished me with some pigeons but a little while ago. They were taken home to Norwood, and shut up for a few days, and well fed, in the hope that they would stay with us; but no sooner were they set at liberty than they soared aloft, made three circles in the sky, and then flew direct for this spot. How I wished on my sick bed that I had their wings, and could hasten hither too. It is so with believers. The devil may put us in captivity and shut us up a while, but give us the opportunity and our heart knows the way back to Jesus. The spouse hath dove's eyes, and she seeth from afar: she makes short work of it, and is back again with all the speed of the chariots of Amminadib.

This puzzle of 'I sleep, by my heart waketh' has been experienced by thousands. I quote no solitary instances, there are hundreds of the same. I lately met with a little poem by Thomas Vaughan, which touched my heart, because it so aptly described my state. I will read it, to show you that the paradox of a believer's life is no fiction of mine, but is the frequent experience of God's people. In a little out-of-the-way poem, which perhaps no one of you has ever seen, Vaughan quaintly sings:

My sweetest Jesus! 'twas thy voice, 'If I
Be lifted up I'll draw all to the sky.'
Yet I am here: I'm stifled in the clay,
Shut up from thee, and the fresh East of day.
I know thy hand's not short; but I'm unfit,
A foul, unclean thing! to take hold of it.
I am all dirt: nor can I hope to please
Unless in mercy thou lov'st a disease.
Diseases may be cur'd, but who'll reprieve
Him that is dead? Tell me, my God, I live.
'Tis true, I live: but I so sleep withal
I cannot move, scarce hear when thou dost call,
Sin's lullabies charm me when I would come,
But draw me after thee, and I will run.
Thou know'st I'm sick: let me not feasted be,
But keep a diet, all prescrib'd by thee.
Should I carve for myself, I would exceed
To surfeits soon, and by self-murder bleed.
I ask for stones and scorpions, but still crost
And all for love: should'st thou grant, I were lost.
Dear Lord, deny me still: and never sign
My will, but when that will agrees with thine.
And when this conflict's past, and I appear
To answer, what a patient I was here,
How I did weep when thou did'st woo: repine
At thy best sweets, and in a childish whine
Refuse thy proffer'd love; yet cry and call,

For rattles of my own to play withal:
Look on thy cross and let thy blood come in
When mine shall blush as guilty of my sin.
Then shall I live, being rescued in my fall,
A text of mercy to thy creatures all.
Who having seen the worst of sins in me,
Must needs confess, the best of love's in thee.

Does not this writer dip his pen into your soul's sorrows?
3. Spare me a minute or two while I dwell on the head of MYSTERY SOLVED. 'I sleep, but my heart waketh.' How doth her heart wake? It is because the voice and knock of her Beloved are heard. Every child of God has a wondrous union with Christ. 'Because I live,' saith Christ, 'ye shall live also.' Ask you why you are alive in such a body of death and grave of sin as your poor nature is? You live because Christ lives; and you cannot die till he does. This is why you cannot sleep as do others, because he does not sleep. 'He that keepeth Israel shall neither slumber nor sleep', and till Christ's spiritual life shall altogether slumber out into forgetfulness and inaction yours never shall. The mystic union between yourselves and him secures you from destruction, which apart from him would sweep you away as with a besom. This is why, dear friends, when you get where you should not be, you cannot be happy because Jesus is not happy when you are there. He groans over your follies; they cost him wounds and bloody sweat and death, and they must cost you something, too, if you indulge them. That field all tangled with the brambles tore the Shepherd when he sought you out, and the briars will tear you also if you wander there. The reason why you are awake at all is because Jesus calls you. His voice rings in your ears through his Word both heard and read. He more than calls, he knocks at your heart by affliction, by mercy, by warning, by comfort. He will do more with you yet if you are his; he will put in his hand by the hole of the door, and then you shall open to him and he will come and sup with you and you with him. The mystery is all solved, the saint would be a sinner if it were not that he is one with the sinner's Saviour; the living believer would be a lump of death and corruption if it were not that he is one with him who is the resurrection and the life, who hath said, 'whosoever believeth in me shall never die' and again, 'though he were dead yet shall he live'. What a blessing is this vital union with the ever-blessed Head, immortal and unslumbering!

4. Now for THE LESSON LEARNED. It is this, *be very careful when you possess great joys*, for in this instance the spouse had been with the Beloved in choice fellowship, and yet was soon drowsy. He had given her to drink abundantly, and he had feasted with her, but no sooner had the sun set than she said, 'I sleep'. We are singular creatures. Our very perfect brethren, although they do not see it, generally exhibit some glaring imperfection if you let them talk for five minutes. If you knock at the door to see if Mr Pride is at home, you need not praise them long before he will show his full-length portrait. We are thankful for these brethren so far as they are saints, for good people are scarce; but I wish they would not tell us so much about their saintliness, for I have noticed that great cry often goes with little wool, and the noisiest thing that goes down the street is the dust-cart. He who makes most noise about his own perfection has the least of it. Let us be careful whenever we rise to the summit of the hill; careful to keep up, careful that we so act when we are up that we do not come down with a run. Whenever the Lord visits you entertain him right heartily. Be careful that nothing grieves him, lest he depart. High joys may produce slumber; the chosen three upon the mount Tabor were soon overcome with heaviness. At the too transporting sight of the transfigured Saviour darkness covered them. Mind what you do when on the mount; be careful to carry a full cup with a steady hand.

Next, *when you are blaming yourselves for your own work, do not forget the work of the Spirit in you.* 'I sleep': smite your heart for that, but do not forget to add if it be true, 'My heart waketh'. Bless God for any grace you have, even if it be but little. What if I am not sanctified as I wish to be and shall be, yet I am perfectly justified! What if I do not exhibit my Father's likeness so completely as I hope to do, yet I am his child! What if as yet I do not produce all the fruits of the Spirit, yet I have the germs of them, the buds and the blossoms, and soon I shall have the ripe fruit. In Aaron's rod we see that the same power that could put the buds and blossoms on a dry stick could put the almonds there too.

Lastly, *make sure above all things that you have that true faith which knows the voice of Jesus.* The spouse had not awaked if it had not been for the charm of Jesus' voice which affected even her drowsy faculties. Some persons can be more easily awakened by the voices of those they love than by any other means. The charm of memory, the charm of intimate affection, the charm of delight, gives music to some tongues: let your ear find all its music in the voice of Jesus. Know his voice. He saith, 'Incline your ear, and come unto me: hear, and your soul shall live. My sheep hear my voice, and I know them, and they follow me, and I give unto them eternal life.' God bless you, dear friends, with a faith that trusts Jesus, knows his voice, and follows him, and may we be aroused out of all our sleepiness, if we are at all drowsy, into a holy wakefulness, so as to serve the Lord our God with all our heart and soul and strength while we live. Come, Holy Spirit, and give us this privilege, for Jesus' sake. Amen.

34

NEARER AND DEARER

'I sleep, but my heart waketh: it is the voice of my beloved that knocketh, saying, Open to me, my sister, my love, my dove, my undefiled: for my head is filled with dew, and my locks with the drops of the night. I have put off my coat; how shall I put it on? I have washed my feet; how shall I defile them? My beloved put in his hand by the hole of the door, and my bowels were moved for him. I rose up to open to my beloved; and my hands dropped with myrrh, and my fingers with sweet-smelling myrrh, upon the handles of the lock. I opened to my beloved; but my beloved had withdrawn himself, and was gone: my soul failed when he spake: I sought him, but I could not find him; I called him, but he gave me no answer. The watchmen that went about the city found me, they smote me, they wounded me; the keepers of the walls took away my veil from me. I charge you, O daughters of Jerusalem, if ye find my beloved, that ye tell him, that I am sick of love' (Song of Solomon 5:2-8).

The most healthy state for a Christian is that of unbroken and intimate fellowship with the Lord Jesus Christ. From such a state of heart he should never decline. 'Abide in me, and I in you' is the loving precept of our ever loving Lord. But, alas! my brethren, as in this world our bodies are subject to many sicknesses, so our souls also, by reason of the body of this death with which we are encompassed, are often sorely afflicted with sin, sickness and an evil heart of unbelief in departing from the Lord. We are not what we might be, we are not what we should be, we are not what we shall be, we are not what we wish to be. I fear that many of us are not walking in the light of God's countenance, are not resting with our heads upon the Saviour's bosom, nor sitting with Mary at the Master's feet; we dwell in Kedar rather than Zion, and sojourn in Mesech rather than Jerusalem.

Spiritual sickness is very common in the church of God, and the root of the mischief lies in distance from Jesus, following Christ afar off, and yielding to a drowsy temperament. Away from Jesus, away from joy. Without the sun the flowers pine; without Jesus our hearts faint. My object, this morning, is to put myself into the hands of the Holy Spirit that he may now come, and, like a physician, prescribe for you, that if any of you in your hearts have become like the spouse in this part of the Song, you may as fully imitate her in that which is good as in that which is blameworthy. If you do not soon find your Beloved to your soul's joy, may you at least, like the spouse declare that you are 'sick of love', and continue to follow his track until you overtake him.

(1) Commencing where the text begins, **we observe that the spouse confesses A VERY COMMON SIN**: she cries, '*I sleep*'.

She had no right to be asleep, for her Beloved knew no rest. He was standing without in the cold street, with his head wet with dew, and his locks with the drops of the night; why should she be at ease? He was anxiously seeking her, how was it that she could be so cruel as to yield to slumber? It is a most unseasonable thing, my brethren and sisters, for any of us to be indolent and indifferent, for we profess to have gone forth to meet the Bridegroom, and it is shameful for us to sleep because for a little while he tarries.

The world is perishing. We are sent into the world instrumentally to be its saviours – how dishonourable, that with such necessities for activity, and with such noble ends to be served by industry, we should fold our arms and delight ourselves in indolence! Nothing can be more inexcusable than for us to sleep, seeing that we are not of the night nor of darkness.

If we had been the children of the night, it might seem according to our nature for us to be sluggards; but we have avowed that the light of the glory of God in the face of Jesus Christ has shone into our eyes. Let us not therefore sleep as do others, but let us watch and be sober, for they that sleep, sleep in the night; and since the night is past to us, it is highly indecent and improper that we should still continue to toss upon the bed of sloth.

No time for slumber, it seems to me, can be more unseasonable to the Christian than the present one, for the world is reeking with wickedness, and superstitions like the frogs of Egypt are covering the land. Everyone who is but so much as half awake can see the enemy industriously sowing tares among the wheat. Shall the watchmen of Zion continue to slumber on their watchtowers when the foe is undermining the bulwarks? Shall the shepherds sleep when the wolf has broken into the fold? Shall the seamen sleep when the gale is furiously driving the vessel upon the rocks?

So far as our own hearts are concerned, we have no private reasons for slumbering, for our daily cares require watchfulness, the temptations which assail us every hour demand of us that we should stand with our loins girt, and our abounding enemies all warn us that our danger is extreme unless we are always fully equipped in our celestial armour.

If we must sleep, let it be in a less dangerous position than these hostile lands, through which we march today; there will be rest enough on the other side of Jordan, where the drawn sword is exchanged for the well-tuned harp; but to be careless now is to sleep in the midst of a bloody conflict, to dream upon the verge of a precipice, and to sport in the jaws of death. From our beds let the Master's voice arouse us, for he cries aloud, 'What I say unto you I say unto all, Watch.'

Do you not find, my brethren, that almost unconsciously to yourselves, a spirit of indifference steals over you? You do not give up private prayer, but alas! it becomes a mere mechanical operation. You do not forsake the assembling of yourselves together, but still your bodily presence is all that is given, and you derive no refreshment from the unspiritual exercise. Have you not sat at the Lord's table spiritually asleep? Has not the heavenly watcher detected your soul nodding when the sacred emblems have been spread before you, or even in your mouth? Have you not been content with the bare symbols, which are barrenness, while the spiritual essence, which is marrow and fatness, you have not tasted?

I find from the very fact that I am always engaged in the Master's service from the early morning till far into the night, that I become dull and carnal, being cumbered with much serving, so that I have to question the vitality of my religion because its freshness and vigour flag. It is grievous to go on like a clock which is wound up, not because you rejoice in the work, but because you must. My soul shudders at the thought of routine religion, formal service, dead devotion, mechanical godliness. What a mercy to reach the fresh springs, to feel a daily renewed youth, an anointing with fresh oil! For this I pine and pant.

One gets driving on in the dark, as coachmen sometimes do when they are asleep on the box: dangerous work, this! I know that I am safe in Christ, but I could fain suffer anything rather than become habitually of a slumbering heart. Better smart under the long whip of affliction, or feel the stings of conscience, or even the darts of the devil, than lie down in carnal security's lap to be shorn of one's locks by the Philistines; yet I fear this has been my case. I do not know how far my confession may be echoed by my brethren today, but I am shrewdly suspicious that the more wakeful you are, the more heartily will you acknowledge a terrible tendency in the other direction.

Again let me remind you that to sleep now is an evil thing, dangerous to yourselves, a cruel thing to others, an ungrateful act towards Christ, and dishonourable to his cause. Shall such a King be served by lie-a-bed soldiers? Shall his midnight pleadings be repaid by our daylight sleepiness? Shall an agony of blood sweat be recompensed by heavy eyelids and yawning mouths? Away, for ever away, O ye who are redeemed by the Well-beloved, with this detestable slumber, of which I fear you must honestly confess yourselves to have been guilty!

(2) The song before us reminds us of A HOPEFUL SIGN – '*My heart waketh.*'

What a riddle the believer is! He is asleep and yet he is awake. His true self, the I, the veritable *Ego* of the man is asleep, but yet his heart, his truest self, his affections, are awake. The believer is a standing paradox; he cannot even understand himself. The wakefulness of the heart, does it not mean just this: 'I sleep, but I am not content to be asleep'? The true believer is not satisfied to slumber. Time was when, if he could have pacified his conscience, he would have been extremely thankful, however deadly might have been the drug which caused the slumber, but now the man starts, shivers, tosses to and fro in his sleep, is unrested by his rest, dreams horribly, and cries to be awakened. The saved man cannot be happy in a false and rotten peace. The divine life within struggles against the monstrous serpent of sin which tries to twist its folds of sleep around it. No renewed heart can enjoy perfect rest while conscious of being an idler in the vineyard, and a loiterer in the race.

Backsliding believer, does you heart wake? If so, you will know it, for it will smite you, it will upbraid you, and demand of you whom thou art, that thou shouldst thus behave thyself? Elect of God, and yet asleep while Jesus is dishonoured! Redeemed by blood, and yet misspending time which belongs to thy Redeemer! Married to Christ, and yet absent from thy Husband, and content without a smile from his dear face! How can it be? Be ashamed and be confounded, and never show thy face any more, for this is ingratitude of the deepest dye.

It is a hopeful sign when a man can conscientiously say as much as the spouse in this case, but remember it is not much to say. Do not pride yourself upon it. Be ashamed that you should be asleep at all. Do not congratulate yourself that your heart is awake. Be thankful that infinite love affords you grace enough to keep your heart alive, but be ashamed that you have no more when more *may* be had and *should* be had. Mere longings and moanings are so small a work of grace, that they should alarm rather than console. It will be a foul temptation of Satan if you are led to say, 'I am content to sleep so long as my heart does but wake.' Firm resolves of amendment are needful, and something more than resolves. Alas! I have need to add those few words, because the most of our resolutions vanish in thin air. We get as far as this, 'I am not quite content to be in such a lukewarm state of mind, and I will therefore by-and-by endeavour to arouse myself, and renounce this downy bed of sloth.' This is not much to say, for it is no more than we ought to do, it is all the less, because we so seldom keep the vow, but like the disturbed sluggard, we turn over to the other side and mutter sullenly, 'A little more folding of the hands to sleep.'

I fear me that there are thousands of God's children who are enough awake to know that they are asleep, enough convinced of their wrong to know that they are wrong, and to hope that they will one day be better, but alas! they continue in the same unhallowed condition. May I invite every believer to make a strict examination of his own spiritual state.

My brother, you may be sleeping through great worldly prosperity, for nothing tends to slumber more surely than a gentle rocking in the cradle of luxury. On the other hand, you may be sleeping because of overwhelming sorrow, even as the twelve fell asleep when our Lord was in the garden. Some make a downy pillow of their wealth, but others fall asleep in their poverty, like Jacob with a stone for his pillow. To be surrounded with constant worldly occupation, to be oppressed with many cares in business, this is to pass through the enchanted ground; and happy is the man who has grace enough to overcome the influence of his position.

Now, if your heart today is sufficiently awake to tell you that you are not living as near to God as you were some years ago, that you have not the love to him you once had, that your warmth and zeal for Christ has departed from you, I beseech you to hear the voice of Jesus Christ: 'As many as I love, I rebuke and chasten: be zealous therefore, and repent.' 'Repent and do thy first works.' Turn unto your Saviour now, that this very day ere the sun goeth down you may rejoicingly exclaim, 'I have found him whom my soul loveth; I will hold him, and will not let him go.'

The third thing in the text is A LOVING CALL.

Asleep as the spouse was, she knew her Husband's voice, for this is an abiding mark of God's people: 'My sheep hear my voice.' A half sleeping saint still has spiritual discernment enough to know when Jesus speaks.

At first the Beloved one simply *knocked.* His object was to enter into fellowship with his church, to reveal himself to her, to unveil his beauties, to solace her with his presence. Such is the object of our blessed Lord, this morning, in bringing us to this house. I hope this sermon will be a knock: I trust my discourse may give many knocks at the door of every backsliding believer here. Jesus cries, 'Open to me! Open to me!' Will you not admit your Saviour? Thou lovest him. He gave himself for thee, he pleads for thee: let him in to thy soul, commune with him this morning.

When you turn to read his Word, every promise is a knock. He saith, 'Come and enjoy this promise with me, for it is yea and amen in me.' Every threatening is a knock. Every precept is a knock. In outward providences every boon which we receive through our Mediator's intercession is a gentle knock from his pierced hand, saying, 'Take this mercy, but open to me! It comes to you through me; open to me!' Every affliction is a knock at our door; that wasting sickness, that broken bone, that consumptive daughter, that rebellious child, that burning house, that shipwrecked vessel, and dishonoured bill – all these are Christ's knockings, saying, 'These things are not your joys, these worldly things can afford no rest for the sole of your foot; open to me, open to me! These idols I am breaking, these joys I am removing; open to me, and find in me a solace for all your woes.'

Knocking, alas! seems to be of little use to us. We are so stubborn, and so ungenerous towards our heavenly Bridegroom, that he, the crucified, the immortal lover of our souls may stand and knock, and knock, and knock again, and the preacher and adversity may be his double hammer, but yet the door of the heart will not yield.

Then the Bridegroom tried his voice. If knocking would not do, he would *speak* in plain and plaintive words, 'Open to me, my sister, my love, my dove, my undefiled.' The Lord Jesus Christ has a sweet way of making the Word come home to the conscience; I mean, not now, that effectual and irresistible power of which we shall speak by-and-by, but that lesser force which the heart may resist, but which renders it very guilty for so doing.

Some of you who are the Lord's people, have heard soft and sweet whispers in your heart, saying, 'You are saved; now, my beloved, live in the light of salvation. You are a member of my mystical body, draw near and enjoy fellowship with me, such as a member ought to have with its Head.' Do you not see the Lord Jesus beckoning to you with gentle finger, and saying, 'Come with me oftener into the closet of secret prayer; get oftener alone to muse on things divine; acquire the habit of walking with me in your business. Abide in me, and I in you'? Do not these admonitions visit you like angels' whispers, and have you not too often resisted them? Have you not been thoughtful for them for the moment, and recorded them in your diary, and then forgotten them and lived as frigidly as you had done before, though the Sun of Righteousness was waiting to arise upon you with healing beneath his wings?

Now, beloved, observe the appeals which the Beloved here makes. He says, 'Open to me', and his plea is the love the spouse has to him, or professes to have, the love he has to her, and the relationship which exists between them.

'Open to me, my *sister*.' Next akin to me, bone of my bone, flesh of my flesh, born of the same mothers'; for Jesus is 'the seed of the woman', even as we are. One with us in our humanity, he takes each human heart that believeth to be his mother and sister and brother. 'Open to me, my sister.' If you are so nearly related to Jesus, why do you act so coldly towards him? If, indeed, he be your closest kinsman, how is it that you live so far remote, and come not to visit him, neither open the doors of your heart to entertain him?

'*My dove*', my gentle one, my favourite, my innocent. Oh, if you be indeed his dove, how can you rest away from the dovecote? How can you be satisfied without your mate? One turtle pines without the other, how is it thou dost not pine to have fellowship with the dear Husband of thy soul?

'*My love*', Jesus calls us what we profess to be. We say we love him; yes, and unless we have been dreadfully deceived, we do love him. It brings the water into my eyes to think of it that I should so often be indifferent to him, and yet I can say it as before him, 'Thou knowest all things, thou knowest that I love thee.' Men and brethren, if we love him, let us crave his presence in our souls. How miserable must it be to live, as some do day after day, without a real soul-stirring heaven-moving prayer. Are there not some who continue week after week without searching the Word, and without rejoicing in the Lord? Oh, wretched life of banishment from bliss! Dear hearer, can you be satisfied to go forth into the world, and to be so occupied with it, that you never have a desire towards heaven? If so, mourn over such backsliding, since it exiles you from your best Beloved's bosom.

The Bridegroom adds another title, '*my undefiled*'. There is a spiritual chastity which every believer must maintain; our heart belongs to no-one but to Christ. All other lovers must be gone; he fills the throne. He has bought us; no other paid a part of the price; he shall have us altogether. He has taken us into personal union with himself; of his mystical body we make up a part; we ought, therefore, to hold ourselves as chaste virgins unto Christ, undefiled with the pollutions of the flesh and the rivalries of earthly loves. To the undefiled Jesus says, 'Open to me.'

Oh! I am ashamed, this morning, to be preaching from such a text, ashamed of myself most of all, that I should need to have such a text applied to my own soul. Why, beloved, if Christ deigns to enter into such a poor miserable cottage as our nature is, ought we not to entertain the King with the best we have, and feel that the first seat at our table is all too poor and too mean for him? What if in the midst of this dark night our Beloved comes to us who profess to love him, shall he have to knock and speak and plead by every sweet and endearing title, and yet shall we refuse to arise and give him the fellowship he craves?

Did you notice that powerful argument with which the heavenly lover closed his cry? He said, 'My head is filled with dew, and my locks with the drops of the night.' Ah, sorrowful remembrances, for those drops were not the ordinary dew that fall upon the houseless traveller's unprotected head. His head was wet with scarlet dew, and his locks with crimson drop of a tenfold night of God's desertion, when he 'sweat as it were great drops of blood falling down to the ground'. My heart, how vile art thou, for thou shuttest out the Crucified. Behold the Man thorn-crowned and scourged, with traces of the spittle of the soldiery, canst thou close the door on him? Wilt thou despise the 'despised and rejected of men'? Wilt thou grieve the 'Man of sorrows, and acquainted with grief'? Dost thou forget that he suffered all this for thee, for thee, when thou deservest nothing at his hands? After all this, wilt thou give him no recompense, not even the poor return of admission to thy loving communings?

I am afraid some of you believers think it a very small thing to live a day or two without fellowship with God in prayer. Probably you have fallen into such a sleepy state that you can read your Bible without enjoyment, and yet you do not feel it to be any very remarkable thing that it is so. You come to and fro to the Tabernacle and listen to the gospel, and it does not come home to you with the power it once had, and yet you do not feel at all alarmed about it. My Master does not treat your state of mind with the same indifference that you do, for it causes him pain, and though as Mediator his expiatory griefs are finished once for all, yet he has anguish still over your indifference and coldness of heart; these sorrows are the drops that bedew his head, these are the dewdrops that hang about his raven locks. O will ye grieve him, will ye open all his wounds and crucify him afresh, and put him to an open shame? Doors of the heart, fly open! Though rusted upon your hinges, open ye at the coming of the sorrowful Lover who was smitten of God and afflicted. Surely the argument of his grief should prevail instanter with every honest heart; he whose head is wet with dew, and his locks with the drops of the night, must not be kept standing in the street, it behoves that he be entertained with our warmest love, it is imperative that he be housed at once.

(4) Yet the spouse hastened not to open the door, and I am afraid the like delay may be charged upon some of us. Our shame deepens as we pursue our theme, and think how well our own character is photographed here by the wise man; for notice, in the fourth place, that **after the knocking and the pleading, the spouse made A MOST UNGENEROUS EXCUSE**.

She sat like a queen and knew no sorrow. She had put off her garments and washed her feet as travellers do in the East before they go to rest. She was taking her ease in full security, and therefore she said to her Beloved, 'I have put off my tunic, I cannot robe myself again. As for my feet, I have washed them, and to tread the floor to open the door would defile them; therefore, I pray thee have me excused.' A bad excuse was in this case far worse than none, because it was making one sin an apology for another.

Why did she put off her coat? The bridegroom had not come; she should have stood with her loins girt about, and her lamp trimmed. Why had she washed her feet? It was right to do so if the emblem had indicated purity, but it indicated carnal ease. She had left holy labour for carnal rest. Why did she so? She thus makes her wicked slumber and inaction to be an excuse for barring out her Husband.

My dear brethren and sisters, there is a temptation which is very cunning on the part of Satan, and perhaps he will exercise that upon some of you this morning. While I have been preaching, you have said, 'Well, that is just like me. The text fully opens up my experience'; and the devil will then say, 'Be satisfied; you see you are just in the same condition as the spouse was, therefore it is all right.' Oh, damnable temptation! What can be more vile than this, that because another has sinned against the Beloved, I am to be content to sin in the same way!

Perhaps you will turn this sad course of conduct in the ancient spouse into an excuse for your own negligence. Shall I English the excuse she made? It is this: 'O Lord, I know that if I am to enter into much fellowship with thee, I must pray very differently from what I have done of late. But it is too much trouble; I cannot stir myself to energy so great. My time is so taken up with my business, I am so constantly engaged that I could not afford even a quarter of an hour for retirement. I have to cut my prayers so short.' Is this the miserable excuse in part? Shall I go on? Shall I tell out more of this dishonourable apology?

It is this: 'I do not want to begin an examination of myself: it may reveal so many unpleasant truths. I sleep, and it is very comfortable to sleep; I do not want to be driven out of my comforts. Perhaps if I were to live nearer to Christ, I should have to give up some of the things which I so much enjoy. I have become conformed to the world of late; I am very fond of having Mr So-and-so to spend an hour with me in the evening, and his talk is anything but that which my Master would approve of, but I cannot give him up. I have taken to read religious novels. I could not expect to have the Lord Jesus Christ's company when I am poring over such trash as that, but still I prefer it to my Bible; I would sooner read a fool's tale than I would read of Jesus' love.'

How ashamed I feel this morning, to have to put it into words like these, the sins of some of you, but my words are literal truth. Do not many of you live as if you had a name to live, and were dead?

Jesus Christ comes and knocks this morning and reminds you that the happiest life is living near to him, that the holiest, purest, sweetest hours you ever had were those in which you threw yourselves upon him, and gave up all beside. He reminds you of your better days.

O do not, I pray you, offer him excuses frivolous and vexatious. O despise not your Lord who died for you, in whose name you live, with whom you hope to reign for ever, who is to wrap you about with glory in the day of his appearing. Let it not be said that he is pushed into a corner, and his love despised, while the vile painted-faced world takes up the love of your life. It should not be so; it is baseness itself on our part when it is so.

Still as a wonder of wonder, although shamefully and cruelly treated, the beloved Husband did not go away. We are told that he 'put in his hand by the hole of the door', and then the bowels of his spouse were moved for him. In the Eastern door there is generally a place near the lock into which a man may put his hand, and there is a pin inside which, if removed, unfastens the door. Each one of these locks is different from another, so that no-one usually understands how to open the door except the master. So the

Master in this case did not actually open the door – you notice the spouse did that, but he pulled out the pin, so that she could see his hand, she could see that the door was not fast closed now he had removed the bar. 'My Beloved put in his hand by the hole of the door.'

Does not this picture *the work of effectual grace*, when the truth does not appeal to the ear alone, but comes to the heart; when it is no longer a thing thought on, and discussed and forgotten, but an arrow which has penetrated into the reins, and sticks fast in the loins to our wounding, and ultimately to our spiritual healing? No hand is like Christ's hand. When he puts his hand to the work it is well done. He 'put *in* his hand': not his hand on me to smite me, but his hand in me to comfort me, to sanctify me. He put in his hand, and straightway his beloved began to pity him, and to lament her unkindness. She thought as she looked at that hand pierced with the nail mark, 'O Jesus, have I no love for thee? Hast thou done all this for me, and have I been a transparent hypocrite after all, and locked thee out when I ought to have admitted thee? I have used no other friend so ill. I should have been ashamed to have thought of such conduct even to a foe. But thou, O though who hast done more for me than mother, brother, husband, friend, could have done, to thee I have been an ingrate most base and wilful.' Her bowels were moved with repentance; her eyes gushed with tears, and she rose to let him in.

As she arose she first buckled on her garments, and then she searched for the alabaster box of precious ointment, that she might anoint his weary feet and dewy locks; no sooner did she reach the door, than see the love of God to her! Her 'hands dropped with myrrh, and her fingers with sweet smelling myrrh'. Here is the Holy Spirit come to help our infirmities. She begins to pray, and the Holy Ghost helps her. She begins already to enjoy the sweetness, not of communion, but of the very desire after communion. For, beloved, when our tears begin to flow because we are far from Christ, those holy drops have myrrh in them. When we begin to pray for grace, there is a blessedness even about our yearnings and longings and sighings and pantings and pinings; our fingers drop with sweet smelling myrrh upon the handles of the lock. An unction from the Holy One descends upon the soul when it is earnestly seeking for its Beloved.

But that ought never to satisfy us. Behold another temptation of the devil. He will say to you, 'On this very morning you felt some sweetness in hearing about Christ, your hands have evidently dropped with myrrh upon the handles of the lock.' Yes, but still it is not the myrrh that will content the loving heart, it is Christ she wants; and if not only hands, but lips and feet and her whole frame had dropped with myrrh, this would never have contented her until she get the Lord himself.

I pray you, beloved, if the life of Jesus be in you of a truth, rest not satisfied with all the graces and the promises and the doctrines and the gifts of the Spirit of God, but seek after this most excellent gift, to know Christ, and to be found in him, to say of him, 'He loved me, and gave himself for me'; and, yet more, 'His left hand is under my head, and his right hand doth embrace me.' It was that effectually putting in of the hand that moved her. O Lord, grant the like unto us.

5. But now, in the fifth place, **observe THE DESERVED CHASTISEMENT which the Bridegroom inflicted**.

When her spouse was willing to commune, she was not; and now that she is willing, and even anxious, what happens? I wish to describe this to you because some of you may have felt it, and others of you who never have, but have preserved your intimacy with Christ up till now, may be warned by it.

The newly awakened one went to the door, and opened it to her Beloved, for though he was gone, she did not doubt of her love, nor of his love to her. 'I opened to my Beloved, but,' says the Hebrew, 'He had gone, he had gone.' The voice of lamentation, the reduplicated cry of one that is in bitter distress. There must have been a sad relief about it to her sinful heart, for she must have felt afraid to look her dear one in the face after such heartless conduct; but sad as it would have been to face him, it was infinitely sadder to say, 'he is gone, he is gone'.

Now she begins to use the means of grace in order to find him. 'I sought him,' said she, 'and I found him not. I went up to the house of God; the sermon was sweet, but it was not sweet to me, for *he* was not there. I went to the communion table, and the ordinance was a feast of fat things to others, but not to me, for *he* was not there. I sought him, but I could not find him.' Then she betook herself to prayer. She had neglected that before, but now she supplicated in real earnest, 'I called him; I said to him, "Come, my Beloved, my heart wakes for thee. Jesus, reveal thyself to me as thou dost not to the world.

I thirst, I faint, I die to prove
The sweetness of redeeming love,
Thy love, O Christ, to me;"

her prayers were many; she kept them up by day and by night. 'I called him, but he gave me no answer.'

She was not a lost soul, do not mistake that. Christ loved her just as much then as before, nay, loved her a great deal more. If there can be any change in Christ's love, he must have much more approved of her when she was seeking him in sorrow, than when she was reclining upon the couch and neglecting him. But he was gone, and all her calling could not bring him back. What did she then?

Why, she went to his ministers, she went to those who were the watchmen of the night, and what said they to her? Did they cheer her? Perhaps they had never passed through her experience; perhaps they were mere hirelings. However it might be, they smote her. Sometimes the truthful preaching of the gospel will smite a child of God when he gets out of his walk with God, and it is right it should be so. But they did more than smite, they 'wounded' her until she began to bleed from the wounds given by the very men whom she hoped would have comforted her. 'Sure,' she might have said, 'you know where the city's King is, for you are the city's guards!' but she received no comfort.

When a poor soul in this case flies to an unsympathising minister, he will say, 'Well, you say you have lost the presence of Christ, you should bestir yourself to find it.'

'Yes,' says the spouse, 'I rose up and opened to him.'

'You should use the means.'

'But I have used the means; I sought him, but I found him not.'

'You should pray.'

'I did pray; I called him, but he gave me no answer.'

'Well then,' perhaps he will add, 'you should wait patiently for him.'

'Oh, but,' she says, 'I cannot, I must have him; I am sick of love.'

And then perhaps the minister will be sharp, and say, 'I fear you are not a child of God.'

Now what is that? Why, that is taking away the veil from the mourning seeker; plucking away the ensign of sincerity from the benighted seeker. No woman went into the streets of Jerusalem without her veil, except she was of the baser sort, and the watchmen seemed to say to this woman, 'You are of ill name, or you would not be here at this time of night crying out for one you have lost.' Oh, cruel work to pull off her veil and expose her, when she was already wretched enough! Sometimes a sharp sentence from a true minister may set a poor soul in the stocks who ought rather to have been comforted.

I hope these hands will never pull away the veil from any of you poor mourning lovers of Christ. Far rather would these lips tell him when I speak with him, that you are sick of love. But it cannot be helped at all times, for when we are dealing with the hypocrite, the tender child of God thinks we mean him; when we are speaking against the formalist, as we must do, the genuine believer writes bitter things against himself. When the fan is in our hand, and we are seeking thoroughly to purge the floor, it sometimes happens that some of the lighter wheat gets blown a little away with the chaff, and so distress is brought to weak but real children of God. If so, recollect it is not our fault, for we would not grieve you; but it is your fault for having lost your Beloved, for if you had not lost him, you would not have been saying, 'Tell me where I shall find him!' Instead you would have been rejoicing in him, and no watchmen would have smitten you, and no keepers of the walls would have taken away your veil from you, for Jesus would have been your Protector and your Friend.

(6) Now, to close. **As the poor spouse did not then find Christ, but was repulsed in all ways, she adopted A LAST EXPEDIENT**. She knew that there were some who had daily fellowship with the King, daughters of Jerusalem who often saw him, and therefore she sent a message by them, 'If ye see my Beloved, tell him that I am sick of love.'

Enlist your brother saints to pray for you. Go with them to their gatherings for prayer. Their company will not satisfy you without Jesus, but their company may help you to find Jesus. Follow the footsteps of the flock, and you may by-and-by discover the Shepherd. And what a message it is to send to Christ!

Do not send it by other people's lips only, send it by your own. Tell him, 'I am sick of love.' This is of all things the main painful, and the most happy thing in all the world. This is a sickness that I should like to die of, but I should like to feel it in rather a different shape from this.

There are two love-sicknesses in Solomon's Song. The one is when the spouse longs for the presence of her Lord, and the second is when she gets that presence, he is so glorious to her, that she is ready to die with excess of joy, and she exclaims, 'Stay me with flagons, comfort me with apples: for I am sick of love.' If you cannot get the second, recollect that the first is the clear way to it. Resolve in your heart, my brother and sister, that you will never be happy till you win the face of Christ. Settle it in your soul that there shall be no end to your cries and tears till you can say with all your heart, 'My Beloved is near me; I can speak to him; I am in the enjoyment of his love.'

If you can be content without it you shall go without it, but if you must have it you shall have it. If your hunger will break through stone walls to reach your Lord, no stone walls shall keep him from you. If you are insatiable after Christ, he will feed you with himself. If you bid goodbye to all the dainties of the world, and all its sweet draughts and its delicacies, and must have Christ, and Christ alone, then no hungering soul shall long be kept without him. He *must* come to you. There are cords that draw him to you at this hour. His love draws you to him, but your love draws him close to you. Be not afraid, your soul shall be like the chariots of Ammi-nadib; perhaps even this morning, and you shall go on your way rejoicing. The Lord grant it may be so for is love's sake. Amen.

35

HEAVENLY LOVE-SICKNESS!

'I charge you, O daughters of Jerusalem, if ye find my beloved, that ye tell him that I am sick of love' (Song of Solomon 5:8).

SICK! that is a sad thing; it moves your pity. Sick of love – love-sick! that stirs up other emotions which we shall presently attempt to explain. No doubt certain sicknesses are peculiar to the saints: the ungodly are never visited with them. Strange to say, these sicknesses, to which the refined sensibilities of the children of God render them peculiarly liable, are signs of vigorous health. Who but the beloved of the Lord ever experience that sin-sickness in which the soul loathes the very name of transgression, is unmoved by the enchantments of the temper, finds no sweetness in its besetting sins, but turns with detestation and abhorrence from the very thought of iniquity. Not less is it for these, and these alone, to feel that self-sickness whereby the heart revolts from all creature-confidence and strength, having been made sick of self, self-seeking, self-exalting, self-reliance, and self of every sort. The Lord afflicts us more and more with such self-sickness till we are dead to self, its puny conceits, its lofty aims, and its unsanctified desires.

Then there is a twofold love-sickness. Of the one kind is that love-sickness which comes upon the Christian when he is transported with the full enjoyment of Jesus, even as the bride elated by the favour, melted by the tenderness of her Lord, says in the fifth verse of the second chapter of the Song, 'Stay me with flagons, comfort me with apples: for I am sick of love.' The soul overjoyed with the divine communications of happiness and bliss which came from Christ, the body scarcely able to bear the excessive delirium of delight which the soul possessed, she was so glad to be in the embraces of her Lord, that she needed to be stayed under her overpowering weight of joy.

Another kind of love-sickness, widely different from the first, is that in which the soul is sick, not because it has too much of Christ's love, but because it has not enough present consciousness of it; sick, not of the enjoyment, but of the longing for it; sick, not because of excess of delight, but because of sorrow for an absent lover. It is to this sickness we call your attention this morning.

This love-sickness breaks out in two ways, and may be viewed in two lights. It is, first of all, the soul longing for a view of Jesus Christ in grace; and then again, it is the same soul possessing the view of grace, and longing for a sight of Jesus Christ in glory. In both these senses we, as accurately as the spouse, may adopt the languishing words, 'If ye find my beloved, tell him that I am sick of love.'

First, then, let us consider our text as the language of a soul LONGING FOR THE VIEW OF JESUS CHRIST IN GRACE.

(1) Do ye ask me concerning the sickness itself: What is it? It is the sickness of a soul panting after communion with Christ. The man is a believer; he is not longing after salvation as a penitent sinner under conviction, for he is saved. Moreover, he has love to Christ and knows it; he does not doubt his evidence as to the reality of his affection for his Lord, for you see the word used is 'My beloved', which would not be applicable if the person speaking had any doubts about her interest; nor did she doubt her love, for she calls the spouse, 'My beloved'. It is the longing of a soul, then, not for salvation, and not even for the certainty of salvation, but for the enjoyment of present fellowship with him who is her soul's life, her soul's all.

The heart is panting to be brought once more under the apple tree; to feel once again his 'left hand under her head, while his right hand doth embrace her'. She has known, in days past, what it is to be brought into his banqueting house and to see the banner of love waved over her, and she therefore crieth to have love visits renewed. It is a panting after communion. Gracious souls, my dear friends, are never perfectly at ease except they are in a state of nearness to Christ; for mark you, when they are not near to Christ, they lose their peace. The nearer to Jesus, the nearer to the perfect calm of heaven; and the further from Jesus, the nearer to that troubled sea which images the continual unrest of the wicked. There is no peace to the man who doth not dwell constantly under the shadow of the cross; for Jesus is our peace, and if he be absent, our peace is absent too. I know that being justified, we have peace with God, but it is 'through our Lord Jesus Chrjst'. So that the justified man himself cannot reap the fruit of justification, except by abiding in Christ Jesus, who is the Lord and Giver of peace. The Christian without fellowship with Christ loses all his life and energy; he is like a dead thing. Though saved, he lies like a lumpish log –

His soul can neither fly nor go
To reach eternal joys.

He is without vivacity, yea, more, he is without animation till Jesus comes; but when the Lord sensibly sheds abroad his love in our hearts, then his love kindles ours; then our blood leaps in our veins for joy, like the Baptist in the womb of Elizabeth. The heart when near to Jesus has strong pulsations, for since Jesus is in that heart, it is full of life, of vigour, and of strength. Peace, liveliness, vigour – all depend upon the constant enjoyment of communion with Christ Jesus. The soul of a Christian never knows what joy means in its true solidity, except when she sits like Mary at Jesus' feet.

Beloved, all the joys of life are nothing to us; we have melted them all down in our crucible, and found them to be dross. You and I have tried earth vanities, and they cannot satisfy us; nay, they do not give a morsel of meat to satiate our hunger. Being in a state of dissatisfaction with all mortal things, we have learned through divine grace, that none but Jesus, none but Jesus can make our souls glad. 'Philosophers are happy without music,' said one of old. So Christians are happy without the world's good. Christians, with the world's good, are sure to bemoan themselves as naked, poor and miserable, unless their Saviour be with them. You that have ever tasted communion with Christ will soon know why it is that a soul longs after him.

What the sun is to the day, what the moon is to the night, what the dew is to the flower, such is Jesus Christ to us. What bread is to the hungry, clothes to the naked, the shadow of a great rock to the traveller in a weary land, such is Jesus Christ to us. What the turtle is to her mate, what the husband is to his spouse, what the head is to the body, such is Jesus Christ to us; and therefore, if we have him not, nay, if we are not conscious of having him; if we are not one with him, nay, if we are not consciously one with him, little marvel if our spirit cried in the words of the Song, 'I charge you, O ye daughters of Jerusalem, if ye find my beloved, tell him that I am sick of love.' Such is the character of this love-sickness.

We may say of it, however, before we leave that point, that it is a sickness which has a blessing attending it: 'Blessed are they that do hunger and thirst after righteousness'; and therefore, supremely blessed are they who thirst after the Righteous One – after him, who in the highest perfection embodies pure, immaculate, spotless righteousness. Blessed is that hunger, for it comes from God. It bears a blessing within it; for if I may not have the blessedness in full bloom of being filled, the next best thing is the same blessedness in sweet bud of being empty till I am filled with Christ. If I may not feed on Jesus, it shall be next door to heaven to be allowed to hunger and thirst after him. There is a hallowedness about that hunger, since it sparkles among the beatitudes of our Lord.

Yet it is a sickness, dear friends, which, despite the blessing, causes much pain. The man who is sick after Jesus will be dissatisfied with everything else; he will find that dainties have lost their sweetness and music its melody and light its brightness and life itself will be darkened with the shadow of death to him, till he finds his Lord, and can rejoice in him. Beloved, ye shall find that this thirsting, this sickness, if it ever gets hold upon you, is attended with great vehemence. The desire is vehement, as coals of juniper. Ye have heard of hunger that it breaks through stone walls: but stone walls are no prison to a soul that desires Christ. Stone walls, nay, the strongest natural barriers, cannot keep a love-sick heart from Jesus.

I will venture to say that the temptation of heaven itself, if it could be offered to the believer without his Christ, would be as less than nothing; and the pains of hell, if they could be endured, would be gladly ventured upon by a love-sick soul, if he might but find Christ. As lovers sometimes talk of doing impossibilities for their fair ones, so certainly a spirit that is set on Christ will laugh at impossibility, and say, 'It shall be done.' It will venture upon the hardest task, go cheerfully to prison and joyfully to death, if it may but find its beloved, and have its love-sickness satisfied with his presence. Perhaps this may suffice for a description of the sickness here intended.

(2) Ye may enquire concerning the cause of this love-sickness, What maketh a man's soul so sick after Christ? Understand that it is the absence of Christ which makes this sickness in a mind that really understands the preciousness of his presence. The spouse had been very wilful and wayward; she had taken off her garments, had gone to her rest, her sluggish slothful rest, when her beloved knocked at the door. He said, 'Open to me, my beloved; for my head is filled with dew, and my locks with the drops of the night.' She was too slothful to wake up to let him in. She urged excuses: 'I have put off my coat; how shall I put it on? I have washed my feet: how shall I defile them?' The beloved stood waiting, but since she opened not, he put in his hand by the hole of the lock, and then her bowels were moved towards him. She went to the door to open it, and to her surprise, her hands dropped with myrrh, and her fingers with sweet-smelling myrrh upon the handles of the lock. There was the token that he had been there, but he was gone.

Now she began to bestir herself, and seek after him. She sought him through the city, but she found him not. Her soul failed her; she called after him, but he gave her no answer, and the watchman, who ought to have helped her in the search, smote her and took away her veil from her. Therefore it is that now she is seeking, because she has lost her beloved. She should have held him fast and not permitted him to go. He is absent, and she is sick till she findeth him.

Mingled with the sense of absence is a consciousness of wrongdoing. Something in her seemed to say, 'How couldst thou drive him away? That heavenly Bridegroom who knocked and pleased hard, how couldst thou keep him longer there amidst the cold dews of night? O unkind heart! what if thy feet had been made to bleed by thy rising? What if all thy body had been chilled by the cold wind, when thou wast treading the floor? What had it been compared with his love to thee?' And so she is sick to see him, that she may weep out her love and tell him how vexed she is with herself that she should have held to him so loosely, and permitted him so readily to depart.

So, too, mixed with this, was great wretchedness because he was gone. She had been for a little time easy in his absence. That downy bed, that warm coverlet, had given her a peace, a false, cruel and a wicked peace, but she has risen now, the watchmen have smitten her, her veil is gone, and, without a friend, the princess, deserted in the midst of Jerusalem's street, has her soul melted for heaviness, and she pours out her heart within her as she pineth after her lord. 'No love but my love, no lord but my lord,' saith she, with sobbing tongue and weeping eyes; for none else can gratify her heart or appease her anxiety.

Beloved, have you never been in such a state, when your faith has begun to droop, and your heart and spirits have fled from you? Even then your soul was sick for him. You could do without him when Mr Carnal-security was in the house, and feasted you, but when he and his house have both been burned with fire, the old love-sickness came back, and you wanted Christ, nor could ye be satisfied till ye found him once again.

There was true love in all this, and this is the very pith of all love-sickness. Had not she loved, absence would not have made her sick, nor would her repentance have made her grieve. Had she not loved, there would have been no pain because of absence, and no sinking of spirits; but she did love, thence all this sickness. It is a delightful thing to be able to know when we have lost Christ's company, that we do love him: ' "Yea, Lord, thou knowest all things; thou knowest that I love thee." I did deny thee, yea, in the moment of thy sorrow, I said, "I know not the man". I did curse and swear that men might think I was no follower of thine, but still thou knowest all things; thou knowest that I love thee.' When you can feel this, dear friends, the consciousness that you love will soon work in you a heart-burning, so that your soul will not be satisfied till you can tell out that love in the Master's presence, and he shall say unto you, as a token of forgiveness, 'Feed my sheep'.

I do not doubt that in this sickness there had been some degree of fear. Sorrowful woman! She was half afraid she might never find him again. She had been about the city – where could he be? She had sought him on the walls and on the ramparts, but he was not there. In every ordinance, in every means of grace, in secret and in public prayer, in the Lord's Supper, and in the reading of the Word, she had looked after him, but he was not there; and now she was half afraid that though he might give his presence to others, yet never to her, and when she speaks, you notice there is half a fear in it. She would not have asked others to tell him if she had any assuring hope that she should meet him herself – 'If ye find him,' she seems to say, 'O ye true converts, you that are the real grace-born daughters of Jerusalem; if he reveals himself to you, thought he never may to me, do me this kindness, tell him that I am sick of love.'

There is half a fear here, and yet there is some hope. She feels that he must love her still, or else why send a message at all? She would surely never send this sweet message to a flinty, adamantine heart: 'Tell him I am sick of love'; but she remembered when the glancings of her eyes had ravished him; she remembered when a motion from her hand had made his heart melt, and when one tear of her eyes had opened all his wounds afresh. She thinks, 'Perhaps, he loves me still as he loved me then, and my moanings will enchain him; my groans will constrain him and lead him to my help.' So she send the message to him – 'Tell him, tell him I am sick of love.'

To gather up the causes of this love-sickness in a few words, does not the whole matter spring from relationship? She is his spouse; can the spouse be happy without her beloved lord? It springs from union; she is part of himself. Can the hand be happy and healthy if the life-floods stream not from the heart and from the head. Fondly realizing her dependence, she feels that she owes all to him, and gets her all from him. If then the fountain be cut off, if the streams be dried, if the great source of all be taken from her, how can she but be sick?

And there is besides this, a life and a nature in her which makes her sick. There is a life like the life of Christ, nay, her life is in Christ, it is hid with Christ in God; her nature is a part of the divine nature; she is a partaker of the divine nature. Moreover she is in union with Jesus, and this piece divided, as it were, from the body, wriggles, like a worm cut asunder, and pants to get back to where it came from. These are the causes of it. You will not understand my sermon this morning, but think me raving, unless you are spiritual men. 'But the spiritual judgeth all things, yet he himself is judged of no man.'

(3) What endeavours such love-sick souls will put forth. Those who are sick for Christ will first send their desires to him. Men use pigeons sometimes to send their messages. Why, what sort of carrier pigeons do they use? The pigeon is of no use to send anywhere but to the place from which it came, and my desires after Christ came from him, and so they will always go back to the place from which they came: they know the way to their own dovecot, so I will send him my sights and my groans, my tears and my moans. Go one, sweet doves, with swift and clipping wings, and tell him I am sick of love.

Then she would send her prayers. Ah! methinks she would say of her desires, 'They will never reach him; they know the way but their wings are broken, and they will fall to the ground and never reach him.' Yet she will send them whether they reach of not. As for her prayers, they are like arrows. Sometimes messages have been sent into besieged towns bound to an arrow, so she binds her desires upon the arrow of her prayers, and then shoots them forth from the bow of her faith. She is afraid they will never reach him, for her bow is slack, and she knoweth not how to draw it with her feeble hands which hang down. So what does she?

She has traversed the street; she has used the means; she had done everything; she has sighed her heart out, and emptied her soul out in prayers. She is all wounds till he heals her; she is all a hungry mouth till he fills her; she is all an empty brook till he replenishes her once again, and so now she goeth to her companions, and she saith, 'If ye find my beloved, tell him I am sick of love.' This is using the intercession of the saints. It is unbelief that makes her use it, and yet there is a little faith mixed in her unbelief. It was an unbelief but not a misbelief. There is efficacy in the intercession of saints. Not of dead saints – they have enough to do to be singing God's praises in heaven without praying for us – but saints on earth can take up our case. The king has his favourites; he has his cupbearers; he has some that are admitted into great familiarity with him: give me a share in a good man's prayers. I attribute under God the success the Lord has given me, to the number of souls in every quarter of the earth who pray for me – not you alone, but in every land there are some that forget me not when they draw near in their supplications. Oh! we are so rich when we have the prayers of saints.

When it is well with thee, speak for me to the Captain of the host, and if he should say to thee, 'What was his message?' I have no other message but that of the spouse, 'Tell him I am sick of love'. Any of you who have close familiarity with Jesus, be the messengers, be the heavenly talebearers between love-sick souls and their divine Lord. Tell him, tell him we are sick of love. And you that cannot thus go to him, do seek the help and aid of others.

But after all, as I have said, this is unbelief though is not misbelief, for how much better it would have been for her to tell him herself. 'But,' you say, 'she could not find him.' Nay, but if she had had faith she would have known that her prayers could; for our prayers know where Christ is when we do not know, or rather, Christ knows where our prayers are, and when we cannot see him they reach him nevertheless. A man who fires a cannon is not expected to see all the way which the shot goes. If he has his cannon rightly sighted and fires it, there may come on a thick fog, but the shot will reach the place; and if you have your hearts sighted by divine grace after Christ, you may depend upon it, however thick the fog, the hot-shot of your prayer will reach the gates of heaven though ye cannot tell how or where.

Be ye satisfied to go to Christ yourself. If your brethren will go, well and good, but methinks their proper answer to your question would be in the language of the women in the sixth chapter, the first verse, 'Whither is thy beloved gone, O thou fairest among women? whither is thy beloved turned aside? that we may seek him with thee.' They will not seek him for us they say, but they can seek him with us. Sometimes when there are six pair of eyes, they will see better than one; and so, if five or six Christians seek the Lord in company, in the prayer-meeting, or at his table, they are more likely to find him. 'We will seek him with thee.'

(4) Blessed love-sickness! we have seen its character and its cause, and the endeavours of the soul under it; let us just notice the comforts which belong to such a state as this.

Briefly they are these – you shall be filled. It is impossible for Christ to set you longing after him without intending to give himself to you. It is as when a great man doth make a feast. He first puts plates upon the table, and then afterwards there cometh the meat. Your longings and desirings are the empty plates to hold the meat. Is it likely that he means to mock you? Would he have put the dishes there if he did not intend to fill them with his oxen and with his fatlings? He makes you long: he will certainly satisfy your longings. Remember, again, that he will give you himself all the sooner for the bitterness of your longings. The more pained you heart is at his absence the shorter will the absence be. If you have a grain of contentment without Christ, that will keep you longer tarrying; but when your soul is sick till your heart is ready to break, till you cry, 'Why tarrieth he? why are his chariots so long in coming?', when your soul fainteth until your beloved speaks unto you, and you are ready to die from your youth up, then in no long space he will lift the veil from his dear face, and your sun shall rise with healing beneath his wings. Let that console you.

Then, again, when he does come, as come he will, oh, how sweet it will be! Methinks I have the flavour in my mouth now, and the fulness of the feast is yet to come. There is such a delight about the very thought that he will come, that the thought itself is the prelude, the foretaste, the antepast of the happy greeting. What! Will he once again speak comfortably to me? Shall I again walk the bed of spices with him? Shall I ramble with him amongst the groves while the flowers give forth their sweet perfume? I shall! I shall! and even now my spirit feels his presence by anticipation: 'Or ever I was aware, my soul made me like the chariots of Amminadib.'

You know how sweet it was in the past. Beloved, what times we have had, some of us. Oh, whether in the body or out of the body, we cannot tell – God knoweth. What mountings! Talk ye of eagles' wings – they are earthly pinions, and may not be compared with the wings with which he carried us up from earth. Speak of mounting beyond clouds and stars! – they were left far, far behind. We entered into the unseen, beheld the invisible, lived in the immortal, drank in the ineffable, and were blessed with the fulness of God in

Christ Jesus, being made to sit together in heavenly places in him. Well, all this is to come again, 'I will see you again, and your heart shall rejoice.' 'A little while, and ye shall not see me: and again, a little while, and ye shall see me.' 'In a little wrath I hid my face from thee for a moment; but with everlasting kindness will I have mercy on thee, saith the Lord thy Redeemer.' Think of this. Why, we have comfort even in this sickness of love. Our heart, though sick, is still whole, while we are panting and pining after the Lord Jesus.

O love divine, how sweet thou art,
When shall I find my willing heart
All taken up with thee?
I thirst, I faint, I die to prove
The fulness of redeeming love –
The love of Christ to me.

And now, secondly, with as great brevity as we can. This love–sickness may be seen in A SOUL-LONGING FOR A VIEW OF JESUS IN HIS GLORY.

(1) And here we will consider the complaint itself for a moment. This ailment is not merely a longing after communion with Christ on earth – that has been enjoyed, and generally this sickness follows that:

When I have tasted of the grapes,
I sometimes long to go
Where my dear Lord the vineyard keeps
And all the clusters grow.

It is the enjoyment of Eshcol's first fruits which makes us desire to sit under our own vine and our own fig tree before the throne of God in the blessed land.

Beloved, this sickness is characterized by certain marked symptoms; I will tell you what they are. There is a loving and a longing, a loathing and a languishing. Happy soul that understands these things by experience. There is a loving in which the heart cleaves to Jesus:

Do not I love thee from my soul?
Then let me nothing love:
Dead be my heart to every joy
When Jesus cannot move.

A sense of his beauty! an admiration of his charms! a consciousness of his infinite perfection! Yea; greatness, goodness and loveliness in one resplendent ray combine to enchant the soul till it is so ravished after him that it crieth with the spouse, 'Yea, he is altogether lovely. This is my beloved, and this is my friend, O ye daughters of Jerusalem.' Sweet loving this – a love which binds the heart with chains of more than silken softness, and yet than adamant more firm.

Then there is a longing. She loves him so that she cannot endure to be absent from him; she pants and pines. You know it has been so with saints in all ages; whenever they have begun to love they have always begun to long after Christ. John, the most loving of spirits, is the author of those words which he so frequently uses: 'Come quickly, even so, come quickly.' 'Come quickly' is sure to be the fruit of earnest love. See how the spouse puts it – 'O that thou wert as my brother, that sucked the breasts of my mother! when I should find thee without, I would kiss thee; yea, I should not be despised.' She longs to get hold of him; she cannot conclude her song without saying, 'Make haste, my beloved, and be thou like to a roe or to a young hart upon the mountains of spices.' There is a longing to be with Christ. I would not give much for your religion if you do not long to be with the object of your heart's affections.

Then comes a loathing. When a man is sick with the first love-sickness, then he does not loathe – it is, 'Stay me with flagons, comfort me with apples.' When a man has Christ, he can enjoy other things; but when a man is longing after Christ and seeking after Christ, he loathes everything else – he cannot bear anything besides. Here is my message to Jesus: 'Tell him –' what? Do I want crowns and diadems? Crowns and diadems are nought to me. Do I want wealth, and health and strength? They are all very well in their way. No – 'Tell him, tell the beloved of my soul that I grieve after himself – his gifts are good, I ought to be more grateful for them than I am, but let me see his face; let me hear his voice. I am sick of love, and nothing but that can satisfy me, everything else is distasteful to me.'

And then there is languishing. Since she cannot get the society of Christ, cannot as yet behold him on his throne nor worship him face to face, she is sick until she can. For a heart so set on Christ will walk about traversing highway and byway, resting nowhere till it finds him. As the needle once magnetized will never be easy until it finds the pole, so the heart once Christianized never will be satisfied until it rests on Christ – rests on him, too, in the fulness of the beatific vision before the throne. This is the character of the love-sickness.

(2) As to its object – what is that? 'Tell him that I am sick of love'; but what is the sickness for? Brethren, when you and I want to go to heaven I hope it is the true love-sickness.

I catch myself sometimes wanting to die and be in heaven for the sake of rest; but is not that a lazy desire? There is a sluggish wish that makes me long for rest. Perhaps, we long for the happiness of heaven – the harps and crowns. There is a little selfishness in that, is there not? Allowable, I grant you; but is not there a little like selfishness? Perhaps, we long to see dear children, beloved friends that have gone before; but there is a little of the earthy there.

The soul may be sick as it will, without rebuke, when it is sick to be with Jesus. You may indulge this, carry it to its utmost extent without either sin or folly.

What am I sick with love for? For the pearly gates? No; but for the pearls that are in his wounds.

What am I sick for? For the streets of gold? No; but for his head, which is as much fine gold. For the melody of the harps and angelic song? No; but for the melodious notes that come from his dear mouth.

What am I sick for? For the nectar that angels drink? No; but for the kisses of his lips. For the manna on which heavenly souls do feed? No; but for himself, who is the meat and drink of his saints; himself, himself – my soul pines to see him.

Oh, what a heaven to gaze upon! What bliss to talk with the man, the God, crucified for me; to weep my heart out before him; to tell him how I love him, for he loves me and gave himself for me; to read my name written on his hands and on his side – yea, and to let him see that his name is written on my heart in indelible lines; to embrace him, oh! what an embrace when the creature shall embrace his God – to be for ever so close to him, that not a doubt, nor a fear, nor a wandering thought can come between my soul and him for ever –

For ever to behold him shine,
For evermore to call him mine,
And see him still before me;
For ever on his face to gaze,
And meet his full assembled rays,
While all the Father he displays
To all the saints in glory.

What else can there be that our spirit longeth for? This seems an empty thing to worldlings, but to the Christian this is heaven summed up in a word – 'To be with Christ, which is far better' than all the joys of earth. This is the object, then, of this love-sickness.

(3) Ask ye yet again what are the excitement of this sickness? What is it makes the Christian long to be at home with Jesus? There are many things. There are sometimes some very little things that set a Christian longing to be at home.

You know the old story of Swiss soldiers, that when they have enlisted into foreign service they never will permit the band to play the 'Ranz des Vaches' – the Song of the Cows, because as soon as ever the Swiss hears the Song of the Cows, he thinks of his own dear Alps, and the bells upon the cow's necks, and the strange calls of the herd-boys, as they sing to one another from the mountains' peaks; and he grows sick and ill with home-sickness. So if you were banished, if you were taken prisoner or a slave, why, to hear some note of one of old England's songs would set your spirit a-pining for home, and I do confess, when I hear you sing sometimes:

Jerusalem! my happy home!
Name ever dear to me;
When shall my labours have an end,
In joy, and peace, and thee?

it makes me say, 'Ye daughter of Jerusalem, if ye find my beloved, tell him, that I am sick of love.' It is the home-song that brings the homesickness. When we remember what he used to be to us, what sweet visits we have had from him, then we get sick to be always with him. And, best of all, when we are in his presence, when our soul is overjoyed with his delights, then the great deep sea of his love has rolled over the mast-head of our highest thoughts, and the ship of our spirit has gone right down, foundering at sea in the midst of an ocean of delights, ah, then its highest, its deepest thought is, 'O that I may always be with him, where he is, that I might behold his glory – the glory which his Father gave him, and which he has given me, that I may be one with him, world without end.'

I do believe, brethren, that all the bitters and all the sweets make a Christian, when he is in a healthy state, sick after Christ; the sweets make his mouth water for more sweets, and the bitters make him pant for the time when the last dregs of bitterness shall be over. Wearying temptations, as well as rapt enjoyments, all set the spirit on the wing after Jesus.

(4) Well now, friends, *what is the cure of this love-sickness?* Is it a sickness for which there is any specific remedy? There is only one cure that I know of, but there are some palliatives. A man that is sick after Christ, longs to be with him, and pants for the better land, singing as we did just now:

Father, I long, I faint to see
The place of thine abode.

He must have the desire realized, before the thirst of his fever will be assuaged. There are some palliatives, and I will recommend them to you.

Such, for example, is a strong faith that realizes the day of the Lord and the presence of Christ, as Moses beheld the promised land and the goodly heritage, when he stood on the top of Pisgah. If you do not get heaven when you want it, you may attain to that which is next door to heaven, and this may bear you up for a little season. If you cannot get to behold Christ face to face, it is a blessed make-shift for the time to see him in the Scriptures, and to look at him through the glass of the Word.

These are palliatives, but I warn ye, I warn ye of them. I do not mean to keep you from them, use them as much as ever you can, but I warn you from expecting that it will cure love-sickness. It will give you ease, but it will make you more sick still, for he that lives on Christ gets more hungry after Christ. As for a man being satisfied and wanting no more when he gets Christ – why he wants nothing but Christ it is true, in that sense he will never thirst; but he wants more, and more, and more, and more of Christ. To live on Christ is like drinking sea-water, the more ye drink the more thirsty ye grow. There is something very satisfying in Christ's flesh, you will never hunger except for that, but the more you eat of it the more ye may; and he that is the heartiest feaster, and hath eaten the most, hath the best appetite for more. Oh, strange is this, but so it is; that which we would think would remove the love-sickness, and is the best stay to the soul under it, is just that which brings it on more and more.

But there is a cure, there is a cure, and you shall have it soon – a black draught, and in it a pearl – a black draught called Death. Ye shall drink it, but ye shall not know it is bitter, for ye shall swallow it up in victory. There is a pearl, too, in it – melted in it. Jesus died as well as you, and as you drink it, that pearl shall take away all ill effect from the tremendous draught. You shall say, 'O death, where is thy sting? O grave, where is thy victory?' When you have once drank that black draught, you are secure against that love-sickness for ever. For where are you? No pilgrimage, no weary flight through cold ether, thou art with him in paradise. Does thou hear that, soul?

Thou art with him in paradise, never to be separated, not for an instant; never to have a wandering thought, not one; never to find thy love waning or growing cold again; never to doubt his love to thee any more; never more to be vexed and tempted by sighing after what thou canst not view. Thou shalt be with him, where he is:

Far from a world of grief and sin,
With God eternally shut in.

Till then, beloved, let us strive to live near the cross. Those two mountains, Calvary and Zion, stand right opposite one another. The eye of faith can sometimes almost span the interval. And the loving heart, by some deep mystery of which we can offer you no solution, will often have its sweetest rapture of joy in the fellowship of his griefs. So have I found a satisfaction in the wounds of a crucified Jesus, which can only be excelled by the satisfaction I have yet to find in the sparkling eyes of the same Jesus glorified. Yes; the same Jesus! Well spake the angels on Mount Olivet: '*This same Jesus*, which is taken up from you into heaven, shall so come in like manner as ye have seen him go into heaven.' This same Jesus! My soul doats on the words; my lips are fond of repeating them. This same Jesus!

If in my soul such joy abounds,
While weeping faith explores his wounds,
How glorious will those scars appear,
When perfect bliss forbids a tear!

Think, O my soul, if 'tis so sweet
On earth to sit at Jesus' feet,
What must it be to wear a crown
And sit with him upon his throne?

Would to God you all had this love-sickness! I am afraid many of you have it not. May he give it to you. But oh! If there be a soul here that wants Jesus, he is welcome. If there is one heart here that says, 'Give me Christ,' you shall have your desire. Trust Jesus Christ, and he is thine; rely upon him, thou art his. God save thee and make thee sick *of* vanities, sick *after* verities; pining even unto sickness for Jesus Christ, the beloved of my soul, the sum of all my hope, the sinner's only refuge, and the praise of all his saints; to whom be everlasting glory. Amen.

36

THE INCOMPARABLE BRIDEGROOM AND HIS BRIDE

'What is thy beloved more than another beloved, O thou fairest among women? What is thy beloved more than another beloved, that thou dost so charge us?' (Song of Solomon 5:9).

This morning, we had the great privilege of preaching the doctrine of substitution, and of directing the minds of God's people to the solid rock of the meritorious sacrifice of Christ whereon all their hopes of heaven must be built. What we have to say tonight is less doctrinal, and more practical; therefore let us guard ourselves at the outset. If we should, with very much earnestness, urge believers to good works, let nobody suppose that, therefore, we imagine that men are saved by works. Let no one for a moment dream that, in urging the believer to bring forth fruit unto righteousness, we are at all teaching that salvation is the work of man.

I have no doubt that all of us who know anything of true religion are of the same opinion as that celebrated Scotch divine, old David Dickson, who was asked when dying, what was the principal subject on which his thoughts were engaged, and he answered: 'I am gathering up all my good works, and all my bad works, tying them into one bundle, and throwing them all alike down at the foot of the cross, and am resting alone upon the finished work of Jesus.' It is related of that mighty master in Israel, James Durham, that his experience at the last was very much akin to that of his friend Dickson, for he said, 'Notwithstanding all my preaching, and all my spiritual experiences, I do not know that I have anything to hang upon excepting this one sentence spoken by Christ, 'Him that cometh to me I will in no wise cast out." "Ah!" replied someone who stood by Mr Durham at the time, "you might well hazard a thousand souls, if you had them, upon the strength of that one precious text." '

Having said so much by way of caution, I want to address some earnest words to the people of God upon certain practical truths that arise out of our text. The first thing I have to say is this, that the daughters of Jerusalem recognized in the spouse an exceeding beauty, which dazzled and charmed them, so that they could not help calling her the 'fairest among women'. This was not her estimate of herself; for she had said, 'I am black, but comely.' Nor was it the estimate of her enemies; for they had smitten her, and wounded her. But it was the estimate of fair, candid, and impartial onlookers.

This leads me to remark, first, that OUR CHARACTER SHOULD GIVE WEIGHT TO OUR PROFESSION OF RELIGION.

You will observe that it was in consequence of thinking her the 'fairest among women' that they asked the spouse: 'What is thy Beloved more than another beloved?' They thought that one so fair might well have her choice of a Bridegroom, that one so lovely herself would be likely to have an eye to loveliness in her Husband, and consequently they considered her judgment to be worth some attention, and they put to her the question why her Beloved was more than another beloved. Take it for granted, dear friends, as a truth which your own observation and experience will make every day more and more clear, that your power to spread religion in the world must mainly depend upon your own personal character – of course, in absolute reliance upon the Holy Spirit. I suppose it is the earnest wish of every Christian to win for Christ some new converts, to bring some fresh province under the dominion of the King of kings. I will tell you how this may be accomplished.

Your power to achieve this noble purpose must largely depend upon your own personal consistency. It little availeth what I say if I do the reverse. The world will not care about my testimony with the lip, unless there be also a testimony in my daily life for God, for truth, for holiness, for everything that is honest, lovely, pure and of good report. There is that in a Christian's character which the world, though it may persecute the man himself, learns to value. It is called consistency, that is, the making of the life stand together, not being one thing in one place and another thing in another, or one thing at one time and quite different on another occasion.

It is not consistency to be devout on Sunday and to be dishonest on Monday. It is not consistency to sing the songs of Zion today and to shout the songs of lustful mirth tomorrow. It is not consistency occasionally to wear the yoke of Christ, and yet frequently to make yourself the serf of Satan. But to make your life all of a piece is to make it powerful, and when God the Holy Ghost enables you to do this, then your testimony will tell upon those amongst whom you live.

It would be ludicrous, if it were not so sorrowful a thing, to be spoken of even with weeping, that there should be professed Christians who are through inconsistency among the worst enemies of the cross of Christ. I heard, the other day, a story which made me laugh. A poor creature, in a lunatic asylum, had got it into his head that he was some great one, and he addressed a person who was visiting the asylum in the following words: 'I am Sir William Wallace; give me some tobacco!' What a ridiculous contrast between his proud assertion and his poor request! Who but a lunatic would have said such a thing? Yet, alas! We know people who say, by their actions, if not in words, 'I am a Christian, but I will take advantage of you when I can. I am one of the blood-royal of heaven, my life is hid with Christ in God, and my conversation is in heaven, but – but – I like worldliness and sensual pleasure and carnal mirth quite as well as other men!' I say again that this kind of thing would be superlatively ludicrous if it were not ineffably sorrowful, and it is, anyhow, utterly contemptible. If your life be not all of a piece, the world will soon learn how to estimate your testimony, and will count you to be either a fool or a knave, and perhaps both.

But it is not enough to be barely consistent; what the world expects in Christians is real holiness as well as consistency. Holiness is something more than virtue. Virtue is like goodness frozen into ice, hard and cold; but holiness is that same goodness when it is thawed into a clear, running, sparkling stream. Virtue is the best thing that philosophy can produce, but holiness is the true fruit of the gospel of Jesus Christ, and of that alone. There must be about us an unworldliness, a something out of the common and ordinary way, or else, mark you, that uncommon gospel, that heavenly gospel, which we hold, will not seem to be bringing forth its legitimate fruit. If you are just barely honest and no more, if you are barely moral and no more, it is of no service that you should try to speak of Christ; the world will not reckon you as the fairest among women, and it will not enquire anything about your Well-beloved.

But, brethren and sisters, I feel as if, instead of exhorting you thus, I might better turn to confession myself, and ask you to join me in confessing how far short we come of being anything like the fairest among women as to character. We do hope that we have something Christ-like about us; but oh, how little it is! How many imperfections there are! How much is there of the old Adam, and how little of the new creature in Christ Jesus!

Archbishop Usher was once asked to write a treatise upon Sanctification; this he promised to do, but six months rolled away, and the good Archbishop had not written a sentence. He said to a friend, 'I have not begun the treatise, yet I cannot confess to a breach of my promise, for, to tell you the truth, I have done my best to write upon the subject; but when I came to look into my own heart, I saw so little of sanctification there, and found that so much which I could have written would have been merely by rote as a parrot might have talked, that I had not the face to write it.' Yet, if ever there was a man renowned for holiness, it was Archbishop Usher; if ever there was a saintly man who seemed to be one of the seraphic spirits permitted to stray beyond the companionship of his kind among poor earthworms here, it was Usher; yet this is the confession that he makes concerning himself!

Where, then, shall we hide our diminished heads? I am sure we may all say, with good Mr Fletcher of Madeley, who was another bright example of seraphic holiness, that what we want is more grace. He had written a pamphlet on some political matter, and Lord North wrote to know what he could give him in return. His answer was, 'I want what your lordship cannot give me – more grace. That is also true of us, we want more grace. It is to be had; and if we had it, and it transformed us into what we should be, oh, what lives of happiness and of holiness we might lead here below, and what mighty workers should we be for our Lord Jesus Christ! How would his dear name be made to sound to the utmost ends of the earth! I fear me it is but a dream; but just conceive that all of you, the members of this church, were made to be truly saintly, saints of the first water, saints who had cast off the sloth of worldliness and had come out in the full glory of newness of life in Christ Jesus. Oh, what a power might this church become in London, and what a power to be felt the wide world over! Let us seek it, let us strive after it, recollecting that it is a truth never to be denied that only in proportion to the sanctity and spirituality of our character will be our influence for good amongst the sons of men.

Advancing now a step, our second remark will be, that WE SHOULD CHARGE OTHERS CONCERNING CHRIST. 'What is thy Beloved more than another beloved, that thou dost so charge us?'

The 'fairest among women' was asked why she had so spoken: 'I charge you, O daughters of Jerusalem, if ye find my Beloved, that ye tell him, that I am sick of love.' By this 'charge' is meant, I suppose, that the spouse adjured them, and spoke solemnly to them about her Beloved.

Christians, be troublesome to the world! O house of Israel, be like a burdensome stone to the world! You are not sent here to be recognized as honourable citizens of this world, to be petted and well-treated. Even Christ himself, the peaceable One, said, 'I am come to send fire on the earth; and what will I, if it be already kindled.' What I mean is this, we are not to be quiet about our religion. The world says to us, 'Hold your tongue about religion, or at least talk about it at fit times; but do not introduce it at all seasons so as to become a pest and a nuisance.' I say again, and you know in what sense I mean it, be a nuisance to the world; be such a man that worldlings will be compelled to feel that there is a Christian in their midst. An officer was walking out of the royal presence on one occasion, when he tripped over his sword. The king said to him, 'Your sword is rather a nuisance.' 'Yes,' was the officer's reply, 'your majesty's enemies have often said so.' May you be a nuisance to the world in that sense, troublesome to the enemies of the King of kings! While your conduct should be courteous, and everything that could be desired as between man and man, yet let your testimony for Christ be given without any flinching and without any mincing of the matter.

This afternoon, I was reading a sermon by a certain divine, whose subject of discourse was why the working-classes do not go to a place of worship. The preacher seems to have made up his mind that whatever is preached in this Tabernacle is especially obnoxious to labouring men and women. The reason he gives why the working-classes do not attend places of worship is that we preach such dreadful doctrines. It is very remarkable that places where these truths are preached are crowded, while places where the opposite things are proclaimed are often empty! It is curious, if the doctrine of the gospel is such a very horrible thing that it drives people away, that at the places where it is preached there are more people than can get in, whereas where some of the modern doctrines are declared you may see more spiders than people! It is a singular circumstance, certainly, yet one for which we can easily account.

A Socinian minister was once asked by one who preached Evangelical truth, 'If I, who proclaim doctrines which you say are obnoxious to common reason, have my place full, and you who preach such pretty, reasonable doctrines can get nobody to hear you, do you not think it is because the people have an idea that what I teach is true, and that what you preach, though it is very pleasant and palatable, is not true, and therefore they do not care to hear it?' It is not by altering our testimony that we are to hope to win an audience, and it is not by hiding the light of the gospel under a bushel that you or I shall discharge our obligations to our Lord. We must speak up for Christ, and so speak up for him that men will be moved to ask us the question, 'What is they Beloved more than another beloved, that thou dost so charge us?'

I have read that Mr Kilpin of Exeter had every pew in the chapel where he preached sketched out on a plan, and the names of all the occupants of the pews written on it, so that he might pray for every one, and, if possible, speak to every one. Such a plan might not be practicable in so large a building as this, but it is an excellent method; and if we cannot adopt it, let this place be mapped out in your own mind, and let every believer, wherever he sits, consider that there is a little district allotted to him, and let him seek to have a word of courteous Christian conversation about divine things with all who sit near him. I suggest this as a very excellent mode of beginning to 'charge' others about Christ. And then in your daily business, in the workshop, at fit times and seasons, at periods when Christian prudence and Christian zeal would give their voice together, introduce Christ and begin to talk of him, and hold him up as the great cure-all for human diseases, the great staff and support for human weakness.

We shall never see as much blessing as we might until the work of the Church becomes far more general than it is at present. There is something which every believer can do for his Lord. He must be able to tell of what he has tasted and handled of the Word of Life, and if he has not tasted and handled it, then he is not a child of God at all. The best teaching in the world is experimental; nothing wins upon men like personal witnessing, not merely teaching the doctrine as we find it in the Book, but as we have felt it in its living power upon our own hearts. When we begin to tell of its effect upon ourselves, it is wonderful what power there is upon others in that testimony.

A person talks to me about a certain medicine, how it is compounded, what it looks like, how many drops must be taken at a dose, and so on. Well, I do not care to hear all that, and I soon forget it; but he tells me that for many months he was bedridden, he was in sore distress and in great pain, and like to die; and, looking at him as he stands before me in perfect health, I am delighted with the change, and he says that it was the medicine which restored him. If I am a sick man in the same state as he was, I say to him, 'Give me the name and address, for I must try that medicine for myself.'

I believe that the simple witness of converted boys and girls, converted lads and lasses, especially the witness of converted fathers and mothers and friends beloved, the witness that comes of the grey head that is backed up by years of godly living, has a wonderful power for the spread of the gospel, and we cannot expect that God will give us any very large blessing until the whole of us shall be at work for our Lord. We need not all climb up the pulpit stairs, but each one of us can proclaim Christ according to our ability, and according to the circumstances in which he has placed us. When we shall do that, then we may expect to see 'greater things than these'. Days that shall make us laugh for very joy of heart, and well nigh make us dance like David did before the ark, will come when all the rank and file of the army, and even those who halt upon their crutches, shall march unanimously against the foe.

Thirdly, it is important for us to MAKE ALL WHO COME IN CONTACT WITH US FEEL THAT CHRIST JESUS IS FIRST AND FOREMOST WITH US.

You perceive that the question of the text is not, 'What is thy Beloved that he should be equal to others?' It is, 'What is thy Beloved more than another beloved?' The idols of the heathen are all made to stand in the Pantheon face to face and there is no quarrelling among them; but as soon as you introduce Christ there, they must all go down, or he will not stay. The principle of the toleration of every form of doctrine – I mean not, of course, civil toleration, which we hold to be always necessary and right, but I mean the principle of mental toleration of all forms of doctrine and all forms and shades of action – is heathenish, for where Christ comes he comes to reign; and when once he enters the soul of a man, it is down, down, down with everything else.

There is a text which is often misunderstood. I heard it read thus only last Sunday: 'No man can serve two masters.' I very much question whether he cannot; I believe he could serve, not only two, but twenty. That is not the meaning of the text; the true reading of it is, 'No man can serve two masters.' They cannot both be masters; if two of them are equal, then neither of them is really master. It is not possible for the soul to be subject to two master-passions. If a man says, 'I love Christ,' that is well; but if he says, 'I love Christ, and I love money, and I love them both supremely,' that man is a liar, for the thing is not possible. There is only one that can be the master-passion; and where Jesus enters the soul, love to him must be the master-passion of the heart.

It strikes me that a Christian, living fully up to his privileges, would be such a man as this. If he had, on one side, the opportunity to enjoy pleasure and, on the other side, a painful opportunity of honouring Christ, he would prefer to honour Christ rather than to enjoy himself. If, on the one hand, there were gain, even lawfully to be had, and on the other hand, Christ could be honoured in a way that would bring no monetary gain, the man would prefer the glorifying of his Master to the obtaining of the advantage in cash which was held out to him. And if it comes to this, that by soft speeches he may get himself into good repute, and that by sternly speaking out and rebuking error he may honour his Master but bring much contempt upon himself, if he be a genuine Christian he will always take the latter course. The first question he will ask will be, 'How can I most honour my Lord? How can I best glorify him?'

It is clear that Christ is not first in every nominal Christian's heart. No, alas! He is not first, and he is not even second, he is very far down in the scale.

Look at them – good honest tradespeople, perhaps, but from the first dawn of Monday morning to the putting up of the shutters on Saturday night, what is the main business of their life? It is only, 'What shall we eat? Or what shall we drink? or wherewithal shall we be clothed?' Now, where is Christ in such as case as that? Look at others; with them the question is, 'Where shall I invest such-and-such an amount of spare cash? How shall I best lay by such-and-such a sum? What field shall I buy next? What house shall I add to my estate?' As for the Lord Jesus, he is put off with the cheese-parings and the candle-ends; he gets a little now and then dropped into the offering-box, but it is only a mere trifle compared with what he ought to receive. The man's words are nine hundred and ninety-nine for himself, and perhaps not much more than half a one for Christ; almost all his time goes to the world, and not to his Lord; his whole self goes to himself, and not to the Saviour to whom he professes to belong.

This is not the case with the truly Christ-like man. With him, Christ is first, Christ is last, Christ is midst, Christ is all in all; and when he speaks about anything connected with Christ, his words come with such a solemn earnestness, that men are impressed with what he says, and they turn round to him and ask, as the daughters of Jerusalem enquired of the spouse, 'What is thy Beloved more than another beloved, that thou dost so charge us?'

(4) Our last thought is this; if ever, through the grace of God, we should possess such a character, and bear such a testimony as we have been talking about, so that men shall ask us the question of the text, IT WILL BE WELL FOR US TO BE PREPARED TO ANSWER IT.

This is an age in which the world asks many questions, and from some Christians it cannot get an answer. I will say one thing which some of you may not like to hear, perhaps, but I cannot help that.

There are some of you who are Baptists; but why? Well, I suppose, because I happen to be one, and you have followed me without carefully studying the teaching of the New Testament upon the question. I fear it is so with some of you, and there are others of you who are Wesleyans or Independents or Church people, but the only reason you can give for being so is that your grandmother or your mother happened to be of that denomination. This is an age in which people do not estimate truth as they should do. A good earnest controversy seems to me to be a very healthy thing, because it turns men's attention somewhat more than usual to divine things.

But you know how it is even with many professing Christian people. They think it would be wicked to read a novel; but if it is written upon a religious subject, it is a very proper thing then. There is hardly a weekly newspaper, nowadays, or even a penny magazine, that can live without having a novel in it;

and there must be a market for all this rubbish or it would not be supplied so plentifully. Why, sirs, in Puritanic times, men read solid books like John Owen's *On the Mortification of Sin*; they studied such works as Richard Gilpin's *On Satan's Temptations* or Stephen Charnock on *The Divine Attributes*. But, in these days, people, who ought to read these solid books so as to be able to give a reason for the hope that is in them, are often wasting their time over poor stuff which only addles the brain, and does the soul no good. I would to God that we could again see a race of sturdy believers, who would hold to nothing but what they had tested by the Word of God; who would receive nothing merely because it was taught by their minister or by their parents or by any human authority, but who would accept with unquestioning faith everything that is revealed in the inspired Book. Our motto still should be, 'To the law and to the testimony: if they speak not according to this word, it is because there is no light in them.' We want to breed again – and oh, may God give us grace to do so! – a race of men who shall be rooted and grounded in the faith, and who, when they are asked for a reason for the hope that is in them, shall be able to give it, not with fear and trembling and hesitation, but with holy boldness and determination, because they have tested and tried the matter for themselves.

See how the spouse does; she does not pause a minute before she gives her reply. She is asked, 'What is thy Beloved more than another beloved?' and she has the answer, as we say, at her fingers' ends, and why was this? Why, because she had it in her heart. So she says, 'My Beloved is white and ruddy, the chiefest among ten thousand.' She does not say, 'Stop a bit, I must read up on that question; I must get myself well-instructed upon it,' but it is such a vital point, and one so dear to her, as it touches the person of her Lord, that she answers an once, 'Is my Beloved better than any other beloved? Certainly he is, and here are the reasons.' She puts them together one after another without a pause, so that the daughters of Jerusalem must have been convinced; and I commend her example to you also, my beloved in Christ Jesus. Do study the Word, that your faith may not stand in the wisdom of men, but in the power of God. I beseech you, if I have taught you anything that is not revealed in the Scriptures, or if you have received anything only as by my authority, give it up until you have tested and tried it by the Word of the Lord. I am not afraid what the result will be, for if in anything I have erred, I pray the Lord to teach me and also to teach you, so that we may grow together in the unity of the Spirit in the bonds of the faith. Do let us all seek to be taught of God; and then, with a holy life added to this divine instruction, and a clear testimony for Jesus Christ constantly borne by us, our witnessing must tell upon the age in which we live.

Oh, that the Lord would send us times of true revival once again! Run your finger down the page of history till you come to the Reformation; what was there in Luther, in Calvin, in Zwingli, that they should have been able to shake the world any more than there is in men who are living nowadays? Nothing but this, that they believed what they did believe, and they spoke with an awful earnestness, like men who meant what they said, and straightway there arose a noble race of men, men who felt the power of faith, and lived it out, and the world was made to feel that 'there were giants in those days'. Then, again, in later times, when the Church had fallen into a fatal slumber, there came the age of Whitefield and Wesley. What was the power of the early Methodists? Why, simply the power of true sincerity combined with holiness! What if I say that it was the power of intruding religion upon men, of forcing men to hear God's voice, of compelling a sleeping world to wake out of its slumbers?

As I sat, last week, in the hall of the Free Church Assembly in Edinburgh, just beneath the Castle, I started in my seat, I thought the whole hall was going to fall, for at one o'clock the gun on the Castle was fired from Greenwich by electricity. It startled every one of us, and I noticed that nearly everybody took out his watch to see whether it was right by the gun. I thought to myself, 'This is just what the Christian Church ought to do. It ought, at the proper time, to give a loud, clear, thundering testimony for God and for truth, so that every man might examine his own conscience, and get himself put right where he is wrong.' Our testimony for Christ ought not to be like the ticking of an ordinary clock or as sounding brass or a tinkling cymbal, but a mighty booming noise that commands and that demands a hearing. Let our soul be but linked with heaven, let the Spirit of the Lord flash the message along the wires, and our life may be just as accurate and just as startling as that time-gun at Edinburgh. So, when men ask us, 'What is they Beloved more than another beloved, that thou dost so charge us?' we shall have an answer ready for them, which may God bless to them, for Christ's sake! Amen.

37

CHRIST'S PERFECTION AND PRECEDENCE

'My beloved is white and ruddy, the chiefest among ten thousand'
(Song of Solomon 5:10).

The spouse in this verse styles her Lord, 'my Beloved,' from which it is easy for us to gather that it is of the utmost importance that our heart's affection should be really and truly set upon Christ Jesus our Lord. We must trust him and we must love him. Christ on the cross saves us when he becomes to us Christ in the heart. It is of small service for us to know of Christ if we do not really trust and love him. It will be of little avail for us to talk of him unless our heart be really welded and knit to him. Let us, therefore, dear friends, commence this evening's meditation with a solemn enquiry made by each one for himself or herself, 'Can I call the Lord Jesus Christ, who was crucified on Calvary, but who now reigns at the right hand of the Father, can I truly call him, 'my Beloved'?'

There may be a question raised in your soul by a natural anxiety lest you should presume, but be not content until you have solemnly and seriously searched your hearts, to know whether in very deed and truth an ardent affection burns within your spirit towards the Lord Jesus. It were better for you that you had never been born than that you should live and die without love to Christ. Remember that startling sentence of the apostle Paul, which is so solemn that I can scarcely quote it without tears: 'If any man love not the Lord Jesus Christ, let him be Anathema Maranatha,' that is, let him be accursed at the coming of the Lord. It will be so with you, dear friends; however shining your moral attributes may have been, however you may have carved your name upon the rock of history, you must go down to endless misery and shame unless your heart has in it a vital sense of true religion, a sincere love to the crucified Christ of Calvary.

If this important personal enquiry has had its due weight upon our minds, it may lead us to another consideration, namely, that it is a blessed thing, if we do love Christ, to be able to speak about our affection for him as a matter of course and a matter of fact; not as a thing that hangs trembling in the balance, but as an ascertained truth and certainty. The spouse does not speak of 'him whom I hope to love by-and-by,' or of 'him whom I trust I shall one day know,' but she calls him, without question or qualification, 'my Beloved.' She is quite sure about this blessed relationship; she raises no doubts and she has no fears concerning it.

I do not say that, if any man has a doubt about his love to Christ, he need therefore necessarily condemn himself; but I do say that he must never be content to continue in such a state. Perhaps they who love the Master best are the very people who will be the most likely to have such a high opinion of the love which he deserves, that they will often chide themselves that they do not love him at all, when they see how little their love is compared with that perfection of affection which he deserves. We must not affirm that the question of anxiety is sinful; it is painful, and anxiety, if it be not divinely removed, will become sinful, but the anxiety is not so in itself.

Yet, beloved, I beseech you to press on beyond this stage of your pilgrim journey. Do not be content to live on hopes and fears and peradventures and surmises. You would not like to think that perhaps you loved your child or your husband or your friend. You would not care to say, 'I hope I love virtue, I hope I love honesty;' but it is a baser thing still for us to allow a question to exist as to whether we love him who is dearer than our own kindred, and who is better than any one moral excellence, seeing that he is the combination of all excellences. O beloved, seek to reach the blessed heights of full assurance, that each one of you may be able to say of Christ, 'This is my Beloved, and this is my Friend; I would as soon doubt my own existence as doubt the love that burns within my heart towards him who has bought me with his precious blood.' Sing, as we have often done:

My Jesus, I love thee, I know thou art mine,
For thee all the follies of sin I resign;
My gracious Redeemer, my Saviour art thou,
If ever I loved thee, my Jesus, 'tis now.

If we have reached that stage in our journey heavenwards, it will be well if we go a step further. Loving our Lord and Saviour in our heart, and being assured of that love in our inmost conscience after earnest heart-searching, it will be well if we have the courage never to hesitate in the avowal of that love. Our love to Christ is so sacred a passion that it is not to be talked of in all companies. We must not cast our pearls before swine; but, on the other hand, it is so ennobling a passion that we need never blush to own it in any company. If we ever are ashamed of loving Christ, we have good reason to be ashamed of such shameful shame. When you have heard his dear name reviled, did you ever start for fear lest you should be called upon to share his reproach? Did you ever sit silent when you ought to have spoken because Christ was being blasphemed? Did you ever try to make it out to yourself that it was a prudent retirement that shunned the conflict when, in very truth, it was a hateful cowardice that turned its back upon the Crucified in the hour of his need? I fear that the charge might be brought against the most of us; if so, let us humbly confess it on our knees alone, and blush before the presence of our blessed Master. Remember what we sang just now:

Jesus! And shall it ever be?
A mortal man ashamed of thee!
Ashamed of thee, whom angels praise,
Whose glories shine thro' endless days.

Ashamed of Jesus! Sooner far
Let evening blush to own a star;
He sheds the beams of light divine
O'er this benighted soul of mine.

Ashamed of Jesus! Just as soon
Let midnight be ashamed of noon:
'Tis midnight with my soul, till he,
Bright Morning Star, bid darkness flee.

Ashamed of Jesus! That dear Friend
On whom my hopes of heaven depend!
No; when I blush, be this my shame,
That I no more revere his name.

What can there be to be ashamed of in loving him whom angels love, whom God loves, whom all holy spirits love? What! Not love him? If he were not in himself God, yet he has been so good to me that I must love him. It is an old proverb that we must speak of friends as we find them, and praise the bridge that carries us over the stream; and here is one in whom we have found such goodness, such kindness, such gentleness, and such disinterested affection, one who has done such wonders for us that if we do not love him, and boldly declare that we love him, we have good reason to be ashamed of ourselves and to hide our heads in confusion for ever and ever.

Young people, you who have lately come to love Christ, do not begin as some of your fathers did, in that half-hearted fashion which has continued with them until this day. Alas! There are some professing Christians who have grown grey and yet have scarcely ever dared to speak the name of Christ in company. Yes, some of them have even been ashamed up to this moment to be baptized and to come to the Lord's table. They say that they love Christ, and I hope they do; yet up to this hour, baptism has been a cross too heavy for them to bear, and the Lord's supper has seemed to them to be an ordeal instead of a means of blessing. Play the man, young Christian; be not ashamed to avow your Lord! If ever there was unfurled in this world a banner which deserved the utmost allegiance of human hearts, it is the blood-stained banner of the cross; and if ever there was a Leader who deserved that men should speak his praises, not 'With 'bated breath, and whisp'ring humbleness,' but with manly enthusiasm, that Leader is the Christ of God, who loved you and gave himself for you. Yes, utter it in the face of a scoffing world, stand to it in the teeth of a ribald infidel generation, declare it before the crowd of gainsayers who will mock you to scorn as you pronounce it, 'This is my Beloved – the Christ that died, the Christ that ever liveth at the right hand of God – this is my Beloved, and I am not ashamed to avow him.'

Suppose that we have come as far as this – and I believe that many of us have come so far – it will be our bounden duty to go a step further. Loving Jesus, knowing that we love him and boldly confessing our love to him, let us, next, so study his person and his character that we shall be able to give a reason for the love that is in us to any who make the enquiry, 'What is thy Beloved more than another beloved?'

You observe that the spouse not only calls him, 'my Beloved,' but she describes the complexion of his countenance, and the details relating to his whole person; she hath a word of praise for all his features and all his members. She knows him so well that she speaks of him with a tongue like the pen of a ready writer. So, beloved, let us study Christ as we come again to this communion table.

You who love and fear him, neglect not your Bibles; neglect not that fellowship which, like the light of a candle, shines upon the page of the Bible. Some of you are studying earthly sciences, perhaps you give your minds to the classics, or you delight to master the mysteries of mathematics; but take care that this most excellent science, the science of Christ crucified, is not made to take a second place with you. Always put this science first; try to understand the glory of your Lord's person, without beginning of days or end of years; search into the purity of his character in all that he was here below from his birth to his death. Be conversant with Christ in all his sacred offices; think much of his precious blood, and of all the holy mysteries that cluster around his cross. Trace him from Bethlehem to Gabbatha, and then from Gabbatha follow him in his resurrection and ascension along the star-bespangled way up to the throne of his glory, and let your soul hopefully linger in the full belief of his second coming, and in all the glory that shall surely follow the day of his august appearing. Study Christ, study Christ, so as to be able to tell others of him, and be not slow to communicate to those of an enquiring mind that which you have yourself heard and seen and handled of the Word of life, for so the spouse doth in the chapter before us.

This much must suffice by way of introduction, or rather, by way of practical exhortation to such of you as are enlisted beneath Christ's royal banner of love.

Now let us proceed to consider the general description of the Bridegroom given by his spouse in this verse. First, she saith, 'My Beloved is white and ruddy.' These words set forth his charming complexion. Secondly, the spouse calls her Beloved 'the chiefest among ten thousand,' and so she describes his personal precedence.

First then, the spouse saith, 'my Beloved is white and ruddy,' and so she sets forth HIS CHARMING COMPLEXION.

It seems to me that the spouse intends by these words to call attention to two chief characteristics of her Lord's most blessed person. Had not Solomon often seen the snow-white lambs – the emblems of purity – brought up to the temple to be offered in sacrifice? 'So,' said he, 'my Beloved is white.' Had he not also seen the uplifted knife in the priest's hand, and then seen the ruby stream as it flowed down at the foot of the altar till the white lamb was stained crimson in its own blood? So he puts the two together, and these two things, whether they are meant in the text or not, are certainly the two essentials of the Christian faith concerning the person of Christ; and he is no Christian, and indeed, cannot be a Christian, who hath not well learned and joyously received the two truths which the white and the red here set forth.

Our Lord is, first of all, in himself white; that is, he has immaculate perfection of character. As God, in him is light and no darkness at all; perfect purity, without a trace of sin. He is very God of very God, the Holy One of Israel. In his Godhead, Jesus Christ is perfection itself. As to his manhood, the term *whiteness* well describes him who was born without natural corruption, or taint of hereditary depravity – 'that holy thing', the Christ of God, who became incarnate, yet without sin. Doth not this word 'white' describe him also in his actual life? There was never any sin in Christ. You may challenge every word of his, and you shall find it pure; you may thrust it into the furnace heated seven times hotter than it is wont to be heated, yet shall it come forth as it went in, for no dross shall be found in it. As to Christ's actions, they are matchless and perfect in every respect; the two great objects of his life were the glory of God and the good of man. So pure, indeed, is the character of Christ, that even those who hated his religion, and have read the writings of the four Evangelists with no design but to find some ground for cavilling, have nevertheless been cowed before the majesty of the perfect life of Christ. In fact, it is today as it was of old, when the officers were sent to take him prisoner; they went back without him, for they said, 'Never man spake like this Man.' There is no spot in him; he is the Lamb of God without blemish, the perfect Christ, and hence it is that we love him.

We love those who possess true excellence, and therefore we must love Christ, for he has every excellence in perfection. If there were no atonement, if we did not regard our Lord Jesus as our Saviour, yet still every true heart ought to love him, and to be won to him. There are such charms in his character that, if our souls were not besotted by the love of sin, we must worship and adore this glorious Son of God, who is the brightness of the Father's glory and the express image of his person. He is so white and pure that we ought to love him.

But, next, we come to the blood-shedding, the sacrificial character of Christ. Alas! That this glorious doctrine of the atoning sacrifice should ever be cast into the background, as it so often is, for the blood-shedding of Christ is the very essence of Christianity. In the fulness of time, Jesus Christ, born of a woman, came into this world as the Substitute for sinners. The vengeance of God against sin was poured out upon him; he suffered death that those who trust him might not die; the Lamb of God was slain in their room and place and stead, that he might render satisfaction to the injured honour and broken law of God. This is the chief reason, after all, why Christ's people love him, because, in his precious blood, they see the pardon of all their sins, they see the lifting of themselves up into the life of God, they see the open way of access unto the Father, they see the gates of heaven opened to all believers.

Beloved, there are some in these days who cry up the glorified Christ, and I will cry him up with them, nor shall they find a word too strong for his praise; yet they would have men trust in the glorified Christ, they preach the doctrine of the second advent as though it were the chief teaching of Holy Scripture, and they seem to look to the second coming of Christ rather than to the first. But let Paul's words be always our motto, 'We preach Christ crucified, unto the Jews a stumbling block, and unto the Greeks foolishness, but unto them which are called, both Jews and Greeks, Christ the power of God, and the wisdom of God.' With that same apostle let us cry, 'God forbid that I should glory, save in the cross of our Lord Jesus Christ.' His throne is glorious, and his glory shall speak for itself; but the despised and crucified Christ is the source of the sinner's salvation, and this truth is ever to be preached and held up as the first and cardinal doctrine of our holy faith.

Brethren, let us thus look at Jesus, 'white' in his spotless innocence, 'ruddy' in his sacrificial suffering. Let us view him as the one sinless Being, and also as the chief of martyrs, the One in whom was no sin, yet upon whom the Lord did cause to meet the iniquity of all his people, with all the suffering it deserved, and all the vengeance and wrath of Almighty God that were rightly due to the transgressors. I must not detain you longer upon this part of the subject, but I cannot pass from it without asking the question, Do we all love this precious One in whom there is all excellence, and in whom there is also this matchless suffering, this sin-atoning grief? Oh! If thy heart be truly set on Christ, thou hast a portion so rich that thou needest not envy even the angels, for

Never did angels taste above,
Redeeming grace and dying love.

If this is thy lot, thou art happy, thrice happy, though poor and sick and unknown. If Christ be indeed thy Beloved, thou art married to One who is the equal of the Eternal God. If thy heart embraceth Christ, and Christ be really thine, thou hast more than the world can ever compass, thou hast more than heaven itself could give if Christ were withdrawn from its courts of glory. Be thou happy, then, be thou joyous in thy Lord, let thy heart go up to him, and rest thou in him; and when thou comest to the communion table, let it be with thine eye and thine heart fixed on thy Beloved, who is 'white and ruddy'.

But, my dear hearer, if thou hast not Christ, oh! how I wish thou hadst him, and thou mayest have him this very night. Many of you are strangers to me. At this time of the year, when so many of our regular hearers take their vacation at the seaside, or in the country, there is room for more strangers. Well, dear friends, we are strangers to one another, but I hope many of you are not strangers to the Master; or if you are, possibly the Lord brought you here that you might meet with him, and that he might meet with you. It would be a blessed Sabbath indeed to your soul if now you could say, 'This perfect Man, I must love him; this suffering Substitute, I must trust him. God has laid him in Zion as a foundation and a chief cornerstone; I will come, and build all my hopes for time and for eternity upon him and his great atoning sacrifice.' Thou art black, poor sinner, but then he is white; and his white shall stand in the place of thy black. Thou art black, but then he is ruddy, and his crimson blood shall wash away every speck and stain of thy sin. All thou hast to do is simply to look to him by faith, for there is life in a look at him. Only trust him, trembler; only trust him, guilty sinner; only trust him, and that simple trust shall bring thee life, health, perfection, heaven, God himself. God grant that so it may be!

2. Now passing on to the remaining words of the text, notice that the spouse saith of her Beloved that he is 'the chiefest among ten thousand'. These words set forth HIS PERSONAL PRECEDENCE.

'The chiefest among ten thousand.' Is it not incorrect to say 'the chiefest'? I care not if it is; and I would not like to see the word altered into 'chief.' Human words at best are such poor things that they stagger under the mighty burden of the perfections of Christ. We seem to need some of those huge pillars and pedestals that we sometimes see outside massive piles of architecture, that we may bear up the ponderous truth of our text; we must have such words as 'chiefest', for common language does not suffice in such a case as this. I suppose that in heaven they have done with our poor imperfect speech, and know how to speak of Christ as he deserves. Anyhow, we believe with good John Berridge:

Living tongues are dumb at best,
We must die to speak of Christ.

He is the chiefest among ten thousand, and it so happens that this word 'chiefest' may mean any one of three or four things. First, take it as it stands – 'Chiefest' – that is to say, Christ is higher, better, lovelier, more excellent than any who are round about him. If you shall bring ten thousand angels, he is the chiefest Angel, the Messenger of the covenant. If you shall bring ten thousand friends, he is the chiefest Friend, the 'Friend that sticketh closer than a brother'. If you shall bring ten thousand physicians, he is the best Physician, for he healeth all diseases. If you find ten thousand shepherds, he is the Good Shepherd, the Great Shepherd, the Chief Shepherd. If you find one, two, a hundred, a thousand, ten thousand, all excellent, they must all give way when he appeareth, as the stars are forgotten when the sun ariseth in his strength. Christ is the chiefest, the best, the highest of all beings; whatsoever excellences there may be in others, they are all eclipsed by the surpassing excellences that are found in him.

Christ is the chiefest among ten thousand; that is to say, he is the Head, the Ruler, the Prince, the King, the Lord over all. There he standeth, with his feet like most fine gold, and all around him are the chariots of God that are twenty thousand, even thousands of angels, and there is not one who lifts his head as high even as his Lord's feet, and amongst all the cherubic and seraphic host there is not one who would not count it his highest heaven to fly at Christ's command to the meanest cottage, or even to a dunghill whereon Lazarus doth lie with the dogs licking his sores. Christ is King of all the angels, and here below, too, there are then thousand forces and powers continually at work, for God hath his hosts and armaments on earth as well as in heaven. Christ is Lord High Admiral of all the seas, the great Commander-in-chief of all the battalions, the mighty King who ruleth over all; and when he cometh into his Church, we know that he is Chief there. Who dare look at him, and claim equality with him?

I tremble at the thought of that dreadful blasphemy which might well have condemned England to the lowest hell for daring to call an earthly monarch 'the head of the Church'. It cannot be, it is sheer impiety, for man or angel ever to dare to steal that title of Christ. He alone is King in the midst of Zion, he is the one and only Head of the Church. It was a brave deed of Cameron and his comrades to lift up their voices against this infamy when first it sought to spread itself in Scotland; and it is ill on our part that we have not lifted up our voices more loudly against it in this our land. A man or a woman, head of the Church? No, never! Let Christ, and Christ alone, wear the crown he bought with his own blood; he alone is King, and let him ever be so proclaimed and acknowledged.

In matters of religion, we want not Caesar's favour, and we fear not Caesar's frown. Christ is the one Head of his Church, and his true Church is free both from the control and the patronage of the State, and so she shall be whenever true hearts beat loyally to Christ, and wherever true lips speak his praises. He is 'the chiefest among ten thousand'. If there be ten thousand fathers, he is 'the Everlasting Father'. If there be ten thousand teachers, yet shall they not be called Rabbis, for One is our Teacher and Rabbi, even Christ, and at his feet the reverent Church adoringly doth bow, hailing him and him alone as Head and Master, 'the chiefest among ten thousand'.

According to the Septuagint, the text has another meaning. Our Lord in Scripture is called the chosen One, the elect of God. As the psalmist puts it, speaking by prophecy, 'I have exalted One chosen out of the people.' Christ is chosen out of ten thousand, as the Mediator to stand between God and men. Whoever else might have been employed by God for this service – and we are not able to think of any other – yet first of all was Christ chosen of God; and today we may call him the chosen One because he is the chosen of his Church. If the question were put to us, and a poll were demanded upon it, 'Of all the Church of Christ, who shall be Head and Lord? Who shall be Master? Who shall be Teacher? Who shall be the Beloved?', would not all of us hold up our hands for him – yea, hands and hearts as well, and we would even lay down our heads on the block if it were necessary to secure his election. Every one of us would, with a burst of acclamation, unconstrained except by his own charms, elect him to be the head and Lord in the midst of Zion.

I put to thee, dear hearer, a more personal question: Hast thou chosen him? If not, wilt thou by his grace put thy hand on thy heart now, and say, 'Now have I chosen him because he has first chosen me'? I pray thee at once to make choice of him; for if thou dost, thou wilt never repent of it. I have stood by a great many deathbeds; but there is one scene I never saw, and never expect to see, and that is a child of God repenting that he ever loved Christ Jesus. May you be able to say what we have often sung:

'Tis done! The great transaction's done;
I am my Lord's, and he is mine;
He drew me, and I followed on,
Charm'd to confess the voice divine.

High heaven, that heard the solemn vow,
That vow renew'd shall daily hear;
Till in life's latest hour I bow,
And bless in death a bond so dear.

May Christ be the chosen of your heart! God grant that no soul here may refuse admission to the Prince of Peace!

Lastly, according to the margin of our Bible, the text bears this meaning, and probably should be thus read, 'He is the Standard-bearer among ten thousand.' The 'ten thousand' we may consider to be the warriors of God, enlisted to fight his battles against error and sin. Who is the Standard-bearer of God's militant host below? The only answer is that 'Christ is the Standard-bearer among ten thousand'. For a standard-bearer, there was need of a select man, with good strong arms, who could firmly grasp the pole that held aloft the standard – a man resolute of heart, who, having once taken charge of the flag, would sooner die than loose his hold of the colours. It needed for a standard-bearer one who was courageous, one who would not be alarmed by the din and strife of battle and turn his back, but would go at the head of the host, carrying the banner into the very thick of the fray, to lead on the militant band till they had put all their foes to the rout. The standard-bearer should be a stronger man than all the rest of the host, for

'If the standard-bearer fall,
As fall full well he may,'

what mischief would come to the host, and what confusion to the hearts of all the warriors! Now, our Lord Jesus Christ has come into this world, and set up a standard because of the truth, and well does he handle it, firmly doth he grasp it. When on the cross, the battle thickened round him; all the hosts of hell and all the bands of cruel ones on earth sought to smite him, and to seize the standard, too, but he bore it still aloft through all the dreadful fray; and this day, though he is now in heaven, yet by his blessed Spirit that standard is still unfurled to the breeze.

In the order of his providence, it seems to me that Christ is always bearing that standard a little farther and a little farther on, and if Christians would but keep nearer to Christ, and be more like him, the victories of his Church would be daily fresh and new. We should soon see this world conquered for Christ if we kept step with the Divine Standard-bearer. He is bearing that standard in front of some of you into that alley at the back of the house where you live; dare you follow him, and go and win some spoil for him? Christ's banner is uplifted in many parts of London tonight; dare you follow it? Dare you stand in the streets, and in the byways, to tell of heaven's accomplished salvation, and of Christ's finished work that saves from death and hell? The nations of the earth want the gospel. Christ is opening the gates of brass to our missionaries, are there no young men here who will follow Christ's banner as it gleams afar? Have I no young John Williams here? Is there no young man here who will be a Robert Moffat or a William Knibb? There is the Standard-bearer; Christ is not in the background; oh! wherefore should we be so slow to follow him? We are not straitened in him, but in ourselves. God give us to be worthy followers of so glorious a Standard-bearer as Christ Jesus our Lord!

Lift up your eyes to heaven and see him there bearing the standard at the right hand of God, and the troops are marshalling, and the bugle soundeth for some of us. Grey-heads, are you ready? Young men and maidens, are you ready? If the trumpet sounds in your ears tonight, are you ready to rally round that standard, and to sing the praises of him who has called you? He is coming soon, and then, when the Standard-bearer is here, shall we have a share in his triumph? Shall we rise to shame and confusion of face, or shall we rise to participate in the splendour of his universal reign? God grant that we may all love and trust the Divine Standard-bearer, and that we may all be found among his faithful soldiers for evermore!

The Lord be with you, beloved, for his dear Son's sake! Amen.

38

SPICES, FLOWERS, LILIES and MYRRH

'His cheeks are as a bed of spices, as sweet flowers: his lips like lilies, dropping sweet smelling myrrh' (Song of Solomon 5:13).

In this chapter the spouse describes in detail the person of her Beloved. She is not satisfied with saying, 'He is altogether lovely'; but she delights to talk of the charms of each part of his sacred person, and to picture the beauties of his divine form and features, so that thereby she may, perhaps, win some other heart first to admire and then to love him.

Dear friends, there are some things about which you will be wise not to go into details. You had better speak in general terms of half the things on earth; for if you once describe them in detail, you will have to confess that they are marred by a thousand imperfections. You may be content to give merely a surface glance at them; for if you dive beneath the surface, you will soon discover much that will alter your opinion of the thing that at first sight looked so lovely. But it is not so with Jesus, our Well-beloved. You may talk of him as long as ever you please, and praise him as much as ever you can, yet you will never discover that you have exaggerated his excellences. You may go into detail about him, and dwell with much minuteness upon everything relating to his character, his offices, his words, his deeds and you shall be made to wonder at the perfection of each one of them. You may apply the microscope to Christ; you may examine his little things, if, indeed, anything can be little that refers to him; you may look into the deep things of Christ, the hidden things of Christ, his secrets, and the more, closely you look, the more you shall be amazed, and astonished, and filled with delight.

It is of Christ, the Heavenly Bridegroom, that we perceive the spouse to be speaking, and mentioning in detail at least ten particulars, dwelling with delight upon the beauties of his head and his locks, his eyes and his cheeks, his lips and his hands, and every part of him; and, beloved friends, I think it shows true love to Christ when we want to speak at length upon everything that concerns him. The general hearer says, 'Oh, yes, yes! of course, Christ is the Son of God, and he is also perfect man, I believe that'; but he does not want you to go into minute particulars concerning your Lord. It is not so with those who truly love the Saviour; they wish to know all that can be known about him. True love likes to become familiar with the object of its affection; its heart is set upon that object, it studies it, and can never know it too well or too closely. True love to Christ thinks of him from morning till night; it is glad to be released from other thoughts that it may follow only its one darling pursuit. True love to Christ seeks to go to him, to live with him, to live upon him, and thus to know him so intimately that things which were unobserved and passed over at the first, stand out in clear light to the increased joy and delight of the contemplative mind. I wish, dear friends, that we had many more of those people about who study Christ from head to foot, that they may learn all that can be learned about him; those who would be able, with the spouse, to talk of his charms and beauties in detail, and to describe them as she does with rapturous delight.

You know how very unacquainted many people are with the Song of Solomon; they shut up this Book of Canticles in despair, and say that they cannot understand its meaning. You will find that it is just the same with every truly spiritual thing. If you put into the hands of any one of them a deeply-spiritual book, he will, say, 'I cannot comprehend what the writer means; the man seems to be in a rapture, and I cannot make out what he is aiming at by such writing.' Just so; unspiritual people are all at sea in spiritual things, and even some of God's children, who do know Christ so as to be saved by him, seem to be altogether out of their depth when you begin to speak of the things which you have made touching the King, or dilate upon those special truths which only experience and fellowship with Christ can reveal to the soul.

In speaking upon our text, I am sure that I shall not say too much in praise of my Lord and Master, my fear is that I shall not say a thousandth part as much as he deserves – and yet, mayhap, it shall seem but trivial talk to some who as yet do not know that one hair of his head is worth more than the whole world, and that one drop of his precious blood has an eternal efficacy about it. On the other hand, I know that I shall not speak too enthusiastically for those whose hearts are warm with love to Christ. May the Lord, in great mercy, make us all to have such hearts, and he shall have all the praise!

There are two things I shall speak of as I may be helped by the Holy Spirit. First, *Christ looked upon is very lovely*: 'His cheeks are as a bed of spices, as sweet flowers.' Secondly, *Christ listened to is very precious*: 'His lips like lilies, dropping sweet smelling myrrh.' There is an important distinction between the two heads of my discourse that I want you to notice before I proceed further; for there is a considerable difference between Christ looked upon and Christ listened to. There are some who listen to Christ's gospel, and they do well; but those who also look with eyes of love upon his sacred person, those who contemplate not only what he says but what he is, those who delight to know not only what he taught but what he is who taught it, these are they who have penetrated yet further into the mysteries of Christ.

With these we begin, as we consider our first point, CHRIST LOOKED UPON IS VERY LOVELY. Note that these saints first see their Lord's loveliness, and then they say concerning him, 'His cheeks are as a bed of spices, as sweet flowers.' But why do they mention his cheeks?

I suppose, first, because *every part of Christ is inexpressibly delightful*. Take any portion of his countenance that you may, and it has surpassing beauty about it. The spouse had already spoken upon her Beloved's head, and locks, and eyes, and now she mentions his cheeks. Any sight of Christ is delightful; a single passing glimpse of him is a foretaste of heaven, the beginning of paradise. Though you see but little of Christ, yet if it be Christ whom you really see, that sight will save you. Though you see Christ, as it were, with but one eye and though that eye be dim, and though that dim eye be filled with tears, yet if you do but see him at all, that sight will save you, and just in proportion as you are able to see him, your delight will increase. But a sight of him in any capacity, and under any form, has great richness of sweetness in it.

Think for a moment what is meant by a sight of 'his cheeks'. Though you may not yet see the majesty, of his brow as King of kings and Lord of lords; though you may not perceive the brightness of the lightning flashes of his eyes, which are as a flame of fire; though you may scarcely be able to imagine at present what will be the glory of his second advent; yet, if you can but see the cheeks that he gave to the smiters, if you do but know something of him as the suffering Saviour, you shall find that there is inexpressible delight in him, and with the spouse you will say, 'His cheeks are as a bed of spices.' To a believing soul, then, there is great delight in every part of the Lord Jesus Christ.

But, methinks, the saints see *great loveliness in those parts of Christ which have been most despised*. Just now, I mentioned the cheek as one of those parts of Christ's blessed body that were exposed to special shame, as Isaiah foretold, using by inspiration the very words of the Messiah in his agony: 'I gave my back to the smiters, and my cheeks to them that plucked off the hair: I hid not my face from shame and spitting.' Oh! if we could but see him now, if we could but gaze upon his face as it is in glory, what a subject of meditation it would be to think that ever the spittle of cruel mockers did run a-down those blessed cheeks, that infinite loveliness was insulted with inconceivable contempt, the holy face of the Incarnate Son of God distained with the accursed spittle of brutal men. O my soul, how low thy Lord has stooped! Canst thou really believe it possible that it should have been so? Yea, thou knowest that, it was so; yet, is it not sad to think that his dear face, which is as the sun shining in his strength, which is indeed the very heaven of heavens, the light of the temple of God above, is it not sad to think that his face should have been spit upon for thy sake, and because of thy sin and thine iniquity? Alas! that each of us had a part in that shameful deed.

My Jesus! who with spittle vile
Profaned thy sacred brow?
Or whose unpitying scourge has made
Thy precious blood to flow?

'Tis I have thus ungrateful been,
Yet, Jesus, pity take!
Oh, spare and pardon me, my Lord,
For thy sweet mercy's sake!

'It was I, with my vain and idle talk, with my false and proud speech, that did spit into that dear face.' How sad that he should ever have been made to suffer so! O glorious love, that he should be willing even to stoop to this terrible depth of ignominy that he might lift us up to dwell with him on high! So, I say again, every part of Christ is lovely, but that which has been most despised and most subjected to suffering and shame for us is the peculiar subject of our delightful contemplation.

And next, my brethren, *those parts of Christ in which we do not immediately see any special office or use* are, nevertheless, peculiarly lovely to the saints. I can gaze by faith on the brow of him who plans for me, and admire his infinite wisdom. I can think of the eye of him who looks in love upon me, and bless him for his care. I can praise the lips that speak for me in heaven, and that speak to me upon earth, and I can bless the matchless eloquence that never ceases to plead for me and with me; but as for the cheeks of Christ, what do they do for me? What peculiar function have they to perform? I fear that we are all too apt to ask concerning Christ, 'How is this to work for our advantage, and how is that to turn out for our profit?' Has it come to this, that we are never to love Christ except when we see that we are profited by him? If there be an abstruse doctrine, as we think it, that does not appear to have a practical outlook, are we, therefore, never to speak of it? If we cannot see that we derive comfort or profit or sanctification from some teaching which may be high, mysterious, sublime, so that we do not see whereunto it tendeth, yet, beloved, are we to refuse to think of it? Until the question '*Cui bono?*' shall have been answered, will we seal up that sacred page and never read it? Do you care only for the lips that speak to you? Have you no love for the cheeks that are silent? Do you care for nothing but for the eyes that are watching over you? If there come to you nothing from those cheeks of your Lord yet shall they not be to you 'as a bed of spice, as sweet flowers'? The fact is, we are not to judge concerning Christ in any such fashion as this; on the contrary, if there is any duty which Christ has commanded, but which, instead of seeming to be easy and profitable to us, is hard, and requireth that we should give so much that Judas will cry out, 'To what purpose is this waste?' let us never mind him, but break our alabaster boxes, and pour out the sweet perfume upon our dear Master. Let the cheeks that seem to have no special office to fulfil, let that part of Christ or of Christianity that seemeth to serve no end that we can see, be nevertheless precious to us. These are his cheeks, therefore are they precious to me; this duty is a command from him, therefore I must perform it; and this doctrine, of which I do not see the practical end, is, nevertheless, a doctrine of his teaching, therefore I accept it with delight.

But further, beloved children of God, the followers of Christ have an intense admiration, an almost infinite love for *that part of Christ by which they are able to commune with him,* and perhaps that is one reason why his cheeks are here specially mentioned. The cheek is the place of fellowship where we exchange tokens of love. What a blessing it is that Christ should have had a cheek for the lips of love to approach, and to kiss! What a privilege it is that ever it should be possible for a loving heart to express its affection to Christ! If he had accepted us, and then put us right away from him, and said, 'There, you may love me, but you must never tell me of it'; if we were conscious that, when we did talk of our love to Christ, he never knew it, for he was far away, and high above us, and did not care for such poor love as ours; in such a case, he would not be half such a Christ as he now is to us. If he had taken himself away to the ivory palaces, and had shut to the door, and if, when we tried to gaze up at him there, he only looked down upon us with his countenance 'as Lebanon, excellent as the cedars', but never stooped to where we were, that he might commune with us, and that we might tell out to him the story of our love, he would not be half so sweet to us as he is now.

Many of you know what it is to pray right into his very ear in the time of your sorrow, and you also know what it is to speak right into his ear in the hour of your joy; and, sometimes, when you have been alone with him (now I am talking of the deep things of Christ, of the pearls which are not to be cast before swine), you know that he has heard what you have said to him. You have been as certainly assured that he has been listening to your declaration as if, like Peter, you had heard him ask, 'Lovest thou me?' and you had answered, 'Lord, thou knowest all things; thou knowest that I love thee'; and you have been delighted with the thought that he did know that you loved him, and that you might tell him that it was so. You rejoiced also that you could go forth into the world, and do something that he would see you do, something that you did not do for the sake of the church, much less for your own sake, but which you did all for him, just as you would give him the kisses of love upon his own cheeks, which are 'as a bed of spices, as sweet flowers'. Those of you who have ever been in communion with Christ know what I mean, and you know that anything by which you come into close contact with Christ is very, very delightful to you.

How greatly we rejoice to think of Christ's humanity, because we feel that it brings him very near to us! He is our Brother, he feels what we feel, and through his humanity this wondrous Man is next of kin unto us. He who is truly God, is also our near Kinsman, bone of our bone, and flesh of our flesh. How the blessed doctrine of the union of the saints with Christ delights us, as we remember that 'we are members of his body, of his flesh, and of his bones'! How the wondrous truth of the indwelling of the Holy Ghost charms us, because the same Spirit that rested upon him rests also upon us, and the holy oil that was first poured upon him who is the Head descends even to us who are as the hem of the garment that reaches even to the ground! It is the same Spirit that is upon him that is upon us, and so again we are one with him. Does not this truth also make prayer very sweet as the means of getting to Christ, and does it not make praise very sweet as another means of communicating with Christ ? And oh! though some do put the sacred table of the Lord out of its proper place, yet is the communion of the body of Christ a dear and blessed ordinance. Often do we know him in the breaking of bread when we have not recognized him, even though he has talked with us by the way. So, you see, the saints delight in those truths concerning Christ which enable them to have fellowship with him, and thus they realise what the spouse meant when she said, 'His cheeks are as a bed of spices, as sweet flowers.'

I have thus tried to show you that the saints see great beauty in Christ when they look upon him; but now I have to remind you that saints also labour to tell others of the loveliness of Christ when they look upon him. In this blessed service, however, they must in part labour in vain, for, as we, have often sung:

> Living tongues are dumb at best,
> We must die to speak of Christ.

I suppose that even he who has seen Christ in heaven could not fully tell us of his beauties. Paul has not told us much of what he heard in paradise, though he told all he could tell after he had been caught up to the third heaven. He 'heard unspeakable words, which it is not lawful (or possible) for a man to utter'. Oh, how one longs for but a moment's sight of Christ in glory! One might be content to have only a dry crust, and to lie in an underground dungeon for the rest of one's life, if one might but gaze on his blessed face for once, and hear him say, 'I have loved thee with an everlasting love.' Perhaps you think you would have a deal to tell if that were your blessed experience; but, beloved, you might not have anything to tell, you would only feel less able to speak than ever you were before. You would be so dazzled, so astonished, so amazed, at the glory of Christ that, peradventure, you might never be able to speak at all.

The spouse, however, in our text tries to speak of the loveliness of Christ by comparisons. She cannot do it with one emblem, she must have two even concerning his cheeks; they are 'as a bed of spices', 'as sweet flowers'.

Notice, in the metaphors used by the spouse, that there is *a blending of sweetness and beauty*: 'as a bed of spices', there is sweetness; and then, 'as sweet flowers', there is beauty. There is sweetness to the nostrils and beauty to the eye, spice for its fragrance and flowers for their loveliness. In Christ, there is something for every spiritual sense, and for every spiritual sense there is a complete satisfaction and delight in him. Look at him, and he is to your sight as sweet flowers.

Get a spiritual taste of him, and then he is as honey and the honeycomb. Take, as it were, a spiritual smell of him, and you shall find that he is 'as a bed of spices'. Touch him, or hear him, and it shall be just the same; you shall find the daintiest, the highest, the most harmonious feelings your spirit ever knew when you do but approach him with any spiritual sense in full exercise. Our blessed Master may be viewed from every side, and yet he is perfect from every aspect. We have seen him far above us. There are few things that look well when set up aloft, and gazed at from below; but he does. We shall one day see him side by side, and I warrant you that we shall count him lovely then even as we reckon him lovely now. Angels have looked down upon him from above, gazing on him when he was here on earth, and he was infinitely lovely to their vision then. Seen by daylight or by moonlight, seen in the crowd or seen in solitude, seen in our days of sorrow or seen in our times of joy, our Lord Jesus possesses all kinds of lovelinesses compacted into one perfect loveliness, all perfections blended to make one perfection, every sweet concocted and distilled to make one perfect sweetness. Well, therefore, may his spouse pile up the metaphors, and blend sweet spices with fragrant flowers in trying to describe his charms.

Notice that, when the spouse is speaking even of the cheeks of her Beloved, she brings in the idea of *abundance* – spices, ay, 'a bed of spices'; flowers – not one or two, but, according to the Hebrew, 'towers of perfume', which I understand to mean those raised beds which we delight to have in our gardens, where there are many flowers set in order, forming charming banks of beauty. No doubt Solomon had some of those in his garden, for 'there is nothing new under the sun'; and those raised beds of dainty flowers are fit emblems of the beauteous cheek of Christ, with its delicate tints of white and red. So in Christ there is infinite abundance.

There is also in Christ infinite *variety*; there is in him all you can want of any one thing, and there is more than all you can want of everything. There is all that your soul could take in of any one thing, and more than your soul could take in if it were multiplied a million times, and could take in a million precious things at once. There is all you ever have wanted, and all you ever will want. Did I say, 'want'? There is in Christ all you can desire, for that is one of his names, 'He is all desires'. When you get to heaven, and have a larger heart than you at present possess, when your soul shall be spacious as the sea, if it could be vast as the universe itself, still he would be able to fill it, and still to be himself overflowing with blessing. There is in him abundance, and there is variety. Oh, what a Christ he is! 'As a bed of spices, and as sweet flowers.'

The spouse's metaphors seem to me also to suggest *use and delight.* She speaks of spices, for which there is practical use in surgery and in medicine, for preservation and for perfume; and she also mentions sweet flowers, for which there may not be any particular use, but which are charming for ornament, and for the delectation of taste. So, dear friends, in Christ Jesus there is all that we want, but there is a great deal more. There is something beside and beyond our actual necessities, there are many spiritual luxuries. I like, at the Lord's table, to think to myself, 'Here is bread, that is the staff of life; but what is that in the cup? Wine! Ah! Why not water? Here is more than I need, for I can live without wine', but the Lord says that I shall not do so. He will not only give his people the best things, but the best of the best; when our Lord keeps house, he does not allow us just so many ounces of bread, and so many ounces of meat, as they do in the workhouse, but he says, 'Eat ye that which is good, and let your soul delight itself in fatness.' The Bridegroom cries, 'Eat, O friends; drink, yea, drink abundantly, O beloved'; and he does not merely bring out wine, but you know how it is described, 'wines on the lees well-refined'. Christianity is not the bond-slave's starvation allowance that some people make it out to be: duty and doing and serving to win Christ and to keep up your position, and I know not what besides. It is heirship with Christ, the possession in him of everything, and the privilege of living up to our royal income – oh, that we could attain to that high style of living! 'All things are yours'; then claim them as your own. God has given you his dear Son, and he has given you himself for he has said, 'I will be their God.' Then, live with the joy that a man ought to have who has Jehovah to be his God, and Jesus Christ to be his Saviour. The Lord has given us everything; then let us live at the rate of joy that a man ought to have who possesses everything. God bring us to that happy state!

'His cheeks' – those features of the Beloved which do not at first seem likely to yield us anything – 'are as a bed of spices, as sweet flowers', inexpressibly precious, yielding to us both what we need and what shall delight and overflow our souls. You see, beloved, what saints think of Christ; let each one of us ask himself and herself, 'Do I think thus of him? Do I thus admire him? Is he everything to me?' These are sure marks of a true Christian, that he does love his Master, and he does praise him. There is many a poor child of God who is half afraid that he is not in the number of God's people; but he says, 'I do love Jesus. Oh! I would do anything to glorify him.' My dear friend, do not you ever get the idea that you love him without his loving you; you may be quite sure that the reason why you love him is because he first loved you; and if you love him very much, you may rest assured that he loves you a greet deal more. If you have but a spark of love to him in your heart, he has a furnace of love to you in his heart. If your love to him is but as a single grain, his love to you is abundant as the richest harvest. His love to you is as much above your love to him as the heavens are higher than the earth.

Oh, that we did but think more highly of Christ! Perhaps it may help us to do so if we consider how worthy he is of that love, and how wondrously his thoughts of us exceed our thoughts of him. I sometimes feel very sad when I think about some who profess to be the Lord's people. Ah, me! there are many who, I hope, may prove to be his people; but they do not reflect much credit on him. Some of God's children are a very queer lot; if we had such sons and daughters as God has, some of us would never be able to bear with them at all; we should be impatient with them, and turn them out of doors, to get on as best they could by themselves. When you get sick and sad and weary of God's people, turn your thoughts to God himself; and if ever you see any spots in the Church, Christ's bride, look at her glorious Husband, and you will only love him the more as you think of his wondrous condescension in having loved such a poor thing as his Church is even at her best. Think how bright he is, how glorious, how surpassing are his charms that they can be seen even through the defects and imperfections of his redeemed ones. We may well marvel that ever such love as his could have been lavished upon such unworthy beings as his people are. Do not get depressed and distressed, dear friends, because of your own imperfections, or the imperfections of others; or if you do, quickly rise again to fight against sin under the blessed conviction that there are no imperfections in him, that he is altogether lovely, altogether sweet, and that the day must come when we, who are one with him even now, shall be like him, for we shall see him as he is. Complete sanctification will be the lot of every redeemed soul. If we have known the Lord, and have already had something of his likeness, we shall go on to know him till we are perfect in that likeness. Let that blessed consummation be the subject of our constant prayer and our confident expectation.

Now, secondly, and but briefly, let us turn to the other part of our text: 'His lips like lilies, dropping sweet smelling myrrh.' **These words teach us that CHRIST LISTENED TO IS VERY PRECIOUS**. When he is silent, and we only look at him, he is lovely to our eyes; but when he speaks, we can see 'his lips like lilies, dropping sweet smelling myrrh'.

Notice, first, that it is well, whenever we hear the voice of Jesus Christ, to *try to see the blessed Person who is speaking*. The gospel is very precious to those of us who know its power; but, beyond all question, Christ himself is even more precious than his gospel. It is delightful to read any promise of the Scriptures, but it is more delightful to come into communion with the faithful Promiser. The time when I can most enjoy a promise from the Word of God is when it seems to me as if it must have been written only yesterday on purpose to meet my case, or as if I could see the eternal pen writing every one of the strokes, and making them all for me. Whenever you hear one of the Lord's promises, think of the divine lips that spoke it, and you will love the promise all the better because you have thought of the lips that uttered it. The spouse does not say in our text, 'His words are sweet', but she speaks of 'his lips like lilies, dropping sweet smelling myrrh'. Why should we not believe more in a personal Christ, and why should we not always see the connection between the mercy and the hand that gives it, and between the promise and the lips that speak it?

Some of you may remember William Huntington's story that I have sometimes quoted to you about an old farmer, who, when one of his daughters was married, gave her a thousand pounds as a wedding present. There was another daughter, and her father did not give her a thousand pounds when she was married, but he gave her something as a wedding present, and then he kept on pretty nearly every day in the week sending her what he called 'the hand-basket portion, with father's love', and so in the long run she received a great deal more than her sister did. It was not given all of a lump, and then done with; but it kept on coming, now a sack of flour, and then this, and that, and the other, always 'with father's love', so she had far more than the thousand pounds, and she also had far more of his love. I do like, when I get a mercy, to have it come to me with my Heavenly Father's love, just my daily portion as I need it; not given all in a lump, so that I might go away with it into a far country, as we are sure to do if we have all our mercy at once, but given day by day, as the manna fell, with our Heavenly Father's love every time, a fresh token of infinite grace and infinite love. So, you see, the mercy leads you to think of the hand that gives it, and of the Father who sends it, as in the text it is not the words of the

Beloved, but his lips which the spouse says are 'like lilies, dropping sweet smelling myrrh'.

Notice the comparison in the text – lilies; not white lilies, of course, but red lilies, crimson lilies, lilies of such a colour as are frequently to be seen, which would be a suitable emblem of the Beloved's lips. Christ's lips are peculiarly delightful to us, for *it is with them that he speaks to us, and intercedes with the Father for us.* When he pleads as the Intercessor on behalf of a poor soul like me, his lips are indeed in God's sight like lovely lilies. The Father looks at his dear Son's lips, and he is charmed with them, and blesseth us because of Christ's intercession. And whenever Christ turns round, and speaks to us, shall we not listen at once, with eyes and ears wide open, as we say, 'I like to watch his lips as he is speaking, for his lips are to me as lilies'?

I suppose this comparison means that Christ's lips are very pure, as the lily is the purest of flowers; and that they are very gentle, for we always associate the lily with everything that is tender and soft and kind. There is not a thorn about it as there is with the rose; we speak not of it as Herbert did of the rose:

> Whose hue, angry and brave,
> Bids the rash gazer wipe his eye.

It is not so; the lily is all tenderness and is without a thorn, though often it may be found growing among thorns. The lily also is inconceivably beautiful, and so is Christ in speaking to his people. 'Never man spake like this Man.' The very words of Christ are the loftiest poetry and the sweetest music. Though they sometimes make us weep, great joy lies deeply hidden beneath the grief he causes to our spirits. 'His lips are like lilies.'

But, dear friends, the spouse's comparison fails for she said, 'His lips like lilies, dropping sweet smelling myrrh'. This lilies do not do, but Christ does. He is more than a lily, or he is a lily of such a sort as never bloomed on earth except once. He was the only lily that ever dropped sweet smelling myrrh. The spouse says that his lips do that; what means this? Does it not mean that his Word is often full of a very sweet, mysterious, blessed influence? You have come here often, and it is not because I have spoken that there has been a blessing to your souls; but when I have set forth Christ to you – and I have no other theme but Christ – there have often come to you mysterious droppings, you have had singular feelings in your spirit caused by the secret exudations of the Word, the outflowings from the Word, and inflowings into your spirit, causing you to say, 'What a change has come over me! I went into God's house very heavy, but I came away quite relieved. I went in there perplexed and worried, and I came away knowing clearly what I ought to do. I went in there cold and chilly, and feeling myself at a distance from God; and I came out ready to dance with the sense of his realized presence.' Ah! that change has been caused by some of the sweet smelling myrrh that has dropped from the lips of Christ.

There are many people who meet with us on the Sabbath who do not care to come out to the weeknight services. I take the weeknight attendance as somewhat of a test of piety; any hypocrite will come out on a Sunday, but it is not every hypocrite who will come out on a Thursday night, though some do, I dare say; but still, the most of them are for a Sunday religion only, but a weekday religion they do not want. That is to say they will feed on the Word after a fashion, and worship God after a fashion, when most other people do; but give me that religion that loves to creep out on a weeknight, and is willing to take a back seat if it may but get a bit of spiritual food. Give me that man who says, 'My soul must be fed. I have been tearing about all this week, almost worn out with fatigue, and perplexed with a great many cares; it is a delightful thing to be able to get into the house of prayer, to hear about Christ, and to feed on him.' Oh, you who eat your morsels in secret behind the door, I believe more in you than in those who sit openly at the table, but who never have a secret feast at all!

'Oh, but!' says one, 'I do not hear the Word to profit.' No, of course you do not. You see, you are looking to the lips of a man; but if you look to the lips of the Master, you will find that 'his lips are as lilies, dropping sweet smelling myrrh'. You may have heard the story of the lady who was present when Mr Ebenezer Erskine preached at a Scotch communion service; she thought she had never heard such a man in all her life, he preached Christ so sweetly that she was charmed. She enquired where he was to preach the next Sabbath, and she left her own place of worship to go to hear Mr. Erskine again; but it was a dreadfully dry discourse, she said, and she was foolish enough to go into the vestry, and to say to the preacher, 'My dear sir, I have been bitterly disappointed in hearing you this morning. I heard you last Sabbath, and you so extolled Christ that I enjoyed the service above measure, and I thought I would come again to hear you, and now I have got nothing.' 'No, madam,' replied the good man, 'last Sabbath you went to worship God, and to feed on Christ, so you received the blessing you sought; today, you came to hear Mr Erskine, and you have heard me, but you have missed the blessing.' Oh, dear friends, beware of going to places of worship merely to hear men! Of course, you must hear a man speaking; but go with this view, that those lips which are as lilies, dropping sweet smelling myrrh, should be the lips to which you really are listening, and be praying all the time, 'Lord, speak to me through the minister, speak to me through the hymn, speak to me through the prayer, speak to me through any part of the service – ay, speak through the speaker's not speaking if thou wilt – only do thou speak to me, let those clear lips of thine drop sweet smelling myrrh into my soul! Pray thus, and you shall not be disappointed, be you sure of that.

This blessing is what you and I must seek after day by day, for we need this myrrh for the healing of the wounds that sin hath made; we need this myrrh in our spiritual worship that we may offer it up unto God; we need this myrrh to perfume us, and make our lives fragrant in the midst of our daily cares ; we need this myrrh to kill the contagion that abounds in this wicked world, and we shall get it through the Word, when it comes fresh from the lips of Christ. O God, bring us all into this blessed state!

I close by saying that if there are any here present who do not prize the Word of God, who have no care to listen to the lips of Christ, I pray God that they may speedily be converted; for if they are not, they shall hear him speak when his lips shall be not as lilies, but as a flaming fire, and his word that shall be spoken then shall burn as an oven, and his enemies shall be consumed thereby. God give grace to such as have not believed in Jesus to look to him and listen to him now! 'Incline your ear,' saith he, 'and come unto me: hear, and your soul shall live.' Yea, he saith, 'Look unto me, and be ye saved, all the ends of the earth: for I am God, and there is none else.' May God give his blessing to these words, for our Lord Jesus Christ's sake! Amen.

39

ALTOGETHER LOVELY

'Yea, he is altogether lovely' (Song of Solomon 5:16).

When the old Puritan minister had delivered his discourse, and dwelt upon firstly, and secondly, and thirdly, and perhaps upon twenty-fifthly, before he sat down he usually gave a comprehensive summary of all that he had spoken. Every one who carefully noted the summary would carry away the essence of the sermon. The summary was always looked upon by the Puritan hearer as one of the most valuable helps to memory, and consequently a most important part of the discourse. In these five words, the spouse here gives you her summary. She had delivered a tenfold discourse concerning her Lord; she had described in detail all his various beauties, and when she had surveyed him from head to foot, she gathered up all her commendations in this sentence: 'Yea, he is altogether lovely.' Remember these words, and know their meaning, and you possess the quintessence of the spouse's portion of the Song of Songs.

Now, as in this allegorical song, the bride sums up her witness in these words, so may I say that all the patriarchs, all the prophets, all the apostles, all the confessors, yea, and the entire body of the church have left us no other testimony. They all spoke of Christ, and they all commended him. Whatever the type, or symbol, or obscure oracle, or open word in which they bore witness, that witness all amounted to this: 'Yea, he is altogether lovely.' Yes and I will add, that since the canon of inspiration has closed, the testimony of all saints, on earth and in heaven, has continued to confirm the declaration made of old. The verdict of each particular saint and of the whole elect host as a body, still is this, 'Yea, he is altogether lovely.' From the sighs and the songs which mingle on the dying beds of saints, I hear this note supreme above all others, 'He is altogether lovely'; and from the songs unmingled with groans, which perpetually peal forth from immortal tongues before the presence of the Most High, I hear this one master note, 'Yea, he is altogether lovely.' If the whole church desired to say with the apostle, 'Now of the things which we have spoken this is the sum', she need not wait for a brief and comprehensive summary, for it lies before her in this golden sentence, 'Yea, he is altogether lovely.'

Looking at my text in this light I felt much humbling of spirit, and I hesitated to preach upon it, for I said in my heart, ' It is high, I cannot attain unto it.' These deep texts show us the shortness of our plumb-line; these ocean verses are so exceeding broad that our skiffs are apt to be driven far out of sight of land where our timid spirits tremble to spread the sail. Then I comforted myself by the thought that though I could not comprehend this text in a measure, nor weigh its mountains in scales, or its hills in a balance, yet it was all mine own, by the gift of divine grace, and therefore I need not fear to enter upon the meditation of it. If I cannot grasp the ocean in my span, yet, may I bathe therein with sweet content; if I cannot describe the king in his beauty, yet may I gaze upon him, since the old proverb saith, 'A beggar may look at a prince.' Though I pretend not so to preach from such a heavenly word as that before us, as to spread before you all its marrow and fatness, yet may I gather up a few crumbs which fall from its table. Poor men are glad of crumbs, and crumbs from such a feast are better than loaves from the tables of the world. Better to have a glimpse of Jesus, than to see all the glory of the earth all the days of our life. If we fail on this subject we may do better than if we succeeded upon another; so we will pluck up courage, seek divine help, and draw near to this wondrous text, with our shoes from off our feet like Moses when be saw the bush aglow with God.

This verse has been translated in another way: 'He is all desires'; and so indeed Jesus is. He was the desire of the ancients, he is the desire of all nations still. To his own people he is their all in all; they are complete in him; they are filled out of his fulness.

All our capacious powers can wish,
In him doth richly meet.

He is the delight of his servants, and fills their expectations to the full. But we will not dispute about translations, for, after all, with such a text, so full of unutterable spiritual sweetness, every man must be his own translator, and into his own soul must the power of the message come, by the enforcement of the Holy Ghost. Such a text as this is very like the manna which fell in the wilderness, of which the rabbis say it tasted after each men's liking. If the flavour in a man's mouth was very sweetness, the angel's food which fell around the camp was luscious as any dainty he had conceived; whatever he might be, the manna was to him as he was. So shall this text be. To you with low ideas of Christ the words shall but glide over your ears, and be meaningless; but if your spirit be ravished with the precious love of Jesus there shall be songs of angels, and more than that, the voice of God's own Spirit to your soul in this short sentence, 'Yea, he is altogether lovely.'

I am an engraver this morning, and I seek somewhat whereon I may engrave this heavenly line. Shall I take unto me ivory or silver? Shall I borrow crystal or gold? These are too common to bear this unique inscription: I put them all aside. Shall I spell my text in gems, with an emerald, a sapphire, a ruby, a diamond or a pearl for each single letter? Nay, these are poor perishable things: we put them all away. I want an immortal spirit to be the tablet for my writing; nay, I must lay aside my graving tool, and ask the Spirit of God to take it; I want a heart prepared of the Holy Ghost, upon whose fleshy tablets there shall be written this morning no other sentence than this, and this shall suffice for a right royal motto to adorn it well: 'Yea, he is altogether lovely.' Spirit of God, find out the prepared heart, and with thy sacred hand write in eternal characters the love of Christ, and all his inimitable perfections.

In handling our text this morning we shall note three points of character, and then we shall show three uses to which we may profitably turn it.

1. We shall consider THREE POINTS OF CHARACTER which are very noticeable in these words, and the first which suggests itself is this: the words are evidently uttered by one who is under the influence *of overwhelming emotion.* The words are rather a veil to the heart than a glass through which we see its emotions. The sentence labours to express the inexpressible, it pants to utter the unutterable. The person writing these words evidently feels a great deal more than any language can possibly convey to us. The spouse begins somewhat calmly in her description: 'My beloved is white and ruddy.' She proceeds with due order, commencing at the head, and proceeding with the divers parts of the person of the Beloved; but she warms, she glows, she flames, and at last the heat which had for awhile been repressed is like fire within her bones, and she bursts forth in flaming words. Here is the live coal from off the altar of her heart: 'Yea, he is altogether lovely.'

It is the utterance of a soul that is altogether overcome with admiration, and therefore feels that in attempting to describe the Well-beloved, it has undertaken a task beyond its power. Lost in adoring wonder, the gracious mind desists from description and cries with rapture, 'Yea, he is altogether lovely.' It has often been thus with true saints; they have felt the love of Jesus to be overpowering and inebriating. Believers are not always cool and calm in their thoughts towards their Lord: there are seasons with them when they pass into a state of rapture, their hearts burn within them, they are in ecstasy, they mount up with wings as eagles, their souls become like the chariots of Amminadib, they feel what they could not tell, they experience what they could not express though the tongues of men and of angels were perfectly at their command. Favoured believers are altogether enraptured with the sight they have of their all-beauteous Lord.

It is to be feared that such raptures are not frequent with all Christians, though I should gravely question his saintship, who has never experienced any degree of holy rapture: but there are some saints to whom a state of overwhelming adoration of their Lord has been by no means an unusual thing. Communion with Jesus has not only entranced them now and then, but it has perfumed all their life with holiness and if it has not caused their faces literally to shine like the face of Moses, it has made the spiritual glory to flash from their countenances, and elevated them among their fellow Christians to he leaders of the host of God, whereat others have admired and wondered. Peradventure, I speak to children of God who know very little of what I mean by the overwhelming emotions created by a sight of our Lord; they have not so seen the Lord as to have felt their souls melting within them while the Beloved spake with them; to such I shall speak with sorrowful sympathy, being, alas I too much like unto them, but my prayer shall go up all the while, 'Lord, reveal thyself to us, that we also may be compelled to say, "Yea, he is altogether lovely." Show us thy hands and thy side till we exclaim with Thomas, "My Lord and my God." '

Shall I tell you why it is, my brethren, that many of you but seldom enjoy the exceeding bliss of Jesus' presence? The cause may lie partly in what is, alas! too common among Christians, *a great degree of ignorance of the person of the Lord Jesus.* Every soul that sees Jesus by faith is saved thereby. If I look to Christ with a bleared eye, that is ever so weak and clouded with tears, and if I only catch a glimpse of him through clouds and mists, yet the sight saves me. But who will remain content with such a poor gleam of his glory as that? Who wishes to see only 'through a glass, darkly'? No, let my eyes be cleansed till they become as doves by the rivers of waters, and I can see my Lord as he is seen by his bosom friends, and can sing of those beauties which are the light and crown of heaven itself. If you do but touch the hem of Jesus' garment, you shall be made whole; but will this always satisfy you? Will you not desire to get beyond the hem and beyond the garment to himself and to his heart, and there forever take up your abode? Who desires to be forever a babe in grace, with a half-awakened dreamy twilight consciousness of the Redeemer? Brethren, be diligent in the school of the cross, therein is enduring wisdom. Study your Saviour much. The science of Christ crucified is the most excellent of sciences; and to know him and the power of his resurrection, is to know that which is best worth knowing. Ignorance of Jesus deprives many saints of those divine raptures which carry others out of themselves, therefore let us be among those children of Zion who are taught of the Lord.

Next to this you shall find *the want of meditation* to be a very serious robber of the wealth of renewed hearts. To believe a thing is, as it were, to see the cool crystal sparkling in the cup; but to meditate upon it is to drink thereof. Reading gathers the clusters, contemplation squeezes forth their generous juice. Meditation is of all things the most soul-fattening when combined with prayer. The spouse had meditated much in this chapter, for otherwise she had not been able to speak in detail concerning her Lord. O saintly hearts, imitate ye her example! Think, my brethren, of our Lord Jesus: he is God, the Eternal, the Infinite, the ever blessed; yet he became man for us – man of the substance of his mother, like ourselves. Meditate upon his spotless character; review the sufferings which he endured on Calvary; follow him into the grave, and from the grave to the resurrection, and from the resurrection up the starry way to his triumphant throne. Let your souls dwell upon each of his offices, as prophet, priest, and king; pore over each one of his characters, and every scriptural title; pause and consider every phase of him, and when you have done this, begin again and yet again. It is good to chew the cud by meditation, then shall the sweetness and fatness of divine truth come to your soul, and you shall burst forth with such rapturous expressions as that of the text, 'Yea, he is altogether lovely.' The most of you are too busy, you have too much to do in the world; but what is it all about? Scraping together dust, loading yourselves with thick clay. O that you were busy after the true riches, and could step aside awhile to enrich yourselves in solitude, and make your hearts vigorous by feeding upon the person and work of your ever blessed Lord! You miss a heaven below by a too eager pursuit of earth. You cannot know these joyful raptures if meditation be pushed into a corner.

Another reason why little of the Lord's beauty is discerned is *the low state of the spiritual life in many a Christian.* Many a believer is just alive and no more. Do you not know such starveling souls? May you not be one such yourself! His eyes are not delighted with the beauties of Christ, he is purblind, and cannot see afar off; he walks not with Jesus in the garden of pomegranates, he is too feeble to rise from the couch of weakness; he cannot feed upon Christ, his appetite is gone – sure sign of terrible decline. For him there are no climbings to the top of Amana, no leaping for joy in the temple, no dancing before the ark with David; no, if he be but carried to the feet of Jesus in an ambulance as a sick man borne of four, it is as much as he has yet received. To be strong in the Lord and in the power of his might, to have the wings of eagles with which to mount above the clouds of earth, to this many are strangers. But beloved, there are noble spirits and better taught, who know something of the life of heaven even while here below. The Lord strengthen us with grace in our inner man, and then shall we drink deeper draughts of the wines on the lees well refined, and then also our eyes being open, we shall see Jesus more clearly, and bear fuller witness that he is 'fairer than the children of men'.

I am afraid that *the visits of to our souls have been disesteemed, and the loss of those visits has not caused us corresponding sorrow.* We did not sufficiently delight in the beauty of the Bridegroom when he did come to us; when our hearts were somewhat lifted up with his love we grew cold and idle, and then he withdrew his conscious presence; but, alas! we were not grieved, but we wickedly tried to live without him. It is wretched work for a believer to try and live without his Saviour. Perhaps, dear brethren, some of you have tried it until at last you have almost succeeded. You were wont to mourn like doves if you had no word from your Master in the morning, and without a love-token before you went to rest you tossed uneasily upon your bed; but now you are carnal and worldly, and careless, and quite content to have it so. Jesus hides his face, the sun is set, and yet it is not night with you. O may God be pleased to arouse you from this lethargy, and make you mourn your sad estate! Even if an affliction should be needful to bring you back from your backsliding it would be a cheap price to pay. Awake, O north wind, with all thy cutting force, if thy bleak breath may but stir the lethargic heart! May the Lord grant us grace so to love Christ that if we have not our fill of him, we may be ready to die with hungering and thirsting after him. May we never be able to find a place to build our nest upon while our wing wanders away from the tree of life. Like the dove of Noah, may we drop into the water and be drowned sooner than find rest for the sole of our foot except upon the ark, Christ Jesus our Saviour.

Beloved, if none of these suggestions should hit the mark, and reveal the cause why so little is known of rapturous love to Christ, let me suggest another. Very often *professors' hearts are vain and frivolous;* they are taken up during the week with their business. This might plead some excuse; but when they have little spaces and intervals these are filled up with very vanity. Now, if the soul has come to look at the mere trifles of this world as all-important, is it any marvel that it should be unable to perceive the exceeding preciousness of Christ Jesus? Who will care for the wheat when he dotes on the chaff? And with this it will often happen that the professor's mind has grown proud as well as vain; he does not remember his natural poverty and meanness, and consequently does not value the riches of Christ Jesus. He has come to think himself an established, experienced Christian; he fancies that he is not like those foolish beginners who are so volatile and so readily led astray; he has acquired the wisdom of years and the stability of experience. O soul, if thou art great, Christ will be little; thou canst never see him on the throne until thou hast been on the dunghill thyself. If thou be anything, so much the less is Christ; for if he be all in all, then there is no room for anything else; and if thou be something, thou hast stolen just so much from the glory of thy Lord Jesus. Lie low in the dust, it is the place for thee.

> The more thy glories strike my eyes,
> The humbler I shall lie.

The humbler I am in myself, the more shall I be capable of seeing the enchanting beauties of Christ.

Let me just say these two or three words. I believe those are the happiest saints who are most overwhelmed with a sense of the greatness, goodness and preciousness of Christ. I believe these to be the most useful saints, also, and to be in the Christian church as a tower of strength. I pray that you and I, walking with God by faith, may nevertheless often have our festival days, our notable seasons, when he shall specially kiss us with the kisses of his love, and we shall drink larger draughts of his love, which is better than wine. Oh! to be carried right away with the divine manifestation of the chief among ten thousand, so that our souls shall cry out in rapture, 'Yea, he is altogether lovely.' This is one characteristic of the text: may it be transferred to us.

A second is this, and very manifest it is upon the surface of the verse – here is *undivided affection*. 'He is altogether lovely.' Note that these words have a world of meaning in them, but chiefly they tell us this, that Jesus is to the true saint the only lovely one in the world. 'He is altogether lovely'; then there is no loveliness anywhere else. It is as though the spouse felt that Christ had engrossed all the beauty and all the loveworthiness in the entire universe. Who among us will say that she erred? Is not Jesus worthy of all the admiration and love of all intelligent beings? But may we not love our friends and kinsfolk? Ay, but in him, and in subservience to him; so, and so only, is it safe to love them. Did not our Lord himself say, 'If any man love father or mother more than me, he is not worthy of me'? Yea, and in another place he put it more strongly still, for he said, 'Except a man hate father and mother', or love them not at all in comparison with me, 'he is not worthy of me.' Except these are put on a lower stage than Jesus is we cannot be his disciples. Christ must be monarch in the breast; our dear ones may sit at his footstool, and we may love them for his sake, but he alone must fill the throne of our hearts. I may see excellences in my Christian brethren, but I must not forget that there would be none in them if they were not derived from him; that their loveliness is only a part of his loveliness, for he wrought it in them by his own Spirit. I am to acknowledge that Jesus is the monopoliser of all loveliness, the engrosser of all that is admirable in the entire universe; and I am, therefore, to give him all my love, for 'he is altogether lovely'.

Our text means, again, that in Jesus loveliness of all kinds is to be found. If there be anything that is worthy of the love of an immortal spirit, it is to be seen in abundance in the Lord Jesus. Whatsoever things are true, whatsoever things are honest, whatsoever things are just, whatsoever things are pure, whatsoever things are lovely, whatsoever things are of good report; if there be any virtue, and if there be any praise, all can be found without measure in Christ Jesus. As all the rivers meet in the sea, so all beauties unite in the Redeemer. Take the character of any gracious man, and you shall find a measure of loveliness, but it has its bounds and its mixtures. Peter has many virtues, but he has not a few failings. John, too, excels, but in certain points he is deficient; but herein our Lord transcends all his saints, for all human virtues, all divine, are harmoniously blended in him. He is not this flower or that, but he is the Paradise of perfection. He is not a star here or a constellation there, he is the whole heaven of stars, nay, he is the heaven of heavens; he is all that is fair and lovely condensed in one.

When the text says again that Jesus 'is altogether lovely', it declares that he is lovely in all views of him. It generally happens that to the noblest building there is an unhappy point of view from which the architecture appears at a disadvantage; the choicest piece of workmanship may not be equally complete in all directions; the best human character is deformed by one flaw, if not with more; but with our Lord all is lovely, regard him as you will. You shall contemplate him from all points, and only find new confirmation of the statement that 'he is altogether lovely.' As the everlasting God before the world was made, angels loved him and adored; as the babe at Bethlehem or as the man at Bethany; as walking the sea or as nailed to the cross; in his grave, dead and buried, or on his throne triumphant; rising as forerunner, or descending a second time to judge the world in righteousness; in his shame, despised and spit upon, or in his glory, adored and beloved; with the thorns about his brow and the nails piercing his hands, or with the keys of death and hell swinging at his girdle; view him as you will, and where you will, and when you will, 'he is altogether lovely'. Under all aspects, and in all offices and in relations, at all times and all seasons, under all circumstances and conditions, anywhere, everywhere, 'he is altogether lovely'.

Nor is he in any degree unlovely; the commendation forbids the idea; if he be 'altogether lovely', where could you find room for deformity? When Apelles painted Alexander, he laid the monarch's finger on an unsightly scar; but there are no scars to conceal when you portray the countenance of Immanuel. We say of our country (and who among us will not say it?), 'With all her faults we love her still'; but we love Jesus, and find no strain put upon our heart, for trace of fault he has none. There is no need of apologies for Jesus, no excuses are required for him. But what is that I see upon his shoulder? It is a hard rough cross; and if I follow him I must carry that cross for his sake. Is not that cross unsightly? Oh, no! he is altogether lovely, cross and all. Whatever it may involve to be a Christian, we count even the reproach of Christ to be greater riches than the treasures of Egypt. The world will honour a half Christ, but a whole Christ it will not acknowledge. The bat's-eyed Socinian saith, 'I admire the man Christ, but I will not adore Jesus the God.' To him the eternal Word is but half lovely, if lovely at all. Some will have Christ in silver slippers – my lord archbishop's religion – but they would not listen to the gospel from a poor gracious Methodist, or think it worth their while to join the unlettered throng whose devout songs rise from the village green. Alas! how much we see of crosses of gold and ivory, but how little do men love the lowly cross of Jesus! Brethren, we think Jesus 'altogether lovely' even in poverty, or when hanging naked on the cross, deserted and condemned. We see unspeakable beauty in Jesus in the grave, all fair with the pallor of death. Jesus bruised as to his heel by the old serpent is yet comely. His love to us makes him evermore 'white and ruddy' to our eye. We adore him anywhere and everywhere, and in any place, for we know that this same Christ whose heel is bruised breaks also the serpent's head, and he who was naked for our sakes is now arrayed in glory. We know that the despised and rejected is also King of kings, and Lord of lords, the 'Wonderful, Counsellor, the Mighty God, the Everlasting Father, the Prince of Peace'. 'Yea, he is altogether lovely.' There are no flaws in him.

The text intends us to know that Jesus is lovely in the highest degree: not lovely positively and then failing comparatively, but lovely superlatively in the highest possible sense. But I leave this for your hearts to enlarge upon. I will close this point by saying, every child of God acknowledges that Christ Jesus is lovely altogether to the whole of himself. He is lovely to my judgment; but many things are so, and yet are not lovely to my affections – I know them to be right, and yet they are not pleasant: but Jesus is as lovely to my heart as to my head, as dear as he is good. He is lovely to my hopes: are they not all in him? Is not this my expectation – to see him as he is? But he is lovely to my memory too: did he not pluck me out of the net? Lovely to all my powers and all my passions, my faculties and feelings. As David puts it, 'My heart and my flesh crieth out for the living God' – the whole of the man seeking after the whole of the Saviour; the whole Saviour sweet and inexpressibly precious to the man's entire being. May it be so with you and with me. But is it so? Do you not set up idols in your hearts? Men of God, do you not need to take the scourge of small cords, and purge the temple of your souls this morning? Are there not buyers and sellers where Christ alone ought to be? Oh, to love him wholly, and to love him only, so that we have no eyes for other beauty, no heart for other loveliness, since he fills our souls, and is to us 'altogether lovely'.

The third characteristic of the text is that to which I desire to draw the most attention, and that is *ardent devotion*. I called the text a live coal from off the altar, and surely it is so. If it should drop into our hearts to set them on a blaze, it would be an unspeakable mercy. Ardent devotion flames from this sentence. It is the language of one who feels that no emotion is too deep when Jesus moves the heart. Do any chide you and say you think too much of your religion? It cannot be, it cannot be. If the zeal of God's house should eat us up until we had no existence except for the Lord's glory, we should not have gone too far. If there be corresponding knowledge to balance it, there cannot be too much of zeal for God. The utterance is that of one whose heart is like a furnace, of which love is the fire. 'He is altogether lovely' – it is the exclamation of one who feels that no language is too strong to commend the Lord. The spouse looked through the Hebrew tongue to find an intense expression, and our translators ransacked the English language for a forcible word, and they have put it in the most weighty way – 'He is altogether lovely.' There is no fear of exaggeration when you speak of Christ; hyperboles are only sober truth when we depict his excellences. We have heard of a portrait painter who owed his popularity to the fact that he never painted truthfully, but always gave a flattering touch or two; here is one who would defy his art, for it is impossible to flatter Jesus. Lay on, ye men of eloquence, spare no colours, ye shall never depict him too bravely. Bring forth your harps, ye seraphs; sing aloud, ye blood-washed ones; all your praises fall short of the glory which is due to him.

It is the language of one who feels that no service would be too great to render to the Lord. I wish we felt as the apostles and martyrs and holy men of old did, that Jesus Christ ought to be served at the highest and richest rate. We do little, very little: what if I had said we do next to nothing for our dear Lord and Master nowadays? The love of Christ doth not constrain us as it should. But those of old bore poverty and dared reproach, marched weary leagues, passed tempestuous seas, bore perils of robbers and of cruel men, to plant the cross in lands where as yet Jesus was not known; labours that nowadays could not be expected of men were performed as daily matters of commonplace by the Christians of the earliest times. Is Christ less lovely, or is his church less loyal? Would God she estimated him at his right rate, for then she would return to her former mode of service. Brethren, we want to feel, and we shall feel if this text is deeply engraven on our hearts, that no gift is too great for Christ, though we give him all we have, and consecrate to him all our time and ability, and sacrifice our very lives to him. No suffering is too great to bear for the sake of the Crucified, and it is a great joy to be reproached for Christ's sake. 'He is altogether lovely.' Then, my soul, I charge thee think nothing hard to which he calls thee, nothing sharp which he bids thee endure.

As the knight of the olden time consecrated himself to the Crusade, and wore the red cross on his arm, fearing not to meet death at the hands of the Infidel, if he might be thought a soldier of the Lord, so we too would face all foes for Jesus' sake. We want, only refined and purified, and delivered from its earthly grossness, we want the chivalrous spirits once again in the church of God. A new crusade fain would I preach: had I the tongue of such a one as the old hermit to move all Christendom, I would say, 'This day Christ, the altogether lovely one, is dishonoured: can ye endure it? This day idols stand where he should be and men adore them; lovers of Jesus, can ye brook it? This day Juggernaut rides through the streets on his bloody way, this day God's Christ is still unknown to millions, and the precious blood cleanses not the nations, how long will ye have it so? We, in England, with ten thousand Christian hearts, and as many tongues endowed with eloquence, and purses weighted with gold, shall we refuse our gifts, withhold our witness, and suffer the Lord to be dishonoured? The church is doing next to nothing for her great Lord, she falls short both of her duty and of the grim need of a perishing world. O for a flash of the celestial fire! Oh, when shall the Spirit's energy visit us again! When shall men put down their selfishness and seek only Christ? When shall they leave their strifes about trifles to rally round his cross! When shall we end the glorification of ourselves, and begin to make him glorious, even to the world's end? God help us in this matter, and kindle in our hearts the old consuming, heart-inflaming fire, which shall make men see that Jesus is all in all to us.

2. Thus I have shown you the characteristics of the text, and now I desire to USE IT IN THREE WAYS FOR PRACTICAL PURPOSES. As time flies, we must use it briefly.

The first word is to you, Christians. Here is very *sweet instruction*. The Lord Jesus 'is altogether lovely'. Then if I want to be lovely, I must be like him, and the model for me as a Christian is Christ. Have you ever noticed how badly boys write at the bottom of the pages in their copybooks? There is the copy at the top; and in the first line they look at that; in the second line, they copy their own imitation; in the third line, they copy their imitation of their imitation, and so the writing grows worse and worse as it descends the page. Now, the apostles followed Christ; the first fathers imitated the apostles, the next fathers copied the first fathers, and so the standard of holiness fell dreadfully; and now we are too apt to follow the very lees and dregs of Christianity, and we think if we are about as good as our poor, imperfect ministers or leaders in the church, that we shall do well and deserve praise. But now, my brethren, cover up the mere copies and imitations, and live by the first line. Copy Jesus; 'he is altogether lovely'; and if you can write by the first line, you will write by the truest and best model in the world. We want to have Christ's zeal, but we must balance it with his prudence and discretion; we must seek to have Christ's love to God, and we must feel his love to men, his forgiveness of injury, his gentleness of speech, his incorruptible truthfulness, his meekness and lowliness, his utter unselfishness, his entire consecration to his Father's business. O that we had this, for depend upon it whatever other pattern we select, we have made a mistake; we are not following the true classic model of the Christian artist. Our master model is the 'altogether lovely' one. How sweet it is to think of our Lord in the double aspect as our exemplar and our Saviour! The laver which stood in the temple was made of brass: in this the priests washed their feet whenever they offered sacrifices; so does Christ purify us from sin; but the tradition is that this laver was made of very bright brass, and acted as a mirror, so that as often as the priests came to it they could see their own spots in it. Oh, when I come to my Lord Jesus, not only do I get rid of my sins as to their guilt, but I see my spots in the light of his perfect character, and I am humbled and taught to follow after holiness.

The second use to which we would put the verse is this, here is a very *gentle rebuke* to some of you. Though very gentle, I beseech you to let it sink deep into your hearts. You do not see the lowliness of Christ, yet 'he is altogether lovely'. Now, I will not say one hard word, but I will tell you sorrowfully what pitiable creatures you are. I hear enchanting music, which seems more a thing of heaven than of earth: it is one of Handel's half-inspired oratorios. Yonder sits a man, who says, 'I hear nothing to commend.' He has not the power to perceive the linked sweetnesses, the delicious harmonies of sounds. Do you blame him? No, but you who have an ear for music, say, 'How I pity him: he misses half the joy of life!' Here, again, is a glorious landscape, hills and valleys, and flowing rivers, expansive lakes and undulating meadows. I bring to the point of view a friend, whom I would gratify, and I say to him, 'Is not that a charming scene?' Turning his head to me, he says, 'I see nothing.' I perceive that he cannot enjoy what is so delightful to me; he has some little sight, but he sees only what is very near, and he is blind to all beyond. Now, do I blame him? Or if he proceed to argue with me, and say, 'You are very foolish to be so enthusiastic about a nonexistent landscape, it is merely your excitement', shall I argue with him? Shall I be angry with him? No, but I shed a tear, and whisper to myself, 'Great are the losses of the blind.' Now, you who have never heard music in the name of Jesus, you are to be greatly pitied, for your loss is heavy. You who never saw beauty in Jesus, and who never will for ever, you need all our tears. It is hell enough not to love Christ! It is the lowest abyss of Tartarus, and its fiercest flame, not to be enamoured of the Christ of God. There is no heaven that is more heaven than to love Christ and to be like him, and there is no hell that is more hell than to be unlike Christ and not to want to be like him, but even to be averse to the infinite perfections of the 'altogether lovely'. The Lord open those blind eyes of yours, and unstop those dear ears and give you the new and spiritual life, and then will you join in saying, 'Yea, he is altogether lovely.'

The last use of the text is that of *tender attractiveness*. 'Yea, he is altogether lovely.' Where are you this morning, you who are convinced of sin and want a Saviour, where have you crept to? Are you hidden away where my eyes cannot reach you? At any rate, let this sweet thought reach you. You need not be afraid to come to Jesus, for 'he is altogether lovely'. It does not say he is altogether terrible – that is your misconception of him; it does not say he is somewhat lovely, and sometimes willing to receive a certain sort of sinner; but 'he is altogether lovely', and therefore he is always ready to welcome to himself the vilest of the vile. Think of his name. It is Jesus, the Saviour. Is not that lovely? Think of his work. He is come to seek and to save that which was lost. This is his occupation. Is not that lovely? Think of what he has done. He hath redeemed our souls with blood. Is not that lovely? Think of what he is doing. He is pleading before the throne of God for sinners. Think of what he is giving at this moment – he is exalted on high to give repentance and remission of sins. Is not this lovely? Under every aspect Christ Jesus is attractive to sinners who need him. Come, then, come and welcome, there is nothing to keep you away, there is everything to bid you come. May this very Sabbath day, in which I have preached Christ and lifted him up, be the day in which you shall be drawn to him, never again to leave him, but to be his for ever and for ever. Amen.

40

THE BEST BELOVED

'Yea, he is altogether lovely' (Song of Solomon 5:16).

No words can ever express the gratitude we owe to him who loved us even when we were dead in trespasses and sins: the *love* of Jesus is unutterably precious and worthy of daily praise. No songs can ever fitly celebrate the triumphs of that salvation which he wrought single-handed on our behalf: the *work* of Jesus is glorious beyond compare, and all the harps of angels fall short of its worthy honour. Yet I do believe, and my heart prompts me to say so, that the highest praise of every ransomed soul and of the entire Christian church should be offered to the blessed *person* of Jesus Christ, our adorable Lord. The love of his heart is excelled by the heart which gave forth that love, and the wonders of his hand are outdone by the hand itself, which wrought those godlike miracles of grace. We ought to bless him for what he has done for us as Mediator in the place of humble service under the law, and for what he suffered for us as Substitute on the altar of sacrifice from before the foundation of the world; and for what he is doing for us as Advocate in the place of highest honour at the right hand of the Majesty on high: but still the best thing about Christ is Christ himself. We prize *his*, but we worship *him*. His gifts are valued, but he himself is adored. While we contemplate, with mingled feelings of awe, admiration and thankfulness, his atonement, his resurrection, his glory in heaven and his second coming, still it is Christ himself, stupendous in his dignity as the Son of God, and superbly beautiful as the Son of man, who sheds an incomparable charm on all those wonderful achievements, wherein his might and his merit, his goodness and his grace appear so conspicuous. For *him* let our choicest spices be reserved, and to him let our sweetest anthems be raised. Our choicest ointment must be poured upon his head, and for his own self alone our most costly alabaster boxes must be broken.

'*He* is altogether lovely.' Not only is his teaching attractive, his doctrine persuasive, his life irreproachable, his character enchanting, and his work a self-denying labour for the common good of all his people, but he himself is altogether lovely. I suppose at first we shall always begin to love him because he first loved us, and even to the last his love to us will always be the strongest motive of our affection towards him; still there ought to be added to this another reason less connected with ourselves, and more entirely arising out of his own superlative excellence; we ought to love him because he is lovely and deserves to be loved. The time should come, and with some of us it has come, when we can heartily say we love him because we cannot help it, for his all-conquering loveliness has quite ravished our hearts. Surely it is but an unripe fruit to love him merely for the benefits which we have received at his hand. It is a fruit of grace, but it is not of the ripest flavour; at least, there are other fruits, both new and old, which we have laid up for thee, O our beloved, and some of them have a daintier taste. There is a sweet and mellow fruit which can only be brought forth by the summer sun of fellowship – love because of the Redeemer's intrinsic goodness and personal sweetness. Oh that we might love our Lord for his own sake, love him because he is so supremely beautiful that a glimpse of him has won our hearts, and made him dearer to our eyes than light. Oh that all true and faithful disciples of our beloved Lord would press forward towards that state of affection, and never rest till they reach it! If any of you have not reached it, you need not therefore doubt your own safety, for whatever the reason why you love Jesus, if you love him at all, it is a sure pledge and token that he loves you, and that you are saved in him with an everlasting salvation. Still covet earnestly the best gifts, and rise to the highest degree of devotion. Love as the purest of the saints have loved; love as John the apostle loved; for still your Lord exceeds all the loving homage you can pay to him. Love his person, love himself; for he is better than all that he has done or given; and as from himself all blessings flow, so back to himself should all love return.

Our text tells us that Christ is altogether lovely. What a wealth of thought and feeling is contained in that exclamation! I am embarrassed to know how to preach on such a subject, and half inclined to wish it had not been laid so much upon my heart. What, I pray you, what is loveliness? To discern it is one thing, but it is quite another thing to describe it. There is not one amongst us but knows how to appreciate beauty, and to be enamoured of its attractions, but how many here could tell us what it is? Stand up, my brother, and define it. Perhaps while you were sitting down you thought you could easily tell the tale, but now you are on your feet you find that it is not quite so easy to clothe in words the thoughts which floated through your brain. What is beauty? Cold-blooded word-mongers answer, *fitness*. And certainly there is fitness in all loveliness. But do not tell me that beauty is mere fitness, for I have seen a world of fitness in this world which, nevertheless, seemed to me to be inexpressibly ugly and unlovable.

A wise man tells me that beauty is *proportion*; but neither is this a full description by many a league. No doubt it is desirable that the features should be well balanced; the eyes should be fitly set, no one feature should be exaggerated, and none should be dwarfed.

In nature what affects our hearts,
Is not th'exactness of peculiar parts:

'Tis not a lip or eye we beauty call,
But the joint force and full result of all.

Harmony is beauty. Yet I have seen the chiselled marble, fashioned with skilful art into a well-nigh perfect form, which did not, could not, impress me with a sense of loveliness. There stands in one of the halls of the Vatican a statue of Antinous. Every feature in that statue is perfect in itself, and in complete harmony with all the rest. You could not find the slightest fault with eye or nose or mouth. It is indeed as much the ideal of male beauty as the Venus is of female charms, yet no one could ever have been enchanted with the statue, or have felt affection to the form which it represents. There is no expression whatever in the features. Everything is so adjusted and proportioned that you want a divergence to relieve you. The materialism is so carefully measured out that there needs a stir, a break in the harmony to give at least some semblance of a soul. Beauty, then, consists not in mere harmony, nor in balancing the features.

Loveliness surely is *attractiveness*. Yes, but that is another way of saying you do not know what it is. It is a something that attracts you, and constrains you to exclaim, 'Nought under heaven so strongly doth allure.' We feel its power, we become its slaves; but we cannot write with pen of cold steel, nor could we write even with a pen of lightning, a description of what it is. How, then, can I – enamoured, entranced, enraptured as I am with him whom my soul loveth – how can I speak of him? He is altogether lovely? Where shall I find words, terms, expressions that shall fitly set him forth? Unless the Eternal Spirit shall upraise me out of myself I must for ever be incapable of setting forth the Well-beloved.

Besides, were I baffled by nothing else, there is this, that the beauty of Christ is mysterious. It surpasses all the comeliness of human form. He may have had great beauty according to the flesh. That I cannot tell, but I should imagine that such a perfect soul as his must have inhabited a perfectly moulded body. Never yet did you or I gaze with satisfaction upon the work of any painter who had tried to picture our Lord Jesus Christ. We have not blamed the great masters, but we have felt that the effort surpassed their powers. How could they photograph the sun? The loftiest conceptions of great artists in this case fall far short of the mark. When the brightness of the Father's glory is the subject the canvas glows in vain. Art sits at her easel and produces diligently many a draught of the sacred features; but they are all failures, and they must be. Who shall ever depict Immanuel, God-with-us? I suppose that, by-and-by, when our Lord had entered upon his active life and encountered its struggles, his youthful beauty was marred with lines of sadness and sorrow. Still his courage so overshadowed his cares, the mercy he showed so surpassed the misery he shared, and the grace he dispensed so exceeded the griefs that he carried, that a halo of real glory must ever have shone around his brow. His countenance must still have been lovely even when surrounded with the clouds of care and grief. How can we describe even the marred visage? It is a great mystery, but a sure fact, that in our Lord's marred countenance his beauty is best seen. Anguish gave him a loveliness which else he had not reached. His passion put the finishing touch upon his unrivalled loveliness.

But, brethren, I am not about to speak of Christ's loveliness after the flesh, for now after the flesh know we him no more. It is his moral and spiritual beauty, of which the spouse in the song most sweetly says, 'Yea, he is altogether lovely.' The loveliness which the eye dotes on is mere varnish when compared with that which dwells in virtue and holiness; the worm will devour the loveliness of skin and flesh, but a lovely character will endure for ever.

1. THIS IS RARE PRAISE. Let that be our first head. This is rare praise. What if I say it is unique? For of no other being could it be said, 'Yea, he is altogether lovely.'

It means, first, that *all that is in him is lovely, perfectly lovely*. There is no point in our Lord Jesus that you could improve. To paint the rose were to spoil its ruddy hue. To tint the lily, for he is lily as well as rose, were to mar its whiteness. Each virtue in our Lord is there in a state of absolute perfection: it could not be more fully developed. If you were able to conceive of each virtue at its ripest stage it would be found in him. In the matter of transparent ingenuousness and sterling honesty, did every man speak or act so truthfully as he? Ask, on the other hand, for sympathising tenderness and love, was ever any so gentle as Jesus? Do you want reverence to God? how he bows before the Father. Do you want boldness before men? how he beards the Pharisees. You could not better anything which you find in Jesus. Wherever you shall cast your eye it may rest with satisfaction, for the best of the best of the best is to be seen in him. He is altogether lovely at every separate point, so that the spouse, when she began with his head, descended to his feet, and then lifting her eyes upward again upon a return voyage of delight, she looked into his countenance and summed up all that she had seen in this one sentence, 'He is altogether lovely.' This is rare praise.

And he is all that is lovely. In each one of his people you will find something that is lovely – in one there is faith, in another abounding love; in one tenderness, in another courage; but you do not find all good things in any one saint, at least not all of them in full perfection – but you find all virtues in Jesus, and each one of them at its best. If you would take the best quality of one saint, and the best quality of another, yea, the best out of each and all the myriads of his people, you would find no grace or goodness among them all which Jesus does not possess in the fullest degree and in the highest perfection. He combines all the virtues and gives them all a sweetness over and beyond themselves. In flowers you have a separate beauty belonging to each; no one flower is just like another, but each one blushes with its own loveliness; but in our Lord these separate and distinct beauties are found united in one. Christ is the posy in which all the beauties of the garden of perfection are bound up. Each gem has its own radiance: the diamond is not like the ruby, nor the ruby like the emerald; but Christ is that ring in which you have sapphire, ruby, diamond, emerald, set in choice order, so that each one heightens the other's brilliance. Look not for anything lovely out of Jesus, for he has all the loveliness. All perfections are in him making up one consummate perfection; and all the loveliness which is to be seen elsewhere is but a reflection of his own unrivalled charms.

In Jesus Christ – this, moreover, is rare praise again – *there is nothing that is unlovely.* You have a friend whom you greatly admire and fondly esteem, of whom, nevertheless, I doubt not you have often said to yourself in an undertone, 'I wish I could take away a little of the rough edge of his manners here and there.' You never thought that of Christ. You have observed of one man that he is so bold as to be sometimes rude; and of another that he is so bland and amiable that he is apt to be effeminate. You have said, 'That sweetness of his is exceedingly good, but I wish that it were qualified with sterner virtues.' But there is nothing to tone down or alter in our divine Lord. He is altogether lovely.

Have you not sometimes in describing a friend been obliged to forget, or omit, some rather prominent characteristic when you wished to make a favourable impression? You have had to paint him as the artist once painted Oliver Cromwell; the great wart over the eyebrow was purposely left out of the portrait. Cromwell, you know, said, 'Paint me as I am, or not at all.' We have, however, often felt that it was kind to leave out the warts when we were talking of those we esteemed, and to whom we would pay a graceful tribute. But there is nothing to leave out in Christ, nothing to hold back, or to guard, or to extenuate. In him is nothing redundant, nothing overgrown. He is altogether lovely.

You never need put the finger over the scar in his case, as Apelles did when he painted his hero. No; tell it all out: reveal the details of his private life and secret thoughts, they need no concealment. Lay bare the very heart of Christ, for that is the essence of love and loveliness. Speak of his death-wounds, for in his scars there is more beauty than in the uninjured comeliness of another; and even when he lies dead in the tomb he is more comely than the immortal angels of God at their best estate. Nothing about our Lord needs to be concealed; even his cross, at which his enemies stumble, is to be daily proclaimed, and it will be seen to be one of his choicest beauties.

Frequently, too, in commending a friend whom you highly appreciated, you have been prone to ask for consideration of his position, and to make excuse for blemishes which you would fain persuade us are less actual than apparent. You have remarked how admirably he acts considering his surroundings. Conscious that someone would hint at an imperfection, you have anticipated the current of conversation by alluding to the circumstances which rendered it so hard for your friend to act commendably. You have felt the need of showing that others influenced him, or that infirmity restrained him. Did you ever feel inclined to apologise for Christ? Did he not always stand unbending beneath life's pressure, upright and unmoved amidst the storms and tempests of an evil world?

The vilest calumnies have been uttered against him, in the age just past which produced creatures similar to Thomas Paine, but they never required an answer; and as for the more refined attacks of our modern scepticism, they are for the most part unworthy even of contempt. They fall beneath the glance of truth, withered by the glance of the eye of honesty. We never feel concerned to vindicate the character of Jesus; we know it to be safe against all comers. No man has been able to conjure up an accusation against Jesus. They seek false witnesses, but their testimony agrees not together. The sharp arrows of slander fall blunted from the shield of his perfectness. Oh, no; he is altogether lovely in this sense – that there is nothing whatever in him that is not lovely. You may look, and look, and look again, but there is nothing in him that will not bear scrutiny world without end.

Taking the Lord Jesus Christ as a whole – this is what our text intends to tell us – he is inexpressibly lovely – *altogether* lovely. The words are packed as tightly as they can be, but the meaning is greater than the words. Some translate the passage 'He is all desires', and it is a good translation too, and contains a grand truth. Christ is so lovely that all you can desire of loveliness is in him; and even if you were to sit down and task your imagination and burden your understanding to contrive, to invent, to fashion the ideal of something that should be inimitable – ay (to utter a paradox) if you could labour to conceive something which should be inconceivably lovely – yet still you would not reach to the perfection of Christ Jesus. He is above, not only all we think, but all we dream of.

Do you believe all this? Dear hearers, do you think of Jesus in this fashion? We speak that we do know, and testify that we have seen. But no man among you will receive our witness until he can say, 'I also have seen him, and having seen him, I set to my seal that he is altogether lovely.'

And now, secondly, as this is rare praise, so likewise IT IS PERPETUAL PRAISE. You may say of Christ whenever you look at him, 'Yea, he is altogether lovely.' He always was so. As God over all, he is blessed for ever, Amen. When in addition to his Godhead, he assumed our mortal clay, was he not inimitably lovely then? The babe in Bethlehem was the most beautiful sight that ever the world beheld. No fairer flower ever bloomed in the garden of creation than the mind of that youth of Nazareth gradually unfolding, as he 'grew, and waxed strong in spirit, filled with wisdom: and the grace of God was upon him'. All the while he lived on earth, what moral perfections, what noble qualities, what spiritual charms were about his sacred person! His life among men is a succession of charming pictures.

And he was lovely in his bitter passion, when as the thick darkness overshadowed his soul he prayed, in an agony of desire, 'Not my will, but thine, be done.' The bloody sweat did not disfigure, but adorn him. And oh, was he not lovely when he died? Without resentment he interceded for his murderers. His patience, his self-possession, his piety, as 'the faithful martyr', have fixed as the meridian of time the hour when he said, 'It is finished', and 'bowed his head', and 'cried with a loud voice, Father, into thy hands I commend my spirit.'

He is lovely in his resurrection from the dead; beyond description lovely. Not a word of accusation did he utter against his cruel persecutors, though he had risen clothed with all power in heaven and in earth. With such tender sympathy did he make himself known to his sorrowing disciples, that despite the waywardness of their unbelief their hearts' instinct told them it was 'the same Jesus'. *He is altogether lovely.*

He will be lovely when he comes with solemn pomp, and sound of trumpet, and escort of mighty angels, and brings all his saints who have departed with him, and calls up those that are alive and remain on the earth till his advent, to meet him in the air. Oh, how lovely he will appear to the two throngs who will presently join in one company! How admirable will his appearance be! How eyes, ears, hearts and voices will greet him! With what unanimity the host redeemed by blood will account their highest acclamations as a trivial tribute to his honour and glory! 'He is altogether lovely.'

Yea, and he shall be lovely for ever and ever when your eyes and mine shall eternally find their heaven in beholding him. 'Jesus Christ, the same yesterday today, and for ever', is always worthy of this word of praise – 'altogether lovely'.

Let us retrace our steps for a minute. The more we study the four Gospels, the more charmed we are with the gospel; for as a modern author has well said, 'The Gospels, like the gospel, are most divine because they are most human.' As followers of Jesus, rank yourselves with those men who companied with him all the time that he went in and out among them; and you shall find him *lovely in all conditions*. Lovely when he talks to a leper, and touches and heals him; lovely by the bedside when he takes the fever-stricken patient by the hand and heals her; lovely by the wayside, when he greets the blind beggar, puts his finger on his eyes and bids him see; lovely when he stands on the sinking vessel and rebukes the waves; lovely when he meets the bier and rekindles the life that had expired; lovely when he visits the mourners, goes with the sisters of Bethany to the new-made grave, and weeps, and groans, and – majestically lovely – bids the dead come forth.

Lovely is he when he rides through the streets of Jerusalem upon a colt, the foal of an ass. Oh, had we been there, we would have plucked the palm branches, and we would have taken off our garments to strew the way. Hosannah, lovely Prince of Peace! But he was just as lovely when he came from the garden with his face all besmeared with bloody sweat; just as lovely when they said, 'Crucify him, crucify him'; just as lovely, and if possible more so, when down those sacred cheeks there dripped the cursed spittle from the rough soldiers' mouths; ay, and loveliest, to my eyes loveliest of all, when mangled, wounded, fainting, bruised, dying, he said, 'My God, my God, why hast thou forsaken me?' uttering a plaintive cry of utmost grief from the felon's gibbet whereon he died.

Yea, view him where you will, in any place soever, is he not – I speak to you who know him, and not to those who never saw him with the eye of faith – is he not in the night and in the day, on the sea and on the land, on earth and in heaven, altogether lovely?

He is lovely in all his offices. What an entrancing sight to see the King in his beauty, with his diadem upon his head, as he now sits in yonder world of brightness! How charming to view him as a Priest, with the Urim and Thummim, wearing the names of his people bejewelled on his breastplate! And what a vision of simple beauty, to see him as a Prophet teaching his people in touching parables of homely interest, of whom they said, 'Never man spake like this man'! The very tones of his voice and the glance of his eyes made his eloquence so supreme that it enthralled men's hearts. Yes, he is lovely, altogether lovely in any and every character. We know not which best beseems him, the highest or the lowliest positions. Let him be what he may – Lamb or Shepherd, Brother or King, Saviour or Master, Foot-washer or Lord – in every relation he is altogether lovely.

Get a view of him, my brethren, from any point and see whether he is not lovely. Do you recollect the first sight you ever had of him? It was on a day when your eyes were red with weeping over sin, and you expected to see the Lord dressed in anger coming forth to destroy you. Oh, it was the happiest sight I ever saw when I beheld my sins rolling into his sepulchre and, when looking up, I beheld him my substitute bleeding on the tree. Altogether lovely was he that day. Since then providence has given us a varied experience and taken us to different points of view that we might look at Christ, and see him under many aspects.

We look at statues from several standpoints if we would criticise them. A great many in London are hideous from all points of view – others are very well if you look at them this way, but if you go over yonder and look from another point the artist appears to have utterly failed.

Now, beloved, look at Jesus from any point you like, and he is at his best from each and every corner. You have been in prosperity: God multiplied your children and blessed your basket and your store – was Jesus lovely then? Assuredly he was the light of your delights. Nothing he had given you vied with himself. He rose in your hearts superior to his own best gifts. But you tell me that you have been very sick, and you have lost one after another of your dear ones; your means have been reduced; you have come down in the world: say, then, is Jesus lovely now? I know that you will reply 'Yes, more than ever is Christ delightful in mine eyes.'

Well, you have had very happy times, and you have been on the mount of hallowed friendship. The other Sunday morning many of us were up there, and thought like Peter that we should like to stay there for ever; and is not Jesus lovely when he is transfigured and we are with him? Yes, but at another time you are down in the depths with Jonah, at the bottom of the sea. Is not Christ lovely then? Yes, even there he hears our prayer out of his holy temple, and brings us again from the deep abyss.

We shall soon lie dying. Oh, my brethren, what brave talk God's people have often given us about their Lord when they have been on the edge of the grave! That seems to be a time when the Well-beloved takes the veil off his face altogether and sits by the bedside, and lets his children look into his face, and see him as he is. I warrant you the saints forget the ghastliness of death when their hearts are ravished with the loveliness of Christ.

Yes, hitherto, up to this point Jesus has been lovely; and now let us add that he will always be so. You know there are persons whom you account beautiful when you are young, but when you grow older in years, riper in judgment, and more refined in taste, you meet with others who look far more beautiful. Now, what think you of your Lord? Have you met with anyone in fact or in fable more beautiful than he? You thought him charming when you were but a babe in grace. What think you of him now? Taste, you know, grows, and develops with education: an article of vertu which fascinated you years ago has no longer any charms for you because your taste is raised. Has your spiritual taste outgrown your Lord's beauties? Come, brothers, does Christ go down as you learn truth more exactly and acquaint yourself more fully with him? Oh no. You prize him a thousand times more today than you did when the first impression of his goodness was formed in your mind.

Some things which look very lovely at a distance lose their loveliness when you get near to them: but is it not true (I am sure it is) that the nearer you get to Christ the lovelier he is? Some things are only beautiful in your eyes for their novelty: you admire them when you have seen them once; if you were to see them a dozen times you would not care much about them. What say you about my Master? Is it not true that the oftener you see him, the more you know him, and the more familiar your intercourse with him, and the more he rises in your esteem? I know it is so; and well, therefore, did the spouse say, 'He is altogether lovely.'

Christ is altogether lovely in this respect – that when men reproach him and rail at him, he is often all the lovelier in his people's eyes. I warrant you Christ has been better known by the burn-side in Scotland by his Covenanting people than ever he has been seen under the fretted roof of cathedral architecture. Away there in lonely glens, amid the mosses and the hills, where Covenanters met for fear of Claverhouse and his dragoons, the Lord Jesus has shone forth like the sun in his strength. We have nowadays to be satisfied with his moonlight face, but in persecuting days his children have seen his sun face, and oh! how glad they have been. Hear how the saints sing in prison! Listen to their charming notes, even on the rack, when the glory of his presence fills their souls with heaven on earth, and makes them defy the torments of the flesh. The Lord Jesus is more lovely to the soul that can bear reproach for him than he is to any other. Put the cross on his back if you will, but we love him all the better for that. Nail up his hands, but we love him all the better for that. Now fasten his feet; ay, but our soul melteth with love to him, and she feels new reasons for loving him when she beholds the nails. Now stand ye around the cross, ye worldlings, and mock him if ye will. Taunt and jest, and jeer and jibe – these do but make us love the better the great and glorious one, who 'made himself of no reputation, and took upon him the form of a servant, and being found in fashion as a man, humbled himself and became obedient unto death, even the death of the cross'.

Beloved, you shall keep on looking at Christ from all these points of view till you get to heaven, and each time you shall be more enamoured of him. When you reach the celestial city and see him face to face, then shall you say, 'The half has not been told us', but even here below Christ is altogether lovely to his people.

3. I leave that head just to notice, in the third place, that though this praise is rare praise and perpetual praise, yet also IT IS TOTALLY INSUFFICIENT PRAISE.

Say ye that he is altogether lovely? It is not enough. It is not a thousandth part enough. No tongue of man, no tongue of angel, can ever set forth his unutterable beauties. 'Oh,' say you, 'but it is a great word, though short; very full of meaning though soon spoken – *altogether lovely*'. I tell you it is a poor word. It is a word of despair. It is a word which the spouse uttered, because she had been trying to describe her Lord and she could not do it, and so she put this down in very desperation: as much as to say, 'There, the task is too great for me. I will end it. This is all I can say, "Yea, he is altogether lovely".' I am sure John Berridge was right when he said:

> Living tongues are dumb at best,
> We must die to speak of Christ.

Brethren, the praise of the text is insufficient praise, I know, because it is praise given by one who had never seen him in his glory. It is Old Testament praise this, that he is altogether lovely: praise uttered upon report rather than upon actual view of him. Truly I know not how to bring better, but *I shall know* one day. Till then I will speak his praise as best I can, though it fall far short of his infinite excellence. Our text is cloth of gold, but it is not fit for our Beloved to put the sole of his foot upon. He deserves better than this, for this is only the praise of a church that had not seen him die, and had not seen him rise, and had not seen him in the splendour at the divine right hand.

'Well,' say you, 'try if you can do better.' No, I will not, because if I did praise him better, the style would not last long, for he is coming quickly, and the best thing the best speaker could ever say of him will be put out of date by the majesty of his appearing. His chariot is waiting at his door now, and he may soon come forth from his secret chambers and be among us, and oh! the glory – oh! the glory! Paul, you know, stole a glance through the lattices one day when he was caught up into the third heaven. Somebody said to me, 'I wonder Paul did not tell us what he saw.' Ay, but what he saw he might not tell, and the words he heard were words which it were not lawful for a man to utter, and yet to live among this evil generation. We shall hear those words ourselves soon, and see those sights not many days hence, so let it stand as it does, 'He is altogether lovely.' But when you have thus summed up all that our poor tongues can express, you must not say, 'Now we have described him.' Oh no, sirs, ye have but held a candle to this glorious sun, for he is such an one as thought cannot compass, much less language describe.

I leave this point with the reflection, that God intends to describe him and set him forth one day. He is waiting patiently, for long-suffering is part of Christ's character; and God is setting forth the long-suffering of Christ in the patient waiting of these eighteen hundred years. But the day shall presently dawn and usher in the everlasting age when Christ shall be better seen, for every eye shall see him, and every tongue confess that he is Lord. The whole earth will one day be sweet with the praise of Jesus. Earth, did I say? This alabaster box of Christ's sweetness has too much fragrance in it for the world to keep it all to itself; the sweetness of our Lord's person will rise above the stars, and perfume worlds unknown. It will fill heaven itself. Eternity shall be occupied with declaring the praises of Jesus. Seraphs shall sing of it; angels shall harp it; the redeemed shall declare it. He is altogether lovely. The cycles of eternity as they revolve shall only confirm the statement of the blood-redeemed that he is altogether lovely. O that the day were come when we shall bow with them and sing with them! Wait a little while and be not weary, and you shall be at home, and then you shall know that I spoke the truth when I said that this was insufficient praise. Earth is too narrow to contain him, heaven is too little to hold him, eternity itself too short for the utterance of all his praises.

(4) So I close with this last thought, which may God bless, for practical uses. **This praise is VERY SUGGESTIVE**.

If Christ be altogether lovely it suggests a question. Suppose I never saw his loveliness. Suppose that in this house there should be souls that never saw anything in Christ to make them love him. If you were to go to some remote island where beauty consisted in having one eye and a twisted mouth, and a sea-green complexion, you would say, 'Those people are strange beings.' Such are the people of this world. Spiritual beauty is not appreciated by them. This world appreciates the man who makes money, however reckless he may be of the welfare of others while scheming to heap up riches for himself. As for the man who slays his fellow-creatures by thousands, they mount him on a bronze horse, put him on an arch, or they pile up a column, and set him as near heaven as they can. He slew his thousands: he died blood-red: he was an emperor, a tyrant, a conqueror: the world feels his power and pays its homage.

As for this Jesus, he only gave his life for men, he was only pure and perfect, the mirror of disinterested love. The vain world cannot see in him a virtue to admire. It is a blind world, a fool world, a world that lieth in the wicked one. Not to discern the beauties of Jesus is an evidence of terrible depravity. Have you, my dear friend, frankly to confess that you were never enamoured of him who was holy, harmless, and undefiled, and went about doing good? Then let this come home to you – that the question is not as to whether Christ is lovely or not, the mistake is here – that you have not a spiritually enlightened eye, a fine moral perception, nor even a well-regulated conscience, or you would see his loveliness at once. You are dark and blind. God help you to feel this.

Do you not love Christ? Then let me ask you why you do not? There was never a man yet that knew Christ that could give a reason for not loving him, neither is there such a reason to be discovered. He is altogether lovely. In nothing is he unlovable. Oh I wish that the good Spirit of God would whisper in your heart, and incline you to say, 'I will see about this Christ. I will read of him. I will look at the four portraits of him painted by the evangelists, and if he be indeed thus lovely, no doubt he will win my heart as he appears to have won the hearts of others.' I pray he may. But do not, I pray you, continue to deny Christ your love. It is all you can give him. It is a poor thing, but he values it. He would sooner have your heart than all the gold in Europe. He would sooner have the heart of a poor servant girl or of a poor humble labourer upon the soil than the queen's diadem. He loveth love. Love is his gem – his jewel. He delights to win it, and if he be indeed altogether lovely, let him have it. You have known people, I dare say, whom you could not help loving. They never had to say to you, 'Love me', for you were captivated at once by the very sight of them. In like manner many and many have only received one beam of light from the Holy Spirit, and have thereby seen who Jesus was, and they have at once said of him, 'Thou hast ravished my heart with one look of thine eyes', and so it has been that all their life long they have loved their Lord.

Now, the praise is suggestive still further. 'Is Christ altogether lovely? Then do I love him? As a child of God, do I love him as much as I ought? I do love him. Yes, blessed be his name, I do love him. But what a poor, cold, chill love it is. How few are the sacrifices I make for him. How few are the offerings that I present to him. How little is the fellowship that I maintain with him.' Brother, is there a rival in your heart? Do you allow anyone to come in between you and the 'altogether lovely'? If so, chase out the intruder. Christ must have all your heart, and let me tell you the more we love him the more bliss we shall have. A soul that is altogether given up to the love of Christ lives above care and sorrow. It has care and sorrow, but the love of Christ kills all the bitterness by its inexpressible sweetness. I cannot tell you how near a man may live to heaven, but I am persuaded that a very large proportion of the bliss of heaven may be enjoyed before we come there. There is one conduit pipe through which heavenly joy will flow, and if you draw from it you may have as much as you will. 'Abide in me,' says Christ; and if you do abide in his love you shall have his joy fulfilled in yourselves that your joy may be full. You will have more capacious vessels in heaven, but even now the little vessel that you have can be filled up to the brim by knowing the inexpressible loveliness of Jesus and surrendering your hearts to it.

Oh that I could rise to something better than myself. I often feel like a chick in the egg; I am picking my way out, and I cannot get clear of my prison. Fain would I chip the shell, come forth to freedom, develop wings, and soar heavenward, singing on the road. Would God that were our portion. If anything can help us to get out of the shell, and to begin to rise and sing, it must be a full and clear perception that Jesus is altogether lovely. Come, let us be married to him afresh tonight. Come, believing hearts, yield again to his charms; again surrender yourselves to the supremacy of his affection. Let us have the love of our espousals renewed. As you come to his table bethink you of the lips of Christ, of which the spouse had been speaking before she uttered my text: 'His mouth is most sweet.' There are three things about Christ's mouth that are very sweet. The first is his word: you have heard that. The second is his breath. Come, Holy Spirit, make thy people feel that. And the third is his kiss. May every believing soul have that sweet token of his eternal love.

Forgive my ramblings. May God bless to all his people the word that has been spoken. May some that never knew my Master ask to know him tonight. Go home and seek him. Read the Word to find him. Cry to him in prayer and he will be found of you. He is so lovely that I should not live without loving him; and I shall deeply regret if any one of you shall spend another four-and-twenty hours without having had a sight of his divine face by faith.

41

THE CHURCH AS SHE SHOULD BE

'Thou art beautiful, O my love, as Tirzah, comely as Jerusalem, terrible as an army with banners' (Song of Solomon 6:4).

There are various estimates of the Christian church. Some think everything of her; some think nothing of her; and probably neither opinion is worth the breath which utters it. Neither Ritualists who idolise their church, nor sceptics who vilify all churches, have any such knowledge of the true spiritual church of Jesus Christ as to be entitled to give an opinion. The king's daughter is all glorious within, with a beauty which they are quite unable to appreciate.

What is usually the most correct character which is obtainable of a woman? Shall we be guided by the praises of those neighbours who are on good terms with her, or by the scandal of those who make her the subject of ill-natured gossip? No; the most accurate judgment we are likely to get is that of her husband. Solomon saith in the Proverbs concerning the virtuous woman: 'Her husband also riseth up, and he praiseth her.' Of that fairest among women, the church of Christ, the same observation may be made. It is to her of small consequence to be judged of man's judgment, but it is her honour and joy to stand well in the love and esteem of her royal spouse, the Prince Emmanuel.

Though the words before us are allegorical, and the whole song is crowded with metaphor and parable, yet the teaching is plain enough in this instance; it is evident that the Divine Bridegroom gives his bride a high place in his heart, and to him, whatever she may be to others, she is fair, lovely, comely, beautiful, and in the eyes of his love without a spot. Moreover, even to him there is not only a beauty of a soft and gentle kind in her, but a majesty, a dignity in her holiness, in her earnestness, in her consecration, which makes even him say of her that she is 'terrible as an army with banners', 'awful as a bannered army'. She is every inch a queen: her aspect in the sight of her beloved is majestic. Take, then, the words of our text as an encomium upon Christ's church, pronounced by him who knows her best, and is best able to judge concerning her, and you learn that to his discerning eye she is not weak, dishonourable and despicable, but bears herself as one of highest rank, consciously, joyously strong in her Lord's strength.

On this occasion let us note, first of all, **WHY IT IS THAT THE CHURCH OF GOD IS SAID TO BE AN ARMY WITH BANNERS**. That she is *an army* is true enough, for the church is one, but many; and consists of men who march in order under a common leader, with one design in view and that design a conflict and a victory. She is the church militant here below, and both in suffering and in service she is made to prove that she is in an enemy's country. She is contending for the truth against error, for the light against darkness; till the day break and the shadows flee away, she must maintain her sentinels and kindle her watch fires; for all around her there is cause to guard against the enemy, and to defend the royal treasure of gospel truth against its deadly foes. But why an army *with banners*?

Is not this, first of all, for *distinction*? How shall we know to which king an army belongs unless we can see the royal standard? In times of war the nationality of troops is often declared by their distinguishing regimentals. The grey coats of the Russians were well known in the Crimea; the white livery of the Austrians was a constant eyesore in bygone days to the natives of Lombardy. No one mistook the Black Brunswickers for French Guards, or our own Hussars for Garibaldians. Quite as effectively armies have been distinguished by the banners which they carried. As the old knights of old were recognised by their plume and helmet and escutcheon, so an army is known by its standard and the national colours. The tricolour of the French readily marked their troops as they fled before the terrible black and white of the Germany army.

The church of Christ displays its banners for distinction's sake. It desires not to be associated with other armies, or to be mistaken for them, for it is not of this world, and its weapons and its warfare are far other than those of the nations. God forbid that followers of Jesus should be mistaken for political partisans or ambitious adventurers. The church unfurls her ensign to the breeze that all may know whose she is and whom she serves. This is of the utmost importance at this present, when crafty men are endeavouring to palm off their inventions. Every Christian church should know what it believes, and publicly avow what it maintains. It is our duty to make a clear and distinct declaration of our principles that our members may know to what intent they have come together, and that the world also may know what we mean.

Far be it from us to join with the Broad Church cry, and furl the banners upon which our distinctive colours are displayed. We hear on all sides great outcries against creeds. Are these clamours justifiable? It seems to me that when properly analysed most of the protests are not against creeds, but against truth, for every man who believes anything must have a creed, whether he write it down and print it or not; or if there be a man who believes nothing, or anything, or everything by turns, he is not a fit man to be set up as a model. Attacks are often made against creeds because they are a short, handy form by which the Christian mind gives expression to its belief, and those who hate creeds do so because they find them to be weapons as inconvenient as bayonets in the hands of British soldiers have been to our enemies. They are weapons so destructive to neology that it protests against them. For this reason let us be slow to part with them. Let us lay hold of God's truth with iron grip, and never let it go.

After all, there is a Protestantism still worth contending for; there is a Calvinism still worth proclaiming, and a gospel worth dying for. There is a Christianity distinctive and distinguished from Ritualism, Rationalism and Legalism, and let us make it known that we believe in it. Up with your banners, soldiers of the cross! This is not the time to be frightened by the cries against conscientious convictions, which are nowadays nicknamed sectarianism and bigotry. Believe in your hearts what you profess to believe; proclaim openly and zealously what you know to be the truth. Be not ashamed to say such-and-such things are true, and let men draw the inference that the opposite is false. Whatever the doctrines of the gospel may be to the rest of mankind, let them be your glory and boast. Display your banners, and let those banners be such as the church of old carried. Unfurl the old primitive standard, the all-victorious standard of the cross of Christ. In very deed and truth – *in hoc signo vinces* – the atonement is the conquering truth. Let others believe as they may, or deny as they will, for you the truth as it is in Jesus is the one thing that has won your heart and made you a soldier of the cross.

Banners were carried, not merely for distinctiveness, but also to serve the purposes of *discipline*. Hence an army with banners had one banner and a central standard, and then each regiment or battalion displayed its own particular flag. The hosts of God, which so gloriously marched through the wilderness, had their central standard. I suppose it was the very pole upon which Moses lifted up the brazen serpent (at any rate, our brazen serpent is the central ensign of the church); and then, besides that, each tribe of the twelve had its own particular banneret, and with these uplifted in the front, the tribes marched in order, so that there was no difficulty in marshalling the armed men. It was believed by the later Jews that 'the standard of the camp of Judah represented a lion; that of Reuben, a man; that of Joseph, an ox; and that of Dan, an eagle. The Targumists, however, believe that the banners were distinguished by their colours, the colour for each tribe being analogous to that of the precious stone for that tribe in the breastplate of the high priest; and that the great standard of each of the four camps combined the three colours of the tribes which composed it.'

So, brethren, in the church of God there must be discipline – the discipline not only of admission and of dismission in receiving the converts and rejecting the hypocrites, but the discipline of marshalling the troops to the service of Christ in the holy war in which we are engaged. Every soldier should have his orders, every officer his troop, every troop its fixed place in the army, and the whole army a regularity such as is prescribed in the rule, 'Let all things be done decently and in order.'

As in the ranks each man has his place, and each rank has its particular place in the battalion, so in every rightly constituted church each man, each woman, will have, for himself or herself, his or her own particular form of service, and each form of service will link in with every other, and the whole combined will constitute a force which cannot be broken. A church is not a load of bricks, remember; it is a house builded together. A church is not a bundle of cuttings in the gardener's hand; it is a vine, of which we are the branches. The true church is an organised whole; and life, true spiritual life, wherever it is paramount in the church, without rules and rubrics, is quite sure to create order and arrangement. Order without life reminds us of the rows of graves in a cemetery, all numbered and entered in the register; order with life reminds us of the long lines of fruit trees in Italy, festooned with fruitful vines. Sunday-school teachers, bear ye the banner of the folded lamb; sick visitors, follow the ensign of the open hand; preachers, rally to the token of the uplifted brazen serpent; and all of you, according to your sacred calling, gather to the name of Jesus, armed for the war.

An army with banners may be also taken to represent *activity*. When an army folds up its colours the fight is over. Little is being done in military circles when the banners are put away; the troops are on furlough, or are resting in barracks. An army with banners is exercising or marching or fighting; probably it is in the middle of a campaign, it is marshalled for offence and defence, and there will be rough work before long.

It is to be feared that some churches have hung up their flags to rot in state, or have encased them in dull propriety. They do not look to do great things, or to see great things. They do not expect many conversions; if many did happen, they would be alarmed and suspicious. They do not expect their pastor's ministry to be with power; and if it were attended with manifest effect they would be greatly disturbed, and perhaps would complain that he created too much excitement. The worst of it is, that do-nothing churches are usually very jealous lest any should encroach on their domains. Our churches sometime ago appeared to imagine that a whole district of this teeming city belonged to them to cultivate or neglect, as their monopolising decree might be. If anybody attempted to raise a new interest, or even to build a preaching station, within half a mile of them, they resented it as a most pernicious poaching upon their manor. They did nothing themselves, and were very much afraid lest anybody should supplant them. Like the lawyers of old, who took away the key of knowledge, they entered not in themselves, and them that were entering in they hindered.

That day, it is to be hoped, has gone once for all; yet too much of the old spirit lingers in certain quarters. It is high time that each church should feel that if it does not work, the sole reason for its existence is gone. The reason for a church being a church lies in mutual edification and in the conversion of sinners; and if these two ends are not really answered by a church, it is a mere name, a hindrance, an evil, a nuisance; like the salt which has lost its savour, it is neither fit for the land nor yet for the dunghill.

May we all in our church fellowship be active in the energy of the Spirit of God. May none of us be dead members of the living body, mere impediments to the royal host, baggage to be dragged rather than warriors pushing on the war. May we, every one of us, be soldiers filled with vigour to the fulness of our manhood, by the eternal power of the Holy Spirit; and may we be resolved that any portion of the church which does not uplift its banner of service shall not long number us among its adherents. Be it ours to determine that whether others will or will not serve God and extend the kingdom of his dear Son, we will, in his name and strength, contend even to the death. Unsheath your swords, ye soldiers of the cross; arise from your slumbers, ye careless ones, gird on your swords and prepare for the war. The Lord has redeemed you by his blood, not that you might sleep, but that you might fight for the glory of his name.

Does not the description, 'an army with banners', imply a degree of *confidence*? It is not an army retiring from the foe, and willing enough to hide its colours to complete its escape. An army that is afraid to venture out into the open, keeps its banners out of the gleam of the sun. Banners uplifted are the sign of a fearlessness which rather courts than declines the conflict. Ho! warriors of the cross, unfurl the gospel's ancient standard to the breeze; we will teach the foeman what strength there is in hands and hearts that rally to the Christ of God. Up with the standard, ye brave men at arms; let all eyes see it; and if the foemen glare like lions on it, we will call upon the Lion of the tribe of Judah to lead the van, and we will follow with his Word like a two-edged sword in our hands:

Stand up! stand up for Jesus!
　Ye soldiers of the cross!
Lift high his royal banner;
　It must not suffer loss:
From victory unto victory
　His army shall he lead,
'Till every foe is vanquish'd,
　And Christ is Lord indeed.

We cannot place too much reliance in the gospel; our weakness is that we are so diffident and so apt to look somewhere else for strength. We do not believe in the gospel as to its power over the sons of men as we should believe in it. Too often we preach it with a coward's voice. Have I not heard sermons commencing with abject apologies for the preacher's daring to open his mouth; apologies for his youth, for his assertions, for his venturing to intrude upon men's consciences, and I know not what else? Can God own ambassadors of this cowardly, cringing breed, who mistake fear of men for humility? Will our Captain honour such carpet-knights, who apologise for bearing arms?

I have heard that of old the ambassadors of Holland, and some other states, when introduced to his celestial majesty, the brother of the sun and cousin of the moon, the Emperor of China, were expected to come crawling on their hands and knees up to the throne; but when our ambassadors went to that flowery land, they declined to pay such humiliating homage to his impertinent majesty and informed him that they would stand upright in his presence, as free men should do, or else they would decline all dealings with him, and in all probability his majesty would hear from a cannon's mouth far less gentle notes than he would care for.

Even thus, though we may well humble ourselves as men, yet as ambassadors of God we cannot crouch to the sons of men, to ask them what message would suit them best. It must not, shall not, be that we shall smooth our tongues and tone our doctrines to the taste of the age. The gospel that we preach, although the worldly wise man despises it, it is God's gospel for all that. 'Ah,' says he, 'there is nothing in it: science has overthrown it.' 'And,' says another, 'this gospel is but so much platitude;

we have heard it over and over again.' Ah, sir, and though it be platitude to you, and you declare it to be contemptible, you shall hear it or nothing else from us; 'for it is the power of God, and the wisdom of God'. In its simplicity lies its majesty and its power. 'We are not ashamed of the gospel of Christ.' God forbid that we should glory save in the cross of our Lord Jesus Christ.' We will proclaim it again with confidence; we will bring forth once more the self-same truth as of old; and as the barley loaf smote the tent of Midian, so that it lay along, so shall the gospel overturn its adversaries. The broken pitcher and the flaming torches and the old war cry, 'The sword of the Lord, and of Gideon', shall yet fill the foeman with dismay. Let us but be bold for Jesus, and we shall see what his arm can do.

The gospel is the voice of the eternal God and has in it the same power as that which brought the world out of nothing, and which shall raise the dead from their graves at the coming of the Son of Man. The gospel, the word of God, can no more return to him void than can the snow go back to heaven, or the raindrops climb again the path by which they descended from the clouds. Have faith in God's Word, faith in the presence of the Holy Ghost, faith in the reigning Saviour, faith in the fulfilment of the everlasting purposes, and you will be full of confidence, and like an army with banners.

Once more, an army with banners may signify the *constancy* and perseverance in holding the truth. We see before us not an army that has lost its banners, that has suffered its colours to be rent away from it, but an army which bears aloft its ancient standard and swears by it still. Let us be very earnest to maintain the faith once delivered to the saints. Let us not give up this doctrine or that, at the dictates of policy or fashion; but whatsoever Jesus saith unto us, let us receive it as the Word of life.

Great injury may be done to a church ere it knows it, if it shall tolerate error here and there; for false doctrine, like the little leaven, soon leavens the whole lump. If the church be taught of the Spirit to know the voice of the Good Shepherd, a stranger it will not follow; for it knows not the voice of strangers. This is part of the education which Christ gives to his people: 'All thy people shall be taught of the Lord.' They shall know the truth, and the truth shall make them free. May we, as a church, hold fast the things which we have learned and have been taught of God; and may we be preserved from the philosophies and refinings of these last days. If we give up the things which are verily believed among us we shall lose our power, and the enemy alone will be pleased; but if we maintain them, the maintenance of the old faith by the Spirit of God shall make us strong in the Lord and in the power of his might. Wrap the colours round you, ye standard bearers, in the day of danger, and die sooner than give them up. Life is little compared with God's lovingkindness, and that is the sure heritage of the brave defender of the faith. Thus resolute for truth, the church becomes an army with banners.

Secondly, the church is said to be TERRIBLE. To whom is she terrible? She should be amiable, and she is. May God grant that our church may never be terrible to young converts by moroseness and uncharitableness. Whenever I hear of candidates being alarmed at coming before our elders, or seeing the pastor, or making confession of faith before the church, I wish I could say to them: 'Dismiss your fears, beloved ones; we shall be glad to see you, and you will find your intercourse with us a pleasure rather than a trial.' So far from wishing to repel you, if you really do love the Saviour, we shall be glad enough to welcome you. If we cannot see in you the evidence of a great change, we shall kindly point out to you our fears, and shall be thrice happy to point you to the Saviour; but be sure of this, if you have really believed in Jesus, you shall not find the church terrible to you. Harsh judgments are contrary to the spirit of Christ and the nature of the gospel; where they are the rule, the church is despicable rather than terrible. Bigotry and uncharitableness are indications of weakness, not of strength.

To what and to whom is the church terrible? I answer, first, in a certain sense she is terrible *to all ungodly men.* A true church in her holiness and testimony is very terrible to sinners. The ungodly care not a rush about a mock church, nor about sham Christians; but a really earnest Christian makes the ungodly abashed. We have known some who could not use the foul language which they were accustomed to when they were in the presence of godly men and women, though these persons had no authority or position or rank. Even in the most ribald company, when a Christian of known consistency of character has wisely spoken the word of reproof, a solemn abashment comes over the majority of those present; their consciences have borne witness against them, and they have felt how awful goodness is.

Not that we are ever to try and impress others with any dread of us; such an attempt would be ridiculed and end in deserved failure; but the influence which we would describe flows naturally out of a godly life. Majesty of character never lies in affectation of demeanour, but in solidity of virtue. If there be real goodness in us – if we really, fervently, zealously love the right, and hate the evil – the outflow of our life almost without a word will judge the ungodly and condemn them in their heart of hearts. Holy living is the weightiest condemnation of sin.

We have heard of an ungodly son who could not bear to live in the house where his departed father had in his lifetime so devoutly prayed; every room and every piece of furniture reproved him for forsaking his father's God. We have read of others who were wont to dread the sight of certain godly men whose holy lives held them more in check than the laws of the land.

The bad part of this is that the terror of the ungodly suggests to them an unhallowed retort upon their reprovers, and becomes the root out of which springs persecution. Those whom the ungodly fear because they condemn them by their character, they try to put out of the world if they can, or to bespatter them with slander if they cannot smite them with the hand of cruelty. The martyrdom of saints is the result of the darkness hating the light, because the light makes manifest its evil deeds. There will be always in proportion to the real holiness, earnestness and Christlikeness of a church something terrible in it to the perverse generation in which it is placed; it will dread it as it does the all-revealing day of judgment.

So is there something terrible in a living church to all *errorists*. Just now two armies have encamped against the host of God, opposed to each other, but confederates against the church of God. *Ritualism*, with its superstition, its priestcraft, its sacramental efficacy, its hatred of the doctrines of grace; and on the other side *Rationalism*, with its sneering unbelief and absurd speculations. These, like Herod and Pilate, agree in nothing but in opposition to Christ; they have one common dread, although they may not confess it. They do not dread those platform speeches in which they are so furiously denounced at public meetings, nor those philosophical discussions in which they are overthrown by argument; but they hate, but they fear, and therefore abuse and pretend to despise, the prayerful, zealous, plain, simple preaching of the truth as it is in Jesus. This is a weapon against which they cannot stand – the weapon of the old gospel. In the days of Luther it did marvels; it wrought wonders in the days of Whitefield and Wesley; it has often restored the ark of the Lord to our land, and it will again. It has lost none of its ancient power, and therefore is it the terror of the adversaries of Christ.

Thine aspect's awful majesty
    Doth strike thy foes with fear;
As armies do when banners fly,
    And martial flags appear.

How does thine armour, glitt'ring bright,
    Their frighted spirits quell!
The weapons of thy warlike might
    Defy the gates of hell.

Even *to Satan himself* the church of God is terrible. He might, he thinks, deal with individuals, but when these individuals strengthen each other by mutual converse and prayer, when they are bound to each other in holy love, and make a temple in which Christ dwells, then is Satan hard put to it. O brethren and sisters, it is not every church that is terrible thus, but it is a church of God in which there is the life of God and the love of God;

a church in which there is the uplifted banner, the banner of the cross, high-held amid those various bannerets of truthful doctrine and spiritual grace, of which I have just now spoken.

We will take a third point; and that is, WHY IS THE CHURCH OF CHRIST TERRIBLE AS AN ARMY WITH BANNERS? Why is it terrible because of the banners? The whole passage seems to say that the church is terrible as an army, but that to the fullest degree she owes her terribleness to her banners. 'Terrible as an army with banners.' I believe the great banner of the Christian church to be the uplifted Saviour. 'I, if I be lifted up from the earth, will draw all men unto me.' Around him then we gather. 'Unto him shall the gathering of the people be.' As the brazen serpent in the midst of the camp in the wilderness, so is the Saviour lifted high, our banner. The atoning sacrifice of Christ is the great central standard of all really regenerate men, and this is the main source of dismay to Israel's foes.

But we shall take the thoughts in order. The church herself is terrible, and then terrible because of her banners. Brethren, the army itself is terrible. Why?

First, because *it consists of elect people*. Remember how Haman's wife enquired concerning Mordecai whether he belonged to the seed of the Jews; for if he did, then she foretold that her husband's scheme would prove a failure. 'If Mordecai be of the seed of the Jews, before whom thou hast begun to fall, thou shalt not prevail against him, but shalt surely fall before him.' Now, the church of God as made up of men and women is nothing more than any other organisation. Look at its exterior and you see in it few persons of great education and a great many of no education; here and there a wealthy and powerful person, but hundreds who are poor and despised. It does not possess in itself, naturally, the elements of strength, according to ordinary reckoning. Indeed, its own confession is that in itself it is perfect weakness, a flock of sheep among wolves; but here lies its strength, that each of the true members of the church are of the seed royal; they are God's chosen ones, the seed of the woman ordained of old to break the head of Satan and all his serpent seed. They are the weakness of God, but they are stronger than men; he has determined with the things that are not to bring to nought the things that are. As the Canaanites feared the chosen race of Israel because the rumour of them had gone forth among the people, and the terror of Jehovah was upon them; so is it with the hosts of evil. They have dreamed their dreams, as the Midianite did, and valiant men like Gideon can hear them telling it; the barley cake shall fall upon the royal tent of Midian and smite it till it lies along; the sword of the Lord and of Gideon shall rout the foe. The elect shall overcome through the blood of the Lamb, and none shall say them nay. Ye are a royal priesthood, a peculiar people, a chosen generation; and in you the living God will gloriously declare his sovereign grace.

The church, again, consists of *a praying people*. Now prayer is that which links weakness with infinite strength. A people who can pray can never be overcome, because their reserve forces can never be exhausted. Go into battle, my brother; and if you be vanquished with the strength you have, prayer shall call up another legion, yea, twenty legions of angels, and the foe shall marvel to see undefeated adversaries still holding the field. If ten thousand saints were burned tomorrow, their dying prayers would make the church rise like a phoenix from her ashes. Who, therefore, can stand against a people whose prayers enlist God in their quarrel? 'The Lord of hosts is with us; the God of Jacob is our refuge.' We cry unto the Lord, and he heareth us; he breaketh through the ranks of the foe; he giveth us triumph in the day of battle: therefore, terrible as an army with banners are those who wield the weapon of all-prayer.

Again, a true church is *based upon eternal truth*. I need not quote to you the old Latin proverb which says that truth is mighty and must prevail. Truth is, and truth shall be. It alone is substance, and must outlast the lapse of ages. Falsehoods are soon swollen to their perfection of development, like the bubbles with rainbow hues which children blow, but they are dispersed as easily as they are fashioned; they are children of the hour, while truth is the offspring and heir of eternity. Falsehood dies, pierced through the heart by the arrows of time, but truth, in her impenetrable mail, bids defiance to all foes. Men who love the truth are building gold and silver and precious stones; and though their architecture may progress but slowly, it is built for eternity. Ramparts of truth may often be assailed, but they will never be carried by the foe. Establish a power among men of the most ostentatious and apparently stable kind, but rest assured that if untruth be at the root of it, it must perish, sooner or later; only truth is invincible, eternal, supreme. The fear of the true church and the dread thereof falls upon the enemy, because they have wit enough left to know that truth has an abiding and indestructible power.

I was very much amused the other day to read a criticism by an eminent infidel, whose name would be well known if I were to mention it, in which he speaks very highly of the exceeding great skill and wisdom and common sense always exhibited in the arrangements of the Roman Catholic Church in opposition to Infidelity, and of the imbecility and childishness manifested by Christian ministers in assailing Rationalism with their dogmatism, etc. I was very glad to receive information so valuable, and I thought: 'I see, my friend, what kind of warfare you like best. You admire the Roman Catholic kind of fighting, but you do not admire that which evangelical ministers have adopted. It is no aim of ours to please our enemies in our mode of warfare, but the reverse; and if we have discovered a weapon which galls you, we will use that same arm more freely than ever.' There is a story of an officer who was rather awkward in his manners, and, upon some great occasion, almost fell over his sword in his haste. His majesty remarked, 'Your sword seems to be very much in the way.' 'So your majesty's enemies have very often felt,' was the reply.

So, when the enemies of the truth are finding fault with our procedure, we accept their verdict when we have turned it the other way upwards. If they do not admire our mode of warfare, we think it is in all probability about the best method we could adopt. We would still, God granting us help, continue preaching the 'foolishness' of the gospel, and deliver again and again the old truth, that God was in Christ reconciling the world unto himself, not imputing their trespasses unto them. Instead of lifting up a new banner (which would better please our adversaries), it shall be the old banner still – 'None but Christ'. 'By grace are ye saved through faith; and that not of yourselves: it is the gift of God.' Salvation is by free favour, through the expiatory sacrifice of Jesus Christ our Lord.

We are now to observe that the chief glory and majesty of the church lies mainly in the banner which she carries. What cause for terror is there in the banner? We reply, the enemies of Christ dread the cross, because they know what the cross has done. Wherever the crucified Jesus has been preached, false systems have tottered to their fall. Dagon has always fallen before the ark of the Lord. Rage the most violent is excited by the doctrine of the atonement, a rage in which the first cause for wrath is fear.

The terribleness of the church lies in her banners, because those banners put strength into her. Drawing near to the standard of the cross the weakest soldier becomes strong; he who might have played the coward becomes the hero when the precious blood of Jesus is felt with power in his soul. Martyrs are born and nurtured at the cross. It is the blood of Jesus which is the lifeblood of self-denial; we can die because our Saviour died. The presence of Alexander made the Greeks more than giants; the presence of our Redeemer makes believers swifter than eagles and stronger than lions.

Moreover, the powers of evil tremble at the old standard, because they have a presentiment of its future complete triumph. It is decreed of God, and fixed by his predestinating purpose, that all flesh shall see the salvation of God. Jesus must reign; the crucified One must conquer. The hands nailed to the wood must sway the sceptre of all kingdoms. Like potters' vessels dashed to pieces must all the might and majesty of men be that shall oppose the crown and sceptre of Christ's kingdom. In Christ preached lies the battle-axe and weapons of war with which the Lord will work out his everlasting decrees. The church with the name of Immanuel emblazoned on her banner, which it is her duty to keep well displayed and lifted high, is sure to be terrible to all the powers of darkness.

We will close with one or two reflections. Will each one here say to himself: 'An army, a company of warriors, am I one of them? Am I a soldier? I have entered the church; I make a profession; but am I really a soldier? Do I fight? Do I endure hardness? Am I a mere carpet-knight, a mere lie-a-bed soldier, one of those who are pleased to put on regimentals in order to adorn myself with a profession without ever going to the war?'

'Am I a soldier of the cross – a follower of the Lamb?'

Pass the question round, my dear brethren and sisters: Are you soldiers who engage in actual fighting for Jesus, under his banner? Do you rally round it? Do you know the standard? Do you love it? Could you die in defence of it? Is the person of Jesus dearest of all things to you? Do you value the doctrine of the atoning substitution? Do you feel your own energy and power awakened in the defence of that, and for the love of that? Let not one go away without making the searching question.

And then 'terrible'. Am I in any way terrible through being a Christian? Is there any power in my life that would condemn a sinner? Any holiness about me that would make a wicked man feel ill at ease in my company? Is there enough of Christ about my life to make me like a light in the midst of the darkness? Or is it very likely that if I were to live in a house the inhabitants would never see any difference between me and the ungodly? Oh, how many Christians there are who need to wear a label round their necks: you would never know that they were Christians without it! They make long prayers and great pretences, but they are Christians in nothing but the name. May your life and mine never be thus despicable, but may we convince gainsayers that there is a power in the gospel of Jesus Christ, and make them confess that they, not having it, are losing a great blessing.

One other thought. If I am not a soldier, if I am not a servant of Christ in very truth, and yet I come to the place of worship where Christians meet, and where Christ is preached, the day will be when the church of God will be very terrible to me. I will suppose that there is a person listening to this sermon who has been hearing the preaching of the Word in this place now for many years. Imagine that the last day is come. You are brought before the great judgment-seat, and this is the question: 'Did this sinner hear the gospel faithfully preached? He is ungodly, he has rejected Christ: does he deserve to be cast away? Did he really hear the gospel, and did he reject it?' If I am asked to give my witness, I must say, 'To the best of my ability, I tried to tell him the gospel of Jesus Christ.' 'Was this sinner prayed for by the church?' There are many of the members of this church who would feel bound to declare, 'Yes, Lord, we did pray for him.' Yes, and all of us would say, 'If we did not pray for him by name, we included him in the general company of those who attended upon the means of grace, for whom we made a constant intercession.' Is there any member of the church who would be able to make an apology for the rejector of Christ? He has wilfully rejected the Saviour, he knowingly continued in sin. Will anybody be an advocate of him? Not one tongue would be able to excuse you at the judgment, or to argue against the righteous sentence of God. When the great Judge condemns the sinner to be taken away to execution, the whole church with whom that sinner has worshipped, and in whose presence that sinner has rejected Christ, will become 'terrible as an army with banners'; for all its voices will say, 'Amen, Amen, Amen! Thou art righteous, O Lord.'

There is no picture drawn here from fancy. Know ye not that the saints shall judge the world? They shall sit as co-assessors with the Son of God at the last great assize, and shall say, 'Amen!' to every verdict which proceedeth from his mouth. O that the thought of this might be blessed of God's Spirit, so as to lead many of you to be reconciled to God. Jesus is still the loving Mediator, and a full surrender of yourselves to him will assuredly save you. Whosoever believeth on him is not condemned; and this is to believe on him – that ye trust in him, and know that God hath given unto us eternal life – and this life is in his Son who suffered in the stead of sinners, that whosoever believeth in him might not perish, but have everlasting life.

The Lord bless you, for the Lord Jesus' sake. Amen.

42

OVERCOMING CHRIST

'Turn away thine eyes from me, for they have overcome me'
(Song of Solomon 6:5).

This is the language of the Heavenly Bridegroom to his spouse. In great condescension, he speaks to her and bids her take note that her eyes have overcome him. This morning our subject was overcoming evil with good. We have a very different subject this evening for we are to talk about overcoming him who is goodness itself, the perfection of everything that is excellent.

Saints first learn the art of overcoming evil and then they learn the way to overcome goodness too. But how different, dear friends, are the weapons employed in these two warfares; for while, this morning, as we spoke of overcoming evil, we saw that there was much for us to do, and I think that we all felt it was more than we could do apart from divine grace, yet here there is nothing to be done but just to give a look. The Heavenly Bridegroom confesses himself to be overcome by the very look of the eyes of his spouse; she has but to gaze steadfastly upon him, and his heart is vanquished by the glances of her eyes.

Now, it must not be supposed because of the language of the text that there is any opposition between Christ and his people which has to be overcome. He loves his bride far too well to allow any division of feeling to separate them in heart from one another. Nor is it to be imagined that the spouse had to gain some blessing from an unwilling hand, and therefore pleaded with her eyes as well as with her lips. Oh, no! There is a holy discipline in Christ's house that sometimes withholds the coveted blessing till we have learned to pray in downright earnest; but the power that wins the victory in prayer has its real basis in the love of Christ himself. It is because he loves us so much that he permits our prayers to conquer him; it is not so much because we love him as because he loves us, that he permits the look of our eyes to overcome his heart.

This, then, is the subject for our meditation now – the way in which God's people overcome the heart of Jesus Christ and make him say, 'Turn away thine eyes from me, for they have overcome me.'

First, dear friends, let us notice that LOOKING ON HIS CHURCH HAS ALREADY OVERCOME THE HEART OF OUR HEAVENLY BRIDEGROOM.

It was so in the far-distant past, not when she looked at him, but when he looked at her, that she overcame him. Ages upon ages ago, or ever the earth was, Christ had conceived in his heart the purpose to redeem from among men a people that should be precious in his sight for ever and ever. Through the glass of divine foreknowledge, he looked at his people, he recognized the person of every one of them, he saw them all ruined in the Fall, all stained with sin, all contaminated in nature by our first parental disobedience and rebellion. As he looked at them, with a steady resolve that he would rescue them, and perfect them, and lift them up to a level with himself, and make them into a race that should praise God for ever in heaven with hallelujahs and hosannas beyond all the harmonies of angels, his heart so moved towards them that he longed for the time when he should enter upon the great work of their redemption. Long ago, he said, 'My delights were with the sons of men.' His heart was always projecting itself forward in anticipation of that happy yet dreadful day when he should be called upon to redeem his people. Every time he thought of them, he was overcome with the very recollection of his great love towards them; and when the long-expected day did at last come,

> Down from the shining seats above
> With joyful haste he fled,

and was found as a babe in Bethlehem's manger, lying among the hornèd oxen feeding in the stable of the village inn. Oh, marvellous mystery! that he, whom the heaven of heavens could not contain, was not satisfied to be God over all, blessed for ever, but for our sakes he must also become man. He was so overcome by the love he had for his chosen that he left his Father's throne of light to become one flesh with his people, and to be made a man like ourselves that so he might be next of kin unto us. Ah, gracious Saviour, thy Church's eyes did indeed overcome thee when they brought thee from amidst the royalties of heaven down to the sins and sorrows of earth!

You know, too, when he lived down here among men, how often his inmost heart was stirred as he looked upon the people whom he loved. And specially do you recollect the scene on that last night when their redemption-price was about to be paid. He took the cup that he was to drink and sipped at it; but his holy soul revolted from it, and with the bloody sweat upon his face he cried, 'O my Father, if it be possible, let this cup pass from me.' Then he went back, and looked upon his people. Truly, there was not much to see in them; he had taken three specially-privileged apostles to be the representatives of all his chosen, and those three were asleep when he was in his terrible agony; yet, somehow, the sight of them seemed to strengthen him for the awful ordeal that he was enduring. Backward and forward thrice he ran to gaze upon them, and they so overcame him that he turned back, and said to his Father: 'Nevertheless not as I will, but as thou wilt'; and he went through with that tremendous work of laying down his life for his people, and drinking the cup of wrath that was their due. They had overcome him as he had looked at them.

And, beloved, now that *our Lord is risen from the dead*, he still feels the power of the sight of his redeemed. The great joy of Christ at this moment is found in gazing at his redeemed ones, Look at him as man, if you will; and what a wondrous Man he is! But remember also that God hath highly exalted him and given him a name which is above every name; and what does the glorified and exalted Christ think as he looks on the myriads in heaven, all of whom would have been in hell but for him? Then he looks down to the saints on earth and sees the myriads who are all trusting in him, all conquering sin by his might, and all spared from going down to the pit by the merit of his precious blood; and he seems again to say, 'Turn away thine eyes from me, for they have overcome me'; as if Christ felt that a glance at his people brought almost too much joy for him.

What a day that will be when he shall descend from heaven with a shout, with the voice of the archangel, and with the trump of God; when all his people – raised from the dead, or changed in the twinkling of an eye – shall admire him, and he shall be admired in them! And what will be the joy of his heart when the 'great multitude, which no man could number, of all nations, and kindreds, and people, and tongues', all redeemed by blood, shall be gathered unto Christ, to be the delight of his heart for ever and ever! That will be a joy sufficient even for the immensity of his infinite heart as he sees in them the reward of his awful agonies, the rich return for the shedding of his precious blood. His benevolence – that great mainspring of all that he has done – will be gratified and satisfied as he looks on each one of his redeemed, and sees the fruit of his travail in every individual child of his grace, in each sinner reclaimed, in each saint preserved and perfected. I can well conceive of him saying in that day, 'Turn away thine eyes from me, for they have overcome me.' The joy that Christ will feel in his own sight of his people, and in the glances of the multitudes that he has saved, must be a delight beyond anything we can even imagine.

Now I must pass to a second point, which is this, **that THE EYES OF CHRIST'S CHOSEN ONES STILL OVERCOME HIM**. This is a practical point upon which we may profitably spend some little time: the eyes of Christ's chosen ones still overcome him.

And, first, the eyes of his chosen overcome him when they look up in deep repentance, glancing at him hopefully through their tears. Let me try to give you a picture of such a case. Here is a poor soul, conscious of having sinned, and sinned deeply. Once, sin was thought to be only a trifle; now, it is seen to be a horrible evil, to be trembled at and hated. Once, God was judged to be too severe in sending men to hell; but now, the convinced one has nothing to say against God's justice, for he is all taken up with speaking against himself and his sin. There stands this poor soul, with red and weeping eyes, saying, 'O God, I have sinned, and I am still sinning; and if thou dost cast me into the abyss, I dare not challenge thy justice; yet have pity upon me, O Lord! God, be merciful to me a sinner!' When those tear-filled eyes are turned to the Lord Jesus, and sin is confessed again and again with deep contrition and childlike repentance, it is not possible that he should long refuse to grant the pardon which we seek. He seems to say to the poor penitent, 'Turn away thine eyes from me, for they have overcome me. I cannot bear to see thee weeping and sorrowing so. Thy sins, which are many, are all forgiven thee, for I have loved thee with an everlasting love. Go, and sin no more.' There is a wondrous power in the penitent eye, in the full confession that makes a clean breast of every sin before the face of the Lord Jesus Christ.

Remember, brethren, that when we have once repented, we do not leave off repenting, for penitence is a grace that is as long-lived as faith; and as long as we are capable of believing, we shall also necessarily need to repent, for we shall be always sinning. So, whenever *the child of God feels that he has gone astray* in any way, that, though he did live near to God, he has gone back and grown cold in heart, he has only to come to Christ again, and cry after him, and confess his folly in having left him, and his ingratitude in having been so indifferent to him, and Christ will receive him back again. You cannot long mourn his absence, and seek to return to him, and feel that you will die if you do not get back the realisation of his sweet love again, you cannot be long in that state before he will be vanquished by your weeping eyes, and he will say to you, 'Turn away thine eyes from me, for they have overcome me.' And if a child of God, who has not lost fellowship with his Lord, is, nevertheless, jealous lest he should do so, if his morning prayer is, 'O my Lord, keep me from everything that would take me off from thy love'; and if at night he looks back over his conduct during the day, and says, 'Cleanse thou me from every secret fault, for

I am jealous of my heart,
Lest it should once from thee depart,

if there be kept up this delightful tenderness of conscience towards Christ, so that our eyes, with weeping for very fear of sin, still look after him, then shall we hold him spellbound, and the deep sorrow of our loving hearts shall vanquish him, and he will bestow the blessing which our soul is seeking.

Another kind of glance that has great power with the Lord Jesus is *when the soul looks to Christ for salvation*. Then it is that the eyes vanquish the Saviour. It is hard at first to look to Christ, and believe that he can save you. I suppose some of you, dear friends, have a distinct recollection of the first faith-glance you ever took at Christ. I well remember mine; it seemed so strangely simple, and yet so sublime and wonderful, that I could scarcely think it true that there was life in a look at him. I did but glance half furtively at first, as if I thought it could not mean that such a sinner as I was could receive mercy from Christ simply by looking at him. Did he really mean me when he said, 'Look unto me, and be ye saved, all the ends of the earth'? I had long sought him and I had prayed to him; but I could not conquer him, nor win mercy from him by my seeking and my praying; but oh! when my eyes, already red with weeping, looked at him with a steady glance which seemed to say,

I do believe, I will believe,
That thou didst die for me,

then did he cry, 'Turn away thine eyes from me, for they have overcome me.' 'I have blotted out, as a thick cloud, thy transgressions, and, as a cloud, thy sins.'

Many times since then, you and I have looked to Jesus Christ *when a sense of sin has been very heavy upon us*. I suppose all of you who are really children of God sometimes get into that state in which you begin to ask, 'Was I ever truly converted? Did my sin ever roll from my shoulders and disappear in the tomb of Christ?' When these questions arise within your heart, go and stand once more at the foot of the cross and look at your suffering Lord. I have looked, and looked, and looked again, until I have seemed to look him all over, and at last I have begun to sing:

Oh, 'tis sweet to view the flowing
Of my Saviour's precious blood,
With divine assurance knowing,
He has made my peace with God.

While the eyes of faith are thus resting upon Jesus, he is overcome by them and he darts inexpressible joy into our hearts as he says to us, 'Turn away thine eyes from me, for they have overcome me.' His heart is carried by storm by the faith-looks of his children.

We also give another overcoming glance *when we look to the Lord Jesus Christ for all things*. Worldlings do not understand the terms on which we are linked with Christ. To them, Christ is a somebody who lived eighteen hundred years ago, and then died; but to us, he is alive, he is our familiar Friend, we are intimately acquainted with him, we are in the habit of taking all our troubles to him, and asking him for all that we need; and he removes our sorrows and grants us the desires of our hearts. There are times with all of us when we get into trouble of one sort or another; and, blessed be his name, he has taught us, when we are in trouble, to lift up our eyes to the hills whence cometh our help. Now, perhaps, dear brother, you have for a while been looking to Christ, and saying, 'Lord, I believe thou wilt help me; didst thou die to save me from hell, and wilt thou not supply me with bread and water while I am in the wilderness? Hast thou covered me with the robe of thy perfect righteousness, and wilt thou not find me clothes to cover my nakedness, and shield me from the weather? Hast thou done the greater, and wilt thou not do the less? '

When another trouble comes, you keep on looking to him still. You will not believe that he can be unkind; you give him credit for loving you, and caring for you, so you look to him, and as you look you submit to his will, and say, 'I will never distrust thee, my Lord.' If he sends yet another rough providence, you continue looking to him, and only say, 'Show me wherefore thou contendest with me. Though thou slay me, yet will I trust in thee. I have known thee too long to doubt thee now, my blessed Lord. Thou hast done too much for me in the past for me to turn away, and say, "I will not trust thee." My Lord and Master, thou canst not make me believe that thou dost not love me, for I know thee better. My inmost soul is assured that thou dost love me, so I look to thee still, and watch the movement of thy countenance; and as I look, my heart says, "My Lord, I cannot tell why thou dost smite thy servant again and again; yet, if it be thy love that makes thee smite, smite on. Whatever is most for thy glory, do with me as thou wilt." ' When thine eyes are like that, full of submission, full of hope, full of trust, it cannot be long before the Lord will, somehow or other, deliver thee, for he will say, 'I cannot hold out against thee any longer. "Turn away thine eyes from me, for they have overcome me.'' "I will deliver thee, and thou shalt glorify me.'' I will bring thee out of the furnace, for I only sit there as Refiner till I see my own image in thee; and when I see my eyes in thy eyes, and my heart in thy heart, and my character in thy character, then will I bring thee out of the furnace as gold seven times purified.' Blessed Spirit, give us such eyes as these which shall overcome even the heart of Christ!

Again, there are the eyes of prayer which often overcome the Lord Jesus Christ, and this victory comes, sometimes, *when we are praying for ourselves*. You know what it is in prayer to come to him and say, 'Lord, I am in great straits, and thou hast thyself brought me there. It has not been through my folly, but it is by thine own act and deed that I am where I am. Now, Lord, thou hast promised that in six troubles thou wilt deliver us, and in seven there shall no evil touch us. Thou hast said, "Thy shoes shall be iron and brass; and as thy days, so shall thy strength be"; now, Lord, thou art God, and thou canst not lie, therefore wilt thou not keep thy promise? Here, Lord, thou seest my difficulty and my trial, and thine inspired apostle has said that "all things work together for good to them that love God, to them who are the called according to his purpose"; thy servant David declared that "many are the afflictions of the righteous: but the Lord delivereth him out of them all"; now, Lord, I look to thee to do this for me.'

It is one of the grandest things in all the world when a godly man, with the simplicity of a child, just believes God and fully trusts him for everything. It has come to be a matter of marvel in this evil age that a man can say that God grants him many mercies in answer to prayer. People hold up their hands and say, 'Dear, dear, what a wonder!' A wonder that God hears prayer? It would be a greater wonder if he did not hear it. Beloved, to me, prayer is a matter of fact; for me to go and take a promise to God and ask him to fulfil it, and to get it fulfilled, is as common and as usual and as much a matter of fact as it is for you who are in business to take cheques, and pass them across the counter at the bank and receive the cash for them. Do you think that God is a fiction? If he is, then all our religion is a farce; but if God is real, then prayer is real, too.

Many of us know that it is real for we have tried it, and still try it every day we live. In every time of trouble, we bring the trouble to God's feet and say, 'Dear Lord, as thou art true and faithful, thou wilt help us through it'; and we find that he does help us through it. We speak what we do know and testify what we have seen many a time. When a child of God, in deep distress, believes in his Father, and steadily looks to him for deliverance, those eyes of his have mighty power and God seems to say to him, 'Turn away thine eyes from me, for they have overcome me.' You cannot look steadily to God and say, 'Lord, I am sure about thy faithfulness, I am sure about thy promise, and I cannot and will not doubt it', but before long you shall see the hand of the Lord made bare for your deliverance, and you also shall be among the happy number who have to bear witness that, verify, there is a God in Israel. Thus does prayer prevail with God when we present it for ourselves.

So does it also overcome him when we pray on behalf of others. Moses, you know, prayed for others and prevailed; do you, dear children of God, know what it is to wrestle with the Lord for the souls of others? I am sure that many of you do; there are your dear children, kinsfolk, friends and neighbours whom you bring before the Lord.

I will tell you when you will win the day, mother, when with tears you say, 'O God, thou hast given me these children; now give them to me according to the Spirit as well as according to the flesh.' You will overcome the Lord, dear father, when you spread your suit before him and say, 'Deny my children what thou wilt, but do save them; let them all be thine in the day when thou makest up thy jewels.' You will succeed when, rising from your knees, you set those children a Christian example; and, having pleaded with God for them, you go and plead with them for God, and feel as if your heart would break if you did not see your boys and girls converted. When, like Hannah, you even come to be a woman of a sorrowful spirit because you feel that you must have your children brought to God, then the Lord Jesus will look at you till he will say to himself, 'I cannot let that poor soul cry and sigh in vain; it is not in my heart – the heart of one who was born of a woman – to let that pleading woman's prayer go without an answer', and to you he will say, 'Turn away thine eyes from me, for they have overcome me. Be it unto thee even as thou wilt.'

And you, dear child of God, who are teaching in the Sunday School class, or you who are preaching in some small village station, when you get to feel inward grief of heart over those with whom you have to deal, when that grief increases till it comes to be a perfect agony and you cannot help crying out for anguish of soul, when you feel as if you must have them saved, as if you would give everything you had if they might but be brought to Christ, when you even wake at night to pray for them, and in the midst of your business cares you get distracted with the thought that some whom you love are perishing, at such times as that your powerful eyes in prayer shall move the heart of Christ and overcome him, and he shall give you these souls for your hire.

Brethren, if we do not pray for sinners, for whom shall we pray? Sisters, if we do not plead for the abandoned, if we do not offer supplication for those who are perverse in heart, we have omitted to pray for the very persons who most need our intercessions. Let us bring these hard hearts beneath the almighty hammer. Let us by prayer bring these lepers beneath the healing touch of him who, despite their loathsomeness, can say to them, 'Be ye clean.' Let no degree of natural or inherited depravity, or of depravity that has come from long continuance in sin, hinder us from praying for all the unsaved whom we know, 'O God, have mercy upon these guilty ones!'

I will not farther enlarge upon this point, for it is settled beyond all question that those who love the souls of men will not be hindered from prayer for them on any account whatever. I conjure you, who have prayed for husband or children or friends, do not leave off pleading for them. If you have prayed for twenty years, and they are not converted, pray twenty years more; and if they have grown more wicked while you have pleaded, still pray on; and if heaven and earth and hell seem to combine together to bid you cease your supplications, still pray on. As long as you live, make intercession for transgressors; and as long as they live, let your cries go up to God on their behalf. So shall you 'overcome heaven by prayer' as you plead for the ungodly.

Once again, there is another time when the eyes of the believer seem to overcome the heart of Christ, and that is *when we have turned right away front the world and looked to him alone*. I have known it so again and again; have not you, beloved? In this world, at present, our Lord is somewhat concealed; he does not fully reveal himself to his people. Here he says to us as he said to Mary, 'Touch me not.' He lets us wait till the veil shall be drawn up, and then we shall see him face to face, and shall be like him. Here we have to live by faith rather than by sight, and it is expectation rather than enjoyment that makes up much of our present bliss; yet, at times, I have known my Lord come wonderfully near to his servants and lay bare his inmost heart to them.

It seemed as if he could not help it; it has been at some such gathering as this, when we have gone right away from the world, and have forgotten its cares and pleasures for a while, and we have sat down to think only of him. Our soul has surveyed him in his Godhead and his manhood, as our Prophet, Priest, King and near Kinsman, living, dying, risen, ascended, soon to come; we have looked him over, and there has not been any part of his character which we have not admired, nor one office in which we have not trusted him, nor one deed for which we have not blessed him. We have come to think, 'He is altogether lovely,' and while we have been admiring him in a perfect rapture, there has been added to it this sweet thought, He is all goodness, and he is all mine, from the crown of his head to the sole of his foot. 'My Beloved is mine, and I am his.' We have not said much, and we could not have said much just then; we have been quite quiet and alone with our Lord, and we have felt that silence was the only eloquence we could use as we looked at him again and again and again. At such seasons, my soul has felt ready to swoon away in his presence.

You remember how John in Patmos, when Jesus appeared to him, said,

'When I saw him, I fell at his feet as dead'; and well he might, for he had a brighter vision of his Lord than you and I can have at present. But even faith's view of him is enough to transport us straight away into heaven itself. Well, brethren, whenever we are thus happily engaged in contemplation of our Lord, not only is he very near to us, but he is greatly moved by our love, and he says to us, 'Turn away thine eyes from me, for they have overcome me.' And, meanwhile, to prove how overcome he is, he begins to reveal himself more fully to us.

You may perhaps have read in the life of holy Mr Flavel, the extraordinary instance he records of the love of Christ being poured into his soul. He says that he was riding on a horse, going to some engagement, and he had such a sense of the love of Christ that he completely lost himself for several hours; and when he came to himself again, he found his horse standing quite still, and discovered that he had been sitting on horseback all those hours, utterly lost to everything but a special revelation of the wonderful love of Jesus. You may also have heard of Mr Tennant, the mighty American preacher, and friend of George Whitefield, who was found, lost and absorbed, in a wood, to which he had retired, and his friends had to call him back, as it were, from the sweet fellowship he had been enjoying with Christ. You may remember, too, John Welsh, the famous Scotch preacher, who had to cry out, 'Hold, Lord, hold! I am but an earthen vessel, and if I feel more of thy glorious love, I must e'en die; so stay thy hand a while.'

There are such experiences as these, I will not enquire whether you have ever known them; but if you have, I will tell you one thing. All the infidels in the world and all the devils in hell will never make you doubt the truth of the Scriptures if you have once been face to face with Christ, and have spoken with your Master as a man speaketh with his friend. Such things have happened unto those whose cloud-piercing eyes have been so fixed upon Christ that he at last has felt the mighty fascination of their loving and believing glances, and has revealed himself in still greater measure unto them and made them even more blest than they were before.

Last of all, sometimes the eyes of Christians have great power in overcoming Christ *when they long for his appearing*. Have you never seen the saints lie dying with such language as this on their lips, 'Why are his chariots so long in coming? Why tarrieth he?'

> Haste, my Beloved, fetch my soul
>   Up to thy bles'd abode:
> Fly, for my spirit longs to see
>   My Saviour and my God.

I have heard them say, with evident regret, 'I thought to have been in heaven long ere now.' I have seen them almost grieve when the doctor has said that they were better, and that there was hope that they might last another month or two. They seemed to say, 'Why should my banishment continue? Why should my release be postponed? These chains of clay which seem so hard to shake off, these fetters of brass, will they never drop from me? Must I still linger in this world of pain and sorrow and sin and suffering? Why not let me go?' And they have been like a poor thrush which I have sometimes seen a boy try to keep upon a little bit of turf; it longed for the broad fields, and beat itself against the wires of its cage. So is it with our dear suffering friends at times; yet they have learned patiently to wait till their change came; but often, their eyes have been so fixed upon their Lord that they have said to him, 'Wilt thou never come?' And, at last, Christ has looked out of heaven so sweetly on those sick ones, and he has said, 'Your eyes have overcome me, come up higher'; and they have leaped out of their body into his bosom, and the pierced hands have received their blood-washed spirits, and they have been 'for ever with the Lord'.

I am looking forward, and I trust we who are believers in the Lord Jesus Christ are all looking forward, to that day when God will let us languish into life, when we shall see the bars of the prison opened once for all, and we shall pass through them, and leave this dying world behind to go to the land of the living, the land of the hereafter, where we, too, shall be 'for ever with the Lord'. Keep your hearts always longing for that blest hour. Keep you eyes ever looking upward, beloved. Set small store by anything here, and be ever ready to depart; and so, full often, shall Jesus say to you, as though he could no longer bear that you should gaze upon him, though indeed he loves it all the while, Turn away thine eyes from me, for they have overcome me.'

God bless you all, beloved, for Christ's sake! Amen.

43

THE CHARIOTS OF AMMI-NADIB

'Or ever I was aware, my soul made me like the
chariots of Ammi-nadib' (Song of Solomon 6:12).

We cannot be quite sure at this date what these chariots of Ammi-nadib were to which the inspired poet refers. Some suppose that he may have alluded to a person of that name who was renowned, like Jehu of old, for his furious driving. Hence it might have been familiar at the time, and afterwards have become proverbial to speak in metaphor of the chariots of Ammi-nadib.

The conjecture seems harmless, still it is only a conjecture and cannot be verified.

It is quite possible, however, that our translators may have retained as a proper name a conjunction of two words, which, taken separately, are capable of being interpreted. You remember the word 'Ammi' as it occurs in the prophet Hosea. 'Say unto your brethren, *Ammi*', which signifies 'ye are my people', even as before he had said, 'Call his name *Lo-Ammi*, for ye are not my people.' The one word, Ammi, thus stands for 'people', and the other word, 'Nadib', means 'willing', so that the two united may be rendered 'willing people' – 'like the chariots of a willing people'. Or the words may be read, I think, more correctly, 'The chariots of the princely people' – the princely chariots, the chariots of the prince.

Some have understood them to mean the chariots of God, of the people that surround the Great Prince himself; that is to say, the chariots of the angels, according as we read, 'The chariots of God are twenty thousand, even thousands of angels.' In this case, the figure would be a very striking one – 'Or ever I was aware, my soul made me like the chariots of the attendants upon the Great King. I was like the cherubim themselves, all aglow with consecrated fire.' In whatever way the critical point is deciphered, the practical solution appears to be this. The writer's soul was quickened because full of life, full of energy, full of might, full of spirit and full of princely dignity too, and not only stimulated to a high degree, but also elevated, lifted up from dulness, indifference and apathy – 'Or ever I was aware, my soul made me like the chariots of Ammi-nadib.'

To whom does this text refer? Probably those of us who would never raise a doubt about the Song being a dialogue between Christ and the spouse – a matter we have no intention to canvass just now, as we take it for granted – might find no small difficulty in determining to which of the two sacred personages this speech belongs, whether it was to Solomon or to Shulamite (the masculine or the feminine variety of the same name) – the prince the husband, or the princess the spouse – whether, in a word, it was Christ or the church.

There is very much to be said for its being Christ himself that is speaking. You will notice in this chapter that, from the fourth verse, he has been referring to his church. 'Thou art beautiful, O my love, as Tirzah, comely as Jerusalem, terrible as an army with banners. Turn away thine eyes from me, for they have overcome me', and so on. He is speaking of his church on to the tenth verse: 'Who is she that looketh forth as the morning, fair as the moon, clear as the sun, and terrible as an army with banners?' Then the eleventh verse proceeds: 'I went down into the garden of nuts to see the fruits of the valley, and to see whether the vine flourished, and the pomegranates budded. Or ever I was aware, my soul made me like the chariots of Ammi-nadib.' May it not be the Lord himself who is speaking here? We may entertain the question for a moment without absolutely fixing upon this as its proper solution.

If it refers to Christ, it means just this, that he had been for a while away from his people. They had grieved him and he had hid his face from them. Out of very love and faithfulness he felt bound to chasten them, by hiding from them the brightness of his countenance. But he began to think tenderly of his people, his heart turned towards his church; and while he was thinking of her, he saw such beauties in her that his soul was melted with her charms. Oh, what an extraordinary thing that he should see loveliness in his poor imperfect church! But he saw such a loveliness about her, as her image rose up before his face that he said, 'Thou hast ravished my heart, my sister, my spouse; thou hast ravished my heart with one of thine eyes.' 'Turn away thine eyes from me, for they have overcome me.' And then, musing upon her still, and coming into her garden, and seeing the various graces like plants and flowers in their different stages of development, his heart began to grow warm again towards her and all that concerned her. It had never really been cold; it only seemed so in the deviation of his wonted manner, but, like Joseph before his brethren, he could not refrain any longer. When he saw some of his people budding with desires, others bursting into the realisation of those desires, when he saw some like ripe and mellow fruit upon the bough, ready for heaven, others just commencing the divine life, he was charmed to be in the garden of nuts; or ever he was aware, he found he must be with his people; he must return in the fulness of his love to his church.

Not her beauties only, but the kindlings of his own soul began to stir him, his free grace sought free scope; his infinite love became more than a match for the temporary prudence that had made him hide his face, and, swift as the chariots of Ammi-nadib, did he speed back to his people, to let them see him again, to let them enjoy fellowship again.

There are other Scripture passages where the Saviour is spoken of as being like a roe or a young hart upon the mountains of Bether (or division) because he is so willing to come to his people, so willing to make matters up with them, and end the days wherein they mourn because the bridegroom is absent. When he has hidden his face for a while out of love for them, and out of desire to reveal to them their faults, I say again, he is so willing to blot out their faults once more, and to return to them again with mercies, that his return is compared for swiftness and irresistibleness to the motions of the chariots of Ammi-nadib.

It is a delightful thought that if communion between our souls and Jesus be suspended, it is not because he takes pleasure therein. His delights are with the sons of men. He a thousand times invites his chosen to abide in him, to continue in his love, and to remain in his company. In this Song he cries again and again, 'Come with me, my spouse.' This should encourage us to seek to him for renewed love-tokens, however serious may have been our departures from him, and however dark our prospects under the hidings of his face. If he who is the aggrieved party is eager to be reconciled, the matter is easy, and we may at once rise to the blessed condition from which our sin has cast us down. Jesus longs to embrace us, his arms are opened wide; do not our hearts warm at the sight? Do we not at once rush to his bosom, and find a new heaven in a fresh sense of his boundless love? Wherefore hesitate? What possible cause can there be for abiding in darkness? Lord, we fall upon thy bosom and our joy returns.

Not that I intend to adopt that view as the groundwork of our present reflections. It appears to me that without in the slightest degree wresting the passage, or deviating from an honest interpretation, we may understand that this is the language of the church concerning Christ. If so, Christ's words conclude at the end of the tenth verse, and it is the church that speaks at the eleventh. There is not an instance in the whole Song, so far as I can remember, of the Prince himself speaking in the first person singular; either, therefore, this would be a solitary exception, or else, following the current plan, where the same pronoun is used, the church is speaking to Christ, and telling him of herself: 'I went down into the garden of nuts, to see the fruits of the valley, and to see whether the vine flourished and the pomegranates budded. Or ever I was aware, my soul made me like the chariots of Ammi-nadib.'

Taking the text, then, as referring to the church in particular, and more generally to the Lord's people, there will be *four observations* which we would pointedly make and prayerfully meditate. May God bless us now in fulfilling this purpose!

Our first observation shall be this. **What is most wanted in all religious exercises is THE MOTION, THE EXERCISE OF THE SOUL**. 'Or ever I was aware, *my soul* made me' – or *my soul* became – 'like the chariots of Ammi-nadib.' Soul-worship is the soul of worship, and if you take away the soul from the worship, you have killed the worship; it becomes dead and barren henceforth. Let us turn over that well-known thought. It may benefit us if we look at the many sides of it.

There are professors in this world who are perfectly content if they have gone through the mechanical part of public devotion. If they have occupied their seats, joined in the hymns and the prayers and listened to the preaching, they go away quite content and easy. They would not like to be absent from the solemn assembly, and their conscience would prick them if they neglected the outward ordinances, but having gone through them and complied with the wonted form, they are perfectly content with themselves and think they have done that which is lawful and right, comely and excellent.

Now, it is never so with the child of God. If his soul be awakened from the torpor of death and his sensibilities quickened into the vigour of life, he will feel that, unless in the song he has really praised God in strains of gratitude with emotions of thankfulness, he has rather mocked his heavenly Father than acceptably adored him. He knows that prayer, if it is not the soul that speaks with God, is but the carcase of prayer, destitute alike of the sweet savour which can find acceptance with God and of the sweet satisfaction that can bring refreshment to one's own breast. When he hears the Word preached, he longs to feel it penetrate his heart, even as the rain soaks into the soul; and if he cannot so receive the truth of the gospel when it breaks on his ear as the engrafted Word that saves his soul, and so feed upon it as the bread of life which nourishes his soul, he goes away sad at heart, deploring that, while others were feasting at the banquet, he was there without appetite, and had not the pleasure or the profit which they derived.

Beloved, in our public services we ought to account nothing truly and rightly done which is not done with the heart. That is one reason why in this Tabernacle we have tried to lay aside everything of outward show or external form, which might distract the thoughts or disturb the simplicity of waiting on the Lord. As far as I can, I try to avoid the use of all symbols, except the two which Scripture has ordained, lest the symbol should tempt you to rest satisfied with itself, as I believe it generally does, and so prevent your reaching the Lord with your heart. We try to lay aside everything that would at all touch your senses in the worship, anything which appeals to the ear in the way of sweet music, anything of the aesthetic that would appeal to the eye. If you do not worship God with your souls, I hope you will get tired of our fellowship.

Yet, be it confessed, I painfully feel that it is almost as easy not to worship God with the bald plainness of Quakerism as it is not to worship God with the studied pomp of Ritualism. In any form, or without any form of worship, the amount of real devotion must be measured by the quantity of soul that is in it, provided the quality be pure, sincere, guileless. If the soul be there, in the full exercise of its powers and passions, knowing what is revealed and feeling what is inspired, I believe God is gracious to pity and forgive a thousand mistakes in outward fashion and skill of execution. The preacher's modulation may be faulty, and the people's singing may be ill-timed to barbarous tunes, without peril of the unpardonable sin. But if the soul be lacking, though ye should have essayed to worship according to the pattern given in the Mount, and have never had a word uttered or a sound made but such as in itself would be accredited by men and acceptable with God had it been quickened by the Spirit, yet without that divine Spirit which alone can give force and fervour to the human soul, it is all null and void. I think every genuine Christian knows it is so, and feels it is so. He says, 'My heart crieth out for God, for the living God', nor can he be satisfied unless he does find God, and draws near before him.

As in public worship, it is precisely the same in our own private and personal transactions with the Most High. The religious worldling will say a prayer when he wakes in the morning, and perhaps, unless he is out late, or too sleepy at home, he will have a bit of prayer at night again, in the way of the repetition of some collect, or something which he has learnt by rote. And very likely he has family prayer too. It is not so much a custom as it was, but there are some who think they cannot go through the day unless they have what they call 'Prayers'. But mark how the Christian prizes private prayers above everything that has to do with the ordering of his daily habits. And see how he esteems family prayer to be a necessity of every Christian household!

At the same time he is not content because he prays for a few minutes unless he draws near to the Lord; he is not satisfied because he gathered his children together and read the Scriptures and prayed with them, if, on adding up the sum total of the day, he is compelled to say, 'It was heartless worship. When I awoke it was heartless worship, when I gathered my children and my servants it was the same, and it was sleepy, heartless worship when I knelt by my bed-side and professed to seek the Lord at nightfall.'

If it is heartless it is unacceptable; God cannot receive it. If we have not thrown our heart into it, depend upon it God will never take it from our heart and be pleased with it. Only that prayer which comes from our heart can get to God's heart; if we pray only from the lips or from the throat, and not low down from the very bowels of our nature, we shall never reach the bowels of our Father who is in heaven. Oh, that we may be more and more scrupulous and watchful in these things! In the diary of Oliver Heywood, one of the ejected ministers, he often says, 'God helped me in prayer in my chamber and in the family.' And once he writes thus: 'In my chamber this morning I met with more than ordinary incomings of grace and outgoings of heart to God.'

I am afraid we may get satisfied with ourselves, especially if we are regular in private Scripture reading, private prayer, family prayer, and public prayer, while instead of being satisfied with these exercises we ought to be weeping over them and deploring the formal and heartless manner in which we are prone to discharge them. Be it always recollected that we do not pray at all, unless the soul is drawn out in pleading and beseeching the Lord. *Si nil curarem, nil orarem*, said Melanchthon, 'Were I without cares, I should be without prayers.'

Now, perhaps, you may know a friend of yours who thinks himself a poet. He can make poetry at any time, all the year round. Just pull him by the sleeve, and he will make you very soon a verse or two at the spur of the moment to show the readiness of his wit and the versatility of his talent. Yet I dare say you think that he is about as far off from being a poet as a sparrow is from being an eagle. You know if he were a poet he would not be able to command the glow of imagination at one time, and at another time he would hardly be able to control it. He would sometimes have a divine afflatus upon him, as some call it, and then noble thoughts in appropriate words would flow from his pen. Otherwise he would be just as dull and insipid as ordinary mortals. He would tell you indignantly that he could not write verses to order like those who scribble rhyme to advertise a tailor's wares. Without the inspiration come upon me, he would say, I cannot compose a line. In like manner a man cannot always pray, and the man who pretends he can doth only utter jargon. He never prays at all, as the other never makes poetry at all. Prayer is a divine art. It is a thing which needs the inspiration not of the muses, but of the Spirit of God himself, and it is when the Spirit comes upon us with divine force, and makes our soul like the chariots of Ammi-nadib that we can pray; and at other times when that Spirit is not with us, we cannot pray as we did before. Every living child of God knows this. We must measure our prayers by the state of the soul that we were in.

Take another illustration from the painter. One person who thinks himself a painter can paint any day you like anything you ask him – a mountain, a river, a horse, an insect, or a flower – it is all the same to him. He takes a brush and soon produces something, which ordinary people might think to be a picture; but send that daub of his to the Royal Academy, and they will tell you that it may do for a tea-tray, but not for the walls of a gallery. But the man that *can* paint, how does he mix his colours? The great painter will tell you that he mixes his brains with his colours; and when he takes his brush and dips it into the paint, he lays it on with his soul. In a great picture, such as sometimes we have seen by a Titian or a Raphael, it is not the colour but the man's heart that he has got out on to the canvas. Somehow he has managed to drop his brush into his soul. That is real painting. And so it is with prayer. The humblest man that prays to God with his soul understands the fine art of prayer; but the man who chants a pompous liturgy, or repeats an extemporaneous effusion, has not prayed. He has dashed off what he thinks to be a picture, but it is not a picture, it is not a prayer. Had it been a prayer it would have had a palpable inspiration in its light and shade. A painting may consist of few lines, but you will see the painter's hand in it; and a prayer may consist of only half a dozen words, but you can see the hand of God in it. The formality repels you in the one case; the vitality attracts you in the other.

So we will come back to the proposition with which we started. We can only pray according to the proportion in which our soul puts forth its force and feeling, and it is the same with praise. We have praised God up to the amount of soul that was in the sense as well as in the sound, be it with an organ or without an organ, with good music or with groanings that cannot be uttered. We may have praised God either way, but only if our soul has been in full swell. With every kind of religious exercise, the soul is the standard of the whole compass of worship.

We proceed to a second remark: **SOMETIMES IT HAPPENS THAT THE HEART IS NOT IN THE BEST STATE FOR DEVOTION**. If religion be a matter of soul, it cannot always be attended to with equal pleasure and advantage. You can always grind a barrel-organ; it will invariably give you the same discordant noise, which people call music, but the human voice will not admit of being wound up in the same fashion, nor will it for the most part discharge the same monotonous functions. The great singer finds that his voice changes and that he cannot always use it with the same freedom.

If the voice is a delicate organ, how much more delicate is the soul! The soul is continually the subject of changes. Ah, how often it changes because of its contact with the body! If we could be disembodied, oh, how we would praise God and pray to him! 'The spirit truly is willing, but the flesh is weak.' I sat among some brethren the other day who were devout, and I tried to be, but I had a splitting headache. I do not know whether you could pray under so grievous a disability; let me confess to you that I could not. At another time, not long ago, I was one of a solemn assembly, when various disturbances occurred in the room – somebody getting up and others coming in late as some of you do – and I could not get into a right frame as I ought to have done. Little things will affect little minds, and our minds, many of them, are little. In that case I could not pray, because my mind was being distracted and my attention was being taken away. Such distractions frequently happen, and bitterly they remind us of our infirmities.

The apostles themselves fell to sleeping when they ought to have been praying; and under Paul's preachings Eutychus went to sleep, and Paul never blamed him. He died as the result of it, but he got raised again from the dead, so I suppose there was no fault in him. We may sometimes, without any wilfulness on our part, as a necessary result of the weakness of our nature, or the stress of our toil and care, have brought ourselves into a condition in which we cannot feel like the chariots of Ammi-nadib, and it is no use for us to attempt it. The body does affect the soul materially; and a thousand outside agencies will tell upon our mental susceptibilities. I have known persons come into this Tabernacle who have, perhaps, been annoyed with somebody in their pew, or somebody outside. It ought not to be so, but it is so. A little fly buzzing about one's face, so small a thing as that, will disturb one's devotion, so that you cannot pray as you would and as you desire.

And then, alas, our sins are a much more serious hindrance to our devotion. A sense of guilt puts us into such a state that we cannot be bold in our faith and childlike in our confidence when we appear before God. Perhaps we have been angry. How can we come before the Lord calmly when our spirit has been just now tossed with tempest? Probably we have been seeking the world, and going after it with all our might. How can we suddenly pull up, and put all our strength into a vigorous seeking of the kingdom of God and his righteousness in a moment? It is possible, too, that there is a sick child at home, or a wife lying suffering, or serious losses and crosses about business and domestic affairs. Perhaps one has a very heavy heart to bring before the Lord. Now God's grace can help us to overcome all these things, and can even make our souls like the chariots of Ammi-nadib. We do want grace for such emergencies. The soul, in its different phases and states, has need of help from the sanctuary to which it repairs.

'Well,' perhaps one will say, 'I always do what I think right every Sunday in much the same manner. I always pray the same, and I don't know but what I can always sing God's praises the same.' Yes, let me answer our good friend, I have no doubts of your thorough sameness, or of your habitual self-content. If you were to ask one of the statues in St Paul's Cathedral how it felt, I have no doubt it would say that it always felt the same, because it never had any feeling. Appeal to anything destitute of life, you will find that it has no change. But where there is life – and that which is intensely delicate – spiritual life, and where it is placed in circumstances so hostile to it as the circumstances which surround us here, you will find that not only the revolutions of the seasons, but the variations of the temperature, affect it. And every man who has this life in him experiences such changes. We have read of those who have no changes and therefore they fear not God. The fact that a believer cannot at all times draw nigh to God as his spirit would desire, becomes accordingly the key which interprets to him the grace and goodness whereby he sometimes gains access after a manner that surprises and delights his spirit.

This leads cheerfully up to our third observation: **THERE ARE SEASONS WHEN OUR HEART IS SWEETLY MOVED TOWARDS GOD**. 'Or ever I was aware, my soul made me like the chariots of Ammi-nadib.' Have ye not proved welcome opportunities when all your thoughts have been quickened, enlivened and stimulated to activity in the highest degree about your highest interests? We have ceased to moan:

> Our souls, how heavily they go
> To reach eternal joys;

and we have been all wings, and could soar and mount aloft. Like David, we could have danced before the ark of God for very joy, and if any had said to us that we might ourselves fall by our enthusiasm while we seemed vile by our hilarity, we should have replied that we purposed to be viler still. All within us was awake; there was not a slumbering faculty. Our memory told us of the goodness of the Lord in days gone by; and our hopes were regaled by the mercy which we had not tasted yet, but which was made sure to us by promise, and brought near to us by faith. Our faith was active and bright of eye. Our love especially shed a clear light over all our prospects. Oh, we have had blessed times, when our soul has been as light and rapid as the chariots of Ammi-nadib!

And at such times we were conscious of great elevation. The chariots of Ammi-nadib were those of a prince. And oh, we were no more mean and low and beggarly and grovelling, but we saw Christ and were made kings and princes and priests with him. Then we longed to crown his head. Then we could have performed martyrs' deeds. Then we were no cowards, we were afraid of no foes, we sat down at the feet of Jesus, and thought everything little compared with him; sufferings for his sake would have been a gain, and reproach would have been an honour. We had princely thoughts then, large, liberal, generous, capacious thoughts concerning Christ and his people, his cause and his conquests; our souls were like the chariots of Ammi-nadib.

At the same time they were full of power; for, when the chariots of Ammi-nadib went forth, who could stop them? Who could lay his hand upon the reins and turn the coursers as they went onward in their mighty tramping? Such was our spirit. We laughed at thoughts of death and poured contempt upon the trials of life. We were 'strong in the Lord and in the power of his might'. Oh, what splendid times we have had when God has been with us. Do you remember when you had them?

I recollect, when newly converted, how full my spirit was of love and holy triumph, like the chariots of Ammi-nadib. Yours, no doubt, were much like mine. The love of your espousals was upon you. With what pleasing rapture you embraced your Lord and said, 'I will never let him go.' Stronger is love than death or hell. You felt it to be so. You flamed and burned and glowed, and though in yourself you were like low brushwood, yet you were like the bush in the desert, that burned with fire because God was in your soul. Do you remember that?

Well, now, since then, in private prayer sometimes, you have had gracious access, and meditation has been added to prayer, and the love of Christ has come in upon you like a great flood tide, and drowned everything in your soul except itself. There have been periods when a sense of the eternal, immutable, never-ending love of God, his electing sovereign favour, that love of God, the love of God in giving his Son for you, have told upon your spirit with a mighty influence that has laid you prostrate for very joy, when you could not speak, because words were too poor to express the emotions of your soul. You had to feel the force of James Thomson's hymn of the seasons: 'Come, then, expressive silence, muse his praise', for you could not speak it.

You know it has been so with you sometimes, and has not it been so sometimes under the Word, when you have been ready to stand up and clap your hands for joy? Have not I seen gratitude and exultation reflected on your faces sometimes when the Lord has been present in the preaching of the gospel, and the truth has come to you like marrow and fatness from the King's own hands, till Dr Watts has proved to be a faithful interpreter of the very scene and circumstance that ravished your heart:

> The King himself draws near,
> And feasts his saints today;
> Here we may sit, and see him here,
> And love, and praise, and pray.

Oh, yes! in God's house you have known the days of heaven upon earth. Might I speak for the rest of you I should pronounce the choicest periods of fellowship to be those we have found at the Lord's table. When the bread has been broken and the wine poured out down in the Lecture Hall, he has been with us in the breaking of bread. If ever we have come near to Christ, surely it has been in that blessed communion. There are the windows of agate and the gates of carbuncle through which Christ comes to his people in the ordinances he has ordained. We will never slight them. We cannot. The Master puts such reality and fulness of joy into them. Apart from him they are idols; but with him, when he is there, when we have the *real presence* – not the superstitious presence some speak about – but the *real* presence which his own Spirit imparts, our waiting souls participate, and then we have said:

> No beams of cedar or of fir
> Can with his courts on earth compare,
> As myrrh new bleeding from the tree,
> Such is a dying Christ to me.

Not unfrequently too have I known that the Lord has appeared to his people and warmed their hearts when they have been working for him. Some idle, indolent, sluggish professors who have used the ordinances have not found benefit in the ordinances, because the Lord has intended to rebuke their sloth; but when they have got up and gone forth among the poor, when they have gone forth to visit the sick, the sorrowful and the dying, they have heard such delightful expressions from the lips of holy, suffering men and women, or felt their hearts so kindled by a sight of divine compassion in the midst of desperate poverty and gracious pardon for grievous sin, that a quickening has come over them; and whereas they did not seem to care before whether souls were lost or saved, they have gone out into the world with zeal to win fresh trophies for the Messiah, their hearts being like the chariots of Ammi-nadib, though the benefits they have received from Christian service.

A great many Christian people never will be happy, and never fully alive to the destinies that wait on their Redeemer, till they get something to do to give them an interest in those mighty issues. The rule of the Christian life is, 'If any man will not work, neither shall he eat.' If you will not serve God as Christians, you shall not feed upon the sweet things of the kingdom to your own soul's comfort. A little more service, and your soul would become like the chariots of Ammi-nadib.

Beloved, there is no need that I should enlarge; I merely say this to bring up your grateful memories that you may thank God for what he has done, for remember whatever he has done in the past he will do again in the future. When the Lord has come once to his people he says, 'I will see you again, I will come to you again, and your hearts shall rejoice.' Of everything he has ever given you, he has got as much in store, and he is quite as able to give it to you now as he was before. You have never gone so high in joy but you may go higher yet; you have never drunk such draughts from the well of Bethlehem as left the well empty; you shall drink again of it. Do not say, 'I had those sweet times when I was young, I shall never have them again.' You shall have precious times again. Get back to your first love, dear brother, dear sister; get forward to a higher love than ever you had, for God will help you. Say you, 'I look back and think

> 'What peaceful hours I once enjoyed!
> How sweet their memory still!
> But they have left an aching void
> The world can never fill.'

Thank God for that ache. Bless God for the aching void. If your soul aches for God, he will be to your relief ere long. Whenever a soul puts up a flag of distress at the mast-head, he may be sure that Christ is on the look-out for just such a soul. He has thrown up the windows of heaven, and wherever he sees a soul that does what is right and longs to find joy and reconciliation with God, he will come to it, and before long it shall be better for you than even the chariots of Ammi-nadib, and more desirable.

4. Our last observation is this: SOMETIMES THE SWEET SEASONS COME TO US WHEN WE DO NOT EXPECT THEM. 'Or ever I was aware, my soul made me like the chariots of Ammi-nadib.' Some poor hearts do not reckon ever to have these joys again. They say, 'No, no, they are all gone; the last leaf has blown from the tree; the last flower has faded in the garden. My summer is past. It is all over with me!' That is the bitter complaint and the hollow murmuring of unbelief. But the Lord for whom ye wait can suddenly appear, and while you are saying hard things of yourself he can refute them with the beams of his countenance. Even at this very moment you may stand like Hannah, a woman of sorrowful spirit, feeling as if you would be sent away empty; yea, and God's servant himself may address you with rough words as Eli did her, and may even tell you that you are drunken, when it is deep grief that enfeebles your steps and chokes your voice; and all the while the Lord may have in store for you such a blessing as you have never dreamed of; and he may say to thee, 'Go thy way, my daughter; I have heard thy petition, thy soul shall have its desire.' Or ever I was aware, while my unbelief led me to think such a thing impossible, thou hast made me like the chariots of Ammi-nadib.

'Or ever I was aware', as if it came upon me almost without my own consent. Glad enough I was when it did come, but it took me by surprise; it led me captive. Now, is not that the way that the Lord dealt with you when you were not aware of it, when you had no reason to expect him, when you found and felt yourself to be utterly lost, ruined and undone? Did he not surprise you with his mercy and prevent you with his lovingkindness? Again, you are minished and brought low through oppression, affliction and sorrow. There is nothing that leads you to expect a season of joy; you are just as empty and unworthy as you can well be; you feel as if your heart were of stone, and you cannot stir it, and you are saying, 'I only wish I could enjoy the freedom that my companions have, and keep the solemn feasts with their holy gladness: but alas for me! I am afraid I have got to be a mere mechanical Christian, without the lively instincts and lofty inspirations of spiritual worship.' Thus are you writing bitter things against yourself. Oh, beloved, the Lord is looking down upon you now as his son or daughter, as his own dear child, and is about to surprise you with his infinite love!

Let me give you one text to put into your mouth and take home with you. The Lord has said concerning every one of his people, 'Thou art all fair, my love; there is no spot in thee.' 'Why, now, I am all covered over with spots and blemishes,' you say, 'and no beauty'; but the Lord Jesus Christ has washed you with his blood and covered you with his righteousness. Do you think he can see any imperfection in that? You are members of his body, united to him. In Christ you are without spot or wrinkle or any such thing. You are all spots in yourself, but he sees you as he intends to make you before he has done with you and he can discern unspeakable beauties in you.

'Oh,' say you, 'does he think that? Surely then I see unspeakable beauties in him! His love to me opens my eyes to see how dear an one he must be. Did he prove his love to me by bleeding on the cross? Oh, then, I must love him, if he will but let me! Shall such a poor worm as I am love infinite perfection? Oh, yes, I must, since infinite perfection deigns to love me, and since the Sun of Righteousness in all his glory deigns to shine on my soul!' You are beginning to warm already, I see you are. Or ever you are aware, your soul is making you like the chariots of Ammi-nadib.

And if you keep on with those holy contemplations, you will leave off all misgivings about your love to him, so deeply absorbed will you be in musing on his love to you. You will forget all the while about your sin, while you recollect the blood that has put that sin away, the perfect righteousness that has made you accepted in the Beloved, and the everlasting covenant which through grace has put your feet upon a rock and saved your eyes from tears and your feet from falling. Engaged in such sweet soliloquies, or ever you are aware, your soul will make you like the chariots of Ammi-nadib. The Lord make it so!

God grant that surprising grace may come likewise even to sinners and lead them to Jesus, and constrain them to look to Jesus. Then, while looking, faith will breathe in their spirit, so that they will sing:

> Thy mercy is more than a match for my heart,
> Which wonders to feel its own hardness depart;
> Dissolved by thy goodness, I fall to the ground,
> And weep to the praise of the glory I've found.

44

INWARD CONFLICTS

'Return, return, O Shulamite; return, return, that we may look upon thee. What will ye see in the Shulamite? As it were the company of two armies' (Song of Solomon 6:13).

This verse is not addressed to the Church in her doubting state, nor while seeking her absent Lord, but it refers to her in her very best condition, when she has lately come from the enjoyment of fellowship with her divine spouse, and when her soul in consequence is like the chariots of Ammi-nadib. Read the context, and you will perceive that believers, who are rejoicing in the Lord, may look upon this text as their own.

Observe *the title* of the person addressed – it is a marriage name. She has been espoused to Solomon and she has taken his name and become *Solyma*, for such is the best rendering of the word rendered Shulamite. This name is appropriate to souls who are united to Christ, to those whom Christ has betrothed unto himself in righteousness, who live in union with their Lord. You who abide in the Lord Jesus are, by a mysterious bond, made one with Christ; and he has conferred upon you his own name – he is Solomon, and you are Solyma.

That is a remarkable expression in the book of Jeremiah: 'This is *her* name whereby *she* shall be called, the Lord our Righteousness.' One would have thought that such a title was incommunicable; but yet so close is the union between Christ and his people, that the Holy Spirit actually transfers that dignified expression 'Lord our Righteousness' to his Israel, his beloved. The title Solyma also signifies both perfection and peace.

There is *perfection* in every child of God, but not a perfection in the flesh. We are perfect in Christ Jesus; complete in him; spotless, by being washed in his blood; glorious, by being robed in his righteousness. Every child of God is right sumptuously arrayed in the wedding dress of the Saviour's righteousness. We may truly say that 'Solomon in all his glory was not arrayed like one of these'. Every believer stands in Christ perfectly accepted.

The sweet name Solyma, signifies also *peace* – 'Therefore being justified by faith, we have peace with God through Jesus Christ our Lord.' The true heir of heaven is not at enmity with God, nor at war with his own conscience. The silver trumpet has proclaimed an everlasting peace; God's sword has been sheathed in the Saviour's heart, and divine justice is on the side of the chosen people.

The request of the text next demands a moment's consideration. It is repeated four times: 'Return, return, O Solyma; return, return, that we may look upon thee.' Does not this request proceed from the daughters of Jerusalem who desire to behold her beauty? Souls that are anxious about their own state may well desire to understand the experience of the true child of God. You want to know whether you also are a Christian, therefore would you know how Christians feel, how they think of Christ, how they are moved by his Spirit, what is their appearance when his love is shed abroad in their hearts. You anxiously desire to see the true Christian that you may measure yourselves and see whether there be the life of God in you.

These daughters of Jerusalem also desire to look upon her for their own delight; for, as to gaze upon beauty is exceeding pleasant, so is it specially delightful to the pure in heart to have fellowship with the pure in heart – to see the fruits which the Spirit has brought forth – to behold the cleanness of the believer's walk, and to know the savour of the believer's conversation. No beauty equals the beauty of holiness; nothing is so comely as uprightness; and therefore we wonder not that four times the request is made.

Perhaps, too, these daughters wanted to look at her as an example to themselves. Saints look upon the beauty of others that they may be enabled to emulate their excellencies. Let us read with affectionate attention the biographies of holy men that they may be a stimulus to ourselves, exciting us to exert ourselves in the Redeemer's cause, and may afford us some hope that the highest Christian attainments are not altogether beyond our reach.

I think this is the reason why the daughters of Jerusalem said, 'Return, return, O Solyma': they would comfort themselves by seeing whether they are like her; they would delight themselves by beholding her perfections; they would also stir up their own souls by seeing her example.

The rest of the text, you will observe, may be considered two ways: either the spouse asks the question, which is the most probable; she says, 'What shall ye see in Solyma?' She thinks that there is no beauty in her, nothing in her that anyone should delight in her, or fix his eyes upon her, or derive any profit from regarding her. 'Why,' says she, 'all that you will see in me is a company of two armies, a conflict between good and evil. If you look upon me you see nothing but good and evil fighting together, darkness and light contending. I am not worthy your looking at'; and so she would fain veil her face and go away if it were not for the earnest request which seems to hold her fast.

Some think this question is asked by bystanders and is answered by the daughters of Jerusalem. 'What shall ye see in the Shulamite?' the giddy crowd enquire; and instructed believers cry, 'We shall see in her the concurrence of two triumphant armies returning as choristers, with music and with dancing, from the field of battle; we shall see in her the King immortal, invisible, with all his hosts of grace; we shall see in her the purified soul co-working with the glorious Saviour; we shall see in the Christian Church the activity of sanctified manhood, combined with the majestic power of deity residing within.' This is what *she* might not say of herself; but what they would see in her. Observe, then, the two meanings, and let us dismiss the second until another occasion. There is in every Christian a sweet composition of Christ's power and of the activity of his own soul; there is the power of God, and there is the creature himself made willing in the day of God's power. There is in the Christian, God working in him to will and to do of his own good pleasure, and the man himself working out his own salvation with fear and trembling. In the Christian Church there is man working for God and God working in man; and all this in such a joyful manner as to be rather resembling the triumph of returning conquerors than the going forth to fight of those who make war. What shall we see in Solyma? We shall see the blessed confluence of the two great armies of sanctified humanity and of God made flesh.

But we are now coming to take the text in the first sense: the Church blushingly declares that there is nothing to be seen in her except conflict, turmoil, the wrestling of two great powers – two mighty armies contending for the mastery. Upon this point may God give us light for the comfort of many who are passing through this stage of Christian experience.

We shall at the outset, this morning, first call upon you who know the Lord to OBSERVE THE FACT OF THE TWO ARMIES IN EVERY CHRISTIAN.

This is very evident, but to aid your reflections, let me remind you, *throughout this very book you see traces of it.* This Canticle is a marriage song, it therefore speaks less of the battlefield than some other portions of Scripture, for at the marriage feast allusions to trial and to warfare ought to be but few. Yet, that the Church is not altogether sanctified is clear, if you note such passages as the fifth verse of the first chapter: 'I am black,' saith she, 'but comely, O ye daughters of Jerusalem, as the tents of Kedar, as the curtains of Solomon.' She is black: here is her natural state; here we have the manifestation of her continued depravity of heart. 'I am black, but comely': here is her spiritual condition; the Spirit of God had clothed her with beauteous graces; Christ has washed her and made her fair in his sight. 'I am like the tents of Kedar,' says she, 'the smoke-dried curtains of those Arab wanderers who dwelt in this country set forth my sinfulness'; and yet in Christ she compares herself to those embroidered curtains, heavy with gold and silver threads, which hang about the throne of Solomon.

In the third chapter she plainly proves that she is not always enjoying fellowship, but is in a mixed condition. 'By night on my bed': here is her slothfulness; 'I sought him whom my soul loveth': here is her activity; 'I sought him': here is her desire; 'but I found him not'; here is her sad experience of his absence.

Then in the fifth chapter, the second verse, there is a singular commixture. 'I sleep' – I am sluggish, cold, dead, lethargic – 'but my heart waketh' - the inward principle is still vital, still panting after something better. We find her in the third verse making vain excuses for not opening to her Lord; but ere long you come to the fifth verse, and you find her opening to her beloved, though her beloved has withdrawn; refusing but soon complying; the two natures battling; the one fast closing the door and the other opening it and seeking the beloved with tearful complaint. Throughout the song there is always this mixture.

But, as I have said, we cannot expect to find much of this in a nuptial ode; turn therefore to the great book of battle songs, *the Book of Psalms*, and here you have in almost every psalm indications of the complexity of the Christian character. So strange are some of the Psalms that it has been well said they might have been written rather by two persons than by one. David will begin out of the very depths calling unto God and then he will end with all the jubilant notes of a conqueror leading captivity captive. I shall not have time to refer to many passages, but the forty-second Psalm will strike you, where the one David seems to be reasoning with another David: 'Why art thou cast down, O my soul? and why art thou disquieted within me? hope thou in God: for I shall yet praise him.' And the next Psalm is much to the same effect.

Perhaps, however, the most eminent and striking paradox of the whole is the seventy-third Psalm, the twenty-second verse. There he says of himself: 'Nevertheless, I am continually with thee: thou hast holden me by my right hand. Thou shalt guide me with thy counsel, and afterward receive me to glory. Whom have I in heaven but thee? and there is none upon earth that I desire beside thee.' Heavy as a stone he lies embedded in the mire, and yet on a sudden he takes to himself wings and outstrips the eagle's flight as he loses himself in the splendour of the Sun of Righteousness, mounting so high as to be entirely lost to all but God.

David's experience, as we find it pictured to us in the Psalms, is but our own written out in large capital characters; and here we see what strange incongruities, what marvellous paradoxes are found in men.

If we need still further instruction upon this matter, let me refer you to *the epistles of our apostle Paul.* I read in your hearing just now that extraordinary passage in the seventh of Romans. How could there have been more graphically described than we have there, the war and the contention which is always going on between the baser nature and the divine life which God has implanted within us? To the like effect is the seventeenth verse of the fifth chapter of the Galatians, where he says: 'For the flesh lusteth against the Spirit, and the Spirit against the flesh: and these are contrary the one to the other: so that ye cannot do the things that ye would'. We are carnal and yet spiritual; lost in self yet saved in Christ; all imperfections and yet perfect; incomplete in all things and yet complete in everything; strange contradictions, but yet most strangely true.

Another evidence of this matter is the concurrent experience of saved souls. I thought of just taking down at random biographies from my library shelves and writing out passages, but I had scarcely time for that; in truth you have but to read the truthful life of any Christian man, and you soon find that he is not all Spirit but also flesh; not all renewed nature but still compassed with infirmity. We have whole volumes upon this subject. There is Bunyan's *Holy War*, describing God's conquest of the town of Mansoul and its subsequent attacks by sins lurking within and foes storming without. Sibbes' book, *The Soul's Conflict*, contains a mass of experimental knowledge. But you will perhaps feel more pleased if I give you, instead of words prose, one or two expressions in the form of rhyme, which will show you that our hymnwriters – they should be among the more joyous of the Christian Church – have been compelled sometimes to sing paradoxes concerning themselves. Ralph Erskine has left us that strange work, *The Believer's Riddle*, the greatest riddle that ever was written, a perfect maze to all but those who have the clue within. He says:

My heart's a mirror, dim and bright,
A compound strange of day and night,
Of dung and diamonds, dross and gold,
Of summer's heat and winter's cold.

Hart, whose hymns come indeed from the heart – rightly named was he – in his hymn called *The Paradox*, says:

How strange is the course that a Christian must steer,
How perplexed is the path he must tread;
The hope of his happiness rises from fear,
And his life he receives from the dead.

His fairest pretentions must wholly be waved,
And his best resolutions be crossed;
Nor can he expect to be perfectly saved
Till he finds himself utterly lost.

When all this is done and his heart is assured,
Of the total remission of sins;
When his pardon is signed and his peace is procured,
From that moment his conflict begins.

We have that hymn of Newton's, which you will find in your Rippon's Selection:

I would, but cannot sing,
I would, but cannot pray;

and so on. Still more remarkable is that hymn:

I ask'd the Lord that I might grow
In faith, and love, and every grace;
Might more of his salvation know,
And seek more earnestly his face.

But I need not repeat it, because you have it in your books. You will there find that instead of God's working in the way in which he expected, the singer was made to feel the hidden evils of his heart, and so he was humbled and brought in true penitence nearer to God. Cowper thus sings of himself in a hymn which is also in your book:

The Love will happiness divine
On contrite hearts bestow;
Then tell me, gracious God, is mine
A contrite heart or no?

I sometimes think myself inclined
To love thee, if I could;
But often feel another mind,
Averse to all that's good.

My best desires are faint and few,
I fain would strive for more!
But, when I cry, 'My strength renew',
I seem weaker than before.

O make this heart rejoice or ache!
Decide this doubt for me;
And, if it be not broken, break,
And heal it, if it be.

Thus, if time did not fail us, we might go through all those men who have at any time served the Church of God, and say of them all that they have experienced, felt and confessed a struggle and a conflict between what God has implanted and what nature has left in them.

Nor do I think, dear friends, that we ought at all to wonder at this. It sounds strange in the carnal ear, but we ought not to marvel, for this is only according to the analogy of nature. If you look abroad, everywhere you will discern contending forces, and out of these contending forces the rule of nature comes. See yonder orbs; moved by a mysterious impulse they seek to fly off into space, but the sun holds them by invisible bands. The bands of the sun's attraction would draw them at once into his heat, but on the other hand the centrifugal force would drive them far away into distant space; between these two they keep the circular orbit which God has at present appointed. So we have a corrupt nature within us which would drive us to sin, and on the other hand the divine power within would draw us into perfect conformity and union with Christ; between those two forces the Christian life becomes much what it is.

Observe, how in this world death and life are contending together. Death crowds his graves, but life wins the victory; death may toll the knell, and this is his note of triumph; but every cry of every new-born infant is another shout of the battle of life in which life claims still to be victorious. Look at your own persons, and in your own bodies you see this duplex action. You breathe, but the same lungs which receive the fresh, pure air, give forth the noxious vapour. There is scarcely an organ of the body which is without an apparatus for the secretion of an injurious substance and its expulsion. The brightest eye that ever swam in light casts forth some defilement; the skin, if it be healthful, has a part of its functions to throw off from us that which would certainly breed disease. There is going on in every human body a strange conflict between life and death; and every moment our life stands as it were in the centre of two great armies who are contending whether we should be the prey of the worm or should still continue to breathe.

Do you wonder, therefore, if the whole world of nature is or has fallen into this state, that man, the little world, should be the same? Wonder or not, certain it is that it is so; and let those who have been staggered because they have felt a battle within, from this time forth rather rejoice, because this is the path which all the people of God have trodden before.

Secondly, concerning THE ORIGIN OF THIS CONFLICT.
There is but a slight battle in an unrenewed man. There is a sort of conflict of a minor kind between conscience and his grosser passions. Even Ovid could speak of this and several heathen writers confess a war within; but there is no conflict to any high degree in the ungodly man; because while the strong man armed keepeth his house, his goods are at peace. While there is one master, a man may cheerfully serve him; but in the moment of regeneration, a new master comes into the house – a stronger than he has come, and he will bind the strong man and, after many conflicts, cast him out for ever, and get that house to be in his own possession.

The new nature which God implants in his people is directly the opposite of the old one. As the old nature comes of Satan, being defiled and depraved by the Fall, so the new nature cometh direct from heaven, pure and without sport. As the old nature is sin, is essentially sin, so the new nature is essentially grace – it is a living and incorruptible seed which liveth and abideth for ever, a seed which cannot sin because it is born of God. When these two, therefore, come into conflict, it is as when fire and water meet – either the one or the other must die. There can be no truce, no parley; the two are deadly foes; the life of the one is the death of the other; the strength of the one the weakness of the other.

Now the old nature has been there beforehand; it is like a tree well rooted; it has been there twenty, thirty, forty, fifty or sixty years, according to the date of conversion, and it is not easily to be torn up by its roots. Even when grace comes into the heart and makes sin to fall, as Dagon did before the ark of God, yet is it true of sin as it was of Dagon, the stump thereof is left, and there is enough vitality in that old stump still to breed pain and confusion without limit. The reigning power of sin falls dead the moment a man is converted, but the struggling power of sin does not die until the man dies. Bunyan said that unbelief had as many lives as a cat, and sin has the same vitality. Until we are wrapped in our winding-sheets, we shall never have that black thread of depravity drawn out from us; it will, it must continue to be there till God shall sanctify us, spirit, soul, and body, and take us home.

When you remember how pure is the new life which God has given you – it is from God himself; an emanation from his Spirit; as pure as deity – and think how sinful, on the other hand, is your corrupt nature, can it be possible that these two should be at peace? Can two walk together except they be agreed? Can these two principles, which are entirely opposed to one another, by any chance patch up a league? It cannot be, and even if it could be, there are allies without who will never be quiet; there is Satan, who will never rest from stirring up our corruptions, and on the other hand there is the Holy Spirit, who will never pause in the putting forth of his divine power till all evil is cast up, root and branch. Since these two – the Spirit of God and the spirit of evil – must fight, so the two principles within, which are their children, must continue in conflict till our dying day. Here, then, is the source of this conflict.

O my dear hearers, some of you do not know anything about this. Remember, you are in the gall of bitterness if you do not. If you are all one way, then are you all the wrong way. If there be in you no conflict, it is because there is no divine power come there to drive the evil one out. The more of these wars and fightings you feel, the more you have cause to thank God and take courage. The battle is not yours, but God's. You go not a warfare at your own charges; you shall overcome, as thousands have done before you, through the blood of the Lamb.

This brings us to the third reflection. Let us for a moment consider THE REALITY OF THIS CONFLICT.

The warfare in the Christian mind is not a thing of imagination, it is most true and real. If you want proof of it you must pass through it. Did you ever kneel down in an agony of spirit, resisting some furious temptation from within? Some of us know what it is to feel the cold sweat running down our brows when we have to fight against ourselves in fearful struggles against black thoughts of unbelief; perhaps it may be that the base heart within has even doubted the existence of a God and dared to prompt us to defy the deity; and we have loathed that thought and hated it so much that our whole spirit was put to the utmost stretch of tension in order to win a victory over ourselves. You must, if you are at all subject to strong emotions, have felt that this struggle was a terrible fact; to you there could be no doubt about it, for your whole soul felt it; your heart was like a field which is torn up and soaked with blood by the fury of battle.

There is a frightful reality in this conflict, when we remember how some Christians fall during it and sin gets the mastery. Recollect, sin may win a battle, though it cannot win the campaign. What! were there no corruptions in David, think you, that made him sin with Bathsheba? Was there no corrupt heart left in Noah when he was naked to his shame? Was there no corruption in Lot when he sinned in the cave? Why, those black things, which have stained the character of these holy men throughout all time, prove to us how dreadful must be the power of sin and how mighty must be the power which keeps sin down. Remember what the joy of a Christian is when he feels that he has triumphed over sin. Ah! there is something real here. If the daughters of Jerusalem praised David when he came back with Goliath's head, so do all our powers bless and praise God when he gives us the neck of our spiritual enemies. Like the songstress of old, we sing, 'O my soul, thou hast trodden down strength.' These are no fictions, imaginations of a poetic and fevered brain; he that has once been along the road to heaven knows that above all things the traveller has need to be on the watch against himself.

In the fourth place, let us notice THE CHANGES WHICH TAKE PLACE IN THIS WARFARE.

The conflict in a Christian is not always carried on with the same fury. There is always war, but there is not always battle; the flesh always hates the Spirit and the Spirit is always the opponent of the flesh; but they are not always fighting, and when they fight it is not always with the same fury. You ask why?

Well, *sometimes the flesh is not so powerful as at other times*. There are moments when, if sin were in the Christian's way, the flesh would not choose it. I may not be able to tell you exactly why, but certain it is, that partly from changes of body, and also from certain phenomena of mind, there are seasons when the propensities to evil, though still as evil, are not so vigorous as they were; their strength is awful, but it sleeps. The young lion is ever a lion; but its claws are concealed and it plays like a lamb. The raging sea is not always in tempest, yet tempests sleep in its waves. Perhaps there is more to be dreaded in the quietness of our depravity than in the raging of it, for sometimes it is the treacherous calm which the Christian ought more to fear than the storm.

Again, it is quite certain that *the Spirit's work within us is not always equally active*. The Spirit of God is always in a Christian; he dwells in the believer as in a temple. 'My Spirit will I not utterly take from him' is true of every saint; but yet you must know that your faith is often weak, that your love is not always like a flame of fire. You cannot pray at all times as you would. Ah! brethren, we can sometimes dash along in service like the chariots of Amminadib, but at other times the wheels are taken off, and we drag the chariots heavily, like Pharaoh in the midst of the Red Sea. A change then in the flesh, or a change in the spirit, may produce a diversity in the present form of the conflict; it is always there, but not always the same.

I suppose that when it is most furious the reason of its fury may be sought for in the strength of both sides. I do not think that when the flesh is strong and the spirit is weak, that there is much conflict, then rather there is a speedy defeat; but when the Spirit of God is gloriously at work in our souls, when faith is vigorous, when hope is bright, when love is flaming, and when, at the same time the corrupt powers put forth all their might, then it is that the conflict is stern. Some Christians do not enter into this state of strong conflict because of two reasons: they are men of weak passions and grace in them is at a low ebb. But when a man is endowed with a strong mental nature, and the Spirit is also vigorous within him, then there will go on a contest something like the combat of two Samsons fighting and struggling together as to who shall get the victory.

Ah! brethren, these things may change as I have said, but the war is never over. Do not any of you say, 'I shall never be tempted again.' Grey-headed brethren, do not think that the old man in you is dead. If professors fall into grave sin and dishonour the Church, they are as often old men as young men; nay, I think I may say that they are oftener elder men than younger ones. It is sad it should be so, but it is so; and there is many a professor who has stood well for forty years, but makes a fool of himself at the last; and though he has been honoured in God's Church, yet he leaves a blot upon his name, and the godly say in a whisper, 'No doubt he was a child of God, but it is best that he should be dead, for in his dotage he fell into sin.' No, we shall never be out of gunshot of the devil till we have crossed the river of death.

Our carnal minds are like a powder magazine, there only wants the spark; and ah, what an explosion there would be with any of us. May the Lord keep the sparks away. Let us be very vigilant and very careful; there is an enemy behind every hedge; there is a foe waiting for us at every step; and ere this Sabbath's hallowed hours may be over, you and I may have slipped and have fallen into sin, to our own perpetual hurt and hindrance, unless almighty grace shall supervene.

Fifthly, a few words now upon THE EFFECTS OF THIS CONFLICT. Some will say, 'But why does not God remove out of the Christian the old nature?' Some uninstructed Christians even think that in conversion the Lord turns the old nature into a new one, which is very far from the fact. The old nature remains in the Christian; it has received a blow, which will ultimately be its death, but it still lives, and the new nature in the Christian comes to struggle with it for the mastery. But why is this? Well, we cannot tell you.

Such a question reminds us of the negro's enquiry to the minister: 'You say that God is omnipotent and therefore he is greater than Satan?' 'Yes.' 'Then why does not God kill the devil and have done with him?' We believe God to be as morally omnipotent as he is physically omnipotent; and if he willed it, we do not doubt but that evil of every form and shape might disappear out of the universe. Why then does he permit it? Ah! why? But there we leave it. Be amazed at the mystery if you will, but do not question God nor cast the blame of sin upon his holy character. There it is, he suffers sin to remain in the universe, and after all we can say, we observe the fact, but the reason we cannot tell.

Still I think we may in some respects see how sin is overruled in the Christian. Sin remaining in the believer drives him humbly to confess his own nothingness, excludes all boasting from his tongue, compels him to trust in his God, takes away from him his propensity to trust in himself, leads him to value the precious blood which cleanses him, to prize the Holy Spirit who sanctifies him, to rejoice in the faithfulness and patience and longsuffering of God who still continueth to be gracious to him.

And oh! what songs will the man of God sing when he gets to heaven! How much sweeter will be the music because of the conflict! How much more glorious the victory because of the warfare! If I could be totally delivered from sin – root and branch – I certainly would; but yet am I conscious that no Christian would glorify God so much in heaven as he now does, if there had not been sin to be contended with. A creature that could not sin could scarcely show forth much of the praise of God by its holiness; but that the creature can sin, nay, that there is a strong drawing towards sin, and yet the divine grace keeps a man from it, and sanctifies him even to perfection, why this will make the song come swelling up of 'Hallelujah! Hallelujah! Hallelujah!' If no adversaries had been tolerated, then no victories could have been won; if there were no temptations for us to struggle with, then there would have been no elbow-room for our faith, no power for the display of the bare arm of God.

Doubtless it is best as it is, and when the winding up of the chapter comes, perhaps we shall see that our sins committed have been made the means of saving us from other sins which would have been our ruin. Many believers would have grown too proud to be borne with, if some infirmity had not plucked the plume from their helmets and made them mourn with brokenness of heart before God. God can bring good out of evil by his overruling grace, while on the other hand our good works have often been the greatest curse we have ever had. Good works have puffed us up, and so have led us into pride; while our sins, though pulling us down, have, through almighty grace, led us to make men work for eternity.

I want your attention to the last point, which is, THE CONCLUSION OF IT ALL.

This contest, is it for ever to continue? Shall we for ever tremble in the balances? Will there be no valley of decision where our souls may take their rest? Yes, brethren, the fight will soon be over, and the victory is guaranteed and glorious. Yea, even at the present day, the Christian is making progress. I do not admire the term 'progressive sanctification' for it is unwarranted by Scripture; but it is certain that the Christian does grow in grace, and though his conflict may be as severe in the last day of his life as in the first moment of conversion, yet he does advance in grace, and all his imperfections and his conflicts within cannot prove that he has made no progress. Let me show you this.

You know that at certain periods in your children's history they pass through diseases incidental to childhood. Here is your babe of a month old and there is your child of three or four years; this child of three or four years of age is suffering from some of those complaints incidental to infancy; it is not in such good health as your child of a month old; it is far weaker, and its life seems far more in danger. Yet you will not say that there is no progress, for this child of three years old has passed through three years of its difficulties and hazards, which this little one newly-born has yet to encounter. We all know that there are certain growing pains which the lad feels when he is verging out into his manhood, but these pains do not prove a want of strength, but the very reverse; the muscles are being braced and the sinews are being strengthened.

Stand by the seashore when the tide is coming up. There rolled up a big wave. Just mark the place in the sand. For the next few minutes no wave comes up so high as that, nay, some waves suck back the rest and you might even think the sea was still retiring. Is there, therefore, no progress made? Why, friend, you will see in a moment, if you will but wait, another great wave will come sweeping up, far outstripping the one that we marked just now; and when you shall come back in an hour's time, and the sea has come to the fulness of its strength, you will see that the receding of any one individual wave is no mark of its retrogression. You have but to mark the whole sea and take time in which to examine it, and then you discover there has been progress, and that progress has been effected by alternate advance and retreat.

Along the coast of Essex the sea is greatly encroaching upon the land, and every time we go to some of the watering-places, we perceive that the cliff has fallen, hundreds or thousands of tons have been carried away; and yet if you are there at a tide which has gone far out, you will often think, 'Why, surely the land is gaining on the sea! I never walked out so far as this before; I never saw these rocks exposed and dry before.' Well, it is a strangely low tide, but at the same time, ask the old fisherman who has lived there all his days, and he will tell you that his mother was married out in a church which stood where that ship is floating, far out to sea, and that all the intervening soil has been washed away. He recollects when this place, which is now a footpath on the cliff's brink, was a quarter of a mile inland; and then you understand, that though on any one occasion the land may apparently have gained, yet, on the whole, there has been a progress in the sea.

And so it is with spiritual life. There are times when it seems as if sin had gained upon you and you were going back in spiritual things; there is cause for alarm, but not despair; cause for watchfulness, but not for terror; go to the Lord and pray to him to send a mightier wave of his irresistible grace, that your soul may be filled with all the fulness of God. The day is often gloomy at eleven o'clock, but that is no proof that you are not getting towards noon. Many a cold wind howls over the days of March and April, colder than there might have been at Christmas, but that is no proof that you are not getting on to summer. There may come a frosty night in May, nipping the flowers, but that is no proof that the frost is all coming back again. So you may feel within yourself such things as cause you to bow your head in sorrow and to cry out to God in grief, but even these things shall but speed you on your way towards your desired haven. The battle will certainly end right. Just anticipate for a moment the glory of the victory. You *shall* be free from sin one day; you *shall* be perfect, even as your Father who is in heaven is perfect; you shall wave the more joyously because you had to contend with flesh and blood, and with spiritual wickedness; you shall join the eternal song, and it shall roll up to the throne all the more gloriously because you have

> To wrestle hard as we do now,
> With sins, and doubts, and fears.

Come, anticipate that triumph, and pluck up the courage! Go forth, all ye servants of God, as Barak went against Sisera; and the day shall come when your foes shall be swept away. That river of death shall do for your enemies what the Kishon did for Jabin; it shall sweep them away for ever. Standing by the Red Sea of the atoning sacrifice, you shall sing unto the Lord who hath triumphed gloriously and cast the horse and the rider into the depths of the sea.

I have preached this morning especially for the comfort of those who are thus exercised, and who are saying, 'If it be so, why am I thus?' You will now see that instead of having cause for distress in all these conflicts, you have only a reason to come to Christ again. Come to Jesus again; look up to him once more, and take him today to be your Saviour and your all. Put your case into his hands, trust him, and you shall be more than conquerors through him who loved you. Trust him, trust him now, and we will meet in heaven at last to sing his praise for ever. Amen.

45

'RETURN, RETURN, O SHULAMITE; RETURN, RETURN!'

'Return, return, O Shulamite; return, return, that we may look upon thee. What will ye see in the Shulamite? As it were the company of two armies' (Song of Solomon 6:13).

The translation into the word 'Shulamite' is unhappy: it is unmusical, and misses the meaning. The Hebrew word is a feminine of 'Solomon'. 'Solomon' may stand for the bridegroom's name, and then the well-beloved bride takes her husband's name in a feminine form of it, which is Shulamith, Salome, or perhaps better 'Solyma'. The King has named his name upon her, and as Caius has his Caiia, so Solomon has his Solyma. He is the Prince of Peace, and she is the Daughter of Peace. Aforetime she was called 'the fairest among women', but now she is espoused unto her Lord, and has a fulness of peace. Therefore is she called the Peace-laden, or the Peace-crowned. You know how truly it is so with the justified in Christ Jesus. Because the sound is sweeter, and the sense is clearer, permit me to read the text thus: 'Return, return, O Solyma: return, return, that we may look upon thee. What will ye see in Solyma? As it were the company of two armies.' May the Holy Spirit, like a dove, rest upon us while we linger amid the verses of this Song of Loves.

A soul redeemed by blood and brought by the Holy Spirit into loving, living, lasting union with the Well-Beloved cannot remain unnoticed. Solomon is known all over the world, Solomon is sought after for his wisdom; and therefore Solyma will shine with something of his brightness, and she will be enquired after too. In the Church of God no man liveth unto himself or travelleth through the world unwatched. If you are interested in Christ, heaven and earth and hell will be interested in you. Some men are but as a chip in the porridge; they have no savour in themselves, and none comes from them; but the believing man, the Christ-communing man, is full of influences both repellent and attractive, and he may be sure that where he comes he will be known and read. As the house of Israel is among the nations like a burning torch in dry stubble, so also are the spiritual Israel. Voices will cry after the bride of Christ, 'Return! Return! Return! Return!'

A pilgrim bound for the Celestial City cannot go through the world, even through the worst part of it, such as Vanity Fair, without being noticed and questioned and sought after, and if possible ensnared. Do not think, thou who hast been made a living man by the quickening of the Holy Ghost, that thou canst glide through this world as the spiritually dead can do, for they may be quietly borne along to the place of corruption; the life within thee is too strange, too operative to be overlooked. Thou art a wonder unto many, and thou mayest well be so, for God hath wrought great marvels in thee and for thee.

Beloved, ye are the Lord's witnesses, and witnesses must not skulk away in the background or remain dumb. When they bear their honest witness it is in open court, where they will be heard and regarded by all who are concerned in the suit, whether *pro* or *con*. Oh, saints of God, you are never unobserved; you are compassed about with a great cloud of witnesses, and none of these witnesses are indifferent to you; they all watch you with steady gaze to see how you run your race. The good are intent that you should so run as to obtain; and there are evil ones who long for your defeat. Solyma is addressed by urgent voices, who plead with her to return to them. For good or evil, multitudes of tongues cry to her, 'Return, return, O Solyma: return, return.'

Will you kindly notice from the connection of my text what state Solyma was in when these calls came to her? She was in her glory and beauty. In admiration the question is asked: 'Who is she that looketh forth as the morning, fair as the moon, clear as the sun, and terrible as an army with banners?' A church or an individual Christian in a low state of grace may escape observation. Who cares about a dead church? Who fights with a lukewarm people? But if Jesus Christ be in the church, or in the heart, he will soon be seen. The evangelist tells us 'he could not be hid'. You may slip down the street in the night without a candle, and like a thief you may pass by unobserved, but if the Lord has lighted your candle, and you bear it with you, the watchmen will notice you, the dogs will bark at you, and others will spy you out. As fire reveals itself, so also will grace. A bundle of lavender proclaims its own whereabouts by its fragrance, and so does the life of God in the soul. You may be sure that if the Lord of Hosts is with you, and in you, you will assuredly arouse the animosity of some and the admiration of others. I pray that you and I may be in a bright, clear, forcible condition, as the bride was in this part of the Canticle; then shall we be sought after, and enquired about.

It appears that the church in her beauty had gone down to attend to her work: 'I went down into the garden of nuts to see the fruits of the valley, and to see whether the vine flourished, and the pomegranates budded.' She did not sit down in the house to admire herself, nor go into the street to show herself; she went down into her Lord's garden to attend to her proper work, and then it was that they cried, 'Return, return.' Neither the world nor Christ himself will call much after us if we go forth to make displays of our own excellences. 'Come, see my zeal for the Lord of Hosts' is a wretched piece of self-consciousness, which disgusts more than it attracts. A diligent life is an attractive life.

Do thou, like an ant, work in thy season, carrying thy due burden upon the ant-hill, and if thou doest this for love of Jesus thou doest nobly. Plod on without courting approbation, and rest content to do thine utmost for the common weal. In fellowship with thy Lord humbly do thy day's work in thy day. Seek not great things for thyself. Ask not to rule in the court, but be willing to work in the field; seek not to recline on the coach, but take thy pruning-knife and go forth among the vines to fulfil thine office, and in that self-forgetting service thy beauty shall be manifested, and voices shall salute thee, crying, 'Return, return.'

It appears, too, that while she was thus engaged, she was the subject of a great stir and emotion of heart. Perhaps she had felt dull and dreary till she entered on her work, but while she was busy with her pomegranates and her nuts, she cries, 'Or ever I was aware, my soul made me like the chariots of Ammi-nadib.' She felt that she could hasten like the chariots of a willing people, who rush to the fight from love of their prince. She felt as if she could run after her Beloved; she could leap, she could fly. Like a chariot that is drawn by Pharaoh's swiftest coursers, her spirit left all behind. Thus vigorous and active, she was watched by many eyes, and soon she heard voices coming from the four quarters of the universe, crying, 'Return, return, O Shulamith; return, return.'

I would, dear friends, that all Christians were what they should be. I am told, but I would not judge, that large numbers of professing people are only half alive, and are altogether asleep. If it be so, I wonder not that they are so inconsiderable in their influence. If they are neither diligent in their Master's business nor fervent in spirit towards him, they are justly despised by those about them. If it be so with you, my brethren, you are losing the joy of Christian life when you might be filled with delight; you are poverty-stricken, where you might be rich; you are as beggars in the city where you are entitled to take up an honourable burgess-ship. May the Lord revive you! May he forgive your coldness and set your souls on fire with love to Jesus! If you have life, may you now have it more abundantly! Doth not your Master desire that the feeblest of you may be as David, and David as the angel of the Lord?

I speak to you who are the beloved of the Lord, to you who labour in holy service, to you who are quickened with a high degree of spiritual life, and feel your souls within you stirred with sacred enthusiasm. You are worth addressing: may the Holy Spirit make my address worthy of your attention! Let us use our text in two ways; may each one be profitable!

First, *she hears the lower voices that cry, 'Return, return, O Solyma; return, return'*, and she answers them with most conclusive negatives. Read the text another way, and in the second place, *she hears voices from above, which cry, 'Return, return, O Solyma: return, return'*, and she answers them by her actions as well as by her words.

Let us listen for a minute or two, but only with our ears, not with our hearts, to THE LOWER VOICES.

Whence came these voices? There are voices from the vasty deep of sin and hell, voices from the tombs which we have quitted, voices from the Egypt from which we have fled. They are crying evermore, like unquiet ghosts, 'Return, return.'

Especially do they call to young souls who are newly wedded to Jesus, in the hope that they have not as yet forgotten their own kindred and their father's house. When we have gone a long way in the divine life, the world feels dubious of our return, and almost gives us up, preferring rather to accuse than to invite. After many years of faithful service, and of resolute nonconformity to the world, many temptations which assaulted our youth are unknown to our maturity. The devil is not altogether a fool, although he is great in that direction; and therefore he does not continue for ever to use nets which have failed to entangle the birds. If he finds that cajolery will not ensnare us, he leaves his old tactics and tries other methods. When 'Return, return' will not woo us, he puts on his lion form and roars till the mountains shake. Upon young believers he very commonly uses very powerful inducements to go back. In the hope that he is dealing with Mr Pliable, he exhibits the hardness of godliness and the pleasantness of sin, and draws the moral that they had better retrace their steps. To them he calls as sweetly as his cruel voice can tone itself, 'Return, return, O Shulamith: return, return.'

By *old companions* he does this. They say, 'You have left us all, we do not know why. You have turned a fanatic; you have joined with gloomy Christian people, and you are not half the good fellow you used to be. Are you not getting a little tired of those dreary ways? Are not the rules of Christ too precise and Puritanic? Are not the ways of God too self-denying? Is not godliness too holy and too heavenly for poor fallible beings like ourselves? If so, the door is open: we will welcome you back. It is true you rent yourself away and said that you must needs go on pilgrimage to the Celestial City, but we will not throw this in your teeth if you will give up such nonsense. Come, be a good fellow with us once more. We have not drunk up all the wine, nor broken all the viols. We are care-for-nothings still, and we shall be glad to make you as lighthearted as ourselves. You were a jolly fellow before you took those blues, and turned so squeamish: Come, shake it off, and be yourself again'. How winningly they put it! How cleverly they mimic the tones of true friendship! One would think they sought our good, and were anxious to be our guardian angels.

Sometimes *the desires of nature* come to their help and the tender passion is enlisted on the side of evil. Bright eyes and gentle lips speak to the natural heart and plead with it to return. The tender love of women has thus played the tempter, and so has the strong affection of men. Courtesy and amiability cry, 'Why do you fight so shy of us? You know what happy times we used to have together. Come, you have tried these Christian people and their faith; you must have found it very moping and melancholy; return and be merry once more. See how much more free we are than they; do not live by rule and order; return to the liberty of sin.' Thus do her former comrades cry, 'Return, return, O Solyma.'

The *old joys* sometimes, in moments of weakness which will come upon us, revive upon the memory and attempt to mislead us. I have known the young Christian remember what he once thought were joys, and though he has clean left them and hates them, yet in the distance which lends enchantment he does not notice so much of their shallowness, baseness and brevity, and he thinks to himself, 'In those days I laughed away the hours right merrily; life was light as a feather; in its froth and foam I saw rainbows of delight. Shall I try these things again? Was I not too hasty in renouncing them?' All the while the voices cry enchantingly, like the songs of the Sirens, 'Return, return, O Solyma; return, return.' They bring out their most melodious music and omit all discordant passages from the sonnet of life. They would have us hark back to what was once our joy. Oh, brothers, 'tis a wretched temptation, and yet some fall before it.

Do you not know how the world will even call us back to our *old cares*? We used to fret and worry until by God's grace we were led to try walking by faith, and then the Lord helped us to rest in his love and wait patiently for him; and now perhaps for years we have had no burdens, for we have cast them on the Lord; we have gone in the morning and told him the fears of the day, and at night we have had little else to do but to bless him for the mercy which has averted all those fears. We have lived in sweet content, rich in joyful expectation, and not poor even in present felicity; and now perhaps the world says, 'You have spent too much of your money on religion; why did you not save it? You wasted a mint of your time upon furthering a kingdom which is imaginary. Oh, if you had given up those energies to the world and stuck to your business, how much richer you might have been! Come now, quit those dreams, shun those prayer-meetings, leave that tiresome office in the Sunday School, give up philanthropic speculations, and follow after your personal interests, like a sensible man, you may get on then; if you mind the main chance you may rise in the social scale.'

There are times when steady, sober people, for whom the temptations of gaiety and vice have no charm at all, stand spell-bound by these more solid but equally degrading offers. Madame Bubble, as you know, offereth to the pilgrim her person, and there are many who turn with loathing from so vile a proffer; but then she also offereth her purse, and there are men like Mr Standfast, who are as poor as an owlet, to whom that offer comes with dangerous force. Her voice has a shrill metallic ring, as she cries, 'Return, return, O Solyma; return, return. Return from generosity to selfishness, from holy zeal to worldliness and prudence. Seek that which all the nations of the world seek after, that which thou canst see with thine eyes and enjoy with thy mouth.'

Many are these calls: I need not go into details, you will hear them soon enough. The Sirens are a numerous and ensnaring sisterhood.

When do these voices come? Their sound is heard full often. 'Return, return, return, return' – four times over the text hath it. They come so often that the word in the epistle to the Hebrews is more than justified: 'And truly, if they had been mindful of that country from whence they came out, they might have had opportunity to have returned.' These opportunities come in our way everywhere and at all times.

If you wish to leave off being a Christian, if you wish to follow the world in its pleasures or in its labours, the doors are always open. It is a wonderfully forgiving world if you will but quit your protest against it. If we have run away from our old master, and wish to return to his service, his yoke is always ready for our neck; he will never deny us employment, even though it be to feed swine. Only too glad is the devil to pardon runaways. He is not ashamed to return with seven others to the house which he aforetime quitted. Often, often the child of God in his early days hears the entreaties of destroyers, as with all subtlety they plead, 'Return, return, O Bride of Solomon; return, return.'

At times these voices come from quarters to which our hearts lie open. Many a man hath been wooed from the ways of holiness by her that lay in his bosom. Samson had his Delilah. Oftener still, the professing Christian woman has been solicited to forsake her Lord by him who should have helped her in her noblest aspirations. Children have been misled by parents, friends by friends; for Satan hath many servitors, and many who do his bidding almost unwittingly. It is a fight to reach to heaven and few there be to help us in it; but the path to hell is downward and multitudes thrust out their hands to urge us to the infernal deeps. These cries are borne to us by every gale, in tones both loud and gentle, 'Return, return.'

And, dear brethren, we shall find that they solicit us in our best moments. I cannot fully account of the fact, but so it is, that I am most liable to speak unadvisedly with my lips when I have just enjoyed the raptures of high fellowship with God. Yonder shines the Mountain of Transfiguration in its unrivalled splendour; but lo, at the very foot of it the devil rages in the lunatic child! Our highest graces are not to be trusted, for, as the most venomous serpents lurk among the brightest flowers, so are temptations most abundant hard by our most spiritual and heavenly joys. Trust not thyself, O child of God, when thou hast seen the invisible, when thou hast stood within the circle of fire, and spoken with God as only his favourites may! Think not thyself secure when thou comest down into thy worldly business, though thou hast bathed thy forehead in the serene light of communion. As pirates distinctly aim to attack the most heavily-laden galleons, so will Satan assail thee when thy vessel has just left the Gold Coast of meditation and prayer. Therefore, watch thou, and pray evermore.

That detestable voice, which dared to ask the Master himself to fall down and worship Satan, will come to thee when thou art most bright and shining with the glory of hallowed fellowship, and it will whisper to thee, 'Return, return. Come down from the mount, and break the commandments to shivers at its foot.' The fiend will call thee Solyma, quoting thy heavenly name – that name of peace and love – and yet he will dare to say, 'Return, return.' He will flatter us for our virtues and yet tempt us to the worst of vices. Get thee behind me, Satan. Avaunt, foul fiend! Even when repulsed he will return to the charge, crouch at our feet, and whine out still, 'Return, return.' The treasures of Egypt and the pleasures of sin are his bait and bribe. We cannot and will not return at his bidding, yet his frequent solicitation puts us to a stand and makes us cry for help.

Notice that our text goes on to say *why they wish us to return*. 'Return, return, that we may look upon thee.' And is that all? Am I to be a traitor to my Lord and quit his holy ways and forfeit heaven to be made a show of by thee, O Satan? Or by thee, O world? Is this a full reward for treachery – 'that we may look upon thee'? Why, their looks are daggers. As the eyes of basilisks are the eyes of the ungodly world; as malignant stars that blast the soul. Whenever you long for ungodly men to see your piety, your piety will wither beneath their glance. Remember how that expression of looking upon Zion is sometimes used in Scripture; in Micah 4:11 we have it, 'Now also many nations are gathered against thee, that say, Let her be defiled, and let our eye look upon Zion.' They wished to spy out her sorrows and weaknesses, that they might jest at her and grieve her; these enemies will do the same with you if you give them the opportunity. Trust a wolf at your throat sooner than worldly men in religious matters. They cannot mean you good, nor do you good should they mean it. They will draw you out, and then expose you;

they will entice you into sin and then report your faults. When the world loves the holy man it is the love of the vulture for the sick lamb. Fear you the worldling, even when he bears you gifts.

Now hear *Solyma's wise answer to her tempters*. She says, 'What will ye see in Solyma?' Dost thou ask me, O world, to come back and show myself to be thy friend? Dost thou promise me approbation? Dost thou vow to look upon me and admire me, and take me for an example? What is there in me that thou canst approve of? What wilt thou see in Solyma?

What can the world see in a believer? The world knoweth us not, because it knew Christ not. A blind man wants to see me: I need not go far to oblige him, for he will get but little out of it if I yield to his request. What a vain reason – 'That we may look upon thee'! They are so blind they cannot even see themselves, nor know that they are blind. What have you and I to do with them? No, let us walk in the light, and have fellowship with God, and then our life shall be hid with Christ in God, only to be manifested when our Lord is manifested; and we shall be well content to have it so.

Listen, O blind world, while we tell you what you would see if we did come to you. 'What will ye see in Solyma?' You would see – we grieve to say it – a conflict within us: 'As it were the company of two armies.' You would see two things in us; and yet neither would give you satisfaction. There is sin in us; but inasmuch as it grieves us to have it there we will not show it you. We do not wish to make mirth for the daughter of Babylon, and when her children ask us to make music for them by singing one of the songs of Zion, we answer, 'How shall we sing the Lord's song in a strange land?' If we must tell you what you would see in us, we will confess our faultiness, but warn you that out of this you would get but little joy. You would see two armies, it is true, but neither of them would yield to you.

You would see in us a nature like your own; but it is mortified, kept under, and laid under condemnation. It would give you no great pleasure to see it, for we reckon it to be dead. The dead are poor company. There is in us, it is true, a capacity for all your worldly joys; but the world is crucified to us, and we are crucified unto the world. There is in us a capacity for all your merriment, but if we were forced to be with you we should be dreadful killjoys to you; you would wonder that we did not laugh when you laugh at sin, and that we should not be as ready as you are to run into excess of riot. We should soon weary you, for the Lord has said, 'I will make Jerusalem a burdensome stone for all people.' You would say by and by, 'Let these slow souls begone: they hinder our mirth.' If we came among you as we are, it would happen with us ere long as it did with Israel, for 'Egypt was glad when they departed'. Our nature that is like your nature is put under restraint, and dies daily, and its expiring groans would be sorry music in your ears.

Then, do you know we have another army in us? That is, there is a new life in us; that life is the indwelling Spirit of God, as it is written, 'I will dwell in them, and walk in them.' If we did return at your request, if we came in the fulness of the blessing of the gospel of Christ, with the Holy Spirit indwelling our bodies, and making them his temples, you would not know what to make of us, and consequently you would scoff at us, as Ishmael did at Isaac, or envy us as his brethren envied Joseph. You would be sure to ridicule us, for you would not understand us, and therefore you would count us hypocrites and sanctimonious fools. As well might oxen commune with men as the wicked with the godly. We have a life beyond you and above you, into which you cannot enter. We are sorry for you that you will not receive the heavenly life which is in Christ Jesus, but as you have it not, we cannot make you our confidants or associates. You would grieve us, and we should provoke you; and therefore we are best apart. You say, 'Return, return, O Solyma; return, return, that we may look upon thee', and our only answer must be, 'What would ye see in Solyma?' Nothing but that which would rebuke and anger you; you would see a company of two armies, both fighting against you.

Come, young brothers and sisters, you that have been tempted to go back; you cannot even tolerate the thought. You have burned your boats behind you, and must conquer or die. Like one of old, you say, 'I have opened my mouth unto the Lord, and I cannot go back.' To go back were to give the lie to the Word of God, to make God himself false, to tell the worldling that there are, after all, no pleasures in Christ like the pleasures of the world; it would be to spit in your Saviour's face, to play the Judas, to sell Christ for pieces of money, or for the filthy lusts of this present evil world. Go back! It were to renounce heaven and all its glories; it were to choose a terrible deathbed, with a guilty conscience ringing the knell of your soul; it were to choose eternal banishment from the presence of God and from the glory of his power. You cannot return; you cannot even look back. If thou art a true Shulamith, thou wilt not even deliberate for a moment about it, but flinging thyself into the Beloved's arms, thou wilt cry, 'Lord, to whom should I go? Thou hast the words of eternal life.'

God help you so to do, for Jesus' sake. That is the first part of our subject.

Now we turn to listen, not with our ears only, but with our hearts too, to the call of THE HIGHER VOICES which cry, 'Return, return'.

Brethren, to go to heaven, to go to Christ, to go towards holiness, is a return to God's people: for God's people are originally his children. Though they are prodigals, and have gone into a far country, they always were his children; even when they spent their substance in riotous living they were still his sons, and each of them could speak of 'My Father's house'. To come to Christ and holiness and heaven is to return.

Besides, all God's people have a new life put into them. Whence came that new life but from heaven and God? Therefore to go towards God is for the quickened ones to return. All God's people are bound for heaven; it is in their charter-party that they should sail for heaven, and therefore to heaven they must go. When the Israelites came out of Egypt to go to Canaan they were not going to a strange land, they were returning to what had always been their inheritance according to the covenant; they were going out of the house of bondage and they were returning to the land that flowed with milk and honey, where their fathers had sojourned before them.

Now, today, as a child of God, I can hear voices out of the yet beyond, ringing out of the glory, and crying to me, 'Return, return.' My Father is in heaven; my Saviour is on the throne; many brethren have gone before; all my heart is with my treasure; therefore I hear the shining ones crying to me every day, 'Return, return, O Solyma; return, return!' Every harp in the heavenly choir is ringing out an invitation to all the Lord's beloved; every palm-bearing hand is beckoning to us; every glorified lip is calling us to come up higher.

To return, I think, means this – come nearer to Christ, nearer to God, nearer to holiness. You are saved; seek to be like your Saviour. You did enjoy splendid days at first, in the love of your espousals; return to them; walk always in the light as God is in the light. You were once in the banqueting-house and the banner over you was love; return to that house of fellowship. Every day seek to lose yourself more in Christ, to live more completely in him, by him, for him, with him. Return, return, to greater heights of holiness, to deeper self-denial, to braver service, to intenser love, to more burning zeal, to more of the Godlike and the Christlike. Return, return.

The holiest and the best call us that way. Every saint in heaven cries, 'Return'; every child of God on earth who is full of the inner life entreats us to return; and chiefly, that dear voice, which once for us cried 'My God, my God, why hast thou forsaken me?' is always calling to us, 'Return, return.' Oh, how sweetly doth he use the name he himself did give us, our marriage name! Hear him beseech us, 'O Solyma, my best beloved, return, return, and come to me!' These are the higher voices.

Notice that in the text that word 'return' is put four times over. Is it not because it is of the highest importance that every child of God should keep returning, and coming nearer to the Father's house? Is it not because it is our highest joy, our strongest security, our best enrichment, to be always coming to Christ as unto a living stone, and getting into closer fellowship with him?

As he calls four times, is it not a hint that we are slow to come? We ought to come to Jesus not only at his first call, but even at the glances of his eyes, when he looks as though he longed for our love; it ought to be our rapture to think only of him, and live wholly to him; but as we fail to answer to first pleas, he cries four times, 'Return, return, O Solyma; return, return. Come to thine own Husband, thine own loving Lord.'

He ceases not to entreat until we do return. Do not the reduplications of this call hint at his strong desire after us, his condescending love for us? It does seem so wonderful to me that Christ should want our fellowship, but he does; he cannot be happy without us. Still he sitteth down upon the well when he is thirsty, and looking across to Samaria's fallen daughter he says to her, 'Give me to drink.' His people are his fulness; he cannot be filled if they are away: I dared not have said this if the Holy Ghost had not declared it, but it is true. Without his people Jesus would be a Head without a body, and that is a ghastly object; a King without subjects, and that would have been a wretched parody of royalty; a Shepherd without sheep, and that would have been a dolorous office, having many pains but no reward. Jesus must have us or he is a Bridegroom without a bride, bereaved and barren. Oh, how he loves us! How he longs for communion with us! Shall he stand and cry, 'Return, return', and will we not come to him at once?

Hear him again in another way. He knocks at our door and he cries, 'Open to me, my sister, my love, my dove, my undefiled: for my head is filled with dew, and my locks with the drops of the night.' Will we not admit him? If he seeks our company and therefore calls us to return, our spirit burst her fetters, she is ashamed of the bonds that hold her on the right and on the left. She cries, 'Let me go; I must be with my Lord; his voice compels me. My soul would leap out of the body rather than not come at him who cries, "Return, return, return, return".'

I have shown you why the call is so oft repeated. Do you not think it is a very instructive call? Permit me to put it thus: 'Return', that is, to your first simple faith. If you have risen to greatness of conceit and pride of knowledge, return to your humble thoughts. Shrink to nothing again in the presence of your God. Come to the cross as you came at first, saying,

> I the chief of sinners am,
> But Jesus died for me.

Return to your first loving intercourse with Christ, for then the days were only bright with his presence, and the night watches were not weary while you could commune with him. Return to the happy love of thine espousals, when thou wentest after him into the wilderness, for those were halcyon days.

Return, return, to your first ardour in service. Nothing was too hot, or too heavy for you then; you were impetuous to be engaged in seeking his redeemed. You have grown lazy now, and you think service for God too severe a strain upon you. Return to your first diligence in joyous service.

Return also to your eagerness for holy growth. Then you desired to have the best that God could give you: in those days you resolved to be a thorough Christian; not barely to live, but to live unto God in the highest degree. Return unto that, and aspire after more. If you have left the best form of consecration, return to it. Oh, sea, rise once more to high-water mark, if thou hast turned or longed for! As the eagle cries, 'higher'; so let it be with thee. Thou art married to him whose blood has bought thee, and he cannot, will not be in heaven without thee; therefore, hasten to obey while he saith to thee, 'Return, return!'

I beg you to observe what the spouse has to say to this when she is thus called upon to return to the Lord. The Lord saith to her, 'Return, return, that we may look upon thee.' Is not that a reason for coming back? The Lord says, 'That I may look upon thee.' He desires your society, and seems gently to hint that you have kept aloof from him. He seems to say: 'You have not been much with me alone lately, you have neglected the reading of the Word, and the hearing of it; I have scarcely seen thy face; therefore return, that I may look upon thee.'

Cover your face and say, 'Lord, why shouldst thou look on me? I am full of sin'; but then draw near to him, that his look of love may bring thee to repentance, and cause thy sin to pass away. Remember he hath power in his eyes to look thee into purity and beauty. Come and say, 'Look upon me, Lord; search me, try me, and know my ways.' Return, that with infinite pity thy Beloved may see what aileth thee, and then with his dear pierced hand may perform a divine surgery upon thee, and make thee well again.

'Return, that we may look upon thee.' I think I may use the phrase to express also that intense satisfaction which Jesus has in every believer. With what pleasure the mother looks upon her child: she remembereth no more the travail for joy that a man is born into the world; but with infinitely greater satisfaction doth Christ see of the travail of his soul in every believer. You ought to show yourselves to Jesus, you have cost him so much; he has loved you even to the death, and loves you still, you ought to abide in him. Return to him that he may look upon you.

And I think, too, when we live near to him, and get into fellowship with him, Jesus feels a sweet complacency towards us. O dear parents, you know the pleasure you have in your loving children; if they have been away from you for years, what a satisfaction it is again to see them within your doors; there is no sight like it! Your Lord loves you so much that it gives him profound pleasure, it swells his heaven to the brim to see you living in his love. What must be his grief when you go fussing about the world, and have no time to talk with him; when you go out sporting and mixing with his enemies, and say that you have no leisure to commune with him! You give delight to him who is Immanuel, God with us, when you frequently approach him, or constantly abide with him. You make him glad with your secret devotion, your heart's affection, your holy boldness, your all absorbing zeal. Oh, do come to your Lord that he may look upon you!

Did I hear you bashfully say, 'What will ye see in Solyma? If Jesus looks on such a dead dog as I am, what will he see in me? I am so full of evil.' He will see in you that which delights him. He will see his own work there; yea, he will see himself there. Did you never see the sun reflected in a little splinter of glass? The mirror was scarcely an inch in diameter, yet you saw the heavens in it. Have you never looked upon a bubble blown by a schoolboy's pipe, and seen a thousand rainbows in it? When the Lord looks on his people, he sees the reflection of himself; he can see himself in our eyes, and therefore those eyes charm him so that he cries: 'Thou hast ravished my heart, my sister, my spouse; thou hast ravished my heart with one of thine eyes, with one chain of thy neck.' The infinite love there is between Christ and us makes him see no sin in Jacob, neither iniquity in Israel; but he looks until he exclaims, 'Thou art all fair, my love; there is no spot in thee.' Be not ashamed to return to your Lord, for he lovingly urges thee to do so. Let your heart and your flesh, like two armies, welcome him; let all your inward conflict aim at coming nearer to him. Rest not till, like Jacob's two bands, you are altogether under the blessing of the covenant angel.

I will turn my text about a little, and give you another rendering which will suit the heart which is welcoming its Lord. Our Mahanaim, our meeting of hosts, shall not be for war, now that the Lord invites us like Jacob to return to the land of milk and honey; but the companies shall be as musical as they are martial. There are within our experiences companies of singing soldiers, choirs of camps. The text exhibits the warring soul, triumphant in her Lord, and meeting him with timbrel and harp.

Spouse of Christ, in arms contending,
Though thy battle-course must run;
Yet with prayers for help ascending,
Shout thy praise for triumphs won.

Oh, if my Lord will come and meet me, he shall see in me whole choirs of songsters! My heart, like Miriam, shall take a timbrel, and all my powers, like the daughters of Israel, shall follow, dancing and singing with glad accord. On the high-sounding cymbals my heart shall play, singing: 'His own right hand and his holy arm have gotten him the victory. Glory! Glory! Where he cometh glory dwelleth.' When shall I come into his presence and behold my God, my exceeding joy? Then will I praise him with body and soul, with heart and with voice. His coming with all his perfections and my coming with all my desires shall make a Mahanaim; and the two hosts, once met, shall encamp together, guarding the King's pavilion, which glitters in the midst. Then shall the warriors become minstrels, and the soldiers shall be singers, as in the valley of Berachah, where all the people triumphed, and they returned to Jerusalem playing upon harps and psalteries and trumpets.

Here I leave you in the joyful presence of the King. We cannot cease speaking at a higher point. The Lord keep us in his presence, for his love's sake. Amen.

46

GOOD WORKS IN GOOD COMPANY

> 'Come, my beloved, let us go forth into the field; let us lodge in the villages. Let us get up early to the vineyards, let us see if the vine flourish, whether the tender grape appear, and the pomegranates bud forth: there will I give thee my loves. The mandrakes give a smell, and at our gates are all manner of pleasant fruits, new and old, which I have laid up for thee, O my beloved.' (Song of Solomon 7:11-13).

The daughters of Jerusalem had been praising the Church as the fairest among women. They spoke of her with admiring appreciation, extolling her from head to foot. She wisely perceived that it was not easy to bear praise; and therefore she turned aside from the virgins to her Lord, making her boast not of her own comeliness, but of her being affianced to her beloved: 'I am my beloved's, and his desire is toward me.' Solomon has said, in his Book of Proverbs: 'As the fining pot for silver, and the furnace for gold; so is a man to his praise:' meaning to teach us that praise is a serious ordeal. Very many men can bear censure and abuse, for their spirit rises so superior to it all, that they are even profited thereby; but to be flattered, or even duly honoured, is not so easy a thing to endure. The sun's warm beams made the traveller unbind his coat, when the wind made him wrap it the more closely about him; the warmth of praise may make us relax our integrity, unless we be very watchful. How many have been foolish enough, when standing upon a pinnacle, to look down and admire their own elevation, and then their brain has reeled, and they have fallen to their own shameful ruin. If we must at any time listen to the praises of our virtues, if we have served God so that the Church recognises and rewards our usefulness, it is well for us to listen just as long as we are obliged to do, but no longer; and then let us turn aside at once to something more practical and more healthful to our own spirits. The spouse seems abruptly to break off from listening to the song of the virgins, and turns to her own husband-Lord, communion with whom is ever blessed and ever profitable, and she says to him, 'Come, my beloved, let us go forth into the field; let us lodge in the villages.'

Communion with Christ is a certain cure for every ill. Whether it be the bitterness of woe, or the cloying surfeit of earthly delight, close fellowship with the Lord Jesus will take the gall from the one and the satiety from the other. Live near to Jesus, Christian, and it is matter of secondary import whether thou livest on the mountain of honour or in the valley of humiliation. Live near to Jesus, and the glowing coals of the furnace cannot consume you, nor the chill blasts of wintry affliction destroy you. Living near to Jesus, you are covered with the wings of God and underneath you are the everlasting arms. If you read the three verses before us with attention, you will see that the Church all through anxiously desires fellowship with her Lord. It is '*Come* with me' – 'let *us*'. She will do nothing except as she is near to her beloved and in the enjoyment of his company.

I think she desires three things in her words; first, *she desires to practise self-examination:* she would go and see whether the vine flourisheth and whether the tender grape appear; but it is self-examination *with him.* She desires next *to go into active service:* it is to this end that she would lodge in the villages and go among the tender plants, that she may labour there, but it is *with him*, 'Let *us* go!' '*Come* with me!' In the third place, *she has a store of fruits laid up for him.* Some things done and some things doing, things old and new, but they are all for him, and she will not mention them except for him, much less bring them out for them to be enjoyed by a rival. 'They are laid up for thee, O my beloved.' Let us try to make a personal matter of the text, this morning, and may God hear the desire of our hearts that we may have true fellowship with his own dear Son.

First, then, IN THE MATTER OF SELF-EXAMINATION.

This is a most desirable and important business, but every believer should desire to have communion with Christ while he is attending to it. *Self examination is of the utmost importance.* No trader who would wish to succeed would neglect to keep his books. No husbandman who wishes to prosper would be careless as to the state of his fields. No flock-master who would see his herds abundantly increase, would leave to his servants the care of them, and fail to tend them with a watchful eye. If thou wouldst have the business prosper, see to it carefully thyself.

In soul-business, it is of no use taking anything for granted where there are so many temptations to self deception in our own hearts; where so many around us are deceived, and are willing to help us to be deceived too; and where Satan sedulously and craftily seeks to cry to us, 'Peace, peace,' where there is no peace; it is of the first and last importance that we should search ourselves whether we be in the faith, and whether, being in the faith, our graces are growing, our faith increasing, and our love deepening. Well does the spouse suggest that she should see whether the vine flourished, whether the tender grape appeared and the pomegranates budded forth; for our spiritual vineyard needs perpetual watchfulness.

While you are attending to this important business, see to it at the same time that you keep up your communion with Christ, for you will never know so well the importance of self-examination as when you see *him*. Mark him there! fastened to the accursed tree, wearing the thorn crown all set with ruby drops of his own blood; look at his griefs, if repenting tears do not blind you; behold his awful agonies; gaze into that visage more marred than that of any man, and stay awhile and listen to the heartrending shriek, '*Eloi! Eloi! Lama sabachthani?*' And did Christ suffer all this that souls might be saved? Then surely, my soul, it should be thy chief business to see that thou hast an interest in him. What! shall I miss that which is purchased with such a price? When such a crimson stream from Christ's own heart flows to cleanse away sin, shall I think it a matter of no account whether I am cleansed or no? When that head, which once was reverenced by angels, is now crowned with the thorns of mockery and cruelty, shall I not use all the thoughts of my head and brain to find out whether I am one with Christ and a partaker of his passion? That cannot be a little heritage which Christ hath purchased with such agonies: let me fear lest I should lose it. That cannot be a slight evil which cost my Saviour such griefs: let me search myself to see whether I am delivered from it.

I am sure, beloved, you cannot have a better candle to look into the secret recesses of your soul than a candle lit at the fire of Jesus' love. Know his love for you, and all his griefs on your behalf, and you will charge your own heart after this fashion: 'See to it, that thou make sure work as to thine interest in Jesus, that thou be really one with him, that thy faith in him be genuine, and that thou shalt be found in him in peace at the day of his appearing.'

Self-examination, however, is very *laborious work*: the text hints at it. It does not say, 'Let us go' but '*Let us get up*'. Self-examination is ever up-hill work. It is by no means a pleasant task; it is one from which flesh recoils, for the flesh cries, 'Let well alone; you are easy and comfortable; you have a hope which affords you much solace; do not dig too deep, the house stands well enough just now; be not too anxious about the foundations; rest assured that it is all right; you would not have all these joys and present comforts if you had built upon the sand.' We need to school ourselves to perform a duty so irksome. But, beloved, if we attempt to examine this, feeling that Christ is with us, and that we are having communion with him, we shall forget all the labour of the deed. There I see him in the garden, sweating great drops of blood in prayer! Can I view him prostrate on that cold winter's night (when the ground was hard with frost), so burning with his soul's travail that huge gouts of blood-red gore are falling upon the frozen earth! and shall I think any toil too great to make sure of my interest in him? Does he, when the cup is put to him, say, 'Not as I will, but as thou wilt', and drink it up with resignation? And shall the far less bitter cup of self-examination, which is so much for my good, be refused by me? No, Saviour of the world, I have not yet resisted unto blood, striving against sin; but if it must be, if all my powers and members must be made to bleed, if my poor heart must be brayed as in a mortar, then let it be, so that I may but be found one with thee, washed in thy blood and covered with thy righteousness. Keep close to the Saviour and the difficulties of self-examination will vanish, and the labour will become light.

Self-examination should always be *very earnest work*. The text says, 'Let us get up early.' It has been well observed that all men in Scripture who have done earnest work, rose up early to do it. The dew of the morning, before the smoke and dust of the world's business have tainted the atmosphere, is a choice and special season for all holy work. In this passage, getting up early signifies that the Church felt she must give her best hour to this necessary work; and as the work might be long, she gets up early that she may have a long day before her; that before the sun goes down, she may have examined every vine and looked to every pomegranate and examined all the mandrakes of the garden. So we must set to work earnestly about self-examination. This is no child's-play. If thou wouldst find out the trickery of thy deceitful heart, thou must be very careful and watchful. If thou wouldst know on what foundation thy hope is built, it is a labourer's work to dig out the rubbish and to find out where the foundation is laid. He who has to prove the title-deeds of his estate doth not always find it an easy business: there are many manuscripts through which he must wade, and numerous title-deeds to be read, verified and collated, before the case will be clear.

And so it must be with you. The great matter, 'Do I believe in Jesus', needs no hours of deliberation, for if I do not, I will now begin again; but to know the growing state of one's graces is not so easy. After all, you may be deceived; therefore come to it with a soul all glowing with zeal, saying, in earnest prayer, 'Search me, O God, and know my heart: try me, and know my thoughts: and see if there be any wicked way in me, and lead me in the way everlasting.' Now, methinks, there is nothing which can make you do this earnest work so well as to say to your Master and your Lord, 'Lord, come with me.' 'While we examine ourselves, abide with us to help us in the work.' I cannot be careless when I hear Christ say, 'My meat and my drink is to do the will of him that sent me.' I cannot be careless in my own Christian career when I see him straining every nerve that he may run the race and win the crown for me. When I see him sitting yonder, above all principalities and powers, pleading for my soul with never-ceasing intercession, I cannot be dull and sluggish. Wake up, ye drowsy powers; be stirred up, ye sleeping passions, to examine yourselves anxiously and carefully, since Christ for Zion's sake doth not hold his peace, and for Jerusalem's sake doth not rest.

And yet again, self-examination, it seems to me (I may be wrong) is not the simple work that some people think, but is *beset with difficulties.* I do believe that the most of self-examinations go on a wrong principle. You take Moses with you when you examine yourself and consequently you fall into despair. He who looks at his own character and position from a legal point of view will not only despair when he comes to the *end* of his reckoning, but he will be a wise man if he despair not at the *beginning*; for if we are to be judged on the footing of the law, there shall no flesh living be justified. The very brightest members of Christ's family, those who wear the most of the Saviour's image, and honour him best among men, may well shrink from the place where even Moses did 'exceedingly fear and quake'.

O brethren, remember to take Jesus with you, and not Moses, lest you dishonour the grace of God, and harbour suspicion against the faithfulness of God, when you ought rather to have suspected yourself. If I take Jesus with me, see on what different principles the examination is carried on! I do not ask, 'Am I perfect?' That question Moses would suggest: 'Am I perfect in myself?' but I ask, 'Am I perfect in Christ Jesus?' That is a very different matter. I do not put it thus, 'Am I without sin, naturally?' but thus: 'Have I been washed in the fountain opened for sin and for uncleanness?' It is not, 'Am I in myself well-pleasing to God?' but it is, 'Am I accepted in the beloved?'

The Christian man sometimes looks at his evidences, and grows ashamed of them and alarmed concerning his own salvation. 'Why,' saith he, 'my faith has no belief in it, it is not able to save me.' Suppose he had looked at *the object* of his faith instead of his faith, then he would have said, 'There is no failure in *him,* and therefore I am safe.'

He looks at his hope: 'Why,' saith he, 'my very hope is marred and dimmed by an anxious carefulness about present things; how can I be accepted?' Yes, but if he had looked at the ground of his hope, he would have seen that the promise of God standeth sure, and that whatever our hope may be, that promise never faileth.

Then he looks at his love: 'Oh!' saith he, 'surely I am condemned, for my love is so cold'; but if he had looked at Christ's love, he would have said: 'No, never shall I be condemned; for many waters cannot quench his love, neither can the floods drown it, and, loving me as he does, he will never condemn me, nor cast me away.'

I do not want you to look at Christ so as to think less of your sin, but to think more of it; for you can never see sin to be so black as when you see the suffering which Christ endured on its behalf. But I do desire you, dear friends, never to look at sin apart from the Saviour. If you gaze at the disease and forget the remedy, you will be driven to despair. If you look at the gathering gangrene and forget the all-gracious Surgeon who is able to remove it, you may well lie down and die. If you see your own emptiness and poverty, and forget his fulness, you will never glorify his name. If you are lost in a sense of your own corruptions, and forget the eternal glory which belongs to you in Christ, so that you are even now raised up together, and made to sit together in heavenly places in him, I say, if you forget this grace-given brightness, and only remember your native blackness, your spirit will turn aside from the path of faith, and you will hang your harp upon the willows, and fail to glorify your God.

Examine yourselves, but let it be in the light of Calvary; not by the blazing fires of Sinai's lightnings, but by the milder radiance of the Saviour's griefs. Am I resting upon thee, thou Son of God? Are thy wounds my hiding place? Have thy nails nailed me to thy cross? Has thy spear pierced my heart, and broken it with grief for sin? And am I now crucified with thee to the world, buried with thee to the power of sin, risen with thee to newness of life, and, like thyself, waiting for the day of manifestation when sin, death and hell shall be trodden under foot, and Jesus shall be all in all? Come, let us look to the vines and pomegranates, but let us make sure that our crucified Lord accompanies us; for else we shall do the work amiss.

It appears, from the words of the spouse, that the work of self-examination should be *carried on in detail*, if it is to be of real service. It is written, 'Let us see if the vine flourish, the tender grape appear and the pomegranates bud forth.' We must not take a general view of the garden, but particularize and give special attention to each point. If a candle be guarded on all sides, if there be but one place left open, the wind will find it out and blow out the light. So in self-examination, if we find ourselves right in many points, it is not enough: we must seek to be right in all points.

The main thing is your *faith*. Is that faith simple? Does it depend upon Jesus only? Is it real? Is it an active living faith? Does it work by love? Does it purify the soul? But when you have examined faith, you may possibly make a mistake; therefore go on to see what your *love* is. Do you love the Saviour? Can you truly say, 'The very thought of thee with rapture fills my breast?' Can you hear the music of his name without feeling your blood leap in your veins? Oh! if you can, methinks, dear friend, you have reason for grave questioning. Try your *active graces*; go from one to the other, and search them all. The worm may be at the root just in that part of the soil where you have not upturned the sod. One leak may sink a ship, therefore search well the vessel before you launch her upon the stormy deep. It is by little and by little that backsliders fall; even Judas doth not betray his Master with a kiss at first. Men are schooled in the downward road. Let us be particularly anxious, therefore, that we do not fall by little and by little; and let us watch that we do not suffer small sins to get force and head till, like little sparks, they have kindled a great fire?

If you wish to be exact in prying into every part and corner, you cannot do better than take Jesus with you. Tempted in all points like as we are, he will know all the points in which we are tempted; and, while we are earnestly examining, his gracious finger will point out the spots where our weakness may lie, and we shall thus fulfil the prayer we have often prayed: 'Search me, O God, and know my heart: try me, and know my thoughts: and see if there be any wicked way in me, and lead me in the way everlasting.' When boys are at school, and have to learn to write, every schoolmaster knows that at the first line they keep their eye upon the copy at the top; the next fine they look at their own writing and their penmanship is not quite so good; and the next line they probably look at the last they have written, and so they write worse and worse as they reach the bottom of the page because they have been imitating themselves and copying their own writing.

It is well for the Christian, if he do not fall into this mistake. He must keep his eye upon his great Exemplar, not upon himself. He will be far more likely to see his own faults by looking to Christ, than by looking at any of his own attainments.

What a delightfully white thing this snow is! When it has newly fallen, take the whitest linen you may have ever seen and put it down, you will find it looks positively yellow by the side of it. Take the fairest sheet of paper that ever came from the mill, and compare it; it does not look white at all. There is no whiteness, that I know of, which can at all emulate the heavenly whiteness of the snow. So if I put my character side by side with another man's, I may say of it, 'It will bear comparison'; but if I put it by the side of Christ's perfections, since his whole life is like the pure and spotless snow, I discover at once my own failures and spots. Oh! to have our great pattern ever before our eye!

Jesus should not be a friend who calls upon us now and then, but one with whom we walk evermore. Thou hast a difficult road to travel; see, O traveller to heaven, that thou go not without thy guide. Thou hast to pass through the fiery furnace; enter it not, unless like Shadrach, Meshach, and Abednego, there is a fourth with thee, like unto the Son of Man. Thou hast to storm the Jericho of thine own deceptions; attempt not the scaling until like Joshua, thou hast seen the Captain of the Lord's host with his sword drawn in his hand. Thou hast to meet the Esau of thy many temptations; meet him not until at Jabbok's brook thou hast laid hold of the angel and wrestled with him and prevailed. In every case, in every condition, thou needest Jesus; but most of all, when thou comest to deal with thine own heart's eternal interests. O, keep thou close to him, lean thy head upon his bosom, ask to be refreshed with the spiced wine of his pomegranate, and then there shall be no fear but that thou shalt be found of him at the last without spot, wrinkle, or any such thing. Seeing thou hast lived with him, and lived in him here, thou shalt live with him for ever.

2. THE CHURCH WAS ABOUT TO ENGAGE IN EARNEST LABOUR, and desires her Lord's company.

It is the business of God's people to be trimmers of God's vines. Like our first parents, we are put into the garden of the Lord for usefulness. Observe that the Church, when she is in her right mind, in all her many labours desires to retain and cheerfully to enjoy communion with Christ.

Some persons imagine that one cannot serve Christ actively and yet have fellowship with him. I think they are very much mistaken. I confess it is very easy to get into Martha's position, and to be cumbered with much serving; you may have to preach here and there so many times a week, to attend committees, to visit sick people, and to do so many other things that you may really, unless you are careful, fritter away your own inward life in outward exercises; you may have to complain with the spouse, 'They made me keeper of the vineyards; but mine own vineyard have I not kept.' I do not think, however, that there is any reason why this should be the case except through our own folly.

Certain is it that a person may do nothing at all and yet grow quite as lifeless in spiritual things as those who are most busy! Mary was not praised for sitting still; no, but for sitting still at Jesus' feet. And so Christians are not to be praised, if they neglect duties, merely because they live in retirement and keep much at home; it is not sitting, I say, *but sitting at Jesus' feet.* Had Martha been sitting still or had Mary been sitting anywhere else, I doubt not that the Master would have given a word of rebuke; he would never have said that mere sitting still was choosing the good part.

Indeed, I know some of you who are none the better for doing nothing, but a great deal the worse; for those who do nothing grow sour and are always willing to find fault with the way in which others serve Christ. Do not think, therefore, that mere activity is in itself an evil; I believe it is a blessing. Taking a survey of Christ's Church, you will find that those who have most fellowship with Christ are not the persons who are recluses or hermits, who have much time to spend with themselves, but they are the useful indefatigable labourers who are toiling for Jesus, and who in their toil have him side by side with them, so that they are workers together with God.

Let me, then, try and press this lesson upon you, that when we as a Church, and each of us as individuals, have anything to do for Christ, we must do it in communion with him. We come up to his house, and what do we come for? It is said that among Church people the prayers are the main thing, and among Dissenters the sermon. I believe that in both cases this would be a fault. Praying should not eclipse preaching; for to preach or to listen to preaching is as true an act of worship as to pray. We never worship God better than when we hear his Word, reverently receive it, and are moved thereby to love and gratitude. To hear preaching is, in a sense, praying; since the true effect of all preaching that is worth the listening to draws us into a spirit of devotion, and makes us ready for prayer and every other form of worship.

But what do we come here for? I am afraid there are some who come merely because it is the time to come, because the hour of worship has come round; and others come only because a certain preacher happens to stand upon the platform. Ah! this is not how God's own beloved ones come up to his house! They desire to meet with *him*. Their prayer as they tread the hallowed courts of God's house will be 'My heart and my flesh crieth out for the living God.' There is no hymn sung so well as when we really do praise Jesus in it. No prayer is so true as that prayer which really comes to the mercy-seat, and spreads itself before the all-seeing eye. There is no preaching like that which is full of Christ, which gives forth a savour of his good ointments.

Worship is not to be commended because of the glorious swell of a Gregorian chant, or because of the equally majestic volume of sound which this great assembly may send forth from that sweet instrument, the human voice. A service is not to be commended because of the eloquence of the preacher, or because of the display of learning which he is able to make in expounding his discourse. No, to the Christian it is, 'Was the Master there?' The question on the Sunday morning is, 'What think ye, will *he* come up to the feast?' Coming to the Lord's table, the child of God's business is not so much with the bread and the wine, as with *his* blood and with *his* flesh. May I feed on *him*? May I see *him*? And if I get to *him*, then it is well with me. If I have then to serve God in the public engagements of his house, let me say, 'Come, my beloved, let us get up to the vineyards.'

You have other service to do, dear friends. This afternoon many of you will be occupied with your Sunday School classes. There will be a lot of lads or girls around you. You will, perhaps, he conducting classes of hundreds of young men and young women. This evening, again, many will be occupied in preaching, or you will be engaged at home with your own children. Oh! how blessed it is to go to the classes, or into the pulpit, having the Master with you! It sometimes happens to the preacher that he is like the butcher at the block; he has a cleaver in his hand, and cuts off large pieces of meat as food for those present, but he himself gets none. But it is otherwise with him when he has his Master with him. Then, whether the rest of the assembly are fed or not, certainly he himself is satisfied as with marrow and with fatness. After what a blessed sort the teacher can teach when the love of God is shed abroad in his heart! You will bear with the rudeness of those boys; you will put up with the inattention of those girls; you will not be angry at the folly of that youth; you will not forget to be in earnest with that poor wanderer, when Jesus Christ stands by your side.

A vision of the Crucified, my brethren, is that which ye want. When we are toiling in his harvest-field, and sit down to wipe the sweat from our brow, we grow very weary; the harvest is plenteous, but the labourers are few; we feel that the edge of our sickle is growing very, very blunt, and we wish we could lie down under the spreading tree from the heat of the sun, and toil no longer. But just then we see the Crucified One coming forward with his mighty sickle, and as we mark the blood-drops streaming from his brow, and see the nail-print in the hand with which he grasps the sickle, when we see how he toils, and how he labours, with what an awful love he sacrifices himself, he has stripped off his very garments, and in all the nakedness of self-denial, gives himself up that he may save others while himself he cannot save; then we pluck up heart again, and take our sickle in the hand which once did hang down, saying, 'Jesus, I will never be weary, for thou wast not weary; and when I shall be faint awhile, I will see thee, whose meat and drink it was to do thy Father's will, and I will make it my meat and my drink to serve thee.' Surely you cannot do God's work so well as when you have Jesus Christ with you.

But it is possible, dear friends, that some of you may be engaged in the service of winning for God *some one soul.* I know those who have one soul laid upon their heart. Perhaps it is the most solemn work under heaven to have to pray for one soul. I have so many to look after, that I cannot but feel I may rightly excuse myself from any very sedulous attention to one. But there are some of you who have only one person to look after – one child, one friend, one soul. You tried to talk to that one person the other day; you burst into tears when you heard the answer you received. You have been praying for months, but instead of seeing any answer to your prayer, the person prayed for is growing worse. You are sure that he was never more vile than when you are most earnest. Friend, I should not wonder if Satan should whisper to thee, 'Give it up!' But let me, I pray thee, urge thee never to do so; and if thou wantest something that will make thee never to give up praying for that soul, see yonder, the eternal Son of God, come into this world to save such a sinner as thou thyself art, and thou wilt never think thou art doing anything too hard when trying to save thy fellow-man from destruction.

O for a vision of the Saviour's face covered with the spittle! See him marred and bruised by the rough Roman soldiers! Behold him as his back smarts beneath the thongs of the cruel whips! See him as Pilate brings him forth, and cries, '*Ecce homo.*' Mark him as he treads the Via Dolorosa! See him while they lift him up on high and dislocate his bones! Why, what is all that you can endure compared with this? When your soul swells with fearful grief, you do not feel such grief as this; you do but sip at the cup which the Saviour drained to the dregs; you do but feel a scratch from those nails which went right through his hands; you do not have but for a moment a flesh wound from that spear which pierced his heart. Courage, thou solitary labourer; let Christ's griefs solace thee. Come with me, my beloved; come with me, my Lord; and my toil shall be easy.

There are some Christians engaged in works of heroism, works of peculiar daring for Christ. I should not like to be misunderstood, but I really think that, amid the gross darkness of the Popish Church, there have been some who have caught the true idea of the Christian life far better than the most of us. Let me tell you to what I refer.

There have been some who have denied themselves all the comforts of life, and have lived in suffering and poverty out of love to Jesus and from a sincere desire to benefit their fellow-men. There have been produced in that Church men whose passionate love no labour or persecution could extinguish, who have fed the poor and nourished the sick; and women who have gone into the hospitals, among diseases the most contagious, and have risked life and lost life for the sake of nursing the sick. There are those living at this present moment upon the tops of such mountain-passes as St Bernard and the Simplon, spending the prime of their life in seclusion in inhospitable frost, where somebody must live, but where nobody ever would live if it were not for the sake of religion, simply that they may serve the poor weary traveller when he comes wading through the snow, or is likely to be lost in the snow-storm. No man shall take precedence of me in my abhorrence of the thrice accursed doctrines of the harlot of Rome; but from our enemies it is right to learn; and I do learn and would teach this, that self-denial and consecration are among the highest of the Christian virtues.

I would to God that our people had the spirit of self-consecration in proportion to the light which they enjoy. I would to God we had true Sisters of Mercy who devoted themselves to going from house to house among the sick. We have some, but we want more; some who would be hospital nurses and who would count it but a small sacrifice even if they gave up themselves for the good of others. Missionaries we want who will face the malaria and deadly fever; our societies cry out for such, but very few are coming forward. We want men of substance, who would take their substance and go out with it to a foreign land to evangelise; men, who having prospered in business, would now count it an honour to spend the rest of their days in some new and special work of charity or piety.

Oh! when I see the Saviour in all his agonies doing so much for us, I cannot but think that we as a Christian people do next to nothing for him. There are no stakes of Smithfield now, thank God; there are no dungeons of the Lollard's Tower; no crowns of martyrdom for suffering brows; but there are still special spheres of labour where we could make the name of Christ illustrious. Let me hold up for your imitation some in modern times, who by works of faith and labours of love, have made us feel that the old spirit of Christianity is not dead. Our beloved friend, Mr. George Muller of Bristol, for instance. There burns a holy devotedness, an intensity of faith, a fervour of perseverance, which I would to God we all possessed. May we have more of this, and so by keeping close to Jesus, we shall produce better fruits, richer clusters and more luscious grapes than are commonly produced upon those vines which are in a less happy part of the vineyard.

3. And now let me close by remarking, that according to the text, THE CHURCH DESIRES TO GIVE TO CHRIST ALL THAT SHE PRODUCES.

She has 'all manner of pleasant fruits', both 'new and old', and they are laid up for her beloved. We have some new fruits. This morning, I hope we feel new life, new joy, new gratitude; we wish to make new resolves and carry them out by new labours. Our heart goes up in new prayers, and our soul is pledging herself to new efforts.

But we have some old things too. There is our first love: a choice fruit that! and Christ delights in it. There is our first faith, that simple faith by which, having nothing, we became possessors of all things. There is our joy when first we knew the Lord; let us revive it. How happy then were we, when the candle of the Lord shone round about us. Old things! why we have the old remembrance of the promises. How faithful has God been! In that sickness of ours, how softly did he make our bed! In those deep waters, how placidly did he buoy us up! In that flaming furnace, how graciously did he deliver us, so that not even the smell of fire passed upon us. Old fruits, indeed! we have many of them, for his mercies have been more than the hairs of our head. Old sins we must regret, but then we have had repentances which he has given us, by which we have wept our way to the cross and learned the merit of his blood. We have fruits, this morning, both new and old; but here is the point – they are all to be for Christ.

Do you not, after doing good service, detect yourself whispering, 'I have done that well'? You intended that nobody should know it; you tried to do it as a secret act of devotion; you were half inclined to tell somebody when it was done; and though it came out, you say it was by accident; but you had a finger in that accident, and you did not altogether regret that you had some of the honour of it. Do not you find when you are really serving your Master, that if somebody does not pat you on the back, you grow cold? I know some Sunday School teachers, who, if thcy are looked after and encouraged, can do well, but who, if they have no encouragement, could not keep on in their work. Oh! it is so easy for us to preach, when there are many souls being fed under us, and the Master honours us in the eyes of men. Would it be quite as easy to serve him without honour? I have known brethren who have met with a little bad feeling among their people, and perhaps they have not always been able to keep their own temper, and they have run away from their charge, left the sheep in the wilderness, because in their inmost heart they were serving themselves, at least to a degree. Truly, beloved, those are the best and most acceptable services, in which Christ is the solitary aim of the soul, and his glory without any admixture whatever, the end of all our efforts. Let your many fruits be laid up only for your beloved; bring them forth when he is with you; bless *his* name for them. Put jewels into his crown, but never say, 'Unto me be honour, and unto my name be praise;' but 'Sing unto Jesus, and to Jesus only be glory, while heaven endures.'

O that strangers to Jesus would believe our testimony concerning him. We are asked sometimes for proofs of our religion. There is one proof which we defy anyone to contradict, and this is the intense joy which the love of Christ gives to us. We are not fools, and I may add, we are not dishonest, and our witness is that there is a joy in love to Christ, and in the enjoyment of his presence, which could not possibly have come to us from any but a divine source. We do not speak because we have not tried other joys; some of us have had our fill of them. We can say of some that their sweet is soon lost in bitterness; of others, that they cloy upon our taste. But communion with Christ has no after-bitterness in it. It never cloys; it is a sun without spots; it is a moon which never wanes; it is an ocean which never ebbs, it is a river which flows on for ever; it is all heaven and all bliss. Oh! if thou didst but know it, thou wouldst never doubt again; thy soul would rest implicitly upon Christ, whom God hath set forth to be a propitiation for sin; and, remember, if you rest upon him and trust him, you are saved, and shall be with him where he is, to behold his glory evermore.

May God bless these words for Jesus' sake. Amen.

47

A CALL FOR REVIVAL

'Come my beloved, let us go forth into the field; let us lodge in the villages. Let us get up early to the vineyard; let us see if the vine flourish, whether the tender grape appear, and the pomegranates bud forth: there will I give thee my loves. The mandrakes give a smell, and at our gates are all manner of pleasant fruits, new and old, which I have laid up for thee, O my beloved' (Song of Solomon 7:11-13).

I remember to have heard it said that when a church is in a right condition, all that it wants on the Sabbath day is that the sermon should be like the orders given by a commanding-officer to his troops: it need not be rhetorical or eloquent, it only needs to be clear and plain – a word of direction for the Lord's servants. If the soldiers be prepared for action, they will not look to be regaled with oratory, but having heard the words of command, they will with all their hearts go about to obey them. Assuredly the church needs instructing, consoling and edifying, as well as directing; but this morning I feel that I have a word from the Captain of our salvation, addressed first to this particular regiment, and next to those other portions of the Grand Army which are represented here this morning. I speak as unto wise men; judge ye what I say.

Travelling along our island just now you see everywhere the sickle, or the reaping machine, in full work; harvest whitens the plains; everywhere the loaded wains are bearing home the precious fruits of the earth. My spirit is stirred within me, and my soul is on flame for I see everywhere a harvest except in the church of Christ. Reapers are busy everywhere except in the fields of our divine Boaz. All fields are ripe, but those of Bethlehem; all barns are filling but those of the Great Husbandman; Christ Jesus has scarce a sheaf ingathered of late; we hear of very few results from the sacred sowing of the Word. Here and there the church, like Ruth, gathers an ear, a very precious ear it is true, for who shall estimate the value of a single soul; but we have no wave-sheaves as in the days of Pentecost, or, if we have them, they are few and far between; and as for the harvest home which we have been expecting, our eyes fail in looking for it in vain.

As a church, constituting a part of the Master's field, we have had for years one continued harvest, but still never such an one as has satisfied our spirits, for our idea of our King is such that the largest increase to his church would not content us, we should still feel that our Lord Jesus deserved far more. As *he* has not yet seen of the travail of his soul so as to be satisfied, so neither are we his servants content on his behalf, but we long and cry and pray for a larger harvest as his reward for the dread sowings of Gethsemane and Golgotha, in bloody sweat and streams of vital blood.

The time when our churches can operate extensively with the greatest convenience will soon be upon us. We do not usually look for any great things during the summer, when congregations are scattered at the seaside, and workpeople are busy many hours in the day. The summer of nature is the winter of the Church, and the earth's winter is our harvest. These warm days will soon be gone and the long evenings will come, and with them abounding opportunities of doing good. Therefore, it seemed to me to be a seasonable thing to give the rallying cry this morning, and bid our friends remember that the harvest of the church comes on apace. I would urge you all to sharpen your sickles, and with good hope and prayerful confidence prepare for the appointed weeks of our harvest. May God, by his Holy Spirit, inspire you with zeal for the work which awaits you, and give you to walk in fellowship with Jesus in all that you do.

We shall, this morning, first of all, call your attention to **the fact which is implied in the words of our text, that LOVE IS THE GREAT MOTIVE FOR ACTION IN THE CAUSE OF CHRIST**.

All through these verses the spouse acts with reference to her beloved. It is for him that she goes forth into the field, for the sake of his company, and the quiet enjoyment of his love, she would lodge in the villages; and all manner of pleasant fruits, new and old, which are stored within her gates she declares to be laid up for her beloved. Love, then, is the fittest and most powerful motive to holy service: 'The love of Christ constraineth us.'

This love has about it certain marked peculiarities. It is first a *love which realises the person of the Beloved.* In the text the spouse speaks of 'my beloved' as of a real personage, whom she sees, upon whom she leans, and with whom she talks. Christ Jesus is to his church no fiction, no myth, no imaginary hero. Throughout the song both the personages are most real to each other, so real that they both enter into graphic descriptions of each other's beauties and present us with portraits drawn by the pencil of admiring love. Now, a church will always be strong when the Lord Jesus is real to her; by this, indeed, may her power be estimated. Jesus must be to us no historical personage who was once on earth, but is now dead and powerless; he must be an actual person living still in our midst.

Imagine, my brethren, with what enthusiasm the present audience would be stirred if I should retire, and in my place there should come forward the very Christ who was nailed to the cross of Calvary. You would know him by his hands and by his feet, the sacred marks of his passion. Oh, how the sight of him would stir your souls! You would be bowing your heads in adoration, but grudging the closing of your eyes even for a second in prayer, for you would desire, without a pause, to drink in the blessed vision. And if the crucified One should stand here, and say, 'My brethren, my blood-bought ones, for whom I laid down my life, there is yet much to be done to extend my kingdom; there are precious souls, brothers and sisters of yours who know not my name who must be brought in; there are ignorant ones to be taught and sinful ones to be restored'; and suppose he should then point with his hand to one of you, and say, 'I send you *there*', and to another, 'I send you *there*.' Why you would feel at once anointed to the appointed work, and go forth to do it with much earnestness, carefulness and joy; you would be right pleased to receive a commission from those dear honey-dropping lips.

My brethren, have you forgotten that you walk by faith, and will you permit it to be thought that sight would have more power over you than faith? I trust you will not have it so. Then, remember, by faith you may realise and ought to realise this morning that Jesus walketh among the golden candlesticks and is in his church now, saying to every one of his people, 'Go and serve me! Seek my blood-bought ones! Help my feeble ones! Feed my sheep and my lambs!' I pray you, let your faith this morning sweeten your duties by the knowledge that they arise out of your Beloved's personal commands. Execute his holy commands as if you had received them, as in very deed you have, directly from himself. Let your heart go with mine, while I say, 'Jesus, my beloved, though I see thee not, and must be content to behold thee by faith alone, yet my faith shall be more influential than my sight. I know that thou art here, and what thou biddest me do my soul shall perform with all her might, because thou sayest it.'

Note next, that *the love here spoken of was well assured of the affection of its Beloved.* Note the verse which precedes our test, 'I am my beloved's, and his desire is towards me.' A Christian is never strong for service when he does not know whether Christ loves him or not. If that be a question, you have put out the fire by which alone the force can be generated which must work the machinery of your spirit. You must know beyond question that Jesus loved you and gave himself for you, you must feel that he is loving you now, that his heart is looking out through those dear eyes which once wept over Jerusalem, and that the meaning of his loving glance is, 'Soul, I love thee, I loved thee so that I gave myself for thee, and I have not repented of the gift. I love thee still as much as I loved thee upon Calvary's bloody tree.' It is strength to feel that still 'his desire is toward me'. Oh, when you feel, 'Jesus loves me, Jesus desires me to show my love to him, Jesus at this moment thinks of me and takes a delight in me', this will make you strong as a giant in the cause of your beloved. Between the very jaws of death a man would venture who felt that the love of Christ was set upon him. Love to Jesus is the fountain of courage, the mother of self denial, and the nurse of constancy. Strive then for a well assured sense of the Saviour's love. Be not content till you possess it, for it will be health to your spirit and marrow to your bones; it will be a girdle of strength to your loins and a chain of honour about your neck.

Observe that *the love of the spouse lived in fellowship with the Well-beloved.* 'Come, my beloved, let us go, let us lodge, let us get up, let us see, there will I give thee my loves.' True love to Jesus grows stronger and stronger in proportion as it abides in him. We are cold in our love because we live at a distance from him. The angel who dwells in the sun has never to complain of an ice-bound heart; and he who lives in Christ and abides in him will blaze and glow with a warmth of love comparable to that of Christ himself. I do not think that the numbers of a church will have so much to do with the work it accomplishes; that depends more upon the degree of love than upon the length of the church roll. A small church inflamed with ardent affection for the divine Lord will do more for him than a great host eaten up by worldliness. Love burns its way by its own vehement flames. Coals of juniper are soon felt. The Enochs are the men – they walk with God and hence they have power over their times. The Johns are the men – they lean on Jesu's bosom, and when they come forth to tell of what they have seen and heard, they speak with authority as sent by the Most High.

The Lord give to us as members of this church to abide in habitual fellowship with Jesus; not to have occasional spasms of delight in God, but one unbroken rest in him. We would not now and then look through the windows of agates and behold the king in his beauty, but we would continue 'looking unto Jesus'. We would have his praise continually in our mouths, and his love burning like the quenchless altar fire of the temple, for ever within our hearts. This is the one thing needful to promote and sustain a revival in a church. If we have abounding love to Jesus we can prosper under disadvantages, but if we have it not we have lost the great secret of success. Love to Jesus teaches our hands to war and our fingers to fight. It sets us side by side with the conquering Immanuel, and makes us share his victories. It yokes us with the strong Son of God, and so makes our infirmities to be but opportunities for the display of his power.

This love leads the church to hold all things in joint possession with Christ. Observe that word, 'at our gates are all manner of pleasant fruits'. Love to Jesus constrains us to make over all that we hold to him, while faith appropriates all that Jesus has to itself. Love will not stand to have divided properties. Such was the love of Jesus that he gave all that he had to us. He could not bear to have anything, not even his throne itself, that should be altogether to himself. He stripped himself to his last rag to clothe us, and then gave us his breath to be our life, his blood to be our health; and now today, if we love him as we should, we are saying:

If I might make some reserve,
And duty did not call;
I love my God with zeal so great,
That I would give him all.

I like to think, in church matters especially, that we are all Christ's, that if we have any ability, it is Christ's ability – to be laid at his feet; if we have any substance, it is Christ's money – to be used in spreading his church: our Sunday School is Christ's nursery, and the little ones are Christ's lambs. Our work out of doors in preaching at the corners of the streets is Christ's mission; it is his trumpet, that is blown when the gospel is preached; and every form of agency is not ours – it is Christ's; or if ours, it is only so because it is his. Oh, to have more and more all things common with our Lord, and no longer to speak of mine or thine. Beloved, we are joint heirs with him; all that we have is his, and all that he has is ours. When the church believes and acts upon this, the hour of her success is close at hand.

Consider once more, the love which is the great motive to Christian action is a *love which looks to Jesus for united operation.* It is, 'Come, my beloved, let us go forth into the field, let us get up early to the vineyard.' Oh, it is glorious when Christ comes with the preacher, not the servant alone, but the Master looking through his servant's eyes, and speaking with his servant's tongue, and pleading with his servant's heart. Oh, it is good teaching in your Sabbath School when Jesus sits there among the boys and girls and speaks to their hearts It is good going into lodging-houses or calling at the people's doors to tell them of the Saviour when Jesus knocks as well as you, and the Crucified goes with you among the fallen, the infidel and the profane. All is well when the Redeemer leads the way. Be not afraid, beloved, for you go in good company. Who among us will be afraid to do anything or go anywhere if Jesus saith 'I will go with you?'

Such was the prayer the spouse put up, and doubtless she was led to pray for that which God will grant. Let us pray with her as she prayed. Come Saviour, come up with us to whatsoever we attempt for thee! If there be any brethren here who are working away for thee in dark places in London, dear Saviour carry the lantern with them, be thou their light! If they are digging for thee and quarrying amidst granite rocks which refuse to yield to their strokes, come thou Almighty One and wield thy hammer, and straightway the stone shall be broken. Come with us, Lord. This is the fellowship we desire of thee, the fellowship of labour and of soul-winning. We would not only sit at thy feet to learn, but we would take up our cross and follow thee. We would go with thee whithersoever thou goest; we would fight or labour or suffer or live or die at thy bidding. Be this the fellowship thou shalt bestow upon us!

Secondly, LOVE LEADS US TO GO AFIELD IN THE SERVICE OF JESUS.

'Come, my beloved, let us go forth into the field.' A *loving church spontaneously puts herself upon widened service.* She has a large heart towards her Lord and longs to see him reign over all mankind. She does not wait to hear again and again the Macedonian's cry, 'Come over and help us,' but she is prompt in mission enterprise. She does not tarry till she is forced by persecution to go abroad everywhere preaching the Word, but she sends forth her champions far and wide. As sure as ever she loves her Lord she asks herself the question, 'What more can I do for him?' When she looks over the plot of ground which she has been tilling, she says, 'It is not large enough: the harvest I can get out of this will not suffice me for my dear Lord'; and she saith to him, 'Let me go to the regions beyond, to break up the fallow ground, and cause the wilderness to blossom.'

Now, beloved members of this church, do you not feel some such desire this morning? It is upon my heart that we should be undertaking larger things for Christ. Keep up the old agencies by all manner of means; quicken them, strengthen them; but does not love suggest that as increasing years add increasing indebtedness to Christ, as we are always receiving fresh mercies, so we should make new and larger returns to our best friend? If by us, as a church, nothing new may be ventured, yet cannot each individual have his own plan and branch out afresh? Will not each man say in his heart, 'What can I do for Jesus today, over and above what I should have done if things had gone on in the ordinary course? Enquire of him you love, and if your hearts are with him, it will not be long before you will discover what he would have you do.

The spouse, when she said, 'Let us go forth into the field', *knew that the proposal would please her Lord*; for the nature of Christ is a large and loving one, and, therefore, he would bless the far off ones. His is no narrow heart; his thoughts of love are far reaching, and when the church says, 'Let us go forth into the field', truly her Lord is not backward to accept the invitation. The spouse does not guess at this, nor does she merely infer it from her Bridegroom's nature, but she has it in express command from his own lips: 'Go ye into all the world and preach the gospel to every creature.' There stand the orders, and when our largest enterprises shall have been fulfilled we shall not have exceeded them. There is no exclusion put upon any tribe or clan, no classes are laid under ban, no individuals are exempted. Therefore, Church of Christ, by the love thou bearest to thy crucified Master, by his wounds and death for thee, and by his living love to thee, seek out the lost and gather together the outcasts. Ye fishers of men, launch out into the deep and let down your nets for a draught. Ye sowers of holy seed, go abroad and sow the untrodden wastes. Ye consecrated builders, break away from old foundations and lay fresh groundwork for a larger temple for your God and King. Surely the Spirit of love in a church will suggest this.

Note that *the spouse is evidently prepared for any discomfort that may come as the result of her labour.* She must needs leave the fair palaces of her royal husband and lodge in rustic cottages. Poor lodgings there for Solomon's fair spouse; but what cares she? Any roof which covers her from the evening dew and shields her from the drops of the night shall quite suffice her; yea, if he be there, the tents of Kedar shall be fair as the curtains of Solomon, for his sake. Brethren and sisters, if you serve the Lord Christ in breaking up fresh ground, you may have to meet difficulties and make sacrifices, but they will be as nothing to you; you will welcome them for his dear sake.

Am I stirring no heart now? Has my linger touched no responsive string? I think I feel in my own soul that some of you are responding. Some brother, some sister is here – I know not to whom the prophetic word is coming – who is saying, 'Lord, I am thy spouse; I will go forth with thee into the field, and I will lodge with thee in the villages, if there I may but glorify thy name.'

Observe, too, *the spouse is quite ready to continue in this uncomfortable service.* She says, 'I will *lodge* in the villages', there will she abide awhile, not paying a flying visit, but stopping until the good work is done, for which her Lord and she went forth. Oh, get ye out, ye Christians, into the distant fields of labour. Many of you – how often have I said it I – sit here Sunday after Sunday, and hear many sermons, when I believe you would be better engaged if you were preaching yourselves and winning souls for the Redeemer. I have often been glad to miss some of my dearest brethren from our assemblies. Your presence gives me great pleasure, but when I know you have been away, seeking after Christ's blood-bought souls, I have had pleasure in your absence. Go, and the Lord go with you; go, more of you; yes, I say, go, more of you. Your empty seats will be occupied by sinners whom God will save; while you, dear comrades, if you be fighting for my Master somewhere else, will do my Master much more service than you could have done by listening to me.

We must not allow a single talent to lie idle; we must not waste an hour of these blessed Sabbaths; we must get us away among the ignorant ones and carry them the light. We must hunt for precious souls. For our Master's sake, and in his strength and company, we must compass sea and land for his redeemed ones. Only, if any of you go, *do not try to go alone.* Stop until you breathe the prayer, 'My beloved, let us go.' You go in vain when you go not with the Master, but when you have secured his company, then go and welcome, for you 'shall doubtless come again rejoicing, bringing your sheaves with you'.

Observe how the spouse says, 'There will I give thee my loves'. As much as to say, if Jesus will thus go with us into active service, then will we reveal to him the love of our hearts. I suppose there may have been times in the Church when a hermit's life would suitably reveal the heart's love to Jesus, but I am certain it is not so now. If there are any here who love contemplation and would fain spend their whole lives in quiet retirement, I am persuaded that such a course would be injurious to their generation and to the cause of truth. Of course, there may be exceptions, and if you have no gifts but such us could be serviceable to Christ in solitude, use them in solitude, but from the most of us the times demand activity. So dark is the world we cannot afford to lose a glow-worm's spark. Men are perishing, can we let them perish? Would we suffer a soul to be lost even though it were given to us in exchange to enjoy the highest fellowship with Christ? Behold this day the sheep have gone astray, and the wolves are howling after them; not even to enjoy the great Shepherd's company, can we, the under-shepherds, dare to leave you wanderers to perish.

The Church today hath her vocation, which is not so much to eat the fat and drink the sweet, as to light her candle and sweep her house, and seek diligently till she find her lost piece of money. Think not that active service prevents fellowship; nay, it is but another form of sitting at his feet, another shape of fellowship quite as true, and because more called for at this era, even more acceptable.

I know I have had as great fellowship with Christ in his service as ever I have had in quiet contemplation. When I have met with a poor soul who has rejected the Lord, I have felt my heart breaking over him like the heart of Christ over obstinate Jerusalem; when I have seen the tears flowing from a penitent's eyes who could not as yet find the Saviour, I have felt sympathy with Jesus when he has looked upon the like, and had compassion upon them; and when I have seen the glow of joy, when the sun of Christ's countenance has shone at last upon the troubled heart, I have entered into the joy of the Lord when he rejoices over one sinner that repenteth.

Laziness never yet had communion with Christ. Those who walk with Christ must walk swiftly. Jesus is no idler or loiterer; he is about his Father's business, and you must march with quick step if you would keep pace with him. As vinegar to the teeth, and as smoke to the eyes, are sluggards to active persons. Those who have much to do have no fellowship with gossips, who drop in to while away the hours with chat. Jesus has no fellowship with you, who care not for souls that are perishing. He is incessantly active, and so must you be if you would know his love. There is a fierce furnace-heat beating upon everything today; men are toiling hard to hold their own, and Jesus must not be served by slothful hearts. I am sure that I err not from his mind when I say to you, beloved, if you would know the Beloved fully you must get up early, and go afield with him to work with him. Your joy shall be in spending and being spent for him.

Thirdly, LOVE LABOURS ALSO AT HOME.

Nearer the palace there were vineyards, and the spouse said, 'Let us get up early to the vineyards.' Note, then, that the Church does her work at home as well as abroad. When she loves her Lord she works with zeal, *she gets up early.* All men in Holy Scripture who loved God much rose early to worship him. We never read of one saint engaged upon sacred service who rose late. Abraham rose early, David rose early, Job rose early, and so did they all. It is put here as the very type and symbol of an earnest, vigorous service of Christ.

Dear brethren, there is such a thing you know as keeping the Sunday School going, and keeping the Tract Society going, and keeping the Evangelists' Society going, and yet nobody is up early, but, after a fashion, everybody is nodding. I know these warm Sunday mornings it is not a very difficult thing for some of you, if you try hard, to go to sleep during a sermon. Well, that is a visible slumber, and is soon got over, but there is an invisible sleep which will come on Sunday afternoon when you are teaching, which is neither so soon discovered nor so easily cured. You are talking, talking, addressing your class, or speaking to your men and women, or whatever else may be your calling, and all the while your soul is nodding. Anybody can wake you up with a push in your side if only your body is sleeping, but when the soul is slumbering it is not so easy. I fear greatly that a large proportion of Christian workers are usually asleep.

What a difference there is between what a man teaches when he is asleep and what he teaches when he is awake. You can see it in a minute. I could not describe the difference, but it is apparent in tone and manner, and in every other way. The man may say and do the self-same thing, but still it is a different thing. The children soon perceive it if it is in your class, your hearers soon perceive it if it is in your pulpit. Oh that God would wake up this church; I do not believe that success so much depends upon what the church does as upon how she does it. You may take your hammer and go tinkering about and not fasten a tin-tack, but if your arm has muscle in it you will soon be driving the nails home to the very head, and clinching them. May the Lord's love so come upon you all, my brethren, that what you do you may do with all your might, plunging your whole soul into his service, and never sparing force in anything.

Notice that God's people, when they are awake, first *look well to the church.* 'Let us see if the vine flourish.' The church is Christ's vine. Let us take stock of it. Beloved, we ought to be each one of us, in a measure, pastors of the church. In so large a church as this, the pastoral office cannot be vested in one, or even in twenty. Each must look after his brother, and thus you must be pastors of one another. Watch over one another; pray for one another. How wonderful is the power of prayer. We do not know what blessings come from our prayers. Ten thousand darts might long ago have pierced the Lord's elect were it not that the prayers of the saints are a shield over their heads, defending the sacramental host from harm.

Then the church *looks after the little ones.* 'Let us see if the vine flourish, whether the tender grape appear.' No earnest church forgets the children of her Sabbath School, and every other agency for the young will be sure to be well minded. An active church seeks to bring Jesus among the children, to see if the tender grape appear. She pays her visits and performs her services, but ever in his dear company. Helpers in the Sabbath school, and workers for Christ, I salute you. The Lord be with you. The Lord give you to see many tender grapes appearing, and may this church have joy of you as hundreds shall be converted to God by your instrumentality.

Then the church also *takes notice of all enquiries.* 'Let us see whether the pomegranates bud forth.' If a church be alive, there will be always many to observe where the first tear of repentance is glistening. In this congregation, every Sabbath day, thank God, some persons are pricked in the heart. Watch them, brethren. Those of you who occupy your seats and do not go a-field, can do the cause great service by watching at home. There is no need to leave those seats in order to be useful. Around you there are unconverted persons. Each Sabbath morning and evening there come in here strangers, and it may be the Lord will deal with them, only be you on the alert; speak with them, and try if you can to use the short-handed claymore, that if my longer bladed sword may not have reached them, you who are near at hand may send a deadly wound into the very heart of their sins.

O my brethren, words fail me to set before you the ways in which you may show your love to Jesus in the church itself, but I am certain that there is no need for me to speak. Love herself, will teach you. Mothers somehow bring up their children, though there are no colleges for mothers. Love with its instincts makes them wise, and so will Christians with their love to Jesus become wise to serve. I do believe the less rule and human direction there is in the church, the better. I do not want to say, 'Brother, do this, and do that'; if you love Christ, you will know what to do better than anybody else can tell you. You will find your own places; the Lord will lead you to them. I might put a square man into a round hole if I had the placing of you, but love always puts the man into the right position, it tells him what suits his qualification, it puts him to his work, and what is more, it keeps him to it. I shall measure your love to Jesus, and measure my own, not by the way in which we can talk, or the way in which we can criticise other workers, but by the way in which we shall henceforth labour for the Lord.

The last point is this, that LOVE IN A CHURCH BRINGS FORTH ALL ITS STORES FOR THE BELOVED. The church of God has in herself, through the rich love of her husband, *all manner of pleasant fruits.* This church is a large one, but the same truth will hold good of the smallest church. The Lord never leaves his church without a suitable measure of gifts and graces. If our spiritual nostril and eye could act this morning, we should discern all the fruits of the Paradise of God in this church, and we should smell the sweet savour of all pleasant things; for some brethren here have the apples of faith, others bear the delicious pomegranates of love, and others yield the charming clusters of hope and joy. There are all manner of pleasant fruits among us. One has one, another another, and in some hearts there are many fruits united. A church of God, if well cultivated, is rich in multiform displays of the fruit of the Spirit of God.

Some of these fruits are *new,* and oh, how full of savour they are. Our new converts, thank God for them, what a freshness and power there is about their love! Certain mouldy old professors have lost their taste altogether; they have passed beyond the time in which they were sweet; they have got into the sleepy pear state, and are getting rotten. They are chips in the porridge, the taste has gone out of them, if they ever had any. Alas! some have acquired a nauseous flavour, they are very naughty figs indeed. The new fruits may be sharp, and have more pungency than mellowness about them, but for all that they are choice to the Lord Jesus, whose soul desireth the first ripe fruits. I thank God for youthful zeal; it might with advantage have a little more knowledge mingled with it, yet the zeal is good, and the fervour is good. May we never be without new-born souls.

Then there are *old* fruits, the experience of believers who are ripening for heaven, the well-developed confidence which has been tried in a thousand battles, and the faith which has braved a lifetime of difficulties. These old fruits – the deep love of the matron to Christ, the firm assurance of the veteran believer – there is a mellowness about them which the Lord delights in.

All these choice things ought to be *laid up.* Every good thing in a church is meant to be stored up, not to be despised and forgotten; and the point of all is that all in the church ought to be laid up *for our Beloved.* And now is the time when I earnestly ask, in the name of the Lord Jesus, by the roes and by the hinds of the field, yea by each sacred token of the love you bear your Master, that each one of you should bring forth his pleasant fruits, whether they be new or whether they be old. We do not bring them forth to buy his love, we know better; for though we should give all the substance of our house for love it would be utterly contemned. We do not bring forth these fruits to secure his love for the future; we know it is an everlasting love that never can be taken away from us. We do not bring them forth because we want to commend ourselves. Ah, no, any beauty we have does not lie in the fruits of our storehouses, but in what he has put upon us, and in what his love sees in us. Neither do we bring forth these pleasant fruits to feed on them ourselves. Old experiences are mouldy things; old manna breeds worms and stinks; and as for any fruits which we have brought forth we take no satisfaction in them ourselves. All we have belongs to him and to him alone, and at his feet we would lay the whole.

I beseech you, brethren, if you have any love pour it out upon him; if you have any faith exercise it for him; if you have any courage be bold for him; if you have any endurance endure hardness for him; if you have any grace, any virtue, any gift of his Spirit, anything that is lovely and of good repute, use it for him. Now is the day, now is the hour, now his love puts in her claim and serves you with her sacred writs. By the espousals which you have not forgotten, by the covenant which you have oft repeated with him, by the seals of his table, by your burial with him in baptism in days gone by, I beseech you now, bring forth all your pleasant things for your Beloved; none for anyone else, but all for him.

I fear we often forget to do all for him. I know if I preach a sermon and have any recollection that such and such a passage might please a learned or wealthy hearer, I have failed to please God. If I have any consideration in my mind as to whether I shall gain esteem for excellence of speech I am weak directly; but if I preach for Jesus only, then whoever finds fault my work is sweet to him. And if you pray in the prayer meeting, or teach in the class, or give your contribution to the Lord's work; if you feel you have done it for him, oh, then you know you have done aright because that is the point which sweetens all.

I believe that many have stolen up to the offering-box and dropped in what they could give for the Lord's sake, and none have known it, and therefore Christ has accepted it; while others may have given large sums ostentatiously because others of their standing were giving as much, and, therefore, they were not accepted. I want your aid for the College and the Orphanage, but do not give for my sake, but for my Lord's sake. Put what you give into the pierced hand; make that your treasury.

Jesus is your Master. No one else has bought you; no one else has died for you; no one else will receive you until his fond embrace at the last; no one else is preparing heaven for you; no one else can say, 'Well done, good and faithful servant.' Serve ye him, then, with both your hands, with all your heart, with every drop of blood in your veins, and every breath in your lungs. Give him yourself, your whole self, from the sole of your foot to the crown of your head, and when you have done that, if he spare you for another half century you will find that you have spent the best life for yourself, though that must not enter into your thoughts.

I have thus spoken to my own dear friends and brethren in Christ, but let me remind those who are not in Christ that nothing of this has anything to do with them. I don't bid you do anything for Christ. I cannot. Christ does not want his enemies to work in his vineyard. I do not ask you either to give to Jesus or to work for him? Why should you? Till you love him your services would be a mockery of him. I hold up no standard to enlist under it men whose hearts are disloyal toward our Captain. Ah, no; but if your service be rejected, and you feel grieved at heart that it is so, let me whisper this word in your ear - thy heart may yet be made right. Thou mayest yet come and serve him. Here is his message to thee: 'Come now and let us reason together, saith the Lord; though your sins be as scarlet they shall be as white as snow; though they be red like crimson they shall be as wool.' 'He that believeth and is baptised, shall be saved.'

There is the point for thee, good friend. Thou must begin with being thyself saved, and then when thou art saved, thou canst serve Christ. Christ will have no man work for him with the view of saving himself; you must first be saved, and then you have not your own salvation to look to. When you have left that with Christ, you can then labour for him. A rich English merchant was requested by Queen Elizabeth to take up certain affairs of hers. 'Your Majesty,' said he, 'I am willing enough, but if I do your bidding my business will be ruined.' 'Sir,' said the Queen, 'You attend to my business, and I will attend to yours.' Now, sirs, give the business of your soul's salvation up to Christ; let him save you; and when that is done you can make it your business to serve him, and he will be glad of such a servant.

The Lord bless you, for Jesus' sake. Amen.

48

LEANING ON OUR BELOVED

'Who is this that cometh up from the wilderness, leaning upon her beloved?' (Song of Solomon 8:5).

Careful readers will have noticed that in the verses which precede my text, the spouse had been particularly anxious that her communion with her Lord might not be disturbed. Her language is intensely earnest, 'I charge you, O daughters of Jerusalem, that ye stir not up, nor awake my love, until he please.' She valued much the fellowship with which her beloved solaced her; she was jealously alarmed lest she should endanger the continuance of it; lest any sin on her part or on the part of her companions should cause the Beloved to withdraw himself in anger.

Now it is a very striking fact that immediately after we read a verse so full of solicitous care concerning the maintenance of communion, we immediately fall upon another verse in which the upward progress of that selfsame spouse is the theme of admiration; she who would not have her beloved disturbed is the selfsame bride who cometh up from the wilderness, leaning herself upon him; from which it is clear that there is a most intimate connection between communion with Christ and progress in grace, and therefore the more careful we are to maintain fellowship with our Lord, the more successful shall we be in going from strength to strength in all those holy graces which are landmarks on the road to glory.

The well-head and fountain of growth in grace is well-sustained communion and manifest oneness with Christ; we may strive after moral virtue if we will, but we shall be like those foolish children who pluck flowers and thrust them into their little garden without roots; but if we strive after increasing faith in Jesus, we shall be as wise men, who plant choice bulbs and living seeds, from which shall in due time uprise the golden cups or the azure bells of lovely flowers, emblems of things that are lovely and of good repute. To live near to Christ is the one thing needful; to keep up that nearness, and never to suffer our fellowship to be interrupted, should be our one great business here below; and all other things, this being sought after in the first place, will be added to us. We shall come up from the wilderness, when we are anxious that our beloved's fellowship with us shall not be disturbed.

That preface strikes the key-note of this morning's discourse. Our real theme, whatever may be the form our meditation shall take, will be communion with Christ as the source of spiritual progress.

1. We shall, without further prefatory remarks, come at once to the consideration of the text, and **we shall notice THE HEAVENLY PILGRIM AND HER DEAR COMPANION.** 'Who is this that cometh up from the wilderness, leaning upon her beloved?'.

Every soul that journeys towards heaven has Christ for its associate. Jesus suffers no pilgrim to the New Jerusalem to travel unattended. He is with us *in sympathy*. He has trodden every step of the way before us; whatever our temptations, he has been so tempted; whatever our afflictions, he has been so afflicted. He is touched with the feeling of our infirmities, having been tempted in all points like as we are.

Nor is Jesus near us in sympathy alone, he is with us *to render practical assistance*. When we least perceive him, he is often closest to us. When the howling tempest drowns his voice, and the darkness of the night hides his person, still he is there, and we need not be afraid. It is no fiction, no dream, no piece of imagination that Christ is really with his people. 'Lo, I am with you *alway*, even to the end of the world' is true of all his saints; and, 'Fear thou not;

for I am with thee: be not dismayed; for I am thy God' is no meaningless assertion, but to be understood as a certain verity and a practical truth.

In every step of this pilgrimage, from the wicket-gate of repentance up to the pearly gate which admits the perfect into paradise, Jesus Christ in sympathy of heart and in actual presence of help is very near to his people. Be this the pilgrim's encouragement this morning.

Dear friends, who among us would not undertake a journey in such company? If he were here today, and said, 'My child, I call you to go on pilgrimage', perhaps you would start back with dark forebodings of the way; but if he added, 'But I will be with thee whithersoever thou goest,' we should each one reply, 'Through floods, or flames, if thou dost lead, we will follow thee where thou goest. Lead the van, O Crucified, and we will follow thee. Let us but see thy footprints in the road, and whether the path winds up the hill of difficulty or descends into the valley of humiliation, it shall be the best road that ever mortal footsteps trod if it be but marked with the tokens of thy most blessed presence.' Courage, then, ye wayfarers who traverse the vale of tears; you come up from the wilderness in dear company, for one like unto the Son of God is at your side.

Note the title that is given to the companion of the spouse: '*her beloved*.' Indeed, he of whom the song here speaks is beloved above all others.

He was the Beloved of his Father or ever the earth was; he was declared to be the Lord's Beloved in the waters of Jordan and at other times when out of the excellent glory there came the voice, 'This is my beloved Son in whom I am well pleased.' Beloved of his Father now, our Jesus sits for ever glorious at God's right hand.

Jesus is the Beloved of every angel and of all the bright seraphic spirits that crowd around the throne of his august majesty, casting their crowns before his feet, and lifting up their ceaseless hymns. They are not merely servants who obey because they must, but reverent admirers who serve because they love.

He is the Beloved of every being of pure heart and holy mind. The hosts triumphant, who have washed their robes and made them white in the blood of the Lamb, sing that word 'Beloved' with an emphasis which our colder hearts as yet have failed to reach, but still is he Beloved of the militant band this side the Jordan. Yes, Lord, with all that we have to confess of hardness and indifference, we do love thee, and thou knowest it.

> Would not our heart pour forth its blood,
> In honour of thy name,
> And challenge the cold hand of death
> To quench the immortal flame?

The adamant is softer than our hearts by nature, and yet the love we bear thee, O divine Redeemer, stimulated by the love which thou hast manifested to us, has made our soul to melt in thy presence;

> Yes, we love thee, and adore;
> O for grace to love thee more.

Note well that the sweetest word of the name is 'leaning on *her* beloved'. That Jesus is beloved is most true, but is he my Beloved? Ah, if this be true, there is a heaven wrapped up in it. Say thou who art listening to the Word this morning, is Jesus thy Beloved? Dost thou love him? Canst thou put forth the finger of thy timid faith and touch the hem of his garment, and receive the virtue which goeth out of him? Dost thou dare to say, 'He is all my salvation and all my desire. Other refuge have I none, my soul hangs in her utter helplessness entirely upon him?' Then is he thy Beloved; and the more thou canst foster the well-grounded belief that Jesus is thine, the more thou canst roll that truth under thy tongue as a sweet morsel, the happier and holier wilt thou be. Realise the fact that Jesus is as actually and truly thine as thy husband, thy wife, thy child, thy mother, or thine own self, then will peace and love reign within thy spirit.

The spouse could not have leaned on Jesus as *the* Beloved, she could only find rest in him as *her* Beloved. Till you get a sense of his being yours you do not dare to lean, but when you come to know that Christ is yours by an act of appropriating faith, then comes the after-result of faith in the consecrated repose which the soul feels in the power and love of him on whom she relies.

Thus, O pilgrim to the skies, thou art reminded that thou hast with thee a companion whose name to thee is 'my Beloved'. Pause thou awhile and look about thee! Dost thou not see him? Canst thou not perceive the marks of his presence? Then rejoice that thou art found in such company, and take care to enjoy the honours and privileges which such society secures thee.

2. We now pass on to something deeper. **We have said that the pilgrim has a dear companion, but that much of the blessedness of the text lies in HER POSTURE TOWARDS HIM**.

'Who is this that cometh up from the wilderness *leaning upon* her beloved?' Her posture then is that of 'leaning'. His relation to her is that of a divine supporter. What does this leaning mean?

Why, first of all, there can be no leaning on another unless we believe in that other's presence and nearness. A man does not lean on a staff which is not in his hand, nor on a friend of whose presence he is not aware. The instincts which lead us to preserve our uprightness would not permit us to lean on a shadow or on a nothing. It behoves thee then, Christian, if thou wouldst be like this wondrous woman in the text, to seek to be conscious of the presence of Christ. It is true thy senses cannot perceive him, but thy senses are less to be relied upon than thy faith, for senses may be mistaken, but the faith of God's elect errs not. God makes that which faith depends upon to be more real than anything which the senses can perceive. Christ Jesus is with thee; though thou hearest not his voice and seest not his face, he is with thee. Try to grasp that truth, and to realise it clearly, for thou wilt never lean until thou dost.

Leaning also implies nearness. We cannot lean on that which is far off and unapproachable. Now, it is a delightful help to us in believing repose if we can understand that Christ is not only with us, but to an intense degree near us. I love that hymn we sang just now concerning our Lord's coming nigh to us, and making his name a common word among us. The Christ of a great many professors is only fit to occupy a niche on the church wall, as a dead, inactive but revered person. Jesus is not a real Christ to many, he is not a Christ who can really befriend them in the hour of grief; not a brother born for adversity, not a condescending companion. But the Christ of the well-taught Christian is one that liveth and was dead and is alive for ever more, a sympathising, practical friend who is actually near, entering into our sorrows, sharing in our crosses, and taking a part with us in all the battle of life.

Come, child of God, see that it be thus with thee. Realise Christ first, and then believe that he is nearer to thee than friend or kinsman can be, for he pours his counsels right into thy heart; being so near that at times when thy secret trouble cannot be shared by any mortal, it is shared by him; so near that when thy heart's inmost recesses must necessarily be locked up to all other sympathy, those recesses are all open to his tenderness; so near to thee that thou livest in him, and he abides in thee, and thou abidest in him. A sacred unity exists between thee and him, so that thou dost drink of his cup, and art baptised with his baptism, and in all thy sorrows and thine afflictions he himself doth take his share.

These two things being attended unto, leaning now becomes easy. To lean implies the throwing of one's weight from one's self on to another, and this is the Christian's life. The first act that made him a Christian at all was when the whole weight of his sin was laid on Christ. When by faith the sinner ceased to carry his own burden, but laid that burden on the great Substitute's shoulder, it was that leaning which made him a Christian. In proportion as he learns this lesson of casting all his burden upon his Lord, he will be more and more a Christian; and when he shall have completely unloaded himself and cast all his matters upon his God, and shall live in the power and strength of God and not in his own, then shall he have attained to the fulness of the stature of a perfect man in Christ Jesus.

To lean, I say, is to throw your weight off from yourself on to another

– being fatigued, to make another fatigued if he can be; being wearied, to make another take your weariness, and so yourself to proceed with your load transferred to a substitute. Yes, I repeat it, this is the true Christian life – to leave every thing that troubles me with him who loves me better than I love myself; to leave all that depresses me with him whose wisdom and whose power are more than a match for all emergencies. Herein is wisdom, never to try to stand alone by my own strength, never to trust to creatures, for they will fail me if I rest upon them, but to make my ever blessed Lord Christ, in his manhood and in his Godhead, the leaning place of my whole soul, casting every burden upon him who is able to bear it. This is what I think is meant in the text by leaning.

One would imagine that there must have been of late years a society for the improvement of texts of Scripture; and if so I cannot congratulate that honourable company upon its success. This text has been a favourite object of the society's care, for I think I never heard it quoted correctly in my life. It is generally quoted, 'Who is this that cometh up from the wilderness, leaning upon *the arm of* her beloved?' But it is not so in the text at all. Here is no distinct reference to an arm at all. There is an arm here undoubtedly, but there is a great deal more – there is a whole person; and the text speaks of leaning upon the whole person of '*her beloved*'.

Observe, then, that the Christian leans upon Christ in his personality and completeness; not merely upon the arm of his strength, as that altered text would have it, but upon the whole Christ. The leaning place of a Christian is, first of all, Christ's person. We depend upon the Lord Jesus as God and as man. As God, he must be able to perform every promise and to achieve every covenant engagement. We lean upon that divinity which bears up the pillars of the universe. Our dependence is upon the Almighty God, incarnate in human form, by whom all things were created, and by whom all things consist. We lean also upon Christ as man; we depend upon his generous human sympathies. Of a woman born, he is partaker of our flesh; he enters into our sicknesses and infirmities with a pitiful compassion, which he could not have felt if he had not been the Son of man. We depend upon the love of his humanity as well as upon the potency of his deity. We lean upon our beloved as God and man. Ah! I have known times when I have felt that none but a God could bear me up; there are other seasons when, under a sense of sin, I have started back from God, and felt that none but the Man Christ Jesus could minister peace to my anguished heart. Taking Christ in the double nature as God and man, he becomes thus a suitable leaning place for our spirit, whatever may happen to be the state in which our mind is found.

Beloved, we lean upon Christ himself in all his offices. We lean upon him as priest; we expect our offerings and our praises and our prayers to be received because they are presented through him. Our leaning for acceptance is on him. We lean upon him as our prophet. We do not profess to know or to be able to discover truth of ourselves, but we sit at his feet, and what he teaches that we receive as certainty. We lean upon him as our King. He shall fight our battles for us, and manage all the affairs of our heavenly citizenship. We have no hope of victory but in the strength of him who is the Son of David and the King of kings.

We lean upon Christ in all his attributes. Sometimes it is his wisdom – in our dilemmas he directs us; at other time it is his faithfulness – in our strong temptations he abides the same. At one time his power gleams out like a golden pillar and we rest on it, and at another moment his tenderness becomes conspicuous and we lean on that.

There is not a trait of his character, there is not a mark of his person, whether human or divine, but that we feel it safe to lean upon, because he is as a whole Christ, perfection's own self, lovely and excellent beyond all description. We lean our entire weight upon HIM, not on his arm; not on any part of his person, but upon himself do we depend.

Beloved, there is no part of the pilgrimage of a saint in which he can afford to walk in any other way but in the way of leaning. He cometh up at the first, and he cometh up at the last, still leaning, still leaning upon Christ Jesus; ay, and leaning more and more heavily upon Christ the older he grows. The stronger the believer becomes, the more conscious he is of his personal weakness; and, therefore, the more fully does he cast himself upon his Lord and lean with greater force on him.

Beloved, it is a blessed thing to keep to this posture in all we do. Oh, it is good preaching when you lean on the Beloved as you preach and feel, 'He will help me, he will give me thoughts and words, he will bless the message, he will fill the hungry with good things, and make the Sabbath to be a delight to his people.' Oh, it is blessed praying when you can lean on the Beloved; you feel then that you cannot be denied; you have come into the King's court, and brought your Advocate with you, and you lay your prayer at the foot of the throne, the Prince himself putting his own sign manual and seal and stamp of love upon your desires.

This is the sweet way to endure and suffer with content. Who would not suffer when Jesus makes the bed of our sickness, and stays us up and gives us tokens of his love? This is the divine method of working. Believe me, no sacred work can long be continued with energy except in this spirit, for flesh flags, and even the spirit languishes except there be the constant leaning upon the Beloved. As for you, men of business, you with your families and with your shops and with your fields and your enterprises, you will find it poor living unless you evermore lean on your Beloved in all things. If your can bring, your daily cares, your domestic troubles, your family sicknesses, your personal infirmities, your losses and your crosses, if you can bring all things to Jesus, it will be easy and happy living. Even the furnace itself, when the coals glow most, is cool and comfortable as a royal chamber spread for banqueting with the King, when the soul reclines on the bosom of divine love.

O ye saints, strive after more of this. We are such lovers of caring for ourselves, we so want to set up on our own account; we pine to run alone while our legs are too weak; we aspire to stand alone when the only result can be a fall. Oh, to give up this wilfulness, which is our weakness, and like a babe to lie in the mother's bosom, conscious that our strength is not in ourselves, but in that dear bosom which upbears us!

I would fain encourage the heir of heaven, who is in trouble, to lean. I can encourage you from experience. The Lord has laid on me many burdens in connection with much serving in his church, and I sometimes grow very weary; but whenever I bring myself, or rather the Holy Spirit brings me to this pass, that I am clear that I cannot do anything of myself, and do not mean to try, but will just be God's obedient servant and ready instrument, and will leave every care with him – then it is that peace returns, thought becomes free and vigorous, and the soul once more having cast aside its burden, runs without weariness and walks without fainting.

I am sure, my dear fellow servants, life will break you down, this London life especially, unless you learn the habit of leaning on Jesus. Be not afraid to lean too much. There was never yet a saint blamed for possessing too much faith; there was never such a thing known as a child of God who was scolded by the Divine Father for having placed too implicit reliance upon his promise. The Lord has said, 'As thy day thy strength shall be.' He has promised, 'I will never leave thee, nor forsake thee.' He has told you that the birds of the air neither sow nor reap, nor gather into barns, and yet are fed. He has assured you that the lilies of the field toil not, neither do they spin, and yet your heavenly Father makes them more beautiful than Solomon in all his glory. Why do you not cast your care on him who cares for ravens and for flowers of the field? Why are you not assured that he will also care for you?

Thus much upon the leaning. 'Who is this that cometh up from the wilderness leaning upon her beloved?'

Our third point shall be, **HER REASONS FOR THUS LEANING**. She was a pilgrim, and she leaned on her beloved; was she justified in such leaning? For every confidence is not wise. There be refuges of lies and helpers of no value. Ahithophels are a numerous race. He that eateth bread with us doth lift up his heel against us. Friends who seemed to be strong and faithful, turn out to be as broken reeds, or as sharp spears to pierce us to our hurt. Did she well then, in leaning on her beloved? What were her reasons? She did well, and her reasons were some of them as follows.

She leaned on her beloved because *she was weak.* Strength will not lean, conscious strength scorns dependence. My soul, dost thou know anything of thy weakness? It is a sorrowful lesson to learn; but oh! it is a blessed and profitable lesson, which not only must be learned, but which it were well for thee to pray to learn more and more, for there is no leaning upon Christ except in proportion as you feel you must. I do believe that as long as we have a grain of self-sufficiency, we never trust in the All-sufficient. While there is anything of self left we prefer to feed on it, and only when at last the mouldy bread becomes too sour for eating, and even the husks that the swine do eat are such as cannot fill our belly, it is only then that we humbly ask for the bread of heaven to satisfy us. My soul, learn to hate every thought of self-sufficiency.

Brethren, do you not find yourselves tempted at times, especially if you have had a happy week and have been free from trials, to think, 'Now, really I am better than a great many. I think I am now growing to be an old experienced saint. I have now escaped the power of ordinary temptations, and have become so advanced in grace that there is no likelihood of my sinning in those directions wherein new converts show their weakness'? There is your weak point, brother. Set a double guard where you think you are strongest.

Just when you are most afraid, and say to yourself, 'O that I might be kept from such a sin – I know that is my besetment, and I am afraid I shall be led into it', you are less likely to sin there than anywhere. Your weakness is your strength, your strength is your weakness. Be nothing, for only so can you be anything. Be poor in spirit, for only so can you be rich towards God. The spouse leaned because she was weak. Brother, sister, is not this a good argument for thee? For me? Are not we also weak? Come then, let us lean wholly upon him who is not weak, but to whom all power belongeth to bear all his people safely through.

She leaned, again, on her beloved, because *the way was long.* She had been going through the wilderness. It was a long journey, and she began to flag, and therefore she leaned; and the way is long with us, we have been converted to God now some of us these twenty years, others these forty, and there are some in this house who have known the Lord more than sixty years, and this is a long time in which to be tempted and tried, for sin is mighty and flesh is weak. If one good spurt would win the race, the most of us would strain every nerve; but to tug on at the weary oar year after year when the novelty has gone, and when there comes besides another sort of novelty, fresh temptations, new allurements which we knew not of before; O soul, to win the crown by pressing on and on and on till we hear the Master's plaudit, this is no mean labour. If we can lean, we shall hold on, not else.

Faith, casting herself upon the power of her Lord, never grows exhausted.

She is like the eagle when it renews its youth. She drinks from the fountain head of all vitality, and her lost vigour comes back to her; such a soul would be strong evermore though she had to live the life of a Methuselah; myriads of years would not exhaust her, for she has learned to cast that which exhausts upon him who is inexhaustible, and therefore keeps on the even tenor of her way. She leaned because the road was long. Aged friends, here is good argument for you; and young men and maidens, who have lately set out on pilgrimage, since the way may be long to you, here also is good reason for your leaning at the beginning and leaning on to the end.

She leaned again, because *the road was perilous.* Did you notice, she came up from the *wilderness*! The wilderness is not at all a safe place for a pilgrim. Here it is that the lion prowls and the howl of the wolf is heard; but she leaned on her Beloved, and she was safe. If the sheep fears the wolf, he had better keep close to the shepherd, for then the shepherd's rod and staff will drive the wolf away. There is no safety for us except in close communion with Christ. Every step you get away from Jesus your danger doubles; and when you have lost the sense of his sacred presence, your peril is at the maximum. Come back, come back, thou wanderer, and get close to thy Great Helper, and then thou mayst laugh to scorn the fiends of hell, the temptations of life, and even the pangs of death – for he is blessedly safe who leans all on Christ.

The careful are not safe, the fretful are not safe, the anxious are not safe; they are tossed to and fro in a frail bark, upon a sea whose waves are too strong for them; but those who leave their cares to the great caring One, those who cast their anxieties upon him who never forgets, these are always safe. 'Trust in the Lord, and do good; so shalt thou dwell in the land, and verily thou shalt be fed.' 'The young lions do lack, and suffer hunger: but they that seek the Lord shall not want any good thing.' There may come a famine, notwithstanding all your industry; you may rise up weary and set up late, and eat the bread of carefulness, and yet have no prosperity; you may keep the city, and the watchman may pass along the walls each hour of the night, and yet it may be taken by assault; but blessed is he that trusteth in the Lord, for neither shall his city be destroyed, nor shall famine come to his land; or, if so it be, in famine he shall be fed, and in the days of peril the angels shall keep watch and ward about him. Lean, then, upon the Beloved, because the way is perilous. This is good reasoning for all of us for we are in danger; tempted on all sides, liable to sin for a thousand causes. O my brethren, in this age of temptation, lean on the Beloved, it is your only safety.

Again, she leaned on the Beloved because *her route was ascending*. Did you notice it? 'Coming up.' The Christian's way is up – never content with past attainments, but up; not satisfied with graces to which he has reached, but up. He is not good who does not desire to be better; he is not gracious who would not be more gracious. Thou knowest not the light if thou dost not desire more light. The heavenly way is upward, upward, upward, upward! This is the way to heaven.

The tendency of man's nature is downward. How soon we descend, and how prone is our soul, from her most elevated condition, to sink back into the dull dead level of her natural estate! If we are to go up, we must lean. Christ is higher than we are; if we lean, we shall rise the more readily to his elevation. He comes down to us that we, leaning upon him, may go up to him. The more we lean, the more truly we cast the weight of our spiritual wrestling, spiritual struggling, spiritual growth, upon him, the more surely shall we gain the wrestling, the struggling, and the growth.

Depend as much for growth in grace upon Christ as for the pardon of sin. He is made of God unto you sanctification as well as redemption. Look for sanctification through the blood, for it is a purifier as well as a pardoner. The same blood which puts away the guilt of sin is by the Holy Ghost applied as a blood of sprinkling to put away from us the reigning power of sin. O that we knew more about this, this going up! But I am afraid we do not go up because we do not lean.

If there be here this morning a poor child of God who cries, 'I the chief of sinners am, and my only hope is in my blessed Lord; I do not feel that I grow in the least. I sometimes think I get worse and worse; but one thing I do know, I trust him more than ever I did, and feel my need of him more.' Dear heart, you are the very one who is going up. I know you are, for you are leaning. But if there be another who boasts, 'I believe I have made distinct advances in the divine life, and I feel that I am growing strong and vigorous, and I believe that one of these days I shall have reached to perfection,' I think it is very likely that this brother is going down; at any rate, I would recommend to him this prayer: 'Hold thou me up, and I shall be safe;' and this caution, 'Let him that thinketh he standeth take heed lest he fall.'

Yet I must detain you another moment, to observe that the spouse leaned on her beloved because *her walk was daily separating her more and more from the whole host of her other companions.* The church is in the wilderness, but this traveller was coming up from the wilderness. She was getting away from the band marching through the desert, getting more and more alone. It is so, and you will find it so; the nearer you get to Christ, the more lonely you must necessarily be in certain respects. The sinner is in the broad way, where thousands walk, the Christian is in the narrow way – there are fewer in this last; but if the believer keeps the centre of the narrow way, and if he presses on with vigour, he will find his companions to be fewer and fewer; I mean the companions of his own stature, those of his own size and his own attainments; and if he continues in rapid advances, he will at last get to such a position that he will see no man save Jesus only, and then he will be sure to lean more heavily than ever, since he will have discovered that all men are vanity, and all confidences in an arm of flesh are but lies and deceit.

The spouse leaned upon her beloved because *she felt sure that he was strong enough to bear her weight.* He upon whom she leaned was no other than God over all blessed for ever, who cannot fail nor be discouraged. She leaned yet again *because he was her beloved.* She would have felt it unwise to lean if he were not mighty; she would have been afraid to lean if he had not been dear to her. So is it, the more you love the more you trust, and the more you trust the more you love. These twin graces of faith and hope live and flourish together. In proportion as that dear crucified Saviour reigns in your soul, and his beauties ravish your heart, in that proportion you feel that all is safe because it is in his hands; and then, on the other hand, in proportion as you trust all to him, and have not a suspicion or a doubt, in that proportion your soul will be knit to him in affection.

I appeal to any here who are the servants of Christ, but have fallen out of the habit of leaning, whether it would not be well to return to it. Was not it better with you when you did lean than it is now? Before you set up for yourselves, were you not happier and better than now? Before you let that wicked pride of yours get the upper hand, you were wont to take every daily trouble and burden to your Lord, but at last you thought you were wise enough to manage for yourselves; I ask you, have you not from that very day met with many sorrows and defeats and downcastings? And there is this pang about all untrustful living, if a man getteth into any troubles through his own wisdom, then he has to blame himself for it; but if any trial cometh upon us direct from God, then we feel we cannot blame ourselves, it belongs to our God to do as he wills; and since he cannot err, we expect that he will justify his own proceedings. It is better to trust in the Lord than to put confidence in man; it is better to trust in the Lord than to put confidence in princes. Wait ye only upon God, and let your expectations be from him, and he shall bring forth your judgment as the light, and your righteousness as the noonday; and in the day when the wicked shall be confounded, and they that trusted in themselves shall be melted away as the fat of rams, you shall shine forth as the sun in the kingdom of your Father.

4. And now let us close. **The last point is this: THE PERSON AND THE PEDIGREE of her who leaned upon her beloved**.

The text says, 'Who is this?' What made them enquire, 'Who is this?' It was because they were so astonished to see her looking so happy and so little wearied. Nothing amazes worldlings more than genuine Christian joy. Holy peace in disturbing times is a puzzle to the ungodly. When they hear the righteous sing, 'God is our refuge and strength, a very present help in trouble; therefore will not we fear, though the earth be removed, and though the mountains be carried into the midst of the sea,' they say one to another, 'Where did these men learn that tune? They are men of like passions with ourselves, how is it they have learned thus to bear trials?' Therefore they enquire, 'Who is this? Who is this?' How fine a thing it would be if we all so leaned upon Christ in all respects as to enjoy unbroken serenity, so that our kinsfolk and neighbours should be led to enquire, 'Who is this?' for then might we have an opportunity of telling them concerning our Well-beloved, who is the stay of our peace and the source of our comfort.

Who then is this that leans on her beloved? I will tell you. Her name was once called 'outcast,' whom no man seeketh after, but according to this old book her name is now Hephzibah, for the Lord delighteth in her. The name of the soul that trusts in God, and finds peace in so doing, was by nature a name of shame and sin. We were afar off from God even as others; and if any soul is brought to trust in Christ, it is not from any natural goodness in it, or any innate propensity towards such trusting; it is because grace has wrought a wondrous transformation, and God the Holy Ghost has made those who were not a people to be called the people of God.

Good news this for any of you who feel your guilt this morning. You have been hitherto serving Satan, but mercy can yet bring you to lean upon the Beloved; grace can bring you up from the wilderness instead of permitting you to go down into the pit.

She who today joyously trusts in her God was once a weeping Hannah, a woman of a sorrowful spirit, but now her soul rejoiceth in the Lord, for he hath remembered her low estate.

She was once a sinful Rahab, dwelling in a city doomed to destruction, but she has hung the scarlet line of faith in the precious blood in her window; and if all others perish, she shall be secure in the day of destruction.

She who is here spoken of as a Ruth. She came from afar as an idolatress; she left the land of her nativity, and she hath entered into union with the Lord and his people. Her cry is, 'Where thou dwellest I will dwell. Thy people shall be my people, thy God shall be my God.' She was once a stranger, but she is now an Israelite indeed; she was once accursed, but she is now blessed; once foul, but now washed; once lost, but now found again.

In a word, the soul that leans upon Christ habitually every day and casts her care upon him is one of a princely race; she has been begotten into the family of God; the blood imperial flows within her veins, and in the day when the crowns of princes and of emperors shall melt into the common dust to which they belong, the crown jewels and the diadems of these believing souls shall glitter with immortal splendour in the kingdom of God.

My dear hearer, dost thou trust Jesus? Does the Holy Spirit move thee to begin to trust him today? If so, though thy journey be in a wilderness of trouble, thou shalt come up out of it to a paradise of bliss, and thy peace and thy comfort shall all spring from leaning on the Well-beloved.

The Lord bless us, and teach us that sacred art of dependence on the Beloved for Christ's sake. Amen.

49

THE SHULAMITE'S CHOICE PRAYER

'Set me as a seal upon thine heart, as a seal upon thine arm: for love is strong as death; jealousy is cruel as the grave: the coals thereof are coals of fire, which hath a most vehement flame. Many waters cannot quench love, neither can the floods drown it' (Song of Solomon 8: 6, 7).

This is the prayer of one who hath the present enjoyment of fellowship with Christ, but being apprehensive lest this communion should be interrupted, she avails herself of the opportunity now afforded her to plead for a something which shall be as the abiding token of a covenant between her and her beloved, when his visible presence shall be withdrawn. You will notice that this is not the cry of a soul that is longing for fellowship, for that cry is: 'Tell me, O thou whom my soul loveth, where thou feedest.' It is not even the cry of the soul that has some fellowship and needs more, for then it would say, 'Oh that thou wert as my brother!' Nor is it the cry of a soul that has had fellowship but has lost it, for that is, 'Saw ye him, whom my soul loveth?' And she goes 'about the streets and in the broad ways', saying, 'I will seek him.' But this is the prayer of the spouse when she has been coming up from the wilderness, leaning upon his bosom. The thought strikes her, that he that has sustained her is about to go from her, to depart and leave her for a season, because it is expedient and more useful for her, and she prays that since he is no more in the earth, but has entered into the ivory palaces where her God dwelleth, that he would be pleased to make a covenant with her never to forget her, and that he would give here some sign and mark by which she might be well assured that she is very near to his heart, and still written upon his arm.

I take it to be the prayer of the Church at the present day, now that Christ is before the Father's throne. The Bridegroom is not with us; he has left us, he has gone to prepare a place for us, and he is coming again. We are longing for his coming; we are saying in the language of the last verse of this song of songs: 'Make haste, my beloved, and be thou like to a roe or to a young hart upon the mountains of spices.' Yet ere he went, it seemed as if his Church did pray unto him: 'Set me as a seal upon thine heart, as a seal upon thine arm.' And this is the cry of the Church tonight, and I trust your cry too, that while he is not present but is absent from you, you may be near to him, and have a sweet consciousness of that blessed fact.

Now without further preface, let me first notice, the prayer, and secondly, the *reasoning with which the spouse argueth her suit*. The prayer is, 'Set me as a seal upon thine heart, as a seal upon thine arm.' The argument is four-fold she pleadeth thus, 'Love is strong as death'; she waxeth bolder – 'Jealousy is cruel as the grave'; she wrestles again – 'The coals thereof are coals of fire, which hath a most vehement flame'; and once again she bringeth forth her choice words: 'Set me as a seal upon thine heart, for many waters cannot quench thy love, neither can the floods drown it.'

1. THE PRAYER, you will notice, is two-fold, although it is so really and essentially one: 'Set me as a seal upon thine heart, as a seal upon thine arm.'

Now I think I can perhaps explain this text best by a reference to the high priest of old. You know that when he put on his holy garments – those robes of glory and beauty – he wore the breastplate of cunning work in which four rows of precious stones were set. If you will turn to Exodus 39:14, you read, 'And the stones were according to the names of the children of Israel, twelve, according to their names, like the engravings of a signet, every one with his name, according to the twelve tribes.' How suggestive of this prayer! 'Set me as a seal or as an engraved signet, as a precious stone that has been carved – set my name upon thy breast.' Let it be always glittering there.

But beside this breastplate, there was the ephod, and we are told that 'they made shoulder pieces for it, to couple it together, by the two edges was it coupled together.' Then in the sixth verse we read: 'And they wrought onyx stones inclosed in ouches of gold, graven, as signets are graven, with the names of the children of Israel; and he put them on the shoulders of the ephod, that they should be stones for a memorial to the children of Israel; so the Lord commanded Moses.' So that it was set as a signet upon his shoulder, or upon his arm, as well as upon his heart. I think these were to indicate that the high priest loved the people, for he bore them on his heart; and that he served the people as a consequence of that love, therefore he bore them upon his shoulders.

And I think the prayer of the spouse is just this: she would know once for all that Christ's heart is entirely hers, that he loves her with the intensity and the very vitality of his being, that his inmost heart, the life-spring of his soul belongs to her. And she would also know that that love moves his arm. She longs to see herself as supported, sustained, strengthened, defended, preserved and kept by that same strong arm which put Orion in its place in the sky, and holds the Pleiades that they should give their light for evermore. She longeth that she may know the love of his heart, and that she may experience the power of his arm.

Can we not, each of us, join the spouse in this prayer to night? Oh! Lord, let me know that my name is engraved on thy heart; not only let it be there, but let me know it. Write my name not only in thy heart, but may it be as a signet on thy heart that I may see it. Doubtless there are the names of very many written upon Christ's heart, who have not yet been able to see their names there; they are there, but not written as on a signet. Christ has loved them from all eternity; his heart has been set on them from everlasting, but as yet they have never seen the signet. They have never had the seal of the Spirit to witness within that they are born of God. While their names may be in his heart, they have not seen them there as a seal upon his heart.

And no doubt there are multitudes for whom Christ has fought and conquered, and whom he daily keeps and preserves, who have never seen their names written as a seal upon his arm. Their prayer is that they may see Christ's love visibly, that they may discover it in their experience, that it may be beyond a question, and no more a matter of doubt, that his hand and his heart are engaged for their eternal salvation. I repeat it, ye can all join in this prayer, ye people of God; it is a cry that you would put up now, and continue to put up till it is fully answered. Oh! let me know, my Lord, that I am thine, bound to thine heart; and let me know that I am thine, protected and preserved by thine arm. This is the prayer; I shall not say more upon it, because I wish to speak more at length upon the arguments with which it is here pleaded.

2. The spouse argues with her Lord thus. It is to my advantage that thou shouldst thus write my name upon thine hand and heart, for I know this concerning thy love, that it is strong, that it is firm; that it has a wondrous intensity; and that it has a sure and unquenchable eternity. With these four pleas she backeth up her suit.

(1) She pleadeth that he would show her his love, because of *the strength of it*. 'Thy love is strong as death.' Some expositors think that this means the Church's love; others say, 'No, it means the love of Christ to his Church.' I am not careful to determine which it meaneth, for they are extremely like each other. Christ's love to his Church is the magnificent image, the affection which his people bear to him is the beautiful miniature. They are not alike in degree and measure, for the Church never loveth Christ so much as Christ loveth her; but they are as much alike as the father in his strength is to the babe in weakness; there is the same image and superscription. The love of the Church to Christ is the child of Christ's love to the Church, and consequently there is something of the same attribute in both, and while it is true that Christ's love to us is so strong that he did defy and endure death for us, it is true also that the love of the Church to him is as

strong as death. Her chosen sons and daughters have endured the pangs of the rack and the pains of the sword, and have gone through a thousand deaths sooner than be turned aside from their chaste fidelity to their Lord.

I shall, however, keep to the first idea, that this is the love of Christ, and shall use it thus, as being the plea of his Church, that because his love is strong she desires to be certified of her interest in it, and to see most visibly the signet and seal of her being really in his heart. 'Love is strong as death.' What a well-chosen emblem this is! What beside love is so strong as death?

With steadfast foot death marches over the world. No mountains can restrain the invasion of this all-conquering king. There is no chalet on the mountain Alp so high that his foot cannot climb to hunt the inhabitant. There is no valley so fair that he doth not intrude and stalk, a grim skeleton across the plain. Everywhere and in every place beneath the moon hast thou sway, O death! The lordly lion bows his neck to thee. Leviathan yields up his corpse which floateth many a rood upon the briny waves. Thou art the great fisher. Thou hast put thy hook into his jaw and dragged him from the sea. Master of all thou art! Thou hast dominion given unto thee. Thou wearest an iron crown, and thou dashest in pieces as though they were but potter's vessels the strongest of the sons of men. None among the sons of Adam can withstand death's insidious advances. When his hour is come, none can bid him delay. The most clamorous prayers cannot move the flinty bowels of death. Insatiable, and not to be appeased, he devoureth and devoureth ever. That scythe is never blunted; that hour-glass never ceases to flow. Mightiest among the mighty art thou, O Death.

But Christ's love is strong as death. It too can climb the mountain and lay hold upon the mountaineer, far removed from the sound of the ministration of the gospel. It too can march into the valley, and though Popery with all its clouds of darkness should cover it, yet the love of Christ can win its glorious way. What can stand against it? The stoutest must yield to it, and adamantine hearts are dashed to shivers by one blow of its golden hammer. As the sun dissolves the chains of frost and bids the rill rush on in freedom, though once bound as if it were stone, so doth this love of Christ wherever it cometh, give life and joy and liberty, snap the bonds and win its way, never being retarded, never being hindered, because it is written 'I will have mercy on whom I will have mercy, and I will have compassion on whom I will have compassion.'

Who can measure the strength of Christ's love? Men have defied it, but their defiance hath been overcome. They have resisted long, but they have been compelled to throw down their weapons; they have crossed it but they have found it hard to kick against the pricks. They have gone on caring for none of these things, but thus the eternal counsel has decreed it – Christ must, he shall have that redeemed man, and he has had him.

Jesus Christ's love is strong as death. Sooner might a man live, after God's will had decreed that he should die, than a sinner remain impenitent one hour after God's love had decreed to melt his heart. Sooner might ye defy the grave and hurl back upon his haunches the pale horse of Death, than turn back the Holy Spirit when he cometh in his divine omnipotence to lay hold upon the heart and soul of man. As all the owls and bats with all their hootings could not scare back the sun when once its hour to rise has come, so all the sins and fears and troubles of man cannot turn back the light of love when God decrees that it should shine upon the heart; stronger than death his love is found.

Death is but weakness itself when compared with the love of Christ. What a sweet reason why I should have a share in it! What a blessed argument for me to use before the throne of God! Lord, if thy love be so strong, and my heart be so hard, and myself so powerless to break it, oh! let me know thy love, that it may overcome me, that it may enchain me with its sure but soft fetters, and that I may be thy willing captive evermore.

But let me notice here that when the spouse says that Christ's love is strong as death, you must remember that she may in faith have foreseen that it would one day be tried which was the strongest. You know, do you not, that these two once entered into the lists to try their strength; and it was a struggle, sure, upon which angels gazed. Jesus – I mean incarnate love – he first seemed to shrink before death: 'He sweat as it were, great drops of blood falling to the ground.' Ye cannot see the brow of his antagonist, but could ye have perceived it, Death – the invaded – was trembling more than Christ, the invader. Christ had the prophecy of victory, but Death – the fates were against it. Well do you remember that story of how the Saviour's back was ploughed, his hands pierced, and his side opened? Death – methinks I see the flush that crossed his pale face as he thought that he had gained the victory, but Jesus triumphed. Love reigned while Death lays prostrate at his feet.

Strong as Death indeed was Jesus' love, for Jesus swallowed up Death in victory, not merely overcame it, but seemed to devour it, to make nothing of it, and put it away once for all. 'O Death' said Love, 'I will be thy plague! O grave, I will be thy destruction!' And Love has kept its word, and proved itself to be 'strong as Death'.

Well, beloved, we may add to these few remarks this word. Rest assured that as Death will not give up its prey, so neither will Love. How hard and firm doth Death hold its captives! Till that resurrection trump shall make him loose their bonds none shall go free. Their ashes he preserves as carefully as a king keeps the jewels of his crown. He will not suffer one of them to escape as did Israel out of the land of Pharaoh. In the house of bondage, there they must lie. And is not Christ's love as strong as this? He shall keep his own. Those who are his he never will let go. Nay, when the archangel's trump shall dissolve the grasp of death, then shall be heard the cry: 'Father, I will that they also whom thou hast given me be with me where I am.' And when Death itself is dead, Love shall prove its eternal strength by taking its captives home.

Love, then, is strong as Death. Lord Jesus, let me feel that love; let me see thine arm nerved with it, and thine heart affected by this strong love which all my enemies cannot defeat, which all my sins cannot overturn, which all my weakness cannot gainsay. I think this is a most sweet and powerful argument to lead you to pray the prayer, and one which you will use when you are pleading before God.

(2) Let us now turn to the second plea: 'Jealousy is cruel as the grave.' Krummacher, in a sermon upon this passage, following the translation of Luther, quotes it as though it ran thus: 'Jealousy is firm as hell'; and I believe that such is the proper translation, at least quite as correct as the present one. 'Jealousy is firm as hell.' Those of you who have Bibles with the margins in them (and the margins are generally like fine gold) will perceive the words in the corner, 'Hebrew, hard' – 'Jealousy is hard as the grave', which is just the idea of firmness, it is as firm as the grave. *Sheol*, I believe the word is here for grave; otherwise we translate it 'Hades' – the place of separate souls, without reference to good or evil – or as Luther translates it – 'hell'. 'Jealousy is hard as hell.'

The idea is just this: that the love of Christ in the form of jealousy is as hard and as sternly relentless as is the grave and hell. Now hell never looses one of its bondslaves. Once let the iron gate be shut upon the soul and there is no escape. When the ring of fire has once girdled the immortal spirit, none can dash through the flaming battlements. The dungeon is locked. The key is dashed into the abyss of destiny and never can be found.

Fixed is their everlasting state,
could they repent 'tis now too late.

'Escape for thy life, look not behind thee' is a cry which may be uttered on earth, but which can never be heard in hell. They who are once there, are there for ever and for ever. That modern doctrine of the restoration of damned souls hath no foundation in the Word of God. It is a dream and they shall find it so who once come into that place. 'Where their worm dieth not, and where their fire is not quenched' – a more perfect picture of an unrelenting seizure could not be found anywhere. The flrmness and hardness of the grave and hell are without abatement. When once they have got their hands upon their prey they hold it with a tenacity which defies resistance.

Well, but such is the love of Christ. If just now we had to speak of its strength, we have now to speak of its tenacity, its hardness, its attachment to those whom it has chosen. You may sooner unlock Hades and let loose the spirits that are in prison there, than ye could ever snatch one from the right hand of Christ. Ye may sooner rob death of its prey, than Jesus of his purchased ones. Ye may spoil the lion's den, but shall the lion of the tribe of Judah be spoiled? Shall the prey be taken from the mighty, and the lawful captive delivered? Ere one child of God shall be lost, ye shall go first and make death relax his grasp, and then next ye shall make hell with all its fury give up its prey. As soon as ever it can be proved that one child of God perishes, it can be proved that the fires of hell can be put out; but until then, there shall never be shadow of a fear of that. As certainly as ever lost souls are lost, so certainly believing souls are saved.

Oh! little do they know the love of Christ who think that he loves today, and hates tomorrow. He is no such lover as that. Even earthly worms would despise such affection. Is Christ's affection a play of fast and loose? Doth he choose and then refuse, doth he justify and then condemn? Doth he press to his bosom and afterwards reject with distaste? It is not so. If ye have seen Niagara in its tremendous strength, leaping from its rock into the depth beneath, ye might conceive some hand bidding it leap back, or staying it in its mid-current. Some mighty imagination might conceive that stream changed in its course, and made to ascend and climb the hills, instead of leaping downwards in its strength; but even then, no imagination can conceive the love of Christ retracing its eternal pathway. The divine fury which is in it, drives it on, and on it must go as it has begun.

The love of Christ is like an arrow which has been shot from the bow of destiny; it flies, it flies, and heaven itself cannot change its course. Christ has decreed it, such men shall be his, and his they shall be, nor will he turn away one of them, or make a new election, or plan a new redemption, or bring those to heaven whom he never intended to bring, or lose those whom he ordained to save. He hath said, and he will do it. He hath commanded his covenant for ever, and it shall stand fast. He will have compassion on whom he will have compassion, and he will have mercy on whom he will have mercy.

You have then, here, another reason why you should pray that your name may be upon Christ's heart, and upon his arm – once there it is there for ever. So surely there, so jealously there, so hardly there, so fixedly there, that it can never be removed come what may. Christ is jealous of his people, he will not let another have his spouse. He will not sit still and see the prince of darkness walking off with her whom he spoused unto himself in the eternal ages. The supposition is absurd. That cruel jealousy of his would make him start up from his heavenly repose, to snatch his chosen spouse from him who would seek to lead her to the hellish altar. She shall not be divorced from him; she must not be married to another.

> Stronger his love than death or hell,
> Its riches are unsearchable;
> The firstborn sons of light
> Desire in vain its depths to see,
> They cannot reach the mystery,
> The length, the breadth, the height.

(3) If the love of Christ is strong as death; if it be such that it can never be moved from its object, yet the question arises, May not the love itself die out? Even should it abide the same in its purpose, yet may not its intensity be diminished? 'No,' says the Shulamite, 'it is an attribute of Christ's love that the coals thereof are coals of fire which hath a most vehement flame.' More forcible is the language of the original – 'The coals thereof are the coals of God' – a Hebrew idiom to express the most glowing of all flames; 'the coals of God' as though it were no earthly flame, but something far superior to the most vehement affection among men.

Some who look carefully at it, think there is an allusion in this sentence to the fire which always burnt at the altar, and which never went out. You remember there were coals of fire which were always kept burning under the Levitical dispensation. The flame was originally kindled by fire from heaven and it was the business of the priest perpetually to feed it with the sacred fuel. You will remember too, that one of the cherubims flew and took a live coal from off this very altar, and said to Isaiah, 'Lo, this hath touched thy lips.' Now, the love of Christ is like the coals upon the altar which never went out.

But the spouse has brought out a fuller idea than this. She seems to say, 'Its vehemence never decreases, it is always burning to its utmost intensity.' Nebuchadnezzar's furnace was heated seven times hotter, but no doubt it grew cool, Christ's love is like the furnace, but it is always at the seven-fold heat, and it always has within itself its own fuel. It is not like fire merely, but like coals of fire, always having that within itself which supports it. Why did Christ love the spouse? What lit the fire at first? He kindled it himself. There was no reason whatever why Christ should love any of us, except the love of his own bowels. And what is the fuel that feeds the fire? Your works and mine? No brethren, no, no, a thousand times no; all the fuel comes from the same place; it is all from his bowels. Now, if the flame of Christ's love depended upon anything we did, if it were fed with our fuel, it would either die out, or else it would sometimes dwindle as the smoking flax, and then again it might kindle to a vehement heat. But since it dependeth on itself, and hath the pure attributes of divinity, it is a self-existent love, absolute and independent of the creature. Well, then, may we understand that it never shall grow less but always be as a vehement flame.

Now I do not want to preach about this, but I wish you would think of it a little. Christian, turn it over in your mind. Christ loveth you, not a little, not a little as a man may love his friend, not even as a mother may love her child for she may forget the infant of her womb. He loves you with the highest degree of love that is possible, and what more can I say, except I add, he loves you with a degree of love that is utterly impossible to man. No finite mind could, if it should seek to measure it, get any idea whatever of the love of Christ towards us. You know, when we come to measure a drop with an ocean, there is a comparison. A comparison I say there is, though we should hardly be able to get at it. But when you attempt to measure our love with Christ's, the finite with the infinite, there is no comparison at all. Though we loved Christ ten thousand times as well as we do, there would even then be no comparison between our love to him and his love to us. Can you believe this now – 'Jesus loves me?' Why to be loved by others here often brings the tear to one's eye. It is sweet to have the affection of one's fellow; but to be loved of God, and to be loved to an intense degree – so loved that you have to leave it as a mystery the soul cannot fathom – you cannot tell how much! Be silent, O my soul! and be ye silent too before your God, and lift up your soul in prayer thus: 'Jesus, take me into this sea of love, and let me be ravished by a sweet and heavenly contentment in a sure confidence that thou hast loved me and given thyself for me.'

(4) We shall now turn to the last argument of this choice prayer, which is equally precious. It is *the unquenchable eternity of this love*. There is that in its very essence which defies any opposite quality to extinguish it. The argument seems to me to run thus: 'Yes, but if Christ's love do not die out of itself, if it have such intensity that it never would of itself fail, yet may not you and I put it out? No, says the text, 'Many waters cannot quench love, neither can the floods drown it.' Christ has endured many waters already – the waters of bodily affliction, the waters of soul travail, the waters of spiritual desertion. Christ was in this world like Noah's ark; the depths came up from beneath; hell troubled him; the great water-floods came from above; it pleased the Father to bruise him. The cataracts leaped on him from either side, he was betrayed by his friends, he was hunted by his foes. But the many waters could no more destroy his love than it could drown the ark of gopher wood. Just as that ark mounted higher and higher and higher, the more the floods prevailed; so then that love of Christ seemed to rise higher and higher and higher, just in proportion to the floods of agony which sought to put it out.

Fixed and resolved to bring his ransomed home, the captain of our salvation becomes perfect through suffering, plunges into the thick of the battle, and cometh out of it more than conqueror. And oh! since then, my beloved, what floods has Christ's love endured! There have been the floods of our sins, the many waters of our blasphemy and ungodliness. Since conversion, there have been the many waters of our backslidings, and the floods of our unbelief. What crime on crime, what transgression on transgression have we been guilty of. Yet he hath never failed us up to this moment. 'By the grace of God we are what we are. And we are persuaded that neither life, nor death, nor things present, nor things to come, nor angels, nor principalities, nor powers, nor height, nor depth, nor any other creature shall be able to separate us from the love of God which is in Christ Jesus our Lord.'

What if we should be tried in circumstances? 'Neither famine, nor persecution, nor nakedness, nor peril, nor sword, shall separate from the love of Christ.' What if we backslide and wander from his ways? 'Though we believe not, he abideth faithful.' And what if in the last black hour we should have bitter sufferings on the dying bed? Still he shall be with us in the last moment, for it is written: 'The last enemy that shall be destroyed is Death.' So you see he is to be destroyed, and we are to be victors over him. Gather up then all the thoughts of how we have tried and how we shall try the Master, and let us set to our seal tonight our own solemn 'Yea and Amen' to this most precious declaration of the Shulamite. 'Many waters cannot quench love neither can the floods drown it.' Then, Lord, write my name on thy heart; engrave my name as a signet on thy arm that I may have a share in this unfailing and undying affection, and be thine now, and thine for ever.

Poor sinner! I know thou hast been saying while I have been preaching thus: 'I wish I had a share in that love.' Well, this prayer you may pray tonight: 'Set me – it is a black name – set me as a seal upon thine heart, as a seal upon thine arm. Love me, Lord. Help me, Lord. Let thy heart move towards me; let thine arm move for me too. Think of me, Lord; set me on thy heart. Work for me, Lord. Set me on thine arm. Lord, I long to have thy love, for I hear it is strong as death, and thou knowest I am chained by Satan, and am his bondslave. Come and deliver me: thou art more than a match for my cruel tyrant. Come with thy strong love and set me free. I hear that thy love is firm too as hell itself. Lord, that is such a love as I want. Though I know I shall vex thee and wander from thee, come and love me with a love that is firm and everlasting. O Lord, I feel there is nothing in me that can make thee love me. Come and love me, then, with that love which finds its own fuel. Love me with those coals of fire which have a vehement flame.'

And since many waters cannot quench thy love, prove that in me, for there are many waters of sin in me; but Lord, help me to believe that thy love is not quenched by them; there are many corruptions in me, but, Lord, love me with that love which my corruptions cannot quench. Here, Lord, I give myself away; take me; make me what thou wouldst have me to be, and keep and preserve me even to the end.'

May the Lord help you to pray that prayer, and then may he answer it for his mercy's sake.

50

UNPURCHASABLE LOVE

'If a man would give all the substance of his house for love,
it would utterly be contemned' (Song of Solomon 8:7).

That is a general truth, applying to all forms of real love; you cannot purchase love. If it is true love, it will not run on rails of gold. Many a marriage would have been a very happy one if there had been a tithe as much love as there was wealth; and, sometimes, love will come in at the cottage door and make the home bright and blest, when it refuses to recline on the downy pillows of the palace. Men may give all the substance of their house and form a marriage bond; the bond may be there, but not that which will make it sweet to wear. 'If a man would give all the substance of his house for love, it would utterly be contemned.'

Who, for instance, could purchase a mother's love? She loves her own child specially because it is her own; she watches over it with sedulous care, she denies her eyes the necessary sleep at night if her babe be sick, and she would be ready to part with her own life sooner than it should die. Bring her another person's child, and endow her with wealth to induce her to love it; and you shall find that it is not in her power to transfer her affection to the son or daughter of a stranger. Her own child is exceedingly precious to her, and another infant, that to an unprejudiced eye might be thought to be a far more comely babe, shall receive tenderness from her, for the woman is compassionate; but it can never receive the love that belongs to her own offspring.

Take, again, even the love of friends; I only instance that just to show how true our text is in relation to all forms of love. Damon loved Pythias; the two friends were so bound together that their names became household words, and their conduct towards one another grew into a proverb. Yet Damon never purchased the heart of Pythias, neither did Pythias think to pay a yearly stipend for the love of Damon. The introduction of the question of cost would have spoilt it all; the very thought of anything mercenary, anything like payment on the one side or receipt upon the other, would have been a death-blow to their friendship. No; if a man should give all the substance of his house even for human love, for the common love that exists between man and man, it would utterly be contemned.

Rest assured that this is pre-eminently true when we get into higher regions, when we come to think of the love of Jesus, and when we think of that love which springs up in the human breast towards Jesus when the Spirit of God has renewed the heart, and shed abroad the love of God within the soul. Neither Christ's love to us nor our love to him can be purchased; neither of these could be bartered for gold or rubies or diamonds or the most precious crystal. If a man should offer to give all the substance of his house for either of these forms of love, it would utterly be contemned.

We will begin at the highest manifestation of love, and commune together upon it. So let me say, first, **that THE LOVE OF OUR LORD JESUS CHRIST IS ALTOGETHER UNPURCHASABLE.** This fact will be clear to us if we give it a moment's careful thought. Indeed, so clear is it that I scarcely like to multiply words upon it, and I do so only that you may dive the deeper into this glorious truth.

It must be quite impossible to purchase the love of Christ, because it *is inconceivable that he ever could be mercenary.* It would be profane, surely, it would amount to blasphemy, and a very high degree of it, to suppose that the love of his heart could be bought with gold or silver or earthly stores. No, if he loves, it must be all free, like his own royal self. If he deigns to cast his eyes so far downward as to view the creatures of an hour, and to set his love upon them so that his delights are with the sons of men, it is not possible that he could gain aught from them. Nay, were we angels, we could not think that he could love us because of some service we could render, or some price we could pay to him. The bare idea runs cross and counter to all we know of Jesus; it is a flat contradiction of all our beliefs and all our knowledge concerning him.

He loves us because he pities us, but not because there is a fee when he comes to us as the great Physician. He instructs us because he grieves over our ignorance, and because he knows the sorrow of it, and would have us learn of him; but his instructions are not given in order that we may each one bring our school pence to him. He labours, it is true; but none shall say that he labours for hire; though if he asked all worlds for his hire, he might well claim them for such labours as those which he has performed. The feats attributed to Hercules are nothing compared with the wonders wrought by Christ. He has cleansed stables far more filthy than the Augean, and slain monsters far more terrible than the hydra-headed demons of the ancient fables. True, 'he *shall* see of the travail of his soul, and *shall* be satisfied'; there was a joy that was set before him, for which he endured the cross, despising the shame; yet the love that lay at the bottom of it all was love unbought, and love unsought, and love in which not so much as a single atom of anything like selfishness could ever be discovered. The pure stream of his love laps like the crystal rill, and there is no sediment that can be found in it; it is altogether unmixed love to us.

Besides, brethren, there is another point that renders this idea of purchasing Christ's love as impossible as the first thought shows it to be incredible; for *all things are already Christ's.* Therefore, what can be given to him wherewith his love could be purchased? If he were poor, we might enrich him; but all things are his. 'He *was* rich,' says the apostle; 'he is rich,' we also may reply. He could say to us, at this moment, if we were so foolish as to attempt to bribe him to win the love of his heart, 'I will take no bullock out of thy house, nor he-goats out of thy folds. For every beast of the forest is mine, and the cattle upon a thousand hills. I know all the fowls of the mountain: and the wild beasts of the field are mine. If I were hungry, I would not tell thee: for the world is mine, and the fulness thereof.' All things are Christ's, not only on this speck of a world, but throughout the universe.

The things that are seen by us are as nothing compared with the things that we have not seen; yet all belong to Christ, and he has the power to create ten thousand times more than ever yet have been formed by him. There is nothing which he conceives in his infinite mind but he could at once fashion it by his almighty power; there is nothing he might desire but he could in an instant command it to appear before him. 'Let it be,' he might say, and it would be even as he had said. Wherewith, then, could you bribe him, and where is the substance of your houses that you would give in exchange for his divine love? O ye who dwell in houses of clay, where is the substance which you could bring to him who is Lord of heaven and earth? Our substance? It is but a shadow. Our wealth? It is a child's plaything in his sight; it is nought compared with his boundless riches.

Let us also note that, if Christ's love could be won by us by something we could bring to him or do for him, it would suppose that there was something of ours that was of equal merit and of equal value with his love; or, at any rate, *something which he was willing to accept as bearing some proportion to his love.* But, indeed, there is nothing of the sort. Gold and silver – I scarcely like to mention them in the same connection with the love of Christ. I am sure our poet was right when he said:

> Jewels to thee are gaudy toys,
> And gold is sordid dust.

Think of the difference between gold and the love of Christ in the hour of pain, in the hour of depression of spirit; what can the strong boxes of the merchant do for us then? But one drop of the love of Christ helps us to bear up, however fast the heart may palpitate, or however much the spirits may have been cast down. What is the use of earthly riches when one comes to die? One laid his money bags close to his heart to see if they could make a plaster that would give him rest, but they were hard and cold; but the love of Jesus, like the touch of the king's hand in the old superstition, healeth even the disease of death itself, and makes it no longer death to die. There is nothing, then, by way of treasure that could be compared with the love of Christ; I will say it, and every believer here will agree with me, that there is no emotion we have ever felt in our most sanctified moments, there is no holy desire that has ever flashed through our soul in our most hallowed times, there is no seraphic longing that has ever been begotten in us when the Spirit of God has been most operative in our hearts, that we should dare to put side by side with the love of Christ and say that it was at all fit to be reckoned as a fair price for it. Our best is not one-thousandth part as good as Christ's worst. Our gold is not equal to his clay. There is nothing that can be found in us, or that ever will be in us, that we should dare to say could for a moment stand in comparison with his love.

Well, then, since there is no coin of metal, or emotion of mental condition, or power of spiritual grace, that could be counted out or weighed as the purchase price of Christ's love, we will not dream of having anything of the kind; for there comes, at the back of this thought, the consciousness that, even if we do possess anything that is really valuable, if there is something about us now that is commendable and pure and acceptable, yet *it all belongs to Christ already*. We have nothing with which we can buy anything of him, because all we have belongs to him.

Under the righteous law of God, all the good of which we are capable is already due to our Creator. His command is, 'Thou shalt love the Lord thy God with all thine heart, and with all thy soul, and with all thy might.' Very comprehensive, very swooping, are the demands of the law of the Lord. You must not imagine that there is the slightest truth in the idea that man may come to do more for Christ than it is his duty to do; this cannot be, for all that is possible for us to do, is already Christ's. 'Ye are not your own,' and yet you talk about giving yourself to him. You belong to him now, you Christians, doubly so; and all men are under obligation to Christ even for the temporal favours he has bestowed upon them.

You, believer, cannot say, ''Now I am going to do for Christ something more than, I think, might absolutely be claimed by him.' Why, if you are really what you claim to be, you are his already, body, soul, and spirit! All your time, all your money, all your faculties, all the possibilities that are in you, are all his now; and therefore, wherewithal shall you come to purchase his love? No, it cannot be purchased; that is certain for many other reasons besides these which I have given you.

But what a blessing it is that *we have the love of Christ, though we could not purchase it!* The Son of God hath loved us; he has bestowed upon us what he never would have sold us; and he has given it to us freely, 'without money and without price.' And, beloved, this love is no new thing. He loved us long before we were born. When his foreknowledge sketched us in his mind's eye, he beheld us in love. He proved his love, too. It was not merely contemplative love, but it was practical love, for he died for us before we knew anything of him, or were even here to learn about him. His love is of such a wondrous kind that he always will love us. When heaven and earth have passed away, and like a scroll the universe shall be rolled up, or be put away like a worn-out vesture, he will still love us as he loved us at the first. The greatest wonder to me is that this unpurchasable love, this unending love is mine; and you, my brethren and sisters, can always say, each one of you, if you have been regenerated, 'This love is mine; the Lord Jesus Christ loves me with a love I never could have purchased.'

Peradventure, someone is saying just now, 'I wish I could say that.' Do you really wish it? Then, let the text serve to guide you as to the way by which you may yet know Christ's love to you. Do not try to purchase it, abandon that idea at once. Perhaps you say, 'I never thought of buying it with money.' Possibly not, but the mass of mankind think of purchasing it in some way or other. They hear from their priests of certain ceremonies, and they attach great importance to them, and offer them as a bribe to Christ; but these things will never buy his love. They then resort to prayers, not prayers from the heart, but prayers said as a sort of punishment; and it is thought by many that surely these will procure his love, but they never will. We have even known some who have punished themselves, tortured themselves, thinking they would get Christ's love in that fashion.

Now, if I knew anybody who tried to win my love by making himself miserable, I should say to him, 'My good fellow, you will never make me love you in that way; be as happy as you can; that method is a great deal more likely to touch my heart than the other.' I don't believe that penance and mortification afford any pleasure to God; I think he would be more likely to say, 'Poor silly creatures; when I make gnats, I teach them to dance in the summer sunshine; when I make the fish of the sea, they leap up from the waves with intense delight; and when I make birds, I show them how to sing.' God hath no delight in the miseries of his creatures, and the flagellations that fools give to themselves they deserve for their folly, but they certainly bring no pleasure to the heart of God. It is vain to think of purchasing the love *of* Christ in such a way.

'But surely, surely, we may do something. We will give up this vice, we will renounce that bad habit, we will be strict in our religiousness, we will be attentive to all moral duties.' So you should; but when you have done all that, do you think you have done enough to win his love? Is the servant, who has only done what he ought to have done, entitled to the love of his master's heart because of that? Thou shalt not win Christ's love so; if thou hast his love shed abroad in thy heart, thou hast infinitely more than thou hast ever earned.

Suppose any person here were to say, 'I do feel so resolved to be saved that I will give all I have in this world to some good cause, and then I will give myself to go abroad into foreign lands, to some fever-stricken place, to die in the service of God.' Ah! shouldst thou do all that, thou wouldst utterly be contemned if thou didst think thus to purchase the love of God. Will he be bartered with? Will he put up his heart to be sold in the market, he whose very temple was defiled by the presence of buyers and sellers? It cannot be. Go thou, and chaffer and bid and barter with thy fellow-men; even they will disdain thee if thou thinkest that love is thus to be procured, but dream not that thou art thus to deal with thy God. I say again, it cannot be.

The text does not merely say that the price would be refused, but 'it would utterly be contemned.' Love would open her bright eyes, and look at the man, and then she would frown, and say, 'How canst thou insult me so? Take back thy gold, and be gone'; and God's great love, even when his pity was in the ascendant, would but weep a tear, and then reply, 'I pity thee, for thou knowest not what thou art doing; and I despise the price thou bringest to me. How couldst thou think that I was such an one as thyself, and that my love could be purchased with paltry pelf that thou canst bring? '

We cannot spare more time for that point, but it is one that you may think over for many a day, and your heart may be charmed with it till you love and bless your Saviour with all your heart, and mind, and soul, and strength.

My second remark is, that, **IN OUR CASE, NOTHING CAN EVER SERVE AS A SUBSTITUTE FOR LOVE**.

If Christ has loved us, or if we are desirous of realising that he has done so, *the one thing needful and essential is that we have true love to him.* God's demand of each one who professes to be his child is, 'My son, give me thine heart.' There are many who would like to be thought to be his sons, and therefore every morning they wickedly say, 'Our Father which art in heaven,' though God is not their Father. If they were to say, 'Our father,' to him who is their father, they would pray to the devil, for God is no father of theirs. Alas! there are many who want to be thought to be God's children, and they will come and bring to him anything but love. Sad, sorrowful truth!

If God would but say to men, 'I will accept *unspiritual service*,' he might be the God of the whole earth at once; or rather, let me more truly say that he would be the demon of the whole earth, for men do not care what the religion is externally so long as it does not trouble their hearts. The last thing some people will do is to think. 'Give you a guinea? Oh, certainly!

Excellent is the charity for which you are pleading. A guinea for the hospital? Certainly. Five guineas for a new place of worship? Certainly. When I have money, I am always glad to give it; but don't you come and bother me with any of your doctrines, for I don't want to hear about them. You religious people are so divided into sects and parties, and you are always controverting and contradicting one another, So I do not want to think about these things.' That is a very poor excuse, is it not? Because this seems to be a matter which requires a great deal of thought, therefore this person will not give it any consideration at all; and because those who do think about it do not exactly agree on all points, therefore this man says, 'I shall not think of it at all.' Because all the charts of an intricate portion of the ocean may not happen to be exactly alike, therefore this man will not even study that part of the sea over which his own vessel must go, although there all the charts do agree! He makes an excuse upon some trivial matter to neglect altogether the steering of his vessel. He will strike upon a rock one day, and he will have no one to blame for it but himself.

'Oh!' says another person, 'I don't mind saying prayers; or I will go to church and listen to the reading of prayers. I don't mind hearing sermons, but don't come and tell me that *I have to repent of my sins*. I cannot do it; I do not understand what you mean. I join in "the General Confession" every Sunday; I say that I am a miserable sinner though I don't know that I am particularly miserable, and I don't know that I am particularly a sinner either; but still, I always say that, and I don't mind saying it. Yet if you come to me, saying, "Repent", I cannot do that.' Men will offer to God anything but that which has to do with the heart. You may call upon them to torment their bodies, as the priests of false religions have done; and they will not object to that. The fakir in Hindustan will pierce himself with knives, or lie upon a bed of spikes, or swing himself up by a hook in his back, and hang there by the hour together in all but mortal agony. A man will do almost anything except bow his heart before his God; he will not confess that Jehovah is Lord of all, and that he himself is a poor sinful creature who deserves to be punished; he will not obey a law that is spiritual, and demand the allegiance of the secret thoughts and intents of his heart; and he will not accept a faith which is so superlatively pure that it demands that sin be given up, and tells him that even when given up it must be washed out in the precious blood of Jesus, and that a man must exercise repentance towards God and faith in the Saviour or he cannot be saved.

The most unpopular truth in the world is this sentence which fell from the lips of Christ, '*Ye must be born again*'; and, consequently, there are all sorts of inventions to get the truth out of those words. 'Oh, yes!' say some, 'you must be born again, but that means the application of aqueous fluid to an infant's brow.' As God is true, that teaching is a lie; there is no grain or shade of truth within it. 'Except a man be born again' (from above), 'he cannot see the kingdom of God.' No operation that can be performed by man can ever regenerate the soul; it is the work alone of God the Holy Spirit, who creates us anew in Christ Jesus. Men do not like that truth; the spiritual still displeases the natural man. They will profess to worship God in Jerusalem or at Gerizim, and fight about the place where he ought to be worshipped, to show how little good their religion has done them! They will not speak to each other, the Jew will have no dealings with the Samaritan, to prove how unlike he is to the God who makes his sun to shine both on the just and on the unjust! But when you utter this message, 'God is a Spirit, and they that worship him must worship him in spirit and in truth,' they are offended, and turn away.

Still, the truth holds good, whatever men think of it. If thou give not to God thy heart, thou hast given him nothing. If thou give not to God thy soul, if thou love him not, if thou serve him not because thou lovest him, if thou come not to him, and surrender to him thy inner self, thou mayest have been baptized – immersed or sprinkled – thou mayest have come to the communion table, thou mayest have bowed thy knees till thy knees have grown horny, thou mayest have prayed till thou art hoarse, sad wept till the fountains of thine eyes are dry, thou mayest have given all thy gold, and lacerated every member of thy body with mortifications, and starved thyself to a skeleton, but thou hast truly done nothing towards obtaining love to Christ. The substance of thy house is utterly contemned if thou dost offer it to the Lord in the stead of the love of thy heart. Love he must have; this is his lawful demand. His people delight to render it; and if thou dost not, then thou art none of his.

This takes us to a third truth, which is, that THE SAINTS' LOVE IS NOT PURCHASED BY CHRIST'S GIFTS.

The love of saints to their Lord is not given to Christ because of his gifts to them; I must explain what I mean, lest at the very outset I am mistaken or misunderstood. We love our Lord, and we love him all the more because of the many gifts he bestows upon us; but *his gifts do not win our love*. I will show you why.

All that he has given me today, he gave me many years ago. The covenant of grace was always mine. I heard the preacher tell about it. He told how Christ had died for me; that he had loved me, and given himself for me. Truly, he had done so; he had poured out his blood for my redemption. I would not believe it to be so, or, believing it, I did not think it was of any consequence. Then the preacher spread out the rare gifts of Christ before me, and I saw that he had given these to such as believed in him; but I did not think them worth examining, and I turned away from them. I should never have loved him if he had not given me much more than the substance of his house. I needed his blessed Spirit to show me the value of the substance of his house, and above all, to show me that for which this day I love my Saviour best of all, namely, *himself*, HIMSELF.

Oh, it is 'Jesus Christ himself' who wins the love of our hearts! *If he had not given us himself, we should never have given to him ourselves.* All else that may be supposed to be of the substance of his house would not have won his people's hearts, until at last they learnt this truth, and the Spirit of God made them feel the force of it: 'He loved me, and gave himself for me.'

'My Beloved is mine, and I am his' is now one of the sweetest stanzas in love's canticle. The spouse does not say, 'His crown is mine, his throne is mine, his breastplate is mine, his crook is mine'; she delights in everything that Christ has as a King and a Priest and a Shepherd; but, above all else, that which wins and charms her heart is this, 'He himself is mine, and I am his.'

But I meant mainly to say, under this head, that *there are some of Christ's gifts that do not win our hearts*, that is to say, our hearts do not depend upon them. And they are, first, his temporal gifts. I am very thankful, and I trust that all God's people are also, for health and strength. I have lost these sometimes, but I did not love my Lord any the less then; neither do I love Christ this day because I am free from pain. If I were not free from pain, I would still love him.

Christ has given to some of you a competence, you have all you want for this world; but is that why you love Christ? Oh, no, beloved! if he were to take all away, I know that you would love him in your poverty. The devil was a liar when he said of Job, 'Doth Job fear God for nought? Hast not thou made an hedge about him and about his house, and about all that he hath on every side? thou hast blessed the work of his hands, and his substance is increased in the land. But put forth thine hand now, and touch all that he hath, and he will curse thee to thy face.' We do not love God altogether for what he gives us in this world; ours is not such poor cupboard-love as that. We love him because he first loved us, and we do not pretend to have climbed to that high state of disinterested love in which there is no gratitude mingled with it. We always must be grateful to him, and love him for that reason; but still, temporal things never win our heart's love to God.

There are numbers of you who have health and wealth and many other things that so many desire, but they never make you love God, and they never will. You love them, and make idols of them very readily, but they do not lead you to love the Lord; while the children of God, who love their dear Saviour, can tell you that they do not love him because of what he gives them, for if he takes from them, they love him all the same. With Job, they say, 'The Lord gave, and the Lord hath taken away; blessed be the name of the Lord.' They do not love him simply because he caresses them, for if he chastens them, they love him still, and kiss the rod with which he smites them.

I meant also to say that *we do not love Christ because of his temporary indulgence of us in spiritual things.* You know, beloved, our Saviour very frequently favours us with manifestations of his presence. We are overjoyed when he comes very near to us, and permits us to put our fingers into the prints of the nails. We have our high days and festivals when the Bridegroom is with us, emphatically with us. He takes all the clouds out of our sky and gives us the bright shining of the sun; or he opens the lattices and shows us himself in a way only second to that in which we shall see him when we behold him face to face. And oh, how we love him then! But, thank God, when he draws the lattice back again, and hides his face, we do not leave off loving him because of that. Our love to our Lord does not depend upon the weather. True, our love is not manifested to him so sweetly when we are in the dark as when he cheers us with his smile, but still it is there all the while. We could not let him go. 'Though he slay me,' – though he slay me – he who loves me, though he turn to be my enemy, and slay me – 'yet will I trust in him.' We will hold to him still, and love him still, not because of the substance of his house, but because of what he himself is.

There are times when we are half inclined to say with the elder brother, 'These many years have I been with thee, privileged to serve thee, and yet thou hast not given me so much as a kid that I might make merry with my friends.' Perhaps we have been long without the light of his countenance, and have had no love-tokens from him; but for all that we will remain in his service, and abide in his house; and even if our Father should answer us roughly, we will tell him that he is our Father still. We do not love him merely for the substance of his house, but for himself, and because his Spirit has made love to him to be an instinct of our new nature, and has put within us such a principle that we cannot help loving him. Even if we should be called to pass through terrible trials and adversities, and should have to walk a long time in clouds and darkness, yet still would we love him and rejoice in him.

The last observation I shall have to make upon our text is this: **THE LOVE OF SAINTS CANNOT BE BOUGHT OFF FROM CHRIST AT ANY PRICE**.

The love of some persons to religion is very cheaply bought, and very speedily sold. It is very lamentable to notice the great numbers of persons who are quite content to go and worship God with Christian brethren, and to hear the gospel preached, while they are themselves poor, or in middling circumstances, but who find, as soon as they have accumulated a little wealth, that *the world has a church of its own,* and they must go there, 'because, you see, everybody goes there; and if you are cut off from Society, where are you?'

I have been asked that question, sometimes, and I have replied, 'Where are you? Why, where Christ would have you to be – 'without the camp, bearing his reproach.' But that place of separation, 'without the camp', is a position which is not always taken up cheerfully by professedly Christian people. It is very sorrowful to see how, because God has entrusted them with wealth, they get drawn away from the gospel, and from the Church of God; and though they are troubled a little at first, they soon get rid of one scruple after another, and subside altogether into worldliness.

Well, now, I am not altogether sorry that there is this test in the world. Every good husbandman keeps a winnowing fan; of course, he that is foolish, when he sees a great heap lying on the barn floor, says, 'All this is my wheat that I have brought in.' He does not want to have it diminished, for it is the result of his labour; but if he is a wise husbandman, he says, 'Though I have brought in a great heap, I know that there is chaff with it,' and he is glad to have the winnowing fan used, and the corn tossed up that the fresh breeze may blow through it. If the mere professors go, let them go. 'They went out from us, but they were not of us; for if they had been of us, they would no doubt have continued with us.'

There are some who go away from Christ's people, and renounce religion and love to Christ, because of business. *It will pay better in certain lines not to be religious*; and therefore, as the main thing with them is to get money – religiously, if they can, but irreligiously, if need be – therefore, by-and-by they are offended, and they sell Christ Jesus. I am pained to see the numbers of persons who go and live in the suburbs of London, and who make that an opportunity for selling their religion, such as it is. It is not long ago that I stood at a dying bed, and a part of what I heard there was, 'O sir, ten years ago, we used to be members of such a church; we came to live out here, but there was no place of worship handy, so we have not been anywhere.' That person was dying without hope, after selling Christ for love of a little country air. That was about all it was, and little more was to be gained by it.

'Oh, but!' asks someone, '*do saints sell Christ like that*?' No, not they; these are only the professors who have mingled with the saints. These are like the mixed multitude that came out of Egypt with the children of Israel; howbeit they are not all Israel that are of Israel. The saints sell Christ? No, they are too much like their Master to do that. You recollect how Satan took their Master to the top of a high mountain, and showed him all the kingdoms of the world, and the glory of them, and said, 'All these things will I give thee, if thou wilt fall down and worship me.' Wicked thief! It was not his to give; yet he tempted Christ in that way, but Jesus answered, 'Get thee hence, Satan: for it is written, Thou shalt worship the Lord thy God, and him only shalt thou serve.' If any of Christ's followers are tempted in the same fashion, let them give the same reply. All the substance of the devil's house could not win the love of that man who has set his affection on Jesus.

'Who shall separate us from the love of Christ? 'The cruel Romanists have taken the martyrs into the lone dungeon of the Inquisition, and tormented them there in such a way that it pains us even to read or hear of what they suffered. But did they give up Christ? No, not they; they never would. At other times, they have taken the Christians into a palace, and said, 'We will clothe you in scarlet and fine linen; you shall fare sumptuously every day; but you must give up Christ.' Yet they would not. All the substance of this world has been laid at the feet of holy men, and they have rejected the price with scorn.

I know men today, and rejoice to know them, who have sacrificed honour and position among men, who have borne abuse and scorn, and have been glad to bear it, and counted it their privilege that they were not only permitted to have Christ as their Saviour, but also that they were allowed to suffer for his sake. O brethren and sisters, may the Lord so clothe us with the whole armour of righteousness that no temptation may ever be able to wound our love to Jesus! Let us feel, 'We can let all else go, but we can never let him go.'

> If on my face for his dear name,
> Shame and reproaches be,

there let them be for his sake. Give me but a vision of the Crucified, let me see that thorn-crowned brow, let me but gaze into his dear languid eyes so full of love for me, and I will then say, 'My Master through floods or flames, if thou shalt lead, I'll follow where thou goest. When the many turn aside, I will still cling to thee, and witness that thou hast the living Word, and that there is none upon earth that I desire beside thee. I will give up the treasures of Egypt for I have respect unto the recompense of the reward. I will let the ingots of gold go, every one of them, I will cast them into the sea without regret; but if thou wilt abide in the vessel, my soul shall be content. Bind me to thy altar, for I am but flesh and blood, and may start aside in the trial-hour. Cast the links of thy love about me; chain me to thyself; ay, crucify me; nail me to thy cross, and let me be dead to the world, for then the world will leave off tempting a corpse. Let me be dead with thee, for then the world, that cast thee out, may cast me out, too, and have done with me; and it were well then to be counted as the off-scouring of all things for thy dear sake, my Lord!'

'If a man should give all the substance of his house to bribe the saints to sell their Lord, it would utterly be contemned. By this test shall we prove you, O professors! By this trial shall it be known whether ye can stand firm in the evil day. God grant that you may, for our Lord Jesus Christ's sake! Amen.

51

THE BRIDEGROOM'S PARTING WORD

'Thou that dwellest in the gardens, the companions hearken to thy voice: cause me to hear it' (Song of Solomon 8:13).

The Song is almost ended: the bride end bridegroom have come to their last stanzas, and they are about to part for a while. They utter their adieux, and the bridegroom says to his beloved, 'Thou that dwellest in the gardens, the companions hearken to thy voice: cause me to hear it.' In other words – when I am far away from thee, fill thou this garden with my name, and let thy heart commune with me. She promptly replies, and it is her last word till he cometh: 'Make haste, my beloved, and be thou like to a roe or to a young hart upon the mountains of spices.'

These farewell words of the Well-beloved are very precious to his chosen bride. Last words are always noticed: the last words of those who loved us dearly are much valued; the last words of one who loved us to the death are worthy of a deathless memory. The last words of the Lord in this canticle remind me of the commission which the Master gave to his disciples or ever he was taken up; when he said to them, 'Go ye into all the world, and preach the gospel to every creature.' Then, scattering benedictions with both his hands, he ascended into the glory, and 'a cloud received him out of their sight.' As the sermon progresses you will see why I say this, and you will detect a striking likeness between the commission connected with the accession and the present adieu, wherein the spiritual Solomon saith to his espoused Solyma, 'Thou that dwellest in the garden, the companions hearken to thy voice: cause me to hear it.'

We will get to our text at once, without further preface, and we notice in it, first of all, **AN APPOINTED RESIDENCE**. The bridegroom, speaking of his bride, says, 'Thou that dwellest in the gardens.' The Hebrew is in the feminine, and hence we are bound to regard it as the word of the Bridegroom to his bride. It is the mystical word of the church's Lord to his elect one. He calls her 'Inhabitress of the gardens' – that is the word. So then, dear friends, we who make up the church of God are here addressed this morning under that term, 'Thou that inhabitest the gardens.'

This title is given to believers here on earth, first, by way of *distinction* – distinction from the Lord himself. He whom we love dwelleth in the ivory palaces, wherein they make him glad; he is gone up into his Father's throne, and has left these gardens down below. He came down awhile that he might look upon his garden, that he might see how the vines flourished, and gather lilies; but he has now returned to his Father and our Father. He watered the soil of his garden with his bloody sweat in Gethsemane, and made it to bear fruit unto life by being himself laid to sleep in the tomb of Joseph of Arimathea; but all this lowly work is over now. He does not dwell in the gardens as to his corporeal presence; his dwelling-place is on the throne. Jesus has not taken us up with him; he will come another time to do that; but now he leaves us among the seeds and flowers and growing plants to do the King's work until he comes. He was a visitor here, and the visit cost him dear; but he is gone back unto the place whence he came out, having finished the work which his Father gave him: our life-work is not finished, and hence we must tarry awhile below, and be known as inhabitants *of* the gardens.

It is expedient that we should be here, even as it is expedient that he should *not* be here. God's glory is to come of our sojourn here, else he would have taken us away long ago. He said to his Father, 'I pray not that thou shouldest take them out of the world, but that thou shouldest keep them from the evil.' He himself is an inhabitant of the palaces, for there he best accomplishes the eternal purposes of love; but his church is the inhabitress of the gardens, for there she best fulfils the decrees of the Most High. Here she must abide awhile until all the will of the Lord shall be accomplished in her and by her, and then she also shall be taken up, and shall dwell with her Lord above. The title is given by way of distinction, and marks the difference between her condition and that of her Lord.

Next, it is given by way of *enjoyment.* She dwells in the gardens, which are places of delight. Once you and I pined in the wilderness, and sighed after God from a barren land. We trusted in man, and made flesh our arm, and then we were like the heath in the desert, which seeth not when good cometh. All around us was the wilderness of this world, a howling wilderness of danger and need and disorder. We said of the world at its very best, 'Vanity of vanities, all is vanity.' Do you remember how you roamed, seeking rest and finding none? Your way was the path of darkness which leadeth unto death. Then you were poor and needy, and sought water and there was none, and your tongue cleaved unto the roof of your mouth for thirst.

Then came the Lord that bought you, and he sought you until he brought you into the gardens of his love, where he satisfied you with the river of the water of life, and filled you with the fruits of his Spirit, and now you dwell in a goodly land: 'The fountain of Jacob shall be upon a land of corn and wine; also his heavens shall drop down dew.' Your portion is with the Lord's saints, yea, with himself; and what can be a better portion? Is it not as the garden of the Lord? You dwell where the great Husbandman spends his care upon you and takes a pleasure in you. You dwell where the infinite skill and tenderness and wisdom of God manifest themselves in the training of the plants which his own right hand has planted; you dwell in the church of God, which is laid out in due order, and hedged about and guarded by heavenly power; and you are, therefore, most fitly said to dwell in the gardens. Be thankful: it is a place of enjoyment for you: awake and sing, for the lines have fallen unto you in pleasant places. Just as Adam was put into the garden of Eden for his own happiness, so are you put into the garden of the church for your comfort. It is not a perfect paradise of bliss, but it has many points of likeness to paradise: for God himself doth walk therein, the river of God doth water it, and the tree of life is there unguarded by the flaming sword. Is it not written, 'I the Lord do keep it: I will water it every moment; lest any hurt it, I will keep it night and day'? See, beloved, although you are distinguished from your Lord by being here while he is there, yet you are made partakers of his joy, and are not as those who are banished into a salt land to die in desolation. The Lord's joy is in his people, and you are made to have a joy in them also: the excellent of the earth, in whom is all your delight, are made to be the comrades of your sojourning

The title is also used by way of *employment* as well as enjoyment. Adam was not put in the garden that be might simply walk through its borders, and admire its flowers, and taste its fruits; but he was placed there to keep it and to dress it. There was sufficient to be done to prevent his stagnating from want of occupation. He had not to toil sufficiently to make him wipe the sweat from his brow, for that came of the curse: 'In the sweat of thy face shalt thou eat bread'; but still he was not permitted to be idle, for that might have been a worse curse. Even for a perfect man unbroken leisure would not be a blessing. It is essential even to an unfallen creature that he should have work to do – fit work and honourable, seeing it is done by a creature for the great Benefactor who had created him.

If we had not our daily tasks to fulfil, rest would corrode into rust, and recreation would soon gender corruption. You and I are set in the garden of the church because there is work for us to do which will be beneficial to others and to ourselves also. Some have to take the broad axe and hew down mighty trees of error; others of a feebler sort can with a child's hand train the tendril of a climbing plant, or drop into its place a tiny seed. One may plant and another may water: one may sow and another gather fruit. One may cut up weeds and another prune vines. God hath work in his church for us all to do, and he has left us here that we may do it. Our Lord Jesus would not keep a single saint out of heaven if there were not a needs-be for his being here in the lowlands, to trim these gardens of herbs, and watch these beds of spices. Would he deny his well-beloved the palm branch and the crown if it were not better for us to be holding the pruning-hook and the spade?

A school-book wherewith to teach the little children may be for a while more to our true advantage than a golden harp. To turn over the pages of Scripture wherewith to instruct the people of God may be more profitable to us than to hear the song of seraphim. I say, the Master's love to his own which prompts him to pray, 'I will that they also whom thou hast given me be with me where I am, that they may behold my glory,' would long ago have drawn all the blood-bought up to himself above, had it not been the fact that it is in infinite wisdom seen to be better that they should abide in the flesh.

Ye are the lights of the world, ye are the salt of the earth: shall the light and the salt be at once withdrawn? Ye are to be as a dew from the Lord in this dry and thirsty land; would ye be at once exhaled? Brothers, have you found out what you have to do in these gardens? Sisters, have you found out the plants for which you are to care? If not, arouse yourselves and let not a moment pass till you have discovered your duty and your place. Speak unto him who is the Lord of all true servants, and say to him, 'Show me what thou wouldest have me to do. Point out, I pray thee, the place wherein I may serve thee.' Would you have it said of you that you were a wicked and slothful servant? Shall it be told that you dwelt in the gardens, and allowed the grass to grow up to your ankles, and suffered the thorns and the thistles to multiply until your land became as the sluggard's vineyard, pointed at as a disgrace and a warning to all that passed by? 'O thou that dwellest in the gardens!' The title sets forth employment constant and engrossing.

Dear friends, it means also *eminence*. I know many Christian people who do not feel that they dwell in the gardens. They reside in a certain town or village where the gospel may be preached, but not in demonstration of the Spirit and in power. A little gospel is made to go a long way with some preachers. In some ministries there is no life or power, no unction or savour. The people who meet under such preaching, are cold of heart and dull in spirit; the prayer-meetings are forgotten; communion of saints has well-nigh died out; and there is a general deadness as to Christian effort.

Believe me, it is a dreadful thing when Christian people have almost to dread their Sabbath days; and I have known this to be the case. When you are called to hard toil through the six days of the week you want a good spiritual meal on the Sabbath, and if you get it, you find therein a blessed compensation and refreshment. Is it not a heavenly joy to sit still on the one day of rest, and to be fed with the finest of the wheat? I have known men made capable of bearing great trials – personal, relative, pecuniary, and the like – because they have looked backward upon one Sabbatic feast, and then forward to another. They have said in their hour of trouble, 'Patience, my heart; the Lord's Day is coming, when I shall drink and forget my misery. I shall go and sit with God's people, and I shall have fellowship with the Father and with the Son, and my soul shall be satisfied as with marrow and fatness, till I praise the Lord with joyful lips.' But what a sorry case to dread the Sunday, and to mutter, 'I shall get nothing next Sunday any more than I did last Sunday except some dry philosophical essay, or a heap of the childish toys and fireworks of oratory, or the same dull mumbling of a mechanical orthodoxy.' Oh, brethren and sisters, my text is scarcely meant for those who dwell in such deserts, but it speaks with emphasis to those who dwell where sweet spiritual fruits are plentiful, where odours and perfumes load the air, where the land floweth with milk and honey. If any of you happen to dwell where Christ is set forth evidently crucified among you, and where your hearts do leap for very joy because the King himself comes near to feast his saints and make them glad in his presence, then it is to you that my text hath a voice and a call: 'Thou that dwellest in the gardens, in the choicest places of all Immanuel's land, let me hear thy voice.'

Yet one more word. The title here employed is not only for eminence but for *permanence*. '*O* thou that *dwellest* in the gardens.' If you are only permitted to enjoy sound gospel teaching now and again, and then are forced to cry, 'It may be another twelve months before I shall be again fed on royal dainties,' then you are in a trying case, and you need to cry to God for help. But blessed are those who dwell in the good land, and daily fill their homers with heavenly manna. 'Blessed are they that dwell in thy house: they will be still praising thee.' No spot on earth is so dear to the Christian as that whereon he meets his Lord.

I can understand why the Jew asked of a certain town that was recommended to him as good for business, 'Is there a synagogue there?' Being a devout man, and finding that there was no synagogue, he said he would rather remain where trade was dull, but where he could go with his brethren to worship. Is it not so with us? How my heart has longed for these blessed assemblies! Give me a crust and a full gospel rather than all riches and a barren ministry. The profitable hearing of the Word is the greatest enjoyment upon earth to godly men. It would be banishment to go where every week's business turned into a mint of money if one were also compelled to be a member of an unhappy, quarrelsome or inactive church. Our greatest joy is in thee, O Jerusalem! Let our tongue cleave to the roof of our mouth if we prefer thee not above our greatest joy!

How charming is the place
    Where my Redeemer God
Unveils the beauties of his face,
    And sheds his love abroad.

Not the fair palaces,
    To which the great resort,
Are once to be compared with this
    Where Jesus holds his court.

Beloved, if you dwell in the gardens you have a double privilege, not only of being found in a fat and fertile place, but in living there continually. You might well forego a thousand comforts for the sake of this one delight, for under the gospel your soul is made to drink of wines on the lees well refined.

This, then, is my first head – appointed residence: 'Thou that dwellest in the gardens.' Is not this a choice abode for the Lord's beloved? I leave you to judge how far this describes yourselves. If it be your case, then listen to what the Bridegroom has to say to you.

Secondly, **let us note the RECORDED CONVERSE**:
'Thou that dwellest in the gardens, the companions hearken to thy voice.' She was in the gardens, but she was not quiet there, and why should she be? God gives us tongues on purpose that they should be used. As he made birds to sing, and stars to shine, and rivers to flow, so has he made men and women to converse with one another to his glory. Our tongue is the glory of our frame, and there would be no glory in its being for ever dumb. The monks of La Trappe, who maintain perpetual silence, do no more than the rocks among which they labour. When God makes bells he means to ring them. It may be thought to be a desirable thing that some should speak less, but it is still more desirable that they should speak better. When the tongue indites a good matter, it is no fault if it be nimble as the pen of a ready writer. It is not the quantity, it is the quality of what we say that ought to be considered.

Now, observe that evidently the spouse held with her companions *frequent intercourse*: 'The companions hearken to thy voice.' She frequently conversed with them. I hope it is so among those of you who dwell in this part of Christ's garden. It should be so: 'Then they that feared the Lord spake often one to another'. They had not now and then a crack, now and then the passing of the time of day, but they held frequent converse. Heaven will consist largely in the communion of saints, and if we would enjoy heaven below we must carry out the words of the creed in our practice: 'I believe in the communion of saints.' Let us show that we do believe in it.

Some persons sit still in their pews till the time to go, and then walk down the aisle in majestic isolation, as if they were animated statues. Do children thus come in and out of their father's house with never a word for their brothers and sisters? I know professors who float through life like icebergs from whom it is safest to keep clear; surely these partake not of the spirit of Christ. It is well when such icebergs are drawn into the gulf stream of divine love and melt away into Christ and his people. There should be among those who are children of the common Father a mutual love, and they should show this by frequent commerce in their precious things, making a sacred barter with one another. I like to hear them making sacred exchanges: one mentioning his trials, another quoting his deliverances; one telling how God has answered prayer, and another recording how the Word of God has come to him with power. Such converse ought to be as usual as the talk of children of one family.

And next, it should be *willing and influential*; for if you notice, it is put here: 'Thou that dwellest in the gardens, the companions *hearken* to thy voice.' They do not merely hear it, and say to themselves, 'I wish she would be quiet,' but they hearken, they lend an ear, they listen gladly. I know some Christians whose lips feed many. I could mention brethren and sisters who drop pearls from their lips whenever they speak. We have still among us Chrysostoms, or men of golden mouths; you cannot be with them for half an hour without being enriched. Their anointing is manifest, for it spreads to all around them. When the Spirit of God makes our communications sweet, then the more of them the better. I like to get sometimes under the shadow of God's best people, the fathers in Israel, and to hear what they have to say to the honour of the name of the Lord. We who are young men feel gladdened by the testimonies of the ancients; and as for the babes in grace, they look up to the grey-beards and gather strength from their words of experience and grace.

If there are any here whose language is such that others delight to listen to it, it is to such that my text is especially addressed; and when I come to open up the later part of it I want you that have the honeyed tongues, I want you who are listened to with pleasure, to notice how the Beloved says to you: 'Thy companions hearken to thy voice: cause me to hear it.' Give thy Lord a share of thy sweet utterances; let thy Saviour's ear be charmed as well as thy companions' ears. Come, speak *to him* as well as to thy brethren, and if there be music in thy voice let that music be for the Well-beloved as well as for thy fellow-servants. This is the very heart of the matter. I cannot help alluding to it even before we have fairly reached that part of the text. The converse of the bride in the gardens was constant, and it was greatly esteemed by those who enjoyed it.

I gather from the text, rather by implication than otherwise, that the converse was *commendable*; for the bridegroom does not say to the spouse, 'Thou that dwellest in the gardens, thy companions hear too much of thy voice.' No; he evidently mentions the fact with approval, because he draws an argument from it why he also should hear that self-same voice. Brothers, I leave it to yourselves to judge whether your communications with one another are always such as they should be. Are they always worthy of you?

What communications have ye had this morning? Can I make a guess? 'Nice and fresh this morning.' 'Quite a change in the weather.' Is not this the style? How often we instruct each other about what we all know! When it rains so as to soak our garments we gravely tell each other that it is very wet. Yes, and if the sun shines we are all eager to communicate the wonderful information that it is warm. Dear me, what instructors of our generation we are! Could we not contrive to change the subject? Is it because we have nothing to say of love and grace and truth that we meet and part without learning or teaching anything? Perhaps so. I wish we had a little more small change of heavenly converse: we have our crowns and sovereigns for the pulpit, we need groats and pence for common talk, all stamped with the image and superscription of the King of heaven. O Holy Spirit, enrich us after this sort. May our communications be such that if Jesus himself were near we might not be ashamed for him to hear our voices. Brethren, make your conversation such that it may be commended by Christ himself.

These communications were, no doubt, very *beneficial*! As iron sharpeneth iron, so does a man's countenance his friend. Oh, what a comfort it is to drop in upon a cheerful person when you yourself are heavy! What a ballast it puts into your ship, when you are a little too merry, to meet with one in sore travail who bids you share his burden and emulate his faith. We are all the better, believe me, when our Lord can praise us, because the companions hearken to our voices.

In fact, our communications with one another ought to be preparatory to higher communications still. The converse of saints on earth should be a rehearsal of their everlasting communion in heaven. We should begin here to be to one another what we hope to be to one another, world without end. And is it not pleasant to rise from communion with your brethren into communion with the Bridegroom? To have such talk to one another that at last we perceive that truly our fellowship is with the Father and with his Son Jesus Christ? We thought that we only communed with our brethren; but, lo! we see that the Lord himself is here: do not our hearts burn within us? We too are talking of him, and now we see that he himself is here, opening to us the Scriptures, and opening our hearts to receive those Scriptures in the power of them.

Beloved, let us try if we cannot make it so, that as we dwell together as church members, and work together in one common vineyard, we may be always making our fellowship with each other a grand staircase of fellowship with the King himself. Let us so talk that we may expect to meet Jesus while we are talking. How sweet to hear and see the Master in the servant, the Bridegroom in the Bridegroom's friend, the Head in the members, the Shepherd in the sheep, the Christ in every Christian! Thus may we rise upon the wings of hallowed intercourse with holy ones to yet more hallowed intercourse with the Holy One of Israel.

Thus have we meditated upon two things: we have noted the appointed residence and the recorded converse. We know what we are talking about.

3. Now comes the pith of the text: **INVITED FELLOWSHIP**

'The companions hear thy voice: cause me to hear it.' It is beautiful to hear the Beloved say in effect, 'I am going away from you, and you see me no more; but I shall see you: do not forget me. Though you will not hear my voice with your bodily ears, I shall hear your voices: therefore speak to me. Unseen I shall feed among the lilies; unperceived I shall walk the garden in the cool of the day; when you are talking to others do not forget me. Sometimes turn aside, and when you have shut to the door, and no eye can see, nor ear can hear, then let me hear thy voice: it has music in it to my heart, for I died to give you life. Let me hear the voice of your prayer and praise and love.'

Now, I note concerning this invitation, first of all, that it is very *loving and condescending* to us that the Lord should wish to hear our voice. I do not wonder that some of you love to hear my voice, because the Holy Spirit has blessed it to your conversion; but what good has Jesus ever derived from any of us? Is it not marvellous that he, the infinitely blessed, should want to hear our voices when all that he hath heard from us has been begging, sighing, and a few poor broken hymns? You do not want to hear a beggar's voice, do you? I expect if the man you have helped a score of times should be tomorrow morning at your door, you would say, 'Dear, dear; there is that man again.' Might not the Well-beloved say the same of you? 'There she is again: come on the same errand. Come to confess some new faults, or to ask fresh favours.' But instead of being tired of us our Lord says, 'Let me hear thy voice.'

O loving Bridegroom! Must he not love us very truly to ask us to speak with him? See, he asks as though he begged it of us as a favour, 'Let me hear thy voice. Thy companions hearken: let me take a share in their intercourse: they find thy voice pleasant, let it be a pleasure also to me. Come, do not deny me, thy heart's best beloved! Do not be silent unto me! Come, speak to me with thine own sweet mouth.'

It is condescending and gracious, and yet how *natural* it is! How like to Christ! Love ever seeks the company of that which it loves. What would a husband say if his wife was seen to be chatty and cheerful to everybody else, but never spoke to him? I cannot suppose such a case: it would make too sorrowful a household. I should pity the poor, broken-hearted man who should be forced to say, 'My beloved, others hear thy voice, and admire it; wilt thou not speak to me, thy husband?' O believer, will you let the Lord Jesus, as it were with tears in his eyes, say to you, 'You talk to everybody but to me: you lay yourself out to please everybody but me: you are a charming companion to everybody but to me'? Oh, our Beloved, how ill have we treated thee! How much have we slighted thee!

In looking back, I fear there are many of us who must feel as if this gentle word of the Lord had also a sharp side to it. I do remember my faults this day. The text goes like a dagger to my soul, for I have spoken all day long to others, and have had scarce a word for him whom my soul loveth. Let us mend our converse, and henceforth show our Lord a truer love.

We may truly add that this invitation to fellowship is a *blessed and profitable* request. We shall find it so if we carry it out, especially those of us who are called by God to use our voices for him among the crowds of our companions. I address some brothers and sisters here who are preachers and teachers. What a relief it is, when you have been letting the companions hear your voice, to stop a bit and let Jesus hear it! What a rest to leave the congregation for the closet, to get away from where they criticise you to one who delights in you. What a relief, I say. And what a help to our hearts! Jesus gives us sweet returns if we commune with him, and such as speakers greatly need.

The apostles said that they would give themselves to the Word of God and to prayer. Yes, we must put those two things together. We shall never fitly handle the Word of God without prayer. When we pray we are taught how to speak the Word to others. Salvation and supplication are a blessed pair. Put the two together, so that when you speak to others about salvation, you do it after having baptized your own soul into supplication. 'The companions hear thy voice: cause me to hear it: before thou speakest with them speak to me; whilst thou art still speaking with them still speak with me; and when thy speaking to men is done, return unto thy rest and again speak with me.'

This invitation is a *many-sided one*; for when the bridegroom says, 'Cause me to hear it,' he means that she should speak to him in all sorts of ways. Frequently we should be heard in praise. If thou hast been praising the Lord in the audience of others, turn aside and praise him to his face. Sing thy song to thy Beloved himself. Get into a quiet place and sing where only he can hear. I wish we had more of that kind of music which does not care for other audience than God. Oh, my God, my heart shall find *thee,* and every string shall have its attribute to sing, while my whole being shall extol *thee*, my Lord. The blessed Virgin had none with her but Elizabeth when she sang, 'My soul doth magnify the Lord, and my spirit doth rejoice in God my Saviour.' Oh, let the Lord hear your voice! Get up early to be alone with him. So let it be with all your complaints and petitions; let them be for Jesus only. Too often we fill our fellow creature's ear with the sad tale of all our care. Why not tell the Lord about it, and have done with it? We should employ our time far more profitably if, instead of murmuring in the tent, we enquired in the Temple.

Speak with Jesus Christ, dear friends, in little broken sentences, by way of frequent ejaculation. The best of Christian fellowship may be carried on in single syllables. When in the middle of business you can whisper, 'My Lord and my God!' You can dart a glance upward, heave a sigh, or let fall a tear, and so will Jesus hear your voice! When nobody observes the motion of your lips you may be saying, 'My Beloved, be near me now!' This is the kind of fellowship which your Saviour asks of you. He says, 'The companions hear thy voice: cause me to hear it. Be sure that when thou speakest with others thou dost also speak with me!'

This is such a blessed invitation that I think, dear friends, we ought to avail ourselves of it at once. Come, what say you? The best Beloved asks us to speak with him, what shall we say at once? Think for an instant! What shall I say? Perhaps I have the start of you, because I have my word ready. Here it is: 'Make haste, my beloved, and be thou like to a roe or to a young hart upon the mountains of spices.' 'Why,' say you, 'that is what the church said in the last verse of the Song.' Exactly so, and that is what we may wisely say at this moment. We cannot improve upon it. 'Come quickly; even so, come quickly, Lord Jesus.' Often and often, then, when you are about your business, say, 'Come, Lord Jesus! Come quickly!' It is a sweet frame of mind to be in to be willing to invite Christ to come; and whenever you cannot do so let it be a warning to you that you are in dangerous waters.

I can imagine a man in business calling himself a Christian about to engage in a doubtful transaction: how is he to discern the danger? Let him ask the Lord Jesus Christ to come while he is doing it. 'Oh, dear no!' cries one, 'I had rather he should not come until that matter had been finished and forgotten.' Then be you sure that you are moving in the wrong direction. Suppose you think of going to a certain place of amusement about which you have a question, it is easy to decide it thus: When you take your seat your first thing should be to bow your head and ask for a blessing, and then say, 'Lord, here I sit waiting for thine appearing.' 'Oh,' say you, 'I should not want the Lord to come there.' Of course you would not. Then do not go where you could not wish your Lord to find you. My text may thus be a monitor to you, to keep you from the paths of the destroyer. Jesus says, 'Let me hear thy voice,' and let thy voice utter these desires: 'Even so, come quickly; come, Lord Jesus!'

Alas, time reproves me; I must hasten on.

I have a fourth head, which shall be very briefly handled. **I find according to the Hebrew that the text has in it a REQUESTED TESTIMONY**.

According to learned interpreters the Hebrew runs thus: '*Cause to hear me.*' Now, that may mean what I have said, 'Cause me to hear'; but it may also mean, 'Cause them to hear me.' Now hearken; you that are in Christ's garden make those who dwell in that garden with you to hear from you much about HIM. In the church everyone has a right to talk about the Head of the church. Some of our brethren in this Tabernacle kindly undertake to speak to individuals about their souls, and now and then they receive very sharp rebuffs. What right has he to put such a question? How dare he intrude with personal remarks? What! Is the man poaching? No: these are the Lord's preserves; and the Lord's gamekeepers have a right to do as they are bidden by him. They are not poaching in this place, for they are on the Master's own land. Anywhere inside these four walls you may speak to anybody about Christ, and no man may forbid you. Speak lovingly and tenderly and prudently; but certainly the law of the house is that here we may speak about the Lord of the house. There are some other things you may not talk about, but about the Lord Jesus you may speak as much as you will. In the garden, at any rate, if not in the wild wilderness, let the Rose of Sharon be sweetly spoken of. Let his name be as ointment poured forth in all the church of God.

Again, you, according to the text, are one that can make people hear, so that 'the companions hearken to thy voice'; then make them to hear of Jesus. You have the gift of speech: use it for Christ crucified. I always feel regret when a powerful speaker espouses any other cause but that of my Lord. Time was when I used to wish that Milton had been a preacher, and instead of writing a poem had proclaimed the gospel to the multitude. I know better now, for I perceive that God doth not use learning and eloquence so much as knowledge of Christ and plain speech; but still I am jealous of any man who can speak well that he should not give my Lord the use of his tongue. Well-trained tongues are rare things, and they should be all consecrated to Christ's glory. If you can speak to the companions – make them hear about Christ; if you can speak well, make them to hear attractive words about Christ.

If you do not speak about Christ to strangers, do speak to your companions. They will hearken to you; therefore let them hearken to the Word of the Lord. I have heard of men who called themselves Christians who yet never spoke to their children about their souls, never spoke to their servants nor to their workpeople about Jesus and his love. This is to murder souls. If tongues can bless and do not, then they in effect curse men by their silence. If you have a voice, make the name of Jesus to be sounded out all around you. Many are the voices that strike upon the ear: the world is full of din, even to distraction, yet the name which is above all other names is scarcely heard. I pray you, my brethren, you that are like silver bells, ring out that name o'er hill and dale. As with a clarion, trumpet forth the saving name of Jesus till the deaf hear the sound thereof. Whatever is left out of your testimony, be sure that Christ crucified is first and last in it. Love Christ and live Christ; think of Christ and speak of Christ.

When people go away from hearing you preach, may they have to say, 'He kept to his subject: he knew nothing but Jesus.' It is ill when a man has to say of preachers, 'They have taken away my Lord, and I know not where they have laid him.' Yet in certain sermons you meet with a little about everything except the one thing. They offer us what we do not need; but the need of the soul is not supplied. Oh, my brethren, cause Christ to be heard. Hammer on that anvil always: if you make no music but that of the harmonious blacksmith it will suffice. Ring it out with sturdy blows: 'Jesus, Jesus, Jesus crucified.' Hammer away at that. 'Now you are on the right string, man,' said the Duke of Argyll, when the preacher came to speak upon the Lord Jesus. It needed no duke to certify that. Harp on that string. Make Jesus to be as commonly known as now he is commonly unknown. So may God bless you as long as you dwell in these gardens, till the day break and the shadows flee away. Amen.

52

COME, MY BELOVED!

'Make haste, my beloved, and be thou like to a roe or to a young hart upon the mountains of spices' (Song of Solomon 8:14)

The Song of Songs describes the love of Jesus Christ to his people, and it ends with an intense desire on the part of the Church that the Lord Jesus should come back to her. The last word of the lover to the beloved one is, 'Speed thy return; make haste and come back.' Is it not somewhat singular that, as the last verse of the Book of love has this note in it, so the last verses of the whole Book of God, which I may also call the Book of love, have that same thought in them? At the twentieth verse of the last chapter of the Revelation, we read, 'He which testifieth these things saith, Surely I come quickly. Amen. Even so, come, Lord Jesus.' The Song of love and the Book of love end in almost the selfsame way, with a strong desire for Christ's speedy return.

Are your hearts, dear friends, in tune with that desire? They ought to be, yet have not some of you almost forgotten that Jesus is to come a second time? Refresh your memories. Others of you, who know that he will come, have you not thought of it as a doctrine that might be laid by on the shelf? Have you not been without any desire for his glorious appearing? Is this right? That Song of Solomon is the central Book of the Bible; it is the innermost shrine of divine revelation, the holy of holies of Scripture; and if you are living in communion with God, you will love that Book, you will catch its spirit, and you will be inclined to cry with the spouse, 'Make haste, my beloved.' If you have no longings for Christ's appearance, no desires for his speedy return, surely your heart is sick, and your love is faint. I fear that you are getting into a lukewarm state. I believe that our relationship to the Second Advent of Christ may be used as a thermometer with which to tell the degree of our spiritual heat. If we have strong desires, longing desires, burning desires, for the coming of the Lord, we may hope that it is well with us; but if we have no such desires, I think, at best, we must be somewhat careless; perhaps, to take the worst view of our case, we are sadly declining in grace.

Well now, to come to our text; I want you to notice, first, **WHAT THE CHURCH HERE CALLS HER LORD**: 'Make haste, *my beloved*.'

I will have only a few words upon this point. I am hardly going to preach tonight, but just to talk familiarly to you, and I want you to let your hearts talk. Observe, the spouse first calls her Lord, 'Beloved,' and secondly, 'My Beloved.'

Christ is our *'Beloved.'* This is a word of affection; and our Lord Jesus Christ is the object of affection to us. If you read the Bible, especially if you read the New Testament, and study the life of Christ, and yet you only admire it, and say to yourself, 'Jesus Christ was a wonderful being', you do not know him yet; you have but a very indistinct idea of him. If, after reading that life, you sit down, and dissect it, and say to yourself, coolly, calmly, deliberately, 'So far as is practicable, I will try and imitate Christ,' you do not yet know him, you have not come near to the real Christ as yet. If any man should say, 'I am near the fire,' and yet he is not warm, I should question the truth of his words; and though he might say, 'I can see the fire; I can tell you the appearance of the coals; I can describe the lambent flames that play about the stove,' yet if he were not warmed at all, I should still think that he was mistaken, or that there was some medium that interposed between him and the fire at which he said he was looking.

But when you really come to see Jesus, and to say, 'I love him; my heart yearns towards him; my delight is in him; he has won my love, and holds it in his own heart,' then you begin to know him. Brethren, true religion has many sides to it; true religion is practical, it is also contemplative; but it is not true religion at all if it is not full of love and affection. Jesus must reign in your heart, or else, though you may give him what place you like in your head, you have not truly received him. To Jesus, beyond all others, is applicable this title of the Beloved, for they who know him love him. Ay, if ever love had emphasis in it, it is the love which true believers give to Christ; and we do well when we sing:

I love thee because thou hast first lovèd me,
And purchased my pardon on Calvary's tree;
I love thee for wearing the thorns on thy brow;
If ever I loved thee, my Jesus, 'tis now.

I will love thee in life, I will love thee in death,
And praise thee so long as thou lendest me breath;
And say when the death-dew lies cold on my brow,
If ever I loved thee, my Jesus, 'tis now.

We may also go beyond that point, as the hymn does, and say,

In mansions of glory and endless delight,
I'll ever adore thee in heaven so bright;
I'll sing with the glittering crown on my brow;
If ever I loved thee, my Jesus, 'tis now.

Our love to Jesus begins with trust. We experience his goodness, and then we love him in return. 'We love him because he first loved us.' They say that love is blind; I should think it is, from what I have seen of it in some people; but love to Christ might have ten thousand eyes, and yet be justified in loving him. The more you see him, the more you know him, the more you live with him, the more reason will you have for loving him. There will never come a time in which you will have to question whether you were right to surrender your heart to him; but even throughout the eternal ages you shall, in the felicities of his blessed company, feel that you were, in fact, more than justified in calling him your Beloved.

That is the first part of the name the spouse gives to her Lord; no, not the *first*; the first part of the name is '*my*', she calls him '*my Beloved*'.

Brethren, this signifies appropriation; so that the two words together mean affection and appropriation: '*My* Beloved'. If nobody else loves him, I do. This is a distinguishing affection; and I love him because he belongs to me; he is mine, he has given himself to me; and I have chosen him because he first chose me; he is 'my Beloved'. I am not ashamed to put him in front of all others; and when men say, 'What is thy Beloved more than another beloved? 'I can tell them that 'My Beloved' is more than all the earthly beloveds put together.

It is a delightful thing to get hold of Christ with both hands, as Thomas did when he said, 'My Lord and my God.' There he held him with a double-handed grip, and would not let him go. It is sweet and saving even to come into contact with him, as the woman did who touched the fringe of his garment; but, oh, to take him up in your arms, to hold him with both hands, and say, 'This Christ is mine; by a daring faith, warranted by the Word of God, I take this Christ to be mine, to have and to hold, for better or worse, and neither life nor death shall ever part me from him who is "my Beloved".'

Now, there is a sweet name for the Lord Jesus Christ. My dear hearers, can you speak of Jesus in that way, 'My Beloved'? He who can, by the Spirit of God, say this, has uttered two words that have more eloquence in them than there is in all the orations of Demosthenes. He who cannot truly say this, though he may speak with the tongues of men and of angels, yet, since he hath not this charity, this divine love in his heart, it profiteth him nothing. Oh, that every one of you could say, 'My Beloved! My Beloved!'

Do you all really know what saving faith is? It is the appropriation to one's own self of Christ in his true and proper character as God has revealed him. Canst thou make this appropriation? 'Oh,' says one, 'I am afraid I should be stealing salvation if I did! 'Listen: so long as thou canst get Christ anyhow, thou mayest have him. There is never any stealing of that which is freely given. The difficulty is not about any rights that thou hast, for thou hast no rights whatever in this matter, but come and take what God gives to thee, though thou hast no claim to it. Soul, take Christ tonight, and if thou takest him, thou shalt never lose him. I was going to say, if thou dost even steal him, so long as thou dost but take him to thyself, he will never withdraw himself from thy grasp. It is written, 'Him that cometh to me, I will in no wise cast out.' Some come properly, and Christ does not cast them out; but there are some who come improperly, they come, as it were, limping on a wooden leg, or perhaps only creeping or crawling. It does not matter how you come to Christ, as long as you really do come to him, he will never cast you out. Get to him anyhow you can; and if you once come to him, you may plead that blessed promise of his, 'Him that cometh to me I will in no wise cast out.'

I have told you before that, some years ago, I felt a great depression of spirit; I knew whom I had believed; but, somehow, I could not get the comfort out of the truth I preached. I even began to wonder whether I was really saved; and, having a holiday, and being away from home, I went to the Wesleyan Chapel, and a local preacher occupied the pulpit that morning. While he preached a sermon full of the gospel, the tears flowed from my eyes, and I was in such a perfect delirium of joy on hearing the gospel, which I so seldom have an opportunity of doing, that I said, 'Oh, yes, there is spiritual life within me, for the gospel can touch my heart, and stir my soul.' When I went to thank the good man for his sermon, he looked at me, and he could hardly believe his eyes. He said, 'Are you not Mr. Spurgeon?' I replied, 'Yes.' 'Dear, dear,' said he, 'why, that is your sermon that I preached this morning!' Yes, I knew it was, and that was one reason why I was so comforted by it, because I felt that I could take my own physic, and I said to myself, 'There now, that which I have seen to have a certain effect upon others has had the same effect upon me.' I asked the preacher to my inn to dinner, and we rejoiced together to think that he should have been led to give the people one of my sermons so that I should be fed out of my own cupboard. I do know this, that, whatever I may be, there is nothing that moves me like the gospel of Christ. Do not many of you feel just as I do?

Now I will lead you on to the second division of my subject. I have shown you what the Church calls her Lord; now, in the second place, **I will tell you WHENCE SHE CALLS HIM**: 'Make haste, my beloved, and be thou like to a roe or to a young hart upon the mountains of spices.' What does that mean? She cries to him to come from the place where he now is, which she calls 'the mountains of spices'.

Readers of Solomon's Song know that there are four mountains spoken of in the Song. The first set of mountains is mentioned in the seventeenth verse of the second chapter of the Song, where we read of *the mountains of division:* 'Until the day break, and the shadows flee away, turn, my beloved, and be thou like a roe or a young hart upon the mountains of Bether', or, the mountains of division, the divided crags, or the mountains that divide. Well now, beloved, this was Christ's first coming. There were mountains of division; our sins and God's justice, like great mountains, divided us. How could God's love ever come to us, or how could we get to it? There were mountains of division; and, as we looked at them, we said, 'They are impassable; nobody can ever climb those lofty crags, or scale those awful precipices, or cross those dread abysses. These mountains effectually separate a guilty soul from a holy God; and, my brethren, there was no way over those hills, till Jesus came like a roe or a young hart. Roes and harts can stand on crags where men's heads turn giddy and they fall; and our Divine Master was able to stand where we could not. He came leaping over the mountains of our sins, and over the hills of divine justice, and he came even to us, and opened up a way over the mountains of Bether, the mountains of division, by which God comes to us and we come to God; and now, instead of division, there is a saved union.

That was Christ's first coming, over the mountains of division.

But there were other mountains beside those, which you read of a little further on in the Song; these were *the mountains of the leopards,* the dens of the lions. Turn to the fourth chapter, at the eighth verse: 'Come with me from Lebanon, my spouse, with me from Lebanon: look from the top of Amana, from the top of Shenir and Hermon, from the lions' dens, from the mountains of the leopards.' When Christ came the first time, he met with fierce opposition from sin and death and hell. These were the lions; these were the leopards; and our great Champion had to go hunting them, and they hunted him. You know how these grim lions met him, and how they tore him; they rent his hands and his feet and his side. Do you not remember how that great lion of the pit came leaping upon him, how he received him upon his breast, like a greater Samson, and though he fell in the death-struggle, he tore that lion asunder, as though he had been a kid, and cast him down? As for his other enemies, he could truly say, 'O death, where is thy sting? O grave, where is thy victory?' Our Well-beloved came to us, over the mountains of the leopards and the dens of the lions, more than conqueror through the greatness of his love. Do you not see him as he comes from Edom, with dyed garments from Bozrah, travelling in the greatness of his strength, speaking in righteousness, mighty to save? In spite of all opposition, he finished the work of our redemption.

So Jesus came to us, over the mountains of separation, and over the mountains of the leopards.

But there is a third mountain mentioned in this wonderful poetical Book and that is *the mountain of myrrh*. In the sixth chapter at the second verse, it says, 'My beloved is gone down into his garden, to the beds of spice, to feed in the gardens, and to gather lilies.' It is called a garden, but in the sixth verse of the fourth chapter it is called a mountain: 'Until the day break, and the shadows flee away, I will get me to the mountain of myrrh, and to the hill of frankincense.' You know the story well. After Jesus had come over the mountains of our sins, after he had killed the lions and the leopards that stood in our way, he gave up his soul into his Father's hands, and loving friends took his body, and wrapped it in white linen, and Joseph of Arimathea and Nicodemus brought myrrh and aloes to preserve his blessed body, that matchless casket of a perfect soul; and, having wrapped him up, they laid him in a new tomb, which thus became the garden or mountain of myrrh. A bitter thing was that grave wherein he buried all our sin, that grave out of which he came victorious over death, that grave out of which he rose that he might justify his people. That was the mountain of myrrh to which Jesus went for a very brief season. Scarcely three days was he there; but I think I can hear his Church standing at the tomb, and saying, 'Make haste, my beloved! Be thou like a roe, or a young hart, and come quickly from thy sleep with the dead in the mountains of myrrh.' It was but a short time that he was there, even as he said to his disciples, 'A little while, and ye shall not see me; and again a little while, and ye shall see me.' Soon was that slumber over, and when he woke, as Samson carried away the gate of Gaza, so Christ arose, and took up the gates of death, posts and bar and all, and carried them away, and neither death nor hell can ever bring them back again. By the resurrection of Christ, the tomb is opened, never to be closed again.

The 'mountain of myrrh' is the third that is mentioned in the Song; but our text refers to *the mountains of spices*. I am not stretching this passage, or drawing a lesson where there is none; the mountains of spices are those places where Jesus dwells at this very moment at the right hand of God. It is from there that we now call him with the spouse when she said, 'Make haste, my beloved, and be thou like to a roe or to a young hart upon the mountains of spices.'

What are these spices? Are they not Christ's infinite merits, which perfume heaven and earth? The foul corruption of our sins is not perceptible, because of the mountains of spices. One single sin would be vile enough to pollute a universe; what, then, were all our sins put together? Behold this wondrous sanitary power of divine grace; these mountains of spices more than nullify the foulness of our sins. Christ's merit is perpetually before the eye of his Father, so that no longer does he perceive our sins.

What shall I say next of these mountains of spices? Are they not our Lord's perpetual and prevailing prayers? He intercedes for his people before the throne of God. He is that great angel from whose swinging censer there goes up continually the incense of intercession. The prayers of saints are presented by him to his Father with all his own merit added to them. These are the mountains of spices, Christ's infinite merits, and his ceaseless prayers, his undying supplications to the great Father on behalf of all his people.

In consequence of this, I think I may say that the praises of his glorified people, the sweet music of the harps of the redeemed, the everlasting symphonies of the spirits of just men made perfect and cleansed by his atoning blood – are not these as sweet spices before God? Yea, all heaven is perfumed with everything that is precious and acceptable, full of a sweet savour unto God, and a delightful fragrance to all his people. Now, this is where Jesus is now; not here in this foul, polluted world, but up yonder he rests in the mountains of spices; and the prayer of his Church continually is, 'Come, my Beloved! Make haste, my Beloved! Be thou like to a roe or to a young hart upon the mountains of spices.'

That brings me to what is really the gist, the main point, the arrow-head of the text. **We have noticed what the Church calls her Lord, and whence she calls him; now, thirdly, note HOW SHE CALLS HIM**. She says, 'Make haste, my Beloved, make haste.'

Why is it that all the Church of God, and each individual Christian in particular, should be found anxious for the speedy coming of our Lord Jesus Christ? I think, surely, that *this is the result of true love*. Does not love always wish to see the object on which its heart is fixed? When your dearest one parts from you for a while, do you not always wish for a speedy return? The parting is painful; it were bitter indeed if you did not expect to meet again. So you say, 'Be no longer absent than you are forced to be. Come home as speedily as you can.' Where there is great love, there gets to be great longing; and that longing sometimes becomes so vehement as to be well-nigh impatient. May not the Church that mourns her absent Lord sigh and cry till he returns? Is not this the very language of intense love, 'Make haste, my Beloved, and return to me'? If we love our Lord, we shall long for his appearing; be you sure of that, it is the natural result of ardent affection.

But, notwithstanding this, beloved, we sometimes need certain incentives to stir up our souls to cry for our Lord's return. One reason that ought to make the believer long for Christ's coming is that it *will end this conflict*. Our lot is cast in a wretched time, when many things are said and done that grieve and vex God's Holy Spirit, and all who are in sympathy with him. Sometimes, it is false doctrine that is proclaimed; and if you preach the truth, they smite you on the mouth, and then you say to yourself, 'Would God the Lord would come! 'At other times, it is sheer blasphemy that is uttered, when men say, 'The Lord delayeth his coming,' or when they talk as if he were not Lord, as if his gospel were no gospel, and his salvation wore worn out. Then we say, 'Make no tarrying, O our God! Come, Lord, and tarry not!' We grow almost impatient then for his coming.

And, dear friend, when you see the oppression of the poor, when you hear the cry of the needy, when you know that many of them are ground down to bitter poverty, and yet are struggling hard to earn a bare pittance, you say, 'Lord, will this state of things always exist? Shall not these wrongs be righted? Oh, that he would come, who will judge the people righteously, and vindicate the cause of the poor and the oppressed!'

Then we look even on the professing church, and we see how lukewarm it is, how honeycombed it is with heresy and worldliness, and how often the church that ought to honour Christ insults him, and he is wounded in the house of his friends. We say, 'Will not this evil soon be at an end? Will not the conflict speedily be over?' Oh, how have I stood, in the midst of the battle, when the deadly shafts have flown about me on the right hand and on the left, and, wounded full sore, I have cried, 'Will not the King himself soon come, and shall I not ere long hear the sound of those blessed feet, whose every step means victory, and whose presence is eternal life?' 'Come, Lord! Make haste, my Beloved! Come to the rescue of thy weak and feeble servants; come, come, come, we beseech thee!' Put yourself into this great fight for the faith; and if you have to bear the brunt of the battle, you will soon be as eager as I am that Jesus should make haste, and come to your relief. You also will cry, 'Make haste, my Beloved', when you think what wonders he will work at his coming.

What will Christ do at his coming? *He will raise the dead.* Mine eyes shall see him in that day. 'I know that my Redeemer liveth, and that he shall stand at the latter day upon the earth, and though after my skin worms destroy this body, yet in my flesh shall I see God.' When Christ shall come the second time, and that blast, of which we sang just now, 'the loudest and the last,' shall ring through earth and heaven, then shall the dead men arise. There are newly-made graves; the mourners' tears are not yet wiped away. There are the graves of many who have gone home long ago, and we remember them, and we say, 'Would God that Christ would come, and spoil death of those precious relics! Oh, that he would re-animate those bodies, and call together the dry bones, and bid them live! 'Come, Lord! Come, Lord! make no tarrying, we-beseech thee!

And when he comes, beloved, remember that *then shall be the time of the glory of his people:* 'Then shall the righteous shine forth as the sun in the kingdom of their Father.' Slander will be rolled away in the day when Christ cometh. 'The wicked shall awake to everlasting contempt, but the righteous to an everlasting justification. They shall be clear of every accusation in that day, and then shall they sit on the throne with their Lord. They were with him in his humiliation; they shall be with him in his glory. They, too, were despised and rejected of men, as he was; but in that day none shall dare to despise them, for every saint shall be seen to be a king, and a son of the King. Oh, the glory that awaits his people in the day of his coming! 'It doth not yet appear what we shall be: but we know that, when he shall appear, we shall be like him; for we shall see him as he is.'

Well may the child of God say, 'Make haste, my Beloved.' Oh, for the sheathing of the sword, and the waving of the palm! Oh, for the drying of the tear, and the handling of the harp of gold! Oh, for the ending of the doubt and the trouble, and the beginning of the everlasting enjoyment and the eternal serenity at the right hand of the Ever-blessed One!

Still, there is another reason why we say, 'Make haste, my Beloved.' It is this. We desire to share in Christ's glory; but *our chief desire is that our Lord may be glorified.* I do believe I shall have the support of every Christian heart when I say that we would a thousand times rather that Christ were glorified than that we should be honoured. Many years ago, after the Surrey Music Hall accident, I well-nigh lost my reason through distress of heart. I was broken down in spirit, and thought that, perhaps, I might never preach again. I was but a young man, and it was a great sorrow that crushed me into the dust through that terrible accident; but one passage of Scripture brought me recovery in a moment. I was alone, and as I was thinking, this text came to my mind: 'Him hath God exalted with his right hand to be a Prince and a Saviour,' and I said to myself, 'Is that so? Is Jesus Christ exalted? Then I do not care if I die in a ditch. If Christ is exalted to be a Prince and a Saviour, that is enough for me.'

I distinctly recollect remembering what is recorded of some of Napoleon's soldiers, who were well-nigh cut to pieces, lying dying, bleeding, suffering, agonizing on the battle-field; but when the Emperor rode by, every man lifted himself up as best he could, some resting on the only arm that was left, just to look at him once more, and shout, '*Vive l'Empereur!*' The Emperor had come along, he was all right, and that was enough for his faithful followers. I think that I felt just like that; whatever happened to me, it was true of Christ, 'Him hath God exalted.' Never mind what becomes of the man, the King lives and reigns, Jesus Christ is glorified; and so long as that is the case, what matters it what becomes of us?

I think I can say for you, as well as for myself, that, if there is anything in this world that will glorify Christ, you will make no hesitation about the bargain. If it will glorify Christ, you say, let it come. Though your name should be cast out as evil, and your body should be left unburied, to be gnawed of dogs, what matters it, so long as he who loved us, and gave himself for us, should ride on conquering and to conquer in the midst of the sons of men?

To every loyal soldier of King Jesus, this is the best thought in connection with his Second Advent, that when he comes, it will be to be admired in his saints, and to be glorified in all them that believe. Then shall there be universal acclamations to him, and his enemies shall hide their heads in shame and dismay. Oh, what will they do then? What will they do in that day of his appearing? They also will live again, and what will they do in that day? Judas, where are you? Come here, man! Sell your Lord again for thirty pieces of silver! What does he say? Why, he flees, and wishes that he could again go out, and destroy himself; but that is impossible. Now Pilate, vacillating Pilate, wash your hands in water, and say, 'I am innocent of the blood of this just person.' There is no water for him to wash his hands in, and he dare not again perform that wicked farce. And now, ye who cried, 'Crucify him, crucify him', lift up your voices again if you dare! Not a dog doth move his tongue; but hearken, they have found their tongues, and what do they say? They are imploring the hills to fall upon them, they are calling on the rocks to hide them. The King has not put his hand upon his sword, he has not sent forth his lightnings to scatter you; why flee ye so, ye cravens? Hear their bitter wail! 'Oh, rocks and hills, hide us from the face, from the face, from the face of him that sitteth upon the throne!' It is the face of Jesus, which they were bidden to look upon, that they might live; but now, in another state, they dare not look upon that face of placid love which, in that day, shall be more stern than the frowning brow of vengeance itself. Yes, they flee, they flee; but you who have trusted Christ, you whom he hath saved, you will draw near to him, you will shout his praises, you will delight in him, it shall be your heaven to bless him for ever and ever. Oh, yes, great Master, 'Make haste, my beloved, and be thou like to a roe or to a young hart upon the mountains of spices', and all his saints, with one voice and heart, will say, 'Amen.'

Oh, that you, who have never trusted him, would trust him now; and if you trust him, you shall live with him for ever and ever. God grant it! Amen.